Lecture Notes in Computer Science 10082

Commenced Publication in 1973
Founding and Former Series Editors:
Gerhard Goos, Juris Hartmanis, and Jan van Leeuwen

More information about this series at http://www.springer.com/series/7410

Yun Qing Shi · Hyoung Joong Kim
Fernando Perez-Gonzalez · Feng Liu (Eds.)

Digital Forensics
and Watermarking

15th International Workshop, IWDW 2016
Beijing, China, September 17–19, 2016
Revised Selected Papers

 Springer

Editors
Yun Qing Shi
New Jersey Institute of Technology
Newark, NJ
USA

Hyoung Joong Kim
Korea University
Seoul
Korea (Republic of)

Fernando Perez-Gonzalez
University of Vigo
Vigo
Spain

Feng Liu
Chinese Academy of Sciences
Beijing
China

ISSN 0302-9743   ISSN 1611-3349 (electronic)
Lecture Notes in Computer Science
ISBN 978-3-319-53464-0   ISBN 978-3-319-53465-7   (eBook)
DOI 10.1007/978-3-319-53465-7

Library of Congress Control Number: 2017931057

LNCS Sublibrary: SL4 – Security and Cryptology

Printed on acid-free paper

This Springer imprint is published by Springer Nature
The registered company is Springer International Publishing AG
The registered company address is: Gewerbestrasse 11, 6330 Cham, Switzerland

Yun Qing Shi · Hyoung Joong Kim
Fernando Perez-Gonzalez · Feng Liu (Eds.)

Digital Forensics and Watermarking

15th International Workshop, IWDW 2016
Beijing, China, September 17–19, 2016
Revised Selected Papers

 Springer

Editors
Yun Qing Shi
New Jersey Institute of Technology
Newark, NJ
USA

Hyoung Joong Kim
Korea University
Seoul
Korea (Republic of)

Fernando Perez-Gonzalez
University of Vigo
Vigo
Spain

Feng Liu
Chinese Academy of Sciences
Beijing
China

ISSN 0302-9743   ISSN 1611-3349   (electronic)
Lecture Notes in Computer Science
ISBN 978-3-319-53464-0   ISBN 978-3-319-53465-7   (eBook)
DOI 10.1007/978-3-319-53465-7

Library of Congress Control Number: 2017931057

LNCS Sublibrary: SL4 – Security and Cryptology

Printed on acid-free paper

This Springer imprint is published by Springer Nature
The registered company is Springer International Publishing AG
The registered company address is: Gewerbestrasse 11, 6330 Cham, Switzerland

Preface

The 15th International Workshop on Digital-Forensics and Watermarking 2016 (IWDW2016), hosted by the State Key Laboratory of Information Security, Institute of Information Engineering, Chinese Academy of Sciences, was held at Beijing Fragrant Hill Hotel, Beijing, China, during September 16–19, 2016. IWDW 2016, following the tradition of IWDW, aimed at providing a technical program covering state-of-the-art theoretical and practical developments in the field of digital watermarking, steganography and steganalysis, forensics and antiforensics, visual cryptography, and other multimedia-related security issues. Among 70 submissions from 10 different countries and areas in the world, the Technical Program Committee selected 45 papers (35 oral and 10 poster presentations) for presentation and publication, including one paper for the best student paper award, and one for the best paper award. Besides these paper presentations, the workshop featured four invited lectures: "Digital Forensics for Network Information Credibility Evaluation" presented by Professor Tieniu Tan, Vice President of the Chinese Academy of Sciences, "Future Directions of Reversible Data Hiding" presented by Professor Hyoung Joong Kim, "The Good, the Bad and the Public: Sensor-Based Device Identification Beyond Media Forensics" presented by Assistant Professor Matthias Kirchner, and "Multimedia Forensics: Source Inference from Uncertainty and Enormity" presented by Professor Chang-Tsun Li. Furthermore, there was a 1.5-hour panel discussion and rump session among all the participants; and eight industrial exhibitions demonstrated the achievements and applications of the field.

We would like to thank all of the authors, reviewers, lecturers, and participants for their valuable contributions to IWDW2016. Our sincere gratitude also goes to all the members of Technical Program Committee, International Publicity Liaisons, and our local volunteers for their careful work and great efforts made in the wonderful organization of this workshop. We appreciate the generous support from the Institute of Information Engineering, Chinese Academy of Sciences. Finally, we hope that the readers will enjoy this volume and that it will provide inspiration and opportunities for future research.

October 2016

Yun Qing Shi
Hyoung Joong Kim
Fernando Perez-Gonzalez
Feng Liu

Organization

General Chair

Dongdai Lin   Institute of Information Engineering, Chinese Academy
                                              of Sciences, China

Technical Program Chairs

Yun Qing Shi   New Jersey Institute of Technology, USA
Hyoung Joong Kim   Korea University, South Korea
Fernando Perez-Gonzalez   University of Vigo, Spain

Technical Program Committee

Lee-Ming Cheng   City University of Hong Kong, SAR China
Claude Delpha   University of Paris-Sud XI, France
Jana Dittmann   University of Magdeburg, Germany
Isao Echizen   National Institute of Informatics, Japan
Guang Hua   Nanyang Technology University, Singapore
Fangjun Huang   Sun Yet-sen University, China
Xinghao Jiang   Shanghai Jiao-Tong University, China
Xiangui Kang   Sun Yat-sen University, China
Mohan S. Kankanhalli   NUS, Singapore
Anja Keskinarkaus   University of Oulu, Finland
Minoru Kuribayashi   Okayama University, Japan
Chang-Tsun Li   University of Warwick, UK
Shenghong Li   Shanghai Jiaotong University, China
Feng Liu   Chinese Academy of Sciences, China
Zheming Lu   University of Zhejiang, China
Bing Ma   Shandong University of Political Science and Law,
                                              China
Jiang Qun Ni   Sun Yat-sen University, China
Michiharu Niimi   Kyushu Institute of Technology, Japan
Akira Nishimura   Tokyo University of Information Science, Japan
Alessandro Piva   University of Florence, Italy
Yong-Man Ro   KAIST, South Korea
Vasiliy Sachnev   Catholic University, South Korea
Pascal Schöttle   University of Münster, Germany
Andreas Westfeld   HTW Dresden, Germany
Xiaotian Wu   Sun Yat-sen University, China
Dawen Xu   Ningbo University of Technology, China

Diqun Yan	Ningbo University, China
Ching-Nung Yang	National Dong Hwa University, Taiwan
Rui Yang	Sun Yet-sen University, China
Xinpeng Zhang	Shanghai University, China
Xianfeng Zhao	Chinese Academy of Sciences, China
Rongrong Ni	Beijing Jiao Tung University, China
Guopu Zhu	Chinese Academy of Sciences, China

International Publicity Liaisons

America

Ton Kalker	Huawei, USA
Min Wu	University of Maryland, USA

Europe

Anthony T.S. Ho	University of Surrey, UK
Stefan Katzenbeisser	TUD, Germany

Asia

Heung-Kyu Lee	KAIST, South Korea
Yao Zhao	Beijing Jiao Tung University, China

Industrial Liaisons

Jing Dong	Institute of Automation, CAS, China

Organizing Committee

Chairs

Feng Liu	Institute of Information Engineering, CAS, China
Xianfeng Zhao	Institute of Information Engineering, CAS, China
Linna Zhou	University of International Relations, China

Members

Jing Dong	Institute of Automation, CAS, China
Gang Shen	Institute of Information Engineering, CAS, China
Qian Zhao	Institute of Information Engineering, CAS, China
Dingyu Yan	Institute of Information Engineering, CAS, China
Wen Wang	Institute of Information Engineering, CAS, China
Yawei Ren	Institute of Information Engineering, CAS, China
Yun Cao	Institute of Information Engineering, CAS, China
Peipei Wang	Institute of Information Engineering, CAS, China

Yanfei Tong   Institute of Information Engineering, CAS, China
Qingxiao Guan   Institute of Information Engineering, CAS, China

Sponsors

Contents

Visual Cryptography

Reversible Data Hiding

Steganography and Steganalysis

Digital Forensics

A Multi-purpose Image Counter-anti-forensic Method Using Convolutional Neural Networks

Jingjing Yu, Yifeng Zhan, Jianhua Yang, and Xiangui Kang[⊠]

Guangdong Key Lab of Information Security, School of Data and Computer Science,
Sun Yat-Sen University, Guangzhou 510006, China
isskxg@mail.sysu.edu.cn

Abstract. During the past decade, image forensics has made rapid progress due to the growing concern of image content authenticity. In order to remove or conceal the traces that forensics based on, some far-sighted forgers take advantage of so-called anti-forensics to make their forgery more convincing. To rebuild the credibility of forensics, many countermeasures against anti-forensics have been proposed. This paper presents a multi-purpose approach to detect various anti-forensics based on the architecture of Convolutional Neural Networks (CNN), which can automatically extract features and identify the forged types. Our model can detect various image anti-forensics both in binary and multi-class decision effectively. Experimental results show that the proposed method performs well for multiple well-known image anti-forensic methods.

Keywords: Convolutional Neural Networks · Counter anti-forensics · Multi-purpose

1 Introduction

With the popularity of digital cameras and powerful image processing software tools, it is easy to record, edit and share photos. In law enforcement, digital image content plays an important role in deciding a case. Since the digital image can be easily altered by the forgers without leaving perceptible artifacts, its authenticity and reliability must be verified. As a result, image forensics has raised more and more attention over the last decade [1]. Various digital forensic techniques [5,7,8,12,13] are proposed to detect the image processing operations, *e.g.*, JPEG compression, median filtering, resampling and contrast enhancement, which are considered in our experiments. On the other hand, the farsighted forgers attempt to fool the investigators by using anti-forensic techniques [2,4,6,9,10,14,15] to remove or hide the traces that they may leave after certain operations. To restore authenticity and rebuild the credibility, many countermeasures [3,11,22–24] have been proposed to detect different anti-forensics.

X. Kang—This work was supported by NSFC (Grant nos. 61379155, U1536204, 61502547, 61332012, 61272453 and NSF of Guangdong province (Grant no. s2013020012788).

© Springer International Publishing AG 2017
Y.Q. Shi et al. (Eds.): IWDW 2016, LNCS 10082, pp. 3–15, 2017.
DOI: 10.1007/978-3-319-53465-7_1

Up to now, most counter-anti-forensic methods focus on a binary decision, which targets only one type of image anti-forensics, and are difficult to extend to counter other diverse image anti-forensics. For example, the method to detect JPEG anti-forensics (anti-JPEG) is not applicable for identifying resampling or contrast enhancement anti-forensic (short for anti-Res and anti-CE) operations. Additionally, some existing detectors assume that they know the possible anti-forensic type of the questionable images, which is not reasonable since no prior information is provided in real-life scenario, the detector needs to have knowledge of as many counter-anti-forensics as possible, which may cost plenty of effort to seek out and then detect the specific anti-forensic technique. Hence, a multi-purpose method is needed in this case.

Convolutional Neural Networks (CNN) [19], which belongs to deep learning [16–21], has recently enjoyed a great success in speech and image recognition. Its shared weights network was inspired by the biological neural network, which reduces both the complexity of models and the numbers of weights. Moreover, CNN can automatically learn features jointly with the classification, while most existing counter-anti-forensic techniques have to separate the feature extraction and classification. The latter may degrade the total detection performance, as they cannot be optimized simultaneously. Therefore, we adopt CNN as our basic architecture in this work.

In this paper, we propose a multi-purpose method to detect various image anti-forensics using Convolutional Neural Networks, which can automatically extract features and identify various image anti-forensics. Compared with some existing specific counter measures, the proposed method can not only achieve better detection performance, but also be used to extend to classify multiple image anti-forensic operations. The rest of this paper is organized as follows. In Sect. 2, we briefly review works on the anti-forensics involved in this paper. Section 3 describes the proposed CNN architecture. Section 4 presents the experimental results, and the conclusions are drawn in Sect. 5.

2   Background

In this section, we briefly review the image anti-forensic processing operations and its traces left.

2.1   JPEG Anti-forensics

JPEG is the most commonly used compression standard in digital cameras and image editing tools. Due to the nature of lossy transform coding, JPEG introduces characteristic traces in the compressed images, e.g., the quantization artifact in the DCT domain and the blocking artifact in the spatial domain. Subsequently, anti-forensics [2,4] have been proposed to erase these traces. To remove the quantization artifact, the authors of [2] added dither in the DCT coefficients to restore the DCT coefficient histogram. The effectiveness of this anti-forensic technique can be seen in Fig. 1. In order to detect the tampered

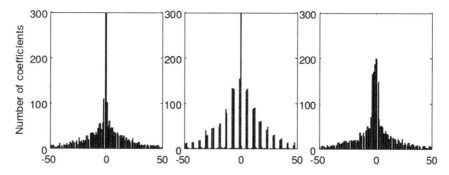

Fig. 1. DCT coefficient histogram of an image (a) before JPEG compression, (b) after JPEG compression, (c) after JPEG anti-forensic operation.

traces, the authors [3] proposed a countering JPEG anti-forensic method. In [4], JPEG blocking artifact is eliminated by median filtering followed by the dither. This method can significantly disguise the traces left by JPEG compression and decrease the detection accuracy of the aforementioned work [3]. To detect such anti-forensic method, another countering method is proposed by estimating the noise level of the questioned images [22].

2.2   Median Filtering Anti-forensics

Median filtering is frequently used in image processing for image enhancement and anti-forensic purposes. Many median filtering detectors [12,13] and anti-forensic (anti-MF) methods [14,15] have been developed to identify or mitigate the operating traces. In [23], a specific countermeasure has been proposed to counter anti-forensics via analyzing the periodicity of the added noise. However, this method loses effectiveness when facing another median filtering anti-forensics [14], which left no periodical footprint.

2.3   Resampling Anti-forensics

Resampling traces are caused by linear dependencies among pixels. Popescu and Farid [5] detect the traces based on its periodic artifacts by a probability map. Subsequently, some farsighted forgers remove the periodic artifacts by irregular sampling [6]. To detect the new clue which leaves behind this anti-forensics, the authors in [24] proposed a new method using partial autocorrelation coefficients.

2.4   Contrast Enhancement Anti-forensics

The evidence left by contrast enhancement can be detected by measuring the impulsive peaks and gaps in the image pixel value histogram [7,8]. As a result, a variety of anti-forensics have been proposed to remove the fingerprints by introducing noise in the contrast enhancement procedure [10] or into the contrast enhanced image [9].

3 The Proposed CNN Model for Countering Anti-forensics

Convolutional Neural Networks (CNN) [17] is a new approach to discover highly correlated information, which includes several types of layers, such as convolutional layers, pooling layers and fully-connected layers. The convolutional layer is the core building block of a CNN, and its output volume can be interpreted as holding neurons arranged in a 3D volume. The parameters of the convolutional layer consist of a set of learnable filters. Each filter is small spatially (along width and height), but extends through the full depth of the input volume. The pooling layer is able to reduce the spatial size of the representation, decrease the amount of parameters and computation on the network, and hence also control overfitting. Neurons in a fully connected layer have full connections to all activations in the previous layer, and their activations can be computed with a matrix multiplication, followed by a bias offset.

It is well-known that CNN shows an extraordinary ability for object recognition [17]. The major difference between object recognition and image anti-forensics is the signal strength, since anti-forensic image detection, unlike object recognition, has very insignificant differences compared to the original image. Thus, some methods should be used during the training process in order to make CNN work for image anti-forensics. In the following, we will explain why using this network in anti-forensic classification.

3.1 Convolution

In this paper, we recall the major concepts of CNN, which is a deep learning network that has proved its efficiency in image classification competitions. The most important operation of CNN is convolution, which is done between the input image and a filter. There are many filters in a convolutional layer, and each one leads to a filtered image. Then the second and third steps are applied, leading to a new image called feature map. Compare to fully connected layer, convolutional layer shows much better performance in extracting feature because

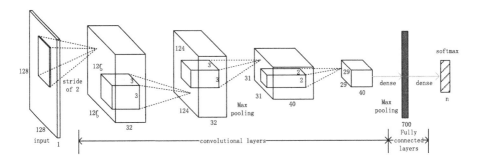

Fig. 2. Overall architecture of the proposed method.

of parameter sharing. Moreover, parameter sharing can dramatically reduce the number of parameters which leads to much less training time. Suppose an input volume had a size of $16 \times 16 \times 20$. If the size of receptive field is 3×3, every neuron in the convolutional layer would have a total of $3 \times 3 \times 20 = 180$ connections (much less than $16 \times 16 \times 20 = 5120$) to the input volume. Filter size is critical for the network, and a more suitable receptive filter results in a better extracted feature. In our experiment, we accept a size of 3×3 filter for each receptive field, which has been proved very efficient in [17], and also shows the satisfied performance in feature extraction in the anti-forensic classification.

CNN can catch the desired feature (anti-forensic operation) by neural network training. The theoretical basis given as follows. Formally, let $I^{(0)}$ denote the input image, $F_k^{(1)}$ denote the kth filter from layer $l = 1, ..., L$ with L being the number of convolutional layers. A convolution from the first layer with the kth field leads to a filtered image, denote $I_k^{(l)}$ which also been called feature maps), such that:

$$I_k^{(l)} = I^{(0)} * F_k^l \tag{1}$$

Generally, a convolutional layer is made of three steps, i.e. convolution, activation, and pooling. These three consecutive steps can be summarized by examining the link from the feature map of one layer to that of its previous layer:

$$I_k^l = pool(f(b_k^{(l)} + \sum_{i=1}^{i=K^{l-1}} I_i^{l-1} * F_{k,i}^l)) \tag{2}$$

with $b_k^{(l)}$ being a scalar used for setting a bias to the convolution, $f()$ being the activation function applied pixel per pixel to the filtered image, and the pooling, $pool()$, which pools a local neighborhood, and K^l being the number of filters the lth layer has. Note that the filter kernel (weights), and the bias have to be learned and are modified by back-propagation of the error.

Since convolution part shows above and anti-forensic operation can both be presented through a combination of linear and non-linear function, the proposed convolutional layer is supposed to be able to extract the anti-forensic feature. In order to see the feature map actually extract useful feature with increasing depth of convolutional layers, the feature maps of the proposed CNN network is displayed in Fig. 3. Figure 3(a)–(d) are the feature maps of an original image obtained from the convolutional layer 1, 2, 3, and 4 respectively. Figure 3(a) and (b) have 32 feature maps, (c) and (d) have 40 feature maps. The bright area in a feature map indicates large weights and vice versa.

The feature maps in Fig. 4 are generated by the 4th convolutional layer with original and anti-forensic images test in our experiments. 40 feature maps are included in one subgraph. We can see perceptible difference of units in the same position of certain feature map between original and anti-forensic images. Median filtering and JPEG operation will cause the image fuzzy phenomenon, and their anti-forensics both altered by adding corresponding noises, thus it will make their images details blurred. As seen in Fig. 4(a)–(c), the features of anti-JPEG and anti-MF are similar and both fuzzy compared to the original image. Anti-CE

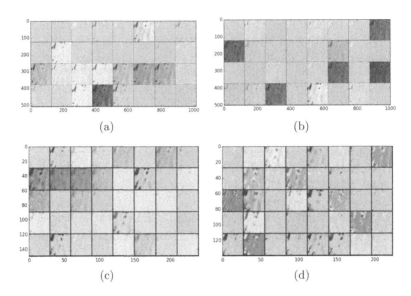

Fig. 3. Feature maps of original image (a)–(d) are obtained from the convolutional layer 1, 2, 3, 4 respectively.

is aimed to falsify the forensics and achieve the effect of contrast enhancement. There is a sharp contrast in the feature maps of anti-CE image compared to the original. In the operation of resampling, the image will resize according to the specified scaling factors. Seen in Fig. 4(e)–(f), the feature of the up-sampling image is just like an amplifier of the original one, while the down-sampling feature includes more textures than the original. The analysis above shows that our network can extract useful and decisive features when dealing the counter-anti-forensic task during the training process.

3.2 Pooling

Pooling layers in CNN summarize the outputs of previous layers and operates independently on each depth slice of the input, as well as resizing it spatially. Pooling layer can not only effectively reduce training complexity by eliminating parameters, but also play an important role in preventing overfitting. Pooling layers usually use MAX operation. Normally, the neighborhoods summarized by adjacent pooling units do not overlap, but when it is applied on image anti-forensics, it is necessary to preserve the adjacent area for better performance. Based on our experiment, overlapping max pooling layers reduce the error rate by 2% or more.

3.3 Activation

The Rectified Linear Units (ReLU) is used in our work due to its fast convergence in large datasets [27]. It also increases the nonlinear properties of the

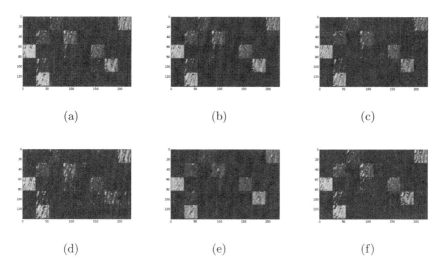

Fig. 4. The feature maps of (a) Original image, (b) Anti-JPEG image, (c) Anti-MF image, (d) Anti-CE image, (e) Anti-RES image (up-sampling) and (f) Anti-RES image (down-sampling) from the last convolutional layer respectively.

decision function and the overall network. The convolutional and non-linearity transformation can be denoted as:

$$x_j^k = g\left(\sum_{i=1}^{n} x_i^{k-1} * w_{ij}^{k-1} + b_j^k\right) \tag{3}$$

where '*' denotes convolutional operation; x_j^k is the jth output feature map in the kth layer; w_{ij}^{k-1} is the weight at layer $k-1$, i, j position; b_j^k is the bias parameter, and g denotes non-linearity transformation where ReLU has been used. ReLU, which has been proved to have better convergence properties than the sigmoid and tanh functions [17], can be expressed as:

$$g(x) = max(0, x) \tag{4}$$

3.4   Dropout

The classification layer consists mainly of two parts: the softmax layer and the fully connected layer. We adopt a widely used technique called dropout to avoid overfitting, which randomly sets certain output of fully connected layers to zero with a probability of 0.5. The softmax layer, trained using a cross-entropy scheme, is used for classification, which is essentially a nonlinear multinomial logistic regression. Back propagation algorithm is used to fine-tune weights and biases for training the parameters in the proposed CNN. Consequently, CNN is able to use the classification result to adjust the extracted features and build a better learning mechanism for measuring and classifying anti-forensic methods automatically.

3.5   Overall Architecture

Figure 2 is the overall architecture of the proposed CNN model, the net contains five layers with weights, the first four are convolutional layers and the fifth is a fully connected layer. Unlike some deep convolutional networks in image classification, the 5-layer architecture can prevent the diffusion of gradients, and performs ably in our experiment. The architecture with less layers cannot extract useful feature base on our experiments. The very small 3×3 receptive fields are used as filters throughout the whole net. The output of the last fully-connected layer is fed to an n-way softmax, which produces a distribution of n-class labels.

4   Experimental Result

In this section, we first show the network settings of the proposed CNN architecture. Then, the proposed method is tested on detecting six anti-forensic methods separately in Sect. 4.2. Finally, the detection performance for the multi-class classification of anti-forensics is given. A total of 10000 original images from BOSS-base [18] are cropped from the center to a size of 128×128 pixels. Without loss of generality, grayscale images are adopted in all of our experiments. The tampered images are created via different anti-forensics manipulations mentioned in Sect. 2.

4.1   Network Settings

In our work, we load images of size 128×128 as input to the CNN model, and the first convolutional layer filters the input data with 32 kernels of size 3×3 and a stride of 1. The second convolutional layer takes the output of the previous layer as input with 32 kernels of size 3×3 and a stride of 1. Subsequently, it follows a max pooling operation. The third and fourth convolutional layers also take the output of their respective previous layers as input but with 40 kernels of size 3×3, and a max pooling operation is used in the fourth convolutional layer, as demonstrated in Fig. 2. Consequently, Fig. 3(a) and (b) have 32 feature maps, (c) and (d) have 40 feature maps. The ReLU is applied to every output of the convolutional layers. The fully connected layer has 700 neurons and each neuron connects to the output layer through a softmax function. In the fully connected layer, the dropout operation is used to delete the neurons randomly to prevent the problem of overfitting. In all of the experiments, four-fifths of the images are used for training and the remainder for testing. All experiments are repeated 10 times and the average results are reported.

4.2   Binary Classification

In the first part, the proposed method is evaluated on detecting the aforementioned anti-forensic operations separately. 20000 images are available for each anti-forensic operation detection, including 10000 original images and 10000 corresponding anti-forensically modified images.

Table 1. Detection accuracy (%) for original and Anti-JPEG images.

Anti-method	Countermeasure		
	[3]	[22]	Proposed
Anti-JPEG [2]	80.0	55.78	98.83
Anti-JPEG [4]	58.02	85.87	99.95

4.2.1 Anti-JPEG Detection

The two measured anti-JPEG databases are created as follows: the original images are first JPEG compressed using a quality factor randomly chosen from 55 to 95 with a step of 10, then modified with corresponding anti-forensics methods [2,4]. The comparative results are shown in Table 1. Seen from Table 1, the proposed method attains better detection accuracy, nearly 14% higher than the two specific counter-anti-forensic methods for comparison. It is also observed that the detection accuracy of the specific counter-anti-forensic method declined rapidly when different anti-forensic method is used by the forger. For example, the detection accuracy of the countermeasure [22] achieves 85.76% when detect the forgery [4], and it degrades to only 55.78% in detecting the anti-JPEG of [2]. According to the experiment results, the proposed method operate well with both the two forged types.

4.2.2 Anti-MF Detection

The original images are first median filtered with a 3×3 window and then modified with the specific anti-forensic methods [14,15] to produce two anti-MF datasets respectively. From Table 2, it is observed that our proposed method achieve almost perfect performance against both anti-MF methods, whereas countermeasure [23] can only detect the case of anti-MF [15]. As mentioned in Sect. 1, many countermeasures target only one kind of image anti-forensics, and the result of [23] exemplifies this statement.

4.2.3 Anti-RES Detection

Anti-Res dataset are created by first selecting a scaling factor from 0.6 to 2.0 randomly, then setting the strength of geometric distortion $\sigma = 0.4$ to generate resampling images [6]. Seen in Table 3, the detection accuracy of the proposed

Table 2. Detection accuracy (%) for original and Anti-MF images.

Anti-method	Countermeasure	
	[23]	Proposed
Anti-MF [14]	-	99.38
Anti-MF [15]	98.45	99.35

Table 3. Detection accuracy (%) for original and Anti-RES images.

Anti-method	Countermeasure	
	[24]	Proposed
Anti-RES [6]	97.67	99.38

method reaches 99.38%, 1.6% higher than the state-of-art specific countermeasure [24].

4.2.4 Anti-CE Detection

Anti-CE dataset are produced by first adding uniform noise and followed by gamma correction [10]. The performance on anti-CE detection is 92.73% in our experiments. To our knowledge, no other countermeasure against this anti-forensics has been proposed.

In conclusion, our proposed method is effective in detecting the aforementioned anti-forensics according, which demonstrates that the CNN model works well to detect anti-forensic operations separately.

4.3 Multi-class Classification

In this experiment, the proposed CNN model is used as a multi-classifier. The results are presented in Table 4. Six kinds of the anti-forensic images mentioned above are included, and a total of 70000 images are used for training and testing. Table 4 presents the accurate prediction and error prediction on our test dataset in one epoch. '*' represents the prediction accuracy below 1%. The horizontal direction denotes the predicted anti-forensics type, and the vertical direction denotes the realistic type. Seen from Table 4, the detection accuracies of these six anti-forensics performs well in the multi-class classification. The total detection accuracy of the multi-class classification is 96.9%. It is clear that our proposed model is effective in detecting the multi-class image anti-forensics.

Table 4. Prediction accuracy (%) for classifying multi-class anti-forensic.

Test/prediction	Original	Anti-JPEG [2]	Anti-JPEG [4]	Anti-MF [15]	Anti-MF [14]	Anti-CE	Anti-Res
Original	94.15	*	*	0	*	2.35	2.5
Anti-JPEG [2]	1.6	97.1	*	0	0	*	*
Anti-JPEG [4]	0	*	99.3	*	0	0	*
Anti-MF [15]	0	*	*	99.4	*	0	*
Anti-MF [14]	*	0	0	0	99.5	*	*
Anti-CE	6.05	*	*	0	*	91.75	0
Anti-RES	*	*	*	*	1	*	97.35

We also test the proposed method when the database is changed. The new test database is created as follows: we use 1000 original images from UCID with the size of 128×128, and create the six corresponding anti-forensic images, 6000 forged images in total. Then we use the model trained with BOSSbase to classify the database created from UCID. The detection accuracy is 94.7% in this case, which demonstrates that the proposed method is not strongly related to the database.

4.4 Practical Cross Database Test

Four different anti-forensic (anti-JPEG [2], anti-MF [15], anti-RES [6], anti-CE are included) images are used to create 10000 forged images, each type responsible for 2500. We first train a classifier with 10000 original images from BOSSbase and the mentioned forged image dataset. Then, we create two test dataset with the anti-forensic methods (anti-JPEG [4] and anti-MF [14], respectively) that are not included in the trained dataset. 1000 original images from UCID and 1000 corresponding anti-forensic images are used to create the test dataset. The accuracy of detecting the forgery of [4] is 98.7%, and the forgery of [14] is 98.65% respectively, which indicates that the proposed method is able to extend to other diverse image anti-forensics without much prior information.

5   Conclusion

In this paper, a CNN-based method is proposed for detecting image anti-forensics, which can automatically extract features and identify various image anti-forensics. Instead of addressing a certain type of manipulations, it provides a multi-purpose approach to detect diverse anti-forensically modified images, which suits numerous scenarios. To the best of our knowledge, it is the first time that a model for detecting image anti-forensic operations based on the CNN architecture has been proposed. Experimental results show that our method achieves satisfactory performance in detecting the six well-known image anti-forensic methods mentioned above. Compared to some state-of-art specific counter-anti-forensic methods, the proposed method achieves better performance. In further studies, we will extend our method to more types of anti-forensic modifications and normal signal processing operations.

References

1. Stamm, M.M.C., Wu, M., Liu, K.J.R.: Information forensics: an overview of the first decade. In: IEEE Access, vol. 1, pp. 167–200, May 2013
2. Stamm, M.M.C., Tjoa, S.K., Lin, W.S., et al.: Anti-forensics of JPEG compression. In Proceedings of IEEE International Conference on Acoustics, Speech, and Signal Processing, pp. 1694–1697, March 2010
3. Valenzise, M.G., Tagliasacchi, M., Tubaro, S.: Revealing the traces of JPEG compression anti-forensics. IEEE Trans. Inf. Forensics Secur. 8(2), 335–349 (2013)
4. Stamm, M.M.C., Liu, K.J.R.: Anti-forensics of digital image compression. IEEE Trans. Inf. Forensics Secur. 6(3), 1050–1065 (2011)

5. Popescu, A.A.C., Farid, H.: Exposing digital forgeries by detecting traces of resampling. IEEE Trans. Signal Process. **53**(2), 758–767 (2005)
6. Kirchner, M.M., Böhme, R.: Hiding traces of resampling in digital images. IEEE Trans. Inf. Forensics Secur. **3**(4), 582–592 (2008)
7. Stamm, M.M.C., Liu, K.J.R.: Forensic detection of image manipulation using statistical intrinsic fingerprints. IEEE Trans. Inf. Forensics Secur. **5**(3), 492–506 (2010)
8. Stamm, M.M.C., Liu, K.J.R.: Blind forensics of contrast enhancement in digital images. In: Proceedings of IEEE International Conference on Image Processing, San Diego, CA, pp. 3112–3115, October 2008
9. Cao, G.G., Zhao, Y., Ni, R., Tian, H.: Anti-forensics of contrast enhancement in digital images. In: Proceedings of ACM Workshop Multimedia and Security, pp. 25–34 (2010)
10. Kwok, C.-W., Au, O.C., Chui, S.-H.: Alternative anti-forensics method for contrast enhancement. In: Shi, Y.Q., Kim, H.-J., Perez-Gonzalez, F. (eds.) IWDW 2011. LNCS, vol. 7128, pp. 398–410. Springer, Heidelberg (2012). doi:10.1007/978-3-642-32205-1_32
11. Valenzise, G.G., Tagliasacchi, M., Tubaro, S.: Revealing the traces of JPEG compression anti-forensics. IEEE Trans. Inf. Forensics Secur. **8**(2), 335–349 (2013)
12. Yuan, H.H.: Blind forensics of median filtering in digital images. IEEE Trans. Inf. Forensics Secur. **6**(4), 1335–1345 (2011)
13. Kirchner, M.M., Fridrich, J.: On detection of median filtering in digital images. In: Memon, N.D., Dittmann, J., Alattar, A.M., Delp, E.J. (Eds.) Media Forensics and Security II, part of the IS&T-SPIE Electronic Imaging Symposium, Proceedings, vol. 7541 of SPIE Proceedings, San Jose, CA, USA, 18–20 January 2010, p. 754110, SPIE (2010)
14. Dang-Nguyen, D.D.T., Gebru, I.D., Conotter, V., et al.: Counter-forensics of median filtering. In: 2013 IEEE 15th International Workshop on Multimedia Signal Processing (MMSP), pp. 260–265, September 2013
15. Wu, Z.Z.H., Stamm, M.C., Liu, K.J.R.: Anti-forensics of median filtering. In: Proceedings of IEEE International Conference on Acoustic, Speech, and Signal Processing, pp. 3043–3047, Vancouver, Canada, May 2013
16. Simonyan, K.K., Zisserman, A.: Very deep convolutional networks for large-scale image recognition. In: Proceedings of ICLR (2015)
17. Krizhevsky, A.A., Sutskever, I., Hinton, G.: Imagenet classification with deep convolutional neural networks. In: Advances in Neural Information Processing Systems, pp. 1097–1105 (2012)
18. Bas, P., Filler, T., Pevný, T.: "Break our steganographic system": the ins and outs of organizing BOSS. In: Filler, T., Pevný, T., Craver, S., Ker, A. (eds.) IH 2011. LNCS, vol. 6958, pp. 59–70. Springer, Heidelberg (2011). doi:10.1007/978-3-642-24178-9_5
19. Lecun, Y.Y., BoUou, L., Bengio, Y., Haffner, P.: Gradient-based learning applied to document recognition. Proc. IEEE **86**(11), 2278–2324 (1998)
20. Srivastava, N., et al.: Dropout: a simple way to prevent neural networks from overfitting. J. Mach. Learn. Res. **15**(1), 1929–1958 (2014)
21. Nair, V., Hinton, G.E.: Rectified linear units improve restricted boltzmann machines. In: Proceedings of the 27th International Conference on Machine Learning (ICML 2010) (2010)
22. Jiang, Y.Y., Zeng, H., Kang, X., et al.: The game of countering JPEG anti-forensics based on the noise level estimation. In: Proceedings of the Asian-Pacific Signal and Information Processing Association Annual Submit Conference (APSIPA ASC) (2013)

23. Zeng, H.H., Qin, T., Kang, X., et al.: Countering anti-forensics of median filtering. In: Proceedings of the IEEE International Conference on Acoustics, Speech, and Signal Processing, pp. 2723–2727 (2014)
24. Peng, A.A., Zeng, H., Kang, X., et al.: Countering anti-forensics of image resampling. In: Proceedings of the 2015 IEEE International Conference on Image Processing (ICIP), pp. 3595–3599, September 2015

Detection of Video-Based Face Spoofing Using LBP and Multiscale DCT

Ye Tian[1] and Shijun Xiang[1,2(✉)]

[1] School of Information Science and Technology, Jinan University, Guangzhou, China
[2] State Key Laboratory of Information Security,
Institute of Information Engineering, Chinese Academy of Sciences, Beijing, China
shijun_xiang@qq.com

Abstract. Despite the great deal of progress during the recent years, face spoofing detection is still a focus of attention. In this paper, an effective, simple and time-saving countermeasure against video-based face spoofing attacks based on LBP (Local Binary Patterns) and multiscale DCT (Discrete Cosine Transform) is proposed. Adopted as the low-level descriptors, LBP features are used to extract spatial information in each selected frame. Next, multiscale DCT is performed along the ordinate axis of the obtained LBP features to extract spatial information. Representing both spatial and temporal information, the obtained high-level descriptors (LBP-MDCT features) are finally fed into a SVM (Support Vector Machine) classifier to determine whether the input video is a facial attack or valid access. Compared with state of the art, the excellent experimental results of the proposed method on two benchmarking datasets (Replay-Attack and CASIA-FASD dataset) have demonstrated its effectiveness.

Keywords: Video-based face spoofing · LBP · Multiscale DCT · Replay-attack · CASIA-FASD

1 Introduction

Spoofing attack is a kind of presentation attack which is targeted towards fooling a biometric system into recognizing an illegitimate user as a genuine one by means of presenting to the sensor a synthetic forged version of the original biometric trait [1]. Currently it is an accepted fact that, many biometric modalities are vulnerable to spoofing attacks [2–8] wherein face spoofing is of paramount importance to be dealt with. For one thing, face is one of the biometric traits with the highest potential impact both from an economic and a social point of view [1]. For another thing, compared with other spoofing attacks, face spoofing is very easy to conduct due to its low-cost and low-tech features. Facial traits are widely available on the Internet including personal websites and social networks. Moreover, an imposter can easily collect photographs or videos from a genuine user at distance.

© Springer International Publishing AG 2017
Y.Q. Shi et al. (Eds.): IWDW 2016, LNCS 10082, pp. 16–28, 2017.
DOI: 10.1007/978-3-319-53465-7_2

Generally speaking, face spoofing attacks can be divided into three categories: photo attacks, video attacks and mask attacks. In the case of a photo attack, the spoofing artefact is a photograph of the genuine client which can be presented to the sensor on a paper or the screen of a digital device. Video attacks are also referred to as replay attacks since they are carried out by replaying a video of the valid user. A mask attack is a fraudulent access attempt using a 3D mask of the legitimate user enrolled in the system.

With the release of several public face spoofing databases [9–12], many publications addressing face spoofing problems have appeared in the last few years. Overlooking methods dealing with mask attacks which are beyond the scope of this paper, the majority of anti-spoofing methods can be classified into two parts, namely photo-based methods and video-based methods. According to [13], photo-based approaches are not suitable for directly detecting video attacks, especially for high resolution videos. It is more difficult to detect video attacks since the dynamics of the video makes the biometric data more realistic. Besides, video attacks tend to have less degradations and fewer artefacts generated during quantization and discretization. Heretofore, while a number of photo-based schemes have been proposed in the literature, the development of research regarding video-based schemes is not up to par.

Motivated by the strong energy compaction property, DCT has been used extensively in image processing tasks. However, it is adopted to extract static information by performing on a frame-by-frame basis in the literature. Heretofore, it has not beed used for dynamic information extraction. In this paper, we propose an innovative way of applying multiscale DCT to LBP features to represent spatial-temporal information. To the best of our knowledge, this is the first attempt of processing video-based face spoofing attacks by performing multiscale DCT on LBP features in the aim of extracting facial dynamic information. While the proposed scheme is very simple and time-saving, our experiments on two benchmarking datasets showed excellent performance which indicated its effectiveness.

The remainder of the paper is organized as follows. Section 2 briefly reviews the existing methods for detecting face spoofing attacks. Section 3 demonstrates the proposed approach, followed by experimental results in Sect. 4. Finally, conclusions and future work are given in Sect. 5.

2   Related Work

Depending on the type of information used, the majority of existing solutions for face spoofing consists of two parts: solutions using spatial information, solutions using both spatial and temporal information. In order to extract spatial information, the first type of solutions are mainly based on the analysis of face texture using different image processing methods. One of the first attempts towards face spoofing was made in [14], where Fourier spectra of a single face image or face image sequences was analysed. Later, Difference of Gaussian (DoG) was adopted to explore specific frequency information in [10,15]. In [16], Gabor wavelet was used to enhance texture representation while Histogram Oriented Gradients (HOG) was utilized to introduce local shape description. Proven as an effective tool, Local Binary Pattern (LBP) and its extensions were employed in many works such as [11, 13, 16–18]. Recently, the authors of [19] created a method for identifying computer-generated facial image which is based on smoothness property of the faces presented by edges and human skin's characteristic via local entropy.

Designed to take advantage of both spatial and temporal information, the second type of anti-spoofing schemes usually achieve very competitive performance, at a cost, in some cases, more time-consuming. An example of such methods is the work in [20] which introduced Local Binary Patterns from Three Orthogonal Planes (LBP-TOP) to combine both space and time information into a single multiresolution texture descriptor. Inspired by the special property of Dynamic Mode Decomposition (DMD), a pipeline of DMD + LBP + SVM was proposed for countering spoof attacks in face anti-spoofing [21]. In [22], the authors combined Multiscale Binarized Statistical Image Features on Three Orthogonal Planes (MBSIF-TOP) and Multiscale Local Phase Quantization Representation on Three Orthogonal Planes (MLPQ-TOP) in the aim of improving the robustness of spoofing attack detector. Recently, a low-level feature descriptor was formed by extracting time-spectral information from the video [23]. Except these texture-based methods, spatial and temporal information are integrated from some other perspectives such as analyzing noise signatures generated by the recapturing process [24].

While the above schemes exploit spatial-temporal information and improve the detection performance, they tend to be more complex and time-consuming. In comparison, the proposed scheme is simple and time-saving. For one thing, the implementations of both LBP and DCT are of high efficiency. For another thing, the proposed method only requires a few of frames instead of the entire frames contained in a video. Furthermore, owing to the strong energy compaction property of DCT, only one or several DCT components are required to form the final descriptor. The scheme as a whole is thus easy to implement and efficient. As for the indispensable classifier in face anti-spoofing task, we use SVM as a back-end classification engine. Our experimental results, strictly following the published experimental protocols, showed that the proposed approach achieved the best performance reported so far. Indeed, we attained zero HTER, i.e., perfect classification, on both the development and test set of Replay-Attack dataset.

3   Proposed Method

In this section, we present an algorithm for video-based attempted spoofing attack detection. The algorithm comprises four main steps: face extraction, low-level descriptor extraction, high-level descriptor extraction, and classification. The overall pipeline is shown in Fig. 1. First, we extract face images from a target video at a fixed time interval. Second, the low-level descriptors, i.e., LBP features are generated for each extracted face image. After that, we perform

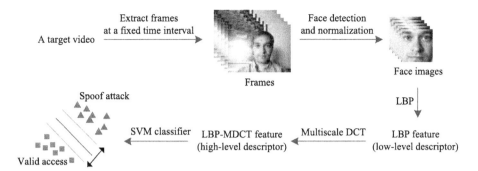

Fig. 1. Flow chart of the proposed method

multiscale DCT on the low-level descriptors to obtain the high-level descriptors (LBP-MDCT features). Finally, the high-level descriptors are fed into a SVM classifier to determine whether the target video is a spoof attack or valid access.

3.1 Face Extraction

Instead of the entire images contained in an input video, only a few of frames are utilized in this work for the sake of efficiency. To this end, we extract frames at a fixed time interval I for each input video. For example, if $I = 1$, the first frame, the third frame, the fifth frame et al. are extracted; if $I = 2$, the first frame, the fourth frame, the seventh frame et al. are extracted. Using the Viola-Jones face detection algorithm [25], we detect face region of each selected frame and then geometrically normalize the face region into 64×64 pixels. Given a video containing M frames, we attain $\lceil \frac{M}{I+1} \rceil$ normalized face images at the end of this stage.

3.2 Low-Level Descriptor Extraction

Local Binary Patterns (LBP), a simple yet a powerful gray-scale invariant texture representation, extracts spatial information based on comparisons of gray values between each pixel and its neighbours. Since it was proposed, many variants have been developed. In this paper, we use the uniform LBP (LBP^{u2}) which only considers labels containing at most two $0-1$ or $1-0$ transitions. Conventionally, uniform LBP is denoted as LBP$^{u2}_{P,R}$, where P and R stand for the number of used neighbourhood pixels and radius respectively. Assuming $N = \lceil \frac{M}{I+1} \rceil$ face images are extracted in total, after we obtain a LBP feature vector of length 59, namely a simple normalized histogram of LBP$^{u2}_{8,1}$ codes for each selected face, all the feature vectors are parallelized, generating a LBP feature matrix of size $N \times 59$ for each video which is adopted as a low-level descriptor in this work.

3.3   High-Level Descriptor Extraction

In this phase, DCT operation is applied to the LBP feature matrix in the aim of extracting temporal information. Figure 2 demonstrates the generation of a LBP-DCT feature. Specifically, after the formation of the $N \times 59$ LBP feature matrix, we perform DCT along its ordinate axis, i.e., the time axis of the entire video, generating many DCT components for each column. Given an input $f(n)$, its 1D-DCT transform can be represented as:

$$F(k) = \alpha(k) \sum_{n=0}^{N-1} f(n) \cos[\frac{(2n+1)k\pi}{2N}] , \tag{1}$$

where $0 \leqslant k \leqslant n - 1$. Since the strong energy compaction property of DCT, the direct component (DC) concentrates the majority of energy. Taking advantage of this special property, there is no need to utilize all the DCT components. With this in mind, only C components are used in this stage. Specifically, in the case of $C = 1$, only the direct component is extracted; in the case of $C = 2$, the direct component along with the first alternating component are extracted. As a result of this process, we end up with a $59 \times C$ LBP-DCT feature matrix. Of particular worth to mention here is the benefits brought by neglecting most of the DCT components which achieves dimension reduction. Not only does dimension reduction decreases computational complexity, it also improves detection efficiency.

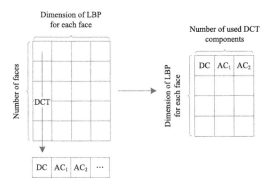

Fig. 2. Demonstration of high-level descriptor extraction

As demonstrated in many previous work [26–28], applying multiscale feature is instrumental in improving performance. Therefore, in order to achieve a better performance, here we perform 3-scale DCT on LBP matrices. In the first scale, we calculate DCT on an entire LBP matrix, generating a $59 \times C$ LBP-DCT feature matrix. In the second scale, the entire LBP matrix is divided into two parts: the first and second part consisting of LBP vectors obtained from the first $\lfloor \frac{N}{2} \rfloor$ frames and the following $\lfloor \frac{N}{2} \rfloor$ frames, respectively. Subsequently,

DCT operation is performed on each part separately, resulting in two LBP-DCT features. Similarly, we obtain four LBP-DCT features in the third scale by partitioning the LBP matrix into four parts. Hence, we end up with seven LBP-DCT features in total through this procedure. Last but not least, the resultant seven LBP-DCT features are concatenated to form a final matrix which is referred to as a high-level descriptor (LBP-MDCT feature) in the present paper.

3.4   Classification

The last step of the proposed algorithm is to use a discriminative machine learning approach to find an appropriate classification model in order to decide whether an input video is an attempted attack or not. In this paper, we choose Support Vector Machine (SVM) [29] algorithm with Radial Basis Function (RBF) kernel. After we feed the high-level descriptors into a SVM, the detection of face spoofing attacks is completed according to the output of the SVM.

4   Experimental Results

In this section, the experimental results of the proposed method are presented and discussed. Prior to proceeding with the experiments, we give an overview of the datasets and experimental protocols employed to evaluate performance of different countermeasures.

4.1   Datasets

In this work, we consider two benchmarking datasets.

Replay-Attack Dataset [11]: This dataset consists of short video recordings of about 10 s of both real access and spoofing attacks to a face recognition system. It contains 1200 videos (200 real access and 1000 spoof attacks) of 50 identities and the samples are taken in 3 different scenarios with 2 different illumination and support conditions.

CASIA-FASD Dataset [10]: This dataset comprises 600 videos (150 real access and 450 attacks) of 50 subjects. It introduces face attacks with a varying degree of imaging quality, namely low quality (captured using an old USB camera with a resolution of 640×480 pixels), normal quality (captured using a new USB camera with a resolution of 480×640 pixels) and high quality (captured using a Sony NEX-5 with a resolution of 1920×1080 pixels). It also considers three different types of attacks including warped photo attacks, cut photo attacks and video attacks.

4.2   Experimental Protocols

In order to fairly measure performance of different face spoofing detection systems, we adopt the widely-used Half Total Error Rate (HTER) as the evaluation parameter. As the following equation shows, HTER is half of the sum of the

False Acceptance Rate (FAR) and the False Rejection Rate (FRR). Since both the FAR and the FRR depend on a threshold τ, increasing one usually decreases the other. For this reason, HTER is conventionally calculated in a specific operating point of the Receiver Operating Characteristic (ROC) curve in which the FAR is equal to the FRR, known as the Equal Error Rate (ERR). Apparently, the lower the HTER value is, the better the approach is.

$$\text{HTER} = \frac{1}{2}(\text{FAR} + \text{FRR}). \qquad (2)$$

Protocol I: In this evaluation protocol, we use the Replay-Attack dataset. This dataset is divided into three partitions: training, development and testing set. The training set is used for training the classifier itself and the development set is used for choosing the threshold τ on the EER. Finally, the testing set is used to report the HTER value.

Protocol II: Herein, we use the CASIA-FASD dataset which is divided into two disjoint subsets for training and testing (240 and 360 videos, respectively). The training subset is used to build a classifier and the testing set is used to report the HTER value.

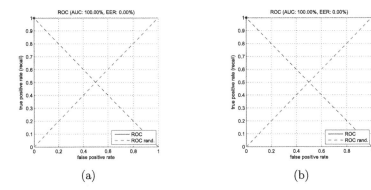

(a)   (b)

Fig. 3. ROC curves of Replay-Attack dataset when $I = 72$ & $C = 1$. (a) Development set (b) Test set

4.3   Effectiveness of the Proposed Scheme on Replay-Attack Dataset

Table 1 shows the performance of this countermeasure on Replay-Attack dataset in terms of HTER with different numbers of used DCT components C and different values of interval I. Note that, there is a limitation for interval I under a specific C. For instance, given $C = 1$, at least 4 frames are required as we perform 3-scale DCT on LBP features. Consequently, when $C = 1$, the maximum value of interval I is 72 due to the minimum number of frames contained in each video in this dataset is 221. Subject to limited space, only part of the parameter sittings are shown in Table 1.

Table 1. Results in HTER (%) of the proposed method on Replay-Attack and CASIA-FASD dataset. Here, C: number of used DCT components, I: interval for extracting frames, Dev: on development set and Test: on test set

C	I	Replay-Attack		CASIA-FASD
		Dev	Test	Test
1	1	0.00	0.00	20.00
	2	0.00	0.00	19.07
	3	0.00	0.00	20.00
	4	0.00	0.00	18.89
2	1	0.00	0.00	20.00
	2	0.00	0.00	19.07
	3	0.00	0.00	20.00
	4	0.00	0.00	19.26
3	1	0.00	0.00	18.89
	2	0.00	0.00	19.26
	3	0.00	0.00	19.07
	4	0.00	0.00	18.43
4	1	0.00	0.00	18.89
	2	0.00	0.00	20.00
	3	0.00	0.00	18.25
	4	0.00	0.00	18.06
5	1	0.00	0.00	18.89
	2	0.00	0.00	19.18
	3	0.00	0.00	19.18
	4	0.00	0.00	18.89

Surprisingly, all the parameter settings lead to HTER values of 0 on both development set and testing set of Replay-Attack dataset. In other words, all the parameter settings achieved perfect classification. Apparently, the greater I is, the fewer frames are involved, thus the faster the detection is and the lower the computational complexity is. Likewise, the less C is, the faster and the simpler the detection is. Therefore, we consider $I = 72$ & $C = 1$ as the best setting for the sake of efficiency and simplicity. Figure 3 shows the corresponding ROC curves when $I = 72$ & $C = 1$.

4.4 Effectiveness of the Proposed Scheme on CASIA-FASD Dataset

Table 1 also shows the HTER of this countermeasure on CASIA-FASD dataset with different numbers of used DCT components C and different interval values I. Same as Replay-Attack dataset, subject to the minimum number of frames contained in each video in CASIA-FASD dataset, there is a maximum value for interval I given a specific C. We also omit some of the results due to limited space.

From Table 1 we notice that while HTER value of the proposed countermeasure on this dataset fluctuates around 19.00%, $I = 4$ & $C = 4$ gives an HTER of 18.06s%, recording the best result on the testing set of CASIA-FASD dataset. Therefore, we consider $I = 4$ & $C = 4$ as the best setting for CASIA-FASD dataset. Figure 4 shows the corresponding ROC curve when $I = 4$ & $C = 4$. As for the relationship between the parameter setting (I and C) and performance fluctuation, it falls into one direction of our future work. Unlike perfect classification attained on Replay-Attack dataset, performance on this dataset is less satisfactory. We believe this is because CASIA-FASD dataset is more challenging than the former dataset. For instance, it incorporates cut photo attack which is a kind of printed 2D attacks. As it simulates eye blinking with perforated eyes, this new kind of attack is difficult to detect. In addition, CASIA-FASD dataset is more heterogeneous than Replay-Attack dataset as it contains three types of attacks (warped photo attack, cut photo attack and reply attack) captured in three different settings (low, normal and high resolutions).

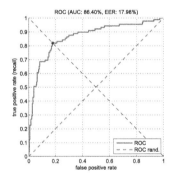

Fig. 4. ROC curve of CASIA dataset when $I = 4$ & $C = 4$

4.5   Comparisons with State of the Art

Finally, Table 2 shows a comparison among state-of-the-art methods. Consistent with our observation that CASIA-FASD dataset is more challenging than Replay-Attack dataset, all the methods show a better performance on Replay-Attack dataset than CASIA-FASD dataset.

We can see from Table 2 that the proposed approach achieves the best performance among other approaches. For Replay-Attack dataset, it recorded zero HTER, i.e., perfect classification. For CASIA-FASD dataset, it recorded 18.06% HTER which also outperforms all the other methods with a minimum superiority of 3.69%. Using LBP for feature extraction, Chingovska et al.'s methods [11] show moderate discriminability with about 15.00% HTER. The best performance

Table 2. Comparison of HTER (%) on test sets for the proposed method with respect to state-of-the-art methods.

	Algorithm	Replay-Attack	CASIA-FASD
Chingovska et al. (2012) [11]	LBP + LDA	13.87	-
	LBP + SVM	18.17	-
Pereira et al. (2013) [30]	Motion Correlation	11.79	30.33
	LBP	15.45	23.19
	LBP-TOP	8.51	23.75
Tirunagari et al.(2015) [21]	DMD + LBP + SVM^E	0.00	-
	DMD + LBP + SVM^F	3.75	21.75
	DMD + SVM^F	7.50	29.50
	PCA + SVM^F	21.50	33.50
	PCA + LBP + SVM^F	17.11	24.50
	PCA + LBP + SVM^E	20.50	-
Proposed method	LBP + MDCT + SVM	0.00	18.06

Here, E: on entire frames and F: on face regions

achieved in Pereira et al.'s work [30] is based on LBP-TOP and the corresponding HTER is 8.51% on Replay-Attack dataset. Although Tirunagari et al.'s method DMD + LBP + SVM^E [21] also gives an HTER of 0% on Replay-Attack dataset, it requires 240 frames from each video while the proposed pipeline only requires 4 frames. As face spoofing detection is aimed for real-time application, the fewer frames the approach uses, the less time the detection takes, thus, the higher the efficiency is and the better the approach is. Therefore, the proposed approach is better than approach DMD + LBP + SVM^E. More importantly, instead of the face regions, pipeline DMD + LBP + SVM^E requires the entire video frames. Once only the face regions are given (DMD + LBP + SVM^F), the performance degrades to 3.75% HTER. This degradation is made by the fact that the backgrounds of videos for different types of attacks in CASIA-FASD dataset are different which may well benefit the detection performance. However, in real life, this difference tends to be non-existent for a certain biometric system. From this point of view, the perfect classification attained by DMD + LBP + SVM^E is meaningless. With all these in mind, the proposed pipeline is superior to all the others including Tirunagari et al.'s method.

In addition to the excellent performance, our approach is of low complexity and high efficiency as it only requires a few of frames rather than the entire frames contained in a video. Besides, the implementation of both LBP and DCT operations are time-saving. For videos from Replay-Attack or CASIA-FASD dataset, it only takes about 0.12 s to obtain a LBP vector for each frame. Given a LBP matrix of a video from the two datasets, the calculation of a LBP-MDCT feature only costs about 0.02 s whatever the parameter sitting is. Moreover, taking advantage of the strong energy compaction property of DCT, only one or several DCT components are used in the stage of high-level descriptor extraction which realises dimension reduction. The scheme as a whole is thus easy to implement and efficient. With low complexity and high efficiency, the proposed method is very competitive and promising for face anti-spoofing which is aimed for real life scenario.

5 Conclusions and Future Work

The present paper addressed the problem of video-based face spoofing detection using LBP and multiscale DCT. $LBP_{8,1}^{u2}$ features are adopted as the low-level descriptors to exact spatial information while multiscale DCT are implemented along the ordinate axis of LBP features in order to take advantage of temporal information at the same time. Therefore, the resultant LBP-MDCT features represents spatial-temporal information. Excellent experimental results demonstrated that multiscale DCT can indeed capture facial dynamic information which makes a significant contribution to distinguish spoof attacks from valid access.

The proposed method was comprehensively evaluated on two benchmarking datasets using standard protocols and shown to be superior to other approaches reported to date. For Replay-Attack dataset, it recorded zero HTER, i.e., perfect classification. For CASIA-FASD dataset, it recorded 18.06% HTER which also outperforms all the other methods with a minimum superiority of 3.69%. We attribute this performance superiority to (1) the capacity of LBP to extract texture information on a frame-by-frame basis, (2) the capacity of multiscale DCT to extract temporal dynamics of video sequences and (3) the choice of pipeline within which multiscale DCT is deployed along the ordinate axis of LBP matrices to capture spatial-temporal information. Note that, instead of the strength of LBP or DCT alone, it is the unique combination of the two descriptors that lead to the superiority of the proposed method. In addition to the excellent performance, our approach is time-saving and very simple to conduct. Taking its outstanding performance, low complexity and high efficiency into account, the proposed method is very competitive and promising for practical application of face anti-spoofing.

Our focus of future research will include a further investigation into the relationship between the skipped frames and detection performance on CASIA-FASD dataset. It would also be interesting to exploit other types of LBP descriptor with the same pipeline and compare the performance. Another future research direction relates to replacing LBP or DCT with other effective operations in the context of using spatial-temporal information.

Acknowledgments. This work was supported by the National Natural Science Foundation of China (61272414) and the research funding of State Key Laboratory of Information Security (2016-MS-07).

References

1. Galbally, J., Marcel, S., Fierrez, J.: Biometric antispoofing methods: a survey in face recognition. IEEE Access **2**, 1530–1552 (2014)
2. Anjos, A., Marcel, S.: Counter-measures to photo attacks in face recognition: a public database and a baseline. In: 2011 IEEE International Joint Conference on Biometrics (IJCB), pp. 1–7. IEEE Press, Washington, DC (2011)
3. Galbally, J., Fierrez, J., Alonso-Fernandez, F., Martinez-Diaz, M.: Evaluation of direct attacks to fingerprint verification systems. Telecommun. Syst. **47**(3–4), 243–254 (2011)
4. Mjaaland, B.B., Bours, P., Gligoroski, D.: Walk the walk: attacking gait biometrics by imitation. In: Burmester, M., Tsudik, G., Magliveras, S., Ilić, I. (eds.) ISC 2010. LNCS, vol. 6531, pp. 361–380. Springer, Heidelberg (2011). doi:10.1007/978-3-642-18178-8_31
5. Chen, H., Valizadegan, H., Jackson, C., Soltysiak, S., Jain, A.K.: Fake hands: spoofing hand geometry systems. In: 2005 Biometrics Consortium Conference (BCC) (2005)
6. Bin, Q., Jian-Fei, P., Guang-Zhong, C., Ge-Guo, D.: The anti-spoofing study of vein identification system. In: International Conference on Computational Intelligence and Security (ICCIS), pp. 357–360 (2009)
7. Akhtar, Z., Fumera, G., Marcialis, G.L., Roli, F.: Evaluation of serial and parallel multibiometric systems under spoofing attacks. In: 5th IEEE International Conference on Biometrics: Theory, Applications and Systems (BTAS), pp. 283–288 (2012)
8. Tome, P., Vanoni, M., Marcel, S.: On the vulnerability of finger vein recognition to spoofing. In: International Conference of the Biometrics Special Interest Group (BIOSIG), pp. 1–10 (2014)
9. Tan, X., Li, Y., Liu, J., Jiang, L.: Face liveness detection from a single image with sparse low rank bilinear discriminative model. In: Daniilidis, K., Maragos, P., Paragios, N. (eds.) ECCV 2010. LNCS, vol. 6316, pp. 504–517. Springer, Heidelberg (2010). doi:10.1007/978-3-642-15567-3_37
10. Zhang, Z., Yan, J., Liu, S., Lei, Z., Yi, D., Li, S.: A face antispoofing database with diverse attacks. In: 2012 5th IAPR International Conference on Biometrics (ICB), pp. 26–31. IEEE Press (2012)
11. Chingovska, I., Anjos, A., Marcel, S.: On the effectiveness of local binary patterns in face anti-spoofing. In: International Conference of Biometrics Special Interest Group (BIOSIG), pp. 1–7. IEEE Press, Darmstadt (2012)
12. Erdogmus, N., Marcel, S.: Spoofing in 2D face recognition with 3D masks and anti-spoofing with kinect. In: 6th IEEE International Conference on Biometrics: Theory, Applications and Systems (BTAS), pp. 1–6 (2013)
13. Pinto, A., Schwartz, W.R., Pedrini, H., de Rezende Rocha, A.: Using visual rhythms for detecting video-based facial spoof attacks. IEEE Trans. Inf. Forensics Secur. **10**(5), 1025–1038 (2015)
14. Li, J., Wang, Y., Tan, T., Jain, A.K.: Live face detection based on the analysis of fourier spectra. Proc. SPIE **5404**, 296–303 (2004)
15. Peixoto, B., Michelassi, C., Rocha, A.: Face liveness detection under bad illumination conditions. In: 2011 18th IEEE International Conference on Image Processing (ICIP), pp. 3557–3560. IEEE Press, Brussels (2011)
16. Maatta, J., Hadid, A., Pietikäinen, M.: Face spoofing detection from single images using texture and local shape analysis. IET Biometrics **1**(1), 3–10 (2012)

17. Kose, N., Dugelay, J.L.: Classification of captured and recaptured images to detect photograph spoofing. In: 2012 International Conference on Informatics, Electronics and Vision (ICIEV), Dhaka, pp. 1027–1032 (2012)
18. Maatta, J., Hadid, A., Pietikäinen, M.: Face spoofing detection from single images using micro-texture analysis. In: 2011 International Joint Conference on Biometrics (IJCB), pp. 1–7. IEEE Press, Washington, DC (2011)
19. Nguyen, H.H., Nguyen-Son, H.-Q., Nguyen, T.D., Echizen, I.: Discriminating between computer-generated facial images and natural ones using smoothness property and local entropy. In: Shi, Y.-Q., Kim, H.J., Pérez-González, F., Echizen, I. (eds.) IWDW 2015. LNCS, vol. 9569, pp. 39–50. Springer, Heidelberg (2016). doi:10.1007/978-3-319-31960-5_4
20. de Freitas Pereira, T., Anjos, A., De Martino, J.M., Marcel, S.: *LBP–TOP* based countermeasure against face spoofing attacks. In: Park, J.-I., Kim, J. (eds.) ACCV 2012. LNCS, vol. 7728, pp. 121–132. Springer, Heidelberg (2013). doi:10.1007/978-3-642-37410-4_11
21. Tirunagari, S., Poh, N., Windridge, D., Iorliam, A., Suki, N., Ho, A.T.S.: Detection of face spoofing using visual dynamics. IEEE Trans. Inf. Forensics Secur. **10**(4), 762–777 (2015)
22. Arashloo, S.R., Kittler, J., Christmas, W.: Face spoofing detection based on multiple descriptor fusion using multiscale dynamic binarized statistical image features. IEEE Trans. Inf. Forensics Secur. **10**(11), 2396–2407 (2015)
23. Pinto, A., Pedrini, H., Schwartz, W.R., Rocha, A.: Face spoofing detection through visual codebooks of spectral temporal cubes. IEEE Trans. Image Process. **24**(12), 4726–4740 (2015)
24. da Silva Pinto, A., Pedrini, H., Schwartz, W., Rocha, A.: Video-based face spoofing detection through visual rhythm analysis. In: 2012 25th SIBGRAPI Conference on Graphics, Patterns and Images, Ouro Preto, pp. 221–228 (2012)
25. Viola, P., Jones, M.J.: Robust real-time face detection. Int. J. Comput. Vis. **57**(2), 137–154 (2004)
26. Arashloo, S.R., Kittler, J.: Class-specific kernel fusion of multiple descriptors for face verification using multiscale binarised statistical image features. IEEE Trans. Inf. Forensics Secur. **9**(12), 2100–2109 (2014)
27. Arashloo, S.R., Kittler, J.: Dynamic texture recognition using multiscale binarized statistical image features. IEEE Trans. Multimedia **16**(8), 2099–2109 (2014)
28. Chan, C.H., Tahir, M.A., Kittler, J., Pietikainen, M.: Multiscale local phase quantization for robust component-based face recognition using kernel fusion of multiple descriptors. IEEE Trans. Pattern Anal. Mach. Intell. **35**(5), 1164–1177 (2013)
29. Cortes, C., Vapnik, V.: Support-vector networks. Mach. Learn. **20**(3), 273–297 (1995)
30. de Freitas Pereira, T., Komulainen, J., Anjos, A., De Martino, J.M., Hadid, A., Pietikäinen, M., Marcel, S.: Face liveness detection using dynamic texture. EURASIP J. Image Video Process. **2014**(2), 1–15 (2014)

Source Cell-Phone Identification Using Spectral Features of Device Self-noise

Chao Jin, Rangding Wang$^{(\boxtimes)}$, Diqun Yan, Biaoli Tao, Yanan Chen,
and Anshan Pei

College of Information Science and Engineering,
Ningbo University, Ningbo, Zhejiang, China
wangrangding@nbu.edu.cn

Abstract. Source cell-phone identification has become a hot topic in multi-media forensics recently. In this paper, we propose a novel cell-phone identi-fication method based on the recorded speech files. Device self-noise is considered as the fingerprint of the cell-phone, and the self-noise is estimated from the near-silent segments of recording. Moreover, two categories of spectral features of self-noise, i.e., spectral shape features (SN-SSF) and spectral dis-tribution features (SN-SDF), are extracted for closed-set classification using SVM classifier. Experimental results show that the self-noise has the ability to identify the cell-phones of 24 different models, and identification accuracies of 89.23% and 94.53% have been obtained for SN-SSF and SN-SDF, respectively. To the best of our knowledge, it is the first attempt to comprehensively define the self-noise of cell-phone and furthermore apply it to source identification issue of audio forensics.

Keywords: Audio forensics · Source cell-phone identification · Self-noise · Noise estimation · Spectral features

1 Introduction

Nowadays, with the development of mobile internet and micro-chip industry, smart terminals become an indispensable part of our daily lives, more than just a communi-cation apparatus [1]. More and more people prefer to use the portable devices (e.g. smart mobile phone, pad) to capture the scene they saw and the sound they heard instead of professional devices such as SLR camera and audio recorder. However, the availability of numerous digital recording devices and massive amount of recording data has brought new issues and challenges concerning the multimedia security [2]. As a tech-nique used for inspecting the originality, authenticity, and integrity of multimedia data, multimedia forensics has become an attractive issue in information security field [3].

One of the most relevant applications of multimedia forensics is to identify the cell-phone used for producing the given digital recorded speech file, a problem called source cell-phone identification. This research direction attracts the interest of forensics community and some significant advances are developed in recent years [4–6]. Hanilci et al. [7] extracted information about the cell-phones from their speech records by using MFCCs and identify their brands and models. They claimed that the identification rates

© Springer International Publishing AG 2017
Y.Q. Shi et al. (Eds.): IWDW 2016, LNCS 10082, pp. 29–45, 2017.
DOI: 10.1007/978-3-319-53465-7_3

can reach 96.42% for a set of 14 different cell-phones in the experiments. Hereafter, their work [8] present a performance comparison of different acoustic features for source cell-phone identification. Mel-frequency, linear frequency and bark frequency cepstral coefficients (MFCC, LFCC and BFCC) and linear prediction cepstral coefficients (LPCC) were assessed and they found the baseline MFCC features was the best one. On the basis of some important researches concerning telephone handset identification [9–11], Kotropoulos [12] considered two raw feature vectors and their corresponding sketches (i.e. feature vectors of reduced size) as the intrinsic device characteristics. One of the feature vectors was obtained by averaging the log-spectrogram of a speech recording, and the other one was extracted from the Gaussian supervectors made by concatenating the mean values of the GMM components modelling the MFCCs. These feature vectors are then used for source phone identification and perfect identification rates was reported for a set of 21 cell-phones of various models from seven different brands. Inspired by Panagakis and Kotropoulos's work, Zou et al. [13] propose a source cell phone verification scheme based on sparse representation. They also employed Gaussian supervectors based on MFCCs to characterize the intrinsic fingerprint of the cell phone. And the experimental results have demonstrated that their scheme was feasible.

However, most existing strategies accomplished cell-phone identification task by using MFCCs or MFCC-based statistics as the classification feature vector. As the name implies, MFCCs are the variables calculated according to the frequency bands equally spaced on the mel-scale instead of the linearly-spaced frequency bands used in the normal cepstrum, which are mainly used in speech recognition application [14]. Although the MFCC-based features achieved satisfactory performance in source device identification, due to the fact that mel-scale bands approximate the human auditory system's response, their classification ability probably be interfered by some uncertain conditions, such as properties of speaker and speech content.

In order to explore a signature which can effectively capture the intrinsic fingerprint of the cell-phone, self-noise is considered as the unique identity for the cell-phones of the same model. Self-noise is referred to as the signal formed by the device itself and its characteristics are mainly influenced by the electronic components and circuit designs of the device. Indeed, the cell-phones of different models do not have exactly the same self-noise because the circuit design and electronics usage of cell-phones varies from a model to another, even though they are produced by the same manufacturers. Consequently, a promising method of cell-phone identification is proposed in terms of the self-noise in this paper. The experimental results demonstrate that the self-noise is capable of recognizing the cell-phones in our database, and the two self-noise-based feature sets SN-SSF and SN-SDF respectively achieve 3.19% and 8.49% improvements of classification rate compared with the features present in [7].

The rest of this paper is organized as follows. Section 2 briefly introduce the self-noise concept and investigate the attributes of self-noise. Then we elaborate on the entire approach of cell-phone identification by using the self-noise in Sect. 3. Section 4 shows how to implement the experiments, and also gives the testing results for 3 different feature sets. Finally, the conclusion is summarized and our future work is discussed in Sect. 5.

2 Self-noise

2.1 Definition of Self-noise

Self-noise of a device or system is the amount of noise generated by the device itself. In electronics all components produce their own noise so long as they are at any temperature above absolute zero [15, 16]. Therefore, the device's self-noise will be recorded as a digital signal, and being a part of the recording provided that the phone VOICE RECODER is working, even though there is no audio signal input. That is, self-noise could be recorded though the device is put in a perfectly silent environment.

Figure 1 shows the processing pipeline of a speech signal going through a cell-phone. It can be observed that the speech signal processing module mainly contains Microphone, A/D converter, Audio DSP, et al., and every unit consists of various electronic components. What's more, the self-noise is dominated by the noise generated by electronic components with no input signal, such as transducer, capacitance, resistance and transistor [17, 18]. Besides, the electromagnetic radio-frequency interference produced by communication module might contribute to the self-noise.

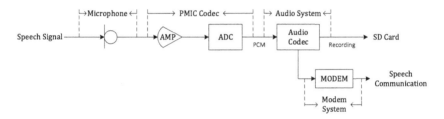

Fig. 1. Diagram of the speech signal processing module in cell-phones.

More specifically, self-noise of a cell-phone can be mainly classified into two categories, indicating the broad physical nature of the noise and their commonly used categorization, as follows: [19].

Electronic noise: (1) Thermal noise is generated by the random movements of thermally energized particles in an electric conductor. Thermal noise is intrinsic to all conductors and is present without any applied voltage. (2) Shot noise consists of random fluctuations of the electric current in an electrical conductor and is intrinsic to current flow. (3) Flicker noise has a spectrum that varies inversely with frequency as $1/f$, which results from a variety of effects in electronic devices. (4) Burst noise consists of step transitions of as high as several hundred millivolts, at random times and durations.

Electromagnetic noise: present at all frequencies and in particular at the radio frequency range (kHz to GHz range) where telecommunication systems operate.

The concept of self-noise indicates that the characteristics of self-noise is closely related to the structure and the constitution of device hardware. So self-noise can be considered as the fingerprint of a cell-phone due to the fact that there must be some differences in circuit design and electronics usage of the cell-phones between different models.

2.2 Properties of Self-noise

In order to figure out the properties of self-noise, we have investigated 25 cell-phones (two iPhone 5 devices) in 24 prevalent models of 7 brands and more details about these phones can be found in Table 1. The audio samples of self-noise were recorded by these devices in an anechoic recording studio with silent environment. To prevent the self-noise from the interference produced by other electric equipment, power source of the whole studio was cut off while the phones were recording.

Table 1. Cell-phones list and specifications.

Class ID	Brand	Model	Class ID	Brand	Model
H_1	HTC	D610t	A_1	Apple	iPhone 4s
H_2		D820t	A_2		iPhone 5
H_3		One M7	A_3		iPhone 5s
W_1	Huawei	Honor 6	A_4		iPhone 6
W_2		Honor 7	A_5		iPhone 6s
W_3		Mate 7	Z_1	Meizu	Meilan note
O_1	OPPO	Find 7	Z_2		MX2
O_2		Oneplus 1	Z_3		MX4
O_3		R831S	M_1	Mi	Mi 3
S_1	Samsung	Galaxy Note2	M_2		Mi 4
S_2		Galaxy S5	M_3		Redmi Note 1
S_3		Galaxy Win GT-I8558	M_4		Redmi Note 2

As we know, most self-noise sounds like hiss, but each of them possesses its own tone and pitch. Figure 2 sketches the self-noise waveforms of 8 cell-phones of 7 different brands, including 2 iPhone 5 devices. It can be seen that every self-noise keeps stable along the time axis. Furthermore, the amplitude of self-noise is so small that almost all sample values fluctuate between −0.002 and 0.002, except for the self-noise recorded by Mi 3.

In addition, we have examined temporal distribution for every self-noise, as shown in Fig. 3, which reveals that, all self-noise follows generalized Gaussian distribution, whereas they are not the same. The self-noise of Huawei honor 6 and Samsung Galaxy Note2 is sparser than the others. More real values used by Meizu Meilan note and OPPO find7 fall into the interval of [−0.001 0.001] when compared with other phones, so that the bars of all intervals in their distribution figures are filled with values. On the other hand, Fig. 3(c) and (d) are seemed to be identical because they belong to the 2 cell-phones of the same model iPhone 5.

For exploring the spectral characteristics of self-noise, a spectrogram is considered as the basic representation to visualize the spectrum of frequencies in the audio signal as they vary with time. Figure 4 presents the spectrograms of the aforementioned 8 cell-phones' self-noise. The self-noise spectrograms of the cell-phone within the same brand, the devices of Apple brand are taken as an example, are given in Fig. 5. From

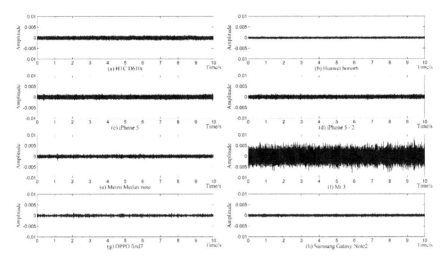

Fig. 2. Waveform of self-noise.

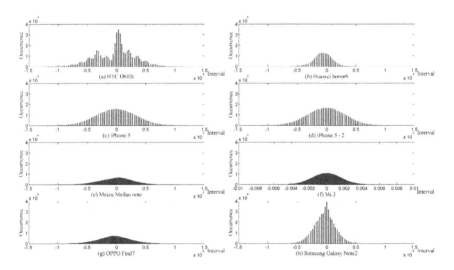

Fig. 3. Histogram of the sample values of self-noise.

the observation of these two figures, it can be found that the self-noises of different brand cell-phones have much differences in spectrograms. For instance, the energies of Mi 3's self-noise are obviously the strongest in all frequency bins spaced from 0–16 kHz; the spectral amplitude curve of Meizu Meilan note's self-noise is altering with a wavy trend along the frequency axis; and there is a severe drop at about 4000 Hz for the spectrogram of HTC D610t's self-noise. On the contrary, the spectrograms of the cell-phones within one brand are similar to some extent, though they are not the

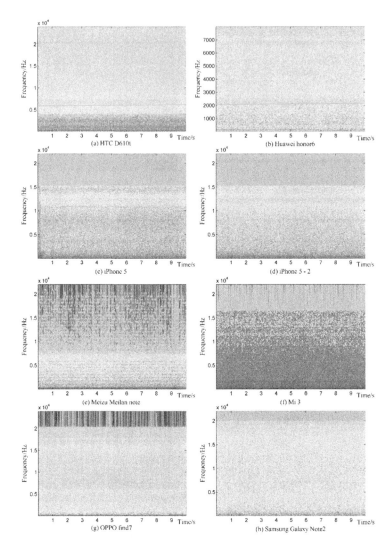

Fig. 4. Spectrograms of the self-noise of the cell-phone with different brands.

same. However, the spectrograms of the same model cell-phones are almost the same, as shown in Fig. 4(c) and (d).

Based on the above analysis, several spectral variables, that reveal the inherent changes in the spectrogram, are taken as the classification features to identify which model of the cell-phone dose a recording file belong to. And the detailed information about the spectral features will be discussed in Sect. 3.2.

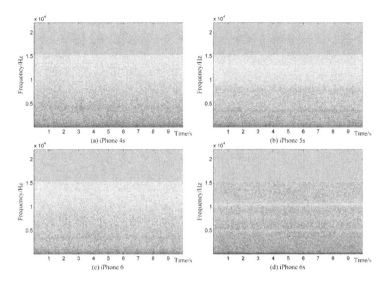

Fig. 5. Spectrograms of the self-noise of the cell-phone with Apple brand.

3 Cell-Phone Identification Using Self-noise

3.1 Self-noise Estimation

Self-noise is utilized as the basic feature for cell-phone source identification in this work. However, self-noise estimation is a challenging task because, instead of self-noise itself, just the recorded audio file is accessible to the examiner in the practical scenario of forensics. So, in this paper, a two-step method is proposed for self-noise estimation, which can be outlined as follows: (1) Near-silent segments extraction, (2) Background noise suppression.

(1) Near-silent Segments Extraction

The reason for estimating self-noise based on near-silent segments is, we think the near-silent part of the recording signal is mainly composed of self-noise and background noise, and it would not be contaminated with the sound response non-uniformity noise which is a dominate part in the comprehensive noise of the speech part [20].

We chose a self-adaptive VAD (Voice Activity Detection) which was developed in work [21] for near-silent segments estimation. As illustrated in Fig. 6(a) and (b), this method can identify the near-silent with a good performance. Note that VAD decision with the label "1" corresponds to speech segment and "0" corresponds to near-silent segment. However, Fig. 6(c) implies that some processed near-silent segments may still incorporate a few speech components due to the fact that no VAD method can perfectly locate the boundary between the speech and no-speech parts so far. To further eliminate the unneeded speech parts, a post-processing scheme is proposed for the near-silent segments $ns(i)$ obtained by the VAD according to the following equation:

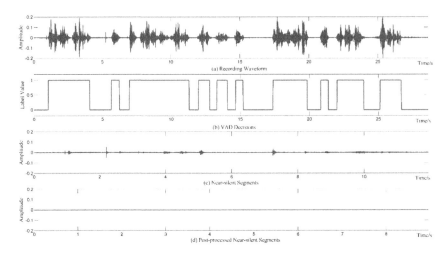

Fig. 6. Example of near-silent segments estimation using VAD.

$$nss(j) = ns(\text{find}|ns(i)|(<5 \times Thr)) \tag{1}$$

where Thr is the mean value of the first 40% samples of the $ns(i)$ after being sorted in ascending order, the function $\text{find}(\cdot)$ is used to locate and output the samples' positions of the $ns(i)$ when their absolute values are smaller than $(5 \times Thr)$.

After being processed by step 1, maybe several near-silent segments of a recording are obtained, and then we concatenate these segments into an integrated signal. Based on the experiments of the database in Sect. 4.1, around 30% samples of every recording is determined as the near-silent signal so the length of the original recording is reduced from 3 s to about 1 s.

(2) Background Noise Suppression

In order to get the actual self-noise from near-silent segments, background noise should be suppressed as good as possible. First, we scrutinized the background noise component for all cell-phones by using a modified spectral subtraction method [22, 23] which is demonstrated according to the pseudo-codes of Algorithm I, as depicted in Fig. 7. Then a universal model of background noise is calculated according to Eq. (2) based on 24000 recording clips of all 24 cell-phones, 1000 audios for each cell-phone.

$$|BN_{mean}(k)| = \frac{1}{24}\sum_{i=1}^{24}\left(\frac{1}{N}\sum_{n=1}^{N}|BN_i(k,n)|\right) \tag{2}$$

where i denotes the cell-phone index; BN_i is defined as the spectrogram of background noise and $BN_i(k,n)$ is the spectral coefficients of the kth $(1 \leq k \leq K)$ frequency bin and n^{th} $(1 \leq n \leq N)$ frame in STFT domain, where K represents the frequency bin number and N means the total frame number of an audio sample. Note, 1024 is set as the number of STFT used through the entire work, which results in a fixed K value equals 513 $(1024/2 + 1)$ owing to the symmetry of STFT output; while N varies with the

---

Algorithm I: Background Noise Calculation
Input: Spectrogram of Near-silent Segment$|NS(k,n)|$, Spectrum of Self-noise$|SN_{mean}(k)|$
Output: Spectrogram of Calculated Background Noise $|BN(k,n)|$
Parameters: Scaling Factor $\alpha_1 = 3$, Gain Compensation Factor $\beta_1 = 0.1$

if$|NS(k,n)| > \alpha_1 \times |SN_{mean}(k)|$
$\quad |BN(k,n)| = |NS(k,n)| - \alpha_1 \times |SN_{mean}(k)|$;
else
$\quad |BN(k,n)| = \beta_1 \times |NS(k,n)|$;
end

Algorithm II:Self-noise Estimation
Input: Spectrogram of Near-silent Segment$|NS(k,n)|$, Spectrum of Calculated Background
Noise $|BN_{mean}(k)|$
Output of Stage 1: Spectrogram of Estimated Self-noise$|SN_{estimated}(k,n)|$
Output of Stage 2: Filtered Estimated Self-noise$|SN_{filtered}(n)|$
Parameters: Scaling Factors$\alpha_2 = 1, \varphi = 3, \omega = 1$, Gain Compensation Factor $\beta_2 = 0.9$
Functions:
$\quad$median($\cdot$):Calculate the median value for every frequency bin along the time axis
$\quad$ifft($\cdot$): Inverse Fast FourierTransform for reconstructing the temporal signal

Stage 1:

if$|NS(k,n)| > \alpha_2 \times |BN_{mean}(k)|$
$\quad |SN_{estimated}(k,n)| = |NS(k,n)| - \alpha_2 \times |BN_{mean}(k)|$;
else
$\quad |SN_{estimated}(k,n)| = \beta_2 \times |NS(k,n)|$;
end

Stage 2:

$|SN_{median}(k)| = $ median($|SN_{estimated}(k,n)|$);

if$|NS(k,n)| \geq \varphi \times |SN_{median}(k)|$
$\quad |SN_{filtered}(k,n)| = \omega \times |SN_{median}(k)|$;
else
$\quad |SN_{filtered}(k,n)| = |SN_{estimated}(k,n)|$;
end

$$|SN_{filtered}(n)| = \text{ifft}(|SN_{filtered}(k,n)|);$$

Fig. 7. Pseudo-code of the algorithms of background noise calculation and self-noise estimation

duration of the given audios. The meaning of k, n, K and N is also applicable to the equations in the rest of this paper.

Therefore, the self-noise of a given cell-phone with unknown source can be acquired by subtracting the universal background noise from near-silent signal. In addition, to make the estimated self-noise not being contaminated with the residual background noise, a filtering scheme is designed. The complete procedure of self-noise estimation is elucidated by the pseudo-code of Algorithm II in Fig. 7.

Figure 8 exemplifies the spectrograms of a near-silent segment and its corresponding self-noise. It can be inspected from Fig. 5(b) and Fig. 8(b) that the true self-noise recorded by iPhone 5s is the most similar one to the estimated self-noise among the Apple series cell-phones, which is illustrated by Fig. 8(c) as well. As a result, the two-step method is qualified for estimating the self-noise of a given recorded speech with unknown source. Note that Figs. 4, 5 and 8 are best viewed in color.

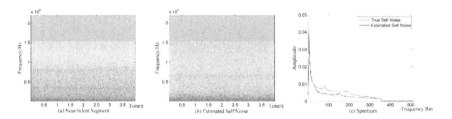

Fig. 8. Comparison of the estimated self-noise and the true self-noise (iPhone 5s).

3.2 Feature Extraction

To achieve the goal of cell-phone source identification, the discriminative features which can capture the differences among all cell-phone self-noise should be constructed. In this paper, spectral distribution features and spectral shape features were extracted for characterizing the spectrogram properties. These spectral features have shown their effectiveness for many applications, including event detection, music retrieval, and sound classification [24, 25]. A brief description of them is provided as follows:

(1) Spectral Distribution Features (SN-SDF):

$$f_{SD}(k) = \frac{1}{N} \sum\nolimits_{n=1}^{N} \log_{10} |SN_i(k,n)| \tag{3}$$

(2) Spectral Shape Features (SN-SSF):

4 Experiments

4.1 Experimental Setup

In our experiment, a speech database was built to effectively evaluate the performance of the proposed method. The database consists of the recorded audio files of

Table 2. Spectral shape features list and specifications.

Feature variable	Equation	Specification
$f_{Cen}(n)$	$\dfrac{\sum_{k=1}^{K}(k-1)\cdot|SN_i(k,n)|^2}{\sum_{k=1}^{K}|SN_i(k,n)|^2}$	Spectral centroid: the center of gravity of the spectral energy
$f_{Spre}(n)$	$\sqrt{\dfrac{\sum_{k=1}^{K}[(k-1)-f_{Cen}(n)]^2\times|SN_i(k,n)|^2}{\sum_{k=1}^{K}|SN_i(k,n)|^2}}$	Spectral spread: the concentration of the power spectrum around the spectral centroid
$f_{Dec}(n)$	$\begin{cases}\dfrac{|SN_i(k,n)|-|SN_i(1,n)|}{\sum_{k=2}^{K}|SN_i(k,n)|}, & k=1 \\[3mm] \dfrac{\sum_{k=2}^{K}\frac{1}{k-1}(|SN_i(k,n)|-|SN_i(1,n)|)}{\sum_{k=2}^{K}|SN_i(k,n)|}, & k>1\end{cases}$	Spectral decrease: the steepness of decrease of the spectral envelop over frequencies
$f_{Slo}(n)$	$\dfrac{\sum_{k=1}^{K}k\cdot|SN_i(k,n)|-\frac{K+1}{2}\sum_{k=1}^{K}|SN_i(k,n)|}{\sum_{k=1}^{K}k(k-K-2)+K\cdot(K+2)^2/4}$	Spectral slope: the slope of the spectral shape
$f_{Cre}(n)$	$\dfrac{\max\limits_{1\le k<K}|SN_i(k,n)|}{\sum_{k=1}^{K}|SN_i(k,n)|}$	Spectral crest factor: the tonalness of the audio signal
$f_{Flat}(n)$	$\dfrac{e^{\frac{1}{K}\sum_{k=1}^{K}\log|SN_i(k,n)|}}{\frac{1}{K}\sum_{k=1}^{K}|SN_i(k,n)|}$	Spectral flatness: how noise like a signal is
$f_{TPR}(n)$	$\dfrac{E_T(n)}{\sum_{k=1}^{K}|SN_i(k,n)|^2}$	Spectral tonal power ratio: the tonalness of signal. $E_T(n)\ge 0.0005$
$f_{Flux}(n)$	$\begin{cases}0, & n=1 \\[2mm] \frac{1}{K}\cdot\sqrt{\sum_{k=1}^{K}\left(|SN_i(k,n)|-|SN_i(k,n-1)|\right)^2}, & n>1\end{cases}$	Spectral flux: the amount of change in the spectral shape
$f_{Roll}(n)$	$i\big|_{\sum_{k=1}^{i}|SN_i(k,n)|=\rho\cdot\sum_{k=1}^{K}SN_i(k,n)}$	Spectral rolloff: the bandwidth of the analyzed frame. $\rho=0.85$
$f_{Ske}(n)$	$E[(|SN_i(\cdot,n)|-\mu/\sigma)^2]$	Spectral skewness: the asymmetry of the distribution of spectral coefficients
$f_{Kur}(n)$	$\dfrac{E[|SN_i(\cdot,n)|-\mu/\sigma)^4]}{(E[(|SN_i(\cdot,n)|-\mu/\sigma)^2])^2}$	Spectral kurtosis: measures the peakedness of the distribution of spectral coefficients

24 cell-phones shown in Table 1. 12 speakers of 6 females and 6 males were invited to participate in our recording project. Each speaker needs to read the given content at normal speed, which lasts about 5 min. The recording environment is a relatively quiet

office and the recorders of the 24 devices were turned on/off simultaneously by the stuff. Hence, 12 speech recordings were recorded for every cell-phone. Then each recording was segmented into 3-second-long clips and 1000 speech clips for each cell-phone were obtained.

Combined with the support vector machine LIBSVM [26, 27], half of the samples was randomly selected for training the model and the remaining was used for testing. It should be noted that all features of the training and testing sets were normalized to the range [0 1] before being loaded into the LIBSVM. In this work, the LIBSVM with RBF kernel implemented in the data mining tool WEKA-3.6 was utilized. Additionally, the two key parameters C (referred to as cost parameter) and γ (referred to as gamma parameter) of LIBSVM were optimized for every feature set by using one of the meta-classifiers CVParameterSelection assembled in WEKA.

4.2   Experimental Results

4.2.1   Result of SN-SSF

All of the spectral shape features were extracted frame by frame for the speech samples. Consequently, the feature dimension depends on the total length of each sample. To avoid feature dimension mismatch, we proposed to use first four moments for temporal feature integration approach. Specifically, first four moments such as mean f_{*_mean}, variance f_{*_var}, skewness f_{*_ske}, and kurtosis f_{*_kur} were calculated over all frames of an individual speech clip, where $*$ represents the spectral shape features defined in Table 2. So, 44 (11×4) dimensional features were constructed for every sample.

Table 3. Classification result of SN-SSF (%).

AL	H_1	H_2	H_3	W_1	W_2	W_3	A_1	A_2	A_3	A_4	A_5	Z_1	Z_2	Z_3	M_1	M_2	M_3	M_4	O_1	O_2	O_3	S_1	S_2	S_3
H_1	85.6	11.2	0.2	0.0	0.0	0.0	0.4	0.4	0.0	0.0	0.0	0.6	0.0	0.6	0.0	0.0	0.0	0.0	0.4	0.0	0.4	0.2	0.0	0.0
H_2	15.0	82.4	1.4	0.0	0.0	0.0	0.2	0.2	0.0	0.2	0.0	0.0	0.0	0.2	0.0	0.0	0.0	0.2	0.0	0.0	0.2	0.0	0.0	0.0
H_3	0.6	0.0	92.4	0.0	0.6	0.0	0.2	0.4	1.0	0.0	0.4	0.0	0.0	0.2	0.2	0.2	0.6	0.2	1.2	0.6	0.6	0.0	0.4	0.2
W_1	0.2	0.0	0.2	86.6	10.4	2.0	0.2	0.0	0.0	0.0	0.0	0.0	0.0	0.2	0.0	0.0	0.0	0.0	0.0	0.0	0.0	0.0	0.2	0.0
W_2	0.0	0.2	0.0	9.8	88.0	1.6	0.0	0.0	0.0	0.0	0.0	0.0	0.0	0.0	0.0	0.0	0.0	0.4	0.0	0.0	0.0	0.0	0.0	0.0
W_3	0.2	0.0	0.0	4.2	3.0	92.4	0.0	0.0	0.0	0.0	0.0	0.0	0.0	0.0	0.0	0.0	0.0	0.0	0.0	0.0	0.2	0.0	0.0	0.0
A_1	0.0	0.0	0.4	0.4	0.0	0.2	77.4	11.2	2.2	6.2	0.2	0.4	0.0	0.4	0.2	0.0	0.2	0.2	0.0	0.2	0.2	0.0	0.2	0.0
A_2	0.0	0.0	0.6	0.0	0.0	0.0	19.8	70.0	2.2	5.2	0.2	0.2	0.0	0.0	0.0	0.0	0.4	0.2	0.2	0.6	0.0	0.4	0.0	0.0
A_3	0.0	0.0	0.2	0.2	0.0	0.0	3.6	4.2	80.0	9.8	0.0	0.0	0.0	0.2	0.0	0.2	0.2	0.4	0.4	0.2	0.2	0.2	0.0	0.0
A_4	0.2	0.2	0.0	0.4	0.2	0.0	13.6	6.6	5.2	71.2	0.6	0.0	0.0	0.2	0.2	0.0	0.2	0.4	0.4	0.0	0.2	0.0	0.0	0.2
A_5	0.0	0.0	1.0	0.0	0.4	0.0	1.8	1.2	1.8	0.0	92.0	0.0	0.2	0.0	0.0	0.0	0.8	0.0	0.0	0.0	0.8	0.0	0.0	0.0
Z_1	0.0	0.0	0.0	0.2	0.0	0.0	0.2	0.2	0.4	0.0	0.0	92.4	0.2	4.8	0.4	0.8	0.0	0.2	0.0	0.0	0.0	0.0	0.2	0.0
Z_2	0.0	0.0	0.0	0.0	0.0	0.0	0.2	0.0	0.0	0.0	0.4	0.0	99.2	0.0	0.0	0.0	0.0	0.0	0.0	0.0	0.0	0.2	0.0	0.0
Z_3	0.0	0.0	0.0	0.0	0.0	0.0	0.0	0.4	0.0	0.0	0.0	5.2	0.2	90.8	0.0	2.2	0.0	0.8	0.0	0.0	0.0	0.2	0.2	0.0
M_1	0.0	0.0	0.2	0.0	0.0	0.2	1.2	0.6	0.4	0.2	0.2	0.0	0.0	0.0	94.4	0.0	0.0	0.4	1.0	0.0	0.8	0.2	0.0	0.2
M_2	0.0	0.0	0.0	0.4	0.0	0.0	0.2	0.2	0.2	0.0	0.2	1.2	0.2	0.4	0.2	96.4	0.0	0.0	0.0	0.0	0.2	0.2	0.0	0.0
M_3	0.0	0.0	0.0	0.0	0.0	0.0	0.6	0.4	0.0	0.2	0.2	0.0	0.2	0.0	0.2	0.0	97.4	0.2	0.0	0.0	0.0	0.4	0.0	0.2
M_4	0.0	0.0	0.0	0.0	0.0	0.0	0.0	0.2	0.6	0.0	0.0	2.2	0.0	3.0	0.0	1.2	0.0	91.6	0.2	0.0	0.0	0.8	0.0	0.0
O_1	0.4	0.2	0.6	0.0	0.0	0.2	0.2	0.0	0.4	0.0	0.0	0.2	0.8	0.0	0.0	0.0	0.2	0.8	92.6	1.8	0.0	0.6	0.0	1.0
O_2	0.0	0.0	0.2	0.0	0.0	0.0	0.0	0.2	0.0	0.0	0.0	0.0	0.8	0.0	0.2	0.0	0.2	0.0	1.6	95.8	0.4	0.0	0.4	0.2
O_3	0.2	0.0	0.4	0.0	0.0	0.0	0.8	1.2	0.6	0.2	0.6	0.0	0.0	0.0	0.0	0.0	0.0	0.2	0.6	0.0	95.0	0.0	0.0	0.2
S_1	0.0	0.0	0.0	0.0	0.0	0.2	0.0	0.8	0.8	0.2	0.0	0.0	0.0	1.0	0.0	0.0	0.2	0.6	0.6	0.0	0.2	94.0	0.2	0.6
S_2	0.0	0.0	0.8	0.4	0.0	0.0	0.0	0.4	0.4	0.0	0.2	0.0	0.4	0.0	0.6	0.0	0.2	0.0	6.6	1.8	0.2	0.0	88.0	0.0
S_3	0.4	0.2	0.2	0.0	0.0	0.0	0.0	0.0	0.2	0.2	0.0	0.0	0.0	0.0	0.0	0.0	0.0	0.6	1.6	0.4	0.0	0.2	0.0	96.0

The 12000 samples were taken as the input data of LIBSVM with $C = 24.9$, $\gamma = 2.2$ for training a model, and the remaining 12000 samples were used for estimating the confusion matrix of these features, as described in Table 2. Herein, the PL and AL are defined as predict label and actual label, respectively. In particular, the first numeric row of Table 3 means that 85.6% of H_1 is classified as H_1, 11.2% of H_1 as H_2, 0.2% of H_1 as H_3, 0.4% of H_1 as A_1, etc. It can be observed that the spectral shape features achieve a satisfactory classification accuracy in total. However, the worst ability of this feature set occurred in identifying the devices of Apple series except iPhone 6s. The average identification rate of these 4 cell-phones just reaches 74.65%. Moreover, about one tenth of HTC D820t and HTC D610t's samples are misclassified as each other, and the similar phenomenon happened to Huawei honor series. This due to the fact that HTC D610t has the similar self-noise with HTC D820t and the self-noise of the two Huawei honor devices are similar as well.

4.2.2   Result of SN-SDF

As mentioned in Sect. 3.1, the number of Fast Fourier Transform is 1024 which leads to 513 dimensional spectral distribution features. The feature set may be too large to guarantee all the features are mutually independent. However, the redundant features do not contribute to improving the detection accuracy, what's worse, they will affect the performance of the feature set. To choose the best subset of spectral distribution features, which is referred to as SN-SDF, the attribute evaluator *CfsSubsetEval* with *BestFirst* search method was used and 50 dimensional features were acquired. Moreover, the parameters C and γ of LIBSVM were set as 24.3 and 2.1, respectively.

Table 4.   Classification result of SN-SDF (%).

AL	\multicolumn{24}{c}{PL (Predict Label)}																							
	H_1	H_2	H_3	W_1	W_2	W_3	A_1	A_2	A_3	A_4	A_5	Z_1	Z_2	Z_3	M_1	M_2	M_3	M_4	O_1	O_2	O_3	S_1	S_2	S_3
H_1	87.0	12.8	0.0	0.0	0.0	0.0	0.0	0.0	0.0	0.0	0.0	0.2	0.0	0.0	0.0	0.0	0.0	0.0	0.0	0.0	0.0	0.0	0.0	0.0
H_2	12.2	87.4	0.4	0.0	0.0	0.0	0.0	0.0	0.0	0.0	0.0	0.0	0.0	0.0	0.0	0.0	0.0	0.0	0.0	0.0	0.0	0.0	0.0	0.0
H_3	0.0	0.0	99.0	0.0	0.8	0.0	0.0	0.0	0.0	0.0	0.0	0.0	0.0	0.0	0.0	0.0	0.0	0.0	0.0	0.0	0.0	0.2	0.0	0.0
W_1	0.0	0.0	0.0	91.6	6.4	0.8	0.2	0.0	0.0	0.0	0.0	0.6	0.0	0.0	0.0	0.4	0.0	0.0	0.0	0.0	0.0	0.0	0.0	0.0
W_2	0.0	0.0	0.4	9.4	89.8	0.0	0.0	0.0	0.0	0.0	0.0	0.0	0.0	0.0	0.0	0.0	0.0	0.0	0.0	0.0	0.0	0.4	0.0	0.0
W_3	0.0	0.0	0.0	0.6	3.2	94.6	0.0	0.0	0.0	0.0	0.0	0.2	0.0	0.0	0.0	0.0	0.0	1.0	0.0	0.0	0.0	0.0	0.0	0.0
A_1	0.0	0.0	0.0	0.2	0.4	0.0	90.8	0.4	3.2	5.0	0.0	0.0	0.0	0.0	0.0	0.0	0.0	0.0	0.0	0.0	0.0	0.0	0.0	0.0
A_2	0.0	0.0	0.0	0.0	0.0	0.0	1.0	97.6	0.4	0.6	0.0	0.0	0.0	0.0	0.0	0.0	0.0	0.0	0.0	0.0	0.0	0.4	0.0	0.0
A_3	0.0	0.0	0.0	0.0	0.0	0.0	7.2	0.2	81.0	11.0	0.0	0.0	0.0	0.0	0.0	0.0	0.0	0.0	0.0	0.0	0.0	0.2	0.4	0.0
A_4	0.0	0.0	0.2	0.0	0.0	0.0	15.4	0.0	6.4	78.0	0.0	0.0	0.0	0.0	0.0	0.0	0.0	0.0	0.0	0.0	0.0	0.0	0.0	0.0
A_5	0.0	0.0	0.0	0.0	0.0	0.0	0.8	0.0	0.0	0.0	99.0	0.0	0.0	0.0	0.0	0.2	0.0	0.0	0.0	0.0	0.0	0.0	0.0	0.0
Z_1	0.0	0.0	0.0	1.0	0.2	0.2	0.0	0.2	0.0	0.0	0.0	96.0	0.0	1.4	0.0	0.4	0.0	0.6	0.0	0.0	0.0	0.0	0.0	0.0
Z_2	0.0	0.0	0.0	0.4	0.0	0.2	0.0	0.0	0.0	0.0	0.0	0.2	99.0	0.0	0.0	0.0	0.0	0.0	0.0	0.0	0.0	0.2	0.0	0.0
Z_3	0.2	0.0	0.0	0.0	0.0	0.0	0.0	0.0	0.0	0.2	0.0	1.6	0.0	96.2	0.0	0.0	0.0	1.8	0.0	0.0	0.0	0.0	0.0	0.0
M_1	0.0	0.0	0.0	0.0	0.6	0.0	0.2	0.0	0.0	0.0	0.0	0.0	0.0	0.0	97.8	0.0	0.0	0.0	0.0	0.0	0.0	1.2	0.0	0.2
M_2	0.0	0.0	0.0	2.4	1.4	0.0	0.0	0.0	0.0	0.0	0.0	0.0	0.0	0.0	0.0	96.0	0.0	0.0	0.0	0.0	0.0	0.2	0.0	0.0
M_3	0.0	0.0	0.0	0.0	0.2	0.0	0.2	0.0	0.2	0.4	0.0	0.0	0.0	0.0	0.0	0.0	99.0	0.0	0.0	0.0	0.0	0.0	0.0	0.0
M_4	0.8	0.2	0.0	0.6	0.0	0.0	0.0	0.0	0.0	0.0	0.0	0.2	0.0	0.8	0.0	0.0	0.0	97.2	0.0	0.2	0.0	0.0	0.0	0.0
O_1	0.0	0.0	0.0	0.0	0.0	0.0	0.0	0.0	0.0	0.0	0.0	0.0	0.0	0.0	0.0	0.0	0.0	0.0	98.6	0.4	0.0	1.0	0.0	0.0
O_2	0.0	0.0	0.0	0.0	0.0	0.0	0.0	0.0	0.0	0.0	0.0	0.0	0.0	0.4	0.0	0.0	0.0	0.0	0.0	99.6	0.0	0.0	0.0	0.0
O_3	0.0	0.0	0.0	0.0	0.0	0.2	0.0	0.0	0.0	0.0	0.0	0.0	0.0	0.0	0.0	0.0	0.0	0.0	0.0	0.0	99.8	0.0	0.0	0.0
S_1	0.0	0.0	0.0	0.0	0.4	0.0	0.0	0.0	0.0	0.0	0.0	0.0	0.0	0.0	0.0	0.0	0.0	0.0	0.0	0.0	0.0	98.4	0.2	1.0
S_2	0.0	0.0	0.0	0.0	0.2	0.0	0.0	0.0	0.0	0.0	0.0	0.0	0.0	0.0	0.0	0.0	0.0	0.0	0.0	0.0	0.0	0.0	95.4	4.4
S_3	0.0	0.0	0.0	0.0	0.0	0.0	0.0	0.0	0.0	0.0	0.0	0.0	0.0	0.0	0.0	0.0	0.0	0.0	0.0	0.0	0.0	0.2	0.0	99.8

Table 4 shows the confusion matrix of SN-SDF and the total identification accuracy 94.53% can be calculated from it. Compared with SN-SSF, of which total identification accuracy is 89.23%, SN-SDF has the better classification ability for all cell-phones. It is dramatic that it compensates for SN-SSF's drawbacks and significantly improves the performance in classifying the cell-phones of Apple brand. For iPhone devices, the averaged improvement of detection rate is 11.16%. In addition, these features gets excellent identification accuracies (higher than 95.4%) for Meizu, Mi, OPPO and Samsung devices. More than 99% samples can be correctly recognized for HTC One M7, iPhone 6s, Meizu MX2, Mi Redmi Note 1, OPPO Oneplus 1, OPPO R831S, and Samsung Galaxy Win GT-I8558.

4.2.3 Comparison

For the sake of assessing the proposed method comprehensively, a typical MFCC-based algorithm [7] for source cell-phone identification reviewed in section Introduction was evaluated based on our database. The features in that work are referred to as 12 dimensional MFCCs and their first-order derivative coefficients of 36 dimensions, which are extracted frame by frame. To solve the problem of feature dimension mismatch, the mean value of every feature was calculated along the time axis and a 48-dimensional feature vector was acquired for each speech sample. What's more, to guarantee that Hanilci's method can achieve the best performance, the parameter C and γ of LIBSVM classifier were set as 8 and 0.3 respectively after applying the same parameter optimization scheme.

Table 5. Classification result of Hanilci's features (%).

AL	H_1	H_2	H_3	W_1	W_2	W_3	A_1	A_2	A_3	A_4	A_5	Z_1	Z_2	Z_3	M_1	M_2	M_3	M_4	O_1	O_2	O_3	S_1	S_2	S_3
H_1	44.0	55.6	0.4	0.0	0.0	0.0	0.0	0.0	0.0	0.0	0.0	0.0	0.0	0.0	0.0	0.0	0.0	0.0	0.0	0.0	0.0	0.0	0.0	0.0
H_2	22.0	78.0	0.0	0.0	0.0	0.0	0.0	0.0	0.0	0.0	0.0	0.0	0.0	0.0	0.0	0.0	0.0	0.0	0.0	0.0	0.0	0.0	0.0	0.0
H_3	1.6	2.0	96.4	0.0	0.0	0.0	0.0	0.0	0.0	0.0	0.0	0.0	0.0	0.0	0.0	0.0	0.0	0.0	0.0	0.0	0.0	0.0	0.0	0.0
W_1	0.0	0.0	0.0	68.4	17.8	12.4	0.0	0.0	0.0	0.0	0.0	0.0	0.0	0.0	0.0	1.4	0.0	0.0	0.0	0.0	0.0	0.0	0.0	0.0
W_2	0.0	0.0	0.0	5.8	93.0	0.8	0.0	0.0	0.0	0.0	0.0	0.0	0.0	0.0	0.0	0.4	0.0	0.0	0.0	0.0	0.0	0.0	0.0	0.0
W_3	0.0	0.0	0.0	4.4	4.8	90.8	0.0	0.0	0.0	0.0	0.0	0.0	0.0	0.0	0.0	0.0	0.0	0.0	0.0	0.0	0.0	0.0	0.0	0.0
A_1	0.0	0.0	0.0	0.0	0.0	0.0	46.8	1.8	20.4	31.0	0.0	0.0	0.0	0.0	0.0	0.0	0.0	0.0	0.0	0.0	0.0	0.0	0.0	0.0
A_2	0.0	0.0	0.0	0.0	0.0	0.0	2.6	97.0	0.0	0.0	0.0	0.0	0.0	0.0	0.0	0.0	0.0	0.0	0.0	0.0	0.0	0.0	0.0	0.0
A_3	0.0	0.0	0.0	0.0	0.0	0.0	10.4	1.4	72.0	16.2	0.0	0.0	0.0	0.0	0.0	0.0	0.0	0.0	0.0	0.0	0.0	0.0	0.0	0.0
A_4	0.0	0.0	0.0	0.0	0.0	0.0	15.4	0.0	28.0	56.6	0.0	0.0	0.0	0.0	0.0	0.0	0.0	0.0	0.0	0.0	0.0	0.0	0.0	0.0
A_5	0.0	0.0	0.0	0.0	0.0	0.0	5.4	0.8	0.0	1.0	91.6	0.0	0.0	0.0	1.2	0.0	0.0	0.0	0.0	0.0	0.0	0.0	0.0	0.0
Z_1	0.0	0.0	0.0	1.8	0.0	0.6	0.0	0.0	0.0	0.0	0.0	97.0	0.2	0.4	0.0	0.0	0.0	0.0	0.0	0.0	0.0	0.0	0.0	0.0
Z_2	0.0	0.0	0.0	0.0	0.0	0.8	0.0	0.0	0.0	0.0	0.0	5.0	92.6	0.0	0.0	0.0	0.0	0.0	1.6	0.0	0.0	0.0	0.0	0.0
Z_3	0.0	0.0	0.0	0.0	0.0	0.0	0.0	0.0	0.0	0.0	0.0	0.2	0.0	96.4	0.0	0.0	0.0	3.2	0.0	0.0	0.0	0.2	0.0	0.0
M_1	0.0	0.0	0.0	0.0	0.0	0.0	0.6	24.4	0.8	0.6	0.4	0.0	0.0	0.0	73.2	0.0	0.0	0.0	0.0	0.0	0.0	0.0	0.0	0.0
M_2	0.0	0.0	0.0	5.4	11.8	4.0	0.0	0.0	0.0	0.0	0.0	0.0	0.0	0.0	0.0	78.8	0.0	0.0	0.0	0.0	0.0	0.0	0.0	0.0
M_3	0.0	0.0	0.0	0.0	0.0	0.0	0.0	0.0	0.2	0.0	0.0	0.0	0.0	0.0	0.0	0.0	99.8	0.0	0.0	0.0	0.0	0.0	0.0	0.0
M_4	0.0	0.0	0.0	0.2	0.0	0.0	0.0	0.0	0.0	0.0	0.0	0.0	0.0	0.0	0.4	0.0	0.0	97.2	0.0	0.0	0.0	2.2	0.0	0.0
O_1	0.0	0.0	0.0	0.0	0.0	0.0	0.0	0.0	0.0	0.0	0.0	0.0	0.0	0.0	0.0	0.0	0.0	0.0	98.2	0.0	0.0	1.8	0.0	0.0
O_2	0.0	0.0	0.0	0.0	0.0	0.0	0.0	0.0	0.0	0.0	0.0	0.0	0.0	0.0	0.0	0.0	0.0	0.0	0.0	98.0	0.0	0.0	0.0	2.0
O_3	0.0	0.0	0.2	0.0	0.0	0.0	0.0	0.0	0.0	0.0	0.0	0.0	0.0	0.0	0.0	0.0	0.0	0.0	0.0	0.0	99.8	0.0	0.0	0.0
S_1	0.0	0.0	0.0	0.0	0.0	0.0	0.0	0.0	0.0	0.0	0.0	0.0	0.0	0.0	0.0	0.0	0.0	0.2	0.0	0.0	0.0	99.8	0.0	0.0
S_2	0.0	0.0	0.0	0.0	0.0	0.0	0.0	0.0	0.0	0.0	0.0	0.0	0.0	0.0	0.0	0.0	0.0	0.0	0.0	0.0	0.0	0.0	99.6	0.4
S_3	0.0	0.0	0.0	0.0	0.0	0.0	0.0	0.0	0.0	0.0	0.0	0.0	0.0	0.0	0.0	0.0	0.0	0.0	0.0	0.0	0.0	0.0	0.0	100.0

Table 5 is the confusion matrix of Hanilci's features. Compared with the 2 aforementioned feature sets, it can be seen that the detection accuracies of several cell-phones are deteriorated seriously, such as HTC D820t, Huawei Honor 6, iPhone 6, Mi 3. Especially for HTC D610t and iPhone 4s, the identification rates have dropped below 50%. But for the cell-phones of Samsung and OPPO brands, Hanilci's features nearly achieve a perfect performance. From the perspective of the total identification accuracy, SN-SDF (94.53%) be the best one and SN-SSF (89.23%) outperforms Hanilci's features (86.04%).

Based on the experimental results and analysis, it can be deduced that device self-noise can be regarded as the fingerprint of a cell-phone and it is a promising feature for source device identification in audio forensics realm.

5 Conclusions

This paper presents an innovative idea on cell-phone identification issue. Self-noise is considered as a kind of fingerprint for the cell-phones with the same model. Because the characteristics of self-noise is mainly decided by the circuit design and electronics usage of the cell-phone itself, it is feasible to take it as the unique identity for cell-phone model identification. The experimental results have verified that the proposed self-noise-based features are able to recognize the cell-phones in our closed-set with impressive performance, and furthermore, more distinguished classification ability can be attained when compared with MFCC-based features.

However, the proposed method is a preliminary study of applying self-noise to recording source identification. There still some limitations need to be further studied. For example, cell-phones' self-noise cannot be perfectly calculated according to the universal model of background noise. This is owing to the fact that, in practice, the background noise varies with different recording environments. Though self-noise estimation is a challenging task, we expect to develop a method in our future work for accurately and adaptively estimating the self-noise. Besides, establishing a comprehensive benchmark database for acquired devices identification is a laborious work, but continually completing this dataset is still our long-term goal.

Acknowledgements. This work was supported by the National Natural Science Foundation of China (Grant No. 61672302, 61300055), Zhejiang Natural Science Foundation (Grant No. LZ15F020010, Y17F020051), Ningbo University Fund (Grant No. XKXL1405, XKXL1420, XKXL1509, XKXL1503) and K.C. Wong Magna Fund in Ningbo University.

References

1. Yang, R., Luo, W., Huang, J.: Multimedia forensic. Sci. China Inf. Sci. **43**(12), 1654–1672 (2013)
2. Jin, C., Wang, R., Yan, D., Ma, P., Zhou, J.: An efficient algorithm for double compressed AAC audio detection. Multimedia Tools Appl. **75**(8), 4815–4832 (2016)

3. Stamm, M., Wu, M., Liu, K.: Information forensics: an overview of the first decade. IEEE Access **1**, 167–200 (2013)
4. Maher, R.: Audio forensic examination (authenticity, enhancement, and interpretation). IEEE Signal Process. Mag. **26**(2), 84–94 (2009)
5. Gupta, S., Cho, S., Kuo, C., et al.: Current developments and future trends in audio authentication. IEEE Multimedia Mag. **19**(1), 50–59 (2012)
6. Bao, Y., Liang, R., et al.: Research progress on key technologies of audio forensics. J. Data Acq. Process. **31**(2), 252–259 (2016)
7. Hanilci, C., Ertas, F., Ertas, T., Eskidere, O.: Recognition of brand and models of cell-phones from recorded speech signals. IEEE Trans. Inf. Forensics Secur. **7**(2), 625–634 (2012)
8. Hanilci, C., Ertas, F.: Optimizing acoustic features for source cell-phone recognition using speech signals. In: Proceedings of ACM Workshop on Information Hiding and Multimedia Security (IH&MMSec 2013), Montpellier, France, pp. 141–148 (2013)
9. Panagakis, Y., Kotropoulos, C.: Automatic telephone handset identification by sparse representation of random spectral features. In: Proceedings of 14th ACM Multimedia and Security Workshop, Coventry, UK, pp. 91–96 (2012)
10. Panagakis, Y., Kotropoulos, C.: Telephone handset identification by feature selection and sparse representations. In: Proceedings of 2012 IEEE International Workshop Information Forensics and Security, Tenerife, Spain, pp. 73–78 (2012)
11. Kotropoulos, C.: Telephone handset identification using sparse representations of spectral feature sketches. In: Proceedings of 1st International Workshop Biometrics and Forensics, Lisbon, Portugal, pp. 1–4 (2013)
12. Kotropoulos, C.: Source phone identification using sketches of features. IET Biom. **3**(2), 75–83 (2014)
13. Zou, L., He, Q., Feng, X.: Cell phone verification from speech recording using sparse representation. In: 2015 IEEE International Conference on Acoustics, Speech and Signal Processing (ICASSP), South Brisbane, QLD, pp. 1787–1791 (2015)
14. Jensen, J., Tan, Z.: Minimum mean-square error estimation of mel-frequency cepstral features-a theoretically consistent approach. IEEE/ACM Trans. Audio Speech Lang. Process. **23**(1), 186–197 (2014)
15. Erich, Z.: Speech processing using digital MEMS microphones. Ph.D. thesis, School of Informatics, University of Edinburgh (2013)
16. Sweetwater: Self-noise. http://www.sweetwater.com/insync/self-noise/. Accessed 27 June 2016
17. Widder, J., Morcelli, A.: Basic principles of MEMS microphones. http://www.edn.com/design/analog/4430264/Basic-principles-of-MEMS-microphones. Accessed 27 June 2016
18. Lewis, J., Schreier, P.: Low self-noise: the first step to high-performance MEMS microphone applications. InvenSense Inc. Doc., 1–4 (2013)
19. Vaseghi, S.: Advanced Signal Processing and Noise Reduction, 4th edn. Wiley Press, Hoboken (2009)
20. Lukáš, J., Fridrich, J., Goljan, M.: Digital camera identification from sensor pattern noise. IEEE Trans. Inf. Forensics Secur. **1**(2), 205–214 (2006)
21. Kinnunen, T., Rajan, P.: A practical, self-adaptive voice activity detector for speaker verification with noisy telephone and microphone data. In: 2013 IEEE International Conference on Acoustics, Speech and Signal Processing (ICASSP), Vancouver, BC, pp. 7229–7233 (2013)
22. Boll, S.: Suppression of acoustic noise in speech using spectral subtraction. IEEE Trans. Acoust. Speech Signal Process. **27**(2), 113–120 (1979)

23. Loizou, P.: Speech Enhancement: Theory and Practice, 2nd edn. CRC Press, Boca Raton (2013)
24. Zhao, H., Chen, Y., Wang, R., Malik, H.: Anti-forensics of environmental-signature-based audio splicing detection and its countermeasure via rich-feature classification. IEEE Trans. Inf. Forensics Secur. **11**(7), 1603–1617 (2016)
25. Lerch, A.: An Introduction to Audio Content Analysis: Applications in Signal Processing and Music Informatics. Wiley-IEEE Press, Hoboken (2012)
26. Chang, C., Lin, C: LIBSVM: a library for support vector machines. ACM Trans. Intell. Syst. Technol. **2**, 27:1–27:27 (2011). http://www.csie.ntu.edu.tw/~cjlin/LIBSVM
27. Faruto, Li, Y.: LIBSVM-farutoUltimateVersion: a toolbox with implements for support vector machines based on LIBSVM (2011). http://www.matlabsky.com

Speech Authentication and Recovery Scheme in Encrypted Domain

Qing Qian, Hongxia Wang$^{(\boxtimes)}$, Sani M. Abdullahi, Huan Wang,
and Canghong Shi

School of Information Science and Technology,
Southwest Jiaotong University, Chengdu 611756, China
hxwang@swjtu.edu.cn

Abstract. This paper proposes a self-embedding fragile watermarking scheme in encrypted speech based on hyper-chaotic system and reference sharing mechanism. Hyper-chaotic system is introduced to hide the feature and improve the confidentiality of original speech. Reference sharing mechanism is used to generate watermark for recovering tampered speech area. Combining the encryption and watermarking technologies, the confidentiality and integrity of original speech can be achieved simultaneously. Analysis and experimental results demonstrate that the proposed algorithm can detect and locate the tampered area. Meanwhile, the self-embedding watermark can be extracted to recover the content of tampered speech with high quality. Additionally, the key space is big enough to resist brute-force attack, while the secure keys are sensitive to slight change.

Keywords: Encryption · Hyper-chaotic system · Fragile watermarking · Speech authentication · Self-embedding

1 Introduction

With the rapid development of network technology and various powerful audio software, the amount of digital speech has been increased sharply. As a popular storage technology, cloud storage such as Microsofts Azure storage service provides customers with scalable, dynamic and hardware-independent storage. Undoubtedly, cloud storage brings a lot of convenience for people, but the open and multi-tenancy cloud storage supplier is not a completely trusted third party, which will introduce significant security and privacy risks. In fact, the biggest hurdle in cloud storage is concern over the confidentiality and integrity [1,2].

As an important aspect of multimedia applications, a lot of speech recordings contain important information, such as instructions in military commanding system, legal evidence in judicature, telephone banking, meeting recording, online voice orders and so on [3]. If these sensitive speech recordings are stored in the cloud, the service provider should not learn any information about speech content. Meanwhile, any unauthorized modification can be detected accurately.

The original version of this chapter was revised. The name of the third author – Sani M. Abdullahi – has been corrected. The erratum to this chapter is available at DOI: 10.1007/978-3-319-53465-7_46

© Springer International Publishing AG 2017
Y.Q. Shi et al. (Eds.): IWDW 2016, LNCS 10082, pp. 46–60, 2017.
DOI: 10.1007/978-3-319-53465-7_4

Therefore, the combination of encryption and data hiding is provided as a new technology for realizing privacy and integrity of digital speech [4,5].

Encryption is an effective method used to protect the privacy and confidentiality by converting ordinary files into unintelligible data. In [6], a speech cryptosystem based on substitution and permutation was presented. Baker map, Henon map and logistic map have been introduced to permutate the transform coefficients of speech signal. In [7], a novel new color image encryption using fractional-order hyper chaotic systems was proposed. Six encryption matrices and one permutation matrix are generated to modify the RGB values of the plain-image pixels and scramble the image pixel-position, respectively. An index-based selective audio encryption scheme was proposed for wireless multimedia sensor networks in [8]. It is a selective encryption that only encrypt the important audio data to reduce the processing delay and energy consumption.

Digital watermarking is a vital technology for multimedia integrity authentication. In [9], a speech content authentication algorithm based on Bessel-Fourier moments was proposed. The scheme was robust to common signal processing and had ability to detect insertion and deletion attacks. In [10], a content-dependent watermarking scheme for protecting the integrity of compressed speech has been proposed. Experimental results show that scheme had ability to identify the attack manners and locate the tampered area. In [11], a semi-fragile speech watermarking scheme based on quantization of linear prediction (LP) parameters was proposed for speech authentication. Meanwhile, an Analysis by Synthesis (AbS) scheme is developed to guarantee the inaudibility in that scheme.

Nowadays, many algorithms have been presented to achieve the confidentiality and data hiding in images simultaneously [12,13]. These algorithms can be classified into two categories: (I) The secret bits are directly embedded into an encrypted multimedia [14,15]; (II) The secret bits are embedded into the vacated space which is not encrypted [16,17]. The second kind of method is an effective way to provide a high payload [18]. Therefore, it is selected to encrypt speech and embed watermark in the proposed paper.

The proposed scheme mainly consists of four phases including speech encryption and decryption, watermark generation and embedding, content authentication and speech tampered recovery. In speech encryption, a hyper-chaotic system [19] is used to encrypt the input speech except the least significant bit (LSB). Note that the LSB of the input speech is reserved for appending extra watermark. In watermark generation and embedding, the watermark bits are generated based on the sampling values of the encrypted speech by using reference sharing mechanism [20]. After that, the generated watermark is inserted into the LSB of the encrypted signal. When a receiver acquires the encrypted and watermarked speech, the tampered area should be located and recovered by the extracted self-embedded auxiliary watermark bits. Experiments show that the proposed scheme provides high security for this system and maintains an excellent inaudibility of the decrypted and marked speech. Additionally, the tamper area can be recovered with high quality.

This paper is organized as follows: Sect. 2 illustrates the proposed algorithm. The performance analysis and experimental results are presented in Sects. 3 and 4, respectively. The conclusions is described in Sect. 5.

2 Proposed Algorithm

In this section, a hyper-chaotic system is introduced to encrypt speech firstly. Then the procedures of watermark generation, watermark embedding, tamper detection, tampered recovery will be elaborated in the following.

2.1 Speech Encryption and Decryption

In order to eliminate the correlation between adjacent sampling points and the statistical characteristic of original speech, a hyper-chaotic system is used to encrypt speech for the confidentiality and privacy in this section.

Suppose that an original speech signal $S = \{s(l)|l = 1, 2, ..., L\}$ containing L samples is quantified in N bits. The details of the speech encryption are elaborated in the following steps.

1. According to a group of secret initial values $\mathrm{x} = (x_1, x_2, x_3, x_4, x_5, x_6)^T$, 6-dimensional hyper-chaotic vectors $\dot{\mathrm{x}} = (\dot{\mathrm{x}}_1, \dot{\mathrm{x}}_2, \dot{\mathrm{x}}_3, \dot{\mathrm{x}}_4, \dot{\mathrm{x}}_5, \dot{\mathrm{x}}_6)^T$ are generated by Eq. (1). Each vector $\dot{\mathrm{x}}_i = (\dot{x}_i^1, \dot{x}_i^2, \dots, \dot{x}_i^L)$ contains more than L values.

$$\dot{\mathrm{x}} = A\mathrm{x} + B \tag{1}$$

A is a nominal matrix used to generate hyper-chaotic sequences. B is a non-linear feedback controller designed to control the hyper-chaotic system. Each element of matrix is described by Eq. (2).

$$A = \begin{pmatrix} -0.5 & -4.9 & 5.1 & 1 & 1 & 1 \\ 4.9 & -5.3 & 0.1 & 1 & 1 & 1 \\ -5.1 & 0.1 & 4.7 & 1 & -1 & 1 \\ 1 & 2 & -3 & -0.05 & -1 & 1 \\ -1 & 1 & 1 & 1 & -0.3 & 2 \\ -1 & 1 & -1 & -1 & -1 & -0.1 \end{pmatrix} \quad B = \begin{pmatrix} f_1(\sigma x_2, \varepsilon) \\ 0 \\ 0 \\ 0 \\ 0 \\ 0 \end{pmatrix} \tag{2}$$

f_1 is a uniformly bounded sinusoidal function as Eq. (3). $\varepsilon = 5.5, \sigma = 20$.

$$f_1(\sigma x_2, \varepsilon) = \varepsilon \sin(\sigma x_2) \tag{3}$$

2. An address index ordered sequence $P = (p_1, p_2, \dots, p_L)$ is obtained by sorting the first vector $\dot{\mathrm{x}}_1 = (\dot{x}_1^1, \dot{x}_1^2, \dots, \dot{x}_1^L)$ in ascending order. Then, the scrambled speech S' is obtained by using the address index sequence P.
3. In order to eliminate the statistical characteristic, pseudo-random secure sequences $\mathrm{K} = \{\kappa_i | i = 1, 2, \dots, 5\}$ and selecting sequence $\bar{\kappa}$ are produced by using $(\dot{\mathrm{x}}_2, \dot{\mathrm{x}}_3, \dot{\mathrm{x}}_4, \dot{\mathrm{x}}_5, \dot{\mathrm{x}}_6)$ to modify the amplitude values of original speech.

$$\kappa_i = \mathrm{mod}((|\dot{x}_{i+1}| - \lfloor |\dot{x}_{i+1}| \rfloor) \times 10^{15}, 2^N) \tag{4}$$

Here, $\kappa_i \in \{0, 1, \dots, 2^N - 1\}$. The operations $|\cdot|$ and $\lfloor \cdot \rfloor$ stand for the absolute value function and the floor function, respectively.

$$\bar{\kappa} = \mathrm{mod}\left(\sum_{i=1}^{5} \kappa_i, 4\right) \tag{5}$$

According to Table 1, the corresponding key sequence can be selected to encrypt the scrambled speech sample by sample in the following way:

$$
\begin{aligned}
C_{4\times(i-1)+1} &= S'_{4\times(i-1)+1} \oplus key(1) \oplus IV \\
C_{4\times(i-1)+2} &= S'_{4\times(i-1)+2} \oplus key(2) \oplus C_{4\times(i-1)+1} \\
C_{4\times(i-1)+3} &= S'_{4\times(i-1)+3} \oplus key(3) \oplus C_{4\times(i-1)+2} \\
C_{4\times(i-1)+4} &= S'_{4\times(i-1)+4} \oplus key(4) \oplus C_{4\times(i-1)+3}
\end{aligned}
\tag{6}
$$

Here, key and IV are selected by $\bar{\kappa}$. S' and C are the scrambled speech and the ciphered speech, respectively. To against Chosen-plaintext attack and improve the security, a feedback in the encryption C_{i-1} and initial vectors are considered. The symbol $\oplus$ denotes the XOR operation.

Table 1. Different sequence selected to encrypt speech

$\bar{\kappa}$	key	IV
0	$(\kappa_1, \kappa_2, \kappa_3, \kappa_4)$	κ_5
1	$(\kappa_1, \kappa_2, \kappa_3, \kappa_5)$	κ_4
2	$(\kappa_1, \kappa_2, \kappa_4, \kappa_5)$	κ_3
3	$(\kappa_1, \kappa_3, \kappa_4, \kappa_5)$	κ_2
4	$(\kappa_2, \kappa_3, \kappa_4, \kappa_5)$	κ_1

In order to obtain the original speech, the downloder need to use the same keystream (formed by the initial condition x) to decrypt the downloaded speech. The decryption process is described in the following.

1. The function in Eq. (7) is used to decrypt the received speech.

$$
\begin{aligned}
S'_{4\times(i-1)+1} &= C_{4\times(i-1)+1} \oplus key(1) \oplus IV \\
S'_{4\times(i-1)+2} &= C_{4\times(i-1)+2} \oplus key(2) \oplus C_{4\times(i-1)+1} \\
S'_{4\times(i-1)+3} &= C_{4\times(i-1)+3} \oplus key(3) \oplus C_{4\times(i-1)+2} \\
S'_{4\times(i-1)+4} &= C_{4\times(i-1)+4} \oplus key(4) \oplus C_{4\times(i-1)+3}
\end{aligned}
\tag{7}
$$

Here, C and S' are the received speech and the decrypted speech respectively. key and IV are selected keystreams by hyper-chaotic sequences as encryption.
2. The same address index sequence P is used to inversely permutate the decrypted speech S' so as to obtain the original speech.

2.2   Watermarking Generation and Embedding

In this section, a reference sharing mechanism is applied to generate the self-embedding watermark. Assume that the encrypted speech $C = \{c_l | l = 1, 2, ..., L\}$ is quantified by N bits. The details of watermark generation and watermark embedding are described as follows:

1. The encrypted signal C is divided into I frames with length $J(I = \lfloor L/J \rfloor)$. Each frame is denoted as $C_i = (c_{i,1}, \ldots, c_{i,j}, \ldots, c_{i,J}), i = 1, 2, \ldots, I$.
2. For each frame C_i, all samples are covered into N bits. The bits from the 1st to $(N-1)$th of all samples are connected to produce a data vector B_i, $B_i = (b_{i,1,1}, \ldots, b_{i,1,N-1}, \ldots, b_{i,j,1}, \ldots, b_{i,j,N-1}, \ldots, b_{i,J,1}, \ldots, b_{i,J,N-1})^T$.
3. Each data vector B_i is fed into a hash function to produce check-bits $V_i = (v_{i,1}, v_{i,2}, \ldots, v_{i,vL})$ with the length of vL.
4. All vectors are connected to obtain a data sequence containing $(N-1) \times I \times J$ bits. The data sequence is denoted as $B = \{B_1, \ldots, B_i, \ldots, B_I\}$.
5. According to the secret key K_1, the sequence B is permuted and re-divided into I groups. Each group is denoted as $B_i' = (b_{i,1}', b_{i,2}', \cdots, b_{i,(N-1) \times J}')^T$.
6. A compressed matrix M is used for compressing each group B_i'. The generated reference-bits R_i with rL bits is calculated by Eq. (8).

$$R_i = \begin{bmatrix} r_{i,1} \\ r_{i,2} \\ \vdots \\ r_{i,rL} \end{bmatrix} = mod(M \cdot \begin{bmatrix} b_{i,1} \\ b_{i,2} \\ \vdots \\ b_{i,(N-1) \times J} \end{bmatrix}, 2), \quad i = 1, 2, \cdots, I. \quad (8)$$

Here, M is a pseudo-random binary matrix sized $rL \times ((N-1) \times J)$. The symbol $\cdot$ is dot-product of two vectors, and $mod(\cdot)$ is a modulo function. R_i is the generated reference bits of the ith group.
7. Connecting all reference-bits, scrambling and dividing those reference-bits into I groups by using the secure key K_2. Each group is denoted as $R_i' = (r_{i,1}', r_{i,2}', \ldots, r_{i,rL}')^T$.
8. The reference-bits R_i' and the check-bits V_i are connected as the final watermark of ith frame and denoted as $W_i = (r_{i,1}', \ldots, r_{i,rL}', v_{i,1}, \ldots, v_{i,vL})$.
9. The generated watermark is embedded into the LSB of each frame signal C_i as Eq. (9).

$$C_{i,j}' = \lfloor C_{i,j}/2 \rfloor \times 2 + w(j), \; j = 1, 2, \ldots, rL + vL. \quad (9)$$

Repeat Step 2 to Step 9 until the process of watermark embedding is finished and the encrypted-watermarked speech CW can be obtained.

2.3 Tampering Location

Suppose $CW' = \{cw^l | l = 1, 2, \ldots, L\}$ is a suspicious encrypted and watermarked speech signal. Define an authentication sequence τ as the location sequence, which has the same length with the frame number. The steps of authentication are illustrated as follows:

1. Dividing the suspicious speech into I frames. Each frame is denoted as $CW_i' = (cw_{i,1}', \ldots, cw_{i,j}', \ldots, cw_{i,J}')$ with J samples.
2. A binary vector $B_i = (b_{i,1,1}, \ldots, b_{i,1,N-1}, \ldots, b_{i,J,1}, \ldots, b_{i,J,N-1})^T$ is obtained by connecting the 1st bit to the (N-1)th bit of all samples in CW_i.

3. The binary data vector B_i is fed into a hash function to reconstruct check-bits $RV_i = (v'_{i,1}, v'_{i,2}, \ldots, v'_{i,vL})$.
4. The embedded watermark bits are extracted by Eq. (10). The previous rL bits are denoted as the extracted reference-bits $ER_i = (r_{i,1}, r_{i,2}, \ldots, r_{i,rL})$. Others are denoted as the extracted check-bits $EV_i = (v_{i,1}, v_{i,2}, \ldots, v_{i,vL})$.

$$w = mod(cw'_{i,j}, 2) \tag{10}$$

5. The reconstructed check-bits RV_i are compared with the extracted check-bits EV_i. If both check-bits are equal, it is proved that the current speech frame is intact, and let $\tau(i) = 0$. Otherwise, it is believed that the current speech frame is tampered and let $\tau(i) = 1$. For the tampered frame, the corresponding binary vector B_i and extract reference-bits ER_i are missing. Thus, each element of B_i and ER_i should be marked as special values.
6. Repeat Step 2 to Step 5 until all frames are detected. After that, each data vector is connected to the next data vector, which contains special values and denotes as $B = \{B_1, \ldots, B_i, \ldots, B_I\}$. Similarly, all extracted reference-bits containing special values are connected as $ER = \{ER_1, \ldots, ER_i, \ldots, ER_I\}$.

2.4 Tampered Recovery

1. Using the secure key K_1, the inverse scrambling is performed on the binary data sequence B to diffuse those special values into the entire data sequence.
2. The scrambled sequence is redivided into I groups. Each group is denoted as $B'_i = (b'_{i,1}, b'_{i,2}, \cdots, b'_{i,(N-1)\times J})^T$.
3. According to the secure key K_2 used in Step 7 of Sect. 2.2, the inverse scrambling and division are performed on the connected reference-bits ER' to diffuse those special reference-bits into different groups. The redivided groups are denoted as $ER'_i = (r'_{i,1}, r'_{i,2}, \cdots, r'_{i,rL})^T, i = 1, 2, \ldots, I$.
4. For each group, the data bits B'_i and the reference-bits are used to obtain the following equation:

$$R_i^* = \begin{bmatrix} r'_{i,1} \\ r'_{i,2} \\ \vdots \\ r'_{i,eL} \end{bmatrix} = M^E \cdot \begin{bmatrix} b'_{i,1} \\ b'_{i,2} \\ \vdots \\ b'_{i,(N-1)\times J} \end{bmatrix}, \quad i = 1, 2, \cdots, I. \tag{11}$$

Here, R_i^* contains the extracted reliable reference-bits $(eL \leq rL)$. The matrix M^E (sized $eL \times (N-1) \times J$) is constituted of some rows in matrix M whose row number is corresponding to those reserved reference-bits.
5. A group of data bits B'_i consists of two parts: the bits of intact frames denoted as B_i^1, and the bits of tampered frames denoted as B_i^2 which need to be recovered. The matrix M^E is also divided into two matrices: The first matrix M^{E1} consists of the columns in M^E corresponding to those reserved data bits B_i^1. While the second matrix M^{E2} consists of the columns in M^E corresponding to those missing data bits B_i^2.

6. The Eq. (11) can be reformulated as Eq. (12).

$$M_i^{E2} \cdot B_i^2 = R_i^* - M_i^{E1} \cdot B_i^1 \tag{12}$$

Here, all parameters are known except B_i^2. If Eq. (12) has a unique solution, all unknown data bits of B_i^2 can be calculated. However, if the number of unknown bits is too large or too many linearly dependent equations exist in Eq. (12), the solution may not be unique. In this case, the calculated B_i^2 may be erroneous.

7. Repeat Step 3 to Step 6 until all missing data bits are recovered. Then those recovered data bits are used to retrieve the tampered sample values of the original speech.

8. Using the decryption algorithm in Sect. 2.1, we can obtain the decrypted and recovered speech.

3   Performance Analysis

3.1   Security

For each encryption algorithm, security level is determined by the protection level of the encrypted data. In this section, several parameters such as key space, key sensitivity and histogram are used to evaluate the security performance of the proposed method.

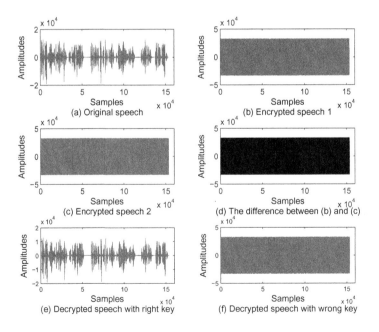

Fig. 1. The sensitivity of key change

Key Space Analysis. Key space is the total number of different keys in a cryptosystem, which should be large enough to make brute-force attacks infeasible. In speech encryption, the secret key is the initial values of Shen's hyper-chaotic which consists of six parameters x_1, x_2, x_3, x_4, x_5 and x_6. According to the IEEE floating-point standard [21,22], the computational precision of a 64-bit double-precision number is about 10^{15}. Therefore, the total number of possible values of that secret key is approximately $(10^{15})^6 = 10^{90}$, which is large enough to resist brute-force attack. Keyspace2

Sensitivity Analysis. Key sensitivity is used to measure the sensitivity of key change, which is evaluated as shown in Fig. 1. For encryption, the hyper chaotic initial values $K_{ey1} = [1.12, 0.34, 1.18, -0.91, 0.2, 1.7]$ is used to obtain the encrypted speech 1 shown in Fig. 1(b). While the key $K_{ey2} = [1.12 + 10^{-15}, 0.34, 1.18, -0.91, 0.2, 1.7]$ with slight change is introduced to obtain the encrypted speech 2 shown in Fig. 1(c). The differential speech between the encrypted speech 1 and the encrypted speech 2 is shown in Fig. 1(d). From Fig. 1(d), we can see that even if just a slight change occurs in encryption key, the encrypted speech will be totally different. For Decryption, we use the right key K_{ey1} and the wrong key K_{ey2} to decrypt the encrypted speech 1. The decrypted speech using the right key K_{ey1} in Fig. 1(e) is totally different with the other one in Fig. 1(f) which uses the wrong key K_{ey2} to decrypt. From the above analysis, it's obvious that the proposed scheme is sensitive to key change.

Statistical Analysis. Admittedly, the distribution of speech samples is regular. Thus, attackers can possibly to get some information by statistical analysis. Histogram of a digital signal shows the distribution of its values. From Fig. 2, it can be seen that the histogram of the encrypted speech is nearly uniform and significantly different with the histogram of the original speech. We can believe that the attacker cannot obtain any useful statistical information from the encrypted speech.

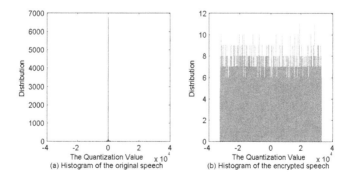

Fig. 2. Histograms of original speech and its encrypted speech

3.2   Performance of Tamper Detection

In watermarking system, the forgery attack is usually undetectable. Therefore, locating the tampered area precisely is the most important issue for speech content authentication and recovery.

For the proposed scheme, if one speech frame is maliciously tampered, the corresponding reconstructed check-bits should be different from the extracted check-bits. Suppose that both check-bits are independent and has equal probability to be the same as each other. When all extracted check-bits match the reconstructed check-bits, the authentication client will declare that attacked frame as intact. Thus, the probability of false detection is computed theoretically as Eq. (13). In that equation, vL is the length of check-bits.

$$P_f = (\frac{1}{2})^{vL} \tag{13}$$

In other words, the attacked frame can be detected correctly with the probability P_c as Eq. (14).

$$P_c = 1 - (\frac{1}{2})^{vL} \tag{14}$$

If vL is large enough, the probability of P_f will be close to zero and the probability of tamper detection P_c will be close to one.

4   Experimental Results

In this section, the well known SQAM files [23] are selected as test speech signals. Every speech signal is a 16-bits monaural file in WAVE format. The sampling frequency of the landline phone and that of 3G codec for cellphones is 8 kHz. Hence, the test signals are down-sampled at 8 kHz. The detailed description of the used signals are listed in Table 2.

Important parameters and initial conditions are set as follows: Each speech frame includes 128 samples ($J = 128$). The numbers of embedded reference-bits and check-bits are 112 bits and 16 bits, respectively ($rL = 112, vL = 16$). The initial vector of the hyper chaotic is x $= (1.12, 0.34, 1.18, -0.91, 0.2, 1.7)$.

Table 2. Test sequences of SQAM database

Index	Signal description	Item (wav)
1	Female speech (English)	Spfe49_1
2	Male speech (English)	Spme50_1
3	Female speech (French)	Spff51_1
4	Male speech (French)	Spmf52_1
5	Female speech (German)	Spfg53_1
6	Male speech (German	Spmg54_1

4.1 Inaudibility

Inaudibility reflects the change degree between two speech signals. In order to evaluate the inaudibility of the proposed scheme, the Signal to Noise Ratio(SNR) [24] is applied to measure the quality of the encrypted watermarked speech and the decrypted watermarked speech.

Table 3. SNR(dB) values of different type voice

Index	Ref. [25]	Ref. [26]	The proposed scheme	
			Encrypted-marked	Decrypted-marked
1	31.99	48.10	−1.59	47.51
2	30.16	44.29	−1.96	46.83
3	26.09	41.12	−1.87	47.39
4	29.76	45.75	−0.90	47.64
5	29.32	44.76	−2.19	47.13
6	29.10	45.84	−1.92	47.44

Table 3 lists the SNR values of the proposed scheme and the algorithms in [25,26]. From Table 3, it's clear that the SNR values between the original speech and the encrypted-watermarked speech are negative. In other words, it indicates that the encryption algorithm has a good encryption effect. According to International Federation of the Photographic Industry(IFPI), the SNR values should be more than 20 dB. The SNR values between the original speech and the decrypted watermarked speech in the proposed scheme are greater than 40 dB which satisfy the IFPI standard. Comparing with other algorithms, it's obvious that the SNR values of the proposed scheme are bigger. We can believe that the proposed watermarking scheme has an excellent inaudibility without affecting the decryption.

4.2 Tamper Location and Recovery

In the following experiment, the speech in Fig. 1(a) is used as the original speech. The encrypted watermarked speech generated by that speech is subjected to mute attack and substitution attack. For the attacked speech, the attacked area is indicated by a rectangle. In the subgraph of the tampered location result, if the tamper location result value is set to one, it means that the corresponding speech frame is maliciously tampered. Otherwise, it means that the corresponding speech frame is intact.

Tamper Location and Recovery Without Attack. Fig. 3(a) shows the waveform of the encrypted watermark speech without attack. In Fig. 3(b), the values of tamper location result are equal to zero, which means all speech frames

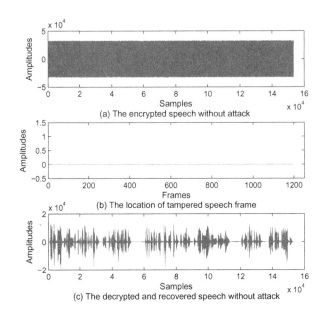

Fig. 3. The location result and decrypted speech without attack

are intact. The decrypted and watermarked speech is shown in Fig. 3(c). It's obvious that the decrypted and watermarked speech has no visual difference with the original speech which is shown in Fig. 1(a).

Tamper Location and Recovery of Mute Attack. Mute attack represents randomly silencing partial samples of the encrypted watermarked speech (from 1285th to 1800th samples, a total of 516 sampling points are muted). The attacked speech, the tampered location result and the decrypted and recovered speech are shown in Fig. 4(a), (b) and (c), respectively. Using the reference sharing mechanism, the tampered frames can be recovered. Hence, the waveform has no visual difference with the decrypted and watermarked speech which is shown in Fig. 3(c).

Tamper Location and Recovery of Substitution Attack. Substitution attack represents replacing partial encrypted watermarked speech signal from other orginal speech. For the substitution attack, the sampling points from 21254th to 23253th are replaced and shown in Fig. 5(a). The tamper location result in Fig. 5(b) shows that the frames from 167 to 182 are tampered frames. In Fig. 5(c), it's clear that the decrypted and recovered waveform has no visual difference with Fig. 3(c).

To measure the quality of recovered speech signals with different attack length objectively, the SNR values between the frames containing the recovered samples and corresponding original frames are calculated. The numbers of tampered samples are 500 samples, 1000 samples, 1500 samples and 2000 samples, respectively.

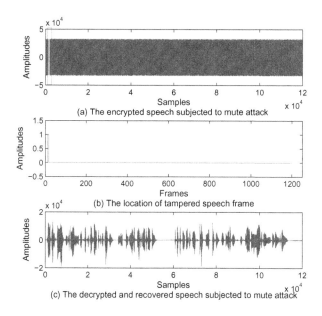

Fig. 4. The location result and recovery speech of mute attack

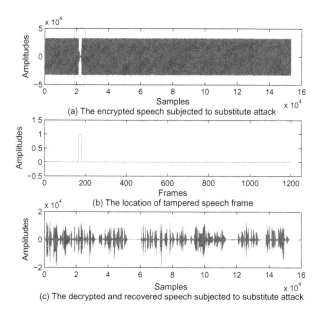

Fig. 5. The location result and recovery speech of substitution attack

Table 4. The SNR(dB) values under attacks with different length

Index	Ref. [25]/Ref. [26]/The proposed scheme			
	500	1000	1500	2000
1	18.71/24.15/47.37	13.24/16.72/47.37	16.23/24.49/47.36	16.28/24.53/47.37
2	24.11/44.25/47.16	19.35/19.53/47.16	19.83/18.02/47.16	16.17/16.95/47.16
3	22.70/28.10/47.67	18.78/20.57/47.67	19.07/19.90/47.68	16.68/18.42/47.67
4	24.97/48.19/46.85	19.11/20.66/46.84	21.37/28.29/46.85	17.80/17.88/46.84
5	26.49/62.20/47.62	17.73/17.19/47.62	23.34/58.31/47.61	17.79/21.64/47.62
6	21.75/43.90/47.44	16.88/18.32/47.44	19.46/23.47/47.43	16.81/16.95/47.45

From Table 4, it can be seen that the proposed scheme has excellent recovery quality than [25, 26].

From what has been discussed in this section, it is concluded that the proposed scheme has strong ability to detect the tampered area. Moreover, those tampered frames can be recovered with excellent quality.

5   Conclusions

The combination of encryption and watermarking is a new technology for confidentiality and integrity. Currently, there are few studies on sensitive speech. In this paper, a hyper-chaotic system is used to encrypt speech except the least significant bit. Meanwhile, self-embedded watermark is generated by reference sharing mechanism and embedded into the LSB of encrypted speech which is reserved space. When a receiver acquires an encrypted and marked speech signal, the tampered area can be located and recovered by the extracted check-bits and self-embedded auxiliary watermark bits, respectively. Experiments show that the proposed scheme provide a high security and it can maintain an excellent inaudibility of the decrypted and watermarked speech. Additionally, the tampered area can be recovered with high quality.

Acknowledgment. This work is supported by the National Natural Science Foundation of China (NSFC) under the grant No. U1536110.

References

1. Kamara, S., Lauter, K.: Cryptographic cloud storage. In: Sion, R., Curtmola, R., Dietrich, S., Kiayias, A., Miret, J.M., Sako, K., Sebé, F. (eds.) FC 2010. LNCS, vol. 6054, pp. 136–149. Springer, Heidelberg (2010). doi:10.1007/978-3-642-14992-4_13
2. Wu, J., Ping, L., Ge, X., Wang, Y., Fu, J.: Cloud storage as the infrastructure of cloud computing. In: International Conference on Intelligent Computing and Cognitive Informatics, pp. 380–383. IEEE Press, Kuala Lumpur (2010)
3. Qian, Q., Wang, H.X., Hu, Y., Zhou, L.N., Li, J.F.: A dual fragile watermarking scheme for speech authentication. Multimedia Tools Appl. **75**(21), 1–20 (2015)

4. Wang, H., Zhou, L., Zhang, W., Liu, S.: Watermarking-based perceptual hashing search over encrypted speech. In: Shi, Y.Q., Kim, H.-J., Pérez-González, F. (eds.) IWDW 2013. LNCS, vol. 8389, pp. 423–434. Springer, Heidelberg (2014). doi:10. 1007/978-3-662-43886-2_30

5. Zhang, X.: Separable reversible data hiding in encrypted image. IEEE Trans. Inf. Forensics Secur. **7**(2), 826–832 (2012)

6. Mostafa, A., Soliman, N.F., Abdalluh, M., El-samie, F.E.A.: Speech encryption using two dimensional chaotic maps. In: 11th International Computer Engineering Conference, pp. 235–240. IEEE Press, Cairo (2015)

7. Wu, X.: A color image encryption algorithm using the fractional-order hyperchaotic systems. In: 2012 Fifth International Workshop on Chaos-Fractals Theories and Applications (IWCFTA), pp. 196–201. IEEE Press, Dalian (2012)

8. Wang, H., Hempel, M., Peng, D., Wang, W., Sharif, H., Chen, H.H.: Index-based selective audio encryption for wireless multimedia sensor networks. IEEE Trans. Multimedia **12**(3), 215–223 (2010)

9. Liu, Z., Wang, H.: A novel speech content authentication algorithm based on Bessel-CFourier moments. Digit. Signal Proc. **24**, 197–208 (2014)

10. Chen, O.T., Liu, C.H.: Content-dependent watermarking scheme in compressed speech with identifying manner and location of attacks. IEEE Trans. Audio Speech Lang. Process. **15**(5), 1605–1616 (2007)

11. Yan, B., Guo, Y.J.: Speech authentication by semi-fragile speech watermarking utilizing analysis by synthesis and spectral distortion optimization. Multimedia Tools Appl. **67**(2), 383–405 (2013)

12. Zhang, W., Ma, K., Yu, N.: Reversibility improved data hiding in encrypted images. Sig. Process. **94**, 118–127 (2014)

13. Qian, Z., Zhang, X., Wang, S.: Reversible data hiding in encrypted JPEG bitstream. IEEE Trans. Multimedia **16**(5), 1486–1491 (2014)

14. Karim, M.S.A., Wong, K.: Universal data embedding in encrypted domain. Sig. Process. **94**, 174–182 (2014)

15. Dixit, S., Gaikwad, A., Gaikwad, S., Shanwad, S.A., Scholar, U.G.: Public key cryptography based lossless and reversible data hiding in encrypted images. Int. J. Eng. Sci. **6**, 3550–3557 (2016)

16. Ma, K.L., Zhang, W., Zhao, X., Yu, N., Li, F.: Reversible data hiding in encrypted images by reserving room before encryption. IEEE Trans. Inf. Forensics Secur. **8**(3), 553–562 (2013)

17. Zhang, X.: Separable reversible data hiding in encrypted image. IEEE Trans. Inf. Forensics Secur. **7**(2), 826–832 (2012)

18. Cao, X., Du, L., Wei, X., Meng, D., Guo, X.: High capacity reversible data hiding in encrypted images by patch-level sparse representation. IEEE Trans. Cybern. **46**(5), 1132–1243 (2016)

19. Shen, C., Yu, S., Lu, J., Chen, G.: A systematic methodology for constructing hyperchaotic systems with multiple positive Lyapunov exponents and circuit implementation. IEEE Trans. Circuits Syst. I Regul. Pap. **61**(3), 854–864 (2014)

20. Zhang, X., Wang, S., Qian, Z., Feng, G.: Reference sharing mechanism for watermark self-embedding. IEEE Trans. Image Process. **20**(2), 485–495 (2011)

21. Kahan, W.: IEEE standard 754 for binary floating-point arithmetic. In: Lecture Notes on the Status of IEEE 754, 94720–1776, 11 (1996)

22. Cowlishaw, M.F.: Decimal floating-point: algorism for computers. In: Proceedings of 16th IEEE Symposium on Computer Arithmetic, pp. 104–111. IEEE Press (2003)

23. EBU, SQAM - Sound Quality Assessment Material. http://sound.media.mit.edu/resources/mpeg4/audio/sqam/
24. Thiede, T., Treurniet, W.C., Bitto, R., Schmidmer, C., Sporer, T., Beerends, J.G., Colomes, C.: PEAQ-The ITU standard for objective measurement of perceived audio quality. J. Audio Eng. Soc. **48**(1/2), 3–29 (2000)
25. Liu, Z., Zhang, F., Wang, J., Wang, H., Huang, J.: Authentication and recovery algorithm for speech signal based on digital watermarking. Sig. Process. **123**(C), 157–166 (2016)
26. Chen, F., He, H., Wang, H.: A fragile watermarking scheme for audio detection and recovery. In: Proceeding of International Congress on Image and Signal Processing, pp. 135–138. IEEE Press, Sanya (2008)

Detecting Double H.264 Compression Based on Analyzing Prediction Residual Distribution

S. Chen[1], T.F. Sun[1], X.H. Jiang[1(✉)], P.S. He[1], S.L. Wang[1],
and Y.Q. Shi[2]

[1] EIEE, Shanghai Jiao Tong University, Shanghai, People's Republic of China
{jdneo,tfsun,xhjiang,gokeyhps,wsl}@sjtu.edu.cn
[2] ECE, New Jersey Institute of Technology, Newark, USA
shi@njit.edu

Abstract. Detecting double video compression has become an important issue in video forensics. A novel double H.264 compression detection scheme based on Prediction Residual Distribution (PRED) analysis is proposed in the paper. The proposed scheme can be applied to detect double H.264 compression with non-aligned GOP structures. For each frame of a given video, the prediction residual is first calculated and the average value of the prediction residual in each non-overlapping 4×4 block is recorded to reduce the influence of the noise. Then the PRED feature is represented by the distribution of the average prediction residual in each frames. After that, the Jensen-Shannon Divergence (JSD) is introduced to measure the difference between the PRED features of adjacent two frames. Finally, a Periodic Analysis (PA) method is applied to the final feature sequence to detect double H.264 compression and to estimate the first GOP size. Fourteen public YUV sequences are adopted for evaluation. Experiments have demonstrated that the proposed scheme can achieve better performance than the state-of-the-art method investigated.

Keywords: Double compression detection · Prediction residual distribution · Non-aligned GOP structure · First GOP estimation

1 Introduction

In order to ensure the authentication of digital videos, researchers have paid much attention to video forensics techniques in the past decade. Generally speaking, video recompression appears in most tampered videos [1] and thus double compression detection is of vital importance in video forensics.

According to whether the GOP structures of the first and the second compression are aligned or not, double video compression can be divided into two corresponding categories. For the case that the GOP structures are aligned, several efficient methods have been proposed, which can be categorized as: (i) DCT coefficient distribution based methods [2–4], (ii) first digit law based methods [5, 6], (iii) Markov statistics based methods [7, 8], and (iv) methods based on other cues [9–11]. For the case that the GOP structures are non-aligned (referred to as non-aligned double video compression), existing methods usually depended on temporal analysis of detection features. For example,

© Springer International Publishing AG 2017
Y.Q. Shi et al. (Eds.): IWDW 2016, LNCS 10082, pp. 61–74, 2017.
DOI: 10.1007/978-3-319-53465-7_5

the prediction residual sequences of MPEG videos have been used to detect double compression in [12–15]. Vázquez-Padín et al. [16] proposed a method based on the variation of macroblock types, which is used to detect double H.264 and MPEG-x video compression. Luo et al. [17] and He et al. [18] proposed double compression detection based on block artifact in double MPEG-x video compression. To sum up, the research on double video compression detection is more focused on MPEG-x standard than H.264 standard, because H.264 standard is more complex than MPEG-x in terms of the compression algorithm and strategy. Since the H.264 coding standard is more popular than other standards in most applications at present, it is important to research on double H.264 video compression.

Therefore, in this work, we have focused on double H.264 compression detection with non-aligned GOP structures. To the best of our knowledge, there is only one method [16] in the literature which aims to solve this challenging problem. In [16], the authors proposed the Variation of Prediction Footprint (VPF) as a tool for double compression detection. However, the experimental results reported in [16] showed that when the videos were rich of texture, the performance of VPF significantly degraded due to the macroblock decision strategy of the encoder. This is because the encoder tends to choose inter prediction to predict texture-rich areas. It is a major limitation of the VPF based scheme.

To overcome the limitation of the VPF scheme mentioned above, a novel method based on the PRED feature is proposed for double H.264 compression detection in this paper. The proposed method is based on the fact that the abnormal increment of prediction residual can be observed in I-P frames (the recompressed P-frame which is encoded as I-frame in single compression) after the second compression. The Jensen-Shannon Divergence (JSD) is introduced to measure the difference between PRED features extracted from I-P frames and other kinds of recompressed P-frames. A new feature sequence is generated from PRED feature by JSD. Then a Periodic Analysis (PA) method is applied to detect double compression and to estimate the first GOP size, which is helpful to provide additional information of the forgery history. The experiments have shown that the proposed scheme has better results than the prior work [16].

The rest of this paper is organized as follows. In Sect. 2, the non-aligned double compression model is analyzed. Section 3 describes the extraction procedure of the proposed PRED feature. Section 4 illustrates the framework of the proposed scheme. In Sect. 5, experiments are presented. Finally, conclusions are drawn in Sect. 6.

2   Theoretical Model of Non-aligned Double Compression Procedure

In H.264 video coding standard, there are three basic types of frames: Intra-coded frame (I-frame), Predictive-coded frame (P-frame) and B-frame (Bi-directionally predictive-coded frame). During the encoding procedure, frames will be grouped into GOPs. In general, each GOP starts with an I-frame, followed by P-frames or B-frames. For simplicity, the H.264 encoder used in this paper is based on the baseline profile, where B-frames are not considered. The number of frames included in a GOP is referred to as the GOP size. In aligned double compression, the GOP size in the first compression (G_1) and the GOP size in the second compression (G_2) are equal. On the other hand, in non-aligned double compression, G_1 and G_2 are different. In this paper, frame deletion and insertion are not taken into consideration in the compression procedure.

An example of non-aligned double compression procedure is illustrated in Fig. 1. A raw video sequence $\mathbb{V}$ of length T can be denoted as:

$$\mathbb{V} \triangleq \{F_1, F_2, \ldots, F_T\}, T \in \mathbb{Z}^+ \tag{1}$$

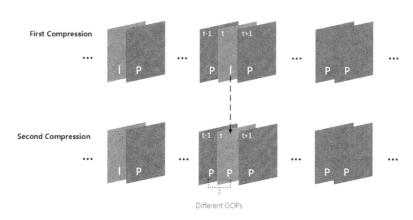

Fig. 1. An example of non-aligned double compression.

where F_t represents the tth uncompressed frame, $\mathbb{Z}^+$ represents the set of positive integers. As shown in Fig. 1, after the first compression, the $(t-1)^{\text{th}}$ image is encoded as a P-frame and the tth image is encoded as an I-frame, which can be expressed as follows:

$$\mathcal{F}_{t-1}^{(1)} = \mathcal{P}\left(\mathcal{F}_{t-2}^{(1)}, F_{t-1}\right) + \mathcal{R}_{t-1}^{(1)} \tag{2}$$

$$\mathcal{F}_t^{(1)} = \mathcal{J}(F_t) + \mathcal{R}_t^{(1)} \tag{3}$$

where $\mathcal{F}_t^{(1)}$ denotes the tth frame after the first compression; $\mathcal{R}_t^{(1)}$ denotes the prediction residual of the tth frame after the first compression; $\mathcal{P}(\cdot, \cdot)$ denotes the motion prediction operator; $\mathcal{J}(\cdot)$ denotes the intra prediction operator. In H.264 coding standard, I-frames also have prediction residual, which is different from MPEG-2 and MPEG-4 coding standard.

After the second compression, the $(t-1)^{\text{th}}$ and t^{th} frame in Fig. 1 are compressed with inter prediction and can be represented as:

$$\mathcal{F}_{t-1}^{(2)} = \mathcal{P}\left(\mathcal{F}_{t-2}^{(2)}, \mathcal{F}_{t-1}^{(1)}\right) + \mathcal{R}_{t-1}^{(2)} \tag{4}$$

$$\mathcal{F}_{t}^{(2)} = \mathcal{P}\left(\mathcal{F}_{t-1}^{(2)}, \mathcal{F}_{t}^{(1)}\right) + \mathcal{R}_{t}^{(2)} \tag{5}$$

where $\mathcal{F}_t^{(2)}$ denotes the tth frame after the second compression; $\mathcal{R}_t^{(2)}$ denotes the prediction residual of the tth frame after the second compression. As shown in Fig. 1, there are two kinds of P-frames in double H.264 compression, including I-P frame and P-P frame, where P-P frame denotes the recompressed P-frame which is encoded as P-frame in single compression. Based on Eqs. (2)–(5), the prediction residual component of the tth and $(t-1)^{th}$ frames after double compression can be described as follows:

$$\mathcal{R}_{t-1}^{(2)} = \mathcal{F}_{t-1}^{(2)} - \mathcal{P}\left(\mathcal{F}_{t-2}^{(2)}, \mathcal{P}\left(\mathcal{F}_{t-2}^{(1)}, F_{t-1}\right) + \mathcal{R}_{t-1}^{(1)}\right) \tag{6}$$

$$\mathcal{R}_{t}^{(2)} = \mathcal{F}_{t}^{(2)} - \mathcal{P}\left(\mathcal{F}_{t-1}^{(2)}, \mathcal{J}(F_t) + \mathcal{R}_{t}^{(1)}\right) \tag{7}$$

According to Eqs. (6) and (7), the prediction residual of I-P frame and P-P frame are different since they have different inputs of the motion prediction operator. Based on the fact that the $(t-1)^{th}$ and t^{th} frame belong to two different GOPs in the first compression, the correlation between these two frames is weak. This effect has further impact on the result of the motion prediction operation in the second compression. Therefore, the prediction residual of I-P frames is usually larger than the prediction residual of P-P frames in general [12]. This phenomenon can be used to detect double compression.

3   PRED Feature Extraction

In this section, the proposed PRED feature is presented in detail. As discussed in Sect. 2, when a video sequence is re-encoded, a larger prediction residual can be observed in the I-P frame. An illustrated example is shown in Fig. 2.

Figure 2 shows three frames from a double encoded video. The video is first encoded with $G_1 = 10$ and then re-encoded with $G_1 = 16$ The bitrate in the first and second compression are both set as 500 kb/s. The encoders for both the first and the second compression are based on the H.264 coding standard. Figure 2(a)–(c) show the video content in frame 20 to frame 22, and Fig. 2(d)–(f) show their corresponding prediction residual in the luminance channel. Since the video is first encoded with $G_1 = 10$, frame 21 becomes I-P frame after re-encoding. It is obvious that the prediction residual of frame 21 is much more significant than those of its adjacent two frames.

In order to represent the abnormal increment of prediction residual in I-P frame, the PRED feature is proposed in this paper. The extraction procedure of PRED is given as follows.

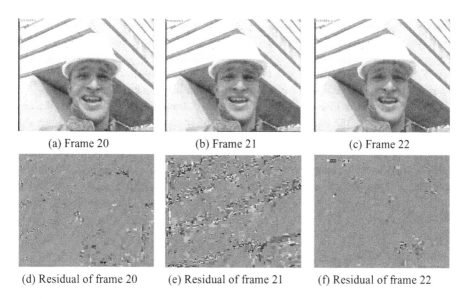

(a) Frame 20   (b) Frame 21   (c) Frame 22

(d) Residual of frame 20   (e) Residual of frame 21   (f) Residual of frame 22

Fig. 2. An illustrated example where prediction residual becomes large in I-P frame.

Firstly, the average prediction residual for each non-overlapping 4×4 block in each frame is calculated as follows:

$$\bar{R}_t(i,j) = \frac{1}{16} \sum\nolimits_{m=1}^{4} \sum\nolimits_{n=1}^{4} |r_{m,n}| \tag{8}$$

where $\bar{R}_t(i,j)$ denotes the average prediction residual for the $(i, j)^{th}$ 4×4 block in the tth frame. $\nabla_{m,n}$ represents the prediction residual locates at the $(m, n)^{th}$ position in the 4×4 block. In H.264 coding standard, both intra-coded macroblocks (I-MB) and inter-coded macroblocks (P-MB) have prediction residual. Besides, the prediction residual in skipped macroblocks (S-MB) is treated as zero since S-MB has no prediction residual in H.264 coding standard. The averaging process is adopted in Eq. (8) to reduce the influence of noise.

Secondly, $\bar{R}_t(i,j)$ will be rounded to its nearest integer. The range of the rounded result is set from 0 to 10 empirically, which covers 99% variations of $R_{round_t}(i,j)$. If the rounding value of $\bar{R}_t(i,j)$ is greater than 10, it will be truncated to 10, which is shown as follows:

$$R_{round_t}(i,j) = \begin{cases} \lfloor \bar{R}_t(i,j) + \frac{1}{2} \rfloor, & \lfloor \bar{R}_t(i,j) + \frac{1}{2} \rfloor < 10 \\ 10, & otherwise \end{cases} \tag{9}$$

where $R_{round_t}(i,j)$ denotes the rounding value of $\bar{R}_t(i,j)$.

Thirdly, by counting the values of $R_{round_t}(i,j)$ for each 4×4 block, the PRED feature for the tth frame $F_{PRED_t}(n)$ can be obtained, which is defined as:

$$F_{PRED_t}(n) = \frac{c_t(n)}{\mathcal{N}_t}, n \in [0, 10] \tag{10}$$

where $\mathcal{C}_t(n)$ is the number of 4×4 blocks whose R_{round_t} value is equal to n in the tth frame. $\mathcal{N}_t$ is the total number of 4×4 non-overlapping blocks in the tth frame.

Figure 3 shows the PRED features for frame 20, frame 21 and frame 22. It can be seen that PRED for frame 20 is similar to that of frame 22, since they are both P-P frames and the video contents are similar. But for PRED for frame 21, the frequency of 0 residual intensity becomes smaller and the frequency of residual ranging from 2 to 5 increases significantly. Such difference is caused by the less correlations between I-P frame and P-P frame, which has been discussed in Sect. 2. So the proposed PRED feature has the ability to identify the difference between I-P frames and P-P frames.

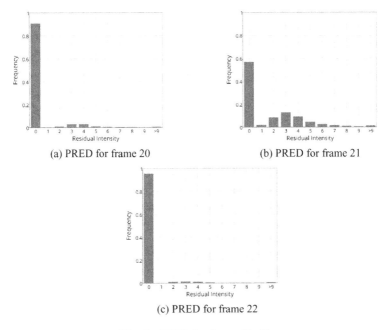

Fig. 3. PRED for frame 20–22.

4   Framework of the Proposed Scheme

The framework of the proposed scheme is given in Fig. 4. For a given video, there are five steps to complete the detection.

Step 1. **Prediction residual extraction**

In the first step, the prediction residual of each frame is extracted from the bitstream directly during the decoding process.

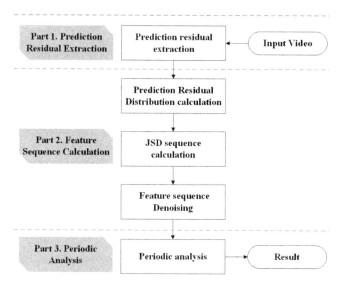

Fig. 4. The framework of the proposed method.

***Step 2.* PRED extraction**

In this step, the PRED feature of each frame is extracted as given in Sect. 3.

***Step 3.* Feature sequence generated**

To reflect the difference between PRED features for adjacent two frames, the Jensen-Shannon divergence is used, which is calculated as follows:

$$S_{JSD}(t) = JSD(F_{PRED_t}(n) || F_{PRED_{t-1}}(n)) + JSD(F_{PRED_t}(n) || F_{PRED_{t+1}}(n)) \qquad (11)$$

where JSD $(\cdot)$ represents the Jensen-Shannon divergence, $F_{PRED_t}(n)$ is the PRED feature for the tth frame. The JSD is a symmetrized version of the Kullback–Leibler divergence. It is defined by:

$$JSD(P||Q) = \frac{1}{2}KLD(P||M) + \frac{1}{2}KLD(Q||M) \qquad (12)$$

where P and Q are two discrete probability distributions and $M = \frac{1}{2}(P+Q)$. The Kullback–Leibler divergence can be calculated as follows

$$KLD(P||Q) = \sum_x p(x)logp(x) - \sum_x p(x)logq(x) \qquad (13)$$

According to Eq. (11), the $S_{JSD}(t)$ can be calculated for the given video.

***Step 4.* Feature sequence de-noising**

After $S_{JSD}(t)$ is calculated for each frame of a given video, median filtering is used to eliminate noise in the sequence, i.e.:

$$S_{MF}(t) = median\{S_{JSD}(t-1), S_{JSD}(t), S_{JSD}(t+1)\} \tag{14}$$

Then the noise can be eliminated according to the following equation:

$$S_{PRED}(t) = max(S_{JSD}(t) - S_{MF}(t), 0) \tag{15}$$

At this point, the final feature sequence $S_{PRED}(t)$ has been obtained. Figure 5(a) shows the $S_{JSD}(t)$ of the video sequence used in Sect. 3. The sequence becomes less noisy after median filtering as shown in Fig. 5(b). Since the GOP size of the first and the second compression is fixed, the peaks appear in a periodic pattern in the final sequence. In Fig. 5(b), basically there is a peak for every 10 frames, which is the first GOP size. Because the video is re-encoded with GOP size 16, the peaks absence for frame 81, 161 and 241 (the common multiple of 10 and 16), since they are I-frames in recompression process.

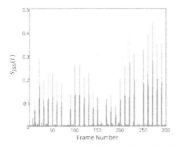
(a) JSD sequence before median filtering

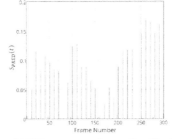
(b) JSD sequence after median filtering

Fig. 5. De-noising for the video feature sequence.

Step 5. **Periodic Analysis**

After calculating the feature sequence, the PA method is introduced to estimate the original GOP size of the video. P is denoted as the set of the frames which has positive value in the feature sequence:

$$\mathbb{P} = \{t \in \{0, \dots, T-1\} : S_{PRED}(t) > 0\} \tag{16}$$

Then a set of possible candidates is first created:

$$\mathbb{C} = \{c \in \{2, \dots, T\} : \exists n_1, n_2 \in \mathbb{P}, \ GCD(n_1, n_2) = c, c < \frac{T}{5}\} \tag{17}$$

where GCD is the greatest common divisors operator, T is the frame number of the given video. The GOP size is assumed to be no more than one-fifth of the frame number of the given video. This assumption is proposed in [15]. The reason is that in a real scenario, the GOP size cannot be too large for the sake of avoiding coding error propagation. To measure which candidates in set C models the periodicity best, a fitness equation is defined:

$$\emptyset(c) = \emptyset_1(c) - \emptyset_2(c) - \emptyset_3(c) \tag{18}$$

where $\emptyset_1(c)$ sums all the value of peaks which appear in multiples of c:

$$\emptyset_1(c) = \sum_{t=kc} S_{PRED}(t), \; with \; t \in \mathbb{P}, k \in \left[0, \left\lfloor \frac{T}{c} \right\rfloor \right] \tag{19}$$

$\emptyset_2(c)$ aims to penalize for the absence of peaks in multiples of c:

$$\emptyset_2(c) = \sum_{t=kc} \beta, \; with \; t \notin \mathbb{P}, k \in \left[0, \left\lfloor \frac{T}{c} \right\rfloor \right] \tag{20}$$

where in this paper $\beta = 0.3 \times max\{S_{PRED}(t)\}$. $\emptyset_3(c)$ aims to penalize the presence of noise:

$$\emptyset_3(c) = max\left\{ \sum_{k=0}^{\lfloor T/z \rfloor} S_{PRED}(kz) \right\}, \; with \; z \in [1, c-1] \tag{21}$$

To classify whether a video is double compressed, a threshold can be used to compare with $\emptyset(c)$. A video is regarded as double compressed, if $\emptyset(c)$ is greater than the threshold. The original GOP is estimated as:

$$\hat{G}_{FIRST} = arg \, max \, \emptyset(c) \tag{22}$$

5   Experiments

In this section, double H.264 compression detection and the first GOP size estimation are both investigated. The experimental results of the proposed approach are compared with those of the VPF method in [16] using the same dataset.

5.1   Dataset Setup

A dataset is established for our experiments. Fourteen YUV sequences (*akiyo, bridge-close, bridge-far, coastguard, container, foreman, hall-monitor, highway, mobile, news, paris, silent, template, waterfall* with CIF resolution) used in [16] are selected in this paper. For those sequences which have more than 300 frames, only the first 300 frames are used. Furthermore, all the sequences are encoded in Constant Bitrate (CBR) mode, which is the same as the encoding mode in paper [16]. The performance for the proposed method on Variable Bitrate (VBR) can be evaluated as a future work. The GOP size is fixed for both first encoding and second encoding. The MPEG-2, MPEG-4 and H.264 coding standards are used to generate singly encoded videos.

Table 1. Parameters explanation for the double compression video dataset

Parameters	First encoding	Second encoding
Encoder	{MPEG-2, MPEG-4, H.264}	{H.264}
Bitrate (kb/s)	{100, 300, 500, 700}	{100, 300, 500, 700}
GOP size	{10, 15, 30, 40}	{9, 16, 33, 50}
Sequence number	672	10752

In recompression process, only H.264 coding standard is considered. Finally, with different combinations of GOP sizes and bitrates, 672 first encoding videos and 10752 s encoding videos are generated. The coding parameters are listed in Table 1.

5.2   Performance Evaluation on Double H.264 Compression Detection

In this section, the proposed method is tested for double H.264 compression detection. AUC (area under the Receiver Operating Characteristic (ROC) curves) is used to evaluate the detection performance. It is worth noting that the AUC can be used to illustrate the performance of a binary classifier system as the discrimination threshold is varied, which is also used in paper [16]. The results are compared with those of Vázquez-Padín et al.'s method [16] (referred to as Vázquez-Padín's method), because their work is the only prior work for the double H.264 compression detection with non-aligned GOP structures in the literature. For each transcoding process, All the 224 singly encoded H.264 videos are chosen as negative samples. In order to make the number of positive samples equal to the number of negative samples, 224 doubly encoded videos which undergo the corresponding transcoding process are randomly selected from our dataset as positive samples. The experiments are conducted 50 times and the average AUC is obtained. Since the PRED feature extraction contains more calculation comparing with the VPF feature, the proposed method cannot be as fast as Vázquez-Padín's method. Some future work may be conducted to reduce the computational effort of the proposed method. The AUC results are investigated according to different encoders in the first compression, which is shown in Table 2.

Table 2. Performance comparisons in AUC

Transcoding process	Proposed	Vázquez-Padín's [16]
MPEG-2 → H.264	0.9791	0.9740
MPEG-4 → H.264	0.9711	0.9573
H.264 → H.264	0.9306	0.9023
Average	0.9603	0.9445

In Table 2, it can be observed that both methods achieve acceptable results when the first encoding process is based on MPEG-x coding standard. It is because more advanced coding standards have better compression efficiency and leave less double compression traces in single compression. It can also be seen that when the encoder used for the first encoding process is based on the MPEG-2 coding standard, the average AUCs of both scheme is above 0.97. When the encoder used for the first encoding process is based on the MPEG-4 coding standard, the AUC of Vázquez-Padín's schemes [16] degraded to 0.9573; however, the AUC of the proposed scheme only decreased 0.008. Besides, when the encoders of the first and the second compression are based on H.264 standard, the AUC of Vázquez-Padín's schemes [16] is 0.0283 less than the proposed scheme.

In all three cases, the average AUCs of the proposed scheme is higher than that of Vázquez-Padín's scheme. The overall average AUC of the proposed scheme is about 0.016 higher than that of Vázquez-Padín's scheme. It demonstrates the proposed scheme is better than Vázquez-Padín's scheme for double compression detection under all the three situations investigated.

5.3 Performance Evaluation on First GOP Size Estimation

In this section, the GOP size estimation performance of the proposed scheme is evaluated in comparison with that of the Vázquez-Padín's scheme [16]. The objective of the GOP size estimation is that it can be used to trace the compression history as well as to provide the original information of the given video. This is helpful to further recognize the double compressed video. All of the 10752 doubly encoded videos in our dataset are used in the experiment. The results are investigated from several different points of view, i.e. different video contents, different bitrate combinations and different transcoding processes.

Analysis on Different Video Contents. The results of GOP estimation with different video contents are shown in Fig. 6. From the results, it can be observed that the proposed method achieves good performance on most videos except for *news* and *silent*. It is because both two videos have strong local movement or scene cuts, causing large prediction residual in several frames. The severe variation of video content degrades the periodicity of the final sequence and makes the GOP estimation more difficult.

Notice that for the video *waterfall*, the performance of the proposed method is much better than Vázquez-Padín's method (improve about 10%). The reason has been discussed in Sect. 2. Since *waterfall* is rich of texture, encoders are more inclined to use

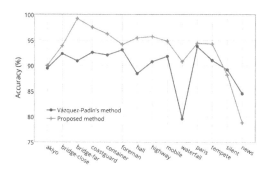

Fig. 6. Estimation accuracy with different video contents

P-MB due to the coding efficiency, while this artifact has less impact on residual based method. Therefore, the proposed method is more robust in the scenario where a video is rich of texture.

To further improve the accuracy of the detection scheme, some works can be conducted such as fusing the two features together to improve the robustness on different kinds of video contents.

Analysis on Different Bitrates Combination. The performance of GOP estimation with different bitrates combination is shown in Table 3, where the better results are highlighted. From Table 3, it can be seen that the proposed method achieves better estimation accuracy in most cases. Especially when the bitrate of the second compression is larger than or equal to that of the first compression, the estimation accuracies of the proposed method are all over 97.9%. On the other hand, when the bitrate of the second compression is less than that of the first compression, the estimation accuracies of both methods drop rapidly. This is because that lower bitrate of the second compression can hide the traces of the first compression, making the estimation more difficult. In general, the proposed method performs better than Vázquez-Padín's method.

Table 3. Estimation accuracy with different bitrates combinations

B_1/B_2		100	300	500	700
100	Proposed	**97.91%**	**99.55%**	**98.95%**	**98.95%**
	Vázquez-Padín's	93.75%	93.30%	92.70%	92.26%
300	Proposed	84.37%	**99.70%**	**99.70%**	**100%**
	Vázquez-Padín's	**86.01%**	94.04%	94.34%	93.60%
500	Proposed	69.49%	**95.83%**	**98.95%**	**99.85%**
	Vázquez-Padín's	**74.85%**	92.55%	94.94%	95.98%
700	Proposed	58.03%	**91.36%**	**97.47%**	**99.25%**
	Vázquez-Padín's	**66.96%**	87.35%	92.11%	94.49%

Analysis on Different Codecs Combination. The performance of GOP estimation with different codecs combinations and the overall accuracy for both methods are reported in Table 4. The experimental results show that the proposed scheme has better performance for the first GOP size estimation with different transcoding processes. Besides, it can be observed that when the first encoding is carried out using MPEG-x coding standard, the results of both schemes are much better. It is because the MPEG-x codecs provide lower encoding performance with respect to H.264 codecs. So the correlation between I-P frame and its previous P-P frame is weaker, which makes higher estimation accuracies for both Vázquez-Padín's scheme and the proposed scheme.

In comparison of the two schemes, the GOP estimation accuracy of the proposed scheme is higher than that of Vázquez-Padín's scheme 1.9%, 3.7% and 2.8% respectively. The overall accuracy of the proposed scheme is 2.8% higher than that of the Vázquez-Padín's scheme.

Table 4. Accuracy comparison of the GOP estimation

Transcoding process	Proposed	Vázquez-Padín's
MPEG-2 → H.264	95.68%	93.78%
MPEG-4 → H.264	94.42%	90.71%
H.264 → H.264	89.17%	86.39%
Overall accuracy	93.09%	90.29%

6 Conclusions

In this paper, a novel double H.264 compression detection scheme is proposed. A new feature, i.e. the PRED feature, is proposed to differentiate the I-P frames from the P-P frames. Then JSD is used to measure the difference between the PRED features of adjacent two frames. After obtaining the feature sequence, a Periodic Analysis method is applied for double compression detection. If the given video is doubly compressed, the Periodic Analysis method can further estimate GOP size of the first compression. Experiments have demonstrated that the proposed scheme is effective for double H.264 compression detection and GOP estimation, especially when the content of the given video is rich of texture.

Acknowledgment. This work was supported by the National Natural Science Foundation of China (Nos. 61572320, 61572321, 61272249, 61272439, 61271319). Corresponding author is X. H. Jiang, any comments should be addressed to xhjiang@sjtu.edu.cn.

References

1. Milani, S., Fontani, M., Bestagini, P., Barni, M., Piva, A., Tagliasacchi, M., Tubaro, S.: An overview on video forensics. APSIPA Trans. Sig. Inf. Process. **1**, e2 (2012)
2. Wang, W., Farid, H.: Exposing digital forgeries in video by detecting double quantization. In: Proceedings of the 11th ACM Workshop on Multimedia and Security, pp. 39–48. ACM (2009)
3. Su, Y., Xu, J.: Detection of double-compression in MPEG-2 videos. In: 2010 2nd International Workshop on Intelligent Systems and Applications (ISA), pp. 1–4. IEEE (2010)
4. Xu, J., Su, Y., Liu, Q.:Detection of double MPEG-2 compression based on distributions of DCT coefficients. Int. J. Pattern Recogn. Artif. Intell. **27**(01)
5. Chen, W., Shi, Y.Q.: Detection of double MPEG compression based on first digit statistics. In: Kim, H.-J., Katzenbeisser, S., Ho, Anthony, T.,S. (eds.) IWDW 2008. LNCS, vol. 5450, pp. 16–30. Springer, Heidelberg (2009). doi:10.1007/978-3-642-04438-0_2
6. Sun, T., Wang, W., Jiang, X.: Exposing video forgeries by detecting MPEG double compression. In: 2012 IEEE International Conference on Acoustics, Speech and Signal Processing (ICASSP), pp. 1389–1392. IEEE (2012)
7. Jiang, X., Wang, W., Sun, T., Shi, Y.Q., Wang, S.: Detection of double compression in MPEG-4 videos based on Markov statistics. IEEE Signal Process. Lett. **20**(5), 447–450 (2013)

8. Ravi, H., Subramanyam, A., Gupta, G., Kumar, B.A.: Compression noise based video forgery detection. In: 2014 IEEE International Conference on Image Processing (ICIP), pp. 5352–5356. IEEE (2014)

9. Subramanyam, A., Emmanuel, S.: Pixel estimation based video forgery detection. In: 2013 IEEE International Conference on Acoustics, Speech and Signal Processing (ICASSP), pp. 3038–3042. IEEE (2013)

10. Liao, D., Yang, R., Liu, H., Li, J., Huang, J.: Double H.264/AVC compression detection using quantized nonzero AC coefficients. In: IS&T/SPIE Electronic Imaging, International Society for Optics and Photonics, p. 78800Q (2011)

11. Huang, Z., Huang, F., Huang, J.: Detection of double compression with the same bit rate in MPEG-2 videos. In: 2014 IEEE China Summit & International Conference on Signal and Information Processing (ChinaSIP), pp. 306–309. IEEE (2014)

12. Wang, W., Farid, H.: Exposing digital forgeries in video by detecting double MPEG compression. In: Proceedings of the 8th Workshop on Multimedia and Security, pp. 37–47. ACM (2006)

13. Qin, Y.-I., Sun, G.-I., Wang, S.-Z., Zhang, X.-P.: Blind detection of video sequence montage based on GOP abnormality. Act Electron. Sin. **38**(7), 1597–1602 (2010)

14. Stamm, M.C., Lin, W.S., Liu, K.R.: Temporal forensics and anti-forensics for motion compensated video. IEEE Trans. Inf. Forensics Secur. **7**(4), 1315–1329 (2012)

15. He, P., Jiang, X., Sun, T., Wang, S.: Double compression detection based on local motion vector field analysis in static-background videos. J. Vis. Commun. Image Represent. **35**, 55–66 (2016)

16. Vázquez-Padín, D., Fontani, M., Bianchi, T., Comesana, P., Piva, A., Barni, M.: Detection of video double encoding with GOP size estimation. In: IEEE International Workshop on Information Forensics and Security (WIFS) (2012)

17. Luo, W., Wu, M., Huang, J.: MPEG recompression detection based on block artifacts. In: Electronic Imaging 2008, International Society for Optics and Photonics, p. 68190X (2008)

18. He, P., Sun, T., Jiang, X., Wang, S.: Double compression detection in MPEG-4 videos based on block artifact measurement with variation of prediction footprint. In: Huang, D.-S., Han, K. (eds.) ICIC 2015. LNCS (LNAI), vol. 9227, pp. 787–793. Springer, Heidelberg (2015). doi:10.1007/978-3-319-22053-6_84

19. Liu, H., Li, S., Bian, S.: Detecting frame deletion in H.264 video. In: Huang, X., Zhou, J. (eds.) ISPEC 2014. LNCS, vol. 8434, pp. 262–270. Springer, Heidelberg (2014). doi:10.1007/978-3-319-06320-1_20

Identification of Electronic Disguised Voices in the Noisy Environment

Wencheng Cao[1], Hongxia Wang[1(✉)], Hong Zhao[2], Qing Qian[1], and Sani M. Abdullahi[1]

[1] School of Information Science and Technology,
Southwest Jiaotong University, Chengdu, China
hxwang@home.swjtu.edu.cn
[2] Department of Electrical and Electronic Engineering,
South University of Science and Technology of China, Shenzhen, China

Abstract. Since voice disguise has been an increasing tendency in illegal application, which brings great negative impact on establishing the authenticity of audio evidence for audio forensics, especially in noisy environment. Thus it is very important to have the capability of identifying whether a suspected voice has been disguised or not. However, few studies about identification in noisy environment have been reported. In this paper, an algorithm based on linear frequency cepstrum coefficients (LFCC) statistical moments and Formant statistical moments is proposed to identify such condition. First, LFCC statistical moments including mean values and variance unbiased estimation values, and Formant statistical moments including mean values are extracted as acoustic features, and then Support vector machine (SVM) classifiers are used to separate disguised voices from original voices. Experimental results verify the excellent performance of the proposed scheme in the noisy environment.

Keywords: Identification · Electronic disguised voices · LFCC · Formant · Noisy environment · SVM

1 Introduction

Voice disguise is a deliberate operation to conceal or forge a speaker's identity by changing his or her voice tone [1]. Disguising methods can be divided into two types: non-electronic and electronic [2]. Non-electronic disguise changes voice tone of a speaker by using mechanical way, and its methods include pinching the nostrils, clenching the jaw, holding the tongue, speaking with an object in mouth, etc. Electronic disguise modifies frequency spectral properties of voice by using audio editing software. Nowadays, the audio editing software such as Audacity, CoolEdit, PARRT can provide disguising tools with a variety of disguising factors. By choosing an appropriate disguised factor, the voice obtained by electronic disguised can easily deceive human auditory system. Such condition add the frequency of criminal in telephone communication, voice chat and other audio applications. But voices in real life are often mixed with noises in different types and intensities, which reduces the audibility and intelligibility of voices and brings negative effect on voices identification accuracy

© Springer International Publishing AG 2017
Y.Q. Shi et al. (Eds.): IWDW 2016, LNCS 10082, pp. 75–87, 2017.
DOI: 10.1007/978-3-319-53465-7_6

rate. Especially in forensic speaker identification (FSI) the correct identification rate can be degraded by the background noise. So it is necessary to study on the effect of disguised voice on FSI [3].

In the literature, previous methods on identifying electronic disguised voices have studied. In [4], MFCC statistical moments as features are extracted for identifying electronic disguised voices based on the TIMIT speech database and SVM [5, 6], which shows good performance in clean voice but does not consider about noisy voices. In [7], MFCC statistical moments as features are extracted for identifying electronic disguised voices based on the TIMIT, NIST, UME speech database and SVM. The experimental results show that the features have good performance using cross-method identification, but noisy voices were not considered. Several related studies have focused on the effect of voice disguise on Automatic Speaker Recognition(ASR) systems. In [3], authors investigated the effect of ten kinds of non-electronic disguised methods on automatic speaker recognition, the ASR is from Reference [8]. A ASR system was designed for speaker recognition evaluation in [9]. References [3, 9] have showed that different disguised voices have a negative effect on the performance of speaker recognition evaluation. The identification of disguised voices can be used as preliminary step before trying to identify a speaker, especially in forensic sciences [10]. Although there were efforts on identification of electronic disguised voices, the results are under clean speech without noisy environment. This may lead to a decrease in effectiveness of identifying realistic voices. Therefore, our study mainly focuses on the performance of identification of electronic disguised voices in noisy environment.

In the proposed approach, statistical moments of linear frequency cepstrum coefficients (LFCC) and formant are computed as the acoustic features, and Support Vector Machine (SVM) [4, 7] method is used for classification. Voices are disguised by Audacity. Noise includes babble noise, factory noise, volvo noise from NoiseX-92 corpus database. The experiments results achieve good performance in different noisy environment.

The remaining of this paper is organized as follows. Section 2 introduces electronic voice disguise. Section 3 is about feature extraction and the approach for detection of disguised voice. Section 4 presents experimental results. Section 5 gives the conclusion and future work.

2 Electronic Voice Disguise

In essence, voice disguise is expected to modify the voice pitch of a speaker to conceal his or her identity [4, 7]. In phonetics, pitch is always measured by 12-semitones-division, indicating that pitch can be raised or lowered by 12 semitones at most [11]. A scaling factor of pitch semitones is the disguising factor. Suppose the pitch of a speech frame to be p_0, the disguising factor to be a semitones and the pitch of the modified speech frame to be p, we have [11]:

$$p = 2^{a/12} \bullet p_0 \tag{1}$$

If a is positive, the spectrum is stretched and pitch is raised. Otherwise, spectrum is compressed and pitch is lowered. In this paper, a disguising factor $+k$ is used to denote a pitch-raise modification with k semitones, while $-k$ is used to denote a pitch-lower modification with k semitones.

3 Identification of Electronic Disguised Voices

Since pitch modification on a speech signal changes LFCC and formant, leaving footprints in statistical moments of LFCC and formant, we use LFCC and Formant statistical moments as the acoustic features for modeling. The detection system is based on SVM [4, 7].

3.1 Features Extraction of LFCC

The features are extracted as follow.

Step 1. A speech signal $x(n)$ is pre-emphasized in advance for compensating the lost of high frequency component. The pre-emphasis filter is

$$H(z) = 1 - a \bullet z^{-1}, 0.9 \leq a \leq 1 \tag{2}$$

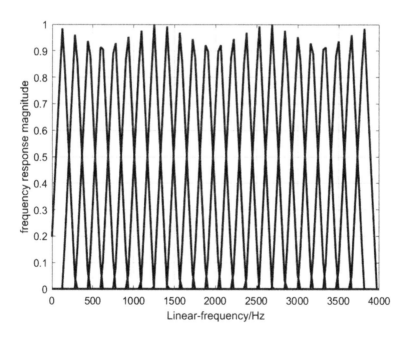

Fig. 1. Linear-filter bank in linear-frequency domain

Step 2. Here $x(n)$ is segmented into N frames. The duration of each frame is m ms and overlap is $m/2$ ms.

Step 3. Voice activity detection (VAD) is performed on the N frames with energy-entropy [12]. Suppose the frequency spectrum $X_i(k)$ of the ith frame $x_i(m)$ is calculated by Fast Fourier Transform(FFT). We have the power spectrum E_i. which is given by Eq. (3):

$$E_i = \sum_{k=0}^{M/2} X_i(k) * X_i^*(k) \tag{3}$$

Where M is the length of FFT, and k refers to the kth spectrum. So the normalized probability density function of each frequency component is $p_i(k)$, given by Eq. 4:

$$p_i(k) = \frac{X_i(k) * X_i^*(k)}{E_i} \tag{4}$$

The energy-entropy of ith frame EEF_i is calculated by Eq. (5):

$$EEF_i = \sqrt{1 + \left| E_i / - \sum_{k=0}^{M/2} p_i(k) \log p_i(k) \right|} \tag{5}$$

Suppose the first frame of a speech does not have human's voice except noise, EEF_1 is used as a threshold. If $EEF_{i \sim i+4, 1 < i < N-3}$ is greater than $EEF_i + thr$(here thr is 0.05), this duration is a sound segment, otherwise, this duration is a silence segment.

Step 4. Frequency spectral $X(j,k)$ of the jth frame of sound segments is calculated by Fast Fourier Transform. The power spectrum filtered by a linear bank B_{lin} is given by Eq. (6):

$$S(j,l) = \sum_{k=0}^{M-1} [X(j,k)]^2 H_l(k), 0 \le l < L, 0 < j < N \tag{6}$$

$H_l(k)$ is given by Eq. (7):

$$H_l(k) = \begin{cases} 0 & k < f(l-1) \\ \frac{k-f(l-1)}{f(l)-f(l-1)} & f(m-1) \le k \le f(l) \\ \frac{f(l-1)-k}{f(l+1)-f(l)} & f(l) \le k \le f(l+1) \\ 0 & k > f(l+1) \end{cases} \tag{7}$$

Here l is the lth linear filter, B_{lin} consists of L triangular band-pass filters, which are located in Linear-frequency in a uniformly spaced way, as shown in Fig. 1. The Discrete Cosine Transform (DCT) is applied to the $S(j,l)$ to calculate the n-dimensional $LFCC$ of $x_j(m)$:

$$lfcc(j,n) = \sqrt{\frac{2}{L}} \sum_{l=0}^{L-1} \log[S(j,l)] \cos(\frac{\pi n(2l-1)}{2L}) \qquad (8)$$

where $lfcc(j,n)$ is $LFCC$ of jth frame, and n is the coefficient of DCT.

Step 5. Suppose there are s sound frames in a speech signal, s n-dimensional $LFCC$ is given by Eq. (9):

$$LFCC = \begin{vmatrix} x_{1,1} & x_{1,2} & \cdots & x_{1,n} \\ x_{2,1} & x_{2,2} & \cdots & x_{2,n} \\ \cdots & \cdots & \cdots & \cdots \\ x_{s,1} & x_{s,2} & \cdots & x_{s,n} \end{vmatrix} \qquad (9)$$

Derivative coefficients $LFCC$ are computed using Eq. (10) to get the $\Delta LFCC$ vectors. $\Delta LFCC$ is given by Eq. (11).

$$\Delta x_{i,j} = \frac{1}{3} \sum_{u=-2}^{2} u x_{i+u,j}, 3 \leq i \leq s-2, 1 \leq j \leq s \qquad (10)$$

$$\Delta LFCC = \begin{vmatrix} \Delta x_{3,1} & \Delta x_{3,2} & \cdots & \Delta x_{3,n} \\ \Delta x_{4,1} & \Delta x_{4,2} & \cdots & \Delta x_{4,n} \\ \cdots & \cdots & \cdots & \cdots \\ \Delta x_{s-2,1} & \Delta x_{s-2,2} & \cdots & \Delta x_{s-2,n} \end{vmatrix} \qquad (11)$$

In this paper, two kinds of statistical moments including mean values (E) and variance unbiased estimation values (VAR) of $LFCC$ and $\Delta LFCC$ in each column are computed as one portion of features. Mean values and variance unbiased estimation values of $LFCC$ are calculated by Eqs. (12) and (13):

$$E_o = E(x_{1,o}, x_{2,o}, \ldots, x_{s,o}), o = 1, 2, \ldots, n \qquad (12)$$

$$VAR_o = VAR(x_{1,o}, x_{2,o}, \ldots, x_{s,o}) \qquad (13)$$

Mean values and variance unbiased estimation values of $\Delta LFCC$ are calculated by Eqs. (14) and (15):

$$\Delta E_o = E(\Delta x_{3,o}, \Delta x_{4,o}, \ldots, \Delta x_{s-2,o}) \qquad (14)$$

$$\Delta VAR_o = VAR(\Delta x_{3,o}, \Delta x_{4,o}, \ldots, \Delta x_{s-2,o}) \qquad (15)$$

The resulting Eo, ΔEo, VAR_O, $\Delta VARo$ are combined to form the statistical moments W_{LFCC}, which is given by Eq. (16):

$$W_{LFCC} = [E_o, \Delta E_o, VAR_o, \Delta VAR_o] \qquad (16)$$

The extraction procedure of LFCC statistical moments is shown in Fig. 2.

Fig. 2. Extraction procedure of LFCC statistical moments

3.2   Features Extraction of Formants

Features on Formants are extracted as in Fig. 3, and the process is as follows:

Fig. 3. Extraction procedure of formant statistical moments

Step 1. Pre-emphasis, framing, VAD are same to extraction of LFCC.

Step 2. Suppose a speech signal $x(n)$, for each sound frame of $x(n)$, p linear predictive coding (LPC) coefficients are calculated to obtain the Formants, here p is set to 9. Roots of p LPC coefficients are used for calculating absolute values and phase angle. Roots are given by Eq. (17). Absolute value and phase angle are given by Eqs. (18) and (19).

$$[root_1, root_2, \ldots, root_p] \tag{17}$$

$$[abs(root_1), abs(root_2), \ldots, abs(root_p)] \tag{18}$$

$$[angle(root_1), angle(root_2), \ldots, angle(root_p)] \tag{19}$$

Here transform the phase angle into frequency by Eq. (20) and the frequency is written as:

$$f\_root_i = angle(root_i)/\pi * fs/2 \tag{20}$$

Step 3. For every roots from each sound frame, if $abs(root_i)$ is bigger than threshold thr2(here thr2 is 0.75), $angle(root_i)$ is smaller than π and f_root_i is bigger than 200, f_root_i is kept as Formant and the number of Formant is 3.

Suppose Formants of $x(n)$ is F given by Eq. (21):

$$F = \begin{vmatrix} x_{1,1} & x_{1,2} & x_{1,3} \\ x_{2,1} & x_{2,2} & x_{2,3} \\ \cdots & \cdots & \cdots \\ x_{s,1} & x_{s,2} & x_{s,3} \end{vmatrix} \tag{21}$$

Mean values calculated is same to Eq. (12) and mean values of Formant are $E_k(k = 1,2,3)$,The statistical moments of Formant $W_{formant}$ is given by Eq. (22):

$$W_{formant} = [E_k] \tag{22}$$

Step 4. Before combining W_{LFCC} and $W_{formant}$ to form the acoustic feature W. $[E_O, \ \Delta E_O]$, $[VAR_O, \Delta VAR_O]$, $[E_k]$ have normalization respective first. The normalization method is given by Eq. (23):

$$H_{i,j} = \frac{S_{i,j} - \min(S)}{\max(S) - \min(S)} \tag{23}$$

After normalization, the final acoustic feature W is given by Eq. (24):

$$W = [E_o, \Delta E_o, VAR_o, \Delta VAR_o, E_k] \tag{24}$$

i and j represent the number of rows and columns, S represents a matrix before normalization, and H represents the matrix after normalization.

3.3 Detection Method

LFCC statistical moments and Formant statistical moments are used in this paper as feature, and SVM classification is adopted. Detection system [4, 7] for disguised noisy voices is given in Fig. 4.

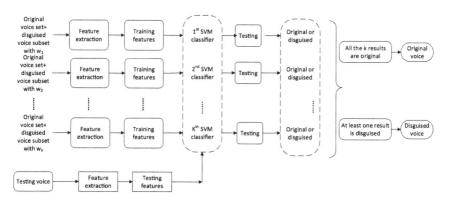

Fig. 4. Generic identification system of disguised voices

In training stage, the data contain two sets of voice data, original voices and disguised voices. According to K different disguised factors, there are K SVM classifiers. Each of the classifiers is used to identify whether a testing voice is disguised or not. In testing stage, the acoustic features are extracted and tested by K classifiers. The conclusion that this voice is not disguised can only be made unless all of the classifier indicate that the tested voices are original. Otherwise it has been disguised.

4 Experimental Results

4.1 Experimental Setup

TIMIT, NOIZEUS and Noise92 are used as corpus in this experiment. TIMIT includes 6300 pieces of voices recorded by 630 persons with the average duration of 3 s. NOIZEUS in our work is composed of 30 voice segments with the average duration of 3 s. The file format is wav, sample frequency is 8000 Hz,16-bit quantization and mono. The TIMIT is divided into two groups in this experiment: one is comprised of 4620 pieces of voices recorded by 462 persons called TIMIT_1 as training group, and the other is called TIMIT_2 which includes 1680 pieces of voices by 168 persons as testing group. Meanwhile, by adding babble noise, factory noise and volvo noise from Noise92 into TIMIT_2 and NOIZEUS makes the signal-noise ratio (SNR) to be 20 dB, 15 dB, 10 dB as testing group too. A Gaussian Radial Basis Function (RBF) kernel method is used in training a SVM classifier.

4.2 Detection Performance

The detection rate (DR) of disguised voices and the False Alarm Rate (FAR) are used in my experimental. Y_D denotes the number of the disguised voices for testing and Y_O denotes the number of the original voices for testing. Y_D' is identified as disguised voices from disguised voices, and Y_O' is identified as disguised voices from original voices. The DR is defined as Y_D'/Y_D, FAR is defined as Y_O'/Y_O.

In this experiment, Audacity is used for disguising voices. The tested disguising factors contain −8, −7, −6, −5, −4, +4, +5, +6, +7, +8. Tables 1 and 2 shows the detection rate of disguised noisy voices with variable disguised factors in TIMIT_2 and NOIZEUS. It can be seen that the detection rate of noisy voices with the babble, factory noise are close to 100%, even the SNR is 10 dB. Detection rate have a significant decrease when voices were added with volvo noise and the SNR equals 10 dB.

Table 3 shows the FAR of original noisy voices in TIMIT_2 and NOIZEUS, FAR_T is the FAR of TIMIT_2, FAR_N is the FAR of NOIZEUS. The FAR of TIMIT_2 is smaller than 3% when SNR is 20 dB or 15 dB. The FAR will have a deterioration when SNR is 10 no matter what noise is added. Most FAR in NOIZEUS are smaller than 10% when the added noise is babble or factory but not volvo. Considering the voices audibility and intelligibility will reduce a lot when SNR is low, making voices disguised meaningless, indicating that the proposed algorithm is still effective to identify disguised voices in noisy environment. Here comparison was just under clean TIMIT voices in the case of [4] only have experiments on that. Table 4 is the comparison between [4] and the proposed algorithm about identification performance of detection rate and FAR with the software Audacity. It can be seen that the proposed algorithm has better detection rate and FAR on clean voices when features have less dimension.

Table 1. Detection rate (DR) of noisy voices with variable disguising factors in TIMIT_2

Disguise factor	Noisy voices								
	Babble			Factory			Volvo		
	SNR = 20 dB	SNR = 15 dB	SNR = 10 dB	SNR = 20 dB	SNR = 15 dB	SNR = 10 dB	SNR = 20 dB	SNR = 15 dB	SNR = 10 dB
−8	100%	100%	100%	100%	100%	100%	100%	100%	100%
−7	100%	100%	100%	100%	100%	100%	100%	100%	97.50%
−6	100%	100%	100%	100%	100%	100%	100%	100%	100%
−5	100%	100%	100%	100%	100%	100%	100%	100%	100%
−4	100%	100%	100%	100%	100%	100%	100%	100%	0.12%
+4	100%	100%	100%	100%	100%	100%	100%	99.82%	72.13%
+5	100%	100%	100%	100%	100%	100%	99.52%	96.69%	99.94%
+6	100%	100%	100%	100%	100%	100%	100%	99.94%	94.88%
+7	100%	100%	100%	99.64%	100%	100%	100%	100%	92.50%
+8	100%	100%	100%	100%	100%	100%	99.94%	99.23%	100%

Table 2. Detection rate (DR) of noisy voices with variable disguising factors in NOIZEUS

Disguise factor	Noisy voices								
	Babble			Factory			Volvo		
	SNR = 20 dB	SNR = 15 dB	SNR = 10 dB	SNR = 20 dB	SNR = 15 dB	SNR = 10 dB	SNR = 20 dB	SNR = 15 dB	SNR = 10 dB
−8	100%	100%	100%	100%	100%	100%	100%	100%	100%
−7	100%	100%	100%	100%	100%	100%	100%	100%	100%
−6	100%	100%	100%	100%	100%	100%	100%	100%	100%
−5	100%	100%	100%	100%	100%	100%	100%	100%	100%
−4	100%	100%	100%	100%	100%	100%	100%	100%	100%
+4	100%	100%	100%	100%	100%	100%	100%	100%	60.00%
+5	100%	100%	100%	100%	100%	100%	100%	100%	36.67%
+6	100%	100%	100%	100%	100%	100%	100%	100%	100%
+7	100%	100%	100%	100%	100%	100%	100%	100%	100%
+8	100%	100%	100%	100%	100%	100%	100%	100%	100%

Table 3. FAR of noisy voices in TIMIT_2 and NOIZEUS

Noisy voices	Babble			Factory			Volvo		
	SNR = 20 dB	SNR = 15 dB	SNR = 10 dB	SNR = 20 dB	SNR = 15 dB	SNR = 10 dB	SNR = 20 dB	SNR = 15 dB	SNR = 10 dB
FAR_T	2.98%	2.62%	28.98%	2.38%	5.18%	42.38%	1.19%	1.19%	79.57%
FAR_N	6.67%	10.0%	6.67%	6.67%	6.67%	13.13%	26.67%	36.67%	33.33%

Table 4. Comparison between proposed and [4] about detection rate and FAR of clean voices

	Disguising factor(semitones)										FAR
	+4	+5	+6	+7	+8	-4	-5	-6	-7	-8	
[4]	98.73%	99.52%	99.94%	100%	100%	100%	100%	100%	100%	100%	3.15%
Proposed	99.94%	99.82%	100%	100%	98.57%	100%	100%	100%	100%	100%	1.61%

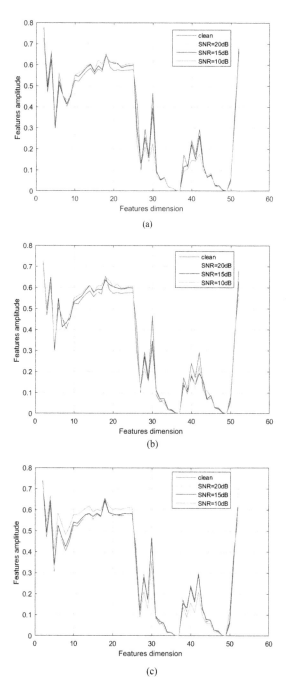

Fig. 5. Features of original clean voice and original noisy voice. (a) Clean voice and noisy voice with babble noise. (b) Clean voice and noisy voice with factory noise. (c) Clean voice and noisy voice with volvo noise

The features of original clean voice and original noisy voice are presented in Fig. 5. It can be seen that when SNR is 20 dB or 15 dB, features from noisy voice are more close to clean voice. However when SNR is 10 dB, the difference between clean voice and noisy voice is more evident.

The features of original clean voice and original noisy voice are presented in Fig. 5. It can be seen that when SNR is 20 dB or 15 dB, features from noisy voice are more close to clean voice. However when SNR is 10 dB, the difference between clean voice and noisy voice is more evident.

5 Conclusions

In this paper, an algorithm for identifying electronic disguised voices in the noisy environment is proposed. LFCC and Formant statistical moments are extracted as acoustic features of speech signals and SVM is used as classification method. In this experiment, four kinds of voices are used for testing, clean voices and three kinds of noisy voices. Detection performance and FAR of the proposed approach is demonstrated to be excellent when SNR is 20 dB and 15 dB when the test corpus is TIMIT_2. However when SNR is 10 dB the performance is not good enough. When test corpus is NOIZEUS, FAR of noisy voices with volvo is not good enough. The future work will focus on the identification of noisy voices with low SNR, taking more noisy environment into considering and the identification between more corpus.

Acknowledgement. This work was supported by the National Science Foundation of China (NSFC) under the grant No. U1536110, partly supported by the National Natural Science Foundation of China under the grant No. 61402219.

References

1. Perrot, P., Aversano, G., Chollet, G.: Voice disguise and automatic detection: review and perspectives. In: Stylianou, Y., Faundez-Zanuy, M., Esposito, A. (eds.). LNCS, vol. 4391, pp. 101–117Springer, Heidelberg (2007). doi:10.1007/978-3-540-71505-4_7
2. Rodman, R.: Speaker recognition of disguised voices: a program for research. In: Proceedings of the Consortium on Speech Technology in Conjunction with the Conference on Speaker Recognition by Man and Machine: Directions for Forensic Applications, pp. 9–22 (1998)
3. Tan, T.J.: The effect of voice disguise on automatic speaker recognition. In: IEEE International Congress on Image and Signal Processing, pp. 3538–3541 (2010)
4. Wu, H.J., Wang, Y., Huang, J.W.: Blind detection of electronic disguised voice. In: IEEE International Conference on Acoustics, Speech and Signal Processing, Brisbane, Australia, pp. 3013–3017 (2013)
5. Gu, B., Sheng, V.S.: A robust regularization path algorithm for ν-support vector classification. In: IEEE Transactions on Neural Networks & Learning Systems, pp. 1–8 (2016)
6. Gu, B., Sheng, V.S., Tay, K.Y., et al.: Incremental support vector learning for ordinal regression. IEEE Trans. Neural Netw. Learn. Syst. **26**(7), 1403–1416 (2014)

7. Wu, H.J., Wang, Y., Huang, J.W.: Identification of electronic disguised voices. IEEE Trans. Inf. Forensics Secur. **9**(3), 489–500 (2014)
8. Jingxu, C., Hongchen, Y., Zhanjiang, S.: The speaker automatic identified system and its forensic application. In: Proceedings of the International Symposium on Computing and Information, vol. 1, pp. 96–100 (2004)
9. Kajarekar, S.S., Ferrer, L., Shriberg, E., et al.: SRI's 2004 NIST speaker recognition evaluation system. In: IEEE International Congress on Acoustics, Pennsylvania USA, pp. 173–176 (2005)
10. Perrot, P., Chollet, G.: The question of disguised voice. J. Acoust. Soc. Am. **123**(5), 3878 (2008)
11. Trehub, S.E., Cohen, A.J., Thorpe, L.A., Morrongiello, B.A.: Development of the perception of musical relations: semitone and diatonic structure. J. Exp. Psychol. Hum. Percept. Perform. **12**(3), 295–301 (1986)
12. Sun, J.N., De-Sheng, F.U., Yong-Hua, X.U.: Speech detection algorithm based on energy - entropy. Comput. Eng. Des. **26**(12), 3429–3431 (2005)

Using Benford's Law Divergence and Neural Networks for Classification and Source Identification of Biometric Images

Aamo Iorliam[1(✉)], Anthony T.S. Ho[1,3,4], Adrian Waller[2], and Xi Zhao[3]

[1] Department of Computer Science, University of Surrey, Guildford, UK
{a.iorliam,a.ho}@surrey.ac.uk
[2] Thales UK Research and Technology, Reading, UK
adrian.waller@uk.thalesgroup.com
[3] School of Computer Science and Information Engineering,
Tianjin University of Science and Technology, Tianjin, China
xi.zhao@tust.edu.cn
[4] Wuhan University of Technology, Wuhan, China
http://www.surrey.ac.uk/cs/people/

Abstract. It is obvious that tampering of raw biometric samples is becoming an important security concern. The Benford's law, which is also called the first digit law has been reported in the forensic literature to be very effective in detecting forged or tampered data. In this paper, the divergence values of Benford's law are used as input features for a Neural Network for the classification and source identification of biometric images. Experimental analysis shows that the classification and identification of the source of the biometric images can achieve good accuracies between the range of 90.02% and 100%.

Keywords: Benford's law · Neural network · Biometric images

1 Introduction

There exist many different types of physical biometric modalities such as fingerprint images, vein wrist images, face images and iris images. If we consider only fingerprint images, there are also different types of fingerprints such as contactless acquired latent fingerprints, optically acquired fingerprints and synthetic generated fingerprints. These fingerprints could be intentionally or accidentally used for a different purpose which could pose a security threat. As such, there exists a possibility that fingerprints could be forged at crime scenes by potentially transferring latent fingerprint to other objects [1].

Recent approaches have been developed to tackle fingerprint forgeries. For example, Iorliam *et al.* [2] used the Benford's law divergence metric to separate optically acquired fingerprints, synthetically generated fingerprints and contact-less acquired fingerprints. The purpose of this study was to protect against insider attackers and against hackers that may have illegal access to

© Springer International Publishing AG 2017
Y.Q. Shi et al. (Eds.): IWDW 2016, LNCS 10082, pp. 88–105, 2017.
DOI: 10.1007/978-3-319-53465-7_7

such biometric data. Hildebrandt and Dittmann [3] used the differences between Benford's law and the distribution of the most significant digit of the intensity and topography data to detect printed fingerprints. Their experiments on 3000 printed and 3000 latent print samples achieved a detection performance of up to 98.85% using WEKA's Bagging classifier in a 10-fold stratified cross-validation. Motivated by approaches in [2,3], this paper investigates the different biometric data using Benford's law divergence metrics. To achieve the Benford's law divergence values, the luminance component of the face images is first extracted and the first digit distributions of the JPEG coefficients is then performed on the face images. For the other datasets described in Sect. 3.2, the first digit distributions of the JPEG coefficients is performed directly on the gray-scale images. Using Eq. (7), the Benford's law divergence values are obtained. The Benford's law divergence values are then used as features fed into a Neural Network (NN) classifier for classification. Therefore an inter-class classification of biometric images using Benford's law divergence and NN is performed. By inter-class classification, we mean separability of biometric images that are not closely related (e.g. fingerprint images, vein wrist images, face images and iris images). We also perform intra-class classification of biometric images using Benford's law divergence and NN. By intra-class classification, we mean separability of biometric images that are closely related (e.g. contact-less acquired latent fingerprints, optically acquired fingerprints and synthetic generated fingerprints). Lastly, both the closely related and non-closely related biometric images are classified using Benford's law divergence and NN.

2   Related Work

2.1   Benford's Law

Benford's law has been reported by Fu *et al.* [13], Li *et al.* [14] and Xu *et al.* [15] to be very effective in detecting tampering of images. Benford's law of "anomalous digits" was first coined by Frank Benford in 1938 [16], is also denoted as the first digit law, considers the frequency of appearance of the most significant digit (MSD), for a broad range of natural and artificial data [17]. The Benford's law as described by Hill [18] can be expressed in the form of a logarithmic distribution, when considering the probability distribution of the first digit from 1 to 9 for a range of natural data. Naturally generated data are supposed to obey this law whereas tampered or randomly guessed data do not follow [19].

When considering the MSD where 0 is excluded, and the datasets satisfy the Benford's law, then the law can be expressed as Eq. (1) [18].

$$p(x) = \log_{10}(1 + \frac{1}{x}) \tag{1}$$

where x is the first digit of the number and $p(x)$ refers to the probability distribution of x.

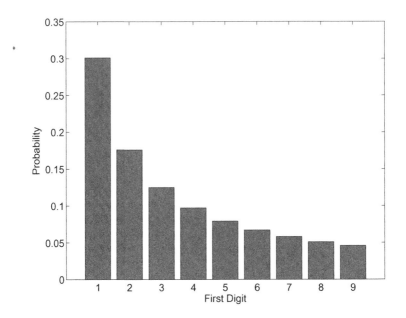

Fig. 1. The first digit probability distribution of Benford's law

The first digit probability distribution of Benford's law is shown in Fig. 1. An extension of the Benford's law by Fu *et al.* [13] is referred to as Generalised Benford's law which closely follows a logarithmic law is defined in Eq. (2) [13].

$$p(x) = N \log_{10}(1 + \frac{1}{s + x^q}) \qquad (2)$$

where N is a normalization factor which makes $p(x)$ a probability distribution. The model parameters in this case are represented by s and q which describe the distributions for different images and different compressions QFs as defined in [13]. Through experiments, Fu *et al.* [13] provided values for N, s and q. They determined these values using the Matlab toolbox, which returns the Sum of Squares due to Error (SSE). The N, s and q values are adopted as shown in Table 1 for our Generalised Benford's law experiments. There have been several developments concerning the Benford's law in image forensics [13,14,17,20–22]. Jolion [21] applied this law to image processing and found that it worked well on the magnitude of the gradient of an image. He also showed that it applied to the laplacian decomposition of images as well. Acebo and Sbert [20] also applied the Benford's law to image processing and showed that when synthetic images were generated using physically realistic method, they followed this law. However, when they were generated with different methods, they did not follow this law. Gonzalez *et al.* [17] proved that when images were transformed by the Discrete Cosine Transform (DCT), their DCT coefficients would follow this law. Moreover, they showed that the Generalized Benford's law could detect hidden data in a natural image [17].

Table 1. Model parameters used for generalised Benford's law [13]

Q-factor	Model Parameters			Goodness-of-fit (SSE)
	N	q	s	
100	1.456	1.47	0.0372	$7.104e - 06$
90	1.255	1.563	-0.3784	$5.255e - 07$
80	1.324	1.653	-0.3739	$3.0683e - 06$
70	1.412	1.732	-0.337	$5.36171e - 06$
60	1.501	1.813	-0.3025	$6.11167e - 06$
50	1.579	1.882	-0.2725	$6.0544e - 06$

Digital images in the pixel domain do not follow the Benford's law because their values fall between 0 (black) and 255 (white). This means we have only 256 values to calculate the Benford's law when considering images in the pixel domain. Thus this will not conform to the Benford's law because this law works better as the dynamic values under consideration tends to be large. By transforming the pixel values using DCT, a single block matrix has 64 DCT coefficients, which when combined together in a whole image, produces dynamic values large enough to follow the Benford's law. Fu *et al.* [13] used this law on DCT coefficients to detect unknown JPEG compression. They used 1,338 images from Uncompressed Image Database (UCID). They also repeated the same experiment on 198 images from Harrison datasets. Qadir *et al.* [22] investigated the Discrete Wave Transform (DWT) coefficients using the Benford's law and analysing the processing history applied to JPEG2000 images, where they observed a sharp peak at the digit five of the Benford's law curve for some images. As a result, they proposed the use of this law to identify unbalanced lighting or glare effect in images with the help of DWT [22]. Li *et al.* [14] used the statistical features of the first digits of individual alternate current and support vector machine (SVM) to detect and locate the tampered region of natural images. Iorliam *et al.* [2] performed experiments on the Benford's law divergence values of biometric data for separability purposes. The results showed that biometric datasets behave differently when analysed using Benford's law divergence metrics. Therefore, we extend the approach in [2], to achieve the Benford's law divergence values from biometric data. We then use these divergence values as features fed into the NN for classification and source identification of biometric images. Hildebrandt and Dittmann [3] main focus was to differentiate between real fingerprints and printed fingerprints. However, our method focuses not only on these two types of datasets but also other biometric datasets such as face images, vein wrist datasets and iris datasets. Furthermore, we use divergence values as features for classification and source identification of biometric images. Whereas their method used the differences between Benford's law and the distribution of the most significant digit of the intensity and topography data to detect printed fingerprints. Additionally, we use NN as a classifier, whereas their method used WEKA's Bagging classifier in a 10-fold stratified cross-validation.

2.2 Neural Networks

NN works by accepting input data, extracting rules based on the accepted inputs and then make decisions. Multi-layer perceptrons (MLP) which is a feed-forward type of NN has one or more hidden layers between the input layer and output layer. Training is usually carried out using back-propagation learning algorithm. MLP has the advantage of modelling functions that are highly non-linear and when trained, it can correctly predict on unknown data sets. Figure 2 shows a pictorial representation of an MLP with two inputs, one hidden layer and two outputs.

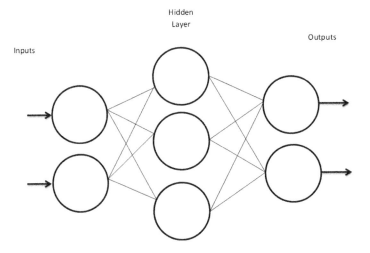

Fig. 2. A multilayer perceptron with one hidden layer

The MLP typically uses the sigmoid hidden neurons which are described by the formula shown in Eq. (3):

$$y = \frac{1}{1 + exp(-s)} \tag{3}$$

where s is an integration function defined by $s = f(x; \theta)$.

Furthermore, the MLP has softmax output neurons which has the formula as shown in Eq. (4):

$$y_i = \frac{exp\,(s_i)}{\sum_j exp\,(s_j)} \tag{4}$$

where s has the same meaning as above.

After the network is trained and tested, there are performance evaluation metrics such as the Cross Entropy (CE) and Percentage Error (% E) that can be used to determine how well the network has achieved in terms of classification. The CE is defined by Eq. (5):

$$CE = -sum(t * log(y))$$ (5)

where t is the target data and y is the output value from the trained network. Whereas the % E is defined by Eq. (6):

$$CE = sum(t \neq y)/(number\ of\ t)$$ (6)

where t and y have the same meaning as above.

Based on the above reasons, we chose NN using MLP for this classification task. For performance evaluation, the CE and % E are used for our experiments in this paper.

3   Experimental Set-Up

The goal of the first experiment is to use the divergence metrics to show how the data samples used for this experiments depart from the Generalised Benford's law. The Benford's law divergence values acquired from physical biometric images (i.e. from the vein wrist images, face images, iris images, optical sensor acquired fingerprints images, artificially printed contact-less acquired latent fingerprint images and synthetic generated fingerprints) are then used as features and fed into an NN for separability purposes. There is a real need to separate biometric images as discussed in the next section.

3.1   Separation of Different Types of Biometric Images

Generally, biometrics is used either for verification (1-to-1 matching) where we seek to answer the question "Is this person who they say they are?" or for identification (1-to-many (n) matching) where we seek to answer the question "Who is this person?" or "Who generated this biometric?" [4]. To achieve identification or verification, biometric modalities are used. For example, fingerprints have been used for identification purposes for over a century [5]. Iris recognition systems use iris modality and it is of importance due to its high accuracy. As such, it has attracted a great deal of attention recently [6]. Vein pattern recognition, which uses vein modality, is a developing field and is a potential research area in the field of biometrics [8].

Fingerprints have different uses. For example, fingerprints captured using optical sensors are used for identification or verification. Whereas synthetic generated fingerprints are used for testing fingerprint recognition algorithms. This requires a large database and collecting real fingerprints for such a large database is very expensive, labour intensive and problematic [7]. The contact-less acquired latent fingerprints are generated for evaluation and research purposes with the aim of avoiding privacy implications [9]. The study of different characteristics of these biometric images is of importance both for biometrics and forensic purposes. This process could assist in the source identification of captured biometric images. This can be achieved by identifying the source hardware that captured the biometric image [10]. This is necessary in cases where the "chain of custody" involving a biometric image has to be properly verified [10].

3.2   Data Sets

As stated in Table 2, for the face modality, the CASIA-FACEV5 is used which consists of 2500 coloured images of 500 subjects [12]. The face images are 16 bit colour BMP files with image resolution of 640 × 480. We use all the face images from CASIA-FACEV5 in this experiment. For the fingerprint modality, we use the FVC2000 which has four different fingerprint databases (DB1, DB2, DB3 and DB4) [11]. DB1, DB2, DB3 and DB4 have 80 gray scale fingerprint images in (tiff format) each. DB1 fingerprint images are captured by a low-cost optical sensor "Secure Desktop Scanner". While DB2 fingerprint images are captured by a low-cost optical capacitive sensor "TouchChip". DB3 fingerprint images are from optical sensor "DF-90". DB4 fingerprint images are synthetically generated fingerprints. However, for the fact that these fingerprints (DB1, DB2, DB3) are captured using different sensors and DB4 is synthetically generated, we treat them as separate fingerprint databases.

An additional fingerprint dataset used in this experiment contains 48 artificially printed contact-less acquired latent fingerprint images. These are grayscale images with 32 bit colour depth [9]. We use 1200 images of wrist pattern from PUT vein database [8]. The iris images used in our experiment are from

Table 2. Summary description of data sets

Data Set	Description	Number of Samples
CASIA-FACEV5 [12]	Coloured face images of 500 subjects	2500
FVC2000 [11]	DB1- Fingerprint images captured by "Secure Desktop Scanner"	80
	DB2- Fingerprint images captured by "TouchChip"	80
	DB3- Fingerprint images captured by "DF-90"	80
	DB4- Synthetically generated fingerprint images	80
Fingerprint data set from Hildebrandt *et al.* [9]	Artificially printed contact-less acquired latent fingerprint images	48
PUT vein database [8]	Images of wrist pattern	1200
CASIA-IrisV1 [6]	Iris images from 108 eyes	756

CASIA-IrisV1 which contains 756 iris images from 108 eyes which are saved in BMP format with resolution of 320×280 [6]. Figure 6 shows some sample biometric images used in these experiments. A summary description of the data sets is given in Table 2.

3.3 Divergence Metric and Separability of Biometric Databases

In order to separate biometric databases, the Benford's law divergence values are obtained from the biometric data. The divergence metric is used to show

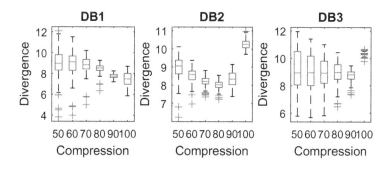

(a)

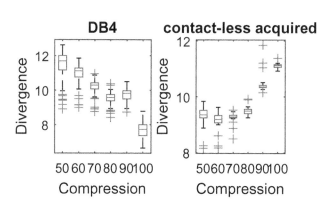

(b)

Fig. 3. Box plot of the divergence for singly compressed: (a) DB1, DB2 and DB3 fingerprints for a $QF = 50$ to 100 in step of 10; (b) DB4 and contact-less acquired latent fingerprints for a $QF = 50$ to 100 in step of 10

how close or far a particular data set is, either with the standard or generalised Benford's law. In all cases, a smaller divergence gives a better fitting. In these experiments, the luminance component of the face images is first extracted and the first digit distributions of the JPEG coefficients is then performed on the face images. For the other datasets described in Sect. 3.2, the first digit distributions of the JPEG coefficients is performed directly on the gray-scale images.

To test for conformity of a particular dataset to the Benford's law, one of the most common criteria used is the chi-square goodness-of-fit statistics test [13, 14, 20, 22, 23]. The chi-square divergence is expressed in Eq. (7).

$$\chi^2 = \sum_{x=1}^{9} \frac{(p_x' - p_x)^2}{p_x} \tag{7}$$

where p_x' is the actual first digit probability of the JPEG coefficients of the biometric images and p_x is the logarithmic law (Generalized Benford's law) as given in Eq. (2). In our experiments, the fingerprint databases are singly compressed at a QF of 50 to 100 in a step of 10. The divergence is calculated as an average on all the data sets as can be seen in Figs. 3(a) and (b). The box plots in Figs. 3(a) and (b) show that DB1, DB2, DB3, DB4 and contact-less acquired latent fingerprints divergence at different QF's from 50 to 100 in a step of 10 are not the same. We repeat the same process on vein wrist images, face images and iris images and results obtained are shown in Fig. 4. In Figs. 3(a), (b) and 4, we observe that the different biometric databases behave differently when anlaysed using the Benford's law divergence metrics.

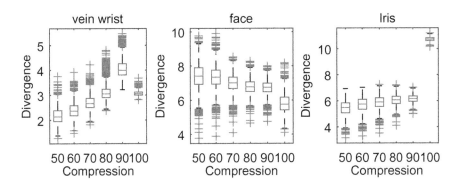

Fig. 4. Box plot of the divergence for singly compressed vein wrist, face images and iris images for a $QF = 50$ to 100 in step of 10

4   Proposed Method

As mentioned earlier, the Benford's law divergence values for different biometric images were found to be different. Hence, there is a need to improve the classification accuracy, as this may assist in source identification of the different biometric images.

4.1 Method Description

The objective of our proposed method is to train an NN to carry out inter-class classification, intra-class classification and a mixture of inter-class and intra-class classification of biometric images. We first obtain the Benford's law divergence values from the biometric images. Divergence values are obtained using the formula in Eq. (7). We then apply compression using a QF of 50 to 100 in a step of 10 to the biometric images, resulting in six rows of Benford's law divergence values with each row representing a QF in the experiment. Thus, we have 6 inputs and 4 outputs (when considering inter-class classification) and we have 6 inputs and 5 outputs (when considering the intra-class classification). For the inter-class classification, our dataset consists of a total of 4536 instances with class 1 (DB1 fingerprints images) having 80 instances, class 2 (vein wrist images) having 1200 instances, class 3 (face images) having 2500 instances and class 4 (iris images) having 756 instances. So the features fed into the NN as input data is a 6×4536 matrix. For our target data, we represent class 1 target as 1 0 0 0, class 2 as 0 1 0 0, class 3 as 0 0 1 0 and class 4 as 0 0 0 1. We therefore, use a 4×4536 matrix as the target data.

For any NN experiment, the choice of hidden layer(s) and hidden neurons is very important. Panchal *et al.* [25] noted that for most NN tasks, one hidden layer is usually adequate for a classification task especially if the data under consideration is not discontinuous.

They further suggested three rules-of-thumb to estimate the number of hidden neurons in a layer, as follows:

– Number of hidden neurons should be between the size of the input layer and size of the output layer
– Number of hidden neurons should be equal to (inputs + outputs) * 2/3
– Number of hidden neurons should be less than twice the size of the input layer

Based on the above rules-of-thumb, we use the Matlab neural network pattern recognition tool with one hidden layer and 4 hidden neurons for this classification task. Training of dataset is carried out using 'trainscg' function because it uses less memory. The input data is randomly divided into 70% training (i.e. 3176 training sample), 15% validation (i.e. 680 validation samples) and 15% testing the NN (i.e. 680 testing samples). The 3176 samples are presented to the NN during the training phase and the network adjusts itself based on its errors. The 680 validation samples are used for generalisation purposes during the validation phase. Testing the NN provides a separate measure of the neural network performance in the course of the training process and after the training process. Based on the 4 hidden neurons, we achieve the CE and %E for our evaluation performance as shown in Table 3. CE usually gives a faster convergence and better results when considering classification error rates as compared to other measures such as Squared Error (SE) [24]. Lower values of CE are better for a classification task. Zero CE means that there is no error in the classification task. The %E is measured to show the proportion of samples that are misclassified for a particular classification task. A zero %E means no misclassification and 100 %E means there exists a maximum misclassification.

5   Results and Discussion

5.1   Inter-class Separability of Biometric Images

After the initial network training setup, we observe it took the network, 1 epoch and 47 iterations to complete the training process. Results for the inter-class classification of biometric images are shown in Table 3.

Table 3. CE and %E for inter-class classification of biometric images

	Samples	CE	%E
Training	3176	2.63644	0.25189
Validation	680	7.44672	0.00000
Testing	680	7.47163	0.44176

We can see from Table 3 that for the training set, the NN has correctly classified approximately 97.36% (when considering CE) and 99.75% (when considering %E). On the validation set, NN has correctly classified approximately 92.55% (when considering CE) and 100% (when considering %E). For the testing set, NN has correctly classified 92.53% (when considering CE) and 99.56% (when considering %E). We see that the best classification result is achieved at the validation sets based on %E (100% classification accuracy) and the least classification accuracy is achieved at the testing sets based on CE (92.53% classification). The confusion matrices for the classification of the biometric images with four classes for this experiment are shown in Fig. 5. The Training Confusion Matrix shows that 48 of the DB1 fingerprint images are correctly classified, five are misclassified as face images. All the vein wrist images are correctly classified. There are 1740 face images correctly classified, whereas five face images are misclassified as DB1 fingerprints images. All the iris images are classified correctly. The overall classification accuracy for the training confusion matrix is approximately 99.7%.

For the Validation Confusion Matrix, all the biometric images are correctly classified at 100%. For the Test Confusion Matrix, 13 DB1 fingerprint images are correctly classified, while two of the DB1 fingerprint images are misclassified

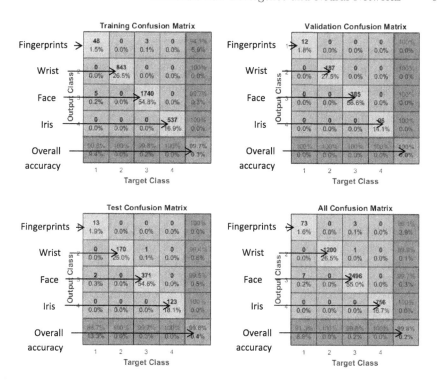

Fig. 5. Confusion matrix for inter-class classification

as face images. For the vein wrist images, they are all classified correctly at 100%. However, for the face images, 371 face images are correctly classified, whereas two of the face images are misclassified as DB1 fingerprint images. All the iris images are correctly classified at 100%. The overall classification accuracy, for the Test Confusion Matrix is approximately 99.6%. We see from the All Confusion Matrix that 73 DB1 fingerprint images are correctly classified, while seven of the DB1 fingerprint images are misclassified as face images. All the vein wrist images are correctly classified at 100%. There are 2496 face images accurately classified, whereas seven are misclassified as DB1 fingerprint images. Lastly, all the iris images are accurately classified. Overall, the All Confusion Matrix achieves approximately 99.8% accuracy for classifying the four biometric images in the experiment.

In the next section, we will investigate the intra-class separability of biometric images following the same process used for inter-class separability as mentioned in this section.

5.2   Intra-class Separability of Biometric Images

In this section, we carry out an intra-class classification of biometric fingerprint images. These fingerprints are DB1, DB2, DB3, DB4 and contact-less acquired latent fingerprints. For the intra-class classification, our dataset consist of a total of 368 instances, with class 1 (DB1 fingerprints images) having 80 instances, class 2 (DB2 fingerprints images) having 80 instances, class 3 (DB3 fingerprints images) having 80 instances, class 4 (DB4 fingerprints images) having 80 instances and class 5 (contact-less acquired fingerprints) having 48 instances. The features fed into the NN as input data is a 6×368 matrix. In this way we have 258 instances for training (70% of the data) purposes, 55 instances for validation (15% of the data) purposes and 55 instances for testing (15% of the data) purposes. For our target data, we represent class 1 target as 1 0 0 0 0, class 2 as 0 1 0 0 0, class 3 as 0 0 1 0 0, class 4 as 0 0 0 1 0 and class 5 as 0 0 0 0 1. We therefore, use a 5×368 matrix as the target data. We repeat the same experiment as in the case of inter-class classification but in this case, we use 8 hidden neurons for this classification task and we have 5 output targets. From the network training setup, we observe that it took the network, 1 epoch and 41 iterations to complete the training process. Results for the intra-class classification of biometric images are shown in Table 4.

Table 4. CE and %E results for intra-class classification of biometric images

	Samples	CE	%E
Training	258	3.31436	0.00000
Validation	55	9.57847	0.00000
Testing	55	9.44136	0.00000

With respect to the results in Table 4, we observe that using the %E, all the fingerprints are correctly classified at 100%. For CE the best classification results achieved using the training set are at approximately 96.69%, followed by the testing set at approximately 90.56% and then the validation set at approximately 90.42%. Overall, for both the CE and %E, the intra-class classification shows a high evaluation performance as shown by the results achieved in Table 4.

From the confusion matrix, we observe that classes (DB1, DB2, DB3, DB4 and contact-less acquired latent fingerprints) are accurately classified at 100%. We observe from the experiments that based on the %E and confusion matrix, the Benford's law divergence values and NN are able to accurately classify all the fingerprint images. In the next section, we will further investigate a mixture of inter-class and intra-class classification of biometric images to compare with individual inter-class and intra-class classification.

5.3 Mixed Inter-class and Intra-class Separability of Biometric Images

We mix the inter-class biometric images (DB1 fingerprints, vein wrist images, face images and iris images) and intra-class biometric images (DB2, DB3, DB4 and contact-less acquired latent fingerprints) for classification evaluation. For this experiment, Table 5 describes the experimental setup. From the table, the number of instances are the corresponding number of biometric images used for this experiment.

Table 5. Experimental setup for mixed classification of biometric images

Classes	Instances	Target data
Class 1 (DB1 fingerprints images)	80	1 0 0 0 0 0 0 0
Class 2 (vein wrist images)	1200	0 1 0 0 0 0 0 0
Class 3 (face images)	2500	0 0 1 0 0 0 0 0
Class 4 (iris images)	756	0 0 0 1 0 0 0 0
Class 5 (DB2 fingerprint images)	80	0 0 0 0 1 0 0 0
Class 6 (DB3 fingerprint images)	80	0 0 0 0 0 1 0 0
Class 7 (DB4 fingerprint images)	80	0 0 0 0 0 0 1 0
Class 8 (contact-less acquired fingerprints)	48	0 0 0 0 0 0 0 1

The features fed into the NN as input data is a 6×4824 matrix. In this way we have 3376 instances for training (70% of the data), 724 instances for validation (15% of the data) and 724 instances for testing (15% of the data). We therefore, use a 8×4824 matrix as the target data. We use the (inputs + outputs) * 2/3 rule-of-thumb and achieve 9 hidden neurons (i.e. $(6 + 8) * 2/3$). So we have a total of 4824 instances with 6 inputs, 9 hidden neurons and 8 outputs for this experiment. From the neural network setup, we observe it took the network, 1 epoch and 37 iterations to complete the training process. The results for the mixed-class classification of biometric images are shown in Table 6.

Table 6. CE and %E results for mixed-class classification of biometric images

	Samples	CE	%E
Training	3376	3.52958	0.740521
Validation	724	9.98217	0.828729
Testing	724	9.95969	0.828729

With respect to the results in Table 6, we observe that the CE accurately classified the mixed biometric images with accuracies of 96.47%, 90.02% and 90.04% for the training, validation and testing, respectively. The %E achieved accuracies of 99.26%, 99.17% and 99.17% for the training, validation and testing, respectively. Based on the classification accuracies, for CE the highest performance of 96.47% is achieved with the training instances and the least evaluation performance of 90.02% is achieved for the validation sets. We also observe that the best classification accuracy of 99.26% is achieved for the training instances. Whereas for the validation and testing instances, our proposed method has achieved the least evaluation performance of 99.17% when considering the %E. Overall, for both CE and %E, the mixed-class classification shows a high evaluation performance.

5.4 Comparative Analysis Between Inter-class, Intra-class and Mixture of Inter-class and Intra-class Classification of Biometric Images

The need for the investigation and classification of inter-class, intra-class and mixture of inter-class and intra-class biometric images is motivated from the concept of mixed biometrics [26]. By mixed biometrics, it means mixing different fingerprints, different faces, or different iris in order to generate joint identities and also to preserve privacy [26]. Mixed biometrics also cover mixing two distinct biometric modalities such as fingerprint and iris to form a joint biometric modality. This means there is a possibility of mixing non-closely related biometric images (inter-class), closely related biometric images (intra-class) and a mixture of inter-class and intra-class biometric images.

Table 7 gives an overall summary of the classification accuracy hierarchy from the best classified class to the least using the Benford's law divergence and NN. For comparison, our work is much wider in scope than the state-of-the-art method developed by Hildebrandt and Dittmann [3] and so we only compare our classification accuracies of fingerprints to [3]. Our highest classification accuracy of 100% exceed the current state-of-the-art method [3] highest detection performance accuracy of 98.85%.

Table 7. Classification accuracy comparison

Classification type	Order of classification
Intra-Class	1 (Best)
Inter-Class	2 (Medium)
Mixture of Intra-Class & Inter-Class	3 (Least)

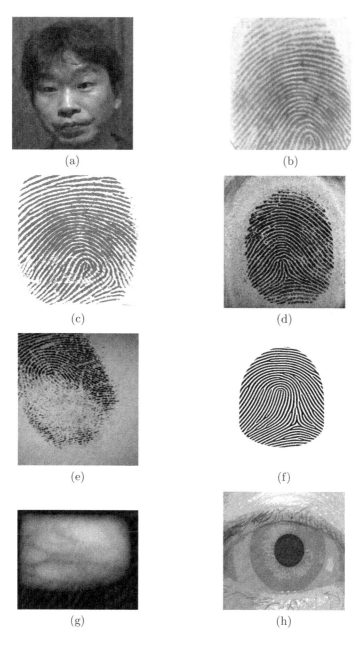

Fig. 6. Sample biometric images from: (a) CASIA-FACEV5, (b) FVC2000 DB1, (c) FVC2000 DB2, (d) FVC2000 DB3, (e) FVC2000 DB4, (f) artificially printed contactless acquired latent fingerprint, (g) PUT vein database, (h) CASIA-IrisV1.

6 Conclusion and Future Work

In this paper, we showed that the Benford's law divergence values could be successfully used with neural networks for classification and source identification of biometric images (DB1 fingerprints, DB2 fingerprints, DB3 fingerprints, DB4 fingerprints, contact-less acquired latent fingerprints, vein wrist images, face images and iris images). The classification accuracy for the biometric images was between the range of 90.02% and 100%. For future work, we plan to investigate other classification techniques such as decision trees and SVM for classification and source identification of biometric images.

References

1. Harper, W.W.: Fingerprint forgery transferred latent fingerprints. J. Crim. Law Criminol. **28**(4), 573–580 (1937)
2. Iorliam, A., Ho, A.T.S., Poh, N.: Using Benford's Law to detect JPEG biometric data tampering. Biometrics 2014, London (2014)
3. Hildebrandt, M., Dittmann, J.: Benford's Law based detection of latent fingerprint forgeries on the example of artificial sweat printed fingerprints captured by confocal laser scanning microscopes. In: IS&T/SPIE Electronic Imaging. International Society for Optics and Photonics, p. 94090A (2015)
4. Yan, Y., Osadciw, L.A.: Bridging biometrics and forensics. In: Electronic Imaging, International Society for Optics and Photonics, p. 68190Q (2008)
5. Jain, A.K., Hong, L., Pankanti, S., Bolle, R.: An identity-authentication system using fingerprints. Proc. IEEE **85**(9), 1365–1388 (1997)
6. Note on CASIA-IrisV1. Biometric Ideal Test. http://biometrics.idealtest.org/dbDetailForUser.do?id=1
7. Maltoni, D., Maio, D., Jain, A.K., Prabhakar, S.: Synthetic fingerprint generation. In: Handbook of fingerprint recognition, pp. 271–302. Springer, London (2009)
8. Vein Dataset. PUT Vein Database Description. http://biometrics.put.poznan.pl/vein-dataset/
9. Hildebrandt, M., Sturm, J., Dittmann, J., Vielhauer, C.: Creation of a Public Corpus of contact-less acquired latent fingerprints without privacy implications. In: Decker, B., Dittmann, J., Kraetzer, C., Vielhauer, C. (eds.) CMS 2013. LNCS, vol. 8099, pp. 204–206. Springer, Heidelberg (2013). doi:10.1007/978-3-642-40779-6_19
10. Bartlow, N., Kalka, N., Cukic, B., Ross, A.: Identifying sensors from fingerprint images. In: IEEE Computer Society Conference on Computer Vision and Pattern Recognition Workshops, pp. 78–84 (2009)
11. FVC2000. Fingerprint Verification Competition Databases. http://bias.csr.unibo.it/fvc2000/databases.asp
12. CASIA-FACEV5. Biometric Ideal Test. http://www.idealtest.org/dbDetailForUser.do?id=9
13. Fu, D., Shi, Y.Q., Su, W.: A generalized Benford's law for JPEG coefficients and its applications in image forensics. In: Electronic Imaging 2007, International Society for Optics and Photonics, p. 65051L (2007)
14. Li, X.H., Zhao, Y.Q., Liao, M., Shih, F.Y., Shi, Y.Q.: Detection of tampered region for JPEG images by using mode-based first digit features. EURASIP J. Adv. Sig. Process. **2012**(1), 1–10 (2012)

15. Xu, B., Wang, J., Liu, G., Dai, Y.: Photorealistic computer graphics forensics based on leading digit law. J. Electron. (China) **28**(1), 95–100 (2011)
16. Benford, F.: The law of anomalous numbers. Proc. Am. Philosophical Soc. **78**(4), 551–572 (1938)
17. Pérez-Gonález, F., Heileman, G.L., Abdallah, C.T.: Benford's law in image processing. In: 2007 IEEE International Conference on Image Processing, ICIP 2007, vol. 1, pp. 1-405 (2007)
18. Hill, T.P.: A statistical derivation of the significant-digit law. Stat. Sci. **10**(4), 354–363 (1995)
19. Durtschi, C., Hillison, W., Pacini, C.: The effective use of Benford's law to assist in detecting fraud in accounting data. J. Forensic Account. **5**(1), 17–34 (2004)
20. Acebo, E., Sbert, M.: Benford's law for natural and synthetic images. In: Proceedings of the First Eurographics Conference on Computational Aesthetics in Graphics, Visualization and Imaging, Eurographics Association, pp. 169–176 (2005)
21. Jolion, J.M.: Images and Benford's law. J. Math. Imaging Vis. **14**(1), 73–81 (2001)
22. Qadir, G., Zhao, X., Ho, A.T.: Estimating JPEG2000 compression for image forensics using Benford's law. In: SPIE Photonics Europe, International Society for Optics and Photonics, p. 77230J (2010)
23. Li, B., Shi, Y.Q., Huang, J.: Detecting doubly compressed JPEG images by using mode based first digit features. In: 2008 IEEE 10th Workshop on Multimedia Signal Processing, pp. 730–735 (2008)
24. Golik, P., Doetsch, P., Ney, H.: Cross-entropy vs. squared error training: a theoretical and experimental comparison. In: Interspeech, pp. 1756–1760 (2013)
25. Panchal, G., Ganatra, A., Kosta, Y.P., Panchal, D.: Behaviour analysis of multi-layer perceptrons with multiple hidden neurons and hidden layers. Int. J. Comput. Theory Eng. **3**(2), 332 (2011)
26. Othman, A.A.: Mixing Biometric Data For Generating Joint Identities and Preserving Privacy. Ph.D. Thesis, West Virginia University (2013)

Source Camera Identification Based on Guided Image Estimation and Block Weighted Average

Le-Bing Zhang[1], Fei Peng[1(✉)], and Min Long[2]

[1] School of Computer Science and Electronic Engineering, Hunan University,
Changsha 410082, China
eepengf@gmail.com
[2] College of Computer and Communication Engineering, Changsha University
of Science and Technology, Changsha 410112, China

Abstract. Sensor pattern noise (SPN) has been widely used in source camera identification. However, the SPN extracted from natural image may be contaminated by its content and eventually introduce side effect to the identification accuracy. In this paper, an effective source camera identification scheme based on guided image estimation and block weighted average is proposed. Before the SPN extraction, an adaptive SPN estimator based on image content is implemented to reduce the influence of image scene and improve the quality of the SPN. Furthermore, a novel camera reference SPN construction method is put forward by using some ordinary images, instead of the blue sky images in previous schemes, and a block weighted average approach is used to suppress the influence of the image scenes in the reference SPN. Experimental results and analysis indicate that the proposed method can effectively identify the source of the natural image, especially in actual forensics environment with a small number of images.

Keywords: Source camera identification · Guided image filtering · Block weighted average · Sensor pattern noise

1 Introduction

With the rapid development of digital imaging devices, portable video camera, digital camera and mobile phone have been widely used in daily life. Digital image acquisition, publishing and sharing are becoming popular information transmission and exchange means in modern social network. Meanwhile, some powerful and easy-to-use digital image processing software provide simple tools to retouch digital images. As it brings convenience to us, the security concerns of the digital image have been attracted wide attention in the past decade, especially in the field of judicial and criminal investigation. Therefore, as a kind of multimedia security technology, digital image forensics can be used to verify the originality, authenticity and reliability of digital images. It is significant for the judicial justice and social order.

Image source identification is an important branch of digital image forensics. It can accurately and reliably match the specific digital image with its source. Typical image

© Springer International Publishing AG 2017
Y.Q. Shi et al. (Eds.): IWDW 2016, LNCS 10082, pp. 106–118, 2017.
DOI: 10.1007/978-3-319-53465-7_8

source identification contains two categories. One is image acquisition pipeline identification. The target is to distinguish images taken from digital camera, images created by computer graphics or images produced by scanners; The other is identification of camera brands or types, and it aims to identify which brand or individual camera is used for a given image. In this paper, the work will be focused on the second type, which is also called as source camera identification.

Natural image is the reflection of the light from the natural scene obtained by the camera. Different digital camera has its own unique properties generated in the process of imaging, which is the key to the identification of image devices. These features include lens aberration [1, 2], CFA interpolation artifacts [3], sensor pattern noise (SPN) [4–13], JPEG compression [14, 15], and etc. In addition, image quality evaluation index and high order statistics in wavelet domain [16, 17] have also been exploited to identify source camera.

Among them, SPN generated by digital camera is widely used in image source camera identification and image tamper forensics [18, 19]. Generally, different camera has different PRNU, and it is not affected by temperature or humidity, just like the unique fingerprint of an individual imaging sensor. Therefore, SPN can be considered to be a unique and stable traces of each camera, and it is well suited for camera source identification. In this paper, extraction of stable and accurate SPN is investigated, and a novel source camera identification scheme based on the guided image estimation and block weighted average is proposed to improve the identification performance.

The main contributions of this paper include:

(1) An effective guided image estimator is used for the extraction of SPN, and it can reduce the influence of image scene and improve the quality of the extracted SPN.
(2) A block weighted average approach is proposed to construct camera reference SPN from arbitrary natural images.
(3) Based on the above SPN extraction and camera reference SPN construction method, an effective source camera identification scheme is proposed, and the experimental results verify the effectiveness of it.

The rest of the paper is organized as follows: the related works are introduced in the Sect. 2. The proposed source camera identification scheme is described in Sect. 3. Experimental results and analysis are provided in Sect. 4. Finally, some conclusions are drawn in Sect. 5.

2   Related Works

Currently, the general idea of source camera identification based on SPN is: a camera reference SPN is first constructed, and then the SPN of testing image is extracted. After that, compare two SPNs and the final decision will be made for whether the testing image is obtained from this camera or not.

Lukas et al. [4] first proposed a method to utilize SPN for source camera identification. Since SPN is a kind of high frequency signal, a wavelet based denoising filter is used to obtain the SPN of the testing image. Meanwhile, camera reference SPN is constructed by averaging multiple SPNs extracted from some images. Based on the correlation between the testing image's SPN and the camera reference SPN, the image source camera can be determined. It provides an effective method for the source camera identification. After that, the researches of camera source forensics based on SPN are mainly focused on two aspects. The first attempts to enhance the quality of the extracted SPN, and the second is to improve the correlation methods. Chen et al. [6] proposed to calculate camera reference SPN by using maximum likelihood estimation, and two preprocessing operations including zero-mean and Wiener filter are implemented to further remove the artifacts of the imaging processing. However, the influence of image scene is still strong. Li [7] assumed that strong signal in SPN is more likely affected by the content of the image, and 6 enhancement models are proposed to suppress the high frequency signal of SPN for reducing the influence of image scene. Recently, Li [9] proposed a spectrum equalization method to reduce the influence of the non-unique artifacts on the reference SPN. It detects and suppresses peaks to equalize the amplitude spectrum of reference SPN based on the local features, and periodic interference is removed. It is similar to the previous SPN enhancement method in [7]. Although it can suppress the image content with high frequency in SPN, it also loses useful high frequency information of SPN. Chierchia et al. [10] proposed a block matched 3D filter (BM3D) [24] to replace the traditional wavelet-based denosing filtering method. Kang et al. [11] proposed a context-adaptive interpolation operator, and Zeng [12] proposed a content adaptive guided image filter for suppressing edge effect of image scene content. Satta [13] proposed a SPN reliability map and then used to weight SPN pixels during matching. All these methods can improve the quality of SPN to a certain degree. However, it is still very difficult to totally remove the image scene in SPN.

For the correlation detection between the testing image's SPN and the camera reference SPN, Lukas et al. [4] proposed normalized cross-correlation (NCC) to detect the similarity. Goljan [20] proposed the peak to correlation energy (PCE) measure to reduce the influence of periodic noise. Kang et al. [21] proposed to use the correlation over circular cross-correlation norm (CCN) to reduce the false positive rate of detection. Different correlation detection methods can be combined with different SPN extraction methods to improve the overall detection accuracy. In addition, fast, accurate and effective camera source identification method based on SPN [22, 23] for large scale dataset is becoming a recent development trend.

Since the SPN is only related to the camera imaging devices, it should be irrelevant to the content of the scene. While the SPN contaminated by the scene cannot accurately reflect the essential characteristics of the camera, which will eventually influence the accuracy of the source camera identification. Therefore, how to effectively eliminate the interference of the image scene to the SPN is important for the source camera identification.

In previous literatures [6, 7, 21], in order to accurately obtain the camera's reference SPN, some blue sky images with no image scene content are generally used for the estimation of the reference SPN. However, in most cases, camera reference SPN can be only extracted from a few ordinary images, which contain different kinds of scene details. Therefore, how to effectively construct the camera reference SPN to identify the source of digital images in actual forensics environment is becoming an urgent problem to be resolved.

To countermeasure the above problems, an effective source camera identification scheme based on guided image estimation and block weighted average is proposed.

3   Description of the Proposed Scheme

Considering the strong dependence between the extracted SPN and the content of the image scene in the traditional methods, a content based adaptive estimator is investigated. By using the difference between the estimated image and the original image, the influence of image scene on the SPN is reduced and the SPN information left by the camera during the imaging process is effectively preserved. Here, guided image filter is implemented to extract the SPN information of the image.

3.1   Guided Image Filter

Guided image filter [25] is a general linear translation invariant filter and its output is a local weighted linear combination of the input image according to a guidance image. The guided image filter exhibits the edge-preserving properties, which can be used as an image content adaptive estimator to estimate the content of the image scene.

3.2   SPN Extraction Based on Guidance-Image Prediction

By employing the property of edge-preserving properties, the SPN can be extracted according to the following steps:

Step 1. To suppress the contents of the image scene, the image I is used as input image and guidance image of the guided image filter. Subsequently, the estimated image $G(I, I)$ is obtained, and the difference R is:

$$R = I - G(I, I), \tag{1}$$

where $G(\bullet, \bullet)$ represents the guided image filtering function, and R represents the residual image.

Step 2. For the residual image R, adaptive Wiener filtering with a window size of 3×3 is performed to it, the SPN of the residual image can be calculated from

$$W(i,j) = R(i,j) \frac{\sigma_0^2}{\hat{\sigma}^2(i,j) + \sigma_0^2}, \tag{2}$$

where $\hat{\sigma}^2$ represents the local variance of the original noise-free image, and σ_0^2 represents the overall variance of the SPN. We follow the work in [11], σ_0^2 is set as 9, and $\hat{\sigma}^2$ is obtained by using the maximum a posteriori probability estimation. It is described as

$$\hat{\sigma}^2(i,j) = \max(0, \frac{1}{m^2} \sum_{(p,q) \in N_m} R^2(p,q) - \sigma_0^2). \tag{3}$$

3.3 Construction of the Reference SPN Based on Block Weighted Average

Currently, there are two conventional methods for constructing a camera's reference SPN. One is Lukas's method [4], which constructs the camera reference SPN through averaging the SPNs of multiple images of the camera.

$$S = \frac{1}{N} \sum_{k=1}^{N} R_k, \tag{4}$$

where S is the camera reference SPN, and R_k is a SPN extracted from the kth image.

Another is Chen's method [6], where Maximum Likelihood Estimator is implemented for the construction of SPN. It can be defined as

$$S = \frac{\sum_{k=1}^{N} R_k I_k}{\sum_{k=1}^{N} (I_k)^2}. \tag{5}$$

For the above methods, the reference SPN usually recommend extracted from more than 50 blue sky images. Therefore, the constructed reference SPN is similar to the ideal SPN. However, considering the actual forensics situations, camera reference SPN can only be extracted from a few existed ordinary images, which contains different kinds of scene details. Thus, the SPN is inevitable disturbed by the content of the scene. Due to the difference of R_k, the conventional methods cannot achieve the minimum mean squared error. For a natural image, it usually contains smooth regions and textural regions. Generally, smooth region is good for the extraction of SPN, while the textural region interfere the calculation of SPN. Meanwhile, the variance in the textural region is usually larger than that of the smooth region. Therefore, by assigning large weight to the smooth region and assigned small weight to the textural region, a novel estimation approach for camera reference SPN is proposed based on block weighted average. It is illustrated in Fig. 1.

Assuming N ordinary images are provided for the construction of camera reference SPN, the details are described as follows:

Step 1. For each image I_k (k = 1,2,…,N), obtain its SPN W_k according to Sect. 3.2. After that, calculate the variance $\sigma_k^2(p,q)$ of each block $BW_k(p,q)$, k = 1,2,…,N, where $BW_k(p,q)$ represents the kth SPN's block located in the pth row q^{th} column.

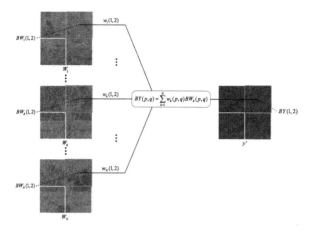

Fig. 1. The diagram for constructing camera reference SPN.

Step 2. The local reference SPN $BY(p,q)$ is constructed by multiplying $BW_k(p,q)$ with the corresponding weights, which is depended on $\sigma_k^2(p,q)$. It is represented as:

$$BY(p,q) = \sum_{k=1}^{N} w_k(p,q)BW_k(p,q). \tag{6}$$

The optimal weight w_k is

$$w_i(p,q) = \frac{\frac{1}{\sigma_i^2(p,q)}}{\sum_{k=1}^{N}\frac{1}{\sigma_k^2(p,q)}}, i = 1, 2, \ldots, N. \tag{7}$$

Step 3. The whole reference SPN y' is acquired by combining these local reference SPN $BY(p,q)$ together.

Step 4. To further suppress the unwanted artifacts caused by camera processing operations such as CFA interpolation and JPEG compression, a pre-procession similar to [6] is adopted. Therefore, the final camera reference SPN y is:

$$y = WF(ZM(y')), \tag{8}$$

where $ZM(\bullet)$ represents zero mean operations in every row and column, and $WF(\bullet)$ represents Wiener filtering in the Fourier domain.

For simplicity, $p = q = 2$ is used in the following experiments.

4 Experimental Results and Analysis

In the following experiments, exclude some particular camera, which contain unexpected artifacts [26], 1350 natural images from 6 cameras are random chosen from Dresden Image Database [27] to form the image dataset. The natural images contain a wide variety of indoor and outdoor scenes, for each camera, random chosen 25 images to estimate reference SPN, and the other 200 were used as test images. The camera model, image format and original resolution are listed in Table 1.

Table 1. Detail of the dataset used in experiment

Brand	Resolution	Number of images
Canon Ixus55	3,264 × 2,448	225
Nikon D200	3,872 × 2,592	225
Olympus Mju 1050SW	3,648 × 2,736	225
Panasonic DMC FZ50	3,648 × 2,736	225
Samsung L74 wide	3,072 × 2,304	225
Sony DSC H50	3,456 × 2,592	225

For simplicity, only the center region of the image is considered. Thus, the testing center sizes include 128×128, 256×256, 512×512 and 1024×1024. Based on this dataset, the performance of the proposed method is compared with the Basic method [4], MLE method [6], Li-Model5 method [7], PCAI8 method [11], and CAGIF method [12]. The camera reference SPN is extracted from a few ordinary images, which contain different kinds of scene details. Meanwhile, the purpose of this work is to verify the effectiveness of eliminating the interference of image scene content on SPN, so NCC is applied to measure the similarity between the camera reference SPN and noise residue of the testing image for each method. It is defined as:

$$\rho(x, y) = corr(x, y) = \frac{(x - \bar{x}) \bullet (y - \bar{y})}{||x - \bar{x}|| \cdot ||y - \bar{y}||}, \tag{9}$$

where $||\cdot||$ represents L_2 norm, and $\bar{x}$, $\bar{y}$ represent the means of the SPN extracted from the testing image x and the camera reference SPN y with the same size $M \times N$, respectively.

To further evaluate the experimental results, ROC curves is implemented for the performance analysis. For a given detection threshold, true positive (TP) and false positive (FP) of each camera are calculated, and then the total true positive and false positive can be achieved. True positive rate (TPR), false positive rate (FPR) and the accuracy are defined as:

$$TPR = \frac{TP}{TP + FN}, \tag{10}$$

$$FPR = \frac{FP}{FP + TN},\tag{11}$$

$$Accuracy = \frac{TP + TN}{TP + TN + FP + FN}.\tag{12}$$

4.1 Experimental Results

In this part, the camera reference SPN is constructed from 25 natural images, which contain different kinds of scene details. The identification accuracies of different methods are listed in Table 2.

Table 2. Accuracy of different methods

Camera/Methods		Image size			
		128 × 128	256 × 256	512 × 512	1024 × 1024
Canon Ixus55	Basic	90.2500%	95.5000%	**99.9167%**	99.9167%
	MLE	89.4167%	96.4167%	99.8333%	**100%**
	Li-Model5	**92.7500%**	**98.2500%**	99.8333%	**100%**
	PCAI8	92.1667%	97.7500%	99.8333%	**100%**
	CAGIF	91.0833%	96.2500%	99.5833%	99.9167%
	Ours	92.1667%	98.0000%	99.8333%	**100%**
Nikon D200	Basic	87.2500%	91.8333%	96.0833%	97.9167%
	MLE	86.1667%	90.7500%	95.4167%	98.1667%
	Li-Model5	**93.4167%**	**95.5833%**	96.4167%	97.0000%
	PCAI8	89.6667%	94.6667%	98.0000%	99.5000%
	CAGIF	87.8333%	90.5000%	96.6667%	99.4167%
	Ours	90.1667%	95.5000%	**98.6667%**	**99.6667%**
Olympus mju1050 W	Basic	86.2500%	90.0000%	93.9167%	94.6667%
	MLE	86.5833%	90.0000%	95.9167%	97.0833%
	Li-Model5	**89.1667%**	91.0833%	92.0833%	94.1667%
	PCAI8	87.3333%	92.1667%	96.0833%	**97.6667%**
	CAGIF	85.5000%	90.9167%	95.9167%	97.3333%
	Ours	88.0000%	**93.0833%**	**96.3333%**	97.5000%
Panasonic DMC-FZ50	Basic	89.9167%	95.7500%	98.0000%	**98.7500%**
	MLE	89.4167%	95.7500%	98.0000%	98.2500%
	Li-Model5	83.3333%	83.3333%	83.3333%	85.6667%
	PCAI8	93.2500%	97.3333%	98.2500%	98.5000%
	CAGIF	89.0000%	94.0833%	97.6667%	98.7500%
	Ours	**93.1667%**	**97.5000%**	**98.3333%**	98.5833%
Samsung L74wide	Basic	86.5833%	91.7500%	98.0000%	99.8333%
	MLE	85.9167%	90.1667%	97.5833%	99.9167%
	Li-Model5	**90.4167%**	**97.0000%**	**99.9167%**	**100%**
	PCAI8	87.9167%	93.6667%	99.1667%	99.9167%

(*continued*)

Table 2. (*continued*)

Camera/Methods		Image size			
		128 × 128	256 × 256	512 × 512	1024 × 1024
	CAGIF	86.0833%	91.3333%	97.4167%	99.9167%
	Ours	88.7500%	93.5833%	98.8333%	**100%**
Sony	Basic	95.1667%	99.0000%	99.5000%	99.8333%
DSC-H50	MLE	96.5833%	99.0833%	**100%**	**100%**
	Li-Model5	94.0833%	96.5833%	97.1667%	97.8333%
	PCAI8	97.1667%	98.9167%	**100%**	**100%**
	CAGIF	96.0000%	98.8333%	99.9167%	**100%**
	Ours	**97.3333%**	**99.1667%**	**100%**	**100%**
Average	Basic	89.2361%	93.9722%	97.5700%	98.4861%
accuracy	MLE	89.0139%	93.6945%	97.7917%	98.9028%
	Li-Model5	90.5278%	93.6389%	94.7917%	95.7778%
	PCAI8	91.2500%	95.7500%	98.5555%	99.2645%
	CAGIF	89.2500%	93.6528%	97.8611%	99.2228%
	Ours	**91.5972%**	**96.1389%**	**98.6667%**	**99.2917%**

From Table 2, it can be found that the average accuracy of the proposed method outperforms the other methods in different image sizes, which indicates the good identification performance of the proposed method.

The ROC curves of CAGIF, PCAI8, Li-Model5, MLE, Basic and the proposed method are shown in Fig. 2.

As seen from Fig. 2, the identification performance is relatively stable when different sizes of the center images are used. This is mainly because the camera reference SPN constructed from natural images contains more residual information of image scenes than that constructed from flat field images, which will impose impacts on the correlation between the reference SPN and the SPN of the testing images, especially for the small size images. However, for large size images, the influence of the noise on the image content is limited.

4.2 Analysis of the Capability of Resisting JPEG Compression

As JPEG compression is generally used for digital images. To evaluate the influence of JPEG compression on the identification performance, all images in the dataset are compressed with quality factor (QF) 90. The ROC curves of these methods are shown in Fig. 3.

As seen from Fig. 3, it is observed that the proposed method can still achieve good performance with JPEG compression. Compared with the images without compression, it can be found that the performance of the proposed methods is almost unaffected by the JPEG compression. However, the performance of PCAI8, CAGIF and MLE methods have declined to a certain degree. Meanwhile, the performance of the Basic and Li-Model5 methods are significant improved compared with the image without compression. The main reason is that JPEG compression with high quality factor

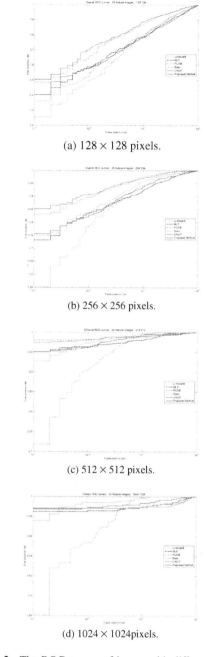

(a) 128×128 pixels.

(b) 256×256 pixels.

(c) 512×512 pixels.

(d) 1024×1024 pixels.

Fig. 2. The ROC curves of image with different sizes.

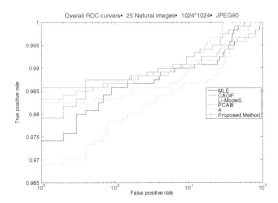

Fig. 3. The ROC curves with JPEG quality factor of 90.

weaken the influence of the irrelevant noise on the extraction of SPN. The results illustrate that the proposed method is stable and robust in resisting JPEG compression with high quality factor compared with the other methods.

5 Conclusion

In this paper, a source camera identification scheme based on the guided image estimation and block weighted average is proposed. It uses a guidance image to reduce the influence of the image scene and improve the quality of the SPN, and the reference SPN is constructed by block weighted average of the extracted SPNs. Experimental results show that the proposed method can achieve fairly good performance compared with some existed schemes. Furthermore, with the situation that camera reference SPN can be only extracted from a few existed ordinary images, it still can get satisfactory performance. Our future work will be concentrated on the research of a more accurate camera reference SPN construction strategy to improve the identification performance.

Acknowledgments. This work was supported in part by project supported by National Natural Science Foundation of China (Grant Nos. 61572182, 61370225), project supported by Hunan Provincial Natural Science Foundation of China (Grant No. 15JJ2007), and supported by the Scientific Research Plan of Hunan Provincial Science and Technology Department of China (2014FJ4161).

The authors thank Prof. Xiangui Kang from Sun Yat-sen University for providing the source code of CAGIF method.

References

1. Choi, S., Lam, E.Y., Wong, K.K.Y.: Source camera identification using footprints from lens aberration. In: Proceedings of SPIE (2006)
2. Johnson, M.K., Farid, H.: Exposing digital forgeries through chromatic aberration. In: ACM Multimedia and Security Workshop, Geneva, Switzerland (2006)

3. Popescu, A.C., Farid, H.: Exposing digital forgeries in color filter array interpolated images. IEEE Trans. Signal Process. **53**(10), 3948–3959 (2005)
4. Lukás˘, J., Fridrich, J., Goljan, M.: Digital camera identification from sensor pattern noise. IEEE Trans. Inf. Forensics Secur. **1**(2), 205–214 (2006)
5. Sutcu, Y., Batram, S.H., Sencar, T., Memon, N.: Improvements on sensor noise based source camera identification. In: Proceedings of IEEE International Conference on Multimedia and Expo, Beijing, China, 2—5 July, pp. 24—27 (2007)
6. Chen, M., Fridrich, J., Goljan, M., Lukás˘, J.: Determining image origin and integrity using sensor noise. IEEE Trans. Inf. Forensics Secur. **3**(1), 74–90 (2008)
7. Li, C.T.: Source camera identification using enhanced sensor pattern noise. IEEE Trans. Inf. Forensics Secur. **5**(2), 280–287 (2010)
8. Fridrich, J.: Sensor defects in digital image forensic. In: Senkar, H.T., Memon, N. (eds.) Digital Image Forensics, pp. 179–218. Springer, Heidelberg (2012)
9. Lin, X., Li, C.T.: Preprocessing reference sensor pattern noise via spectrum equalization. IEEE Trans. Inf. Forensics Secur. **11**(1), 126–140 (2016)
10. Chierchia, G., Parrilli, S., Poggi, G., Sansone, C., Verdoliva, L.: On the influence of denoising in PRNU based forgery detection. In: Proceedings of 2nd ACM Workshop on Multimedia Forensics, Security and Intelligence, pp. 117–122, New York, NY, USA (2010)
11. Kang, X., Chen, J., Lin, K., Anjie, P.: A context-adaptive SPN predictor for trustworthy source camera identification. EURASIP J. Image Video Process. **2014**(1), 1–11 (2014)
12. Zeng, H., Kang, X.: Fast source camera identification using content adaptive guided image filter. J. Forensic Sci. **61**(2), 520–526 (2016)
13. Satta, R.: Sensor Pattern Noise matching based on reliability map for source camera identification. In: Proceedings of 10th International Conference on Computer Vision Theory and Applications (VISAPP 2015), Berlin, Germany (2015)
14. Sorrell, M.J.: Digital camera source identification through JPEG quantisation. In: Multimedia Forensics and Security Information Science Reference, Hershey (2008)
15. Alles, E.J., Geradts, Z.J.M.H., Veenman, C.J.: Source camera identification for heavily JPEG compressed low resolution still images. J. Forensic Sci. **54**(3), 628–638 (2009)
16. Sankur, B., Celiktutan, O. Avcibas, I.: Blind identification of cell phone cameras. In: Proceedings of SPIE, Electronic Imaging, Security, Steganography, and Watermarking of Multimedia Contents IX, vol. 6505, San Jose, CA, 29 January–1 February, pp. 1H–1I (2007)
17. Sutthiwan, P., Ye, J., Shi, Y.Q.: An enhanced statistical approach to identifying photorealistic images. In: Ho, A.T.S., Shi, Y.Q., Kim, H.J., Barni, M. (eds.) IWDW 2009. LNCS, vol. 5703, pp. 323–335. Springer, Heidelberg (2009). doi:10.1007/978-3-642-03688-0_28
18. Chierchia, G., Parrilli, S., Poggi, G., Verdoliva, L., Sansone, C.: PRNU-based detection of small-size image forgeries. In: International Conference on Digital Signal Processing (DSP), pp. 1–6 (2011)
19. Chierchia, G., Poggi, G., Sansone, C., Verdoliva, L.: A Bayesian-MRF approach for PRNU-based image forgery detection. IEEE Trans. Inf. Forensics Secur. **9**(4), 554–567 (2014)
20. Goljan, M.: Digital camera identification from images — estimating false acceptance probability. In: Kim, H.-J., Katzenbeisser, S., Ho, Anthony, T.,S. (eds.) IWDW 2008. LNCS, vol. 5450, pp. 454–468. Springer, Heidelberg (2009). doi:10.1007/978-3-642-04438-0_38
21. Kang, X., Li, Y., Qu, Z., Huang, J.: Enhancing source camera identification performance with a camera reference phase sensor pattern noise. IEEE Trans. Inf. Forensics Secur. **7**(2), 393–402 (2012)
22. Goljan, M., Chen, M., Comesana, P., Fridrich, J.: Effect of compression on sensor-fingerprint based camera identification. In: Proceedings of Electronic Imaging, Media Watermarking, Security Forensics, San Francisco, CA (2016)

23. Valsesia, D., Coluccia, G., Bianchi, T., Magli, E.: Compressed fingerprint matching and camera identification via random projections. IEEE Trans. Inf. Forensics Secur. **10**(7), 1472–1485 (2015)
24. Dabov, K., Foi, A., Katkovnik, V., Egiazarian, K.: Image denoising by sparse 3-D transform-domain collaborative filtering. IEEE Trans. Image Process. **16**(8), 2080–2095 (2007)
25. He, K., Sun, J., Tang, X.: Guided image filtering. IEEE Trans. Pattern Anal. Mach. Intell. **35**(6), 1397–1409, (2013)
26. Gloe, T., Pfennig, S., Kirchner, M.: Unexpected artefacts in PRNU-based camera identification: a 'Dresden image database' case-study. In: Proceedings of ACM Workshop Multimedia Secur. pp. 109–114 (2012)
27. Dresden Image Database, (Technische Universitaet Dresden, Dresden, 2009–2014). http://forensics.inf.tu-dresden.de/ddimgdb. Accessed 3 May 2013

Recapture Image Forensics Based on Laplacian Convolutional Neural Networks

Pengpeng Yang, Rongrong Ni[(✉)], and Yao Zhao

Beijing Key Laboratory of Advanced Information Science and Network Technology,
Institute of Information Science, Beijing Jiaotong University, Beijing 100044, China
{rrni,yzhao}@bjtu.edu.cn

Abstract. Recapture image forensics has drawn much attention in public security forensics. Although some algorithms have been proposed to deal with it, there is still great challenge for small-size images. In this paper, we propose a generalized model for small-size recapture image forensics based on Laplacian Convolutional Neural Networks. Different from other Convolutional Neural Networks models, We put signal enhancement layer into Convolutional Neural Networks structure and Laplacian filter is used in the signal enhancement layer. We test the proposed method on four kinds of small-size image databases. The experimental results have demonstrate that the proposed algorithm is effective. The detection accuracies for different image size database are all above 95%.

Keywords: Recapture images forensics · Laplacian Convolution Neural Networks · Laplacian filter

1 Introduction

With the rapid development of the multimedia technology, a variety of image processing software are springing up in modern society, such as Adobe Photoshop, Meitu, and CorelDRAW, which make editing images easy. Everyone can tamper an image by means of these software and then deliver it to the Internet, which leads to a serious problem for image content security. In order to deal with the problem, digital image forensics has been studied by a number of scholars. Many algorithms have been proposed focusing on forensic issues of different operations, such as recapture, double JPEG compress, median filter, and copy-move.

As a common and facilitating operation, recapture has drawn much attentions in public security forensics. Recapture operation denotes that the original images are projected on some media, such as computer screen, mobile screen, paper and shot again using a camera. A multimedia content security event related to recapture images should be mentioned. In 2007, a villager lived in Shanxi Province claimed that he found the Wild South China Tiger, a kind of endangered animal, and published several groups of photos containing the Wild

© Springer International Publishing AG 2017
Y.Q. Shi et al. (Eds.): IWDW 2016, LNCS 10082, pp. 119–128, 2017.
DOI: 10.1007/978-3-319-53465-7_9

South China Tiger, which had aroused general concern by Forestry Department of Shanxi Province and the public. However, these photos provided by the villager turned out to be fake and the experts identified that these photos were the recaptured images from a New Year painting.

The key point of recapture image forensics is to discriminate between recaptured and original images. For recapture images obtained from different media, researches have proposed various algorithms based on the differences of image statistical characteristics between the original and the recapture images. For recapture images projected on paper, T.T. Ng et al. [1] discovered that the recapture images showed the mesostructure of the high-frequency spatial variations in the specular component. For recapture images shown on mobile screens, T.T. Ng et al. [2] presented a physical model and extracted a series of features from the model, such as background contextual information, spatial distribution of specularity, surface gradient and so on. For recapture images obtained from the original images shown on computer (LCD) screen, H. Cao et al. [3] proposed three kinds of statistical features to detect good-quality recapture images, namely local binary pattern (LBP), multi-scale wavelet statistics (MSWS), and color features (CF). R.H. Li et al. [4] found the physical traits of recaptured images on LCD screens and proposed two kinds of features: the block effect and blurriness effect due to JPEG compression, screen effect described by wavelet decomposition.

For the case of recaptured Images Shown On Lcd Screen, Despite Of The Good Detect Performance Of The Existing Algorithms, It Is Still A Great Challenge To Detect Small-Size Recapture Images. Because That, In General, There Is Less Information Available For Small-Size Images. In This Work, we propose an effective method based on convolutional neural networks with Laplacian filter layer. Considering that applying the convolutional neural networks model to forensics field directly can not achieve the best detect performance, we put signal enhancement layer into convolutional neural networks structure. Laplacian filter is used in the signal enhancement layer, which strengthens the differences between the original images and the recapture images. We realize the proposed method on four kinds of small-size image databases. The size of the images are 512*512, 256*256, 128*128, 64*64, respectively. The experimental results demonstrate that the proposed method outperforms the Li's [4] method. The rest of the paper is organized as follows: Sect. 2 describes details of our method. Section 3 includes the experimental results and analysis; conclusions are given in Sect. 4.

2   Laplacian Convolution Neural Networks

Convolutional Neural Networks (CNNs) have achieved amazingly good performance in computer vision field. From the AlexNet [6] in 2012 to ResNet [7] in 2015, the top-5 error on the ImageNet classification challenge has been decrease from 15% to 3.8%. What's more, CNNs has universality and expansibility. For example, the ResNet in 2015 achieved 3.57% error on the ImageNet test set and

won the 1st prize on the ILSVRC 2015 classification task. Besides the classification task, the ResNet also won several 1st places on the tasks of ImageNet
detection, ImageNet localization, COCO detection, and COCO segmentation. In
addition, it is a remarkable fact that the size of images used in computer vision
field is small. For example, the mnist dataset is a dataset of handwritten digits
and its images size is 32×32 only.

Differing from the traditional schemes that extracts feature handcrafted,
CNNs automatically learn features and combine feature extraction with feature
classification, which make CNNs to get enough information about the image even
for small-size image [5]. In general, the unit of Convolutional neural networks
structure consists of two parts: feature extraction and classification. For the unit
of feature extraction, there are 4 kinds of general layers: convolution layer, pooling layer, ReLU layer, Batch-normalization layer. For the unit of classification,
fully connected layer and softmax layer are common layers.

Considering that CNNs model can automatically learn features and use more
informations of the images, we utilize the CNNs to create a generalized model for
small-size recapture images forensics. However, just putting the CNNs into the
problem of recapture image forensics may not be a good way and the experimental results illustrate that it really is. The reason is that, unlike visual recognition
task, there is a little difference on two classifications of recapture image forensics. So we add the signal enhancement layer into CNNs structure in order to
strengthen the difference.

The architecture of our Laplacian Convolutional Neural Networks model is
shown in Fig. 1., which include two parts: signal enhancement layer and general
Convolutional Neural Networks structure. Firstly, we put the R, G, B channels of
the image into the model. In part of signal enhancement layer, Laplacian filter is
executed to amplify the difference between the original images and the recapture
images. Then, the five basic units are used in feature extraction layers. Lastly,
the softmax layer is used in classification layer.

2.1   Signal Enhancement Layer

The recapture operation would introduce some noise into the images. For the
case of recaptured images shown on LCD screen, the noise introduced would
cause wave effect. We try to stress this effect by detecting edge.

The Laplacian operator of an image finds the regions of rapid intensity change
and is often used for edge detection. The Laplacian transform $L(i, j)$ of an image
I is given by:

$$L(i, j) = \frac{\partial^2 I}{\partial i^2} + \frac{\partial^2 I}{\partial j^2} \tag{1}$$

The Laplacian transform of an image can be achieved using a Laplician filter.
The common used Laplician filter is as follows:

$$LF = \begin{bmatrix} 0, & -1, & 0 \\ -1, & 4, & -1 \\ 0, & -1, & 0 \end{bmatrix} \tag{2}$$

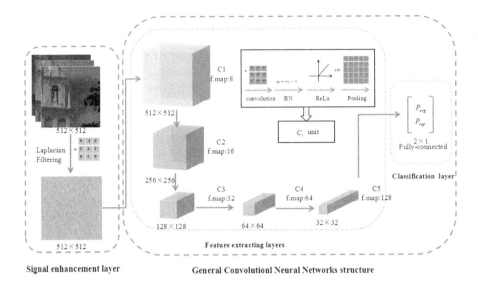

Fig. 1. The structure of the proposed method

The Laplacian operator is sensitive to noise, which has an bad influence on edge detection. However, for the detection of recapture images, we consider the attribute of sensitivity quite suitable. Because that after the processing of the Laplacian filter, the wave effect resulted from the recapture operation will be projected and the differences between the original images and the recaptured images will be amplified. To validate the effectiveness of the Laplacian filter, we random select four pairs of images from the image database provided in [4]. The gray versions of the original image and the recapture image after filtering are shown. In Fig. 2, the left column represents the original images and the right column denotes the recapture images. The difference in Fig. 2 between the original images and the recapture images is slight. Subsequently, these images in Fig. 2 are firstly converted to gray images. Then Laplacian filtering is implemented to the gray images, which results in the images in Fig. 3. It is intuitive to find that the difference between the original and recaptured image is amplified through the processing of the Laplacian filtering. The recaptured images after the Laplacian filtering have obvious stripes, which result from the noise introduced by LCD screen during reccapture operation.

2.2   General Convolutional Neural Networks Structure

In order to simplify the description, we only show the details of the structure for the case that the size of input images is equal to 512. For the other cases, the same operations will be executed and the difference is the size of input images and feature maps.

The general Convolutional Neural Networks structure consists of two parts: feature extraction layers and classification layer. Feature extraction layers

Fig. 2. Images samples. The left column represents the original images and the right column denotes the recapture images

include five basic unit and the softmax layer is applied to classification layer. There are four operations in basic unit: convolution, Batch Normalization, ReLu, and average pooling. The kernels size in convolution layer is 3*3 and step size is 1. In the average pooling layer, the kernels size is 5*5 and step size is 2. In particular, global average pooling is used in average pooling layer of C_5. The numbers of feature maps in five basic unit are 8, 16, 32, 64, 128 respectively. The sizes of feature maps are 515*512, 256*256, 128*128, 64*64, 32*32.

Fig. 3. Signal enhancement by Laplacian kernel for the gray version of the images.

3 Experimental Results

To evaluate the effectiveness of the proposed algorithms, we construct a image database including 20000 images: 10000 original images and 10000 recapture images. The size of the images is 512×512. The images derive from the image databases provided in [3,4]. All images from the two image libraries are used. We crop a square with size of 1024*1024 from the center of the images. In particular, if the height or width of the image is less than 1024, we crop the image to 512*1024 or 1024*512. Then the images are cut into non-overlopping blocks of 515*512. We randomly select 10000 original images and 10000 recapture images as the image database used in this work. The training data contains 4000 original images and 4000 recapture images. The validation set consists of 1000 original images and 1000 recapture images. The rest belongs to the test set. We compare the proposed method with the work in [4] and the detection accuracies are averaged over 3 random experiments.

The experiments about the proposed method are conducted on a GPU and performed based on an open source framework of deep leaning: Caffe [8].

3.1 Experiment 1

To test the effectiveness of the proposed method for small-size recapture images, the images in the image database that we build are cropped to 256, 128, 64 from the center of the image respectively. The experiments are conducted for four different sizes of images. The results of the experiments are given in Table 1. As shown in Table 1, the detection accuracies of proposed method are higher than LBP method and Li's method in all cases.

Table 1. The Detection accuracy (%) for small-size recapture images. The best results are highlighted in bold.

Image size	Method	Accuracy (%)
512×512	LBP [3]	95.02
	Li [4]	91.9
	Proposed method	**99.74**
256×256	LBP [3]	92.54
	Li [4]	90.55
	Proposed method	**99.30**
128×128	LBP [3]	89.01
	Li [4]	88.49
	Proposed method	**98.48**
64×64	LBP [3]	79.5
	Li [4]	85.41
	Proposed method	**95.23**

3.2 Experiment 2

To verify the effectiveness of the signal enhancement layer, we test the network structure without the signal enhancement layer for th case that image size is equal to 64×64. The experiment results in Table 2 show that the detection accuary of proposed method using the signal enhancement layer is higher than the method dropped out the signal enhancement layer (in the case of NON in Table 2).

In the other hand, the filter used in the signal enhancement layer has an impact on the detection accuracy. We test five kinds of common filters, namely HF, VF, HVF, GF, LF. The definitions of these filter are as follows.

$$HF = \begin{bmatrix} 1, -1 \end{bmatrix} \tag{3}$$

$$VF = \begin{bmatrix} 1 \\ -1 \end{bmatrix} \tag{4}$$

$$HVF = \begin{bmatrix} 1, & -1 \\ -1, & 1 \end{bmatrix} \tag{5}$$

$$GF = \begin{bmatrix} -1, & 2, & -2, & 2, & -1 \\ 2, & -6, & 8, & -6, & 2 \\ -2, & 8, & -12, & 8, & -2 \\ 2, & -6, & 8, & -6, & 2 \\ -1, & 2, & -2, & 2, & -1 \end{bmatrix} \tag{6}$$

$$LF = \begin{bmatrix} 0, & -1, & 0 \\ -1, & 4, & -1 \\ 0, & -1, & 0 \end{bmatrix} \tag{7}$$

In Fig. 4, the images after different filtering operations are shown. From the second row to the last row, the filter used is HF, VF, HVF, GF, LF respectively. In order to highlight the effect introduced by filtering operation, we randomly chose one image patch. Then it is magnified and displayed in Fig. 4. These five filters both enhence the difference between the original image and the recapture image. The results in Table 2 indicate that the case of LF (using the Laplacian filter) has the best detection accuracy. It is clear that using Laplacian filter in signal enhencement layer is a good choise for recapture image forensics.

Table 2. The Detection accuracy (%) for different choise in signal enhencement layer. The best result are highlighted in bold

Image size	The choise in signal enhencement	Accuracy (%)
64 × 64	NON	91.23
	HF	93.98
	VF	93.47
	HVF	93.78
	GF	92.61
	LF	**95.23**

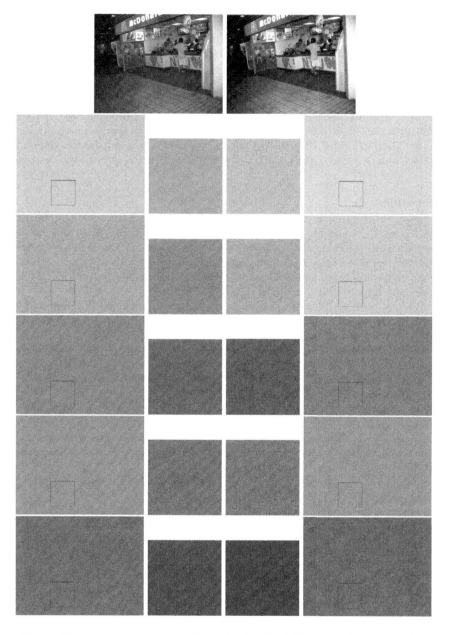

Fig. 4. The images are processed by using kinds of filters for the gray version

4   Conclusions

In this paper, we propose a generalized model for small-size recapture image forensics based on Laplacian Convolutional Neural Networks. In particular, the signal enhencement layer was added into Convolutional Neural Networks structure and Laplician filter was applied to signal enhencement layer. The Laplician filter used in signal enhencement layer plays a important role for the improvement of the detection performance. The experimental results has proven that the detect performance of our method is great.

Acknowledgments. This work was supported in part by National NSF of China (61332012, 61272355, 61672090), Fundamental Research Funds for the Central Universities (2015JBZ002), the PAPD, the CICAEET. We greatly acknowledge the support of NVIDIA Corporation with the donation of the Tesla K40 GPU used for this research.

References

1. Yu, H., Ng, T.T., Sun, Q.: Recapture photo detection using specularity distribution. In: 15th IEEE International Conference on Image Processing, pp. 3140–3143 (2008)
2. Gao, X., Ng, T.T., Qiu, B., Chang, S.F.: Single-view recaptured image detection based on physics-based features. In: 2010 IEEE International Conference on Multimedia and Expo (ICME), pp. 1469–1474. IEEE (2010)
3. Cao, H., Alex, K.C.: Identification of recaptured photographs on LCD screens. In: IEEE International Conference on Acoustics, Speech and Signal Processing, pp. 1790–1793 (2010)
4. Li, R., Ni, R., Zhao, Y.: An effective detection method based on physical traits of recaptured images on LCD screens. In: Shi, Y.-Q., Kim, H.J., Pérez-González, F., Echizen, I. (eds.) IWDW 2015. LNCS, vol. 9569, pp. 107–116. Springer, Heidelberg (2016). doi:10.1007/978-3-319-31960-5_10
5. Chen, J., Kang, X., Liu, Y., Wang, Z.J.: Median filtering forensics based on convolutional neural networks. IEEE Signal Process. Lett. **22**(11), 1849–1853 (2015)
6. Krizhevsky, A., Sutskever, I., Hinton, G.E.: Imagenet classification with deep convolutional neural networks. In: Advances in Neural Information Processing Systems, pp. 1097–1105 (2012)
7. He, K., Zhang, X., Ren, S., Sun, J.: Deep residual learning for image recognition. arXiv preprint arXiv:1512.03385 (2015)
8. An open source framework of deep learning. http://caffe.berkeleyvision.org/

Concealing Fingerprint-Biometric Data into Audio Signals for Identify Authentication

Sani M. Abdullahi, Hongxia Wang$^{(\boxtimes)}$, Qing Qian,
and Wencheng Cao

School of Information Science and Technology, Southwest Jiaotong University,
Chengdu 610031, People's Republic of China
hxwang@swjtu.edu.cn

Abstract. Numerous security issues are raised through the transmission and storage of biometric data due to its high sensitivity and extremely crucial purpose. However, it might be impossible to recover if lost, counterfeited or hacked, thereby ruining the general aim of securing it. In this paper, an 8-layered feature enhancement algorithm is proposed. A centroid based semi-fragile audio watermarking is used to conceal the enhanced fingerprint biometric data into audio signals. The algorithm starts by encrypting our enhanced/extracted fingerprint template and converting it into binary bits prior to watermarking. It hence proceeds with computing the centroid of each audio frame and once more encrypting the obtained watermark using a Logistic map operation. DWT and DCT are performed on the sub-band which carries the centroid of audio thereby embedding the encrypted watermark bits into the domain signal. ODG and SDG analysis are performed on both the original and watermarked signal and the results signify the efficiency of the proposed scheme. Moreover, some signal processing operations are finally carried out on the watermarked signal and the outcome was intriguing as all attacks are counteracted.

Keywords: Biometrics · Fingerprint feature · Embedding · Identity authentication · Watermarking

1 Introduction

Over decades, fingerprints still remain the most widely used and acceptable biometric technique due to their uniqueness and permanence throughout the entire human lifespan. However, the security of fingerprint biometric data is a major concern due to the fact that they can easily be attacked in various ways, either intentional or accidental. Security holes can be identified in the fingerprint biometric system right from data capture up to data storage into the biometric database. Meanwhile, the process of transmitting the extracted feature to the matcher module, database or receivers end will definitely be more prone to attacks than every other stage [1]. For this reason, fingerprint images can be watermarked so as to be secured throughout the transmission process.

All crucial designing criteria of the watermark embedding/extraction system i.e. imperceptibility, robustness and security [2]; were given topmost consideration at every

© Springer International Publishing AG 2017
Y.Q. Shi et al. (Eds.): IWDW 2016, LNCS 10082, pp. 129–144, 2017.
DOI: 10.1007/978-3-319-53465-7_10

stage of our proposed system. In the history of watermarking systems, we are aware of the trade-offs that exits between imperceptibility and robustness [2]. Even with that, our proposed scheme tries to establish a balance between the two.

Biometric data security is recently gaining more attention by researchers from different security realms; being it in steganography, encryption, watermarking, [3] etc. A few amongst the published techniques in multimedia watermarking includes; Bas and Furon [4], in their work, they introduced a new measure of watermarking security known as "the effective key length". The approach captures the difficulty for an adversary to get access to the watermarking channel, thereby making the system more robust and secure irrespective of the trade-off that exist between them.

Recently, Chunlei et al. [5] introduced a self-recoverable watermarking scheme for face image protection. They came up with a technique of using the Principal Components Analysis (PCA) coefficient to generate the watermarks hence reducing the amount of embedding watermarks.

In 2013, Mohammed et al. [6] proposed a new fingerprint image watermarking approach using Dual-Tree Complex Wavelet Transform (DTCWT). Their method expatiates more on the effect of watermark on fingerprint biometric features after the watermark embedding process. Both fingerprint and watermark images are decomposed into real and imaginary parts. This might thus lead to a major hitch on their system with regards to the trade-offs between its robustness and security even though the template was successfully retrieved without corrupting the minutiae.

The concept of using a QR based decomposition was introduced by Arashdeep et al. [7]. Their technique presents a high payload watermarking method for audio speech signals to accommodate biometric based watermarks generated from iris images.

Our proposed scheme enhances the fingerprint image before embedding. It uses double encryption; first to encrypt the extracted feature template before watermarking and the second applied after watermarking thus providing an optimum system security and robustness against attacks. The simulation results achieved from our experiments accomplishes a high perceptual transparency after hiding the fingerprint template by exploiting the masking effects of the human auditory system (HAS).

The remaining part of this paper is organised as follows: In Sect. 2 we gave a step-by-step process of the proposed fingerprint enhancement scheme. In Sect. 3 we gave an explanation about the embedding scheme; both the template embedding and feature extraction procedures are covered in this section. Section 4 evaluates the performance of our proposed system by carrying out an inaudibility test on the watermarked audio signal. In Sect. 5 we outlined the experimental results achieved through different signal processing operations done on the watermarked signal and finally in Sect. 6 is a brief conclusion.

2   Fingerprint Enhancement and Extraction Processes

In our proposed scope, we made use of watermarking in security framework rather than copyright protection or digital rights management purposes considering our sole aim is to protect the fingerprint feature even though it serves as the watermark. We used centroid based semi-fragile watermarking as it is best suited for our fingerprint feature embedding because the receiver already has the knowledge of the watermark/fingerprint feature, thereby mainly focusing on matching it with the extracted version before further processes.

In the same vein, we want our fingerprint feature to yield a very efficient result when matched to the fingerprint database during the process of authentication since the fingerprint matching accuracy always depends on the image quality as well as the algorithm involved in the enhancement or extraction processes [8, 9].

Therefore, in this section, we introduce a fast fingerprint enhancement algorithm which will adaptively improve the clarity of ridges and valleys structures of input fingerprint images based on 8-layered enhancement process.

The stages involved in the fingerprint enhancement and extractions procedure are given as follows:

Step 1. Normalization
The main purpose of normalization is to reduce the variations in grey-level values along ridges and valleys which facilitates the subsequent stages. We use the traditional normalization technique in [22] to reduce the dynamic range of ridges and valleys of our fingerprint images.

Step 2. Binarization
Binarization is performed by a simple threshold applied on the normalized fingerprint image. We obtain a binary image through the ridge extraction procedure on a gray scale fingerprint image as follows:

1. Divide the normalised image $N(x, y)$ into small blocks of size 16×16 pixels.
2. Then, calculate the threshold t of the block and check the value of each pixel in the block. If pixel value is greater than threshold value, assign binary 1 to pixel value; else assign 0 to pixel value as represented in Eq. (1).

$$I(x, y) = \begin{cases} 1 & if\ I(x, y) \geq t, \\ 0 & otherwise \end{cases} \tag{1}$$

3. Binary 1/white represents ridge and binary 0/black represents valley.
4. The gray scale pixel intensity value is transformed to a binary intensity of black (0) or white (1).

Step 3. Thinning
Thinning is performed on the normalized binary image. It is done in order to simplify the extraction of minutiae since the ridges obtained in the previous stage are few pixels wide. A morphological operation is performed so as to erode the ridges until they are one pixel wide. We used the standard thinning algorithm proposed by Giang et al. in [21] to apply the thinning operation.

Step 4. Smooth Orientation
Orientation Smoothing is performed after the thinning process. It helps to eliminate sensitive noise (ridges and valleys damages, image area scars, creases cuts etc.) in the fingerprint image. We obtain the smooth orientation field according to the following procedure in [15]:

1. Compute the gradients $d_x(x, y)$ and $d_y(x, y)$ at the pixel (x, y) and divide image into non overlapping blocks with size $w \times w$.
2. Then estimate the local orientation of each block centered at pixel (x, y) using the equation below:

$$V_x(x, y) = \sum_{u=x-\frac{w}{2}}^{x+\frac{w}{2}} \sum_{v=y-\frac{w}{2}}^{y+\frac{w}{2}} 2d_x(u, v)d_y(u, v), \tag{2}$$

Subsequently,

$$\theta(x, y) = \frac{1}{2} tan^{-1}\left(\frac{V_y(x, y)}{V_x(x, y)}\right), \tag{3}$$

where $\theta(x, y)$ is the least square estimate of the local ridge orientation at the block centered at pixel (x, y).

3. Low pass filtering is introduced in order to modify the incorrect local ridge orientation by converting the orientation image into continuous vector field defined as:

$$\Phi_x(x, y) = \cos(2\theta(x, y)), \tag{4}$$

and

$$\Phi_y(x, y) = \sin(2\theta(x, y)), \tag{5}$$

where Φ_x and Φ_y are the x and y components of the vector field respectively. The low pass filter is then reduced to;

$$\Phi'_x(x, y) = \sum_{u=-w_\Phi/2}^{w_\Phi/2} \sum_{v=-w_\Phi/2}^{w_\Phi/2} W(u, v)\Phi_x(x - uw, y - vw) \tag{6}$$

$$\Phi'_y(x, y) = \sum_{u=-w_\Phi/2}^{w_\Phi/2} \sum_{v=-w_\Phi/2}^{w_\Phi/2} W(u, v)\Phi_x(x - uw, y - vw) \tag{7}$$

Finally, the smooth orientation at (x, y) is calculated as follows:

$$\theta'(x, y) = \frac{1}{2} tan^{-1}\left(\frac{\Phi'_y(x, y)}{\Phi'_x(x, y)}\right) \tag{8}$$

Step 5. Making mask

Masking distinguishes between the recoverable and unrecoverable portions of the fingerprint image. Three features are used to characterize the sinusoidal-shaped wave formed by the local ridges and valleys. They are amplitude (A), frequency (f), and variance (Var).

1. Let $X[1], X[2], \ldots X[l]$ be the x-signature of a block centered at (x, y).
2. The three features corresponding to the pixel(block) (x, y) are computed as;
(a) $A = (average\ height\ of\ the\ peaks - average\ depth\ of\ the\ valleys)$.
(b) $f = \frac{1}{T(x,y)}$, where $T(x, y)$ is the average number of pixels between two consecutive peaks.
(c) $Var = \frac{1}{l} \sum_{x=1}^{1} (X[x] - (\frac{1}{l} \sum_{x=1}^{1} X[x]))^2$
3. If a block centered at (x, y) is recoverable, then $R(x, y) = 1$, else $R(x, y) = 0$
4. After the image R is obtained, the percentage of recoverable region is computed.
5. If the percentage of recoverable regions is smaller than the threshold, then the input fingerprint image is rejected. The accepted image is then passed through minutiae finding stage.

Step 6. Finding minutiae
At this stage, the minutiae are extracted from the masked image. We apply the crossing number method in [13] to find the minutiae as thus;

1. First, label the ridges in accepted masked image.
2. Select a ridge and scanned neighbors of each pixel in ridge using a 3×3 matrix.
3. Central element of matrix must be pixel value under operation. Figure 1 is a mask used to identify ridge endings and ridge bifurcations of a minutiae.
4. If central element is 1 and have only one neighbor pixel with value 1, mark it as a ridge termination.
5. If central element is 1 with exactly 3 neighbors with pixel value 1, mark it as a bifurcation.

1	0	1
0	1	0
0	1	0

0	0	1
0	1	0
0	0	0

(a) Ridge bifurcation   (b) Ridge termination

Fig. 1. Ridge termination and ridge bifurcation

Step 7. Core point selection
The core point is such a consistent point in the fingerprint image. It has a diverse applicability in both fingerprint classification, registration and matching. We use the geometry of region technique (GR) in detecting the core point using the following procedure.

1. Start by computing the smoothed orientation field in $\theta'(x, y)$ by using Eq. (8) above.
2. Compute $\varepsilon(x, y)$, which is a sine component of $\theta'(x, y)$.

$$\varepsilon(x, y) = \sin(\theta'(x, y)) \tag{9}$$

3. We initialize a label image A which is used to indicate the core point.
4. Then assign the corresponding pixel in A the value of integrated pixel intensity of each region.

$$A(x, y) = \sum_{R1} \varepsilon(x, y) - \sum_{R2} \varepsilon(x, y) \tag{10}$$

5. The region $R1$ and $R2$ were empirically determined and their geometry are also designed to capture the maximum curvature in concave region.
6. Find the maximum value in A and assign its coordinate as the core point.
7. If the core isn't located yet, the steps (1–6) should be iterated while decreasing window size in i.

Step 8. Filtering false minutiae
False ridge breaks and false ridge cross-connections might not be completely eliminated in the previous stages. Therefore, we use the procedure below to remove all false minutiae.

1. Calculate the average inter-ridge width (I) using the steps below;
    (a) Scan a row of thin ridge image and add up all pixels whose value is 1.
    (b) Divide row lengths by above summation to get the ridge width (I).
2. Proceed to select the minutiae pair and calculate the distance between selected minutiae using the distance formula;

$$D = \sqrt{(x_2 - x_1)^2 + (y_2 - y_1)^2} \tag{11}$$

2. If the distance D between one termination and one bifurcation is less than the average inter-ridge width I and both the minutiae are on the same ridge, discard both.
4. If the distance D between two bifurcations is less than the average inter-ridge width I and both the minutiae are on the same ridge, remove both.
5. If the distance D between two terminations is less than the average inter-ridge width I and both the minutiae are on the same ridge, remove both.
6. Finally, if two terminations are on a ridge and the length of the ridge is less than the average inter-ridge width I, then discard both of the minutia's.

After filtering all false minutiae, the fingerprint image is enhanced and its minutiae is also extracted. Then we can proceed to embed the extracted feature into an audio signal. However, we can notice that our proposed fingerprint enhancement and extraction algorithm in Fig. 2, introduces more additional layers of enhancement better than those in [10–13], which will henceforth increase the overall efficiency of the matcher. Similarly, Fig. 3 shows the visualized output of each enhanced stage of the proposed 8-layered enhancement technique. We use a minutiae based recognition system which undergoes three main stages of enhancement and extraction processes,

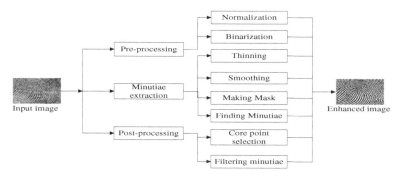

Fig. 2. Flowchart of the proposed algorithm depicting the 8 stages involved in our fingerprint enhancement process

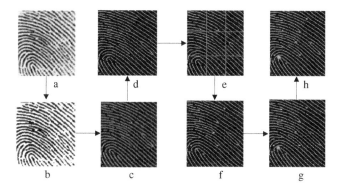

Fig. 3. (a) Normalized image, (b) binarized image, (c) thinned image, (d) smoothed image, (e) masked image, (f) detected minutiae, (g) selected core point, and (h) filtered minutiae

namely Pre-processing, Minutiae extraction and Post-processing [11, 14, 15] as represented in Fig. 2.

With this enhancement of our fingerprint image, we are certain of yielding a top notch quality feature that can easily pass the matcher module.

3   Watermark Embedding and Extraction Algorithm

The watermark embedding/extraction algorithm is a refined version of [16]. It is used to embed and extract our enhanced fingerprint feature into an audio signal.

An increased security and robustness of the system is noted due to the use of double Chaotic Logistic encryption in the embedding process. Figure 4 depicts the entire stages involved in the embedding process.

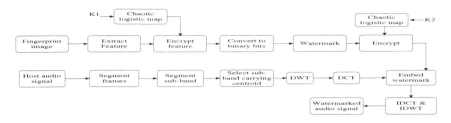

Fig. 4. Proposed fingerprint feature watermark embedding process (client side)

3.1 Template Embedding Process

Step 1. Encrypting template using chaotic logistic map

1. First, we start by converting our 8-bit template of size $M \times N$ into a one-dimensional array of pixels $P_i = (P_1, P_2, \ldots, P_n)$ where $i = 1, 2, 3, \ldots, n$ and $n = M \times N$.
2. The binary image pixels P_i are XORed using a key sequence generated by logistic chaotic with K_1 so as to obtain the encrypted pixel E_i. Thus we have;

$$E_i = P_i \oplus K_i \tag{12}$$

3. Repeat step 2 to encrypt all image pixels.
4. Finally, we transform all encrypted digits $E_i' = (E_1', E_2', E_3', \ldots, E_n')$ into an array of size $M \times N$ to obtain the encrypted template T_E.

Step 2. Convert template to binary bits

1. Let our encrypted template T_E represents a $m \times n$ matrix of two dimensions. Note that n in this step is one part of the matrix dimension of our template which differs from the n in step 1.

$$T_{E_{m \times n}} = \begin{pmatrix} a_{11} & \cdots & a_{1n} \\ \vdots & \ddots & \vdots \\ a_{m1} & \cdots & a_{mn} \end{pmatrix}$$

2. Let say an array of real numbers T_E needs to be converted to binary. Each number will be represented by k bits. Therefore, we will have a $m \times n \times k$ representation as thus:

$$T_{E_{m \times n}} = \begin{pmatrix} a_{11} & \cdots & a_{1n} \\ \vdots & \ddots & \vdots \\ a_{m1} & \cdots & a_{mn} \end{pmatrix} = \begin{pmatrix} a_{111} \cdots a_{11k} & \cdots & a_{1n1} \cdots a_{1nk} \\ \vdots & \ddots & \vdots \\ a_{m11} \cdots a_{m1k} & \cdots & a_{mn1} \cdots a_{mnk} \end{pmatrix}_2$$

3. Our template can be converted into one dimension as the generated watermark which is denoted as thus:

$$W = [a_{111} \cdots a_{11k} \cdots a_{1n1} \cdots a_{1nk} \cdots a_{m11} \cdots a_{m1k} \cdots a_{mn1} \cdots a_{mnk}] \quad (13)$$

Step 3. Encrypting the watermark using chaotic sequence which is generated by a secure key K_2.

1. By the use of chaotic system so as to generate a stream cipher sequence R_C with the same length of watermark W.
2. The encrypted watermark W_c can be obtained as represented below;

$$W_c = W \oplus R_c \quad (14)$$

Step 4. Host audio frame and sub-band segmentation.
The host signal is split into non-overlapping frames M containing N samples. Then each audio frame is further divided into non-overlapping sub-bands M_1 containing N/M_1 samples. Each sub-band is represented as $S_1(p,q)$, $p = 1, 2, \ldots, M$, $q = 1, 2, \ldots, M_1$.

Step 5. Computing the centroid of each audio frame
We use the log power spectrum equation to compute the centroid by calculating its square root as in Eq. (15) below:

$$P(p,q) = \sqrt{\frac{\sum_{t=1}^{N/M_1} \log_2(|S'_t(p,q)|)^2 + \alpha}{N/M_1}}, \quad (15)$$

where $S'_t(p,q)$ denotes the tth FFT domain coefficient of $S_1(p,q)$ and $\alpha > 0$ is a deviation value, though, $\alpha = 1.01$ is adopted. Hence the centroid of each audio frame is given as thus:

$$C(p) = \left\lfloor \frac{\sum_{q=1}^{M_1} q \times P(p,q)}{\sum_{q=1}^{M_1} P(p,q)} \right\rfloor, \quad p = 1, 2, \ldots, M, \quad (16)$$

However, the largest integer more than the original value is returned by $\lfloor . \rfloor$.

Step 6. Embedding watermark feature
At this stage, the watermark bits are embedded into the audio sub-band $S_1(p,q_c)$ which carries the centroid of audio frame. This last phase of watermark embedding process is itemized in Step 5 of [16].

Step 7. Generating watermarked audio
To obtain the final watermarked audio T', we perform the inverse DCT and D-level inverse DWT on the coefficients of DWT-DCT which contains watermark bit respectively.

At the end of this embedding process, the watermarked audio signal T' can be wirelessly transmitted securely to the receiver's end, hence the fingerprint feature can be extracted and authenticated for further verification and/or identification of an individual.

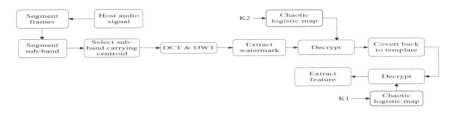

Fig. 5. Proposed feature watermark extraction process (server side)

3.2   Watermark Extraction Process

Figure 5 depicts the stages involved in the watermark extraction process.

Step 1: We perform the operation in step 3 of Sect. 3.1 to obtain the audio sub-band from each audio frame.

Step 2: Watermark extraction

1. The DCT coefficients denoted as $G^*_{pq_c}$ is obtained by performing D-level DWT and DCT on the audio sub-band $S^*_2(p, q_c)$ that carries the centroid of audio frame.
2. The feature watermark bits are finally extracted from the anterior n/n_1 DCT domain coefficients according to the criterion below:

$$w'(i) = \begin{cases} 0, & \left\lfloor G^*_{pq_c}/\Delta \right\rfloor \bmod 2 = 0, \\ 1, & \left\lfloor G^*_{pq_c}/\Delta \right\rfloor \bmod 2 = 1. \end{cases} \tag{17}$$

Step 3: Using the same key to obtain the stream cipher sequence R_c as in step 3 of Sect. 3.1, we generate the decrypted watermark W'' as:

$$W'' = W' \oplus R_C \tag{18}$$

Step 4: Convert watermark binary bits to template

Perform the inverse of the operation in Eq. (13), step 2 of Sect. 3.1 to convert binary bits to template.

Step 5: We decrypt the fingerprint template by performing reverse of the encryption process as in Step 1 of Sect. 3.1.

After this final decryption, we will obtain back the fingerprint template for further authentication. Here the matcher module will authenticate the template by comparing it against the pre-stored fingerprint template in the database using the matching algorithm in [17].

4   Performance Evaluation

In most cases, audio watermarking is used for protecting the host audio [18], but in our case the main objective is protecting the watermark feature. Ideally, throughout the watermark embedding and extraction process, we expect users to be oblivious as to whether the image is watermarked or not, but most importantly, the watermarked audio quality should not be reduced after embedding the watermark, which will henceforth aid in making the watermark template to be indistinguishable or be like a replica of same template prior to watermarking [19]. With this regard, we conducted few experiments on the watermarked audio before extracting the fingerprint template as well as on the extracted template itself.

Various experiments were carried out to test the inaudibility and robustness of the scheme. Subjective difference grade (SDG) and Objective difference grade (ODG) are the criteria through which the evaluation was carried out. The meaning of each score for the SDG and ODG is provided in [16]. In evaluating the ODG, we adopt the PEAQ system measurements in [20], while for the SDG, listeners were provided with both the host audio signals and watermarked audio signals for evaluation and the average is finally taken as the SDG. The result of the ODG and SDG is depicted in Table 2.

5   Experimental Results

In terms of robustness and imperceptibility of the scheme, a series of experiments were carried out on the watermarked audio signal that contains the hidden fingerprint template. The experiments include; MP3 compression set at 64 kbps, 96 kbps and 128 kbps respectively. Re-sampled at 22050 Hz, re-quantized from 16 to 8 and back to 16 bits, low pass filtering at 21.5 kHz, noise addition of 40 db and tampering by replacing the watermarked audio signal with a partial audio signal at the 325000th to 345000th samples. Both the host and watermarked signals are mono signals set at the sampling frequency of 44.1 kHz, sample resolution of 16 bits and a length of 1 m 34 s. Figures 6 and 7 depicts waveforms and amplitude spectrum of both signals. So far, no slight difference is noticed between the two.

The system evaluation is attained by calculating the signal-to-noise-ratio (SNR), mean squared error (MSE) and bit error rate (BER) of the watermarked signal using the afore mentioned operations. The mathematical formulations of SNR, MSE and BER are respectively represented in [23]. So also, from the detailed experimental results in Table 1, we can see that our algorithm achieved 100% accuracy without any attack, with a compression attack at 128 kbps and low-pass filtering at 22.05 kHz. However, all other attacks were also close to accurate as non has achieved below 98.95% accuracy rate. Note that the accuracy rate is attained by calculating the BER which is used to measure the reliability and robustness of the watermarked signal against attacks.

In the ODG and SDG test, we introduced a second signal. Same fingerprint feature was embedded in the signal. It is quite evident from the results in Table 2, that even

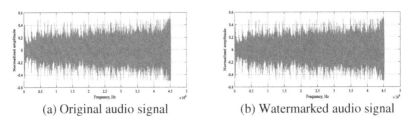

(a) Original audio signal   (b) Watermarked audio signal

Fig. 6. Waveform of audio signals

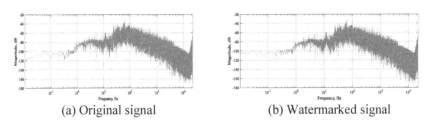

(a) Original signal   (b) Watermarked signal

Fig. 7. Amplitude spectrum of audio signal

though both signals are entirely different, the watermarked feature didn't change the audibility of the signals. However, we should also note that only the first audio signal was used in other evaluations.

The fingerprint image dataset contains a combination of fingers collected from public domain and some that were voluntarily volunteered by students from our research lab. A total of 80 fingerprint images were gathered from both parties. Each finger is captured and set at a resolution of 512 dpi with a size of 374 × 388 pixels. Figure 8(a) shows the original fingerprint feature without enhancement. Figure 8(b) depicts the extracted feature with enhancement. We will notice that all ridges and orientation of the feature are very clear and can easily be matched through all authentication processes (verification and identification). Likewise, Fig. 8(c) depicts the extracted feature after watermarking. No visible difference can be noticed between Fig. 8(b) and (c). Therefore, it is evident that the feature enhancement wasn't reduced

(a) Original image   (b) Enhanced image   (c) Extracted image

Fig. 8. (a) Original fingerprint feature before enhancement, (b) enhanced fingerprint feature before embedding (c) extracted feature after watermarking

during the embedding and extraction processes and thus very effective to match and pass all authentications without hitches.

5.1 Comparison with a Related Scheme

Our proposed algorithm is compared with a related scheme that uses Chaos and NDFT-based spread spectrum for biometric data concealment [23]. The comparison was carried out on each evaluation parameter with different attacks, set at different rates.

Table 3 depicts a comprehensive comparison of the SNR, MSE and BER values under different types of attacks. From the table, we can see that all attacks evaluated under SNR, MSE and BER in our proposed algorithm achieved a significantly better results than Khan's approach. This signifies how robust and efficient our proposed algorithm is to that of Khan's. However, we can also see that Khan's results doesn't cover other attacks at different rates, such as; MP3 compression at 64 kbps and 96 kbps, re-sampling at 22.05 kHz, low-pass filtering at 21.05 kHz, noise addition at 40 dB and tampered replacement from 325000th to 345000th samples.

In all carried out experiments, evaluations and comparisons, our proposed scheme proved very efficient, robust and secured against common signal processing operations.

Table 1. The SNR and MSE values under some signal processing attacks on audio signal

Signal processing attacks	SNR (dB)	MSE	Accuracy (%)
No attack	43.1470	1.4988e-05	100
MP3 compression (64 kbps)	42.7411	1.4701e-05	99.87
MP3 compression (96 kbps)	42.6652	1.4975e-05	99.88
MP3 compression (128 kbps)	42.7142	1.4808e-05	100
Re-sampling (22.50 kHz)	40.1907	1.4759e-05	99.31
Re-sampling (96 kHz)	42.9811	1.5022e-05	99.85
Re-quantization (16-8-16 bits)	41.2501	1.5622e-05	99.94
Low-pass filtering (21.5 kHz)	42.9120	1.4902e-05	99.86
Low-pass filtering (22.05 kHz)	42.9718	1.5301e-05	100
Noise addition (40 dB)	41.8652	1.5220e-05	98.95
Tampering(325000th–345000th)	41.7650	1.5361e-05	99.21

Table 2. ODG and SDG values of different audio signals

Signal type	ODG	SDG
Music 1 (rhythms and blues)	−0.028	0
Music 2 (melody beats)	−0.025	0

Table 3. Comparison of SNR, MSE and BER under different attacks

Attacks	SNR(dB)		MSE		Accuracy (%)	
	Ref. [23]	Proposed Scheme	Ref. [23]	Proposed Scheme	Ref. [23]	Proposed Scheme
Without attack	34.9622	43.147	3.41E-04	1.50E-05	100	100
MP3 compression (64 kbps)	-	42.7411	-	1.50E-05	-	99.87
MP3 compression (96 kbps)	-	42.6652	-	1.47E-05	-	99.88
MP3compression (128 kbps)	34.5602	42.7142	3.74E-04	1.48E-05	100	100
Re-sampling (96 kHz)	34.8861	42.9811	3.47E-04	1.50E-05	99.80	99.85
Re-sampling (22.05 kHz)	-	40.1907	-	1.48E-05	-	99.31
Re-quantization (16-8-16)	34.8991	41.2501	3.46E-04	1.56E-05	100	99.94
Low-pass filtering (22.05 kHz)	34.8085	42.9718	3.53E-04	1.53E-05	99.8	100
Low-pass filtering (21.50 kHz)	-	42.912	-	1.49E-05	-	99.86
Noise addition	32.775	41.8652 (40 dB)	5.64E-04	1.52E-05 (40 dB)	99.41	98.95 (40 dB)
Tampering (325000th–345000th)	-	41.765	-	1.54E-05	-	99.21

6   Conclusion

In this paper, we proposed an 8-layered fingerprint enhancing scheme by combining different techniques. We also introduced a refined version of centroid based semi-fragile audio watermarking for biometric data hiding. The algorithm protects and secretly transmit our biometric data to the receiving party without being corrupted. The main features of our scheme are summarized as follows: (1) Enhancing the fingerprint image before watermarking is applied. (2) Segmenting the host audio signal into multiple audio frames gives room for a high embedding capacity of the scheme without any distortion. (3) The centroid of each audio frame is computed and encrypted so as to obtain the watermark. (4) The use of double chaotic logistic encryption will enhance the security of the proposed scheme. (5) Fingerprint template watermark bits are embedded into the audio sub-band carrying the centroid of the audio frame thus improving the robustness of the system against malicious manipulations. We performed a series of experiments to evaluate the system's performance and the experimental results were second to none. Hence we can deduce that an optimum balance between imperceptibility, security and robustness of the system is achieved.

Acknowledgement. This work was supported by the National Science Foundation of China (NSFC) under the grant No. U1536110.

References

1. Gaurav, B., Wu, Q.M.J.: Chaos-based security solution for fingerprint data during communication and transmission. IEEE Trans. Instr. Meas. **61**(4), 876–887 (2012)
2. Hua, G., Huang, J., Shi, Y.Q., Goh, J., Vrizlynn, L.L.T.: Twenty years of digital audio watermarking-a comprehensive review. Sig. Process. **128**, 222–242 (2016)
3. Anil, K.J., Arus, R., Sharath, P.: Biometrics: a tool for information security. IEEE Trans. Inf. Forensics Secur. **1**(2), 125–143 (2006)
4. Bas, P., Furon, T.: A new measure of watermarking security: the effective key length. IEEE Trans. Inf. Forensics Secur. **8**(8), 1306–1317 (2013)
5. Chunlei, L., Ruimin, Y., Zhoufeng, L., Jianjun, L., Zhenduo, G.: Semi-fragile self-recoverable watermarking scheme for face image protection. Comput. Electr. Eng. **54**, 484–493 (2016)
6. Mohammed, A., Fengling, H., Ron, V.: Fingerprint image watermarking approach using DTCWT without corrupting minutiae. In: IEEE 6th International Congress on Image and Signal Processing (CISP), vol. 3, pp. 1717–1723 (2013)
7. Arashdeep, K., Malay, K.D., Soni, K.M., Nidhi, T.: A secure and high payload digital audio watermarking using features from iris image. In: IEEE International Conference on Contemporary Computing and Informatics (IC3I), pp. 509–512 (2014)
8. Anil, K., Arun, A., Karthik, N.: Introduction to Biometrics. Springer, Heidelberg (2011). ISBN 978-0-387-77325-4
9. Anush, S., Mayank, V., Richa, S.: Latent fingerprint matching: a survey. IEEE Access. IEEE Biom. Compendium RFIC Virtual J. **2**, 982–1004 (2014)
10. Kai, C., Eryun, L., Anil, K.: Segmentation and enhancement of latent fingerprint. IEEE Trans. Pattern Anal. Mach. Intell. **36**(9), 1847–1859 (2014)
11. Josef, S., Mikael, N., Benny, S., Ingvar, C.: Adaptive fingerprint image enhancement with emphasis on preprocessing of data. IEEE Trans. Image Process. **22**(2), 644–656 (2013)
12. Milos, V., Brankica, M., Andelija, M., Dragan, R.: Improving minutiae extraction in fingerprint images through robust enhancement. In: IEEE Conference on 21st Telecommunication Forum (TELFOR), pp. 506–509 (2013)
13. Ravi, K., Sai, K., Rajendra, P., Subba, R., Ravi, P.: Fingerprint minutia match using bifurcation technique. Int. J. Comput. Sci. Commun. Netw. **2**(4), 478–486 (2012)
14. Gnanasivam, P., Muttan, S.: An efficient algorithm for fingerprint preprocessing and feature extraction. Procedia Comput. Sci. **2**, 133–142 (2010)
15. Maltoni, D., Maio, D., Jain, A., Prabhakar, S.: Handbook of Fingerprint Recognition, pp. 141–144. Springer, New York (2003)
16. Wang, H., Fan, M.: Centroid-based semi-fragile audio watermarking in hybrid domain. China Sci. Inf. Sci. **53**(3), 619–633 (2010)
17. Abraham, J., Kwan, P., Gao, J.: Fingerprint matching using a hybrid shape and orientation descriptor. State of the Art in Biometrics (2011). ISBN 978-953-307-489-4
18. Hua, G., Goh, J., Thing, V.L.L.: Time-spread echo-based watermarking with optimized imperceptibility and robustness. IEEE/ACM Trans. Audio Speech Lang. Process. **23**(2), 227–239 (2015)
19. Xiang, Y., Natgunanathan, I., Rong, Y., Guo, S.: Spread spectrum-based high embedding capacity watermarking method for audio signals. IEEE/ACM Trans. Audio Speech Lang. Process. **23**(12), 2228–2237 (2015)

20. International Telecommunication Union. Method for objective measurements of perceived audio quality (PAEQ) ITU-RBS.1387-1, Geneva, Switzerland (1998–2001)
21. Giang, M., Wu, X., Hua, Q.: A fast thinning algorithm for fingerprint image. In: 1st International Conference on Information Science and Engineering (ICISE), pp. 1039–1042 (2009)
22. Jianchun, H., Jinjun, B.: Normalization of fingerprint image using the local feature. In: International Conference on Computer Science and Service System, pp. 1643–1646 (2012)
23. Khan, M.K., Xie, L., Zhang, J.: Chaos and NDFT-based spread spectrum concealing of fingerprint-biometric data into audio signals. J. Digit. Sig. Process. **20**, 179–190 (2009)

A Novel Robust Image Forensics Algorithm Based on L1-Norm Estimation

Xin He[1,2], Qingxiao Guan[1,2]([✉]), Yanfei Tong[1,2], Xianfeng Zhao[1,2], and Haibo Yu[1,2]

[1] State Key Laboratory of Information Security,
Institute of Information Engineering, Chinese Academy of Sciences,
No. 89A, Minzhuang Road, Beijing 100093, China
{hexin,guanqingxiao,tongyanfei,zhaoxianfeng,yuhaibo}@iie.ac.cn
[2] University of Chinese Academy of Sciences, Beijing, China

Abstract. To improve the robustness of the typical image forensics with the noise variance, we propose a novel image forensics approach that based on L1-norm estimation. First, we estimate the kurtosis and the noise variance of the high-pass image. Then, we build a minimum error objective function based on L1-norm estimation to compute the kurtosis and the noise variance of overlapping blocks of the image by an iterative solution. Finally, the spliced regions are exposed through K-means cluster analysis. Since the noise variance of adjacent blocks are similar, our approach can accelerate the iterative process by setting the noise variance of the previous block as the initial value of the current block. According to analytics and experiments, our approach can effectively solve the inaccurate locating problem caused by outliers. It also performs better than reference algorithm in locating spliced regions, especially for those with realistic appearances, and improves the robustness effectively.

Keywords: Image splicing · L1-norm estimation · Noise variance · Image forensics

1 Introduction

With the rapid development of the Internet and the widely use of the electric device, digital images, as a kind of media information carrier, are being spread broadly in the daily life. However, the ease of the image-editing software brings not only the great convenience, but also some security problems such as much easier forgery by image processing. Digital image forgery can cause adverse effects, for example, serious misleading and misjudgment will occur if tampered images are used as key evidences by media or the legal departments. It may have serious impacts on society and public opinion. Therefore, image forensics becomes an urgent problem.

There are various ways to tamper images, the most typical one is image composition. There are two ways to composite images: image copy-move and image splicing. Both methods leave no visual abnormality and their difference

Y.Q. Shi et al. (Eds.): IWDW 2016, LNCS 10082, pp. 145–158, 2017.
DOI: 10.1007/978-3-319-53465-7_11

lies on whether the tampered regions are from the same picture. The former aims to erase parts of contents in an image by padding them with patches from other regions, while the later tampers the image by pasting the forgery region copied from another image. Compared to image copy-move, spliced images are more harmful and detecting them is more complicated owing to diverse spliced regions. Thus, it is more difficult to find an effective method for detecting this kind of forgery. Therefore, in this paper, we focus on the image forensics for splicing images.

In recent years, a growing attention has been paid to image forensics. Currently, there are three main kinds of algorithms to image forensics. They are based on the Color Filter Array (CFA), lighting and noise respectively. For the CFA algorithm [1,2], the main idea is the camera with different CFA model and CFA interpolation algorithm makes pixels have particular correlation relationship. And for spliced images, regions from different images will destroy such relationship. Therefore the spliced region can be classified through the consistency of pixels. However, CFA based method is unable to locate the spliced regions and is not robust to image resize operation. Besides, this method requires other prior-knowledge of CFA. Another kind of method utilizes the light condition in the image. Johnson [3,4] proposed the approach that exposing image forgery by detecting inconsistencies in lightings. It first extracts the closed boundaries from the image and clips them into several blocks. Then, it estimates the lighting direction of every block and calculates the lighting direction consistency to determine whether the image is tampered. This approach could detect spliced images efficiently, but if the object surface does not follow Lambert radiator, or the weather is cloudy or the object is inside the room, it could hardly detect the lighting source. Therefore, its usage is limited. To solve the limitations of the two algorithms, some researchers proposed the new detection algorithm with the image noise. It uses intrinsic noises of the image to distinguish the normal region and spliced region. Furthermore, since the universal existence of the camera noise, this kind of approach needs less prior knowledge and doesn't need any training samples. Accordingly, this kind algorithm has universal applicability and advantages. Gou et al. [5] used image denoising, wavelet analysis, and neighborhood prediction to obtain statistical features of noise. This approach is easy to implement but needs filters with high performance. If images have many intensive variant areas, it may have errors. Amer [6] presented a method to estimate the variance of additive white noise in images and frames. The method finds intensity-homogeneous blocks first and then estimates the noise variance in these blocks taking image structure into account. It uses eight high-pass operators to measure the high-frequency image components.

Existing methods have drawbacks of high complexity and low robustness. In order to solve these problems, we propose a new method based on L1 norm estimation to detect the forgery region. This approach can be viewed as an improved extension of noise variance estimation based forgery detection methods proposed by Pan et al. [7]. In our method, we first show that the noise variation estimation can be described as a linear regression, and then convert it to a L1-norm regression problem to increase the robustness. In this paper, we use the linear program to solve L1 norm regression to estimate the variance level of noise for each block. Since the adjacent blocks in the image have many overlapping pixels, we design an acceleration strategy of the iterative calculation in block-wise noise variance estimation. This method reduces the computation complexity.

The rest of this paper is organized as follows: Sect. 2 describes the camera noise estimation method, and in that section we review the relationship between kurtosis and noise variance, which is proposed in [7]. It lies the foundation of our work. Section 3 is the main part of this paper. It analyzes and summarizes the general form of noise variance estimation, and proposes L1 norm based variance estimation method and an acceleration strategy. The experiment result and analysis will be described in Sect. 4. The last section is the summary and future work.

2   Noise Estimation Based Forgery Detection

Pan proposed an approach to detect image splicing region with inconsistent local noise variances. The foundation of the approach is that tampered region in a spliced image is copied from another image, and noise level of two images are different. In fact, noise in a digital image can be generated through many factors in the real world, including camera sensor, quantization, and JPEG compression. It is common that noise distribution and level of two images are different, which may leave the artifact in spliced image. Thus, we can determine the images integrity and locate the spliced regions by taking advantages of the inconsistent noise variance. On the other head, since the image is mixed by noise and image content, we cannot directly obtain the noise. Therefore, using high-pass filters to obviate the image content first, then modeling the kurtosis and noise variance to estimate the noise variance of regions.

In this section, we first introduce the definition of kurtosis, from which we can find the relationship between variance and kurtosis in a filtered image region. Then we briefly summarize and review the noise variance estimation method proposed in [7] along with it's analysis.

2.1   Kurtosis

Kurtosis is a statistical measure defined by (1):

$$\kappa = \frac{E[(x - E(x))^4]}{(E(x - E(x))^2)^2} - 3. \tag{1}$$

Provided we have n identical independent distribution samples $x_i, i = 1, 2, ...n$, drawing from certain distribution, we can estimate their kurtosis by (2):

$$\kappa = \frac{\frac{1}{n-1}\sum_{i=1}^{n}(x_i - \overline{x})^4}{\left[\sum_{i=1}^{n}(x_i - \overline{x})^2\right]^2} - 3, \tag{2}$$

where $\overline{x} = \sum_{i=1}^{n} x_i/n$ is the mean value of samples. Kurtosis is used for describing the probability density function of the random variable. The kurtosis of

Gaussian distribution is 0. If the kurtosis is bigger than 0, it suggests a distribution with a high peak, which is called leptokurtic. While if it is less than 0, the shape of the distribution is flat and is called platykurtic.

According to some research [8–10], the kurtosis of high-pass filtered natural images is positive, and it tends to be a constant, which is called kurtosis concentration.

2.2   Noise Variance Estimation

Although it is obvious that regions from different image source have different noise variance, we are unable to directly model the noise by the variance of pixels. There are two obstacles:

1. Image noise is coupled with the image content, and such content signal is much more intensive than the noise components, which causes the failure of estimating the true variance of noise.
2. Noise may come from different distributions. It is improper to assume that types of noise are all zero mean Gaussian. For some other distributions, only using variance is insufficient to describe them since they may be also determined by other parameters.

Pan's method solves these two problems by using high-pass filters. According to the procedure of linear filtering, high-pass filters not only depresses image content but also adds up noise from pixels with it's weight, which makes noise component in filtered images approximately conforms to Gaussian distribution. Such property results from the Laplacian Central Limit Theorem.

After filtering, the kurtosis and noise variance of each local region in filtered images can be calculated. Because this method aims to estimate the noise variance of candidate image, it uses the relationship between kurtosis and noise variance from candidate image and filtered images to build the estimation model. More specifically, by the definition of kurtosis and variance, we can deduce (3):

$$\widetilde{\kappa_k} = \kappa_k \left(\frac{\widetilde{\sigma}_k^2 - \sigma^2}{\widetilde{\sigma}_k^2} \right)^2, \tag{3}$$

where κ, σ^2 denote the kurtosis and noise variance of candidate image, respectively. While $\widetilde{\kappa_k}$, $\widetilde{\sigma}_k^2$ represent those of filtered image with the k-th filter, which is computed from regional pixels in filtered image. As mentioned above, considering the kurtosis is positive, we can take square root of (3) to yield (4):

$$\sqrt{\widetilde{\kappa_k}} = \sqrt{\kappa_k} \left(\frac{\widetilde{\sigma}_k^2 - \sigma^2}{\widetilde{\sigma}_k^2} \right). \tag{4}$$

Suppose we have K filters in total, we have to utilize $\widetilde{\kappa_k}$, $\widetilde{\sigma}_k^2$ to estimate κ and σ^2 $(k = 1, 2, ..., K)$. However, it is important to note that (3) and (4) are built in the case of pure noise signal, and $\widetilde{\kappa_k}$, $\widetilde{\sigma}_k^2$ are calculated from filtered images, which means κ, σ^2, $\widetilde{\kappa_k}$, $\widetilde{\sigma}_k^2$ would not rigorously follow to (3) for two reasons:

1. Although the filter somehow can depress image content, it is impossible to eliminate the influence of image content. Thus it may cause inaccuracy of calculating $\widetilde{\kappa_k}$ and $\widetilde{\sigma}_k^2$.
2. $\widetilde{\kappa_k}$ and $\widetilde{\sigma}_k^2$ are calculated from a local region with size of 32×32 in the filtered image. Since the number of pixels in the local region is finite, these statistics inevitably suffer from some instability.

For these two reasons, this method converts the estimation task into a regression problem as in (5):

$$\underset{\sqrt{\kappa}, \sigma^2}{argmin} \sum_{k=1}^{K} \left[\sqrt{\widetilde{\kappa_k}} - \sqrt{\kappa} \left(\frac{\widetilde{\sigma}_k^2 - \sigma^2}{\widetilde{\sigma}_k^2} \right) \right]^2 . \tag{5}$$

Obviously the regression model jointly utilizes result from K filtered images, and we can infer the closed form of the optimal solution of (5) as (6) shows:

$$\sqrt{\kappa} = \frac{\langle \sqrt{\widetilde{\kappa_k}} \rangle_k \langle \frac{1}{(\widetilde{\sigma}_k^2)^2} \rangle_k - \langle \frac{\sqrt{\widetilde{\kappa_k}}}{\widetilde{\sigma}_k^2} \rangle_k \langle \frac{1}{\widetilde{\sigma}_k^2} \rangle_k}{\langle \frac{1}{(\widetilde{\sigma}_k^2)^2} \rangle_k - \langle \frac{1}{\widetilde{\sigma}_k^2} \rangle_k^2} \tag{6}$$

and

$$\sigma^2 = \frac{1}{\langle \frac{1}{\widetilde{\sigma}_k^2} \rangle_k} - \frac{1}{\sqrt{\kappa}} \frac{\langle \sqrt{\widetilde{\kappa_k}} \rangle_k}{\langle \frac{1}{\widetilde{\sigma}_k^2} \rangle_k},$$

where the bracket $\langle \cdot \rangle_k$ denotes the mean value of variables of all the K filters.

To locate the tampered region, it's necessary to analyze the consistency of noise variance across multiple regions of the image. Therefore, the global noise variance estimation needed to be extended to local estimation, which means computing the noise variance of overlapping blocks using the method above. Since the computing is aimed at all the overlapping blocks, the complexity of the algorithm is high. The integral image can be used to accelerate the computing process [11]. That is, we can compute the m-th order raw moment taking advantage of the integral image firstly. Then it is possible to use the initial definition to estimate the kurtosis and noise variance of each region. By now, the aim to get the local noise variance estimation has been realized.

Pan used the 2D DCT basis as the filter bank, and he pointed out that any other high-pass filters can be also chosen for this task, such as wavelet or Fast Independent Component Analysis (FastICA). In this paper, we use the DCT basis as the filter bank.

2.3   Analysis

The experiment shows that the algorithm can locate the spliced region efficiently in most case. However, (4) is applied to the ideal noise environment. In the practical application, the influence caused by the image content can't be entirely eliminated. So the value of $\widetilde{\kappa_k}$ and $\widetilde{\sigma}_k^2$ got by some filtering channels will deviate from (4), which cause the incorrect consequence. These are called outliers. If there are many outliers in the image, the detection result will be influenced greatly. It may even cause false detection as the Fig. 1 shown:

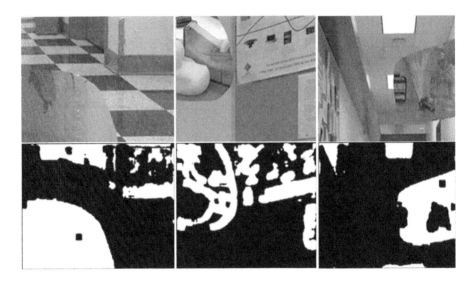

Fig. 1. Pan's detection. (Top: Tampered images, Bottom: Pan's results.)

3   Robust Noise Estimation Model

In this section, we first reformulate Pan's method as a linear regression problem, and then we apply L1-norm to this problem to increase it's robustness. The solution of our method and acceleration strategy is also proposed in this section.

3.1   Linear Regression Model for Noise Variance Estimation

From the second section, we can know that the critical step of the algorithm is to compute the solution of (5) to get the noise variance. We will analyze the property of (5) firstly, and then show our optimization method in the following passage. In order to be clearer, we rewrite (5) here:

$$\underset{\sqrt{\kappa},\sigma^2}{argmin} \sum_{k=1}^{K} \left[\sqrt{\widetilde{\kappa_k}} - \sqrt{\kappa}(\frac{\widetilde{\sigma}_k^2 - \sigma^2}{\widetilde{\sigma}_k^2}) \right]^2 .$$

Next, we reformulate the problem (5) simply by describing it's variables in another form.

Let $w_1 = \sqrt{\kappa}$, $w_2 = \sigma^2\sqrt{\kappa}$, $w = [w_1 \ w_2]^T$, $x_k = [-1 \ 1/\widetilde{\sigma}_k^2]^T$, $b = \sqrt{\widetilde{\kappa_k}}$, then substitute these new variables into (5). Because x_k, b are known and w is unknown, we get the new objective function as follows:

$$\underset{w}{argmin}\, F(w) = \sum_{k=1}^{K}(w^T x_k + b)^2. \tag{7}$$

Now we can solve $\sqrt{\kappa}$ and σ^2 in (5) by solving (7). Since the solution of (5) can be denoted as $w^* = [w_1^*\ w_2^*]^T$, the solution of (5) can be solved as follows:

$$\sqrt{\kappa} = w_1^*, \ \sigma^2 = w_2^*/w_1^*. \tag{8}$$

Actually the problem shown by (7) refers to the relationship between w_1 and w_2, and it is obvious that (7) is a linear regression problem respecting to variable w. It is of significance that we build the equivalent relationship between (5) and a linear regression problem, which facilitates our further works on noise estimation model.

After reformulating it into a linear regression problem, we can get the detection algorithm with noise in more general sense. That is we can use a general form of the distance function $D(w^T x, \sqrt{\widetilde{\kappa_k}})$ to estimate the solution, which means we can transfer the estimation problem to forms of regression problem with other distance metrics in (9):

$$\underset{w}{argmin} \sum_{k=1}^{K} D(w^T x, \sqrt{\widetilde{\kappa_k}}). \tag{9}$$

Moreover, (9) can use various distance metric function for better results, which is presented in the next subsection.

3.2   L1-Norm Based Noise Variance Estimation

As mentioned in the previous subsection, the original method proposed by Pan is actually based on L2 loss regression. However, L2 loss suffers from instability of outlies. Because we employ filters of different frequency bands, some of them may produce extraordinary high response caused by image contents in the local region. For these cases, $\widetilde{\kappa_k}$, $\widetilde{\sigma}_k^2$ deviate so much from the true value of noise distribution. We call these data outliers. L2 loss is sensitive to outliers. In other words, for a region, when outliers occur for few filters, the solution of (5) will greatly be influenced by them due to the properties of L2 loss. Since image contents are complex, it is usual that we should deal with such outliers for better estimation.

In order to improve the robustness of noise estimation, we replace the L2 loss in (7) with L1 loss. Comparing to L2 loss, the advantages of L1 loss is obvious. It uses absolute value instead of square value, which makes less compromise with abnormal error caused by these outliers in regression. The estimation model in our method is presented in (10):

$$\underset{w}{argmin}\ F(w) = \sum_{k=1}^{K} |w^T x_k + b|, \tag{10}$$

where w, x, b are defined the same as those in (7).

This problem is the linear least absolute regression problem. Unlike (7), (10) does not have a close form solution due to the L1 loss, thus we have to find an accurate approach to solve it. In this paper, we use linear programming to solve (10), this method were proposed in some literatures [12,13], and we present it in the following message to make readers clearer.

In order to adopt linear programming method to solve (10), we introduce $2K$ auxiliary variables $\xi_1^+, \xi_1^-, \xi_2^+, \xi_2^-, ..., \xi_K^+, \xi_K^-$, and formulate the following linear programming problem:

$$\begin{aligned} &\underset{w,\xi}{argmin}\, F(w) = \sum_{k=1}^{K}(\xi_k^+ + \xi_k^-) \\ &\quad s.t. \qquad w^T x_k + b = \xi_k^+ - \xi_k^-, \quad \xi_k^+ \geq 0, \xi_k^- \geq 0, \ k = 1, 2, ..., K, \end{aligned} \tag{11}$$

where $\xi = \{\xi_1^+, \xi_1^-, \xi_2^+, \xi_2^-, ..., \xi_k^+, \xi_k^-\}$.

In above problem, there are $2K + 2$ variables to be solved. The objective function and constraint condition are in form of linear, thus (11) can be solved by standard linear programming method.

It is crucial to prove that w in the solution of (11) equals to solution of (10). Assume $\widehat{w}, \widehat{\xi_1^+}, \widehat{\xi_1^-}, \widehat{\xi_2^+}, \widehat{\xi_2^-}, ..., \widehat{\xi_K^+}, \widehat{\xi_K^-}$ is the optimal solution of (11). Because of the constraint condition in (11), we have $\widehat{w}^T x_k + b = \widehat{\xi_k^+} - \widehat{\xi_k^-}, \widehat{\xi_k^+} \geq 0, \widehat{\xi_k^-} \geq 0, \ k = 1, 2, ..., K$. Next we prove that for any k, at most only one of $\widehat{\xi_k^+}$ and $\widehat{\xi_k^-}$ is larger than 0, and the other is zero, which implies $\widehat{\xi_k^+} + \widehat{\xi_k^-}$ equals to the absolute value of $\widehat{w}^T x_k + b$. That is:

$$if\ \widehat{w}^T x_k + b > 0\ then\ \widehat{w}^T x_k + b = \widehat{\xi_k^+}, \tag{12}$$

$$if\ \widehat{w}^T x_k + b < 0\ then\ \widehat{w}^T x_k + b = -\widehat{\xi_k^+}. \tag{13}$$

Otherwise, if there is l that $\widehat{\xi_l^+} > 0$, $\widehat{\xi_l^-} > 0$, we can construct another feasible solution $\widetilde{w}, \widetilde{\xi}$ for problem as (14) shows:

$$\begin{aligned} &\widetilde{w} = \widehat{w}, \\ &\widetilde{\xi_1^+} = \widehat{\xi_1^+}, \ \widetilde{\xi_1^-} = \widehat{\xi_1^-}, \\ &\widetilde{\xi_2^+} = \widehat{\xi_2^+}, \ \widetilde{\xi_2^-} = \widehat{\xi_2^-}, \\ &\qquad\qquad \vdots \\ &\widetilde{\xi_{l-1}^+} = \widehat{\xi_{l-1}^+}, \ \widetilde{\xi_{l-1}^-} = \widehat{\xi_{l-1}^-}, \\ &\widetilde{\xi_l^+} = \max{(0, \widehat{\xi_l^+} - \widehat{\xi_l^-})}, \widetilde{\xi_l^-} = \min{(0, \widehat{\xi_l^-} - \widehat{\xi_l^+})}, \\ &\qquad\qquad \vdots \\ &\widetilde{\xi_K^+} = \widehat{\xi_K^+}, \ \widetilde{\xi_K^-} = \widehat{\xi_K^-}. \end{aligned} \tag{14}$$

From above construction we know that $\widetilde{\xi}_l^+ - \widetilde{\xi}_l^- = \widehat{\xi}_l^- - \widehat{\xi}_l^+$, $\widetilde{\xi}_l^+ > 0$, $\widetilde{\xi}_l^- > 0$ and only one of $\widetilde{\xi}_l^+$, $\widetilde{\xi}_l^-$ can be positive to ensure $\widetilde{w}$, $\widetilde{\xi}$ is a feasible solution. However, $\widetilde{\xi}_l^+ + \widetilde{\xi}_l^- < \widehat{\xi}_l^+ + \widehat{\xi}_l^-$ and consequently:

$$\sum_{k=1}^{K}(\widetilde{\xi}_k^+ + \widetilde{\xi}_k^-) = \sum_{k,k \neq l}(\widehat{\xi}_k^+ + \widehat{\xi}_k^-) + \widetilde{\xi}_l^+ + \widetilde{\xi}_l^- < \sum_{k=1}^{K}(\widehat{\xi}_k^+ + \widehat{\xi}_k^-). \tag{15}$$

Equation (15) contradicts with the assumption that $\widehat{w}$, $\widehat{\xi}$ is the optimal solution of the problem. Thus, it can be concluded that the solution with $\widehat{\xi}_l^+ > 0$, $\widehat{\xi}_l^- > 0$ cannot be the optimal solution.

3.3 Acceleration Strategy for Consecutive Blocks

The proposed approach is to solve the linear programming problem of each overlapping blocks, whereas there is no simple analytical solution of this problem. Thus, it demands to solve the problem by iterative computation. To solve the problem that computational complexity in iterative process is high, we design a strategy to accelerate it. We notice that the adjacent blocks are different only in one row or one column of the block. For example, if the block is 32×32, there will be $31/32 = 96.8\%$ overlapping pixels for two adjacent blocks. Therefore, the noise variance between them is highly similar when they both belong to tampered regions or authentic regions. Therefore, we can sequentially estimate the noise variance of blocks in the row scan manner, and accelerate the iterative process by setting the noise variance of the previous block as the initial value of the current block. This operation fully utilizes the previous result from adjacent block to reduce the iterations in linear programming.

3.4 Procedure of Our Method

The process of image forensics algorithm based on L1-norm estimation is as follows:

1. Using 64 AC filters from DCT decomposition to filter the image to be detected. Then we will get 63 high-pass channel images.
2. Dividing each high-pass channel image with overlapping windows of 32×32 pixels. Then computing the raw moments of first to forth order and computing the corresponding integral image. After this step, we will get 4 integral images for each high-pass channel image.
3. According to the kurtosis and noise variance defined by the raw moments, computing the kurtosis and noise variance of all overlapping blocks for each high-pass channel images.

4. Computing the kurtosis and noise variance of all channels, then using (10) and (11) to compute the kurtosis and noise variance of candidate image in all channels. This step can be accelerated by using the strategy mentioned above. Finally, we will get an estimated noise variance image and a kurtosis image.

5. Using K-means to cluster pixels by their variance value, which will segment the image into authentic regions and the forged regions.

The process is shown by Fig. 2:

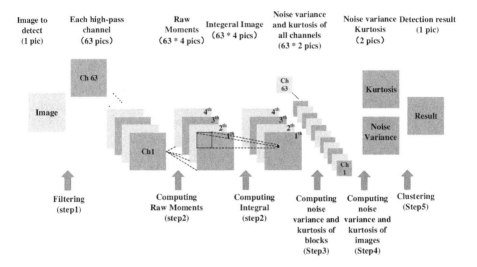

Fig. 2. Our algorithm process.

4   Experiment Result and Analysis

To test our approach, we use two data sources: the Columbia uncompressed image splicing detection evaluation dataset and the CASIA 2.0 spliced image library from Institute of Automation, Chinese Academy of Science. The Columbia's dataset consists of 183 real images and 180 spliced images [14]. The forged image spliced by two original images are stored in uncompressed TIF format and the image size ranges from 757×568 to 1152×768 pixels. There are many different scenarios in the CASIA 2.0. Some of spliced images are pretty hard to be distinguished by people, which close to the spliced images in the real world. The image format of this database includes JPG and TIF. We use these two databases in the experiments so that we can verify the effectiveness and adaptability of our algorithm in a more comprehensive way.

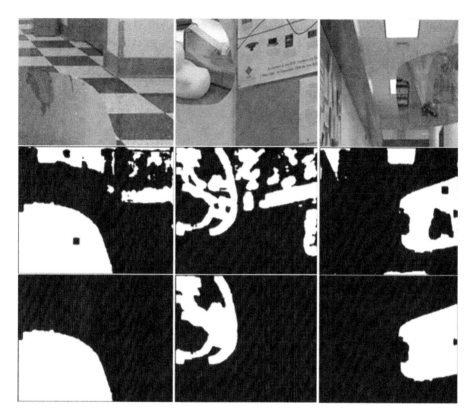

Fig. 3. Detection results on Columbia's dataset. (Top: Tampered images. Middle: Pan's results. Bottom: Our results.)

Figure 3 is the detection result of Pan's algorithm compared to ours which performed on the uncompressed images with TIF format over Columbia's dataset.

From these results, compared to Pan's algorithm, our approach reduces the influence caused by outliers in the background. For example, in the first image of Fig. 3, our approach is more robust and can detect the tampered area more accurately since the impact of the wall has been removed mostly.

Figure 4 shows the comparison result of Pan's method and ours in CASIA 2.0. These images are randomly chosen from CASIA 2.0, and they were converted into JPG format from TIF. From the result, it can be seen that even though the tampered images are manipulated pretty carefully which cannot be identified, our algorithm can still expose the forged area effectively. The result also indicates that our algorithm not only behaves better for spatial images such as TIF format, but also performs well in JPG image. Thus, it can be widely used. However, for the image with large smooth areas, such as grass in the fourth image of Fig. 4, the detection result of our algorithm will also be influenced slightly and may wrongly classify the smooth area into the tampered area. This is mainly due to the noise distribution in the smooth area is different largely from other areas.

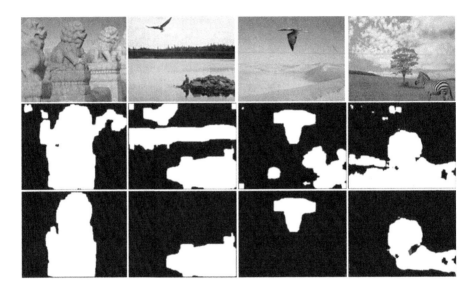

Fig. 4. Detection results on CASIA 2.0. (Top: Tampered images. Middle: Pan's results. Bottom: Our results.)

Table 1 is the evaluation of two algorithms with the True Positive Rate (TPR) and Probability of False Acceptance (FPA). The value in the table is the average value of multiple experiments' results performed on the Columbia's dataset and CASIA 2.0.

Table 1. The performance comparison between Pan's and Ours.

Database	Ours TPR	Pan's TPR	Ours FPA	Pan's FPA
Columbia's dataset	91.8%	90.5%	10.36%	10.33%
CASIA 2.0	90.3%	88.2%	8.67%	8.62%

5   Conclusion and Future Works

To improve the low robustness of the typical image forensics with the noise variance, we propose a novel image forensics approach that based on L1-norm estimation. By transforming noise estimation model to the linear regression form and applying L1-norm to it, our algorithm increases the robustness efficiently. Besides, we also propose an acceleration algorithm that takes advantage of the similarity of adjacent blocks to make it more applicable in real applications. According to analytics and experiments, our approach can effectively solve the inaccurate locating problem caused by outliers.

The future work about forgery detection based on noise estimation includes:

1. Extending the algorithm to GPU acceleration, which will increase the efficiency greatly.
2. Incorporating image segmentation methods to forgery detection for better robustness. For example, when there are many smooth regions in the image, the exposed tampered regions may deviate. It's necessary for us to design more effective algorithm to solve this problem.
3. Using other robust estimation function for computing the noise to improve the true detection rate furtherly.

Acknowledgments. This work was supported by the NSFC under U1536105 and 61303259, National Key Technology R&D Program under 2014BAH41B01, Strategic Priority Research Program of CAS under XDA06030600, and Key Project of Institute of Information Engineering, CAS, under Y5Z0131201.

References

1. Dirik, A.E., Memon, N.D.: Image tamper detection based on demosaicing artifacts. IEEE Trans. Image Process., 1497–1500 (2009)
2. Cao, H., Kot, A.C.: Manipulation detection on image patches using FusionBoost. IEEE Trans. Inf. Forensics Secur. **7**(3), 992–1002 (2012)
3. Johnson, M.K., Farid, H.: Exposing digital forgeries by detecting inconsistencies in lighting. In: Proceedings of the ACM 7th Workshop on Multimedia and Security, pp. 1–10 (2005)
4. Johnson, M, K., Farid, H.: Exposing digital forgeries through specular highlights on the eye. In: International Workshop on Information Hiding, pp. 311–325 (2007)
5. Gou, H., Swaminathan, A., Wu, M.: Intrinsic sensor noise features for forensic analysis on scanners and scanned images. IEEE Trans. Inf. Forensics Secur. **4**(3), 476–491 (2009)
6. Amer, A., Dubois, E.: Fast and reliable structure-oriented video noise estimation. IEEE Trans. Circ. Syst. Video Technol. **15**(1), 113–118 (2005)
7. Pan, X., Zhang, X., Lyu, S.: Exposing image splicing with inconsistent local noise variances. In: IEEE International Conference on Computational Photography, pp. 1–10 (2012)
8. Bethge, M.: Factorial coding of natural images: how effective are linear models in removing higher-order dependencies. J. Opt. Soc. Am. A **23**(6), 1253–1268 (2006)
9. Lyu, S., Simoncelli, E.P.: Nonlinear extraction of independent components of natural images using radial Gaussianization. Neural Comput. **21**(6), 1485–1519 (2009)
10. Zoran, D., Weiss, Y.: Scale invariance and noise in natural images. In: IEEE International Conference on Computer Vision, pp. 2209–2216 (2009)
11. Viola, P., Jones, M.: Robust real-time object detection. Int. J. Comput. Vision **21** (2001)

12. Chen, X.: Least absolute linear regression. Appl. Stat. Manage. **5**, 48 (1989)
13. Li, Z.: Introduction of least absolute deviation method. Bull. Maths **2**, 40 (1992)
14. Hsu, Y.F., Chang, S.F.: Detecting image splicing using geometry invariants and camera characteristics consistency. In: IEEE International Conference on Multimedia and Expo, pp. 549–552 (2006)

Detection of Copy-Move Forgery in Flat Region Based on Feature Enhancement

Weiwei Zhang[1], Zhenghong Yang[1], Shaozhang Niu[2(✉)],
and Junbin Wang[1]

[1] School of Science, China Agricultural University, Beijing 100083, China
zhangweiwei2012@126.com, yangjohn@cau.edu.cn,
wangjunbin34@163.com
[2] Beijing Key Lab of Intelligent Telecommunication Software and Multimedia,
Beijing University of Posts and Telecommunications, Beijing 100876, China
szniu@bupt.edu.cn

Abstract. A new Feature Enhancement method based on SURF is proposed for Copy-Move Forgery Detection. The main difference from the traditional methods is that Contrast Limited Adaptive Histogram Equalization is proposed as a preprocessing stage in images. SURF is used to extract keypoints from the preprocessed image. Even in flat regions, the method can also extract enough keypoints. In the matching stage, g2NN matching skill is used which can also detect multiple forgeries. The experimental results show that the proposed method performs better than the state-of-the-art algorithms on the public database.

Keywords: Copy-move forgery detection · Feature enhancement method · CLAHE algorithm · Flat regions

1 Introduction

With the widespread use of digital image editing software, such as Photoshop, ACDSee and Meitu Xiu Xiu, the manipulation of digital images is becoming much easier. Due to the simplicity, copy-move forgery (CMF) becomes one of the most common tampering method. In CMF, one or more regions in an image are copied and pasted to another place of the same image in order to conceal or enhance some important objects. The duplicated regions can also be created with geometrical or illumination adjustment to make convince for forgery and sometimes pasting is done multiple times. There are mainly two type of approaches used for copy-move forgery detection (CMFD), which are block-based and keypoint-based methods.

Fridrich et al. [1] initially proposed the concept of passive copy move forgery detection. The authors divided the image into overlapping blocks and used DCT coefficients of the image blocks for matching. Later on, in [2, 3], Principal Component Analysis (PCA) based technique is used to reduce the dimension of feature vector. In [4], the authors obtained the low frequency coefficients using DWT and the reduced feature vector representation by applying SVD on each sub-block of low frequency coefficients. In [5], Fourier Mellin Transform (FMT) is applied on each image blocks.

© Springer International Publishing AG 2017
Y.Q. Shi et al. (Eds.): IWDW 2016, LNCS 10082, pp. 159–171, 2017.
DOI: 10.1007/978-3-319-53465-7_12

In [6], Zernike moments based algorithm is described which is invariant to different operations like JPEG compression, rotation, blurring and AWGN. In [7], the authors used MPEG-7 image signature tools for copy move forgery detection. The technique is quite difficult but minimizes false positives by employing the procedure of multi-hypothesis matching. In [8], circular blocks are extracted and rotation invariant uniform local binary patterns (LBP) are applied on the blocks for feature extraction. The comparison among some methods mentioned above has been reported in [9].

All of the above methods are block-based methods, which divide the image into overlapping blocks and use different features for matching. However most of the existing block-based methods are failed to detect forgery with post-processing operations including Gaussian noise, JPEG compression, rotation, scaling etc. Another obvious drawback of this category algorithm is time-consuming. Keypoint-based methods such as Scale Invariant Features Transform (SIFT) and Speed up Robust Features (SURF) are used to avoid these problems. Pan [10] used SIFT features to localize the copied region by means of regional correlation diagram. But this method cannot detect multiple forgeries. Amerini et al. [11] used clustering to detect multiple forgeries and then proposed a method [12] based on J-linkage clustering algorithm which can localize the manipulated patches precisely. Compared with SIFT, SURF is the speed-up version of SIFT. Bo et al. [13] and Shivakumar [14] detect CMF based on SURF which is faster than SIFT.

However, local feature descriptors such as SIFT and SURF typically locate at textured areas, while the smooth or flat regions are ignored. The question that SIFT or SURF-based methods cannot find reliable keypoints in uniform texture regions is considered a well-known open issue [11]. In this paper, this issue is investigated. Contrast Limited Adaptive Histogram Equalization (CLAHE) algorithm is used to improve contrast in images and then extract features based on SURF. After enhanced by CLAHE, keypoints are covered all over the image even in flat or smooth regions. In the matching stage, g2NN matching skill [11] is used which can also detect multiple forgeries. A clustering of the keypoints coordinates are used in order to separate different copied areas.

The rest of the paper is structured as follows: Sect. 2 offers an overview of SURF and CLAHE algorithms, Sect. 3 gives the proposed approach in detail, while experimental results and conclusion are given in Sect. 4 and Sect. 5, respectively.

2   Backgrounds of SURF and CLAHE

This section gives a brief introduction to the relevant knowledge that can help to understand the analysis method of SURF algorithm based on CLAHE.

2.1   Speed up Robust Features

The SURF algorithm is originally proposed by Bay et al. [14]. As a practical implementation method of SIFT algorithm, which utilizes BOX filter instead of Gaussian filter. Compared with SIFT, SURF algorithm needs relatively lower amount of calculation.

Generally, classic SURF algorithm has two major steps: Hessian matrix-based keypoints detection and keypoints description based on sum of Haar wavelet responses. The detailed overview and implementation of SURF is provided in [14].

2.2 CLAHE

CLAHE algorithm which limits the amplification by clipping the histogram at a user-defined value called clip limit was originally developed for enhancement of low contrast medical images [15]. It enhances the contrast of an image by transforming values in the intensity of it. Unlike Histogram Equalization, CLAHE operates in small areas (tiles), rather than the entire image. Each tile's contrast is enhanced, so that the histogram of the output region approximately matches the specified histogram. The neighboring tiles are then combined using bi-linear interpolation in order to eliminate artificially induced boundaries. The contrast, especially in homogeneous areas, can be limited in order to avoid amplifying the noise which might be present in the image.

One of the histogram clips that normally used is Rayleigh distribution which produces a bell-shaped histogram. The function is given by Rayleigh distribution:

$$g = g_{min} + [2(\alpha^2) \ln(1 - \frac{1}{1 - p(f)})]^{0.5}. \tag{1}$$

where g_{min} is the minimum pixel value, $p(f)$ is the cumulative probability distribution and α is the distribution parameter which satisfies $\alpha > 0$. [M, N] specifies the number of tile rows and columns. The total number of image tiles is equal to $M \times N$.

3   The Proposed Method

Although keypoint-based methods guarantee geometric invariance, there are always less keypoints detected in flat or smooth regions. In this section, we present an efficient method to detect CMF especially when an object is covered with flat regions. Given a suspectable test image, CLAHE is used to enhance the contrast of the image. And then SURF algorithm is applied to extract keypoints and coordinate descriptors. In matching stage, generalized 2 Nearest Neighbor (g2NN) algorithm is applied. The flow chart for the proposed algorithm is shown in Fig. 1.

The algorithm can be summarized as:

Step 1: If the test image is color image, convert it into gray scale, else turn to Step 2;
Step 2: Preprocessing the image by CLAHE algorithm;
Step 3: Compute keypoints and descriptors using SURF algorithm;
Step 4: Apply g2NN matching skill;
Step 5: Clustering with single linkage and filtering using distance and RANSAC;
Step 6: Join the matched keypoints using a line to represent the suspect region.

The detailed explanation of the algorithm is given in the following subsections.

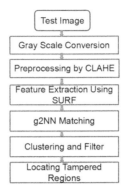

Fig. 1. Flow chart of the proposed algorithm

3.1 Preprocessing by CLAHE

First, the test image is converted into gray scale if it is in RGB format. And then CLAHE algorithm using Rayleigh distribution is employed in this work to improve the detection performance. This step is necessary to overcome the flat region problem in CMFD which influence the feature extraction. Figure 2 gives the comparison of images before and after enhanced. Specifically, Fig. 2(a) is an original image named 'japan_tower' (with 3264 2448 pixels) from database [16]; (a)' is the coordinate tampered (test) image named 'japan_tower_copy' in which the tower is concealed by part of the sky; the ground truth map is shown in (c). White regions denote copy-moved pixels; (a)'' is the enhanced image of (a)' by CLAHE in which the details are clearly visible especially in smooth region like the sky; (b), (b)' and (b)'' are the coordinate histogram of (a), (a)' and (a)'', respectively. (c)' and (c)'' show the SURF keypoints set of image (a)' and (a)'', respectively. We can clearly see that after enhanced by CLAHE, keypoints in (c)'' are distributed all over the image, even in smooth regions, such as the sky and walls.

3.2 SURF Features Extraction

Once the image preprocessing is done, the enhanced test image will be analyzed by SURF algorithm. By using SURF mentioned in Sect. 2.1, keypoints and their corresponding 64 dimensional descriptors are obtained. Let $X = \{x_1, \cdots, x_n\}$ be a set of keypoints with corresponding descriptors $\{f_1, \cdots, f_n\}$ (where n is the number of keypoints). We define a similarity vector $D = \{d_1, d_2, \cdots, d_n\}$ that represents the sorted Euclidean distances with respect to the other (n − 1) descriptors.

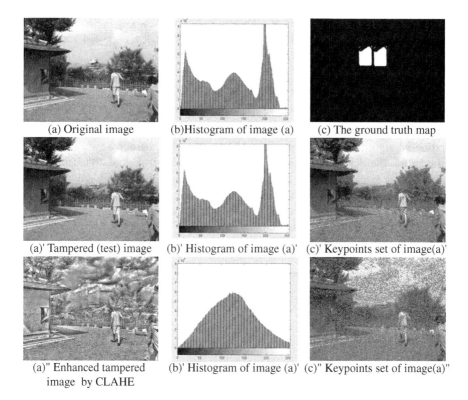

(a) Original image	(b)Histogram of image (a)	(c) The ground truth map
(a)' Tampered (test) image	(b)' Histogram of image (a)'	(c)' Keypoints set of image(a)'
(a)'' Enhanced tampered image by CLAHE	(b)' Histogram of image (a)'	(c)'' Keypoints set of image(a)''

Fig. 2. Comparison of images before and after enhanced

3.3 Keypoints Matching

In Matching, g2NN matching skill [11] is performed among the f_i descriptors of each keypoint to identify similar local patches in the test image. The idea of the g2NN skill is that if the ratio of d_i/d_{i+1} is less than or equal to threshold T and k (where $1 \leq k < n$) is the value in which the procedure stops, each keypoint in correspondence to a distance in $\{d_1, d_2, \cdots, d_k\}$ is considered as a match for the inspected keypoint.

3.4 Clustering and Filtering

In filtering, the mismatched keypoints should be eliminated. Due to strong correlation between adjacent pixels in the natural image, their corresponding descriptors may be very similar. If the distance between two matched keypoints is too small, this pair of matched keypoints possibly is a mismatch. In this paper if the distance between two keypoints is less than threshold $Dis_{\min}$, they will be deleted.

After that, to identify possible cloned areas, hierarchical cluster is performed on spatial locations of the matched points [11].

After clustering, we also apply the RANdom SAmple Consensus algorithm (RANSAC) [17] to delete mismatched points.

At the last step, if the number of matching between classes is not less than three pairs, the image is considered tampered. Then the copied and pasted regions are localized by joining the matched keypoints with a line.

4 Experiments

In this section, Chrislein et al.'s database [16] is employed to test the performance of the proposed algorithm. The image manipulation dataset is a ground truth database for benchmarking the detection of image tampering artifacts. It includes 48 base images and the average size of an image is about 3000×2300 pixels. In total, around 10% of the pixels belong to tampered image regions.

In this paper, the experiment has been implemented using Matlab R2013a a computer of CPU 3.60 GHz with memory of 16 GB.

4.1 Threshold Determination

Through large number of experiment tests, the optimal parameters of the proposed algorithm are set as follows:

Threshold used in CLAHE.

Clip limit is set to 0.5 and α is set to 0.4. An image tile of 16×16 pixels, 16-bits wide falls in line with previous implementations where it has been judged that sufficient detail is retained through this tile size.

Threshold T used in g2NN matching is set to 0.5.
Minimum Euclidean distance.

In our experiments the minimum Euclidean distance mentioned in 3.4 is set to $Dis_{min} = 50$.

Single linkage method is used in clustering, with the cutoff threshold $T_h = 30$.
Threshold used in RANSAC algorithm.

The number of iterations used in RANSAC is set to 1000 and the threshold which used to cataloged inliers and outliers is set to 0.05.

4.2 Plain Copy-Move Forgery Detection

Precision and recall rate is used to evaluate the performance. They are defined as:

$$p = \frac{T_p}{T_p + F_p} \tag{2}$$

$$r = \frac{T_p}{T_p + F_N} \tag{3}$$

Where T_p, F_p, F_N are the number of correctly detected forged images, the number of images that have been erroneously detected as forged, and the falsely missed forged images, respectively.

The score F_1 is also used as a measure which combines precision and recall in a single value. It is defined as follows:

$$F_1 = 2 \cdot \frac{p \cdot r}{p + r} \tag{4}$$

In this paper, the 'orig' and 'nul' subsets are applied to evaluate the performance of the proposed algorithm for plain copy-move forgery without any post-processing operations. Table 1 shows the comparison result for the plain copy-move forgeries.

Table 1. Comparison test results for plain copy-move forgeries

Method	Precision (%)	Recall (%)	F1 Score (%)
[11]	88.4	79.2	83.5
[14]	91.1	85.4	88.2
Our method	**93.3**	**87.5**	**90.3**

The detection result of tampered image 'japan_tower _copy' is shown in Fig. 3, while [11, 14] fail to detect.

Fig. 3. The detection result of the proposed method

Some other plain copy-move forgery examples in Christlein et al.'s database which can be detected by the proposed algorithm, while [11] and/or [14] fail to detect are given in Figs. 4, 5 6 and 7. In these examples, cloned are the smooth regions where SIFT and SURF features rarely covers. Figure 4 is two single forgery examples, while Fig. 6 is two multiple forgery examples. The test results are shown in Figs. 5 and 7, respectively.

Figure 4 gives schematic diagram of single tampering. In particular, Fig. 4(a) are original images named 'four_babies' (upper) and 'scotland' (lower). Figure 4(b) shows tampered images and Fig. 4(c) outlines the ground truth map. The comparison test results of these examples are shown in Fig. 5.

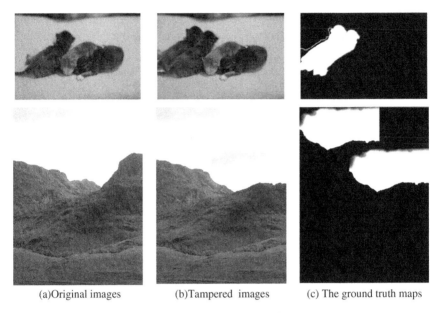

| (a)Original images | (b)Tampered images | (c) The ground truth maps |

Fig. 4. The schematic diagram of single forgery

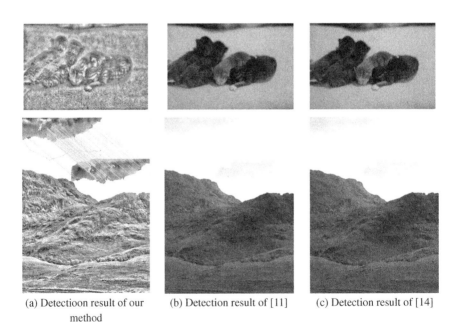

| (a) Detectioon result of our method | (b) Detection result of [11] | (c) Detection result of [14] |

Fig. 5. Comparison test results of single forgery

Figure 5 gives comparison results of single forgery detection and we can see that the forgeries can be correctly detected by the proposed method, while [11, 14] are failed to detect.

The proposed algorithm is not only effective for a single CMF, but also can detect multiple cloning.

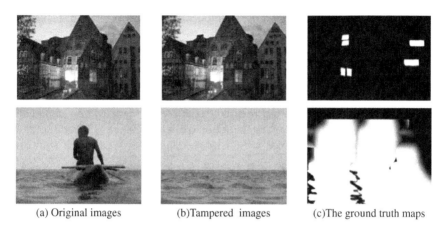

(a) Original images   (b)Tampered images   (c)The ground truth maps

Fig. 6. Schematic diagrams of multiple forgeries

Multiple attack is used to create more than one forged regions on the image. Figure 6 is similar to Fig. 4, the only difference is that Fig. 4 is single CMF while Fig. 6 is multiple cloning. Figure 6(a) is original images named 'dark_and_bright' (upper) and 'malawi' (lower). Figure 6(b) shows the tampered images and Fig. 6(c) outline the ground truth map. The results of multiple forgeries detection is shown in Fig. 7.

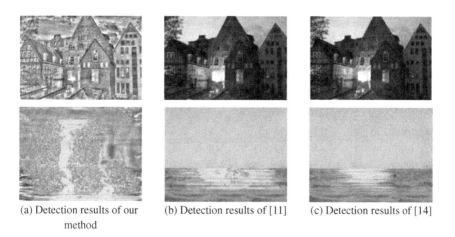

(a) Detection results of our   (b) Detection results of [11]   (c) Detection results of [14]
method

Fig. 7. Comparison test results of multiple forgeries

In Fig. 7, although one of the three copied regions can be detected by [11] and/or [14], the result is far less than satisfactory, and moreover, there is a false positive.

4.3   CMFD with Post-processing

The proposed methodology has also been tested CMF in terms of detection performance about robustness with post-processing operations such as rotation, scaling and JPEG compression.

Figures 8, 9 and 10 are a set of detection results of tampered images with different post-processing operations.

1. Rotation

The proposed method can detect rotation of the copied region with a small angle.

Figure 8 gives an example of tampered image with rotation. Figure 8(a) is the tampered image where the copied region rotated angle 6°. Figure 8(b) shows the detection results.

(a) Rotation with 6 degree   (b) Detection result of (a)

Fig. 8.   Detection result with rotation

2. Scaling

Figure 9 shows detection results with scaling. Figure 9(a) is the tampered image where the copied region has undergone 105% scaling. Similarly, in Fig. 9(a)′, copied region is scaled with 91%. Figure 9(b) and (b)′ are the coordinate detection result of (a) and (a)′.

3. JPEG compression

Figure 10(a) shows the tampered image with addition of global (i.e. full-image) JPEG compression artifacts of quality 90. Figure 10(b) gives the detection result of image (a).

Although the number of matched keypoints is comparatively less after difference attack such as rotation, scaling and JPEG compression, the proposed method still give reliably detects result with sufficient number of matched keypoints.

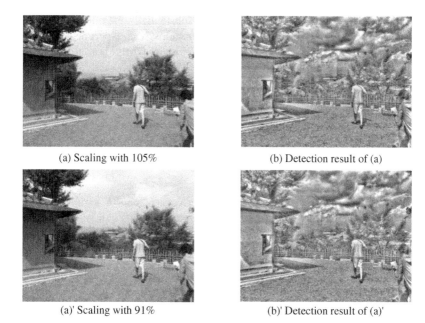

(a) Scaling with 105%   (b) Detection result of (a)

(a)' Scaling with 91%   (b)' Detection result of (a)'

Fig. 9. Detection results with scaling

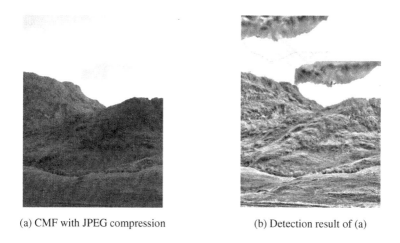

(a) CMF with JPEG compression   (b) Detection result of (a)

Fig. 10. Detection result with JPEG compression

5 Conclusions

In this paper, a new method for CMFD based on feature enhancement is highlighted. CLAHE algorithm is used for image tampering forensics for the first time. Compared with existing work, the paper integrates the CLAHE algorithm into the SURF based framework to detect copy move forgery. Using these enhancement pattern images, the values obtained are highly favorable, increasing substantially the number of keypoints found in the images especially in flat or smooth regions. The experiment results show that the proposed method not only can detect plain CMF, but also has certain robustness to rotation, scaling and compression.

Acknowledgements. This work was supported by National Natural Science Foundation of China (No. 61370195, U1536121).

References

1. Fridrich, B.A.J., Soukal, B.D., Lukáš, A.J.: Detection of copy-move forgery in digital images. In: Proceedings of Digital Forensic Research Workshop (2003)
2. Popescu, A.C., Farid, H.: Exposing digital forgeries by detecting duplicated image regions. In: Computer Science Dartmouth College Private Ivy League Research University, 646 (2004)
3. Mahdian, B., Saic, S.: Detection of copy–move forgery using a method based on blur moment invariants. Forensic Sci. Int. **171**(2–3), 180–189 (2007)
4. Li, G., Wu, Q., Tu, D., et al.: A sorted neighborhood approach for detecting duplicated regions in image forgeries based on DWT and SVD. In: IEEE International Conference on Multimedia and Expo, ICME 2007, 2–5 July 2007, Beijing, pp. 1750–1753 (2007)
5. Bayram, S., Sencar, H.T., Memon, N.: An efficient and robust method for detecting copy-move forgery. In: IEEE International Conference on Acoustics, pp. 1053–1056 (2009)
6. Ryu, S.-J., Lee, M.-J., Lee, H.-K.: Detection of copy-rotate-move forgery using Zernike moments. In: Böhme, R., Fong, P.W.L., Safavi-Naini, R. (eds.) IH 2010. LNCS, vol. 6387, pp. 51–65. Springer, Heidelberg (2010). doi:10.1007/978-3-642-16435-4_5
7. Kakar, P., Sudha, N.: Exposing postprocessed copy–paste forgeries through transform-invariant features. IEEE Trans. Inf. Forensics Secur. **7**(3), 1018–1028 (2012)
8. Li, L., Li, S., Zhu, H., et al.: An efficient scheme for detecting copy-move forged images by local binary patterns. J. Inf. Hiding Multimed. Signal Process. **4**, 46–56 (2013)
9. Mahmood, T., Nawaz, T., Ashraf, R., et al.: A survey on block based copy move image forgery detection techniques. In: International Conference on Emerging Technologies. IEEE (2015)
10. Pan, X., Lyu, S.: Region duplication detection using image feature matching. IEEE Trans. Inf. Forensics Secur. **5**(4), 857–867 (2010)
11. Amerini, I., Ballan, L., Caldelli, R., et al.: A SIFT-based forensic method for copy-move attack detection and transformation recovery. IEEE Trans. Inf. Forensics Secur. **6**(3), 1099–1110 (2011)
12. Amerini, I., Ballan, L., Caldelli, R., et al.: Copy-move forgery detection and localization by means of robust clustering with J-linkage. Signal Process. Image Commun. **28**(6), 659–669 (2013)
13. Bo, X., Wang, J., Liu, G., et al.: Image copy-move forgery detection based on SURF. In: International Conference on Multimedia Information Networking & Security. pp. 889–892 (2010)
14. Shivakumar, B.L., Baboo, S.: Detection of region duplication forgery in digital images using SURF. Int. J. Comput. Sci. Issues **8**(4), 199–205 (2011)

15. Pisano, E.D., Zong, S., Hemminger, B.M., DeLuca, M., Johnston, R.E., Muller, K., Braeuning, M.P., Pizer, S.M.: Contrast limited adaptive histogram equalization image processing to improve the detection of simulated spiculations in dense mammograms. J. Digit. Imaging **11**, 193–200 (1998)

16. Christlein, V., Riess, C., Jordan, J., et al.: An evaluation of popular copy-move forgery detection approaches. IEEE Trans. Inf. Forensics Secur. **7**(6), 1841–1854 (2012)

17. Fischler, M.A., Bolles, R.C.: Random sample consensus: a paradigm for model fitting with applications to image analysis and automated cartography. In: Readings in Computer Vision: Issues, Problems, Principles, and Paradigms, pp. 726–740. Morgan Kaufmann Publishers Inc., San Francisco (1987)

A Local Derivative Pattern Based Image Forensic Framework for Seam Carving Detection

Jingyu Ye$^{(\boxtimes)}$ and Yun-Qing Shi

Department of Electrical and Computer Engineering,
New Jersey Institute of Technology, Newark, NJ 07102, USA
{jy58,shi}@njit.edu

Abstract. Seam carving is one of the most popular image scaling algorithms which can effectively manipulate the image size while preserving the important image content. In this paper, we present a local derivative pattern (LDP) based forensic framework to detect if a digital image has been processed by seam carving or not. Each image is firstly encoded by applying four LDP encoders. Afterward, 96-D features are extracted from the encoded LDP images, and the support vector machine (SVM) classifier with linear kernel is utilized. The experimental results thus obtained have demonstrated that the proposed framework outperforms the state of the art. Specifically, the proposed scheme has achieved 73%, 88% and 97% average detection accuracies in detecting the low carving rate cases, i.e., 5%, 10% and 20%, respectively; while the prior state-of-the-arts has achieved 66%, 75% and 87% average detection accuracy on these cases.

Keywords: Seam carving detection · Image forensics · Local derivative pattern · Support vector machine

1 Introduction

Digital images have been playing an important role in our daily life in the past several decades. Due to the rapid development on image processing technologies as well as on the hardware such as personal computers and smartphone, editing a digital image has become an easy and joyful thing to do for each individual. As a result, the authenticity of a digital image can no longer be guaranteed. In such a situation, more advanced digital image forensic techniques are always in great demand by the entire society and the research of digital image forensics [1] is attracting more and more attentions. In this paper, an LDP based image forensic framework is proposed to detect the most popular image scaling algorithm which is known as 'seam carving' in digital image processing.

Seam carving was first proposed by Avidan and Shamir in 2007 [2]. In order to shrink a digital image, and meanwhile to preserve the important image content, the optimal way is to delete pixels with low energy which are considered as unnoticeable or less important image content from the target image. Therefore, by recursively removing a series of optimal seams, where each seam is a path of 8-connected pixels

© Springer International Publishing AG 2017
Y.Q. Shi et al. (Eds.): IWDW 2016, LNCS 10082, pp. 172–184, 2017.
DOI: 10.1007/978-3-319-53465-7_13

traversing the image horizontally or vertically and the optimal seam has the minimum accumulative energy, the desired image size could be achieved and the main image content could be protected as well. Because of its significant performance, seam carving has been one of the most popular image scaling algorithm in using these days. On the other hand, seam carving is also a powerful technique for image tampering [2] since it can be used to remove any certain object from a target image without leaving perceptible traces. Therefore, detecting seam carving is a very important topic in digital image forensics.

A few papers on detecting seam carving operation in digital images have been published so far, and most of them are passive approaches. They are described as follows. By applying Markov transition probabilities as features to the SVM classifier, the first method on detecting the traces of seam carving in JPEG images was reported in [3]. In [4–11], a series of statistical features were proposed to be effective on detecting seam carving in JPEG images or uncompressed images. In [7], eighteen energy based statistical features, which are to measure the energy distribution and noise level of an image, were introduced to determine whether an uncompressed image has been seam carved or not. Later, the features presented in [7] and other six similar features were proposed to be extracted from Local Binary Pattern (LBP) encoded image instead of from the original image, and the improved detection accuracy is reported in [9]. Besides the above mentioned passive approaches, an active approach which is based on a pre-embedded forensic hash was suggested in [12].

In this paper, we propose to utilize a local derivative pattern (LDP) [13] based forensic framework to detect the operation of seam carving in uncompressed images. In the proposed framework, four LDP encoded images are first generated from the original image, then 94 features are extracted from the four LDP images for the classification. The experimental results, which are based on the linear SVM classifier, have indicated a significant improvement over the prior state of the arts. The rest of paper is organized as follows. Section 2 briefly introduces the proposed algorithm of seam carving. The proposed forensic framework is presented in Sect. 3. In Sect. 4, the experimental results are reported and the conclusion is made in Sect. 5.

2 Background

Interpolation and cropping are two commonly used image scaling techniques. While the interpolation often has a satisfactory performance on the uniform image resizing, the cropping can perfectly provide local content of an image. However, as shown in Fig. 1, the image interpolation is insufficient for the non-uniformly image scaling since severe distortion could be introduced, and the same is true for the cropping as well. To overcome the disadvantages of aforementioned standard image scaling techniques, seam carving has been therefore proposed, which is shown in Fig. 1(d). Compared with Fig. 1(b) and (c), Fig. 1(d) does show the whole image better than Fig. 1(b) and (c) clearly from our human vision point of view.

Seam carving, also known as content-aware image resizing (CAIR), is an image resizing algorithm aiming at shrinking the image without destroying the main image content. By removing multiple seams with lower cumulative energy cost, which can be

(a)

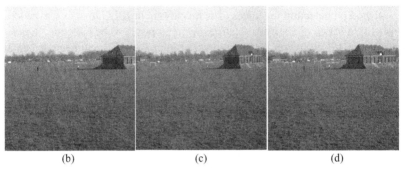

(b)   (c)   (d)

Fig. 1. (a) A sample image from UCID. (b), (c) and (d) are resized versions of (a) by using cropping, cubic interpolation and seam carving, respectively. The image size of (a) is 384×512 and 384×359 for each of the resized copy.

considered as 'less important' information of the image, from the image, the geometric constraints can be fulfilled while the image's important content can be well preserved. A seam is defined as a set of 8-connected pixels either horizontally from left to right, or vertically from top to bottom. For a given image I with the size of $m \times n$, the energy of each pixel can be evaluated by an energy function such as Eq. 1,

$$e(I(x,y)) = \left| \frac{\partial}{\partial x} I(x,y) \right| + \left| \frac{\partial}{\partial y} I(x,y) \right|. \tag{1}$$

In order to keep the rectangular shape of the image, each horizontal seam can be defined as,

$$s^H = \left\{ s_i^H \right\}_{i=1}^n = \left\{ (x(i), i) \right\}_{i=1}^n, \; s.t. \, \forall i, \; |x(i) - x(i-1)| \leq 1, \tag{2}$$

where s_i^H is the coordinates of each pixel in the horizontal seam and $x(i)$ is the row coordinate corresponding to the pixel in column i. Vertical seams can be defined similarly. Therefore, pixels in each seam are 8-connected. Moreover, each horizontal seam includes only one pixel in each column, and each vertical seam evolves only one pixel in each row.

Fig. 2. Sample image (a) from UCID and its resized copies (c), (e), (g) and (i) generated by seam carving. (c) and (e) are with same width as (a) but 5% and 20% less of the height, respectively. (g) and (i) are with same height as (a) but 5% and 20% less of the width, respectively. (b), (d), (f) and (h) are with the same size as the original image (a) and the red lines in (b), (d), (f) and (h) indicate the deleted seams in order to generate (c), (e), (g) and (i).

Assume the height of I is to be reduced which means the horizontal seam with lowest energy is to be deleted. Let $E(s)$ be the cumulative energy of seam, s, then the optimal seam, s^*, which has the minimum energy is defined as,

$$s^* = \min_s E(s) = \min_s \sum_{i=1}^{n} e\left(I\left(s_i^H\right)\right). \tag{3}$$

By applying dynamic programming, the minimum energy M of each pixel (i,j) for all possible connected seams can be calculated by,

$$M(i,j) = e(i,j) + \min(M(i-1,j-1), M(i-1,j), M(i-1,j+1)). \tag{4}$$

With the obtained M matrix, each element of the right most column $M(i,n)$ is the minimum cumulative energy of each possible horizontal seam end at $I(i,n)$, and the element with minimum value is the energy of s^*. Then, each pixel in s^* could be located by backward searching and the entire seam could be removed. By recursively doing the above-mentioned process, the height of I can be reduced. Similarly, we can shrink the width as well. As shown in Fig. 2, it is difficult for human eyes to discriminate if an image has been manipulated by seam carving or not with a large carving rate, i.e., 20%.

3 Proposed Framework

Seam carving is to delete low energy area within a given image, which is considered as the less important image content, so as to resize the image and preserve the more important image content. Therefore, the energy of seam carved image could have difference with the original one, and this change can be utilized for seam carving detection. In [7], 18 energy based features were proposed to discriminant seam carved images from images without seam carving. Once the image content is removed by seam carving, the distortion will be introduced in the manipulated local area. Consequently, the local descriptor which depicts certain area could also vary compared with before seam carving operation. In [9], the idea of combining local texture pattern and energy based feature was addressed. Then, 24 energy based features extracted from the LBP encoded image were applied to detect the operation of seam carving. In this paper, an LDP based forensic framework is proposed as illustrated in Fig. 3. For each input image, four LDP encoded images are generated and 24 energy based features are extracted from each LDP image. Consequently, each input image is represented by a $24 \times 4 = 96$–D feature vector. By applying an SVM classifier, a decision of whether the input image is seam carved or not could be made. According to the experimental results, the proposed framework outperforms the prior state of the arts significantly. The proposed framework for detecting seam carving in digital images is illustrated in Fig. 3. In the following of this section, the proposed framework are introduced in detail.

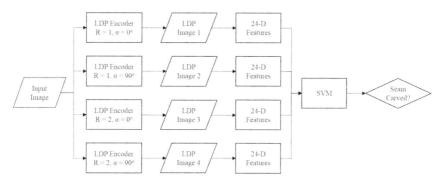

Fig. 3. The proposed framework

3.1 Local Derivative Pattern Image

Local Derivative Pattern (LDP) is one type of local descriptor, similar to Local Binary Pattern (LBP), which encodes the local information of an image into a set of binary patterns. Different with LBP and other variants of LBP, LDP encodes the directional derivatives of local regions instead of encoding the original pixel intensities applied by LBP which could be more sensitive to the manipulation of seam carving since seams are always deleted either horizontally or vertically which could change the relationship of local pixels, especially the directional derivatives within a local region.

Consider a local 5×5 region in a given image I as shown in Fig. 4. There, the 1st order derivative of pixel Z_0 on 4 directions, i.e., $\alpha = 0°$, $45°$, $90°$ and $135°$, can be derived and expressed as follows,

$$I'_{\alpha=0°}(Z_0) = I(Z_0) - I(Z_4), \tag{5}$$

$$I'_{\alpha=45°}(Z_0) = I(Z_0) - I(Z_3), \tag{6}$$

$$I'_{\alpha=90°}(Z_0) = I(Z_0) - I(Z_2), \tag{7}$$

$$I'_{\alpha=135°}(Z_0) = I(Z_0) - I(Z_1), \tag{8}$$

where $I(.)$ represents the intensity of each corresponding pixel, and Z_i, $i = 1...8$, are the eight neighboring pixels of Z_0. Then, the 2nd order LDP of Z_0 is encoded by,

$$LDP^2_\alpha = \left\{ f\left(I'_\alpha(Z_0), I'_\alpha(Z_1)\right), f\left(I'_\alpha(Z_0), I'_\alpha(Z_2)\right), ..., f\left(I'_\alpha(Z_0), I'_\alpha(Z_8)\right) \right\}, \tag{9}$$

where $f(.,.)$ is a binary coding function which encode the co-occurrence of derivative directions at adjacent points with the following rule,

$I(Z_9)$	$I(Z_{10})$	$I(Z_{11})$	$I(Z_{12})$	$I(Z_{13})$
$I(Z_{24})$	$I(Z_1)$	$I(Z_2)$	$I(Z_3)$	$I(Z_{14})$
$I(Z_{23})$	$I(Z_8)$	$I(Z_0)$	$I(Z_4)$	$I(Z_{15})$
$I(Z_{22})$	$I(Z_7)$	$I(Z_6)$	$I(Z_5)$	$I(Z_{16})$
$I(Z_{21})$	$I(Z_{20})$	$I(Z_{19})$	$I(Z_{18})$	$I(Z_{17})$

Fig. 4. Local 5×5 block with central pixel at Z_0 in image I.

$$f\left(I'_\alpha(Z_0), I'_\alpha(Z_i)\right) = \begin{cases} 0, & \text{if } I'_\alpha(Z_0) \cdot I'_\alpha(Z_i) > 0 \\ 1, & \text{otherwise} \end{cases}, i = 1\ldots8. \qquad (10)$$

By doing so, each pixel is encoded and can be represented by its LDP^2_α along direction α, which is an 8-bit binary number. Then, for direction α, the corresponding LDP image can be generated by converting the 8-bit LDP^2_α of each pixel to a decimal number, specifically within the range of [0, 255]. In our paper, we only considered $\alpha = 0°$ and $90°$ because seams are always removed from the images horizontally or vertically by the seam carving, therefore more significant changes could be introduced in the horizontal and vertical LDP images than other directions. At the meantime, since LDP is derivative based, which is the intensity difference of each pair of pixels, LDP could be easily changed during the operation of seam carving thus more sensitive to seam carving than the LBP, which directly applies the pixel intensity value. Therefore, it is expected that the LDP image contains more discriminative information than the LBP image, which has been verified in the experimental works shown below in this paper.

By applying multi-resolution [14] of LDP, we can not only monitor the changes at adjacent locations but also monitor the changes at the locations with certain distance. For example, if we set the radius equal to 2, the 8 neighboring pixels will be $\{Z_i \mid i = 9, 11, 13, 15, 17, 19, 21, 23\}$ shown in Fig. 4. Then, we can compute the corresponding LDPs and thus LDP images. Moreover, the circular sampling is utilized instead of the rectangular sampling because rectangular sampling could cause information loss when the number of sampled pixels is less than the total number of pixels in the local area. As shown in Fig. 5(b), the information of the eight unselected pixels are lost when D = 2

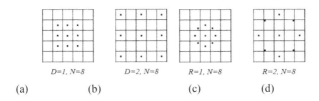

(a)	(b)	(c)	(d)
$D=1, N=8$	$D=2, N=8$	$R=1, N=8$	$R=2, N=8$

Fig. 5. (a) and (b) are the 8 rectangular symmetric neighbors with distance, denoted as D, equal to 1 and 2, respectively; (c) and (d) are the 8 circular symmetric neighbors with radius, denoted as R, equal to 1 and 2, respectively. N is the number of sampled neighbors.

(a) Original image

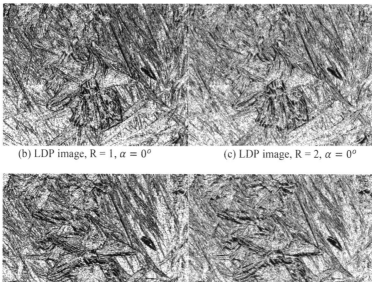

(b) LDP image, R = 1, $\alpha = 0^o$ (c) LDP image, R = 2, $\alpha = 0^o$

(d) LDP image, R = 1, $\alpha = 90^o$ (e) LDP image, R = 2, $\alpha = 90^o$

Fig. 6. Sample image (a) from UCID and its four LDP encoded images (b), (c), (d), and (e).

and rectangular sampling is applied. However, those information could be covered by circular sampling since the pixels not necessarily in the center of each box are interpolated by adjacent four pixels as shown in Fig. 5(d). Therefore, based on these considerations, discussed above, we propose to use the LDP images generated by the 2nd order LDP with radius equal to 1 and 2, $\alpha = 0°$ and 90°, respectively. As shown in Fig. 6, four LDP images are visually distinct from each other, because each of them depicts a particular relationship between the pixels in the original image. And thus, it is believed that the information carried by these LDP images are complementary and can lead to a better performance than any individual. This expectation has been verified by the experimental works reported in Sect. 4.

3.2 Energy Based Features

As seam carving is to remove low energy seams so as to manipulate the image size, it is expected that the energy distribution of an un-touched (not seam carved) uncompressed digital image and its seam carved copy are different. Therefore, features measuring the energy of an image could be used to detect the traces of seam carving. Inspired by [7, 9], we propose to utilize 96-D features to detect seam carved images. The proposed 96-D features consist of four groups of 24-D features where each group of 24-D features is extracted from one of the four above-introduced LDP images. In the following, a group of the 24-D features are summarized in Table 1, and they will be briefly introduced.

Table 1. Description of 24-D features

Feature	Description
1. Average horizontal energy	$\frac{1}{m\times n}\sum_{i=1}^{m}\sum_{j=1}^{n}\left|\frac{\partial}{\partial x}I(i,j)\right|$
2. Average vertical energy	$\frac{1}{m\times n}\sum_{i=1}^{m}\sum_{j=1}^{n}\left|\frac{\partial}{\partial y}I(i,j)\right|$
3. Sum of feature #1 and #2	$\frac{1}{m\times n}\sum_{i=1}^{m}\sum_{j=1}^{n}\left(\left|\frac{\partial}{\partial x}I(i,j)\right|+\left|\frac{\partial}{\partial y}I(i,j)\right|\right)$
4. Difference of feature #1 and #2	$\frac{1}{m\times n}\sum_{i=1}^{m}\sum_{j=1}^{n}\left(\left|\frac{\partial}{\partial x}I(i,j)\right|-\left|\frac{\partial}{\partial y}I(i,j)\right|\right)$
5. Horizontal Seam$_{max}$	$max_{i=1}^{m}M(i,n)$
6. Horizontal Seam$_{min}$	$min_{i=1}^{m}M(i,n)$
7. Horizontal Seam$_{mean}$	$\frac{1}{m}\sum_{i=1}^{m}M(i,n)$
8. Horizontal Seam$_{std}$	$\sqrt{\frac{1}{m}\sum_{i=1}^{m}(Horizontal\,Seam_{mean}-M(i,n))^2}$
9. Horizontal Seam$_{diff}$	$Horizontal\,Seam_{max}-Horizontal\,Seam_{min}$
10. Vertical Seam$_{max}$	$max_{i=1}^{n}M(m,i)$
11. Vertical Seam$_{min}$	$min_{i=1}^{n}M(m,i)$
12. Vertical Seam$_{mean}$	$\frac{1}{n}\sum_{i=1}^{n}M(m,i)$
13. Vertical Seam$_{std}$	$\sqrt{\frac{1}{n}\sum_{i=1}^{n}(Vertical\,Seam_{mean}-M(m,i))^2}$
14. Vertical Seam$_{diff}$	$Vertical\,Seam_{max}-Vertical\,Seam_{min}$
15. Half-horizontal Seam$_{max}$	$max_{i=1}^{m}M\left(i,\frac{n}{2}\right)$
16. Half-horizontal Seam$_{min}$	$min_{i=1}^{m}M\left(i,\frac{n}{2}\right)$
17. Half-horizontal Seam$_{mean}$	$\frac{1}{m}\sum_{i=1}^{m}M\left(i,\frac{n}{2}\right)$
18. Half-vertical Seam$_{max}$	$max_{i=1}^{n}M\left(\frac{m}{2},i\right)$
19. Half-vertical Seam$_{min}$	$min_{i=1}^{n}M\left(\frac{m}{2},i\right)$
20. Half-vertical Seam$_{mean}$	$\frac{1}{n}\sum_{i=1}^{n}M\left(\frac{m}{2},i\right)$
21. Noise$_{mean}$	$\frac{1}{m\times n}\sum_{i=1}^{m}\sum_{j=1}^{n}N(i,j)$
22. Noise$_{std}$	$\sqrt{\frac{1}{m\times n}\sum_{i=1}^{m}\sum_{j=1}^{n}(N(i,j)-Noise_{mean})^2}$
23. Noise$_{skewness}$	$\frac{1}{m\times n}\sum_{i=1}^{m}\sum_{j=1}^{n}\left(\frac{N(i,j)-Noise_{mean}}{Noise_{std}}\right)^3$
24. Noise$_{kurtosis}$	$\frac{1}{m\times n}\sum_{i=1}^{m}\sum_{j=1}^{n}\left(\frac{N(i,j)-Noise_{mean}}{Noise_{std}}\right)^4$

Considering the low energy pixels are removed by the seam carving, it is clear that the overall energy distribution has been changed. Therefore, four average energy based features, i.e., average horizontal energy, average vertical energy, the summation and the difference of the former two features, are extracted to differentiate the seam carved images from the un-touched images. Besides, since each optimal seam which has the lowest accumulative energy will be deleted by the seam carving, the energy of the remaining seams will be different. Thus, sixteen seam energy based features are extracted to capture changes of seams energy during the seam carving. By constructing the M matrix shown in Eq. 4, the minimum cumulative energy matrix, for each image where the bottom row is the energy of each possible vertical seam, five statistic values called min, max, mean, standard deviation, and the difference between min and max are applied as the features. Also, the other five features of horizontal seams are calculated accordingly as well. Furthermore, with the M matrix generated by half of the image, six half-seam energy features including min, max and mean for both horizontal seams and vertical seams can be derived similarly.

Furthermore, because the image content has been manipulated by the seam carving, the noise level of the seam carved image could be differed from the original image. To obtain the noise residue N of each image I, the Wiener filter with 5×5 window, denoted as F, is applied to generate the de-noised copy and the noise residue can be derived by,

$$N = I - F(I). \tag{11}$$

Then, the mean, standard deviation, skewness and kurtosis of the noise residue are extracted as the features for detecting seam carving. Consequently, for each of the four LDP image aforementioned, 24-D features can be obtained. Therefore, the total 96-D features are utilized for the classification of seam carving in this paper.

4   Experimental Results

In this section, we first introduce the establishment of image database which are utilized to evaluate the proposed method. Then, a comprehensive series of experiments based on Matlab are introduced, and finally the results are reported and compared with the state of the art. In the experiments, Lib-SVM [15] is selected as the classifiers and linear kernel with default parameters is utilized. Moreover, in order to validate the performance, each reported result is the average detection accuracy over 10 iterations of 6-fold cross validation.

4.1   Setup of Seam Carving Database

Since there is no other image database available for the performance evaluation of forensic research on seam carving, our utilized image database is based on the UCID (Uncompressed Color Image Database) [16]. It is a benchmark image database for image forensic researches and widely used in the prior seam carving forensics.

The UCID contains 1338 uncompressed color images with varieties of image contents. To build the image database, each color image of UCID was converted to grayscale image to form the un-touched image set. Afterward, the seam carving technique proposed in [2] was implemented on Matlab, and the magnitude of gradient calculated by Sobel operator [17] was utilized as the energy function $e(\cdot)$ in Eq. 1. Then, 12 seam carved copies of each image are generated according to various carving rates, i.e., 5%, 10%, 20%, 30%, 40%, and 50%, and two carving directions, i.e., horizontal and vertical. The carving rate means C% of the image size are reduced. Consequently, 12 seam carved image sets are built which represent 12 different seam carving scenarios. To test each seam carving scenario, the un-touched image set and one of the 12 seam cared image sets are selected to form the 12 experimental datasets.

4.2   Performance of Proposed Framework

In order to evaluate the performance of the proposed framework, the experimental works have been conducted on the pre-built 12 different seam carving datasets. Meanwhile, the approaches presented in [7–9] which represent the state-of-the-art have been implemented and tested to make a fair comparison. As shown in Table 2, the first row stands for each type of seam carving, e.g. '5%H' means the image size is reduced by 5% after deleting the horizontal seams and '5%V' means vertical seams are removed in order to shrink the image by 5%. The results have indicated that the proposed method outperforms the three approaches on all 12 seam carving scenarios. And from Table 3, it is easy to observe that the average detection accuracies achieved by the proposed framework are significantly higher than that achieved by the state-of-the-arts. Especially on the low carving rate cases, i.e., 5%, 10% and 20%, the proposed method can achieve 5%–10% higher classification rates than that by the state-of-the-arts, respectively.

The contribution of each LDP image has also been evaluated. Each group of 24-D features extracted from each LDP image has been tested on the 12 seam carving

Table 2. Detection accuracy of proposed method versus the state-of-the-arts

	5%H	5%V	10%H	10%V	20%H	20%V	30%H	30%V	40%H	40%V	50%H	50%V
Ref. [6]	62.55%	69.23%	71.86%	78.44%	83.14%	88.43%	90.37%	93.84%	94.25%	96.27%	96.63%	97.86%
Ref. [7]	53.03%	51.77%	54.24%	55.36%	59.86%	60.87%	63.51%	67.86%	67.93%	75.47%	71.91%	82.45%
Ref. [8]	59.52%	57.91%	71.85%	68.58%	88.61%	86.12%	96.44%	94.81%	98.82%	98.33%	99.44%	99.58%
Proposed	72.26%	73.80%	88.65%	89.10%	97.85%	97.71%	99.42%	99.45%	99.82%	100.00%	99.92%	100.00%

Table 3. Average detection accuracy of proposed method versus the state-of-the-arts

	5%	10%	20%	30%	40%	50%
Ref. [6]	65.89%	75.15%	85.79%	92.11%	95.26%	97.25%
Ref. [7]	52.40%	54.80%	60.37%	65.69%	71.70%	77.18%
Ref. [8]	58.72%	70.22%	87.37%	95.63%	98.58%	99.51%
Proposed	73.03%	88.88%	97.78%	99.44%	99.91%	99.96%

Table 4. Detection accuracy of features extracted from each LDP image

	5%H	5%V	10%H	10%V	20%H	20%V	30%H	30%V	40%H	40%V	50%H	50%V
h1	62.38%	65.06%	77.96%	80.74%	93.28%	93.79%	98.06%	98.58%	99.25%	99.73%	99.61%	100.00%
h2	65.12%	67.17%	80.46%	82.94%	93.91%	95.35%	98.20%	98.61%	99.23%	99.93%	99.72%	100.00%
v1	62.35%	62.25%	77.95%	76.84%	92.44%	91.89%	98.15%	96.98%	99.47%	98.85%	99.76%	99.66%
v2	63.39%	62.16%	80.83%	80.19%	94.78%	94. 62%	98.51%	98.40%	99.50%	99.32%	99.90%	99.89%

scenarios respectively, and the test results are reported in Table 4. In Table 4, the first column stands for each LDP image. The 'h1' is the LDP image 1 as shown in Fig. 3 which is encoded by LDP operator with $\alpha = 0°$ and radius $R = 1$; the 'h2' is the image encoded with $\alpha = 0°$ and $R = 2$. Similarly, 'v1' and 'v2' are the images encoded by LDP operator with $\alpha = 90°$ and radius equal to 1 and 2, respectively. It can be observed that the individual performance of the features extracted from each LDP image is much lower than the performance achieved when all features are combined even though the individual performance is not bad at all. This demonstrates that the information carried by each LDP image are complementary and it supports our previous assumption.

To further test the robustness of the proposed framework, another test on a mixed seam carving image set has been conducted. By randomly selecting 1/12 samples from each of the 12 different seam carved image sets previously established, while each sample is generated from different original image, the mixed seam carving image set is formed. Then, the proposed framework has been tested on this mixed set and a more than 90% detection accuracy is achieved while the best result achieved by the three compared approaches is only 86%, which was achieved by [9].

5   Conclusion

In this paper, we have presented an LDP based image forensic framework for detecting the operation of seam carving. By converting each image to four LDP encoded images, 96 features are extracted to discriminate if a given image is seam carved or un-touched. According to the experimental results, the proposed method can successfully detect seam carving and outperform the state-of-the-art on the various seam carving scenarios. In particular, the proposed framework has achieved 73%, 88% and 97% average detection accuracies on low carving rate cases, i.e., 5%, 10% and 20%, respectively, which is 5%–10% higher than the performance achieved by the previous state of the arts. And the test results on the mixed test sets also indicate the proposed method is more robust than the previous state-of-the-arts.

References

1. Piva, A.: An Overview on Image Forensics. ISRN Signal Processing, vol. 2013, Article ID 496701, 22 pp. (2013)
2. Avidan, S., Shamir, A.: Seam carving for content-aware image resizing. ACM Trans. Graph. 26(3), July 2007

3. Sarkar, A., Nataraj, L., Manjunath, B.S.: Detection of seam carving and localization of seam insertions in digital images. In: Proceedings of the 11th ACM workshop on Multimedia and Security, MM&Sec 2009, New York, USA, pp. 107–116 (2009)

4. Fillion, C., Sharma, G.: Detecting content adaptive scaling of images for forensic applications. In: SPIE Proceedings of the Media Forensics and Security, p. 75410 (2010)

5. Chang, W., Shih, T.K., Hsu, H.: Detection of seam carving in JPEG images. In: Proceedings of the iCAST-UMEDIA (2013)

6. Liu, Q., Chen, Z.: Improved approaches with calibrated neighboring joint density to steganalysis and seam-carved forgery detection in JPEG images. ACM Trans. Intell. Syst. Technol. 5(4) (2014)

7. Ryu, S., Lee, H., Lee, H.: Detecting trace of seam carving for forensic analysis. IEICE Trans. Inf. Syst. **E97-D**(5), 1304–1311 (2014)

8. Wei, J., Lin, Y., Wu, Y.: A patch analysis method to detect seam carved images. Pattern Recogn. Lett. **36**, 100–106 (2014)

9. Ying, T., Yang, G., Li, L., Zhang, D., Sun, X.: Detecting seam carving based image resizing using local binary patterns. Comput. Secur. **55**, 130–141 (2015)

10. Wattanachote, K., Shih, T., Chang, W., Chang, H.: Tamper detection of JPEG image due to seam modification. IEEE Trans. Inf. Forensics Secur. **10**(12), 2477–2491 (2015)

11. Li, J., Zhao, Y., Ni, R.: Detection of seam carving and contrast enhancement operation chain. In: International Conference on Intelligent Information Hiding and Multimedia Signal Processing (IIH-MSP), pp. 235–238 (2015)

12. Lu, W., Wu, M.: Seam carving estimation using forensic hash. In: Proceedings of the Thirteenth ACM Multimedia Workshop on Multimedia and Security, MM&Sec 2011, New York, pp. 9–14 (2011)

13. Zhang, B., Gao, Y., Zhao, S., Liu, J.: Local derivative pattern versus local binary pattern: face recognition with high-order local pattern descriptor. IEEE Trans. Image Process. **19**(2), 533–544 (2010)

14. Ojala, T., Pietikäinen, M., Mäenpää, T.: Multiresolution gray-scale and rotation invariant texture classification with local binary patterns. IEEE Trans. Pattern Anal. Mach. Intell. **24**(7), 971–987 (2002)

15. Chang, C.C., Lin, C.J.: LIBSVM: A library for support vector machines. ACM Trans. Intell. Syst. Technol. **2**, 27:1–27:27 (2011). http://www.csie.ntu.edu.tw/ ~ cjlin/libsvm/

16. Schaefer, G., Stich, M.: UCID - An uncompressed colour image database. In: 2004 Proceedings of the SPIE, Storage and Retrieval Methods and Applications for Multimedia, vol. 5307, pp. 472–480 (2004)

17. Sobel, I.: An isotropic 3×3 gradient operator. In: Freeman, H. (ed.) Machine Vision for Three - Dimensional Scenes, pp. 376–379. Academic Press, New York (1990)

Visual Cryptography

Privacy Monitor

Teng Guo[1]([⊠]), Feng Liu[2,3], Wen Wang[2,3], and BingTao Yu[1]

[1] School of Information Science and Technology,
University of International Relations, Beijing 100091, China
`guoteng.cas@gmail.com, bintoyu@126.com`
[2] State Key Laboratory of Information Security,
Institute of Information Engineering, Chinese Academy of Sciences,
Beijing 100093, China
[3] University of Chinese Academy of Sciences, Beijing 100190, China
`{liufeng,wangwen}@iie.ac.cn`

Abstract. This paper first proposes a design for privacy monitor that only users at the right angle viewpoint can see the screen clearly, while users at a large enough deviated angle viewpoint cannot see any useful information on the screen. The space where users from that viewpoint can see the screen is called visible space in this paper. Then the visible space of the proposed privacy monitor is completely characterized for IPS screen. By adjusting the distance between the two liquid crystal layers, the size of the visible space can be controlled in such a way that larger distance will result in a smaller visible space, while smaller distance will result in a larger visible space.

Keywords: Privacy monitor · Visible space · Screen

1 Introduction

Visual cryptography is a special method to implement secret sharing, which is first formally defined by [1]. In a (k, n) visual cryptography scheme $((k, n)$-VCS) [2–7], a secret image is divided into n share images in such a way that the stacking of any k share images can reveal the secret image, while any less than k share images provide no information about the secret image. There are two "stacking models" in visual cryptography: 1, OR-based approach [8–15], which abstracts the physical stacking of two transparencies that have ink dots on them; 2, XOR-based approach [16–20], which abstracts the physical stacking of two liquid crystal layers that can rotate the light that passes through them.

In the OR-based approach, a pixel on the transparency either has ink dot on it or does not. If it has ink dot, we denote its state by 1; otherwise, we denote its state by 0. The stacking rule is summarized by the OR operation on the set of Boolean numbers $\{0, 1\}$: $0 + 0 = 0, 1 + 0 = 1, 0 + 1 = 1, 1 + 1 = 1$. Only the stacking of two transparent pixels will result in a transparent (white) pixel. All other cases will result in a black pixel.

© Springer International Publishing AG 2017
Y.Q. Shi et al. (Eds.): IWDW 2016, LNCS 10082, pp. 187–197, 2017.
DOI: 10.1007/978-3-319-53465-7_14

In the XOR-based approach, the beam of light passing through the liquid crystal unit is either rotated 180° or not. If it is rotated 180°, we denote this state of liquid crystal unit by 1, otherwise, we denote this state of liquid crystal unit by 0. The stacking rule is summarized by the XOR operation on the set of Boolean numbers $\{0,1\}$: $0 + 0 = 0, 1 + 0 = 1, 0 + 1 = 1, 1 + 1 = 0$. The total effect of two rotating operations is $360°$ and it is equivalent to no rotation $0°$, which indicates a white pixel.

(a) S

Fig. 1. The original secret image, of image size 425×425.

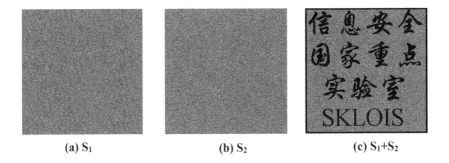

(a) S₁   **(b) S₂**   **(c) S₁+S₂**

Fig. 2. The experimental results for (2,2)-VCS in the OR model, where (a) S_1 is the first share image and (b) S_2 is the second share image and (c) $S_1 + S_2$ is the stacking result of S_1 and S_2, all of image size 600×600. The results are presented in an aspect ratio invariant framework [21].

The encoding rules for a (2,2)-VCS in the OR model are as follows:

$$C_0 = \left\{ \begin{bmatrix} 10 \\ 10 \end{bmatrix}, \begin{bmatrix} 01 \\ 01 \end{bmatrix} \right\}, C_1 = \left\{ \begin{bmatrix} 10 \\ 01 \end{bmatrix}, \begin{bmatrix} 01 \\ 10 \end{bmatrix} \right\}$$

The stacking of two rows of a matrix from C_0 will result in a decoded block that contains one black pixel and one white pixel, while the stacking of two

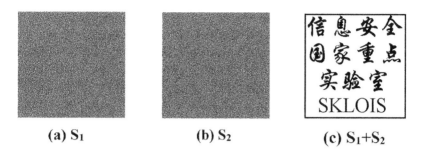

(a) S₁   **(b) S₂**   **(c) S₁+S₂**

Fig. 3. The experimental results for (2,2)-VCS in the XOR model, where (a) S_1 is the first share image and (b) S_2 is the second share image and (c) $S_1 + S_2$ is the stacking result of S_1 and S_2, all of image size 425×425.

rows of a matrix from C_1 will result in a decoded block that contains two black pixels. Thus from an overall view, the white secret pixels are decoded as half gray and the black secret pixels are decoded as black, referring to Fig. 2. The contrast between white pixels and black pixels of the decoded image has 50% loss compared to that of the original secret image (resp. Fig. 1).

The encoding rules for a (2,2)-VCS in the XOR model are as follows:

$$C_0 = \left\{ \begin{bmatrix} 1 \\ 1 \end{bmatrix}, \begin{bmatrix} 0 \\ 0 \end{bmatrix} \right\}, C_1 = \left\{ \begin{bmatrix} 1 \\ 0 \end{bmatrix}, \begin{bmatrix} 0 \\ 1 \end{bmatrix} \right\}$$

The stacking of two rows of a matrix from C_0 will result in a decoded block that contains one white pixel, while the stacking of two rows of a matrix from C_1 will result in a decoded block that contains one black pixel. Hence the white secret pixels are decoded as white and the black secret pixels are decoded as black, referring to Fig. 3. The contrast between white pixels and black pixels of the decoded image has no loss compared to that of the original secret image (resp. Fig. 1).

The secret image is generally encoded line by line, from left to right. If the current secret pixel is white, we randomly choose a matrix from C_0 and distribute its i-th row to party i, else if the current secret pixel is black, we randomly choose a matrix from C_1 and distribute its i-th row to party i. In Fig. 1, (a) is the original secret image for the two (2, 2)-VCSs in the OR model and the XOR model respectively. In Figs. 2 and 3, (a) and (b) are the first and second share images respectively, and (c) is the decoded image.

The proposed privacy monitor adopts an XOR-based approach and has two operating modes: 1, normal browsing mode; 2, private browsing mode. According to the surrounding environment, the users can choose to use normal browsing mode or private browsing mode by setting the security configuration module. In the normal browsing mode, the proposed privacy monitor works the same way as a common computer screen. In the private browsing mode, the users can adjust the distance parameter d between the first liquid crystal layer and the second liquid crystal layer. If d is set larger, the users will have a smaller visual space, while if d is set smaller, the users will have a larger visual space. The size of the visual space can be adjusted on the basis of personal preferences at any time.

Nowadays the screen becomes an important channel for users to access information. However, ordinary screens are vulnerable to side peepers, and sensitive information has the risk of disclosure when it is displayed on a screen. Furthermore, with constantly evolving technology, the volume of miniature cameras becomes smaller and smaller, which facilitates hacker's stealing of confidential information and user's privacy data. A common technology that prevents such leakage of information on screens is by pasting an anti-peep protection membrane. This method costs little and generally causes the screens to be darkened, affecting the visual quality. Besides, an anti-peep protection membrane determines a fixed size of visual space. Once the users want to adjust the visual space, they need to replace the old anti-peep protection membrane with a new one. This is inconvenient and harms the screen as well. On the other hand, the proposed privacy monitor can easily adjust the size of the visual space by setting the parameter d. Furthermore, the characteristic of double liquid crystal layers will facilitate the deployment of optical encryption scheme [22], which is a multidisciplinary topic.

This paper is organized as follows. In Sect. 2, we give a detailed description of the proposed privacy monitor. In Sect. 3, we formally analyze the visual space of the proposed privacy monitor. In Sect. 4, we present the simulation results. The paper is concluded in Sect. 5.

2   The Proposed Privacy Monitor

The proposed privacy monitor contains the following modules: encryption module 1, encryption module 2, synchronous clock module, security configuration module, visible space configuration module, display interface card 1, display interface card 2, liquid crystal layer 1 and liquid crystal layer 2, referring to Fig. 4.

The security configuration module accepts user's setting information of whether using normal browsing mode or using private browsing mode. In normal browsing mode, the security configuration module opens display interface card 1 and sends encryption signal to encryption module 2. In private browsing mode, the security configuration module closes display interface card 1 and sends no encryption signal to encryption module 2. Then the visible space configuration module accepts user's configuration parameter d, and controls the physical distance d between liquid crystal layer 1 and liquid crystal layer 2, adjusting the size of the visible space. Generally, larger d will result in a smaller visible space and on the contrary, smaller d will result in a larger visible space. The synchronous clock module has no input, and sends clock synchronization signals to the encryption module 1 and the encryption module 2, where both encryption modules have a preset pseudo-random number generation algorithm PRNG. After that, the output of encryption module 1 is sent to display interface card 1, and the output of encryption module 2 is sent to display interface card 2. Display interface card 1 controls the liquid crystal units on liquid crystal layer 1 according to its input, and display interface card 2 controls the liquid crystal units on liquid crystal layer 2 according to its input similarly. Liquid crystal layer 1 and liquid crystal layer 2 are physically parallel with each other, where liquid crystal layer 1 is installed on the inside position, and liquid crystal layer 2 is installed on the outside position.

The privacy monitor in normal browsing mode works the same way as an ordinary screen. The privacy monitor in private browsing mode works as follows:

Workflow 1

Input: *A binary secret image m.*

Output: *Two share images S_1 and S_2 are displayed separately on two liquid crystal layers.*

Step 1. *Synchronous clock module sends a clock signal CLK to encryption module 1 and encryption module 2 simultaneously;*

Step 2. *Encryption module 1 computes image S_1 by the formula $S_1 = PRNG(CLK)$, and sends S_1 to display interface card 1.*

Step 3. *Encryption module 2 computes pixels on image S_2 by the formula $S_2[i] = m[i] \otimes PRNG(CLK)[i]$, where $S_2[i]$ represents the i-th pixel value on image S_2, which is an 1-bit value; $m[i]$ represents the i-th pixel value on image m, which is an 1-bit value; $PRNG(CLK)[i]$ represents the i-th pixel value on pseudorandom image $PRNG(CLK)$, which is also an 1-bit value.*

Step 4. *Encryption module 2 sends S_2 to display interface card 2.*

Step 5. *Display interface card 1 controls the liquid crystal units on liquid crystal layer 1 according to S_1.*

Step 6. *Display interface card 2 controls the liquid crystal units on liquid crystal layer 2 according to S_2.*

Outcome: *Users can observe the secret image m in visible space, while users cannot observe any meaningful information in non-visible space.*

Remark 1. There are many technologies that can achieve PRNG, like stream ciphers: Rabbit, Salsa20/12, Grain v1. For an intuitive idea, one can refer to Fig. 4. Figure 5 gives an example of the screen, which considers black and white (resp. 1 and 0) pixels.

3 The Visible Space

In Fig. 6, each pixel is square shaped and of equal size. Both liquid crystal layers contain 4 pixels. Denote the side length of a pixel by 1. The viewpoint of the front observer is just in the z direction, in which the corresponding pixels on the two liquid crystal layers align precisely. Suppose the viewpoint of the side peeper deviates from the z direction, α degree in the x component and β degree in the y component. The superimposed area of two corresponding pixels is $(1-xf)(1-yf)$, where $xf = d\tan\alpha$, $yf = d\tan\beta$ and the overall area of a pixel is 1. Hence $(1 - d\tan\alpha)(1 - d\tan\beta)$ proportion of the area is superimposed for each pixel in the side peeper's viewpoint, referring to Fig. 7.

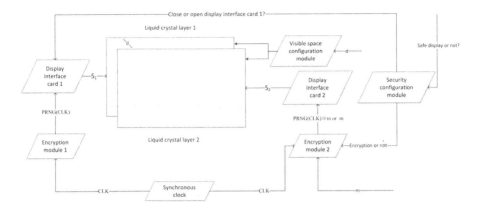

Fig. 4. The working principle of the proposed privacy monitor.

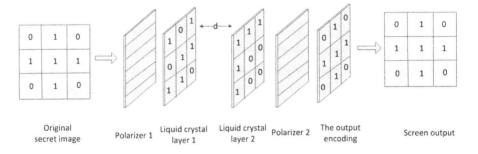

Fig. 5. An example of the displaying process, only considering black and white (resp. 1 and 0) pixels.

3.1 A Concrete Analysis for IPS Screen

An IPS pixel is square shaped and contains three equal size subpixels. If we denote the side length of a pixel by 1, then the length of a subpixel is $\frac{1}{3}$ and the height of a subpixel is 1, referring to Fig. 8. Figure 9 gives an intuitive view of the display of a single IPS pixel. Denote the horizontal offset component from the z direction by α and the vertical offset component from the z direction by β. In such a case, the horizontal offset is $xf = d\tan\alpha$ and the vertical offset is $yf = d\tan\beta$, referring to Fig. 10. The superimposed area of two corresponding subpixels is $(1/3 - d\tan\alpha)(1 - d\tan\beta)$, where the overall area of a subpixel is $1/3$. Hence $(1/3 - d\tan\alpha)(1 - d\tan\beta)/(1/3) = (1 - 3d\tan\alpha)(1 - d\tan\beta)$ proportion of the area is superimposed for each subpixel. The misaligned part does not contribute to the contrast of the screen.

Table 1 summarizes some specific implementation parameters for IPS screen. For example, if the user sets the distance between the liquid crystal layers $d = 1$, then users at viewpoint that is equal or larger than $18.4°$ in the horizontal offset component can perceive no content on the screen, and users at viewpoint that

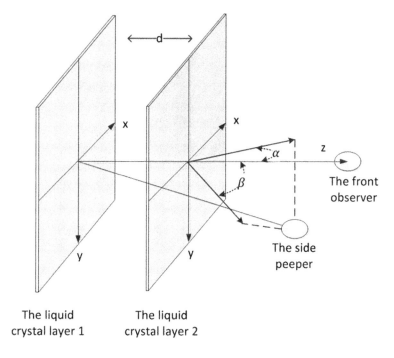

Fig. 6. The schematic diagram of the visible space.

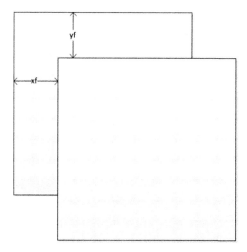

Fig. 7. The superimposition of two corresponding square pixels.

Fig. 8. The arrangement of subpixels on an IPS screen.

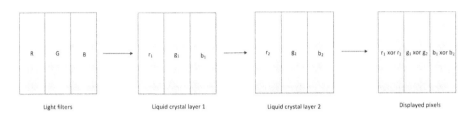

Fig. 9. The display of a single IPS pixel.

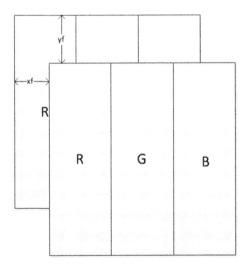

Fig. 10. The superimposition of two corresponding IPS pixels.

Table 1. For gradually increasing distance parameter d, the smallest value of horizontal offset component α that makes the overlay area of corresponding subpixels exactly 0, and the smallest value of vertical offset component β that makes the overlay area of corresponding sub-pixels exactly 0.

	$d = 0.5$	$d = 1$	$d = 1.5$	$d = 2$	$d = 2.5$	$d = 3$	$d = 3.5$
Horizontal offset component α	33.7°	18.4°	12.5°	9.5°	7.6°	6.3°	5.4°
Vertical offset component β	63.4°	45.0°	33.7°	26.6°	21.8°	18.4°	15.9°

is equal or larger than 45.0° in the vertical offset component also can perceive no content on the screen.

4   Simulation Results

Figure 11 summarizes the simulation results for the proposed privacy monitor, where the distance parameter is set to 1.10.

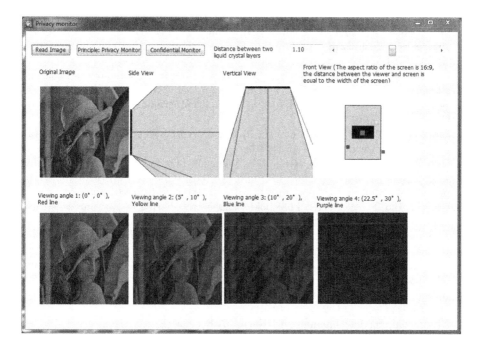

Fig. 11. The simulation results for the proposed privacy monitor.

5   Conclusions

We proposed a privacy monitor that can limit the visible space of the screen. By increasing the distance between the two liquid crystal layers, we can decrease the visible space. Furthermore, we give a concrete analysis of the IPS screen, which is widely used in LG P880, iphone 4/4s.

Acknowledgements. This work was supported by the "Fundamental Research Funds for the Central Universities" grant No. 3262016T47 and the NSFC grant No. 61671448 and the key project of NFSC grant No. U1536207 and the "Strategic Priority Research Program" of the Chinese Academy of Sciences No. XDA06010701. Besides, many thanks to the handling editor and anonymous reviewers for their valuable comments that help us to improve this paper.

References

1. Naor, M., Shamir, A.: Visual cryptography. In: Santis, A. (ed.) EUROCRYPT 1994. LNCS, vol. 950, pp. 1–12. Springer, Heidelberg (1995). doi:10.1007/BFb0053419
2. Hofmeister, T., Krause, M., Simon, H.U.: Contrast-optimal k out of n secret sharing schemes in visual cryptography. In: Jiang, T., Lee, D.T. (eds.) COCOON 1997. LNCS, vol. 1276, pp. 176–185. Springer, Heidelberg (1997). doi:10.1007/BFb0045084
3. Hofmeister, T., Krause, M., Simon, H.U.: Contrast-optimal k out of n secret sharing schemes in visual cryptography. Theor. Comput. Sci. **240**(2), 471–485 (2000)
4. Bose, M., Mukerjee, R.: Optimal (2, n) visual cryptographic schemes. Des. Codes Crypt. **40**, 255–267 (2006)
5. Bose, M., Mukerjee, R.: Optimal (k, n) visual cryptographic schemes for general k. Des. Codes Crypt. **55**, 19–35 (2010)
6. Guo, T., Liu, F., Wu, C.K., Ren, Y.W., Wang, W.: On (k, n) visual cryptography scheme with t essential parties. In: Padró, C. (ed.) ICITS 2013. LNCS, vol. 8317, pp. 56–68. Springer, Heidelberg (2014). doi:10.1007/978-3-319-04268-8_4
7. Guo, T., Liu, F., Wu, C.K.: Threshold visual secret sharing by random grids with improved contrast. J. Syst. Softw. **86**, 2094–2109 (2013)
8. Ateniese, G., Blundo, C., De Santis, A., Stinson, D.R.: Visual cryptography for general access structures. Inf. Comput. **129**, 86–106 (1996)
9. Blundo, C., De Santis, A., Stinson, D.R.: On the contrast in visual cryptography schemes. J. Cryptol. **12**(4), 261–289 (1999)
10. Blundo, C., De Bonis, A., De Santis, A.: Improved schemes for visual cryptography. Des. Codes Crypt. **24**, 255–278 (2001)
11. Arumugam, S., Lakshmanan, R., Nagar, A.K.: On (k, n)*-visual cryptography scheme. Des. Codes Crypt. **71**, 153–162 (2014)
12. Liu, F., Guo, T., Wu, C.K., Qian, L.N.: Improving the visual quality of size invariant visual cryptography scheme. J. Vis. Commun. Image Represent. **23**, 331–342 (2012)
13. D'Arco, P., Prisco, R.: Secure two-party computation: a visual way. In: Padró, C. (ed.) ICITS 2013. LNCS, vol. 8317, pp. 18–38. Springer, Heidelberg (2014). doi:10.1007/978-3-319-04268-8_2

14. Shyu, S.J., Jiang, H.W.: General constructions for threshold multiple-secret visual cryptographic schemes. IEEE Trans. Inf. Forensics Secur. **8**(5), 733–743 (2013)
15. Shyu, S.J., Chen, M.C.: Optimum pixel expansions for threshold visual secret sharing schemes. IEEE Trans. Inf. Forensics Secur. **6**(3), 960–969 (2011)
16. Biham, E., Itzkovitz, A.: Visual cryptography with polarization. In: The Dagstuhl seminar on Cryptography, and the RUMP Session of CRYPTO 1998, September 1997
17. Tuyls, P., Hollmann, H.D.L., Lint, J.H.V., Tolhuizen, L.: A polarisation based visual crypto system and its secret sharing schemes (2002). http://eprint.iacr.org
18. Tuyls, P., Hollmann, H.D.L., Lint, J.H.V., Tolhuizen, L.: XOR-based visual cryptography schemes. Des. Codes Crypt. **37**, 169–186 (2005)
19. Schrijen, G., Tuyls, P., Kevenaar, T., Johnson, M.: Secure visual message communication method and device. In: US20050117748 (2004)
20. Evans, A., Tillin, M., Walton, E.: Display having particular polarisation modifying layer. In: US7400377 (2008)
21. Liu, F., Guo, T., Wu, C.K., Yang, C.-N.: Flexible visual cryptography scheme without distortion. In: Shi, Y.Q., Kim, H.-J., Perez-Gonzalez, F. (eds.) IWDW 2011. LNCS, vol. 7128, pp. 211–227. Springer, Heidelberg (2012). doi:10.1007/978-3-642-32205-1_18
22. Rajput, S.K., Nishchal, N.K.: Fresnel domain nonlinear optical image encryption scheme based on Gerchberg—Saxton phase-retrieval algorithm. Appl. Opt. **53**(3), 418–425 (2014)

Information Security Display Technology with Multi-view Effect

Wen Wang[1,2](✉), Feng Liu[1,2], Teng Guo[3], Yawei Ren[1], and Gang Shen[4]

[1] State Key Laboratory of Information Security,
Institute of Information Engineering, Chinese Academy of Sciences, Beijing, China
wangwen@iie.ac.cn
[2] School of Cyber Security, University of Chinese Academy of Sciences,
Beijing, China
[3] School of Information Science and Technology,
University of International Relations, Beijing, China
[4] Zhengzhou Information Science and Technology Institute, Zhengzhou, China

Abstract. Information security is arousing wide attention of the world. Apart from the traditional attack on transmission process, threats specific to display terminals should not be ignored as well. In this paper, we investigate the color mixture model of a well-known psychophysical phenomenon: "persistence of vision", and propose a new display technology which presents secret and cheating information at the same time. Unauthorized viewers only see the cheating information from display, while authorized viewers can obtain the secret information with the help of synchronized glasses. Experimental results show the rationality and effectiveness of the technology.

Keywords: Information security display · Persistence of vision · Synchronized glasses

1 Introduction

In modern era, information is playing an increasingly important part of our lives. Meanwhile, the security problem has aroused widespread attention of the world. Traditionally, much more efforts have been put on the encryption technology, which aims at defensing hostile attack on information transmission process. However, threats specific to display terminals may also cause a great deal of damage to our lives, for example, unauthorized peeping or photography to the display terminals may leak some valuable information or our privacy, which is hardly to be found in traditional situation.

On account of the great importance of display terminals, a few technologies have been proposed to protect the information displayed on a screen. Privacy filter [1,4] is the most common solution to the problem which limits the viewing angles by closely spaced louvers. However, the visible space of the method is fixed and it can't prevent unauthorized peeping around the visible space completely.

Y.Q. Shi et al. (Eds.): IWDW 2016, LNCS 10082, pp. 198–208, 2017.
DOI: 10.1007/978-3-319-53465-7_15

Recently, [3] develops a displaying technology called temporal psychovisual modulation (TPVM) which makes use of a well-known phenomenon in psychophysics, "persistence of vision". Physiologically, our human visual system (HVS) can't resolve temporally rapidly changing optical signals beyond critical fusion frequency (CFF) [10]. Based on this technology, they construct another kind of information security display system. The system is built upon a 120 Hz LCD display and a pair of active shutter glasses that synchronize with the display. In the system, a secret image I and its luminance-reversed image I' (Supposing the luminance value ranges from 0 to 255, then the luminance-reversed value is calculated by $I' = 255 - I$) are displayed alternately on screen at refresh rate of 120 Hz. Under normal conditions, the CFF of our HVS is about 60 Hz [5]. Hence, viewers with no synchronized glasses only see a gray image that has uniform luminance. While for the authorized viewers, they can see the secret information with the help of synchronized glasses. Compared with the privacy filter, [3] provides larger visible space for authorized viewers and hides secret information on the display completely for unauthorized viewers.

In this paper, we investigate the color mixture model based on "persistence of vision" and propose a new implementation method of information security display system. Compared with [3], our method can provide meaningful information for the unauthorized and authorized viewers at the same time, which provides better cheating effect than the former design.

The rest of this paper is organized as follows. In Sect. 2, we will introduce some preliminaries of the paper. In Sect. 3, we will show the design and implementation of our method. In Sect. 4, the performance of our method and some analysis will be presented. Finally, we conclude and indicate some future work in Sect. 5.

2   Preliminaries

In this section, we will introduce the color mixture model based on "persistence of vision" firstly. It is the foundation of our design. Then, we show a common issue on the luminance value of a display terminal. Finally, we give the construction of the information security display system [3].

2.1   Color Mixture Model Based on "Persistence of Vision"

"Persistence of vision" is an optical illusion whereby multiple luminance signals blend into a single one in our mind when the frequency exceeds the CFF of our HVS. It reflects our subjective perception of luminance that changes with time.

Let $L(t)$ be the function that luminance changes with time. T is the period of time in which the light signals can be perceived as single one. L denotes the intensity of luminance perceived by our HVS in this period. Then,

$$L = \frac{1}{T} \int_0^T L(t)dt. \tag{1}$$

Supposing L_1 and L_2 are two luminance signals of one period T, both of them lasts $T/2$. L is the luminance value perceived by our HVS in this period. We have,

$$L = \frac{1}{T}\left(\int_0^{\frac{T}{2}} L_1 dt + \int_{\frac{T}{2}}^T L_2 dt\right) = \frac{L_1 + L_2}{2}. \qquad (2)$$

2.2   Conversion Between Gray Value and Luminance Value

Generally, when an image is displayed on a screen, the luminance value perceived by our HVS and the gray value of the image are not linear correlated. The luminance value are usually exponential correlated with the gray value where the exponent is called gamma value of the screen.

Let I_n and L_n be the normalized gray and luminance value of a display terminal. γ is the gamma value. Then there is a relation as follows,

$$L_n = I_n^\gamma. \qquad (3)$$

Normally, the gray level of a display is often represented by a 8-bit value of the computer system. Therefore, the gray value is usually scaled into $[0, 255]$. In this paper, we normalize the luminance value and multiply it by 255, then it is also in the range of $[0, 255]$. Let I and L be the gray and luminance values which are in $[0, 255]$, then, the gray and luminance value can be converted mutually by the following relations:

$$L = 255 \times \left(\frac{I}{255}\right)^\gamma. \qquad (4)$$

$$I = 255 \times \left(\frac{L}{255}\right)^{\frac{1}{\gamma}}. \qquad (5)$$

2.3   Information Security Display System of [3]

Construction 1. I is the secret image that will be hided on the display, then the system works as follows:

1. Making a mapping table $g2l$ for gray value to luminance;
2. Making a mapping table $l2g$ for luminance value to gray;
3. Mapping the secret image I to luminance image L by mapping table $g2l$;
4. Generating luminance image L_a by inverting the luminance value of L, $L_a = 255 - L$;
5. Generating the auxiliary gray-scaled image I' from L_a by mapping table $l2g$;
6. Displaying images I and I' on the screen alternately at $120\,\mathrm{Hz}$.

Principle of [3] is shown in Fig. 1. Given a secret image I, the system generates an auxiliary image by reversing the luminance value. Then, these two images are displayed in turn at high frequency that is over CFF of our HVS. The luminance views of these two images are blended into a single one in our mind. Therefore, we can only see an uniform gray image from the screen without the help of synchronized glasses.

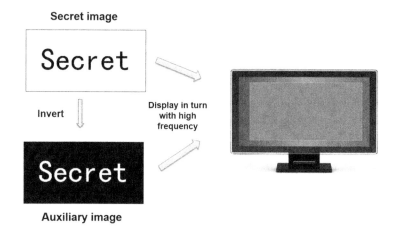

Fig. 1. Principle of information security display system [3]

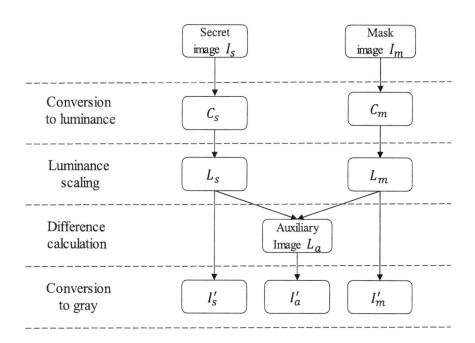

Fig. 2. Design of our scheme. $C_s, C_m, \ldots, L_a$ are temporary images generated by the processes between dotted lines; I'_s and I'_m are secret and auxiliary images that to be displayed on screen; I'_m is the mask image perceived by naked eye viewers.

3   Design and Construction of Our Scheme

Information security display system [3] has the advantage that it only shows secret information for authorized viewers, while the unauthorized get nothing. But if the system presents a mask image for the unauthorized viewers, it will have better cheating effect. Moreover, the system that has mask image allows viewers with different access authorities to watch different contents simultaneously from a single display. Built upon the facilities of [3], we design a new construction of information security display technology which allows meaningful contents for naked eye viewers.

Considering the CFF of our HVS is about 60 Hz, and the refresh rates of modern stereoscopic display is confined to 120 Hz. Only two images are allowed to be blended by our HVS without flicker. The principle of our design is to generate appropriate secret and auxiliary images which can be blended into the mask image by our HVS. Figure 2 shows the details of our design. Specifically, our design is divided into four steps:

Step 1: Conversion to luminance

This step is to calculate the luminance views of secret and mask images which are perceived by our HVS. From the former section, the luminance space of a screen is usually exponential correlated with the gray value. Therefore, to achieve better visual quality, the secret and mask images should be converted to value of luminance space.

Providing the gamma value of the display is γ, then we can covert the gray scaled secret and mask images to luminance space by formula (4).

Step 2: Luminance scaling

Actually, the mask image for unauthorized viewers is not displayed on the screen directly, it is a result of "persistence of vision". Moreover, the luminance space of a screen ranges from 0 to 255. Considering the following cases, if the luminance value of a pixel P_s in secret image is 255, but the luminance value of the pixel P_m in mask image (which has the same position) is 0. According to the color mixture model of our HVS introduced in formula (2), if we want to see luminance view of 0 degree by our HVS, the luminance value of the pixel P_a in auxiliary image should be -255, which is impossible to display. Hence, to ensure the secret and auxiliary images can be displayed, we have to scale the initial luminance space of the images properly.

Supposing the original luminance space of an image ranges from r_l to r_u, and the adjusted luminance space is in $[s_l, s_u]$. Let V_r be a value of the original luminance space, and V_s is the corresponding value of the adjusted luminance space. Then V_s is obtained from V_r by the following relation:

$$V_s = (s_u - s_l)\frac{V_r - r_l}{r_u - r_l} + s_l. \tag{6}$$

Seeing from Fig. 2, by luminance scaling, we get two adjusted luminance views of images, L_s and L_m. L_s is luminance scaled secret image which is also the final view perceived by authorized viewers. While L_m is the adjusted luminance view of mask image, and it is the final view perceived by unauthorized viewers.

Step 3: Difference calculation

The purpose of this step is to generate the luminance view of auxiliary image according to the adjusted views of secret and mask images.

Providing that the luminance space of the adjusted secret image is $[s_l, s_u]$, while the space of the adjusted mask image is $[m_l, m_u]$. V_s, V_m are luminance values of the adjusted secret and mask images respectively. V_a is the luminance value of auxiliary image. Then, according to formula (2), V_a is calculated by:

$$V_a = 2V_m - V_s. \tag{7}$$

Besides, since the luminance value of the auxiliary image generated by the adjusted secret and mask images should be in the range of $[0, 255]$ as well. As a consequence, we have constraint conditions on the range of luminance as follows:

$$\begin{cases} 0 \leqslant 2m_l - s_l \leqslant 255 \\ 0 \leqslant 2m_l - s_u \leqslant 255 \\ 0 \leqslant 2m_u - s_l \leqslant 255 \\ 0 \leqslant 2m_u - s_u \leqslant 255 \\ 0 \leqslant s_l \leqslant s_u \leqslant 255 \\ 0 \leqslant m_l \leqslant m_u \leqslant 255 \end{cases}$$

From the conditions above, we obtain the following relations:

$$(s_u - s_l) + 2(m_u - m_l) \leqslant 255 \tag{8}$$

$$\frac{s_u}{2} \leqslant m_l \leqslant m_u \leqslant \frac{s_l + 255}{2} \tag{9}$$

Hence, if the luminance space of the secret and mask images is scaled into proper range which satisfies formulas (8) and (9), the auxiliary image can be always generated by formula (7).

Step 4: Conversion to gray

See from Fig. 2, by the former steps, we obtain the luminance views of secret image L_s, mask image L_m and auxiliary image L_a. Then, by formula (5), the luminance views can be converted to gray scaled images of display system. I_s' and I_a' are the secret and auxiliary images that displayed on screen; I_m' is the mask image that perceived by naked eye viewers.

Based on the design, we give the formal construction as follows.

Construction 2. I_s is the secret image for authorized viewers, while I_m is the mask image prepared for unauthorized people. γ is the gamma value of the display terminal. Our scheme is implemented by the following steps.

1. Converting secret image I_s and mask image I_m to the corresponding luminance views of images, C_s and C_m, by Eq. (4);

2. Traversing the values of C_s and C_m, and finding the ranges of luminance space respectively, which are denoted as $[cs_l, cs_u]$ and $[cm_l, cm_u]$.
3. Selecting proper values s_l, s_u, m_l and m_u which satisfy formulas (8) and (9);
4. Scaling the luminance values of C_s and C_m from $[cs_l, cs_u], [cm_l, cm_u]$ to $[s_l, s_u]$ and $[m_l, m_u]$ by Eq. (6). The scaled secret and mask images are denoted as L_s and L_m resp.
5. Generating the luminance view of auxiliary image L_a from L_s and L_m by Eq. (7);
6. Converting the luminance views of secret image L_s, auxiliary image L_a and mask image L_m to gray scaled images by Eq. (5) which are denoted as I'_s, I'_a and I'_m resp.
7. Displaying images I'_s and I'_a on the screen alternately at 120 Hz.

Remark. Images I'_s and I'_a displayed on the screen can be perceived as the mask image I'_m by our HVS due to the phenomenon of "persistence of vision". Hence, only viewers wearing synchronized glasses can see the secret image I'_s from display, while the naked eye viewers just observe the mask image I'_m.

4   Experimental Results and Analysis of the Proposed Scheme

In this section, we implement and show the experimental results of our scheme. Here, we use the $NEC^{\circledR}L102W+$ projector as the display system which works at the refresh rate of 120 Hz. Besides, to capture the real visual effect of our HVS, the exposure time of photographic equipment should be adjustable. We choose mobile phone Huawei P9 to capture the experimental results which is confirmed to simulating our HVS well. To illustrate the effectiveness of our scheme, we conduct three experiments in this section. Images for experiments can be seen in Fig. 3.

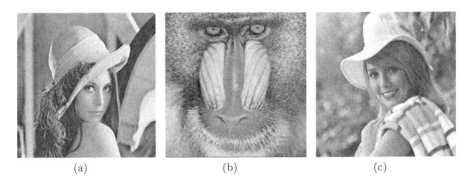

(a)   (b)   (c)

Fig. 3. Three original images used in the experiments: (a) 512×512 "Lena", (b) 512×512 "Baboon", (c) 512×512 "Elaine"

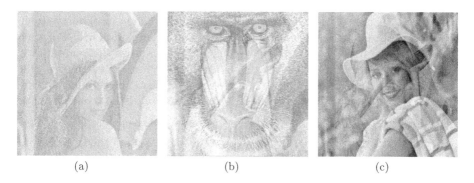

Fig. 4. Secret and auxiliary images: (a) is generated secret image to be displayed on a screen, (b) is the generated auxiliary image in the first case, (b) is generated auxiliary image in the second case.

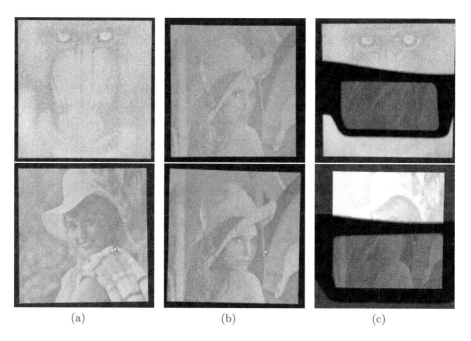

Fig. 5. Visual effect of our scheme. (a) Mask images for unauthorized viewers, seeing by naked eye. (b) Secret images for authorized viewers, photographing through a synchronized glass. (c) Comparison on the visual effect between the two kinds of viewers.

Experiment 1. This experiment is designed to show the rationality and effectiveness of our scheme. The experiment is carried out twice. Here, we use color image "Lena" as the secret information. But selecting different mask image each time. Picture "Baboon" represents color image while "Elaine" is on behalf of gray image. By testing different types of mask images, we can prove the adaptability of our scheme better. Except for the difference in the type of mask images, the parameter settings of the two times are same to each other. The gamma value of display is 2.2. The four luminance values s_l, s_u, m_l and m_u (step 3 of Construction 2) are set as 85, 170, 85 and 170. Exposure time of the camera is $\dfrac{1}{30}$ s. The final secret and auxiliary images generated in the two cases are shown in Fig. 4. Actually, the obtained secret images are the same in these two cases, so we only present one. The real visual effect of our scheme can be seen from Fig. 5.

Experiment 2. In step 3 of Construction 2, we have to select proper luminance values s_l, s_u, m_l and m_u to satisfy formulas (8) and (9). Actually, it is a common sense that when the luminance space of an image is reduced, the contrast will be decreased which may bring down its visual quality. Hence, to take full advantage of the luminance space of a monitor, we only need to select the s_l and s_u in step 3. Other two parameters can be calculated by formulas (8) and (9), then m_l achieves its minimum value while m_u gets its maximum value.

In this experiment, we mainly focus on the influence of luminance values s_l and s_u. We keep the difference of these two values unchanged, and gradually change the value of s_l. Then we will investigate its effect on the visual quality of secret and mask images. The gamma value of display is 2.2. The difference of s_u and s_l equals to 85 which remains unchanged during the experiments. The results of this experiment is shown in Fig. 6.

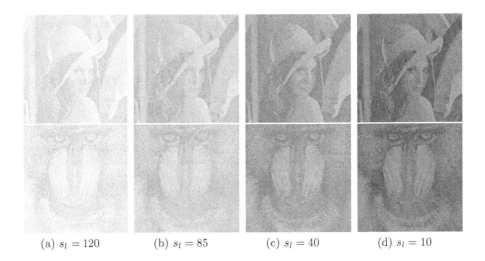

(a) $s_l = 120$ (b) $s_l = 85$ (c) $s_l = 40$ (d) $s_l = 10$

Fig. 6. Influence of luminance value s_l on the visual quality of secret and mask images.

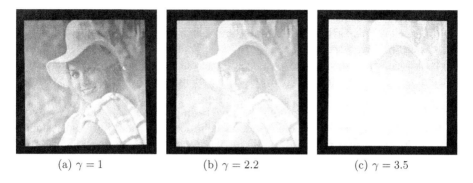

(a) $\gamma = 1$ (b) $\gamma = 2.2$ (c) $\gamma = 3.5$

Fig. 7. Effect of gamma value γ on the visual quality of mask image.

Experiment 3. According to the former design, there are two steps involved with conversion between gray value and luminance value. Here, we experiment on this issue and show the effect of gamma value on the visual quality of mask image. In this experiment, we select "Lena" and "Elaine" as the secret and mask images resp. When the types of secret and mask images are different, our HVS can find the leakage of secret information easier. The four luminance values s_l, s_u, m_l and m_u in step 3 of Construction 2 are set as 85, 170, 85 and 170. Exposure time of the camera is $\dfrac{1}{15}$ s. We can see the experimental results from Fig. 7 for details.

Analysis of the Experimental Results The effectiveness of our scheme is verified by Experiment 1. Seeing from Fig. 5, authorized viewers can get secret information by wearing a pair of synchronized glasses, while the unauthorized only perceive the cover information. Besides, by experimenting with different type of images, our scheme has proved its good adaptability in hiding different kinds of information.

In Experiments 2 and 3, we test the parameters that may influence the visual quality of our scheme. From Fig. 6, we can see that decreasing the value of s_l can improve the visual quality of secret and mask images simultaneously. Hence, when we take full advantage of the luminance space of a screen, we can further improve the visual quality by reducing the minimum luminance value of the secret image. Figure 7 illustrates the importance of luminance conversion. If we don't convert the secret and mask images to the corresponding luminance space according to gamma value of the display terminal properly, the secret information may be at the risk of being perceived by unauthorized viewers.

5   Conclusion and Future Work

In this paper, we investigate the color mixture model based on "persistence of vision" and put forward a new construction method of information security display system. Our method can provide secret and faked information for viewers with different authorization at the same time, which enhances the safety of secret information at a large extent.

The information security display system is one application of "persistence of vision", which combines the characteristics of human vision with the redundancy of high-frequency display well. Based on this typical phenomenon in psychophysics of vision, several technologies have been proposed in recent years. For example, the multi-view technology allows collaborative view port on a single display [6,7,9,11,12]. Moreover, $2 \times 3D$ display technology can provides 2D and 3D images simultaneously with one screen [2,8]. Techniques based on the psychovisual redundancy of high-frequency display bring extraordinary experience to us and may have a wide application prospect in the future.

Acknowledgments. Many thanks to the anonymous reviewers for their valuable comments to improve our work. This work was supported by the National Key R&D Program of China with No. 2016YFB0800100, CAS Strategic Priority Research Program with No. XDA06010701, and NSFC No. 61671448.

References

1. Austin, R.R.: Privacy filter for a display device. US Patent 5,528,319, 18 June 1996
2. Fujimura, W., Koide, Y., Songer, R., Hayakawa, T., Shirai, A., Yanaka, K.: 2x3D: real time shader for simultaneous 2D/3D hybrid theater. In: SIGGRAPH Asia 2012 Emerging Technologies, p. 1. ACM (2012)
3. Gao, Z., Zhai, G., Min, X.: Information security display system based on temporal psychovisual modulation. In: IEEE International Symposium on Circuits and Systems (ISCAS), pp. 449–452. IEEE (2014)
4. Janick, J.M., Locker, H.J., Resnick, R.A.: Privacy filter apparatus for a notebook computer display. US Patent 6,765,550, 20 July 2004
5. Kalloniatis, M., Luu, C.: Temporal resolution (2007)
6. Karnik, A., Mayol-Cuevas, W., Subramanian, S.: MUSTARD: a multi user see through AR display. In: Proceedings of the SIGCHI Conference on Human Factors in Computing Systems, pp. 2541–2550. ACM (2012)
7. Kulik, A., Kunert, A., Beck, S., Reichel, R., Blach, R., Zink, A., Froehlich, B.: C1x6: a stereoscopic six-user display for co-located collaboration in shared virtual environments. ACM Trans. Graph. (TOG) **30**(6), 188 (2011)
8. Scher, S., Liu, J., Vaish, R., Gunawardane, P., Davis, J.: 3D+ 2DTV: 3D displays with no ghosting for viewers without glasses. ACM Trans. Graph. (TOG) **32**(3), 21 (2013)
9. Shoemaker, G.B., Inkpen, K.M.: Single display privacyware: augmenting public displays with private information. In: Proceedings of the SIGCHI Conference on Human Factors in Computing Systems, pp. 522–529. ACM (2001)
10. Wu, X., Zhai, G.: Temporal psychovisual modulation: a new paradigm of information display [exploratory DSP]. IEEE Signal Process. Mag. **30**(1), 136–141 (2013)
11. Ye, G., State, A., Fuchs, H.: A practical multi-viewer tabletop autostereoscopic display. In: 9th IEEE International Symposium on Mixed and Augmented Reality (ISMAR), pp. 147–156. IEEE (2010)
12. Zhai, G., Wu, X.: Multiuser collaborative viewport via temporal psychovisual modulation [applications corner]. IEEE Sig. Process. Mag. **31**(5), 144–149 (2014)

Random Grids-Based Threshold Visual Secret Sharing with Improved Visual Quality

Xuehu Yan$^{(\boxtimes)}$, Yuliang Lu, Lintao Liu, and Song Wan

Hefei Electronic Engineering Institute, Hefei 230037, China
`publictiger@126.com`

Abstract. Visual secret sharing (VSS) by random grids (RG) has gained much attention since it avoids the pixel expansion problem as well as requires no codebook design. However, most of the previous RG-based threshold VSS still suffer from low visual quality or worse reconstructed secrets when more shares are stacked. In this paper, a new RG-based VSS with improved visual quality is proposed. The random bits are utilized to improve the visual quality as well as to decrease the darkness of the reconstructed secret image in the proposed scheme. Experimental results and analyses show the effectiveness of the proposed scheme.

Keywords: Visual cryptography · Visual secret sharing · Random grids · Contrast · Progressive evaluation

1 Introduction

Visual cryptography scheme (VCS) also called visual secret sharing (VSS) [1,2] shares user data into different shares (also called shadows) and distributes them among multiple participants. The decryption of VSS is based on stacking without the needs of cryptographic knowledge and computational devices. It has attracted the attention from scientists and engineers.

Naor and Shamir [1] first proposed the threshold-based VCS [2–9]. In their scheme, a binary secret image is shared by generating corresponding n noise-like shadow images. And any k or more noise-like shadow images are stacking to recover the secret image visually based on human visual system (HVS). However, less than k participants cannot reveal any information of the secret image by inspecting their shares. The main advantage of VCS by [1] is simple recovery, which means the decryption of secret image is completely based on stacking or HVS without any cryptographic computation. However, the scheme suffers from codebook (basic matrices) design and pixel expansion [2]. In order to solve the pixel expansion problem, some previous VCSs without the pixel expansion were proposed. Ito *et al.* [10] proposed the probabilistic VCS by equally selecting a column from corresponding basic matrix. Probabilistic VCS for different thresholds was presented by Yang [4]. Cimato *et al.* [5] further extended the generalization probabilistic VCS.

© Springer International Publishing AG 2017
Y.Q. Shi et al. (Eds.): IWDW 2016, LNCS 10082, pp. 209–222, 2017.
DOI: 10.1007/978-3-319-53465-7_16

VSS by random grids (RG) [11–18] has gained much attention since it can avoid the pixel expansion problem as well as requires no codebook design. Encryption of binary secret images based on RG was first presented by Kafri and Keren [19], each of which is generated into two noise-like RGs (also called shadow images or share images) that have the same size as the original secret image. The decryption operation is the same as traditional VCS. However, the relative RG-based VSS schemes [19–21] are only for cases $(2, 2)$, $(2, n)$ or (n, n).

To achieve the case (k, n), Chen and Tsao [22] proposed a RG-based (k, n) threshold VSS by applying $(2, 2)$ RG-based VSS repeatedly for the first k bits and generating the last $n - k$ bits randomly. Unfortunately, Chen and Tsao's scheme has the limitation of low visual quality of recovered secret image. Then, following Chen and Tsao's work, some RG-based VSS schemes were given to improve the visual quality [15,16,18,23]. Specifically, Guo et $al.$ [23] applied (k, k) threshold for every k bits and $N_k = \lfloor n/k \rfloor$ times, and set the last $n - N_k \times k$ bits randomly. However, since both the last $n - N_k \times k$ bits in Guo et $al.$'s scheme [23] and the last $n - k$ bits in Chen and Tsao's scheme [22] are random, darker reconstructed secrets, poor and unprogressive visual quality will be illustrated when more shares are stacked. Furthermore, in their schemes, (k, k) threshold is generated by serial computation, which may lead to low computational efficiency.

In this paper, a new RG-based VSS approach with improved visual quality is proposed. First, in our design, we performed the (k, k) threshold in parallel to obtain the first k bits. Then, to improve the visual quality, to decrease the darkness as well as to achieve progressive visual quality of the reconstructed secret image, in the proposed scheme, the last $n - k$ bits are set to be equal to the first k bits or white (0). Experimental results and analyses show the effectiveness of the proposed scheme.

The result obtained by the proposed scheme is overall better than those obtained by [22,23]. In addition, the idea of our scheme may be suitable for other schemes.

The rest of the paper is organized as follows. Section 2 introduces some basic requirements and related works for the proposed scheme. In Sect. 3, the proposed scheme is presented in detail. Section 4 is devoted to experimental results. Finally, Sect. 5 concludes this paper.

2   Preliminaries

In this section, we give some preliminaries and related works, i.e., RG-based [22,23] VSS, as the basis for the proposed scheme. In what follows, symbols $\oplus$ and $\otimes$ denote the Boolean XOR and OR operations. $\bar{b}$ is a bitwise complementary operation of a bit b. The binary secret image S is shared among n shadow images, while the recovered secret image S' is recovered from $t(2 \leq t \leq n, t \in Z^+)$ shadow images by stacking. In RG-based VSS, shadow images covered secret after sharing are denoted as SC_p. Here 0 denotes a white pixel and 1 denotes a black pixel.

For a certain pixel x in binary image X with size of $M \times N$, the probability of pixel color is transparent or white (0), is denoted as $P(x = 0)$, and the same for pixel color is opaque or black (1). Besides, $P(S = 0) = 1 - \frac{1}{MN} \sum_{i=1}^{M} \sum_{j=1}^{N} S(i,j), 1 \leq i \leq M, 1 \leq j \leq N$. $AS0$ (resp., $AS1$) denotes the white (resp., black) area of original secret image S defined as $AS0 = \{(i,j)|S(i,j) = 0, 1 \leq i \leq M, 1 \leq j \leq N\}$ (resp., $AS1 = \{(i,j)|S(i,j) = 1, 1 \leq i \leq M, 1 \leq j \leq N\}$).

Definition 1 (Contrast). *The visual quality, which will decide how well human eyes could recognize the recovered image, of the recovered secret image S' corresponding to the original secret image S is evaluated by contrast defined as follows [24]:*

$$\alpha = \frac{P_0 - P_1}{1 + P_1} = \frac{P(S'[AS0] = 0) - P(S'[AS1] = 0)}{1 + P(S'[AS1] = 0)} \tag{1}$$

where α denotes contrast, P_0 (resp., P_1) is the appearance probability of white pixels in the recovered image S' in the corresponding white (resp., black) area of original secret image S, that is, P_0 is the correctly decrypted probability corresponding to the white area of original secret image S, and P_1 is the wrongly decrypted probability corresponding to the black area of original secret image S.

Definition 2 (Visually recognizable). *The recovered secret image S' could be recognized as the corresponding original secret image S if $\alpha > 0$ when $t \geq k$ [1].*

Definition 3 (Security). *The scheme is secure if $\alpha = 0$ when $t < k$ [1], which means no information of S could be recognized through S'.*

Generally speaking, a valid VC construction should satisfy two conditions:

(1) Security condition corresponding to Definition 3: Security condition means that insufficient shares give no clue about secret, i.e., $P_0 = P_1$.
(2) Contrast condition corresponding to Definition 2: Contrast condition indicates that sufficient shares reveal the secret, i.e., $\alpha > 0$.

In addition, traditional VSS has the property of All-or-Nothing, i.e. the secret information could be revealed only when k or more shares are stacked together, and nothing if less than k shares are obtained. In many applications like pay-per-view videos, Pay- TV/Music and art-work image vending, video on demand (VoD), the following feature namely "progressive" is very useful. Progressive visual secret sharing (PVSS) can improve the clarity of a secret image progressively by stacking more and more shares. Although some PVSS schemes [25, 26] were proposed, the progressivity is evaluated only by HVS from the image illustration, the formal definition and evaluation metrics are laked. Thus, the formal definition and evaluation of progressive secret sharing (PSS) will be introduced here based on mathematical differential and expectations, which can be referred by related studies.

Definition 4 (PSS). *A secret sharing scheme is progressive on t in interval $[T_1, T_2]$, if $f(x, t_2) > f(x, t_1) > 0$ when $T_1 \leq t_1 < t_2 \leq T_2$.*
where $f(x, t)$ denotes the quality of the recovered secret image with t shadow images and x indicates other parameters, such as: k or n.

Definition 5 (Progressive rate). *The progressive rate, which will decide how much the quality of the recovered secret image can increase, is defined as follows:*

$$r(x, t) = \frac{\partial f(x, t)}{\partial t} \tag{2}$$

In Definition 5, for mathematical analysis, we assume that $f(x, t)$ is derivable at t although it is not continuous in VSS.

For a certain threshold case x, e.g. (k, n), a scheme may owe different quality of the recovered secret image when t is different, thus we may utilize the contrast mathematical expectations to evaluate the quality of the recovered secret image for case x with t shadow images.

Definition 6 (Quality expectation). $f(x) = \sum_{t=2}^{n} P(x, t) f(x, t)$

where $P(x, t)$ denotes the probability for t, which can be set according to the importance in applications.

In particular, for (k, n) RG-based VSS, we may have $f(x, t) = f(k, n, t) = \alpha(k, n, t)$, $r(x, t) = r(k, n, t) = (\alpha(k, n, t + 1) - \alpha(k, n, t))/1 = \alpha(k, n, t + 1) - \alpha(k, n, t)$. From experience, when $r(k, n, t) \geq 0.05$ we may say $\alpha(k, n, t)$ achieves good progressive performance on t. And $P(x, t) = P(k, n, t)$. If we assume $P(k, n, t) = \frac{1}{n-k+1}$, i.e., different t has the same importance, then

$\alpha(k, n) = \frac{\sum_{t=k}^{n} \alpha(k, n, t)}{n-k+1}$.

The generation and recovery phases of original $(2, 2)$ RG-based VSS are described below.

Step 1: Randomly generate 1 RG SC_1.
Step 2: Compute SC_2 as in Eq. (3).
Recovery: $S' = SC_1 \otimes SC_2$ as in Eq. (4). If a certain secret pixel $s = S(i, j)$ of S is 1, the recovery result $SC_1 \otimes SC_2 = 1$ is always black. If a certain secret pixel is 0, the recovery result $SC_1 \otimes SC_2 = SC_1(i, j) \otimes SC_1(i, j)$ has half chance to be black or white since SC_1 are generated randomly.

$$SC_2(i, j) = \begin{cases} SC_1(i, j) & if\ S(i, j) = 0 \\ \overline{SC_1(i, j)} & if\ S(i, j) = 1 \end{cases} \tag{3}$$

$$S'(i, j) = SC_1(i, j) \otimes SC_2(i, j) = \begin{cases} SC_1(i, j) \otimes SC_1(i, j) & if\ S(i, j) = 0 \\ SC_1(i, j) \otimes \overline{SC_1(i, j)} = 1 & if\ S(i, j) = 1 \end{cases} \tag{4}$$

In fact, Eq. (3) is equal to $sc_2 = sc_1 \oplus s$ or $s = sc_1 \oplus sc_2$. Since if $s = 0 \Rightarrow sc_2 = sc_1 \oplus 0 \Rightarrow sc_2 = sc_1$, and if $s = 1 \Rightarrow sc_2 = sc_1 \oplus 1 \Rightarrow sc_2 = \overline{sc_1}$. The same equation could be extended to $s = sc_1 \oplus sc_2 \oplus \cdots \oplus sc_k$ and the same approach can be extended to (k, n) threshold scheme by applying the above process repeatedly for the first k bits and generating the last n - k bits randomly. (k, n) RG-based VSS is described as follows:

Algorithm 1. Chen and Tsao's (k, n) RG-based VSS

Input: A $M \times N$ binary secret image S, the threshold parameters (k, n)

Output: n shadow images $SC_1, SC_2, \cdots SC_n$

Step 1: For each position $(i, j) \in \{(i, j) | 1 \le i \le M, 1 \le j \le N\}$, repeat Steps 2–6

Step 2: Select $b_1, b_2, \cdots b_k \in \{0, 1\}$ randomly.

Step 3: If $S(i, j) = b_1 \oplus b_2 \cdots \oplus b_k$, go to Step 5; else go to Step 4

Step 4: Randomly select $p \in \{1, 2, \cdots, k\}$ flip $b_p = \overline{b_p}$ (that is $0 \rightarrow 1$ or $1 \rightarrow 0$).

Step 5: Select $b_{k+1}, b_{k+2}, \cdots b_n \in \{0, 1\}$ randomly.

Step 6: Randomly rearrange $b_1, b_2, \cdots b_n$ to $SC_1(i, j), SC_2(i, j), \cdots SC_n(i, j)$

Step 7: Output the n shadow images $SC_1, SC_2, \cdots SC_n$

In addition, Guo et al. [23] improve the visual quality of Chen and Tsao's scheme by computing every k bits by applying (k, k) mechanism for $N_k = \lfloor n/k \rfloor$ times, and setting the last $n - N_k \times k$ bits randomly. Guo et al.'s scheme [23] is described as follows:

Algorithm 2. Guo et al.'s (k, n) RG-based VSS

Input: A $M \times N$ binary secret image S, the threshold parameters (k, n)

Output: n shadow images $SC_1, SC_2, \cdots SC_n$

Step 1: For each position $(i, j) \in \{(i, j) | 1 \le i \le M, 1 \le j \le N\}$, repeat Steps 2–5

Step 2: Select $b_1, b_2, \cdots b_{N_k \times k} \in \{0, 1\}$ randomly, repeat Step 3 for $w = 1, 2, \cdots, N_k = \lfloor n/k \rfloor$

Step 3: If $S(i, j) \ne b_{(w-1)k+1} \oplus b_{(w-1)k+2} \cdots \oplus b_{(w-1)k+k}$, randomly select $p \in \{(w - 1)k + 1, (w - 1)k + 2, \cdots, (w - 1)k + k\}$ flip $b_p = \overline{b_p}$ (that is $0 \rightarrow 1$ or $1 \rightarrow 0$).

Step 4: Select $b_{N_k \times k+1}, b_{N_k \times k+2}, \cdots b_n \in \{0, 1\}$ randomly.

Step 5: Randomly rearrange $b_1, b_2, \cdots b_n$ to $SC_1(i, j), SC_2(i, j), \cdots SC_n(i, j)$

Step 6: Output the n shadow images $SC_1, SC_2, \cdots SC_n$

Based on the above RG-based VSS schemes, both the last $n - N_k \times k$ bits in Guo et al.'s scheme [23] and the last $n - k$ bits in Chen and Tsao's scheme [22] are random, which may lead to darker reconstructed secrets, poor and unprogressive visual quality when more shares are stacked. In addition, (k, k) threshold is generated by serial computation, which may obviously lead to low computational efficiency in their schemes. In this paper, these random bits will be utilized to improve the visual quality by setting them to be equal to the first k bits or white (0), among which (k, k) threshold will be performed by parallel.

3   The Proposed Scheme

There are some random bits, such as the middle $(N_k - 1) \times k$ bits and the last $n - k$ bits in the previous schemes [22,23], which are applied for improving the visual quality in the proposed scheme. Thus the proposed scheme can improve the visual quality.

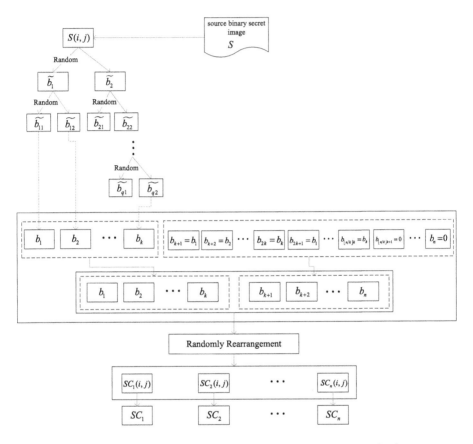

Fig. 1. Shadow images generation architecture of the proposed scheme

The shadow images generation architecture of the proposed scheme is illustrated in Fig. 1, consists of three phases.

1. Generate (k, k) threshold in parallel.
2. Set the next $N_k \times k - k + 2$ bits to be distinct one of the first k bits, the last $n - N_k \times k - 1$ to be 0.
3. Rearrange the generated n bits randomly to corresponding n shadow images bits

---

Algorithm 3. The proposed scheme

Input: A $M \times N$ binary secret image S, the threshold parameters (k, n)

Output: n shadow images $SC_1, SC_2, \cdots SC_n$

Step 1: For each position $(i, j) \in \{(i, j) | 1 \le i \le M, 1 \le j \le N\}$, repeat Steps 2–4

Step 2: To obtain $b_1, b_2, \cdots b_k$ from $S(i, j)$ in parallel one by one repeatedly using Eq. (3) where $\tilde{b}_x$ denotes the temporary pixel

Step 3: Compute $N_k = \lfloor n/k \rfloor$, set $b_{k+1} = b_1, b_{k+2} = b_2, \cdots b_{2k} = b_k, b_{2k+1} = b_1, \cdots b_{N_k \times k} = b_k$ and $b_{N_k \times k+1} = b_{N_k \times k+2} = b_n = 0$

Step 4: Randomly rearrangement $b_1, b_2, \cdots b_n$ to $SC_1(i, j), SC_2(i, j), \cdots SC_n(i, j)$

Step 5: Output the n shadow images $SC_1, SC_2, \cdots SC_n$

The algorithmic steps are described below.

The secret recovery of the proposed scheme is also based on stacking ($\otimes$) or HVS.

The idea of our Algorithm is described precisely as follows:

There are random bits in the last $n - k$ bits. The random bits could be utilized to gain better properties, such as threshold mechanism, and improving the visual quality. In step 2, the k bits are utilized in parallel to gain threshold mechanism, i.e., when less than k shadow images are collected, the secret will not be revealed. While in Step 3, first we set the next $N_k \times k - k + 2$ bits to be distinct one of the first k bits to improve the probability of covering $b_1, b_2, \cdots b_k$ so as to improve the visual quality of recovered secret image. Then the last $n - N_k \times k - 1$ are set to be 0, aiming to decrease the darkness of the reconstructed secret image, in the proposed scheme. As a result, progressive visual quality of the revealed secret image will be gained. In step 4, in order to make all the shadow images be equal to each other, the generated n bits are randomly rearranged to corresponding n shadow images bits.

We note that, for pages limitation, we omit theoretical analysis about security and contrast.

4   Experimental Results and Analyses

In this section, we conduct experiments and analyses to evaluate the effectiveness of the proposed scheme. In the experiments, two secret images are used: original binary secret image1 as shown in Fig. 2(a), and original binary secret image2 as shown in Fig. 3(a) are used as the binary secret images, with size of 512×512, to test the efficiency of the proposed scheme.

4.1   Image Illustration

To test $(3, 4)$ (i.e. $k = 3, n = 4$) threshold of our scheme with secret image1, Fig. 2 (b–e) show the 4 shadow images SC_1, SC_2, SC_3 and SC_4, which are noise-like. Figure 2 (f–j) show the recovered secret images with any 3 or 4 shadow images with stacking recovery, from which the secret image recovered from $k = 3$ or more shadow images could be recognized based on superposition. Figure 2 (k–p) show the recovered secret image with any less than $k = 3$ shadow images based on stacking recovery, from which there is no information could be recognized.

The next experiments, we only give the results by the first t th shadow images for saving pages.

Secret image2 is used to do the test for case (2,5). Figure 3 (b) shows one of the 5 shadow images, which is noise-like. Figure 3 (c–f) show the recovered binary secret image with any t ($2 \leq t \leq 5$) (taking the first t shadow images as an example) with stacking recovery, from which better visual of the recovered secret will be gained by superposing more shadow images.

Based on the above results we can conclude that:

1. The shadow images are noise-like, every single shadow image can not disclose the secret image.
2. When $t < k$ shadow images are collected, there is no information of the secret image could be recognized, which shows the security of the proposed scheme.
3. When $t(k \leq t \leq n)$ shadow images are recovered by stacking, the secret image could be recognized by HVS, which indicates our scheme is visually recognizable.
4. The progressive visual quality of the recovered secret can be achieved when more shares are superposing.

4.2   Visual Quality of the Recovered Secret Images

The visual quality of the recovered secret images is evaluated by contrast in Definition 1. The same original binary secret image as shown in Fig. 3(a) is used to do the experiments of contrast.

Table 1. Average contrast of the proposed scheme

(k, n)	Average contrast of proposed scheme			
	$t = 2$	$t = 3$	$t = 4$	$t = 5$
$(2, 2)$	0.49953			
$(2, 3)$	0.12626	0.50168		
$(3, 3)$		0.25197		
$(2, 4)$	0.28578	0.50008	0.50008	
$(3, 4)$		0.05314	0.25084	
$(4, 4)$			0.124	
$(2, 5)$	0.1555	0.3656	0.50216	0.50216
$(3, 5)$		0.02154	0.08948	0.2525
$(4, 5)$			0.02571	0.12773
$(5, 5)$				0.06275

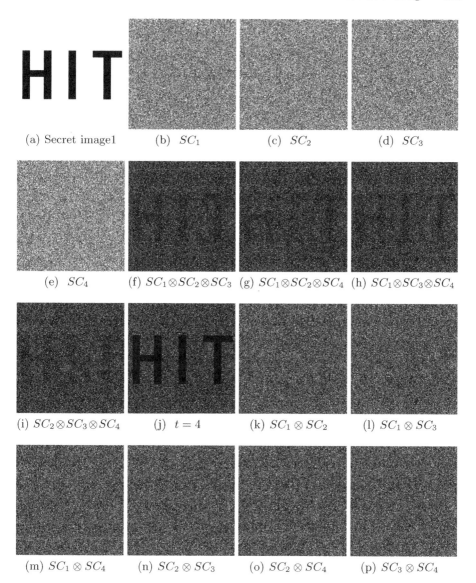

Fig. 2. Experimental example of the proposed (3, 4) scheme

Average contrast for different shadow images combinations of the proposed $(k, n)(2 \leq k \leq n)$ scheme is shown in Table 1, where t denotes the number of recovered shadow images.

From Table 1, we can find that, in the proposed scheme, $\alpha > 0$ when $t \geq k$ and contrast increases as t increases for a certain (k, n) by superposing when $2 \leq n \leq 5$. Thus, for case (k, n), our scheme is progressive on t in

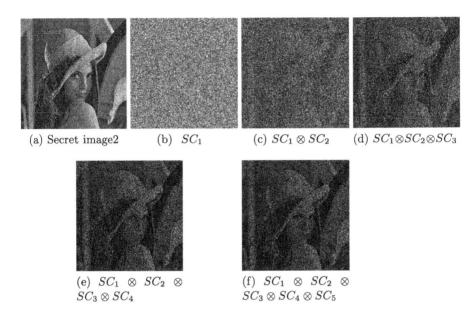

(a) Secret image2   (b) SC_1 (c) $SC_1 \otimes SC_2$ (d) $SC_1 \otimes SC_2 \otimes SC_3$

(e) $SC_1 \otimes SC_2 \otimes$ (f) $SC_1 \otimes SC_2 \otimes$
$SC_3 \otimes SC_4$ $SC_3 \otimes SC_4 \otimes SC_5$

Fig. 3. Experimental example of the proposed (2, 5) scheme

interval $[k, n]$ or $[k, n-1]$. The experimental results of the contrast further verify the validity of our scheme.

4.3 Comparisons with Related Schemes

Herein, we compare the proposed scheme with other related schemes especially Chen and Tsao's scheme [22] and Guo *et al.*'s scheme [23] in terms of image illustration and contrast. since both the proposed scheme and [23] are a continuous and extension work of the scheme in [22]. In addition, schemes in [22,23] have good features in VSS, such as no codebook design, no pixel expansion and so on.

Image Illustration Comparison. Here, (2, 5) threshold with $k \leq t \leq n$ is also applied for comparison. The simulation results of Chen and Tsao's scheme and Guo *et al.*'s scheme are illustrated in Figs. 4 and 5, respectively. We can see that Guo *et al.*'s scheme improves the visual quality of Chen and Tsao's scheme. From Figs. 3, 4 and 5, Guo *et al.*'s scheme and Chen and Tsao's scheme are darker, while the darkness of the proposed scheme is acceptable, since $sc_1 \otimes sc_2 \otimes \cdots \otimes sc_k \cdots \otimes sc_{n-1} \otimes sc_n = sc_1 \otimes sc_2 \otimes \cdots \otimes sc_k$ in the proposed scheme. Hence, the proposed scheme overall outperforms the other two in terms of darkness and progressive property for the case.

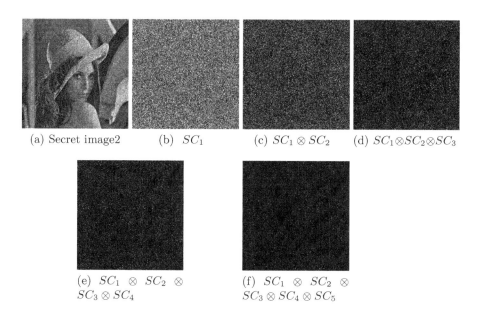

(a) Secret image2   (b) SC_1 (c) $SC_1 \otimes SC_2$ (d) $SC_1 \otimes SC_2 \otimes SC_3$

(e) $SC_1 \otimes SC_2 \otimes SC_3 \otimes SC_4$

(f) $SC_1 \otimes SC_2 \otimes SC_3 \otimes SC_4 \otimes SC_5$

Fig. 4. Experimental example of Chen and Tsao's $(2, 5)$ scheme

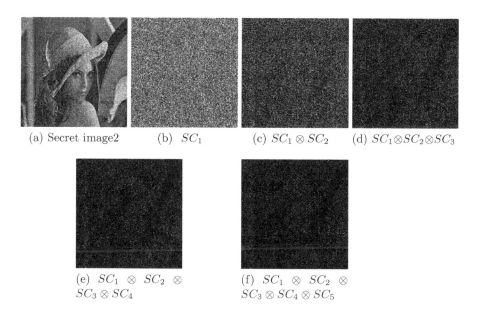

(a) Secret image2   (b) SC_1 (c) $SC_1 \otimes SC_2$ (d) $SC_1 \otimes SC_2 \otimes SC_3$

(e) $SC_1 \otimes SC_2 \otimes SC_3 \otimes SC_4$

(f) $SC_1 \otimes SC_2 \otimes SC_3 \otimes SC_4 \otimes SC_5$

Fig. 5. Experimental example of Guo *et al.*'s $(2, 5)$ scheme

Contrast Comparison. Table 2 shows contrast of Chen and Tsao's scheme and Guo *et al.*'s scheme with all $(k, n)(2 \leq n \leq 5, 2 \leq k \leq n, k \leq t \leq n)$. Remark: The theoretical contrast of the proposed scheme is not given directly by k, t and n, hence the contrast comparisons are given by experiments. In addition, Definition 1 is a statistical result. Thus, the experimental results are close to the theoretical contrast.

Based on Tables 1 and 2, we have the following conclusions:

Table 2. Contrast of Chen and Tsao's scheme and Guo *et al.*'s scheme

(k, n)	Chen and Tsao's scheme				Guo *et al.*'s scheme			
	$t = 2$	$t = 3$	$t = 4$	$t = 5$	$t = 2$	$t = 3$	$t = 4$	$t = 5$
$(2, 2)$	0.50283				0.49995			
$(2, 3)$	0.14466	0.2519			0.1445	0.2526		
$(3, 3)$		0.25119				0.2503		
$(2, 4)$	0.06847	0.11742	0.12501		0.14274	0.2499	0.24992	
$(3, 4)$		0.05717	0.1255			0.0581	0.12632	
$(4, 4)$			0.12499				0.12474	
$(2, 5)$	0.04237	0.07034	0.07415	0.06311	0.08419	0.1434	0.15017	0.12493
$(3, 5)$		0.0237	0.04916	0.06317		0.0224	0.04801	0.06222
$(4, 5)$			0.02535	0.06391			0.02347	0.0616
$(5, 5)$				0.06301				0.06264

1. The contrast of the proposed scheme is overall similar as or greater than others except case $(2, 3)$ with $t = 2$.
2. In our scheme for case $(2, 3)$, two bits of b_1, b_2, b_3 are 0, thus P_1 will be increased. As a result, from Definition 1 contrast will be decreased.
3. If $t = n$ for case (n, n), the contrast of the proposed scheme is nearly the same as that of the others, since they reduce to the same algorithm.
4. The proposed scheme is overall greater than others for the other (k, n) cases when $n - k \geq 0$. Especially for cases $(2, 4)$ and $(2, 5)$, the contrast of the proposed scheme achieves 0.5. Tacking case $(2, 5)$ as an example, our $\alpha(2, 5) = \frac{\sum_{t=2}^{5} \alpha(k,n,t)}{4} = 0.38136$ according to Definition 6, while that of Chen and Tsao's scheme and Guo *et al.*'s scheme are 0.0625 and 0.1257, respectively, Thus, our contrast expectation is greater than theirs. Furthermore, by Definition 5, our $r(2, 5, 2) = \alpha(2, 5, 3) - \alpha(2, 5, 2) = 0.2101$, while that of Chen and Tsao's scheme and Guo *et al.*'s scheme are 0.02761 and 0.05921, respectively. Hence, our Progressive rate is better than theirs. Because the probability of correctly collecting the first k bits of the proposed scheme is larger than that of the others.

5. The contrast of stacking $t = n - 1$ is the same as that of stacking $t = n$ for cases $(2,4)$ and $(2,5)$, since $sc_1 \otimes sc_2 \otimes \cdots \otimes sc_k \cdots \otimes sc_{n-1} \otimes sc_n = sc_1 \otimes sc_2 \otimes \cdots \otimes sc_k$ in the proposed scheme.
6. The idea of our scheme may be applied in Guo *et al.*'s scheme and other schemes to improve their visual quality.

5 Conclusion

This paper proposed a new RG-based progressive VSS with improved visual quality as well as less darkness by in parallel utilizing the last $n - k$ bits are set to be equal to the first k bits or white (0), which outperformed relative schemes in terms of image illustration and contrast. The probability of correctly reconstructing the secret pixels is improved, whose successful points lie in: (1) (k, n) threshold by parallel, (2) requiring no codebook design, (3) avoiding the pixel expansion problem, (4) setting the random bits to be equal to the previous bits or white to achieve larger visual quality and less darkness than the previous related schemes. However, the contrast of the proposed scheme is not given directly by k, t and n, which is left as an open problem for further studies. The idea of our scheme in the future may be extended to other schemes to improve the visual quality.

Acknowledgement. The authors would like to thank the anonymous reviewers for their valuable comments. This work is supported by the National Natural Science Foundation of China (Grant Number: 61602491).

References

1. Naor, M., Shamir, A.: Visual cryptography. In: Santis, A. (ed.) EUROCRYPT 1994. LNCS, vol. 950, pp. 1–12. Springer, Heidelberg (1995). doi:10.1007/BFb0053419
2. Weir, J., Yan, W.Q.: A comprehensive study of visual cryptography. In: Shi, Y.Q. (ed.) Transactions on Data Hiding and Multimedia Security V. LNCS, vol. 6010, pp. 70–105. Springer, Heidelberg (2010). doi:10.1007/978-3-642-14298-7_5
3. Yan, X., Wang, S., El-Latif, A.A.A., Niu, X.: Visual secret sharing based on random grids with abilities of AND and XOR lossless recovery. Multimedia Tools Appl., 1–22 (2013)
4. Yang, C.N.: New visual secret sharing schemes using probabilistic method. Pattern Recognit. Lett. **25**(4), 481–494 (2004)
5. Cimato, S., De Prisco, R., De Santis, A.: Probabilistic visual cryptography schemes. Comput. J. **49**(1), 97–107 (2006)
6. Wang, D., Zhang, L., Ma, N., Li, X.: Two secret sharing schemes based on Boolean operations. Pattern Recognit. **40**(10), 2776–2785 (2007)
7. Wang, Z., Arce, G.R., Di Crescenzo, G.: Halftone visual cryptography via error diffusion. IEEE Trans. Inf. Forensics Secur. **4**(3), 383–396 (2009)
8. Li, P., Ma, P.J., Su, X.H., Yang, C.N.: Improvements of a two-in-one image secret sharing scheme based on gray mixing model. J. Visual Commun. Image Represent. **23**(3), 441–453 (2012)

9. Yan, X., Wang, S., El-Latif, A.A.A., Niu, X.: Random grids-based visual secret sharing with improved visual quality via error diffusion. Multimedia Tools Appl., 1–18 (2014)
10. Kuwakado, H., Tanaka, H.: Image size invariant visual cryptography. IEICE Trans. Fundam. Electron. Commun. Comput. Sci. **82**(10), 2172–2177 (1999)
11. De Prisco, R., De Santis, A.: On the relation of random grid and deterministic visual cryptography. IEEE Trans. Inf. Forensics Secur. **9**(3–4), 653–665 (2014)
12. Yang, C.N., Wu, C.C., Wang, D.S.: A discussion on the relationship between probabilistic visual cryptography and random grid. Inf. Sci. **278**, 141–173 (2014)
13. Fu, Z., Yu, B.: Visual cryptography and random grids schemes. In: Shi, Y.Q., Kim, H.-J., Pérez-González, F. (eds.) IWDW 2013. LNCS, vol. 8389, pp. 109–122. Springer, Heidelberg (2014). doi:10.1007/978-3-662-43886-2_8
14. Wu, X., Sun, W.: Extended capabilities for XOR-based visual cryptography. IEEE Trans. Inf. Forensics Secur. **9**(10), 1592–1605 (2014)
15. Yan, X., Liu, X., Yang, C.N.: An enhanced threshold visual secret sharing based on random grids. J. Real-Time Image Process., 1–13 (2015)
16. Wu, X., Sun, W.: Improved tagged visual cryptography by random grids. Signal Process. **97**, 64–82 (2014)
17. Lee, Y.S., Wang, B.J., Chen, T.H.: Quality-improved threshold visual secret sharing scheme by random grids. Image Process. IET **7**(2), 137–143 (2013)
18. Yan, X., Wang, S., Niu, X.: Threshold construction from specific cases in visual cryptography without the pixel expansion. Signal Process. **105**, 389–398 (2014)
19. Kafri, O., Keren, E.: Encryption of pictures and shapes by random grids. Opt. Lett. **12**(6), 377–379 (1987)
20. Shyu, S.J.: Image encryption by multiple random grids. Pattern Recogn. **42**, 1582–1596 (2009)
21. Guo, T., Liu, F., Wu, C.: K out of K extended visual cryptography scheme by random grids. Signal Process. **94**, 90–101 (2014)
22. Chen, T.H., Tsao, K.H.: Threshold visual secret sharing by random grids. J. Syst. Softw. **84**(7), 1197–1208 (2011)
23. Guo, T., Liu, F., Wu, C.: Threshold visual secret sharing by random grids with improved contrast. J. Syst. Softw. **86**(8), 2094–2109 (2013)
24. Shyu, S.J.: Image encryption by random grids. Pattern Recogn. **40**(3), 1014–1031 (2007)
25. Hou, Y.C., Quan, Z.Y.: Progressive visual cryptography with unexpanded shares. IEEE Trans. Circ. Syst. Video Tech. **21**(11), 1760–1764 (2011)
26. Yan, X., Wang, S., Niu, X.: Threshold progressive visual cryptography construction with unexpanded shares. Multimedia Tools Appl., 1–18 (2015)

Halftone Visual Cryptography
with Complementary Cover Images

Gang Shen[1]($\boxtimes$), Feng Liu[2,3], Zhengxin Fu[1], Bin Yu[1], and Wen Wang[2]

[1] Zhengzhou Information Science and Technology Institute,
Zhengzhou 450001, China
shengang_zisti@163.com
[2] State Key Laboratory of Information Security,
Institute of Information Engineering, Chinese Academy of Sciences,
Beijing 100093, China
[3] School of Cyber Security, University of Chinese Academy of Sciences,
Beijing 100093, China

Abstract. By the addition of halftone techniques, halftone visual cryptography scheme (HVCS) embeds a secret image into halftone shares taking meaningful visual information. In this paper, we propose a (k, n)-HVCS using complementary cover images. Before the halftone processing of the cover images by error diffusion, secret information pixels (SIPs) are prefixed based on the underlying (k, n)-VCS. In the halftone processing, several pairs of complementary cover images are adopted and two halftone methods on the cover images are designed for different (k, n) threshold access structures. The proposed scheme removes the share's cross interference from other shares and obtains better visual quality. Furthermore, the proposed scheme eliminates the burden that each participant may carry multiple shares.

Keywords: Visual cryptography · Visual secret sharing · Extended visual cryptography · Halftone visual cryptography · Meaningful shares

1 Introduction

Naor and Shamir [5] introduced a variant form of secret sharing, called visual cryptography scheme (VCS) that is usually referred to as visual secret sharing. Particularly in a (k, n)-VCS, each pixel of the black-and-white secret image is encoded into m subpixels, referred to as pixel expansion, for each of the n shares (distributed to n participants respectively) by designing two collections of $n \times m$ Boolean matrices C^0 and C^1. To encode a white pixel, the dealer randomly chooses one of the matrices in C^0, and to encode a black pixel, the dealer randomly chooses one of the matrices in C^1. The chosen matrix defines the color of the m subpixels in each of the shares. If any k or more shares are stacked together, our eyes can perceive the secret information due to the darkness difference, referred to as contrast, between black pixels and white pixels in the

© Springer International Publishing AG 2017
Y.Q. Shi et al. (Eds.): IWDW 2016, LNCS 10082, pp. 223–237, 2017.
DOI: 10.1007/978-3-319-53465-7_17

stacked result, while if fewer than k shares are superimposed it is impossible to perceive the secret information.

In a VCS, all shares consisting of random pixel patterns do not take any visual information and may lead to suspicion of secret information encryption. Moreover, managing an increasing number of meaningless shares is challenging since the shares are difficult to manage or use and require careful labeling and storage. Shares showing meaningful images are more desirable in terms of the steganography aspects.

To cater for this need, several extended VCSs (EVCSs), where the shares contain both visual information of the cover images and the secret information, were presented by manipulating the basis matrices [1,2,8]. Then, Nakajima et al. [4] extended the $(2,2)$-EVCS to natural grayscale images. Tsai et al. [6] proposed a transformation method that can transfer any basis matrices of VCSs to generate meaningful shares, where its shares are simply generated by replacing the white and black subpixels in a traditional VCS share with transparent pixels and pixels from natural colourful images, respectively. Yang and Yang [11] developed an EVCS by using the range distribution instead of the fixed pattern. The major shortcomings with these methods are poor visual quality of the shares, no (k,n) threshold, unsatisfied security or contrast conditions, or cross interference from the shares on the reconstructed secret image.

To avoid the above drawbacks, halftone VCS (HVCS) is proposed, where the secret image is embedded into meaningful shares obtained by the halftone processing of the grayscale cover images. Generally, a share in an HVCS is made up of two parts: secret information pixels (SIPs) carrying the secret information and non-SIPs carrying the visual information of cover images. First, Zhou et al. [12] used complementary cover images to avoid the cross interference from the shares on the reconstructed secret image, however, for general access structures multiple shares may be hold by each participant, which is a burden on the share management. Then, three HVCSs were developed by Wang et al. [9] based on error diffusion. Just as the way proposed in [12], Wang et al.'s first method also faces the same drawback. Wang et al.'s second method introduces auxiliary black pixels (ABPs), a part of the non-SIPs, to avoid the cross interference from the shares on the reconstructed secret image, but more ABPs are imported so that the visual quality of shares is degraded. In Wang et al.'s third method, less ABPs are imported, whereas the share's cross interference from other shares is introduced due to the ABPs' selection relying on the image content of the shares. Liu et al. [3] proposed an HVCS by using the special design of dithering matrix to avoid the cross interference from the shares on the reconstructed secret image, however, the cover images are darkened before the halftone processing, which inevitably affects the visual quality of the shares. Recently, Yan et al. [10] generalized Wang et al.'s third method [9], but decreasing the share's cross interference from other shares still remains to be solved.

In this paper, to avoid the share's cross interference from other shares and improve the visual quality of shares, we propose an HVCS with complementary cover images through error diffusion. Before the halftone processing, the location of SIPs is prefixed. In the halftone processing, complementary cover images are adopted to avoid the cross interference from the shares on the reconstructed secret image. Moreover, two halftone methods on the cover images for different (k, n) cases are put forward to ensure each participant receive only one share. Finally, the additional quantization errors introduced by SIPs and non-SIPs are diffused away by error diffusion to the neighboring grayscale pixels, and hence better visual quality of the halftone shares is achieved.

The rest of this paper is organized as follows. Section 2 introduces some preliminaries for the proposed scheme. In Sect. 3, the proposed scheme is presented in detail. Section 4 proves the validity of the proposed scheme and analyzes the visual quality of the halftone shares theoretically. To show the effectiveness and advantages of our scheme, experimental results and comparisons are given in Sect. 5. Finally, this paper is concluded in Sect. 6.

2   Preliminaries

This section provides the model of VCS where some terms and concepts will be referenced in subsequent sections. An introduction of error diffusion is also provided.

2.1   The Model of VCS

The secret image of this paper consists of a collection of black and white pixels. A white pixel is identified as 0 while a black pixel is identified as 1. Each pixel is shared separately. To understand the sharing process consider the case where the secret image consists of just a single black or white pixel. On sharing, this pixel appears in the n shares distributed to the participants. Generally, a secret pixel is encrypted into m subpixels in each share and thus the size of each share is m times the size of the secret image. This m is called the pixel expansion. We further assume that the subpixels are sufficiently small and close enough so that human visual system averages them to some shade of gray. In order that the recovered image is clearly discernible, it is important that the gray level of a black pixel be darker than that of a white pixel. Actually, to construct a VCS, it is sufficient to construct the basis matrices corresponding to the black and white pixel. The collections of matrices C^0 and C^1 are obtained by giving all possible column permutations to the basis matrices S^0 and S^1 respectively. As a result, the dealer has to store only the two basis matrices S^0 and S^1, making the scheme efficient space-wise. In the following, we formally define what is meant by basis matrices.

Notations: Suppose $P = \{1, 2, \ldots, n\}$ be a set of participants. Let M be an $n \times m$ Boolean matrix and $X = \{i_1, i_2, \ldots, i_p\} \subseteq P$. Then M_X denotes the $|X| \times m$ submatrix obtained from M by considering its restriction to rows corresponding to the elements in X. $\otimes(M_X)$ denotes the stacking (Boolean OR) operation to the rows of M_X. $\omega(\otimes(M_X))$ denotes the Hamming weight of the row vector $\otimes(M_X)$, which denotes the number of 1's in the vector $\otimes(M_X)$.

Definition 1. *Two $n \times m$ basis matrices S^0 and S^1 constitute a (k, n)-VCS if the following conditions are satisfied:*

1. *Any k or more participants can recover the secret image. Formally, for $|X| \geq k$, we have $\omega(\otimes(S_X^1)) > \omega(\otimes(S_X^0))$.*
2. *Any less than k participants have no information on the shared image. Formally, for $|X| < k$, S_X^1 and S_X^0 are identical up to a column permutation.*

The first property is related to the contrast of the reconstructed secret image. It states that when a qualified set of participants stack their shares they can perceive the secret information due to the darkness difference. Usually, the contrast is defined as follows:

$$\alpha = \frac{\omega(\otimes(S_X^1)) - \omega(\otimes(S_X^0))}{m}, \tag{1}$$

where α $(0 \leq \alpha \leq 1)$. It is lucid that for a valid VCS, $\alpha = 0$ if $|X| < k$ and $\alpha > 0$ when $|X| \geq k$. From the point of view of participants, the contrast α is expected to be as large as possible.

The second property is called security, since it implies that, even by inspecting all their shares, a forbidden set of participants cannot gain any information in deciding whether the shared pixel was white or black.

2.2 Error Diffusion

Error diffusion is a simple, yet efficient algorithm to realize the halftone processing of a grayscale image. The error means the difference between the original grayscale pixel value and its final halftone pixel value. The quantization error at each pixel is diffused away to the neighboring grayscale pixels. Figure 1 shows the flow chart of error diffusion where $C(i, j)$ represents the (i, j)th pixel of the input grayscale image, $D(i, j)$ is the sum of the input pixel value and the diffused past errors, and $HS(i, j)$ is the output quantized pixel value. Error diffusion consists of two main components. The first component is the thresholding block where the output $HS(i, j)$ is given by

$$HS(i, j) = \begin{cases} 1, & if \ D(i, j) \geq T(i, j) \\ 0, & otherwise. \end{cases} \tag{2}$$

The threshold $T(i, j)$ can be position-dependent and the threshold modulation shown in Eq. (3), which tries to adjust the current threshold by using the information of three preceding halftone pixels, is adopted in this paper,

$$T(i, j) = 0.25 + 0.33 \times 0.25 \times [HS(i, j-1) + HS(i, j-2) + HS(i, j-3)]. \tag{3}$$

The second component is the error diffusion matrix $H(k, l)$ whose input $E(i, j)$ is the difference between $D(i, j)$ and $H(i, j)$. Herein, the widely used Floyd-Steinberg error diffusion matrix in Eq. (4) is applied in this paper,

$$H(k, l) = \begin{bmatrix} 0 & (i, j) & \frac{7}{16} \\ \frac{3}{16} & \frac{5}{16} & \frac{1}{16} \end{bmatrix}. \tag{4}$$

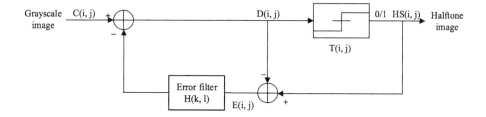

Fig. 1. The flowchart of error diffusion.

Finally, we can compute $D(i, j)$ as

$$D(i, j) = C(i, j) - \sum_{k,l} H(k, l)E(i - k, j - l). \tag{5}$$

The recursive structure of error diffusion indicates that the quantization error $E(i, j)$ depends not only on the current input and out but also on the entire past history. The errors introduced by SIPs and non-SIPs of Sect. 3 in this paper are high frequency or blue noise in nature, and they are diffused away by the error diffusion matrix $H(k, l)$, leading to visually pleasing halftone shares.

3   The Proposed Scheme

The proposed HVCS with complementary cover images is built upon the fundamental principles of VCS. Given a binary secret image and multiple grayscale cover images including some complementary pairs, n halftone shares are generated such that the resultant shares are no longer random patterns, but take meaningful visual images. Stacking at least k shares will reconstruct the secret, while stacking less than k shares gives no clue about the secret.

3.1   Problem Description

In a (k, n)-HVCS, each halftone share is divided into non-overlapping halftone cells of size $q = v_1 \times v_2$, where $q > m$. For a secret pixel, the encoded m pixels by a (k, n)-VCS is embedded into one halftone cell in each share. Within the q pixels in a halftone cell, only the m pixels are called secret information pixels (SIPs), which really carry the secret information. The remaining $q - m$ pixels, called non-SIPs, carry the visual information of the cover images. From the point of view of information coding theory, $q \geq 2m$ is suggested to obtain good visual quality of shares.

In general, it is required that when all qualified shares are stacked together, only the secret visual information is revealed. Thus, to prevent the cross interference from shares on the reconstructed secret image, it should be satisfied for non-SIPs to be all black in the reconstructed halftone cell. To the best of our knowledge, there are four methods to achieve this goal, which are analyzed as follows:

1. With the aid of auxiliary black pixels [9]. Over the non-SIPs, There are some pixels that are forced to be black (value 1) called auxiliary black pixels (ABPs), while the remaining pixels are responsible for carrying the information of halftone shares. ABPs are deliberately introduced into the shares so that the visual information of one share is completely blocked by the ABPs on the other shares. But, a sufficient number of ABPs are usually needed and hence less pixels carry the information of halftone shares, leading to a poor visual quality of the shares.

2. Exploiting parallel halftone processing [9,10]. This method is based on the fact that the halftone processing of grayscale images alone may generate a sufficient number of black pixels to block the share visual information from showing on the reconstructed image. Within the halftone processing, all the shares are checked at each non-SIP position to see if a sufficient number of black pixels have been produced. If a sufficient number of black pixels have not yet been generated, black pixels are deliberately inserted at that position. Obviously, the decision to insert a black pixel or not depends on the image content of the shares. Thus, there exists the share's cross interference from other shares.

3. Designing dithering matrix [3]. By the special design of dithering matrix, the grayscale cover images are converted into halftone shares, where the stacking results of the qualified shares are all black images. This method requires that the gray-levels of all the pixels in each grayscale cover image have to be not too large. Images that do not satisfy this requirement need to be darkened before the halftone processing, which will inevitably cause the loss in the visual quality of the shares.

4. Using complementary pairs of halftone shares [9,12]. A pair of complementary shares can be employed to block all the share's visual information from showing on the reconstructed image. The generated halftone shares in the general scheme must satisfy that any qualified set of shares contains at least one pair of complementary halftone shares. This requirement, however, may not be satisfiable for all access structures unless each participant is distributed more than one share.

According to the above analysis, there is a natural question we can ask: can we put forward such a method that the cross interference from shares on the reconstructed secret image, the share's cross interference from other shares, poor visual quality of shares and multiple shares per participant will be avoid in all?

3.2   SIP Assignment

In the embedding process of SIPs, for security purposes, the distribution of SIPs should be independent of their values. Moreover, to achieve good quality of shares, it is also desirable to distribute the SIPs homogeneously so that one SIP is maximally separated from its neighboring SIPs. Since the SIPs are maximally separated, the quantization error caused by an SIP will be diffused away before the next SIP is encountered leading to visually pleasing halftone shares. To the best of our knowledge, we adopt the void and cluster algorithm (please refer to [7] for details) to distribute the SIPs in this paper.

After the distribution of SIPs is generated, the next step is to assign the values to all the SIPs. This procedure only depends on the underlying VCS. Under the (k,n)-VCS, the basis matrices S^0 and S^1 are constructed first. Then construct a pair of collections of matrices (C^0, C^1) from the basis matrices. For each m SIPs of a halftone cell, a matrix M is randomly selected from C^0 and C^1 according to the value of the corresponding secret image pixel. The values of SIPs in the uth share are then replaced with the uth row of M.

In summary, the distribution and values of the SIPs can be fixed prior to the generation of halftone shares.

3.3   Non-SIP Assignment

To answer the question raised in the first subsection, in this subsection we use the complementary cover images and propose two non-SIP assignments for different (k,n) thresholds to block all the share's visual information from showing on the reconstructed image.

Suppose there are n grayscale cover images $C_1, C_2, \ldots, C_n$ including λ, $1 \leq \lambda \leq \lfloor \frac{n}{2} \rfloor$, pairs of complementary grayscale images and $n-2\lambda$ arbitrary grayscale images. Let c_u $(0 \leq c_u \leq 1)$ denote a pixel value in the grayscale cover image C_u, $1 \leq u \leq n$. Without loss of generality, the pixels of n grayscale cover images are listed in sequence as $\{c_1, \overline{c_1}, c_3, \overline{c_3}, \ldots, c_{2\lambda-1}, \overline{c_{2\lambda-1}}, \ldots, c_n\}$, where $(c_{2v-1}, \overline{c_{2v-1}})$, $1 \leq v \leq \lambda$, is the vth complementary pair of grayscale cover pixels. We call $A = [a_1, a_2, \ldots, a_n]^T$, where $a_u \in \{c_1, \overline{c_1}, c_3, \overline{c_3}, \ldots, c_{2\lambda-1}, \overline{c_{2\lambda-1}}, \ldots, c_n, 1\}$, an assignment column vector for the n halftone shares. The non-SIP assignments of the proposed (k,n)-HVCS are described according to various k and n as follows.

Assignment 1: For (k,n)-HVCS, $k > \lceil \frac{n}{2} \rceil$, on sharing a secret pixel, we input $\lambda = n - k + 1$ pairs of complementary grayscale pixels and $n - 2\lambda$ arbitrary grayscale pixels and set

$$A = [c_1, \overline{c_1}, \ldots, c_{2\lambda-1}, \overline{c_{2\lambda-1}}, c_{2\lambda+1}, \ldots, c_n]^T. \tag{6}$$

Assignment 2: For (k,n)-HVCS, $k \leq \lceil \frac{n}{2} \rceil$, on sharing a secret pixel, we input $\lambda = \lfloor \frac{n}{2} \rfloor$ pairs of complementary grayscale pixels and $n - 2\lambda$ arbitrary grayscale pixels and randomly select one of $t = \lceil \frac{n}{2(k-1)} \rceil$ assignment column vectors $A_1, \ldots, A_t$ set as follows:

$$\begin{cases} A_l = [\underbrace{1, \ldots, 1}_{n_1}, \underbrace{c_{2(l-1)(k-1)+1}, \overline{c_{2(l-1)(k-1)+1}}, \ldots, c_{2l(k-1)-1}, \overline{c_{2l(k-1)-1}}}_{n_2}, \underbrace{1, \ldots, 1}_{n_3}]^T, \\ A_t = [\underbrace{1, \ldots, 1}_{n_4}, \underbrace{c_{2(t-1)(k-1)+1}, \overline{c_{2(t-1)(k-1)+1}}, \ldots, c_{2\lambda-1}, \overline{c_{2\lambda-1}}}_{n_5}, \underbrace{c_{2\lambda+1}, \ldots, c_n}_{n_6}]^T, \end{cases} \tag{7}$$

where $l = 1, \ldots, t-1$, $n_1 = 2(l-1)(k-1)$, $n_2 = 2(k-1)$, $n_3 = n - 2l(k-1)$, $n_4 = 2(t-1)(k-1)$, $n_5 = 2(\lambda - (t-1)(k-1))$ and $n_6 = n - 2\lambda$.

3.4   Generation of Halftone Shares via Error Diffusion

Once the assignments of SIPs and non-SIPs are determined, a halftoning algorithm can be applied to generate the halftone shares from grayscale cover images.
Error diffusion is used in this paper as it is a computationally efficient way to
generate halftone shares.

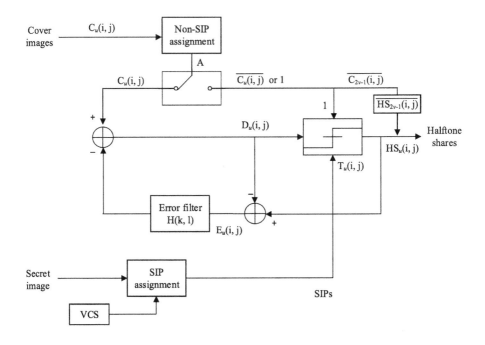

Fig. 2. The flowchart of the proposed HVCS.

In the proposed (k,n)-HVCS, the generation of halftone shares based
on error diffusion is shown in Fig. 2, where the SIPs are prefixed in the
halftone shares. By the non-SIP assignment, we are first able to know the
grayscale cover images to be input. Suppose we need to input λ pairs
of complementary grayscale images and $n - 2\lambda$ arbitrary grayscale images
$\{C_1, \overline{C_1}, C_3, \overline{C_3}, \ldots, C_{2\lambda-1}, \overline{C_{2\lambda-1}}, \ldots, C_n\}$. To produce the halftone share pixel
$HS_u(i,j)$, a grayscale cover image pixel $c_u = C_u(i,j)$ is provided. Then we can
get the input and output to the threshold block as follows:

$$D_u(i,j) = C_u(i,j) - \sum_{k,l} H(k,l)E_u(i-k,j-l), \tag{8}$$

$$HS_u(i,j) = \begin{cases} 1, & if\ D_u(i,j) \geq T_u(i,j) \\ 0, & otherwise, \end{cases} \tag{9}$$

where $E_u(i,j) = HS_u(i,j) - D_u(i,j)$.

Given a non-SIP assignment column vector $A = [a_1, a_2, \ldots, a_n]^T$ where $a_u \in \{c_1, \overline{c_1}, c_3, \overline{c_3}, \ldots, c_{2\lambda-1}, \overline{c_{2\lambda-1}}, \ldots, c_n, 1\}$, the above procedure is applied only when $HS_u(i,j)$ is a non-SIP and $a_u \in \{c_1, c_3, \ldots, c_{2\lambda-1}, \ldots, c_n\}$. Otherwise, if $HS_u(i,j)$ is a SIP, the value of $HS_u(i,j)$ is set equal to the value of the corresponding predetermined SIP. If $HS_u(i,j)$ is a non-SIP and $a_u = 1$, the value of $HS_u(i,j)$ is set to be 1. For the above two cases, the error $E_u(i,j)$ is calculated as the difference between the input to the thresholding block and the SIP value or the value 1. The quantization error caused by the introduction of the SIPs and black pixels is diffused away to the neighboring grayscale pixels, as illustrated in Fig. 2, and will lead to visually pleasing halftone shares. If $HS_u(i,j)$ is a non-SIP and $a_u \in \{\overline{c_1}, \overline{c_3}, \ldots, \overline{c_{2\lambda-1}}\}$, the value of $HS_u(i,j)$ is just set equal to the value obtained by reversing the corresponding $HS_{2v-1}(i,j)$, $1 \leq v \leq \lambda$. In summary, the SIPs are seamlessly embedded into the generated halftone shares and the halftone share is structured taking meaningful visual information.

4   Discussions

In this section, we first prove that the proposed HVCS is a valid construction of VCS by Theorem 1. Then visual quality of meaningful shares generated by the proposed HVCS is discussed.

4.1   Proof of Validity

In general, a valid construction of VCS means that the contrast and security conditions of Definition 1 should be satisfied. To prove the proposed HVCS is a valid VCS, we first give the following lemmas.

Lemma 1. *For* Assignment 1, *any k halftone shares include at least one pair of complementary grayscale cover pixels.*

Proof. When selecting all the arbitrary grayscale cover pixels and all single pixels of each pair of complementary grayscale cover pixels, only $n - k + 1 + n - 2(n - k + 1) = k - 1$ pixels are included. Therefore, any k halftone shares include at least one pair of complementary grayscale cover pixels.   □

Lemma 2. *For* Assignment 2, *any k halftone shares include at least one pair of complementary grayscale cover pixels or at least one black pixel.*

Proof. For $k \leq \lceil \frac{n}{2} \rceil$, there are $t = \lceil \frac{n}{2(k-1)} \rceil$ assignment column vectors $A_1, \ldots, A_t$. For A_l, $l = 1, \ldots, t - 1$, each includes only as many as $k - 1$ different pairs of complementary grayscale cover pixels and $n - 2(k - 1)$ black pixels. Therefore, any k halftone shares include at least one pair of complementary grayscale cover pixels or at least one black pixel. For A_t, if n is even, $n_6 = 0$, and hence there is $\frac{n_5}{2} \leq (k-1)$ different pairs of complementary grayscale cover pixels and $n - n_5$ black pixels; else $n_6 = 1$, and hence there is $\frac{n_5}{2} \leq (k-2)$ different pairs of complementary grayscale cover pixels and $n - n_5 - 1$ black pixels. Therefore, any k halftone shares also include at least one pair of complementary grayscale cover pixels or at least one black pixel.   □

Theorem 1. *The proposed HVCS is a valid VCS.*

Proof. For each halftone cell, since the distribution of SIPs is independent of the values of SIPs, no secret can be inferred from the locations of SIPs which can be detected by comparing the original halftone image and the corresponding halftone share. In addition, since the values of SIPs are only determined by the underlying (k, n)-VCS, no secret information can be obtained by looking at the values of SIPs of fewer than k halftone shares. Therefore, the security condition of Definition 1 is satisfied.

Now consider the stacking result of any k or more halftone shares. Note that, in our generation of halftone shares, one of the complementary grayscale cover pixels is processed by error diffusion and the other is processed by reversing the former one. Hence, by Lemmas 1 and 2, when stacking together shares of any k participants, the non-SIPs in each reconstructed halftone cell are always black as a result of the OR operation. If a secret pixel is white (resp. black), let the reconstructed halftone cell be denoted as Q_0 (resp. Q_1). Then we have

$$w(Q_0) = q - m + w(\otimes(S_{X_k}^0)), \tag{10}$$

$$w(Q_1) = q - m + w(\otimes(S_{X_k}^1)), \tag{11}$$

where X_k is a set of any k or more participants for the underlying (k, n)-VCS. Thus, we have

$$\alpha^h = \frac{w(Q_1) - w(Q_0)}{q} = \frac{w(\otimes(S_{X_k}^1)) - w(\otimes(S_{X_k}^0))}{q} = \frac{\alpha m}{q} > 0, \tag{12}$$

where the contrast α^h is for the proposed (k, n)-HVCS and the contrast α is for the underlying (k, n)-VCS. Therefore, the contrast condition of Definition 1 is satisfied.   □

4.2   Visual Quality of Halftone Shares

In our HVCS, the non-SIPs are responsible for carrying the visual information of the cover images and preventing all the share's visual information from showing on the reconstructed image. Specifically, in an assignment column vector A, with the exception of 1's, all pixels are assigned to carry the share visual information. The proportion of these pixels governs the image quality of the resultant halftone shares. The quantity β is called the quality index of the halftone share and is represented as

$$\beta = \frac{q - m - e}{q}, \tag{13}$$

where e is the number of 1's assigned in each halftone cell. A large β leads to good image quality of the halftone share. However, β cannot be arbitrarily large for all non-SIP assignments. For Assignment 1, $e = 0$ and hence $\beta = \frac{q-m}{q} < 1$, where $k > \lceil \frac{n}{2} \rceil$. For Assignment 2, $e = \frac{q-m}{t}$ and hence $\frac{1}{2} \frac{q-m}{q} \leq \beta = \frac{q-m}{q}(1 - \frac{1}{t}) < \frac{q-m}{q} < 1$, where $t = \lceil \frac{n}{2(k-1)} \rceil$ and $k \leq \lceil \frac{n}{2} \rceil$; moreover, if $n \gg k$, the quality index β achieves the optimal value $\frac{q-m}{q}$ approximately.

HVCS
secret

(a)   (b)   (c)

Fig. 3. Original images used in this paper. (a) The binary secret image with size of 170×170; (b)–(c) two grayscale cover images with size of 510×510, which will be zoomed to their proper size if necessary.

Remark: Note that the pixel expansion m and contrast α of the underlying VCS is predetermined by k and n. Thus, if we fix k and n, then better visual quality of halftone shares can be obtained in larger halftone cells according to Eq. (13). On the contrary, larger halftone cell sizes lead to lower contrast of the reconstructed secret image by Eq. (12). Therefore, a tradeoff exists between the visual quality of the halftone shares and the contrast of the reconstructed secret image. It should be also noted that we use complementary cover pixels or black pixels to block all the share's visual information from showing on the reconstructed image. Besides allowing complementary halftone shares, we remove the share's cross interference from other shares, since the decision to insert the black pixels, according to Assignment 2, is independent of the content of cover images.

5 Experiment and Comparison

In this section, experiments and comparisons are given to demonstrate the effectiveness and advantages of the proposed HVCS. In addition, the original images that will be used in this paper are shown in Fig. 3.

5.1 Experiment

To demonstrate the effectiveness of our HVCS, we design three experiments, involving the two non-SIP assignments, for answering the following questions.

1. Whether or not the proposed HVCS is a valid VCS?
2. Whether or not the proposed HVCS generates meaningful shares? If so, is there a tradeoff between the visual quality of the halftone shares and the contrast of the reconstructed secret image.
3. Whether or not the cross interference from the share images on the reconstructed secret image is avoided?
4. Whether or not the share's cross interference from other shares is avoided?

Experimental results by the proposed HVCSs for $(2, 3)$ and $(3, 4)$ threshold cases are shown in Figs. 4, 5 and 6, respectively, where the basis matrices of

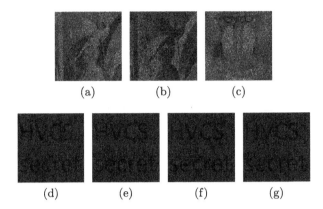

Fig. 4. Experimental results of the proposed $(2,3)$-HVCS, where $m = 3$, $q = 9$. (a)–(c) Three meaningful shares, where $\beta = \frac{3}{9}$; (d)–(f) stacking results by any two of the three shares, where $\alpha^h = \frac{1}{9}$; (g) stacking result by three shares, where $\alpha^h = \frac{1}{9}$.

$(2,3)$-VCS are $S^0 = \begin{pmatrix} 1\,1\,0 \\ 1\,1\,0 \\ 1\,1\,0 \end{pmatrix}$ and $S^1 = \begin{pmatrix} 1\,1\,0 \\ 1\,0\,1 \\ 0\,1\,1 \end{pmatrix}$, and the basis matrices of

$(3,4)$-VCS are $S^0 = \begin{pmatrix} 0\,0\,1\,1\,1\,0 \\ 0\,0\,1\,1\,0\,1 \\ 0\,0\,1\,0\,1\,1 \\ 0\,0\,0\,1\,1\,1 \end{pmatrix}$ and $S^1 = \begin{pmatrix} 1\,0\,0\,0\,1\,1 \\ 0\,1\,0\,0\,1\,1 \\ 0\,0\,1\,0\,1\,1 \\ 0\,0\,0\,1\,1\,1 \end{pmatrix}$.

All of Figs. 4(a)–(c), 5(a)–(c) and 6(a)–(d) show visually pleasing halftone cover images, where the shares cross interference from other shares does not happen with the exception of some complementary shares. From Figs. 4(a)–(c),

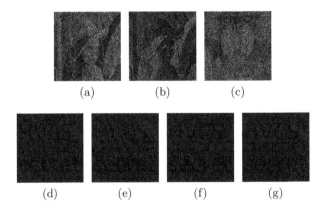

Fig. 5. Experimental results of the proposed $(2,3)$-HVCS, where $m = 3$, $q = 16$. (a)–(c) Three meaningful shares, where $\beta = \frac{13}{32}$; (d)–(f) stacking results by any two of the three shares, where $\alpha^h = \frac{1}{16}$; (g) stacking result by three shares, where $\alpha^h = \frac{1}{16}$.

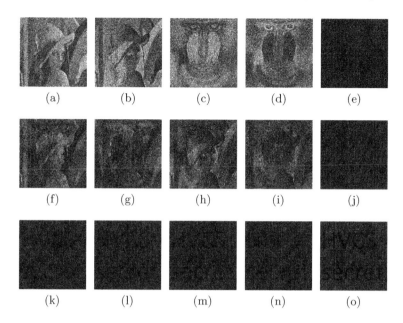

Fig. 6. Experimental results of the proposed $(3,4)$-HVCS, where $m = 6$, $q = 16$. (a)–(d) Four meaningful shares, where $\beta = \frac{10}{16}$; (e)–(j) stacking results by any two of the four shares; (k)–(n) stacking results by any three of the four shares, where $\alpha^h = \frac{1}{16}$; (o) stacking result by four shares, where $\alpha^h = \frac{2}{16}$.

5(a)–(c) and 6(a)–(j), we see that any less than k shares give no clue about the secret image, however, from Figs. 4(d)–(g), 5(d)–(g) and 6(k)–(o), we see that any k or more shares can reconstruct the secret image, where the cross interference from the shares on the reconstructed secret image is removed. In addition, comparing Fig. 4 with Fig. 5, we conclude that the content of each meaningful share in Fig. 5 is recognized more clearly with a quality index $\beta = \frac{13}{32}$ while the content of the reconstructed secret image in Fig. 4 is perceived more easily with a contrast $\alpha^h = \frac{1}{9}$. The above result illustrates the tradeoff between the visual quality of the halftone shares and the contrast of the reconstructed secret image.

5.2   Comparison

To show the advantages of our HVCS, we compare our scheme with related EVCSs or HVCSs [1–4,6,8–12] as follows:

1. The EVCSs proposed in [1,2,11] can only deal with binary input share images, while our proposed scheme can deal with grayscale input images.
2. The pixel expansion of the proposed scheme is less than that of [1,2,8], which is clearly discussed in [3].
3. The EVCS proposed in [4] is only for the $(2,2)$ threshold access structure, and the scheme may have security issues when relaxing the constraint of the

dynamic range as already noted in [4]. Our proposed scheme can be applied to (k, n) access structure for all k and n, and is always unconditionally secure which is inherited from the corresponding VCS.

4. For the HVCS proposed in [12] and the first HVCS proposed in [9], the participants are required to take more than one share for some access structure, while our proposed scheme does not have such a requirement and each participant only needs to take one share.

5. Compared with the EVCSs [6,11], the third HVCS [9] and the HVCS [10], the cross interference from the share images on the reconstructed secret image and the share's interference from other shares, which may increase the suspicion of secret image encryption and decrease the visual quality, are both avoided in our proposed scheme.

6. Compared with the HVCS [3], our proposed scheme does not require the dealer to choose carefully or darken the input grayscale images, which will inevitably cause the loss in the visual quality of the shares.

7. The second HVCS [9] achieves the quality of halftone shares $\beta^* \leq \frac{k-1}{n}\frac{q-m}{q}$, while our proposed scheme achieves better quality of halftone shares, where $\beta = \frac{q-m}{q} \geq \frac{k-1}{n}\frac{q-m}{q} \geq \beta^*$ for $k > \lceil\frac{n}{2}\rceil$ and $\beta = \frac{q-m}{q}(1 - \frac{1}{\lceil\frac{n}{2(k-1)}\rceil}) > \frac{k-1}{n}\frac{q-m}{q} \geq \beta^*$ for $k \leq \lceil\frac{n}{2}\rceil$.

8. The proposed scheme is flexible in the sense that there exists a trade-off between the visual quality of the halftone shares and the contrast of the reconstructed secret image. This flexibility allows the dealer to choose the proper parameters, k, n, q and β, for different applications.

6   Conclusion

In this paper, we have proposed an HVCS with complementary cover images by error diffusion. The main questions existing in previous EVCSs and HVCSs, including the cross interference from shares on the reconstructed secret image, the share's cross interference from other shares, poor visual quality of shares and multiple shares per participant, are solved in all. Extending the proposed scheme from (k, n) to general access structures will be our future work.

Acknowledgments. We would like to thank the anonymous reviewers for their important and helpful comments. This work was supported by the National Natural Science Foundation of China with No. 61602513 and No. 61671448, the Strategic Priority Research Program of the Chinese Academy of Sciences with No. XDA06010701, and the National Key R&D Program of China with No. 2016YFB0800100.

References

1. Ateniese, G., Blundo, C., De Santis, A., Stinson, D.R.: Extended capabilities for visual cryptography. ACM Theor. Comput. Sci. **250**, 143–161 (2001)
2. Droste, S.: New results on visual cryptography. In: Koblitz, N. (ed.) CRYPTO 1996. LNCS, vol. 1109, pp. 401–415. Springer, Heidelberg (1996). doi:10.1007/3-540-68697-5_30

3. Liu, F., Wu, C.K.: Embedded extended visual cryptography schemes. IEEE Trans. Inf. Forensics Secur. **6**, 307–322 (2011)
4. Nakajima, M., Yamaguchi, Y.: Extended visual cryptography for natural images. In: WSCG 2002, pp. 303–412. CSRN, Plzen (2002)
5. Naor, M., Shamir, A.: Visual cryptography. In: Santis, A. (ed.) EUROCRYPT 1994. LNCS, vol. 950, pp. 1–12. Springer, Heidelberg (1995). doi:10.1007/BFb0053419
6. Tsai, D.S., Chen, T., Horng, G.: On generating meaningful shares in visual secret sharing scheme. Imaging Sci. J. **56**, 49–55 (2008)
7. Ulichney, R.A.: The void-and-cluster method for dither array generation. In: Human Vision, Visual Processing, and Digital Display IV, San Jose, CA, vol. 1913, pp. 332–343. SPIE (1993)
8. Wang, D.S., Yi, F., Li, X.: On general construction for extended visual cryptography schemes. Pattern Recogn. **42**, 3071–3082 (2009)
9. Wang, Z., Arce, G.R., Di Crescenzo, G.: Halftone visual cryptography via error diffusion. IEEE Trans. Inf. Forensics Secur. **4**, 383–396 (2009)
10. Yan, X.H., Shen, W., Niu, X.M., Yang, C.N.: Halftone visual cryptography with minimum auxiliary black pixels and uniform image quality. Digital Sig. Process. **38**, 53–65 (2015)
11. Yang, C.N., Yang, Y.Y.: New extended visual cryptography schemes with clearer shadow images. Inf. Sci. **271**, 246–263 (2014)
12. Zhou, Z., Arce, G.R., Di Crescenzo, G.: Halftone visual cryptography. IEEE Trans. Image Process. **15**, 2441–2453 (2006)

Collusive Attacks to Partition Authentication Visual Cryptography Scheme

Yawei Ren[1,2,3]([✉]), Feng Liu[1,3], and Wen Wang[1,3]

[1] State Key Laboratory of Information Security,
Institute of Information Engineering, Chinese Academy of Sciences,
Beijing 100093, China
renyawei@iie.ac.cn
[2] School of Information Management,
Beijing Information Science and Technology University, Beijing 100192, China
[3] University of Chinese Academy of Sciences, Chinese Academy of Sciences,
Beijing 100190, China

Abstract. In order to preventing cheating attack, partition authentication visual cryptography scheme (PAVCS) was proposed, in which each authentication pattern can be revealed on the stacked result of the corresponding partitions of any two shares. Without needing extra share, a PAVCS not only accomplishes sharing a secret image, but also provides mutual authentication of every two shares. In this paper, we propose two types of collusive attacks to (k,n)-PAVCS. The aim of the first type of attack is to destroy the integrity of the secret image revealed by victims, while the second type of attack belongs to cheating attack. Experimental results and theoretical analysis show that the two types of collusive attacks are successful attacks. Furthermore, we put forward the suggestion to devise partition authentication visual cryptography scheme for resisting the proposed two types of collusive attacks.

Keywords: Visual cryptography scheme · Visual secret sharing · Cheating prevention visual cryptography scheme (CPVCS) · Partition authentication visual cryptography scheme (PAVCS) · Collusive attack

1   Introduction

Naor and Shamir [1] firstly proposed visual cryptography scheme (VCS), namely visual secret sharing (VSS), in which a secret image is encrypted into n shares and these shares are distributed to n participants. Any k or more participants can reveal the secret image by stacking their shares, whereas fewer than k participants cannot obtain any secret information through their shares. It is worth mentioning that the secret image is decrypted only by human visual system, rather than complex computation.

During the past more than twenty years, many researchers have concentrated on the construction of VCS. Many VCSs have been proposed such as general

© Springer International Publishing AG 2017
Y.Q. Shi et al. (Eds.): IWDW 2016, LNCS 10082, pp. 238–250, 2017.
DOI: 10.1007/978-3-319-53465-7_18

access structure VCS(GASVCS) [2], extended VCS(EVCS) [3,4], tagged VCS [5–7], progressive VCS [8–10], random grid based VCS [11–14].

Cheating problem in VCS was firstly presented by Horng et al. [15]. Victims who receive some shares forged by cheaters cannot identify whether the revealed image is genuine or not such that victims obtain fake information. In order to preventing cheating attacks, many schemes were proposed [15–25]. In general, these cheating prevention visual cryptography schemes (CPVCSs) mainly adopt two technologies: modifying codebooks and authenticating shares. The former can perplex cheaters' speculation about sub-pixels blocks through adding some columns in codebooks [15–17,20]. The latter can identify genuine shares by the revealed authentication patterns or the authentication results, which comprises whole-share authentication visual cryptography scheme (WAVCS) [16,19,22], random authentication visual cryptography scheme (RAVCS) [21,23] and partition authentication visual cryptography scheme (PAVCS) [24,25].

In this paper, we review the model of partition authentication visual cryptography scheme (PAVCS) and the encryption algorithm of Lin et al.'s PAVCS. We propose two types of collusive attacks to Lin et al.'s PAVCS. The aim of the first type of attack is to destroy the integrity of the secret image revealed by victims, while the second type of attack belongs to the cheating attack. Experimental results and theoretical analysis show that the two types of collusive attacks are successful attacks. In the end, we analyze the resistance property of some cheating prevention visual cryptography schemes (CPVCSs). Furthermore, we suggest to apply random authentication in partition authentication visual cryptography scheme for resisting the two proposed types of collusive attacks.

The remainder of the paper is organized as follows: the preliminary knowledge of (k,n)-conventional visual cryptography scheme $((k,n)$-CVCS) and cheating attack in visual cryptography scheme are reviewed in Sect. 2. We propose two types of collusive attacks to Lin et al.'s PAVCS in Sect. 3. Section 4 gives experimental results and discussion. At last, we give short conclusions about this paper in Sect. 5.

2 Preliminaries

2.1 (k,n)-Conventional Visual Cryptography Scheme $((k,n)$-CVCS)

In a conventional (k,n)-VCS, the binary secret image SI is encoded in n shares $S_1, S_2, \cdots, S_n$. Each pixel of SI is substituted by $n \times m$ white pixels and black pixels. A conventional (k,n)-VCS consists of two collections C_0 and C_1 of $n \times m$ Boolean matrices, where 0 (resp. 1) stands for white (resp. black) pixel. For sharing a white (resp. black) pixel, a $n \times m$ Boolean matrix M is randomly selected from C_0 (resp. C_1) and the jth row of M denoted by M_{L_j} is distributed to the jth share S_j, $1 \le j \le n$.

A conventional (k,n)-VCS is considered to be valid if the following two conditions are satisfied.

1. (Contrast condition) For any $M \in C_0$ (resp. C_1), $OR(M_{L_{j_1}}, M_{L_{j_2}}, \cdots, M_{L_{j_k}})$ is denoted by $\mathbf{v}$, which satisfies $\mathbf{W}(\mathbf{v}) \leq l$ (resp. $\mathbf{W}(\mathbf{v}) \geq h$), where $1 \leq j_1 < j_2 < \cdots < j_k \leq n$, $1 \leq l < h \leq m$.
2. (Security condition) For any subset $\{j_1, j_2, \cdots, j_q\}$ of $\{1, 2, \cdots, n\}$ with $q < k$, the two collections of $q \times m$ matrices obtained by restricting each matrix in C_0 and C_1 to the $j_1, j_2, \cdots, j_q$ rows are indistinguishable in the sense that they contain the same matrices with the same frequencies.

In the above definition, $\mathbf{W}(\mathbf{v})$ denotes the hamming weight of the vector $\mathbf{v}$ and OR denotes the operation of the corresponding rows of M. h (resp. l) denotes the "blackness" of a black pixel (resp. white pixel). m represents the pixel expansion. The contrast α reflects visual quality of the revealed secret image. In [1], $\alpha = \frac{h-l}{m}$ is defined. In some (k, n)-CVCSs, two collections C_0 and C_1 of $n \times m$ binary matrices can be formed by permutating the columns of the $n \times m$ basis matrices B_0 and B_1. At this point, C_0 and C_1 can be presented by B_0 and B_1.

2.2 Cheating Attack to VCS

Horng et al. firstly pointed out the cheating problem in VCS [15]. In their paper, $(2,3)$-CVCS is taken as an example to show two participants' collusive attack. The basis matrices of $(2,3)$-CVCS are

$$B_0 = \begin{pmatrix} 1\,0\,0 \\ 1\,0\,0 \\ 1\,0\,0 \end{pmatrix}, B_1 = \begin{pmatrix} 1\,0\,0 \\ 0\,1\,0 \\ 0\,0\,1 \end{pmatrix}. \tag{1}$$

Assumed that participant A and participant B have known construction matrices and try to cheat the participant C. Because participant A and participant B can reveal the secret image by stacking their shares, they are aware of every secret pixel exactly. If the secret pixel is white pixel and the corresponding sub-pixels blocks of share A and share B are $1\,0\,0$ and $1\,0\,0$, the corresponding sub-pixels block of share C is also $1\,0\,0$. If the secret pixel is black pixel and the corresponding sub-pixels blocks of participant A and participant B are $1\,0\,0$ and $0\,1\,0$, the corresponding sub-pixels block of participant C is $0\,0\,1$. The participant A and participant B can alter the sub-pixels blocks of the original shares according to the white or black pixel of the fake image. If the pixels of the fake image are as same as those of the original secret image, the corresponding sub-pixels blocks are not altered. If the pixel of the fake image is white pixel and the corresponding pixel of the secret image is black pixel, the corresponding sub-pixels block is replaced by the sub-pixels block of the participant C's share. On the contrary, the corresponding sub-pixels block is chosen from the participant A's share or the participant B's share. Finally, the fake share is forged such that the collusive attack has been accomplished successfully. Then the following definition is given:

Definition 1 *([15]). A successful cheating is that a fake image is revealed in the reconstruction phase owing to the cheaters presenting fake shares, and the victims cannot tell whether the revealed image is the original one, that is, the victims cannot tell whether the cheaters presented fake shares or genuine ones.*

Prisco and Santis [17] firstly proposed an explicit definition of cheating prevention visual cryptography scheme as the following.

Definition 2 *([17]). A VCS is cheating prevention if and only if the probability of the successful cheating in any pixel is less than 1.*

Since Definition 2 is relatively weak, Chen et al. [23] presented the definition of ϵ-cheating prevention visual cryptography scheme.

Definition 3 *([23]). A VCS is ϵ-cheating prevention if and only if the probability of the successful cheating in any pixel is equal to ϵ.*

Two types of cheaters in VCS. Hu and Tzeng [19] presented two types of cheaters in VCS: malicious participant (MP) and malicious outsider (MO). The former is a legitimate participant and the latter is not. The collusive attacks we will propose in next section refer to the malicious participants' (MPs') attacks.

3   Collusive Attacks to Partition Authentication Visual Cryptography Scheme (PAVCS)

In (k, n)-PAVCS, the secret image is encrypted into n verifiable shares. Authentication pattern can be revealed by partially stacking any two shares. Meanwhile, the secret image can be revealed visually by stacking any k or more verifiable shares, while no information of the secret image is leaked from fewer than k verifiable shares. Then, we review the model of PAVCS.

3.1   The Model of Partition Authentication Visual Cryptography Scheme (PAVCS)

Let SI denote the secret image and $VS_1, VS_2, \cdots, VS_n$ denote n verifiable shares. Let $\mathbf{R}(VS_{j_1}, VS_{j_2}, \cdots, VS_{j_t})$ denote the revealed result by completely stacking t shares $VS_{j_1}, VS_{j_2}, \cdots, VS_{j_t}$, where $1 \le j_1 < j_2 < \cdots < j_t \le n$. Let $\widetilde{\mathbf{R}}(VS_{j_x}, VS_{j_y})$ denote the revealed result by partially stacking two shares VS_{j_x} and VS_{j_y}, where $1 \le x \ne y \le n$. The model of partition authentication visual cryptography scheme (PAVCS) is described as the following.

(1) $\mathbf{R}(VS_{j_1}, VS_{j_2}, \cdots, VS_{j_t}) = \emptyset$, where $1 \le t < k$.
(2) $\mathbf{R}(VS_{j_1}, VS_{j_2}, \cdots, VS_{j_t}) = SI$, where $k \le t \le n$.
(3) $\widetilde{\mathbf{R}}(VS_{j_x}, VS_{j_y}) = \mathbf{V}$, where $\mathbf{V}$ is the authentication pattern.

3.2   Review of Lin et al.'s Partition Authentication Visual Cryptography Schemes (PAVCS)

In Lin et al.'s PAVCS [25], the secret image SI is firstly encoded in n original shares $S_1, S_2, \cdots, S_n$ by using a (k, n)-CVCS. Let the size of each original share S_j be $W \times H$, where $j = 1, 2, \cdots, n$. The authentication image is a $(W/2) \times (H/(n-1))$ binary image, which contains a valid authentication pattern $\mathbf{V}$. Each original share is divided horizontally into $(n-1)$ equal-sized, non-overlapping partitions, and numbered from partition 1 to partition $(n-1)$ sequentially from top to bottom. The original share is represented in its share partitions given below:

$$S_j = \{P_j^i\}$$

where P_j^i is the ith partition of the original share S_j. The construction procedure of this scheme is described as below.

The construction of Lin et al.'s PAVCS ([25])

Input: n original shares $S_1, S_2, \cdots, S_n$ generated in a (k, n)-CVCS, with each share having the scale of $W \times H$.
Output: n verifiable shares $VS_1, VS_2, \cdots, VS_n$.
Step 1. Generate a $(W/2) \times (H/(n-1))$ binary authentication image on which a valid authentication pattern $\mathbf{V}$ is designated.
Step 2. Divide each of the n original shares $S_1, S_2, \cdots, S_n$ horizontally into $n-1$ equal-sized, non-overlapping partitions.
Step 3. Pick a pair of original shares S_u and S_v. Apply the stamping algorithm in [25] to stamp a copy of the authentication pattern $\mathbf{V}$ on the right half of partition P_u^{v-1} and the left half of partition P_v^u, and stamp a copy of authentication pattern $\mathbf{V}$ on left half of partition P_u^{v-1} and the right half of partition P_v^u.
Step 4. Repeat Step 3 until a copy of authentication pattern $\mathbf{V}$ is stamped in each pair of original partitions P_u^{v-1} and P_v^u, for all $1 \le u, v \le n, u \ne v, u < v$. At last, n stamped shares are the n verifiable shares $VS_1, VS_2, \cdots, VS_n$.

The steps of stamping a copy of verification pattern $\mathbf{V}$ on the two share-partitions Q and R are described as follows:

The stamping algorithm in [25]

Input: The authentication image $\mathbf{V} = \{v_{x,y}\}$ and the two share partitions, $Q = \{q_{x,y}\}$ and $R = \{r_{x,y}\}$, all have the scale of $w \times h$. The probabilities of a white pixel and a black pixel on share partitions Q and R are p_0 and p_1, respectively.
Output: Two stamped share-partitions, i.e., Q_0 and R_0.
Step 1. Take a pixel $v_{x,y}$ from $\mathbf{V}$ in scan order, (i.e., from left to right and from top to bottom), and encode the two corresponding pixels, i.e., $q_{x,y}$ and $r_{x,y}$, on Q and R, respectively, using one of the following encoding rules:

(a) If the color of $v_{x,y}$ is black and the colors of $q_{x,y}$ and $r_{x,y}$ are both white, one of $q_{x,y}$ and $r_{x,y}$ is selected with equal probability, and the selected pixel is set to black.

(b) If the color of $v_{x,y}$ is black and the colors of $q_{x,y}$ and $r_{x,y}$ are one white and one black, the white pixel is selected and set to black with the probability of $1/2$.

(c) If the color of $v_{x,y}$ is white and if the corresponding pixel $q_{x,y}$ on Q is white, it is set to black with the probability of $1/2$; similarly, if the corresponding pixel $r_{x,y}$ on R is white, set it to black with the probability of $1/2$.

Step 2. Repeat Step 1 until all of the pixels on the authentication image $\mathbf{V}$ have been processed. The two stamped partitions Q_0 and R_0 are obtained.

There are $2C_n^2$ authentication images in the above scheme, which have the same authentication pattern $\mathbf{V}$. Figures 1 and 2 show stamp arrangement of the authentication patterns in $(k,3)$-PAVCS and $(k,4)$-PAVCS, respectively. In Fig. 1, V_1 and V_2, V_3 and V_4, V_5 and V_6 are the revealed authentication images by partially stacking share 1 and share 2, share 1 and share 3, share 2 and share 3. In Fig. 2, V_1 and V_2, V_3 and V_4, V_5 and V_6, V_7 and V_8, V_9 and V_{10}, V_{11} and V_{12} are the revealed authentication images by partially stacking share 1 and share 2, share 1 and share 3, share 1 and share 4, share 2 and share 3, share 2 and share 4, share 3 and share 4.

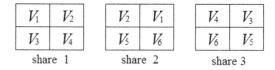

Fig. 1. Stamp arrangement of the authentication patterns in $(k,3)$-PAVCS

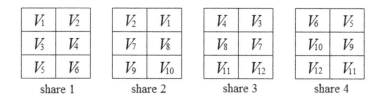

Fig. 2. Stamp arrangement of the authentication patterns in $(k,4)$-PAVCS

3.3   The Proposed Collusive Attacks

In Lin et al.'s PAVCS, each verifiable share can authenticate only one partition of other verifiable shares. Illustrated as Fig. 1, the top half partition is the mutual authentication partition for VS_1 and VS_2 and the bottom half partition is the mutual authentication partition for VS_2 and VS_3. Thus, we propose two types of collusive attacks to Lin et al.'s (k, n)-PAVCS. Because one MO or one MP holds no information about authentication patterns, the fake shares they provide would be detected definitely. The proposed collusive attacks are based on the following conditions all participants having known:

1. The authenticated sets of a PAVCS.
2. The encryption algorithm of a PAVCS.

Then, t $(t \geq max(k, n - k))$ MPs can implement the following attacks to Lin et al.'s PAVCS.

Collusive Attack 1:

Step 1. Obtain the authentication partitions by partially stacking every two of t shares. Randomly select $k - 1$ verifiable shares and replace their mutual authentication partitions with equal-scaled blank images.
Step 2. Distribute different-darkness sub-pixels blocks to the blank partitions of the above $k - 1$ verifiable shares according to the probability distribution of different-darkness sub-pixels blocks in PAVCS.
Step 3. Send the forged $k - 1$ verifiable shares to one victim.

The collusive attack 1 differs from cheating attack in its aim that partial secret information cannot be revealed to the victim.

In Lin et al.'s PAVCS, the probability of z-darkness sub-pixels block is $\frac{C_{m-p}^{z-p}}{2^{m-p}}$, where $z = p, p + 1, \cdots, m$ and p is the number of black pixels in one sub-pixels block of (k, n)-CVCS. According to the probability of z-darkness sub-pixels blocks, distribute different-darkness sub-pixels blocks to the blank partitions of $k - 1$ verifiable shares. Thus, the distribution of the sub-pixels blocks in the forged verifiable shares are uniform. Though the authentication patterns can still be revealed by partially stacking the forged $k - 1$ verifiable shares and the victim's share, the revealed secret image by completely stacking the forged $k - 1$ verifiable shares and the victim's share is incomplete.

Then, we give the detailed steps of Algorithm 1 and the collusive attack 2 to $(2, n)$-PAVCS.

Algorithm 1

Input: Fake image FI and t MPs' verifiable shares $VS_{j_1}, VS_{j_2}, \cdots, VS_{j_t}, 1 \leq j_1 < j_2 < \cdots < j_t \leq n$.
Output: The fake share FS.

Step 1. Obtain the revealed secret image by completely stacking t verifiable shares $VS_{j_1}, VS_{j_2}, \cdots, VS_{j_t}$ and infer the secret image SI.

Step 2. For $1 \leq r \leq W, 1 \leq s \leq H$, do the Steps 3–5:

Step 3. **If** $FI(r,s)$ and $SI(r,s)$ are two pixels with the same colour, **then** let $FS(B_{(r,s)}) = VS_{j_i}(B_{(r,s)})$;

Step 4. **If** $FI(r,s)$ is black pixel and $SI(r,s)$ is white pixel, **then**
(1) let $FS(B_{(r,s)}) = VS_{j_i}(B_{(r,s)})$, when $\mathbf{W}(VS_{j_i}(B_{(r,s)})) = n$;
(2) let $FS(B_{(r,s)}) = \overline{VS_{j_i}(B_{(r,s)})}$ with the probability of $min(P_e, P_{n-e})$ when $\mathbf{W}(VS_{j_i}(B_{(r,s)})) = e$ or $n - e$, $e = 1, 2, \cdots, \lfloor \frac{n}{2} \rfloor$;

Step 5. **If** $FI(r,s)$ is white pixel and $SI(r,s)$ is black pixel, **then**
(1) let $FS(B_{(r,s)}) = VS_{j_i}(B_{(r,s)})$, when $\mathbf{W}(VS_{j_i}(B_{(r,s)})) = n$;
(2) let $FS(B_{(r,s)}) = RCS(VS_{j_i}(B_{(r,s)}), d), d = 1, 2, \cdots, n - 1$ with the probability of $\frac{1}{n-1}$, when $\mathbf{W}(VS_{j_i}(B_{(r,s)})) = 1, 2, \cdots, n - 1$.

Step 6. Output the fake share FS.

In Algorithm 1, $SI_{(r,s)}$ denotes the (r,s) pixel in SI. $FI_{(r,s)}$ denotes the (r,s) pixel in FI. $B_{(r,s)}$ stands for the sub-pixels block corresponding to the (r,s) pixel. VS_{j_i} is one of the t MPs' verifiable shares. The sub-pixels block corresponding to $SI(r,s)$ in the verifiable share VS_{j_i} is represented by $VS_{j_i}(B_{(r,s)})$. The sub-pixels block corresponding to $FI(r,s)$ in the fake share FS is represented by $FS(B_{(r,s)})$. The probability of $\mathbf{W}(VS_{j_i}(B_{(r,s)})) = e$ is denoted by P_e, where $e = 1, 2, \cdots, n - 1$. $\overline{VS_{j_i}(B_{(r,s)})}$ denotes the "NOT" operation of the vector $VS_{j_i}(B_{(r,s)})$. $RCS(VS_{j_i}(B_{(r,s)}), d)$ denotes the d-right circle shift of the vector $VS_{j_i}(B_{(r,s)})$. Algorithm 1 ensures that the probability distribution of z-darkness sub-pixels block in the fake share is unanimous. In Lin et al.'s $(2, n)$-PAVCS, the probability of z-darkness sub-pixels block is $\frac{C_{n-1}^{z-1}}{2^{n-1}}$, where $z = 1, 2, \cdots, n$. The fake image can be revealed by completely stacking the forged share and the victim's share.

Collusive Attack 2:

Step 1. Obtain the authentication partitions by partially stacking every two of t shares. Modify the content in SI corresponding to the position of mutual authentication partitions and form the fake image FI.

Step 2. Apply Algorithm 1 to construct the fake share FS.

Step 3. Send the forged share FS to one victim.

Since t MPs cannot accurately guess the sub-pixels blocks of one victim's verifiable share, the collusive attack 2 is actually a probabilistic cheating attack. However, the probabilistic cheating attack is different from Definitions 2 and 3 in that the probability of the successful cheating in each pixel is different. Collusive attack 2 conforms to Definition 1 in that the victim cannot tell whether the cheater presented fake share or genuine one.

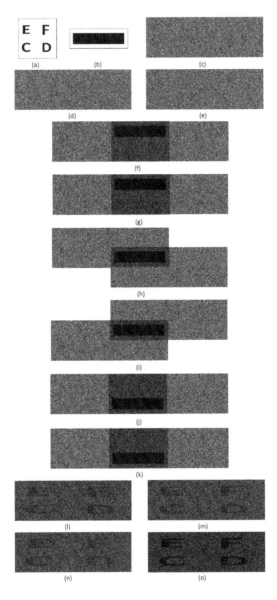

Fig. 3. Experimental results of Lin et al.'s PAVCS: (a) secret image SI; (b) authentication image; (c)–(e) three verifiable shares VS_1, VS_2, VS_3; (f)–(g) the revealed authentication patterns by partially stacking VS_1 and VS_2; (h)–(i) the revealed authentication patterns by partially stacking VS_1 and VS_3; (j)–(k) the revealed authentication patterns by partially stacking VS_2 and VS_3; (l)–(n) the revealed secret images by completely stacking VS_1 and VS_2, VS_1 and VS_3, VS_2 and VS_3; (o) the revealed secret image by completely stacking VS_1, VS_2 and VS_3.

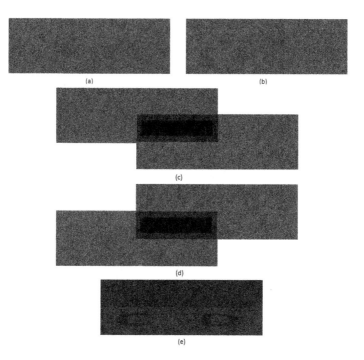

Fig. 4. Experimental results of collusive attack 1 to Lin et al.'s PAVCS: (a) fake share FS_1; (b) verifiable share VS_3; (c)–(d) the revealed authentication patterns by partially stacking FS_1 and VS_3; (e) the revealed secret image by completely stacking FS_1 and VS_3.

4   Experimental Results and Discussion

4.1   Experimental Results

We firstly give the experimental results of Lin et al.'s $(2, 3)$-PAVCS based on $(2, 3)$-CVCS. Figure 3(a) shows the secret image SI with 512×512 pixels and Fig. 3(b) shows the authentication image with 256×768 pixels. Figure 3(c)–(e) show three verifiable shares VS_1, VS_2, VS_3 with 512×1536 pixels. Figure 3(f)–(k) show the revealed authentication patterns by partially stacking any two verifiable shares. Figure 3(l)–(n) show the revealed secret images by completely stacking any two verifiable shares. Figure 3(o) shows the revealed secret image by completely stacking all three verifiable shares.

Figure 4 shows the experimental results of the proposed collusive attack 1 to Lin et al.'s $(2, 3)$-PAVCS. Without loss of generality, we assume that participant 1 and participant 2 are two MPs. As shown in Fig. 3, the mutual authentication partitions of VS_1 and VS_2 are P_1^1 and P_2^1. We select share 1 and replace P_1^1 with one equal-sized blank image. After the blank partition is filled up by different darkness sub-pixels blocks, the fake share FS_1 is obtained. Figure 4(a)–(b) show the fake share FS_1 and the verifiable share VS_3. The authentication patterns revealed

248 Y. Ren et al.

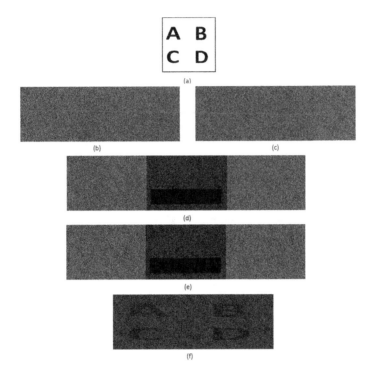

Fig. 5. Experimental results of collusive attack 2 to Lin et al.'s PAVCS: (a) fake image FI; (b) fake share FS_2; (c) verifiable share VS_3; (d)–(e) the revealed authentication patterns by partially stacking FS_2 and VS_3; (e) the revealed secret image by completely stacking FS_2 and VS_3.

by partially stacking FS_1 and VS_3 are shown in Fig. 4(c)–(d). Figure 4(e) shows the revealed secret image by completely stacking FS_1 and VS_3. We can observe that the secret image revealed on the stacked result of FS_1 and VS_3 is incomplete. Therefore, participant 3 can only obtain the partial secret image.

Experimental results of the proposed collusive attack 2 to Lin et al.'s $(2,3)$-PAVCS are shown in Fig. 5. Figure 5(a) shows the fake image FI, which differing from the secret image SI is the top half partition. The forged share FS_2 and the verifiable share VS_3 are shown in Fig. 5(b)–(c). The authentication patterns revealed by partially stacking FS_2 and VS_3 are illustrated in Fig. 5(d)–(e). Figure 5(f) shows the revealed secret image by completely stacking FS_2 and VS_3.

4.2 Discussion

The proposed collusive attack 1 is a new type of attack, which can destroy the integrity of the secret image revealed by the victims. Though the previous proposed cheating prevention visual cryptography schemes (CPVCSs) can resist the cheating attack, some of them cannot stand up to the collusive attack 1.

Because cheating prevention visual cryptography schemes (CPVCSs) [15–17,20] adopt the technology of modifying codebooks, they provide no authentication to every share so that the collusive attack 1 can be performed successfully. In addition, whole-share authentication visual cryptography schemes (WAVCSs) [16,19,22] give authentication to every sub-pixels block and random authentication visual cryptography schemes (RAVCSs) [21,23] randomly authenticate some sub-pixels blocks or regions of every share. Therefore, the above two types of visual cryptography schemes can resist the collusive attack 1.

In conclusion, our suggestion for improving partition authentication visual cryptography scheme is applying both random authentication and partition authentication concurrently to devise visual cryptography scheme.

5 Conclusions

In general, partition authentication visual cryptography scheme (PAVCS) belongs in the category of cheating prevention visual cryptography scheme. Without extra verification shares, a PAVCS can provide mutual authentication of any two shares. In this paper, we propose two types of collusive attacks to Lin et al.'s PAVCS, which are proved to be successful attacks experimentally and theoretically. Our future work is combining random authentication with partition authentication to devise visual cryptography scheme for resisting the proposed two types of collusive attacks.

Acknowledgements. Many thanks to the anonymous reviewers for their valuable comments. This work was supported by NSFC No. 61671448, the "Strategic Priority Research Program" of the Chinese Academy of Sciences grant No. XDA06010701, the National Key R&D Program of China with No. 2016YFB0800100 and the Scientific Research Project of Beijing Municipal Educational Committee grant No. 71E1610972.

References

1. Naor, M., Shamir, A.: Visual cryptography. In: Santis, A. (ed.) EUROCRYPT 1994. LNCS, vol. 950, pp. 1–12. Springer, Heidelberg (1995). doi:10.1007/BFb0053419
2. Ateniese, G., Blundo, C., Santis, A.D., Stinson, D.: Visual cryptography for general access structures. Inf. Comput. **129**, 86–106 (1996)
3. Ateniese, G., Blundo, C., Santis, A.D., Stinson, D.: Extended capabilities for visual cryptography. Theor. Comput. Sci. **250**(1–2), 143–161 (2001)
4. Liu, F., Wu, C.K.: Embedded extended visual cryptography schemes. IEEE Trans. Inf. Forensics Secur. **6**(2), 307–322 (2011)
5. Wang, R.Z., Hsu, S.F.: Tagged visual cryptography. IEEE Signal Process. Lett. **18**(11), 627–630 (2011)
6. Ou, D., Wu, X., Dai, L., Sun, W.: Improved tagged visual cryptograms by using random grids. In: Shi, Y.Q., Kim, H.-J., Pérez-González, F. (eds.) IWDW 2013. LNCS, vol. 8389, pp. 79–94. Springer, Heidelberg (2014). doi:10.1007/978-3-662-43886-2_6

7. Ren, Y., Liu, F., Lin, D., Feng, R., Wang, W.: A new construction of tagged visual cryptography scheme. In: Shi, Y.-Q., Kim, H.J., Pérez-González, F., Echizen, I. (eds.) IWDW 2015. LNCS, vol. 9569, pp. 433–445. Springer, Heidelberg (2016). doi:10.1007/978-3-319-31960-5_35

8. Hou, Y.C., Quan, Z.Y.: Progressive visual cryptography with unexpanded shares. IEEE Trans. Circ. Syst. Video Technol. **21**(11), 1760–1764 (2011)

9. Yan, X.H., Wang, S., Niu, X.M.: Threshold construction from specific cases in visual cryptography without the pixel expansion. Signal Process. **105**, 389–398 (2014)

10. Yang, C.N., Wu, C.C., Lin, Y.C., Kim, C.: Constructions and properties of general (k, n) block-based progressive visual cryptography. ETRI J. **37**, 979–989 (2015)

11. Shyu, S.J.: Image encryption by random grids. Pattern Recogn. **40**, 1014–1031 (2007)

12. Chen, T., Tsao, K.: Threshold visual secret sharing by random grids. J. Syst. Softw. **84**, 1197–1208 (2011)

13. Guo, T., Liu, F., Wu, C.K.: Threshold visual secret sharing by random grids with improved contrast. J. Syst. Softw. **86**(8), 2094–2109 (2013)

14. Wu, X., Sun, W.: Improving the visual quality of random grid-based visual secret sharing. Signal Process. **93**, 977–995 (2013)

15. Horng, G., Chen, T.H., Tsai, D.S.: Cheating in visual cryptography. Design. Code. Crypt. **38**, 219–236 (2006)

16. Yang, C.N., Laih, C.S.: Some new types of visual secret sharing schemes. In: Proceedings of National Computer Symposium, vol. 3, pp. 260–268 (1999)

17. Prisco, R., Santis, A.: Cheating immune (2, n)-threshold visual secret sharing. In: Prisco, R., Yung, M. (eds.) SCN 2006. LNCS, vol. 4116, pp. 216–228. Springer, Heidelberg (2006). doi:10.1007/11832072_15

18. Tsai, D.S., Chen, T.H., Horng, G.: A cheating prevention scheme for binary visual cryptography with homogeneous secret images. Pattern Recogn. **40**(8), 2356–2366 (2007)

19. Hu, C.M., Tzeng, W.G.: Cheating prevention in visual cryptography. IEEE Trans. Image Process. **16**(1), 36–45 (2007)

20. De Prisco, R., De Santis, A.: Cheating immune threshold visual secret sharing. Comput. J. **53**(9), 1485–1496 (2010)

21. Liu, F., Wu, C.K., Lin, X.J.: Cheating immune visual cryptography scheme. IET Inform. Secur. **5**, 51–59 (2011)

22. Chen, Y.C., Horng, G., Tsai, D.S.: Comment on "cheating prevention in visual cryptograph". IEEE Trans. Image Process. **21**(7), 3319–3323 (2012)

23. Chen, Y.C., Tsai, D.S., Horng, G.: A new authentication based cheating prevention scheme in Naor-Shamir's visual cryptography. J. Vis. Commun. Image R. **23**, 1225–1233 (2012)

24. Lin, C.H., Chen, T.H., Wu, Y.T., Tsao, K.H., Lin, K.S.: Multi-factor cheating prevention in visual secret sharing by hybrid codebooks. J. Vis. Commun. Image R. **25**, 1543–1557 (2014)

25. Lin, P.Y., Wang, R.Z., Chang, Y.J., Fang, W.P.: Prevention of cheating in visual cryptography by using coherent image. Inf. Sci. **301**, 61–74 (2015)

On the Robustness of Visual Cryptographic Schemes

Sabyasachi Dutta[1], Partha Sarathi Roy[2(⊠)],
Avishek Adhikari[1(⊠)], and Kouichi Sakurai[2]

[1] Department of Pure Mathematics, University of Calcutta, Kolkata, India
saby.math@gmail.com, avishek.adh@gmail.com
[2] Faculty of Information Science and Electrical Engineering,
Kyushu University, Fukuoka, Japan
royparthasarathi0@gmail.com, sakurai@csce.kyushu-u.ac.jp

Abstract. In this paper, we consider the robustness of a special type of secret sharing scheme known as visual cryptographic scheme in which the secret reconstruction is done visually without any mathematical computation unlike other secret sharing schemes. Initially, secret sharing schemes were considered with the presumption that the corrupted participants involved in a protocol behave in a passive manner and submit correct shares during the reconstruction of secret. However, that may not be the case in practical situations. A minimal robust requirement, when a fraction of participants behave maliciously and submit incorrect shares, is that, the set of all shares, some possibly corrupted, can recover the correct secret. Though the concept of robustness is well studied for secret sharing schemes, it is not at all common in the field of visual cryptography. We, for the first time in the literature of visual cryptography, formally define the concept of robustness and put forward $(2, n)$-threshold visual cryptographic schemes that are robust against deterministic cheating. In the robust secret sharing schemes it is assumed that the number of cheaters is always less than the threshold value so that the original secret is not recovered by the coalition of cheaters only. In the current paper, We consider three different scenarios with respect to the number of cheaters controlled by a centralized adversary. We first consider the existence of only one cheater in a $(2, n)$-threshold VCS so that the secret image is not recovered by the cheater. Next we consider two different cases, with number of cheaters being greater than 2, with honest majority and without honest majority.

Keywords: Basis matrices · Robustness · Deterministic cheating · Visual cryptography

Avishek Adhikari—Research is partially supported by National Board for Higher Mathematics, Department of Atomic Energy, Government of India, Grant No. 2/48(10)/2013/NBHM(R.P.)/R&D II/695. The authors are also thankful to DST, Govt. of India and JSPS, Govt. of Japan for providing partial support for this collaborative research work under India Japan Cooperative Science Programme (vide Memo no. DST/INT/JSPS/P-191/2014 dated May 27, 2014.

© Springer International Publishing AG 2017
Y.Q. Shi et al. (Eds.): IWDW 2016, LNCS 10082, pp. 251–262, 2017.
DOI: 10.1007/978-3-319-53465-7_19

1   Introduction

Secret sharing, originally introduced by Shamir [19] and Blakely [7], is a central cryptographic primitive at the heart of a wide variety of applications. Robust secret sharing scheme [9,18] is a stronger notion of secret sharing which deals with the situation when some parties do not submit their original shares during the reconstruction of the secret. Formally, it is required, for a secret sharing scheme to be robust, that if all the players (say n many) pool together their shares, but up to $k - 1$ of them are incorrect (and it is not known which ones), then the shared secret can still be reconstructed (except maybe with small probability). Such robust schemes are building blocks of many cryptographic protocols, particularly for distributed computing.

From the theory of Reed-Solomon error correcting codes it follows that Shamir secret sharing scheme [19] is robust if $k - 1 < \frac{n}{3}$ [6] and so no increase in the share size is needed to obtain robustness. On the other hand, the robust secret sharing is impossible if $k - 1 \geq \frac{n}{2}$. The threshold access structure requires at least k correct shares for the recovery of the original secret.

A traditional (k, n)-threshold Visual Cryptographic Scheme (VCS) for a set of n participants $\mathcal{P} = \{1, 2, \ldots, n\}$ is a variant of secret sharing, that encodes a secret image SI into n shares which are distributed by the dealer among n participants (also known as parties) in the form of transparencies on which the shares are photocopied. Such shares have the property that only those subsets of participants whose cardinalities are greater than or equal to k can visually recover the secret image by carefully stacking the transparencies. Such subsets of parties are called qualified sets. On the other hand, any subset of parties with cardinality strictly less than k does not have any information about the secret. These subsets are called forbidden sets. We properly define these concepts in Sect. 2. The first VCS was proposed by Naor and Shamir [16] where they considered the threshold access structure. In the literature of (k, n)-threshold VCS most of the constructions are realized by constructing so called basis matrices (S^0, S^1) where S^0 is used to share (and reconstruct) a white secret pixel and S^1 is used to share (and reconstruct) a black secret pixel. One may refer to [1–5,8,10–12,20] for more general studies. It is however assumed in all theses papers that while reconstructing the secret the participants behave honestly. They produce the exact shares i.e. the transparencies given to them by the honest dealer. Horng et al. [13] first showed that cheating is, in fact possible in visual cryptography. They proposed two different methods to resist cheating in visual cryptography. Later [14,15,21,22] forwarded this idea of cheating and proposed cheating immune visual cryptographic schemes. First rigorous mathematical formalization of the cheating model was given by De Prisco and De Santis [17]. They have introduced the idea of "deterministic cheating" and put forward $(2, n)$ and (n, n)-threshold cheating immune visual cryptographic schemes. In their model existence of $n - 1$ many cheaters was assumed. The coalition of cheaters, in the reconstruction phase produces "fake but valid shares" so that when the honest party stacks his share with one of the cheater(s) he sees a white pixel (false recovery) instead of a black pixel (original share) and vice versa. The cheaters are said to cheat a honest participant successfully if they can force the honest party into wrong recovery of each secret pixel with probability 1. However in order to construct a cheating immune $(2, n)$-VCS the pixel expansion becomes abnormally high, namely $n + 2^n + 1$.

1.1 Our Contribution

In this work we study the notion of robustness in the area of visual cryptography. We follow the model of deterministic cheating as given in [17] and propose, for the first time in the literature of visual cryptography, a formal definition of *robustness* of a visual cryptographic scheme. By robustness of a VCS we mean that in presence of cheaters when all the participants come together in the secret reconstruction phase, the cheaters can not deceive the honest parties with probability 1. In usual robust secret sharing schemes, apart from some negligible probability, correct secret must be reconstructed. But, in case of robust visual cryptographic schemes, we put some relaxation. That is, at the reconstructed phase, wrong secret should not be reconstructed. This relaxation provides the power of tolerance of arbitrary number of cheating participants which is not possible in usual robust secret sharing schemes. We first consider the situation when number of cheaters does not exceed the threshold value of a threshold VCS. That is, in a (k, n)-VCS number of cheaters is less than or equal to $k - 1$. Later on we deal with situations where the number of cheaters exceeds the threshold value of the scheme. In the work of [17], the coalition of cheaters focuses on finding deterministic strategy to adjust their shares coming from S^b in such a way that when the honest party produces his share, the entirety of fake share and honest share seems to be coming from S^{1-b} for $b \in \{0, 1\}$. If the cheaters can do it with probability 1 then, according to the work of [17], the cheating is said to be *successful*. However, this is a very restrictive model for cheating. In our work, we relax the model and show that it is possible for just one single cheater to cheat whole lot of honest parties.

Remark 1. The model of cheating and robustness that we are considering here makes it possible to apply robust visual cryptographic schemes to the scenario of consensus on the expert-advice. Consider a situation where a group of individuals relies on an expert's advice while making a binary decision e.g. to buy or not to buy shares in a stock market. Suppose it requires the principles of at least two individuals to buy a certain stock. The expert also wants to make sure that it should not be possible for his clients individually to know whether he is suggesting to buy or not to. The majority should be able to know what his decision is but in a collective manner. The expert could take the shares (corresponding to pixel 0 if his decision is not to buy and to pixel 1 otherwise) of a robust VCS and sends one share each to the clients and publishes an integer value $\gamma \in \mathbb{N}$. The "OR" of the shares produced by the clients is a vector of 0s and 1s. If this vector has hamming weight less than γ then the clients know that the expert's advice is not to buy the shares and if greater than γ then the decision is to buy. Now some parties may behave maliciously and submit false shares to take majority of the parties off the course which may result in a big financial loss. Robust visual cryptographic schemes may be used to prevent this type of cheating.

2   Robustness of Visual Cryptographic Schemes

We follow standard notations and symbols through out. Let $\mathcal{P} = \{1, 2, 3, \ldots, n\}$ denote a set of participants. Let $2^{\mathcal{P}}$ denote the set of all subsets of $\mathcal{P}$. Let $\mathcal{Q}$ and $\mathcal{F}$ be subsets of $2^{\mathcal{P}}$, where $\mathcal{Q} \cap \mathcal{F} = \emptyset$. We will refer to members of $\mathcal{Q}$ as *qualified sets* and the members of $\mathcal{F}$ as *forbidden sets*. The pair $(\mathcal{Q}, \mathcal{F})$ is called the *access structure* of the scheme.

Let $\mathcal{Q}_{min} = \{A \mid A \in \mathcal{Q} \wedge \forall A' \subset A, A' \notin \mathcal{Q}\}$ be the collection of all minimal qualified set. A (k, n)-VCS is a particular type of VCS where there are n many parties and any k many of them constitute a minimal qualified set. The maximal forbidden sets are those subsets which contain exactly $k - 1$ many parties. Thus in this case $\mathcal{Q}_{min} = \{A \subset \mathcal{P} : |A| = k\}$.

We further assume that the secret image consists of a collection of black and white pixels, each pixel being shared separately. In each share the pixel is subdivided into m *subpixels* that is, for one pixel of original secret there are m pixels in each share. This m is called the pixel expansion i.e., the number of pixels, on the transparencies corresponding to the shares (each such pixel is called subpixel), needed to represent one pixel of the original image. The shares are printed on transparencies. So a "white" subpixel is actually an area where nothing is printed, and left transparent. We assume that the subpixels are sufficiently small and close enough so that the eye averages them to some shade of grey.

Notations: Let S be an $n \times m$ Boolean matrix and let $X \subseteq \mathcal{P}$. By $S[X]$ we denote the matrix obtained by restricting the rows of S to the indices belonging to X. Further, for any $X \subseteq \mathcal{P}$ the vector obtained by applying the boolean OR operation "$\vee$", to the rows of $S[X]$ is denoted by S_X. The Hamming weight of the row vector which represents the number of ones in the vector S_X is denoted by $w(S_X)$.

Any visual cryptographic scheme can be implemented by means of basis matrices. However we restrict ourselves to the threshold visual cryptographic schemes. We now give the definition.

Definition 1. *Let us consider a (k, n)-threshold access structure on the set $\mathcal{P}$ of n participants. A (k, n)-threshold VCS is realized using two $n \times m$ basis matrices S^0 and S^1 if the following two conditions hold:*

1. *If $X = \{i_1, i_2, \ldots, i_k\}$, then S_X^0 and S_X^1, the "OR" of the rows $i_1, i_2, \ldots, i_k$ of S^0 and S^1 respectively, satisfy $w(S_X^1) - w(S_X^0) > 0$. The same also holds when $X = \mathcal{P}$.*

2. *If $F = \{j_1, j_2, \ldots, j_p : p < k\}$ be a forbidden set, the two $p \times m$ matrices obtained by restricting S^0 and S^1 to rows $j_1, j_2, \ldots, j_p$ are equal up to a column permutation.*

In this case, if the secret pixel is $b \in \{0, 1\}$ then the dealer gives a random permutation to the columns of S^b and distributes the rows of the resulting matrix as shares to the parties.

Remark 2. The first condition in Definition 1 is called the contrast condition. The principle on which it is based is that there is a positive difference between the hamming weights of OR-ed rows (corresponding to a minimal qualified set) in S^0 and corresponding OR-ed rows in S^1. Many constructions of basis matrices depend on this fact e.g., the formulation of VCS as a solution to an integer programming problem [20]. Therefore, if there is a difference in the hamming weights of OR-ed rows corresponding to a qualified set of parties, the image is clearly discernible, that is if $w(S^1_X) - w(S^0_X) > 0$ where $X \in \mathcal{Q}_{min}$ or $X = \mathcal{P} = \{1, \ldots, n\}$. But if it so happens that $w(R^0_1 \vee R^0_2 \vee \cdots \vee R^0_n) - w(R^1_1 \vee R^1_2 \vee \cdots \vee R^1_n) > 0$ where some of the parties have produced fake shares, then a cheating has occurred. Because now the OR of tampered and honest shares corresponding to a secret white pixel appears darker than that corresponding to secret black pixel. Here, R^b_j denotes the share of the jth party corresponding to the pixel $b \in \{0, 1\}$. If j is a honest party, R^b_j is the true share given by the dealer and if the party is dishonest then the share is perhaps modified. We shall make use of this fact in the rest of the paper.

2.1   The Model for Cheating

Following the basic motivation of robust secret sharing, we only concentrate on the recovery of the secret. Cheating identifiability or immunity are not within the scope this work. In our model we put only the restriction that at least a qualified set of parties submit honest shares. This assumption takes care of the scenario when the cheaters refuse to participate in the reconstruction of the secret image. **To develop the model of cheating and of robustness, it is sufficient to assume that the secret image consists of only one black or white pixel.** Thus each share consists of m subpixels from which the reconstruction must take place. So here the analysis that we are going to discuss is only for one pixel. However, it is to be noted that the decryption process in a visual scheme is completely dependent on the visual perception of the participants. That a recovered pixel corresponds to white or black secret pixel depends on the number of black subpixels recreated by "OR"-ing the shares of the parties. Suppose the secret pixel is white and the honest dealer has generated and distributed the corresponding shares to the parties. Now if a coalition of cheaters has a deterministic strategy to permute the subpixels of their shares such that "OR" of all shares corresponding to a secret white pixel has more black subpixels than that in the OR of all shares corresponding to a secret black pixel then we can say that the coaliton is successful in cheating the honest parties. To make the point more rigorous let us consider a (k, n)-VCS where a coalition of c many cheaters can cheat by forming a coalition and producing "*fake but valid*" shares. By "fake but valid" shares we mean that the tampered shares have the same hamming weights as the original shares. Thus the validity checking power of the reconstructor (or participants) is that he can only check that the hamming weight of a share produced by a party is equal to the weight of the original share produced by the honest dealer. A cheating is said to be successful if the coalition of cheaters can have the following with probability 1:

– the secret pixel is white (black) and the reconstructed pixel is black (white) when all parties stack their shares.

We now formally define the concepts.

Definition 2. *Let s_j^b denote the original share produced by the honest dealer for the participant j while sharing the pixel $b \in \{0,1\}$. A fake but valid share, denoted by FSH_j^b, for a participant j is a binary vector such that*

– *length $(FSH_j^b) = length(s_j^b)$*
– *FSH_j^b may or may not be equal to s_j^b*
– *Hamming weight of $FSH_j^b = $ Hamming weight of s_j^b.*

Definition 3. *(adapted from [17])*
  In a (k,n)-threshold VCS and for a coalition $\mathcal{G}$ of c many cheaters, we define the probability of cheating by the group $\mathcal{G}$, denoted by $Pr(\mathcal{G}, \mathcal{P}, 0 \longleftrightarrow 1)$ as the probability that given the fact that secret pixel is $b \in \{0,1\}$, the cheaters have a deterministic strategy to produce c many fake but valid shares such that superimposing them with the rest $n - c$ of the (honest) shares the pixel $1 - b$ is "realized" instead of b.

Remark 3. The visual recovery of the secret image is a visual perception of the participants who have come to recover the secret. Whether a black pixel is recovered or a white pixel is recovered depends on the realization of the participants. This realization solely depends on the hamming weight of the OR-ed shares produced by the participants. We refer to Examples 1 and 2 to properly understand the meaning of the word "realized" used in the above definition.

Now maximizing over all possible groups of c cheaters we get $Pr(0 \longleftrightarrow 1)$, which we call the cheating probability of a VCS. This cheating may be implemented by the cheaters in certain regions of the transparency sheets so that the recovered image is partially destroyed. In light of Remark 2 there can be another possible deterministic way of cheating for the coalition of the cheaters $\mathcal{G}$ namely, even after superimposing all the shares, the participants cannot distinguish between a white pixel and a black pixel. This happens if in the notations of Remark 2, $w(R_1^0 \vee R_2^0 \vee \cdots \vee R_n^0) - w(R_1^1 \vee R_2^1 \vee \cdots \vee R_n^1) = 0$. We denote the probability of this situation by $Pr(\mathcal{G}, \mathcal{P}, 0 \rightleftharpoons 1)$ and maximizing over all possible groups of c cheaters we get $Pr(0 \rightleftharpoons 1)$. This is the worst kind of cheating in which even partial recovery of the secret image is hindered.

Definition 4. *In a (k,n)-threshold VCS and for a coalition of c many cheaters, the VCS is said to be not-robust if either $Pr(0 \longleftrightarrow 1)$ or $Pr(0 \rightleftharpoons 1)$ equals 1 when all n parties (which means at least all the honest parties) stack their shares.*

We can now define the concept of robust visual cryptographic scheme.

Definition 5. *A VCS is said to be robust if the c cheaters can not make the honest parties to reveal a wrong secret (which includes no secret at all) with probability 1 even if the cheaters produce fake but valid shares during the reconstruction phase.*

3   Realization of Robust Visual Cryptographic Schemes

In this section we first provide some examples of visual cryptographic schemes that are not robust in the sense of Definition 4. These examples give sufficient motivation to study the concept of robustness in the field of visual cryptography. Later we provide some concrete construction methods to achieve robustness.

3.1   Motivation: Some Examples

To make Definitions 3 and 4 more clear let us consider the following examples.

Example 1. Let us consider the $(2,3)$-VCS which is realized by the following basis matrices:

$$S^0 = \begin{bmatrix} 001 \\ 001 \\ 001 \end{bmatrix} \ \& \ S^1 = \begin{bmatrix} 100 \\ 010 \\ 001 \end{bmatrix}.$$

The threshold value is 2 and we assume there is only one cheater. Suppose without loss of generality, the first party P_1 is the corrupt one. He does not have any information whatsoever about the secret pixel. Still he can make the VCS non-robust with probability 1 by choosing the following (deterministic) strategy: P_1 has as his share a vector with hamming weight 1. He interchanges between a 0 and the 1. Thus the tampered share is fake but valid. Now if all the participants stack their shares then it is easy to see that $2 = w(S^0_{\{P_1,P_2,P_3\}}) = w(S^1_{\{P_1,P_2,P_3\}})$. Thus, $Pr(\{P_1\}, \{P_1, P_2, P_3\}, 0 \rightleftharpoons 1) = 1 = Pr(0 \rightleftharpoons 1)$.

Let us consider another example.

Example 2. The basis matrices of a $(2,2)$-VCS are as follows:

$$S^0 = \begin{bmatrix} 01 \\ 01 \end{bmatrix} \ \& \ S^1 = \begin{bmatrix} 10 \\ 01 \end{bmatrix}.$$

Suppose the first party is corrupted and tampers his share by interchanging 0 and 1. Then it is easy to see that $Pr(0 \longleftrightarrow 1) = 1$ and hence the VCS is not robust. The construction (which adjoins one single all-zero column to both the basis matrices) as given in [17] applied to $(2,2)$-VCS can not be made robust, if one participant is cheating. A deterministic strategy of cheating would be to interchange between the $1s$ and $0s$ so that the hamming weight of the share remains the same. This strategy will always give $Pr(0 \longleftrightarrow 1) = 1$.

The two examples show that even if the corrupted participants do not get the secret pixel and can not guess the share of the honest parties, they can make a visual cryptographic scheme non-robust. Indeed, there are some canonical schemes [8] where each participant's share has exactly same number of 0s as the number of 1s. In those cases just one single participant can make the scheme non robust just by interchanging the 0s and 1s. Thus sometimes existence of one single corrupt participant can make a VCS non-robust in light of Definition 4.

3.2   Robust $(2, n)$-Visual Cryptographic Schemes

In this section we provide concrete constructions of robust visual cryptographic schemes. For that consider the following example.

Example 3. Let us begin with the $(2, 3)$-VCS described in Example 1. Suppose instead of taking the basis matrices as in Example 1, the dealer adds one more all zero columnn to both S^0 and S^1, so that the new matrices are

$$S^0_{new} = \begin{bmatrix} 001|0 \\ 001|0 \\ 001|0 \end{bmatrix} \ \& \ S^1_{new} = \begin{bmatrix} 100|0 \\ 010|0 \\ 001|0 \end{bmatrix}.$$

It is easy to check that S^0_{new} and S^1_{new} are basis matrices realizing $(2, 3)$-VCS. However, for a single cheater the probability of cheating all the parties is $Pr(0 \rightleftharpoons 1) = \frac{2}{3} < 1$. Note that $Pr(0 \longleftrightarrow 1) = 0$ in this case. Hence the new scheme is robust against deterministic cheating. Moreover, the cheating probability can be reduced upto whatever degree of accuracy one needs simply by adding more all-zero columns. For example, adding r many all-zero columns reduces the cheating probability to $\frac{2}{r+2}$.

Let us consider Naor-Shamir construction [16] of the basis matrices realizing $(2, n)$-VCS for $n \geq 4$. The basis matrices are as follows:

- The white basis matrix S^0 consists of one all-one column and $n - 1$ many all-zero columns, where the columns are of length n.
- The black basis matrix S^1 is the identity matrix of size $n \times n$.

Example 4. The basis matrices for a $(2, 4)$-VCS obtained by Naor-Shamir construction are as follow

$$S^0 = \begin{bmatrix} 0001 \\ 0001 \\ 0001 \\ 0001 \end{bmatrix} \ \& \ S^1 = \begin{bmatrix} 1000 \\ 0100 \\ 0010 \\ 0001 \end{bmatrix}.$$

Let $\mathcal{P}$ denote the set of all participants. Now if there is one cheater and he produces a fake but valid share then when all the shares of all participants are stacked together, the minimum possible weight $w(S^1_{\mathcal{P}})$ is $n-1$ and the maximum possible weight $w(S^0_{\mathcal{P}})$ is 2. Now since $n \geq 4$ therefore $n - 1 > 2$ always and the image is perceptible. Hence we have the following theorem.

Theorem 1. *For $n \geq 4$, the Naor-Shamir construction of $(2,n)$-VCS is robust in the presence of 1 faulty share. For $n = 3$, there exists a modification of Naor-Shamir construction with pixel expansion 4 (see Example 3) so that $(2,3)$-VCS is robust when one party is cheating.*

Remark 4. The above discussion shows that the Naor-Shamir construction of $(2,n)$-VCS is robust in the presence of one single cheater for $n \geq 4$. If we make the adversarial model more powerful by considering the existence of $1 < c < n$ many cheaters then we see that the basis matrices S^0_{new} and S^1_{new} for $(2,3)$-VCS is still not robust. If we consider c many cheaters where c is greater than 2 then it is easy to see that the maximum weight (when all n shares are stacked) that is achievable by the cheaters from the Naor-Shamir white basis matrix S^0 is $c + 1$. On the other hand the minimum weight (when all n shares are stacked) that is achievable by the cheaters from the Naor-Shamir black basis matrix S^1 is $n - c$. Thus when all the parties stack their shares then $w(S^1_P) \geq n - c$ and $w(S^0_P) \leq c-1$. If $n-c > c+1$ i.e. $n > 2c+1$ then the $(2,n)$-VCS is automatically robust.

We summarize this in the following theorem.

Theorem 2. *If there is a honest majority then Naor-Shamir construction of $(2,n)$-VCS is robust for all $n \geq 4$.*

We point out that when there are $n - 2$ many cheaters where $n \geq 4$, the construction of basis matrices as given in *Construction* 6.1 of [17] does not achieve the robustness. We now have just one minimal qualified set of parties who are honest and thus submit correct shares. Let us consider the basis matrices of cheating immune $(2,4)$-VCS given in [17].
The matrices are $W_4 = [I_{2^4}||\mathbf{0}||S^0_{NS}]$ and $B_4 = [I_{2^4}||\mathbf{0}||S^1_{NS}]$ where I_{2^4} denotes 4×2^4 matrix containing all possible columns of length 4, $\mathbf{0}$ denotes an all-zero column and S^b_{NS} denotes Naor-Shamir basis matrix for $(2,4)$-VCS. Suppose the first two cheaters (who can actually recover the secret) produce two fake shares by replacing all $[1,1]^t$ columns by new $[0,0]^t$ columns and placing those $1's$ in the existing old $[0,0]^t$ columns so that these are transformed into columns with at least one 1. Now the scheme is no more robust as $Pr(0 \rightleftharpoons 1) = 1$.

However, a closer look at the argument reveals that if there are more $[0,0]^t$ columns than the number of $1's$ appearing in the $[1,1]^t$ columns then the cheaters can cheat the honest parties only with a probability strictly less than 1. We modify the constructions of the basis matrices as follows
$W_n = [I_{2^n}||[0]_{n \times 2^n}||S^0_{NS}]$ and $B_n = [I_{2^n}||[0]_{n \times 2^n}||S^1_{NS}]$. Then with respect to these basis matrices we have the following theorem.

Theorem 3. *There exists a robust $(2,n)$-VCS in presence of $n-2$ cheaters with pixel expansion $2^{n+1} + n$.*

We emphasize that the increase in number of cheaters forces the pixel expansion of a VCS to be very large in order to achieve robustness.

4 Conclusion

We have defined the notion of robustness for visual cryptographic schemes and studied the robustness of $(2, n)$-VCS. We maintain the fact that at least one minimal qualified set of parties has to produce honest shares for achieving robustness. It is an interesting problem to construct general (k, n)-VCS that are robust against deterministic cheating and at the same time minimize the pixel expansion.

Appendix

For illustration we provide the following Figures. The Fig. 1 shows the secret black and whie image while the Fig. 2 shows three shares $S1$, $S2$, $S3$ obtained through the construction method of Naor-Shamir [16] for a $(2, 3)$-VCS and MS3 is the fake but valid share produced by the third participant. Stacking of the shares are shown in Fig. 3. It shows that while superimposing the Shares 1, 2 and 3, we get the secret image back. However, if we replace S3 by $MS3$, we do not get the secret back. Figure 4 considers the same access structure but with our modified basis matrix construction method. Note that in the modified scheme, the superimposition of the two shares $S1$ and $S2$ over the modified share $MS3$ provides the secret even though MS3 produces fake but valid share.

CRYPTO

Fig. 1. Secret image

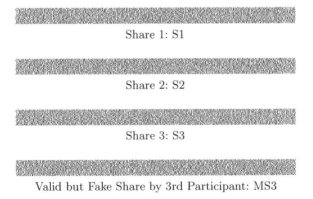

Share 1: S1

Share 2: S2

Share 3: S3

Valid but Fake Share by 3rd Participant: MS3

Fig. 2. 4 Shares: S1, S2, S3, MS3

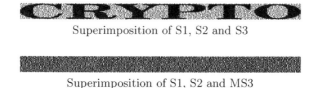

Superimposition of S1, S2 and S3

Superimposition of S1, S2 and MS3

Fig. 3. Superimposed images

CRYPTO
Secret Image

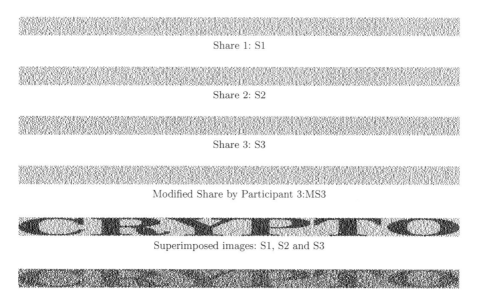

Share 1: S1

Share 2: S2

Share 3: S3

Modified Share by Participant 3:MS3

Superimposed images: S1, S2 and S3

Superimposed images: S1, S2 and MS3

Fig. 4. Robust VCS

References

1. Adhikari, A.: Linear algebraic techniques to construct monochrome visual cryptographic schemes for general access structure and its applications to color images. Des. Codes Crypt. **73**(3), 865–895 (2014)
2. Adhikari, A., Dutta, T.K., Roy, B.: A new black and white visual cryptographic scheme for general access structures. In: Canteaut, A., Viswanathan, K. (eds.) INDOCRYPT 2004. LNCS, vol. 3348, pp. 399–413. Springer, Heidelberg (2004). doi:10.1007/978-3-540-30556-9_31
3. Adhikari, A., Bose, M.: A new visual cryptographic scheme using latin squares. IEICE Trans. Fundam. **E87−A**(5), 1998–2002 (2004)
4. Adhikari, A., Kumar, D, Bose, M., Roy, B.: Applications of partially balanced and balanced incomplete block designs in developing visual cryptographic schemes. IEICE Trans. Fundam. Japan **E-90A**(5), 949–951 (2007)

5. Arumugam, S., Lakshmanan, R., Nagar, A.K.: On (k, n)*-visual cryptography scheme. Des. Codes Crypt. **71**(1), 153–162 (2014)
6. Ben-Or, M., Goldwasser, S., Wigderson, A.: Completeness theorems for non-cryptographic fault-tolerant distributed computation (extended abstract). In: STOC 1988, pp. 1–10. ACM (1988)
7. Blakley, G.R.: Safeguarding cryptographic keys. In: AFIPS 1979, pp. 313–317 (1979)
8. Blundo, C., Darco, P., De Santis, A., Stinson, D.R.: Contrast optimal threshold visual cryptography. SIAM J. Discrete Math. **16**(2), 224–261 (2003)
9. Cevallos, A., Fehr, S., Ostrovsky, R., Rabani, Y.: Unconditionally-secure robust secret sharing with compact shares. In: Pointcheval, D., Johansson, T. (eds.) EUROCRYPT 2012. LNCS, vol. 7237, pp. 195–208. Springer, Heidelberg (2012). doi:10.1007/978-3-642-29011-4_13
10. Droste, S.: New results on visual cryptography. In: Koblitz, N. (ed.) CRYPTO 1996. LNCS, vol. 1109, pp. 401–415. Springer, Heidelberg (1996). doi:10.1007/3-540-68697-5_30
11. Dutta, S., Adhikari, A.: XOR based non-monotone t-$(k, n)^*$-visual cryptographic schemes using linear algebra. In: Hui, L.C.K., Qing, S.H., Shi, E., Yiu, S.M. (eds.) ICICS 2014. LNCS, vol. 8958, pp. 230–242. Springer, Heidelberg (2015). doi:10.1007/978-3-319-21966-0_17
12. Dutta, S., Rohit, R.S., Adhikari, A.: Constructions and analysis of some efficient t-$(k, n)^*$-visual cryptographic schemes using linear algebraic techniques. Accepted at the J. Des. Codes Crypt. **80**(1), 165–196 (2016). doi:10.1007/s10623-015-0075-5 (Springer, US)
13. Horng, G., Chen, T.H., Tsai, D.S.: Cheating in visual cryptography. Des. Codes Crypt. **38**(2), 219–236 (2006)
14. Hu, C., Tzeng, W.: Cheating prevention in visual cryptography. IEEE Trans. Image Process. **16**(1), 36–45 (2007)
15. Liu, F., Wu, C.K., Lin, X.J.: Cheating immune visual cryptography scheme. IET Inf. Secur. **5**(1), 51–59 (2011)
16. Naor, M., Shamir, A.: Visual cryptography. In: Santis, A. (ed.) EUROCRYPT 1994. LNCS, vol. 950, pp. 1–12. Springer, Heidelberg (1995). doi:10.1007/BFb0053419
17. De Prisco, R., De Santis, A.: Cheating immune threshold visual secret sharing. Comput. J. **53**(9), 1485–1496 (2010)
18. Rabin, T., Ben-Or, M.: Verifiable secret sharing and multiparty protocols with honest majority (extended abstract). In: STOC 1989, pp. 73–85. ACM (1989)
19. Shamir, A.: How to share a secret. Comm. ACM **22**(11), 612–613 (1979)
20. Shyu, S.J., Chen, M.C.: Optimum pixel expansions for threshold visual secret sharing schemes. IEEE Trans. Inf. Forensics Secur. **6**(3(pt. 2)), 960–969 (2011)
21. Tsai, D.S., Chen, T.H., Horng, G.: A cheating prevention scheme for binary visual cryptography with homogeneous secret images. Pattern Recogn. **40**(8), 2356–2366 (2007)
22. Xiaotian, W., Sun, W.: Random grid-based visual secret sharing for general access structures with cheat-preventing ability. J. Syst. Softw. **85**(5), 1119–1134 (2012)

Reversible Data Hiding

Optimal Distortion Estimation for Prediction Error Expansion Based Reversible Watermarking

Aniket Roy$^{(\boxtimes)}$ and Rajat Subhra Chakraborty

Secured Embedded Architecture Laboratory (SEAL),
Department of Computer Science and Engineering
Indian Institute of Technology Kharagpur, Kharagpur 721302, West Bengal, India
aniketroy@iitkgp.ac.in, rschakraborty@cse.iitkgp.ernet.in

Abstract. *Reversible Image Watermarking* is a technique to losslessly embed and retrieve information (in the form of a watermark) in a cover image. *Prediction Error Expansion* based schemes are currently the most efficient and widely used reversible image watermarking techniques. Estimation of the minimum achievable (optimum) distortion for a given payload and a given cover image, is an important problem for reversible watermarking schemes. In this paper, we first show that the *bounded capacity distortion minimization problem* for *prediction error expansion* based reversible watermarking schemes is NP-hard, and that the corresponding decision version of the problem is NP-complete. We then propose a low computational overhead heuristic to estimate the minimal distortion. Our estimation technique first estimates (for a given image) the prediction error distribution function without explicit use of any prediction scheme, and then minimizes the distortion for a given payload by solving a convex optimization problem to estimate an embedding threshold parameter. Experimental results for common benchmark images closely match the predictions from our technique, and thus verify the consistency of our approach.

1 Introduction

Reversible Watermarking constitutes a special class of digital watermarking, where during watermark extraction both the watermark and the cover medium need to be recovered losslessly. The cover medium can be text, image, audio or video, but in this paper we exclusively consider the cover medium to be image. Reversible watermarking is widely used for sensitive information transmission in medical, military and legal industries [1,2].

Initial works on reversible image watermarking applied *lossless compression* [3]. But such schemes have low embedding capacity, as well as high image degradation. Ni et al. [4] introduced *histogram-bin-shifting* based reversible

---

This work is supported by *Science and Engineering Research Board (SERB)*, Govt. of India under Research Grant No. SB/FTP/ETA-0191/2013.

Y.Q. Shi et al. (Eds.): IWDW 2016, LNCS 10082, pp. 265–279, 2017.
DOI: 10.1007/978-3-319-53465-7_20

watermarking technique. A *Difference Expansion* based reversible watermarking scheme was first proposed in [5], and the fundamental principle of this scheme was later generalised as *Prediction Error Expansion* (PEE) scheme in [6]. In PEE based schemes, pixel values are predicted leveraging the spatial correlation of pixel values in natural images, and the watermark information is embedded and extracted from the pixel prediction errors. It has been found that PEE schemes are most efficient in providing high embedding capacity, as well as better embedding distortion control, and hence currently PEE is the principle choice for reversible image watermarking. Several variants of PEE schemes are currently known, viz. weighted mean based prediction [7], weighted median based prediction [8], rhombus based prediction [9], local prediction based methods [10], etc.

In PEE based schemes, the prediction error histogram can be modelled reasonably accurately as a zero-mean *Laplacian probability distribution* with a scaling parameter [11]. *Embedding threshold parameters* can then be chosen to divide the histogram into inner and outer regions. Prediction errors in the inner region are used to embed the watermark, while in the outer region prediction errors are shifted but not used for embedding. Eventually, in PEE based reversible watermarking, capacity and distortion both can be modelled, given the *embedding threshold parameter* and the prediction error histogram. In [11], the bounded capacity distortion minimization problem for PEE based reversible watermarking was formulated as a convex optimization problem. The authors in [12] estimate both the optimal histogram scaling parameter and embedding threshold parameters for the prediction error (assuming it to be zero mean Laplacian probability distribution) using optimization techniques. Then, the watermark bits are embedded into the estimated optimal prediction error histogram according to the estimated embedding threshold parameters. This technique is elegant; however, it requires the solution of multiple relatively complex interrelated optimization problems, making the scheme relatively computationally expensive.

In this paper we have employed an alternative technique of error histogram modelling that employs the discretized *Discrete Cosine Transform* coefficient histogram for the image, scaled by the image entropy. For the optimal embedding threshold parameter estimation to minimize distortion, we used the convex optimization formulation proposed in [11]. Since our proposed technique requires the solution of only a single optimization problem, it is relatively computationally efficient. Experimental results show that our simplified model gives results which are quite consistent with those obtained from the more complicated technique used in [12].

Although there exist numerous published reversible watermarking algorithms, and efforts have been made to estimate the maximum embedding capacity and the corresponding distortion in closed form [13], yet the theoretical algorithmic complexity analyses of the corresponding optimal capacity distortion estimation problem for the schemes are rare in the literature. In [14], the authors considered the decision version of the *steganography embedding problem*: given a distortion bound for the stego-object and a lower bound on the payload size, does a steganographic embedding scheme meeting these capacity and distortion constraints exist? The authors proved this problem to be NP-complete. However, to the best of our knowledge, similar analyses for reversible watermarking algorithms have not yet been published.

The *Bounded Capacity Distortion Minimization (*BCDM*) problem* for a PEE based reversible watermarking scheme can be defined as follows: given a cover image and a lower bound on the payload size, what should be the frequency distribution of the prediction errors (i.e. the prediction error histogram), such that the overall distortion is minimized? The corresponding decision problem provides a YES/NO answer to the following question: given a cover image, a minimum payload size constraint, and an embedding threshold parameter value, does there exist any prediction scheme for the PEE based reversible watermarking, which generates a prediction error distribution that minimizes the overall distortion?

In this context, we make the following contributions in this paper:

- We formally prove that the bounded capacity distortion minimization problem for prediction error expansion (PEE) based reversible watermarking scheme for a given value of the embedding threshold parameter is NP-hard, through a polynomial-time reduction from the *Integer Linear Programming* (ILP) problem.
- We then demonstrate that the corresponding decision version of the problem is NP-complete.
- We propose to model the prediction error histogram of a given cover image as the discretized *Discrete Cosine Transform* (DCT) coefficient histogram scaled by the image entropy, and then using a previously proposed convex optimization scheme to minimize the distortion by estimating an optimal value of the embedding threshold parameter. Our technique gives similar estimate compared to previously proposed technique at lesser computational effort, since the prediction error histogram construction is much simpler and does not need the solution of any additional optimization problem. Another unique advantage of our proposed scheme is that the prediction error histogram construction scheme does not employ any particular prediction scheme, and is thus generic in nature.
- The distortion vs. payload characteristics predicted by our techniques shows good match with that obtained experimentally for two different state-of-the-art reversible watermarking techniques.

We would keep our treatment confined to grayscale images, although similar techniques can be applied to colored images also.

The rest of the paper is organized as follows. The general principles and formulation of the distortion function for PEE based reversible watermarking is described in Sect. 2. The theoretical complexity analysis of the bounded capacity distortion minimization problem for PEE based reversible watermarking and its dual is performed in Sect. 3. In the same section we also describe the convex optimization approach for the embedding threshold parameter estimation to minimize distortion. Our proposed simplified prediction error histogram modelling is described in Sect. 4. Experimental results and related discussions are presented in Sect. 5. Section 6 concludes the paper.

2   Prediction Error Expansion Based Reversible Watermarking

General PEE based reversible watermarking consists of the following steps:

2.1   Embedding Algorithm

– Predict the pixels of the cover image using an efficient *prediction function*, leveraging the spatial correlation in pixel values. Let $\mathcal{P}$ be the set of cover image pixels; $(x_1, x_2, .., x_N)$ be the cover image pixel values, where x_i is the value of the i-th pixel, and N be the total number of pixels, i.e., $|\mathcal{P}| = N$. Let $\hat{x}_i$ be the corresponding predicted values, obtained after applying a prediction function $\mathrm{Predict}(\cdot)$, $i = 1, 2, \ldots N$, i.e.,

$$\hat{x}_i = \mathrm{Predict}\,(\mathcal{P}_i) \tag{1}$$

where $\mathcal{P}_i \subseteq \mathcal{P}$ is the subset of pixels used to predict the value of the i-th pixel. Usually, $\mathcal{P}_i$ consists of pixels in the neighbourhood of the i-th pixel, and the exact locations of the member pixels of $\mathcal{P}_i$ depend on the prediction scheme being used.
– Next, calculate the prediction error e_i corresponding to x_i as:

$$e_i = x_i - \hat{x}_i \tag{2}$$

for $i = 1, 2, \ldots N$.
– Generate the histogram of the prediction errors. The prediction error histogram is based on a partition of the set of given image prediction errors, with each set corresponding to exactly one pixel prediction error value. Given this partition, each value $H(k)$ in the histogram is the cardinality of the set of pixel prediction errors of value k, $0 \leq H(k) \leq N$, and,

$$H(k) = |\{e_i : e_i = k, i = 1, 2, \ldots N\}| \tag{3}$$

where $|A|$ denotes the cardinality of set A. For example, for an 256×256 8-bit grayscale image, $0 \leq H(k) \leq 65536$.
– Embed data by expansion and shifting of prediction error e_i:

$$\begin{aligned} e'_i &= 2e_i + b \quad \text{if} \quad e_i \in [-T, T) \\ &= e_i + T \quad \text{if} \quad e_i \in [T, +\infty) \\ &= e_i - T \quad \text{if} \quad e_i \in (-\infty, -T) \end{aligned} \tag{4}$$

where for $i = 1, 2, \ldots N$, $b \in \{0, 1\}$ is the watermark bit to be embedded, and T is the embedding threshold parameter to control the embedding capacity. Prediction errors in the range $[-T, T)$ are expanded to embed data into the prediction error histogram, and those outside this range (i.e. in the range $(-\infty, -T) \cup [T, +\infty)$) are shifted "outwards" to create vacant bins.

– Finally, the modified error e_i' is added with the predicted value $\hat{x}_i$, to get the watermarked pixel sequence x_i':

$$x_i' = \hat{x}_i + e_i' \tag{5}$$

for $i = 1, 2, \ldots N$.

2.2 Extraction Algorithm

– Applying the same prediction method, the predicted value $\hat{x}_i$ corresponding to each watermarked pixel x_i' for $i = 1, 2, \ldots N$ is obtained as:

$$\hat{x}_i = \text{Predict}\,(\mathcal{P'}_i) \tag{6}$$

where $\mathcal{P'}_i$ consists of pixels in the neighbourhood of the i-th watermarked pixel (i.e., x_i').
– The prediction error e_i' is calculated as:

$$e_i' = x_i' - \hat{x}_i \tag{7}$$

for $i = 1, 2, \ldots N$.
– The original prediction error is retrieved from the watermarked prediction error as:

$$
\begin{aligned}
e_i &= \lfloor e_i'/2 \rfloor & \text{if} \quad e_i' \in [-2T, 2T) \\
&= e_i' - T & \text{if} \quad e_i' \in [2T, +\infty) \\
&= e_i' + T & \text{if} \quad e_i' \in (-\infty, -2T)
\end{aligned}
\tag{8}
$$

for $i = 1, 2, \ldots N$.
– Then, the cover image pixels are recovered as:

$$x_i = \hat{x}_i + e_i \tag{9}$$

for $i = 1, 2, \ldots N$.
– Finally, the watermark bits are recovered as:

$$b = e_i' - 2\lfloor e_i'/2 \rfloor \quad \text{if} \quad e_i' \in [-2T, 2T) \tag{10}$$

In this paper, for simplicity we have ignored the issue of overflow/underflow, since they are easily avoided in practical PEE based schemes, and ignoring them does not affect our main results.

2.3 Average Distortion for PEE Based Reversible Watermarking

In the prediction error expansion based scheme discussed, prediction errors in the range $[-T, T)$ are expanded and allowed to embed watermark bits. So embedding capacity will be:

$$C = \sum_{k=-T}^{T-1} H(k) \tag{11}$$

where H denotes prediction error histogram and $H(k)$ denotes number of occurrence of prediction error k. Now, after embedding, prediction errors e_i in the range $[-T, T)$ undergo distortion dependent on the watermark, and e_i in the range $e_i \in (-\infty, -T) \cup [T, +\infty)$ undergo fixed distortion of magnitude T due to constant shifting. If we consider the square of the error distortion, i.e., $D(x_i, x_i') = ||x_i - x_i'||^2$, then the average (squared) distortion for the i-th pixel is given by:

$$D(x_i, x_i') = ||x_i - x_i'||^2 = ||e_i - e_i'||^2$$
$$= \begin{cases} \frac{1}{2} \sum_{b \in \{0,1\}} (e_i + b)^2 = e_i^2 + e_i + \frac{1}{2} & \text{if } e_i \in [-T, T) \\ T^2 & \text{otherwise} \end{cases}$$

Hence, the average (squared) distortion is given by [15]:

$$D_{av} = \sum_{k=-T}^{T-1} \left(k^2 + k + \frac{1}{2} \right) H(k) + \left(\sum_{k=-\infty}^{-T-1} H(k) + \sum_{k=T}^{+\infty} H(k) \right) T^2 \qquad (12)$$

3 Optimization of Distortion Under Capacity Constraint

We now consider the theoretical complexity of the bounded capacity distortion minimization problem. Note that the dual of the problem can be stated as: given a bound of the maximum allowable distortion, how to optimize the embedding capacity.

3.1 Algorithmic Complexity of Bounded Capacity Distortion Minimization: Optimization and Decision Problems

We will need the concept of the *Integer Linear Programming* (ILP) problem and its theoretical complexity in proving our main result. The ILP is a common optimization problem that can be stated in the following form [16]:

$$\begin{aligned} & \text{minimize} \quad b_1 x_1 + b_2 x_2 + \ldots + b_N x_N \\ & \text{subject to:} \\ & a_{11} x_1 + a_{12} x_2 + \ldots + a_{1N} x_N \geq K_1 \\ & a_{21} x_1 + a_{22} x_2 + \ldots + a_{2N} x_N \geq K_2 \\ & \quad \vdots \\ & a_{N1} x_1 + a_{N2} x_2 + \ldots + a_{NN} x_N \geq K_N \end{aligned} \qquad (13)$$

where all b_i, a_{ij}, x_i (to be determined), $K_i \in \mathbb{Z}$ for $i = 1, 2, \ldots N$. It is well-known that the ILP problem is NP-hard [16].

We are now ready to prove our main result of this paper:

Theorem 1. *The* Bounded Capacity Distortion Minimization (*BCDM*) *Problem for PEE based reversible watermarking schemes, for given values of the embedding threshold T, is NP-hard.*

Proof. The proof proceeds by a polynomial-time reduction of the ILP problem to the BCDM problem. The BCDM for PEE based reversible watermarking can be framed as:

$$\begin{aligned} \text{minimize} \quad & D_{av} \\ \text{subject to:} \quad & C - c \geq 0 \end{aligned} \tag{14}$$

for some given positive constant c, which represents the given payload size, and C represents the embedding capacity of the cover image.

Multiplying the objective function by the constant factor 2, the optimization problem equivalently reduces to:

$$\begin{aligned} \text{minimize} \quad & 2D_{av} \\ \text{subject to:} \quad & C - c \geq 0 \end{aligned} \tag{15}$$

We consider a finite range of the prediction error histogram, i.e., in the range $[-T_\infty, T_\infty]$, where $-T_\infty$ and T_∞ denote the feasible limits of the embedding threshold. Suppose, the actual embedding threshold range $[-T, T)$ used for embedding is given. Now, we can represent the embedding capacity C as a linear combination of the pixel count distribution over feasible prediction error values, i.e., as a linear combination of the prediction error histogram values. Average distortion D_{av} can be expressed similarly, as a part of the shifted histogram results in constant distortion, and the rest of the histogram will give some scaled distortion due to embedding. Therefore,

$$C = \sum_{i=-T_\infty}^{T_\infty} c_i H(i) \quad \text{and} \quad 2D_{av} = \sum_{i=-T_\infty}^{T_\infty} d_i H(i) \tag{16}$$

Comparing the above expressions with Eq. (11) and (12) we have:

$$c_i = \begin{cases} 1 & \text{if } i \in [-T, T) \\ 0 & \text{otherwise} \end{cases} \tag{17}$$

and,

$$d_i = \begin{cases} 2i^2 + 2i + 1 & \text{if } i \in [-T, T) \\ 2T^2 & \text{otherwise} \end{cases} \tag{18}$$

We observe that c_i, d_i are non-negative integers. Since these parameters can be computed in polynomial-time for a given embedding threshold parameter T, hence, we can reduce the ILP problem of Eq. (13) to the BCDM problem in Eq. (16) in polynomial-time by setting:

$$\begin{aligned} b_i &= d_i \\ a_{1i} &= c_i \\ a_{ii} &= 1 & 2 \leq i \leq N \\ a_{ij} &= 0 & 2 \leq i \leq N, i \neq j \\ x_i &= H(i) \\ K_1 &= c \\ K_i &= 0 & 2 \leq i \leq N \end{aligned} \tag{19}$$

Since this transformation is polynomial-time, and since the ILP problem is known to be NP-hard, hence, the bounded capacity distortion minimization problem is itself NP-hard.   □

We now prove the corresponding result about the decision version of the problem:

Theorem 2. *The decision version of the BCDM problem is NP-complete.*

Proof. Recall that the decision version of the BCDM problem answers the feasibility question of the existence of an optimal prediction scheme for PEE based reversible watermarking, given a cover image and the embedding threshold parameter value. In other words, the decision version of BCDM problem can be stated as: does there exist any prediction scheme that will produce the prediction error histogram, estimated by the optimization version of the BCDM problem? It can be observed that the BCDM optimization problem is polynomial-time reducible to the corresponding decision problem – any feasible solution to the BCDM optimization problem implies the decision problem has an answer "YES", while the infeasibility of the solution implies that the corresponding answer is "NO". Hence, the decision version of the BCDM problem is also NP-hard.

We would demonstrate the polynomial-time verifiability of a solution obtained from the corresponding optimization problem, with the corresponding answer from the decision problem. Suppose, the BCDM optimization problem is solved and results in a polynomial-length "certificate" consisting of an encoding of the optimal $H(i)$ values. Now, if a particular prediction scheme produces a prediction error distribution that is identical to the prediction error distribution obtained by solving the optimization problem, then the answer to the corresponding decision problem is "YES", i.e., that particular prediction scheme is also optimal. Otherwise, if the produced prediction error distribution is not identical to that obtained by the optimization version, then it would return "NO", i.e., the particular prediction scheme is not optimal. This answer can be verified in polynomial time using Eq. (16). Hence, the decision version of the BCDM problem is in NP.

Thus, the decision version of the BCDM problem is both NP-hard and in NP. Combining, it is NP-complete.   □

3.2   Convex Optimization Based Capacity Threshold Parameter Estimation

Since the bounded capacity distortion minimization problem for PEE based reversible watermarking algorithms, given an embedding threshold value, is NP-hard, it is practically difficult to come with a provably optimal pixel prediction scheme that will result in the correct values of the $H(i)$ terms, to achieve the minimal distortion value. However, an alternative approach of looking at the distortion minimization problem is to pay attention to the fact that the distortion also depends on the embedding threshold parameter T, which was "given" to us in the optimization problem above. If we assume that T is unknown, and if we can construct a reasonably accurate model of the pixel prediction error histogram to get estimates of the $H(i)$ terms, then the distortion can be attempted to be minimized by trying to optimize the T parameter.

There are some well-accepted polynomial time complexity approaches of estimating the embedding threshold parameter (T) that minimizes the total distortion, for a given payload size. In the existing literature the prediction error is assumed to approximately follow a zero-mean Laplacian probability distribution [11]:

$$p(x) = \frac{1}{2b} \exp\left(-\frac{|x|}{b}\right) \tag{20}$$

The scaling parameter b is optimally estimated by *maximum likelihood decoding*:

$$b = \frac{1}{N} \sum_{i=1}^{N} |e_i| \tag{21}$$

where e_i is the i-th sample of prediction error and N denotes the total number of prediction errors. Assuming the prediction errors lying in the range $[-T, T-1]$ are used for embedding, [11] framed the optimal embedding threshold parameter (T) selection for distortion minimization, as an optimization problem as follows:

$$\text{minimize}_L \quad 2b^2 L \ln L - (2b^2 + 0.5)L$$
$$\text{subject to:} \quad L \leq (N - \tau)/N \tag{22}$$

and,

$$T = \lfloor b \ln L \rfloor \tag{23}$$

where τ is the given payload size and L is a parameter (whose upper bound is related to the given payload size) over which the objective function is to be minimized. The problem is proved to be convex optimization problem if $b \geq 0.5$, and this constraint on the value of b was experimentally verified by the authors in [11]. Since convex optimization problems are amenable to polynomial-time solution techniques [17], we have a polynomial-time heuristic to solve the NP-hard problem.

4   Our Approach: Simplified Modelling of Prediction Error

The approach described above has the limitation that the parameter b for the Laplacian distribution in Eq. (20) is estimated as mean of the prediction errors, which is dependent on the prediction scheme used. Hence, without prediction we cannot estimate the parameter b for modelling the prediction error histogram. **One of the main goals of this paper is to minimize the distortion independently of the prediction scheme used, by exploiting the image statistics.** In this paper we model the prediction error histogram as the discretized image DCT coefficient distribution scaled by image entropy (justification of this approach would be provided shortly). For grayscale images we consider prediction error histogram from $H(-127)$ to $H(127)$, as in practice and for all the test images we considered, the prediction error histogram values are zero for prediction errors outside the range $e \in [-127, 127]$. It should be noted that considering a larger range of prediction errors would not affect the analysis that follows.

We make the following assumptions:

- The prediction error histogram is symmetric, i.e., $H(-T) = H(T)$, and,
- the right half of the prediction histogram is equal to the (discretized) value of histogram of the (discretized) DCT coefficients of the image scaled by the *image entropy*, i.e.:

$$H[0 : 127] = \left\lfloor \frac{\text{Histogram } \lfloor \text{DCT}(img) \rfloor}{\text{Entropy}(img)} \right\rfloor \qquad (24)$$

This modelling scheme for the prediction error histogram image works independently of the prediction scheme. *Image entropy* [18] is an information theoretic measure of image randomness, and is defined as:

$$H = -\sum_{k=0}^{M-1} p_k \log_2 p_k \qquad (25)$$

where M is the number of gray levels and p_k is the probability associated with gray level k.

The DCT coefficients [19] for an $M \times N$ image A are defined as:

$$I_{pq} = \alpha_p \alpha_q \sum_{m=0}^{M-1} \sum_{n=0}^{N-1} A_{mn} \cos \frac{\pi(2m+1)p}{2M} \cos \frac{\pi(2n+1)q}{2N} \qquad (26)$$

for $0 \le p \le M-1$, $0 \le q \le N-1$. A_{mn} denotes the (m, n)-th pixel of the image A, and I_{pq} represents the (p, q)-th DCT coefficient of image A. The constants α_p and α_q are defined as:

$$\alpha_p = \frac{1}{\sqrt{M}} \quad \text{if} \quad p = 0$$

$$= \sqrt{\frac{2}{M}} \quad \text{if} \quad 1 \le p \le M-1 \qquad (27)$$

And

$$\alpha_q = \frac{1}{\sqrt{N}} \quad \text{if} \quad q = 0$$

$$= \sqrt{\frac{2}{N}} \quad \text{if} \quad 1 \le q \le N-1 \qquad (28)$$

Since the DCT coefficients and entropy of an image are real numbers, but the histogram function takes only integer arguments, we consider the floor of the ratio of the DCT coefficient and entropy to approximate the prediction error histogram.

4.1   Justification for Prediction Histogram Modelling Using DCT Coefficients and Entropy

The following observations and previously reported results justify our approach:

- In [20] it was mathematically derived that the distribution of the DCT coefficient resembles a zero-mean Laplacian distribution, using a doubly stochastic model of images. This previous result is the main theoretical justification of our approach.
- Relatively "smooth" images (e.g. "*Lena*") have higher spatial redundancy, resulting in higher decorrelation, hence has entropy reduction, and finally produces sharper DCT coefficient histogram. On the contrary, textured images (e.g. "*Mandrill*") produces flatter DCT coefficient histogram with higher variance, as well as prediction error histogram, as shown in Fig. 2. This physically justifies the DCT coefficient histogram being similar in form to a Laplacian distribution.
- The *Energy Compaction Property* of DCT [18] states that it packs maximum energy of the input image into a few coefficients, i.e., a few transform coefficients have larger magnitudes, and most of them have negligibly low values. Hence, the histogram of DCT coefficients has a peak at zero, and decreases gradually with higher transform values. Hence, its distribution is similar to a zero-mean Laplacian distribution, similar to the prediction error histogram. This is reflected in the prediction error histograms for the test images we considered.
- Entropy is an information theoretic measure of randomness of an image. We have modelled prediction histogram to consist of (discretized) DCT coefficient divided by image entropy. So, smooth images having lower image entropy will produce sharper prediction error histogram, while textured images will produce histograms of the opposite nature.
- Finally, our experimental results show good agreement with the predicted trends obtained from the proposed modelling technique.

4.2   Bounded Capacity Distortion Estimation

We now summarize the steps of our proposed approach to estimate the minimum distortion for reversible embedding of a given payload in a given cover image:

- Prediction error histogram is assumed to be a Laplacian distribution of the discretized DCT coefficient of the image, scaled by its entropy. Algorithm 1 shows the histogram construction. The zero-mean Laplacian probability distribution function is of the form:

$$p(x) = \frac{1}{2b} \exp\left(-\frac{|x|}{b}\right) \qquad (29)$$

where we take parameter b to be the entropy of the image, as given by Eq.(25)

Algorithm 1. *PREDICTION ERROR HISTOGRAM MODELLING*

/* Prediction Error Histogram Estimation using DCT Coefficients and Image Entropy
*/

Input: Grayscale image (A).
Output: Modelled Prediction Error Histogram (H)
1: $I = \lfloor DCT(A) \rfloor$
2: $Hist_{DCT} = Histogram(I)$ /* $Hist_{DCT}$ is histogram of I
3: $H(0) = Hist_{DCT}(0)$ /* H[-127,..,0,...,127] is the modelled histogram
4: **for** $i = 1$ *to* 127 **do**
5:     $H(i) = Hist_{DCT}(i)$
6:     $H(-i) = H(i)$
7: **end for**
8: $H = \lfloor \frac{H}{entropy(A)} \rfloor$

– Optimum embedding threshold parameter (T) to minimize distortion for a given payload size (τ) is estimated by solving the following convex optimization problem:

$$\text{min imize}_L \quad 2b^2 L \ln L - (2b^2 + 0.5)L$$
$$\text{subject to:} \quad L \leq (N - \tau)/N \tag{30}$$

and,

$$T = \lfloor b \ln L \rfloor \tag{31}$$

and N denotes the size of image (in pixels).
– Prediction errors $e_i \in [-T, T)$ are used for watermark embedding, and $e_i \in (-T_\infty, -T) \cup [T, T_\infty)$ are shifted by a constant amount T. Hence total estimated distortion:

$$D_{est} = \sum_{k=-T}^{T-1} \left(k^2 + k + \frac{1}{2} \right) H(k) + \left(\sum_{k=-\infty}^{-T-1} H(k) + \sum_{k=T}^{+\infty} H(k) \right) T^2 \tag{32}$$

Here for grayscale images we have taken $T_\infty = 127$, since higher prediction error histogram values are practically zero.

(a)   (b)   (c)   (d)   (e)

Fig. 1. Test images: (a) Lena; (b) Mandrill; (c) Barbara; (d) Boat; (e) Goldhill.

In this way, for a given payload (τ), distortion D_{est} can be estimated.

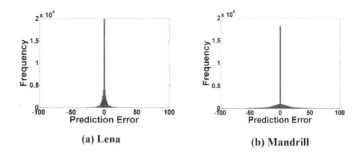

Fig. 2. Estimated Prediction Error histograms for (a) *Lena* and (b) *Mandrill* test images.

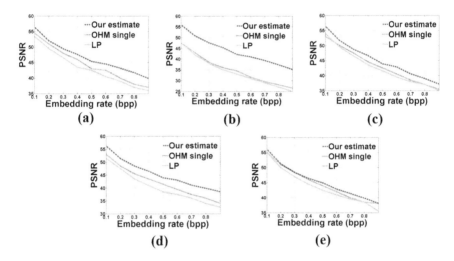

Fig. 3. Distortion vs. payload size comparison with LP [10] and OHM Single [12] reversible watermarking schemes.

5   Results and Discussion

Our estimated optimal distortion is compared with two state-of-the-art reversible watermarking schemes. These are: *minimum rate prediction and optimized single histogram modification schemes* ("OHM Single") [12], and *reversible watermarking through local prediction based difference expansion* ("LP") [10]. We have experimented with 512×512, 8-bit grayscale versions of several standard test images: *Lena, Mandrill, Barbara, Boat* and *Goldhill*, as shown in Fig. 1. All algorithms were implemented in *Matlab*, and the CVX library [21] was used to solve convex optimization problems. Distortion was estimated as *Peak Signal to Noise Ratio* (PSNR), measured in dB, and defined as:

$$PSNR = 10 \log_{10} \left(\frac{MAX^2}{MSE} \right) dB = 10 \log_{10} \left(\frac{255^2}{MSE} \right) dB \qquad (33)$$

where MAX is maximum possible pixel value of the image, which is 255 in the case of an 8-bit grayscale image, and the *Mean Square Error (MSE)* is calculated as:

$$MSE = \sum_{i=1}^{M}\sum_{j=1}^{M} \frac{(X_{org}(i,j) - X_{wm}(i,j))^2}{M \times N} \qquad (34)$$

where $X_{org}(i,j)$ and $X_{wm}(i,j)$ are the (i,j)-th pixel of the original and the watermarked image correspondingly. Payload size was measured in bits-per-pixel (bpp) embedded.

Our estimated prediction error histograms constructed using Algorithm-1 for the *Lena* and *Mandrill* test images are shown in Fig. 2; the other prediction error histograms obtained were of similar nature. It can be observed that the estimated prediction error histograms resemble zero-mean Laplacian distributions. Moreover, smooth images like *Lena* have sharper prediction error histograms, compared to textured image like *Mandrill* having flatter prediction error histograms, as expected.

Figure 3 shows that our estimated distortion vs. payload size characteristic plots generally agree with state-of-the-art reversible watermarking schemes considered, except the *Mandrill* image. It seems that state-of-the-art prediction methods find it difficult to fully exploit the spatial pixel value redundancies of textured images like *Mandrill*, that is indicated by the gap between our estimated distortion levels, and that achieved by the state-of-the-art in Fig. 3. Better prediction mechanisms for textured images may help to reach our estimates of optimal (minimum) distortion levels (i.e. higher PSNR). In general, smooth images like *Lena* have lower distortion at the same payload size, than the images with textured features like *Mandrill*.

6   Conclusion

In this paper we have proved that the bounded capacity distortion minimization problem for PEE based reversible watermarking schemes, given an embedding threshold value, is NP-hard, and the corresponding decision problem is NP-complete. We have simplified the prediction error distribution estimation, and estimated the optimal embedding threshold parameter using a convex optimization method. Experimental results with test images shows our estimate is quite consistent with the performance achieved by state-of-the-art schemes for most test images. Our future work will be directed to extend the analysis for color images, and for developing better prediction schemes to reach the optimal distortion levels, and investigating the computational complexity of the bounded distortion capacity maximization problem (the dual of the problem considered in this paper).

References

1. Cox, I., Miller, M., Fridrich, J., Kalker, T.: Digital Watermarking and Steganography. Morgan Kaufmann, Jeffrey Bloom (2007)

2. Roy, A., Chakraborty, R.S., Naskar, R.: Reversible color image watermarking in the YCoCg-R color space. In: Jajodia, S., Mazumdar, C. (eds.) ICISS 2015. LNCS, vol. 9478, pp. 480–498. Springer, Heidelberg (2015). doi:10.1007/978-3-319-26961-0_28
3. Celik, M.U., Sharma, G., Tekalp, A.M., Saber, E.: Reversible data hiding. In: International Conference on Image Processing, Proceedings, vol. 2, p. 157. IEEE (2002)
4. Ni, Z., Shi, Y.-Q., Ansari, N., Wei, S.: Reversible data hiding. IEEE Trans. Circ. Syst. Video Technol. 16(3), 354–362 (2006)
5. Tian, J.: Reversible data embedding using a difference expansion. IEEE Trans. Circuits Syst. Video Technol. 13(8), 890–896 (2003)
6. Thodi, D.M., Rodríguez, J.J.: Reversible watermarking by prediction-error expansion. In: 6th IEEE Southwest Symposium on Image Analysis and Interpretation, pp. 21–25. IEEE (2004)
7. Luo, L., Chen, Z., Chen, M., Zeng, X., Xiong, Z.: Reversible image watermarking using interpolation technique. IEEE Trans. Inf. Forensics Secur. 5(1), 187–193 (2010)
8. Naskar, R., Chakraborty, R.S.: Reversible watermarking utilising weighted median-based prediction. IET Image Process. 6(5), 507–520 (2012)
9. Sachnev, V., Kim, H.J., Nam, J., Suresh, S., Shi, Y.Q.: Reversible watermarking algorithm using sorting, prediction. IEEE Trans. Circ. Syst. Video Technol. 19(7), 989–999 (2009)
10. Dragoi, I.-C., Coltuc, D.: Local-prediction-based difference expansion reversible watermarking. IEEE Trans. Image Process. 23(4), 1779–1790 (2014)
11. Zhou, J., Au, O.C.: Determining the capacity parameters in pee-based reversible image watermarking. IEEE Signal Process. Lett. 19(5), 287–290 (2012)
12. Xiaocheng, H., Zhang, W., Li, X., Nenghai, Y.: Minimum rate prediction and optimized histograms modification for reversible data hiding. IEEE Trans. Inf. Forensics Secur. 10(3), 653–664 (2015)
13. Naskar, R., Chakraborty, R.S.: A technique to evaluate upper bounds on performance of pixel-prediction based reversible watermarking algorithms. J. Signal Process. Syst. 82(3), 373–389 (2015)
14. Chandramouli, R., Trivedi, S.P., Uma, R.N.: On the complexity and hardness of the steganography embedding problem. In: International Society for Optics and Photonics Electronic Imaging, pp. 496–500 (2004)
15. Bo, O., Li, X., Zhao, Y., Ni, R., Shi, Y.-Q.: Pairwise prediction-error expansion for efficient reversible data hiding. IEEE Trans. Image Process. 22(12), 5010–5021 (2013)
16. Cormen, T.H., Leiserson, C.E., Rivest, R.L., Stein, C.: Introduction to Algorithms, vol. 6. MIT press, Cambridge (2001)
17. Ben-Tal, A., Nemirovski, A.: Lectures on Modern Convex Optimization: Analysis, Algorithms, and Engineering Applications, vol. 2. Siam (2001)
18. Gonzalez, R.C., Woods, R.E.: Digital Image Processing. Prentice Hall, Upper Saddle River (2002)
19. Jain, A.K.: Fundamentals of Digital Image Processing. Prentice-Hall Inc., Englewood Cliffs (1989)
20. Lam, E.Y., Goodman, J.W.: A mathematical analysis of the DCT coefficient distributions for images. IEEE Trans. Image Process. 9(10), 1661–1666 (2000)
21. Grant, M., Boyd, S., Ye, Y.: Cvx: Matlab software for disciplined convex programming (2008)

Blind 3D Mesh Watermarking
Based on Sphere-Shape Template

Hak-Yeol Choi, Jeongho Son, Han-Ul Jang, and Heung-Kyu Lee[(✉)]

School of Computing, Korea Advanced Institute of Science and Technology,
371-1 Guseong-dong, Yuseong-gu, Daejeon, Republic of Korea
{hychoi,hanulj,hklee}@mmc.kaist.ac.kr, sonjh@kaist.ac.kr

Abstract. In this paper, we propose a novel blind 3D mesh watermarking scheme based on synchronization using a template. The proposed template has a sphere shape with a basis point and scale information for the watermarking. The template is invariant to translation, rotation, and scale. In the extraction process of the template, the post-processing, which sorts out the genuine template vertices from many candidate vertices, greatly increases the extracting accuracy. The proposed watermarking method is designed to extract the watermark from the rest of the region even if part of the mesh information is cropped. According to the experimental results, the proposed method has a higher robustness against not only cropping but also general signal processing attacks than the previous methods.

Keywords: 3D mesh watermarking · Template base synchronization · Sphere-shape template

1 Introduction

Next-generation technologies like virtual reality, augmented reality, holography and 3D printing will improve the utilization of 3D data beyond what is available today. In the future, the utilization and value of 3D data will be as high as 2D images are now. Such 3D data needs copyright protection because it has artistic and commercial value in itself. Although digital rights management (DRM) technology is widely studied as copyright protection, the DRM technology is limited to the extent that the protection of content is absolutely impossible if the DRM system is penetrated only once.

3D mesh watermarking technology has been actively studied as a complementary copyright protection technology for 3D model data. 3D mesh watermarking is a technology that subtly changes the 3D mesh data to hide secret information. Unlike DRM technology, with 3D mesh watermarking it is possible to protect the 3D model throughout the entire process of distribution. Therefore, the watermarking technology can complement the security hole of DRM technology.

3D mesh watermarking has been studied in a variety of ways, but a watermarking method that protects against cropping attacks is rare. The cropping

© Springer International Publishing AG 2017
Y.Q. Shi et al. (Eds.): IWDW 2016, LNCS 10082, pp. 280–295, 2017.
DOI: 10.1007/978-3-319-53465-7_21

issue of the 3D mesh is a problem that must be solved for real applications. There are two reasons why the cropping issue is important. First, the 3D model has artistic and commercial value in itself [1]. Therefore, an attacker can illegally distribute only a cropped part. Second, the previous watermarking systems could be easily evaded with cropping of less than 5%. Therefore, the cropping issue is a challenging problem in the 3D mesh watermarking field [3].

Only a few methods have been designed considering the cropping issue. However, such methods are robust against only a small amount of cropping and are generally weak to common signal processing attacks. Existing studies do not tolerate more than 10% of cropping on average. Basically, in the watermark extraction phase, the watermarking method needs robust synchronization that is identical to the embedding phase. Such robust synchronization in a blind environment is the key to solving the cropping problem. Until now, robust synchronization has not been solved.

Previous 3D mesh watermarking schemes can largely be divided into nonblind methods and blind methods. The non-blind approach has the advantage of acquiring robustness because of the ease of synchronization, but also it has a limitation in utilization because it needs the original model in the extraction process [4–6,8], while the blind method requires only a secret key in the watermark extraction process [2,7,9–18,20]. For this reason, the blind method has better utilization. However, it is difficult to obtain high robustness for the blind method. In particular, it is significantly vulnerable to local deformation such as in cropping attacks.

Watermarking methods can also be categorized by the type of domain used. First, there are watermarking methods that use a geometric domain [2,9–17,20]. The geometric domain-based watermarking methods are simple and effective because they change the vertex location directly during the watermarking process. Second, there are spectral domain-based watermarking methods [4–7,18]. In general, the spectral domain-based methods tend to have a higher robustness and invisibility than the geometric domain-based methods.

Watermarking methods that are robust to cropping attacks are as follows. Alface et al. [2] proposed a method that watermarks the local region that is acquired based on targeted feature points prong. The method is highly dependent on the robustness of that prong feature. However, the prong is determined only in a region that has a sharp part. In addition, it is difficult to obtain the feature precisely because it changes before and after the watermarking. Mun et al. [16] proposed a method that watermarks the segments of the model using a shape diameter function (SDF). The SDF is not highly rigid because it is changed by signal processing and cropping attacks. In addition, each segment does not have enough robustness because the amount of vertex information is small. The size of a segment is an area of about 10% of the entire model. Xavier et al. [10] proposed a resynchronization method. In the proposed resynchronization method, the landmarks are constructed on the basis of the parametric surface. Since it is a resynchronization method, not a watermarking method, the authors tried to combine the method with the existing watermarking method. However, without improving the watermarking method, acquiring enough robustness against cropping attacks was hard.

Our proposed method is blind mesh watermarking based on a sphere-shaped template that is resilient to cropping attacks. The proposed method modifies the ring information of vertices in the circle shape. In the extraction process of the template, the method extracts the candidate vertices of the template using the weighted residual error based on least-squares 3D circle fitting. We finally obtain the template sphere by distinguishing the template vertex among the candidate vertices. Such a template sphere, including the basis point and scale information, is used for synchronization in the watermark extraction. In addition, the watermarking method is designed to resist the loss of mesh information.

The rest of the paper is organized as follows. In Sect. 2, we introduce the histogram-based 3D mesh watermarking that inspired the proposed watermarking method. The proposed method is described in Sect. 3. In Sect. 4, the experimental results are provided. Section 5 concludes the paper and introduces topics for future study.

2   3D Mesh Watermarking Based on Radial Information

In this section, we introduce the watermarking method using a histogram of the vertex norm [17]. The method construct the histogram of vertex norm as a first step, and divide it into the bins. The number of bins determined as the number of watermark bits N. Thus the 1-bit watermark is embedded in to each bin. The watermarking part in the proposed method is based on this method. The method is very fast and robust and works in a blind way.

2.1   Watermark Embedding Process

In this method, the watermark information is embedded by modifying the vertex norm information. First, let's define the mesh M as $M = (V, F)$. Here, V is a set of vertices and F is set of faces. Also, v_i represents i-th vertex. i-th vertex norm ρ_i is defined by distance of center of mass C and each vertex v_i. It could be described as follows:

$$\rho_i = |v_i - C|, \text{ for } 0 \leq i \leq N_V - 1 \tag{1}$$

where N_V is the number of vertices.

At first, the watermarking method construct the histogram of the vertex norm. As mentioned before, the watermark bits are embedded into the bin B which is a segment of whole histogram. The i-th bin is defined as follows:

$$B_i = \{v_j | \rho_{\min} + (i) \cdot (\rho_{\max} - \rho_{\min})/N \leq \\ \rho_j \leq \rho_{\min} + (i+1) \cdot (\rho_{\max} - \rho_{\min})/N\}, \text{ for } 0 \leq i \leq N \tag{2}$$

where $\rho_{\max}$ and $\rho_{\min}$ are maximum, minimum value of vertex norms ρ_i, respective.

Each i-th bin and j-th vertex norm is normalized into the range $(0, 1)$ for embedding of the watermark as follows:

$$\hat{\rho}_{i,j} = \frac{\rho_{i,j} - \min \rho \in B_i}{\max \rho \in B_i - \min \rho \in B_i} \tag{3}$$

where $\max \rho \in B_i$, $\min \rho \in B_i$ are maximum, minimum vertex norm in i-th bin B_i.

After the process, the vertex norm information included in each bin is modified for a 1-bit of the watermark embedding. That is based on the observation shown in [17] that the shape of the bins in the normalized histogram is similar with the uniform distribution. Since the expectation value of uniform distribution is $1/2$, the embedding process changes the expectation value μ in accordance with α on the basis of $1/2$. Here, α value means the strength of watermark and higher α value brings higher distortion on the 3D mesh. The watermarking method is as follows:

$$\hat{\mu} = \begin{cases} 1/2 + \alpha \text{ if } w_i = +1 \\ 1/2 - \alpha \text{ if } w_i = -1 \end{cases} \tag{4}$$

where w_i is i-th watermark bit. Each normalized vertex norm information is modified by applying the histogram mapping function into the bin. The embedding method through the histogram mapping function is a method used widely in the existing watermarking method [15,20]. The histogram mapping function is designed as follows:

$$\hat{\rho}'_{i,j} = \hat{\rho}^{\beta}_{i,j}, \text{ for } 0 < \beta < \infty, \ \beta \in \Re \tag{5}$$

The histogram mapping function is applied iteratively to modify the vertex norm slightly in every iteration. The β value is set as $(0, 1)$ to embed bit 0 and $(1, \infty)$ to embed bit 1. If the β value is in $(0, 1)$, the mean value of the bin decreases gradually. Likewise, if β value is in $(1, \infty)$, the mean value of the bin increases gradually. In every iteration, the β value is changed by $\Delta \beta$ to reach into the target mean value.

After the watermarking, each bin is denormalized again for the last step of embedding as follows:

$$\hat{\rho}''_{i,j} = \frac{1}{2}(\hat{\rho}'_{i,j} + 1)(\max \rho \in B_i - \min \rho \in B_i) + \min \rho \in B_i \tag{6}$$

2.2   Watermark Extraction Process

The extraction process is similar with the embedding but is much simpler. The only needed information is the number of bits N, since the entire extraction process is works in a blind way. For the first step of extraction, the bins are constructed using the histogram of vertex norm as Eq. 2 which is same as the embedding process.

Since the mean value is changed on the basis of $1/2$ in the embedding phase, the extraction phase is also based on $1/2$ value. The watermark extraction process could be represented as follows:

$$w_i = \begin{cases} +1 \text{ if } \mu > 1/2 \\ -1 \text{ if } \mu < 1/2 \end{cases} \tag{7}$$

3 Proposed Method

The proposed scheme includes template embedding/extracting for synchronization and the robust watermark embedding/extracting based on the template. Figure 1 describes the entire process of the proposed method. Note that the proposed method embeds the template after the watermark is embedded. Since the extraction process works in a blind way, the other information (i.e., the original model) is not needed except for the secret key in the extraction phase.

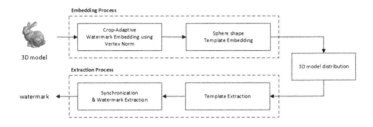

Fig. 1. The entire process of the proposed method

The template can be defined as a set of vertices v_t that represent the specific sphere, including the center point and scale information. In the extraction, v_t are extracted to recover the sphere, and the synchronization goes along with the sphere.

As mentioned before, the proposed watermarking method is inspired by the histogram-based watermarking method introduced in Sect. 2. Although the watermarking method is robust again common signal processing, it is greatly vulnerable to cropping attacks. We propose a histogram-based watermarking method that is designed to be adaptive against cropping attacks. The method is highly robust against cropping attacks when it is combined with the proposed template.

3.1 Watermark Embedding

The robustness of the watermarking method is highly associated with the robust template embedding/extraction. Therefore, the proposed scheme embeds the template after the watermark is embedded to avoid interference by the watermark.

The three pieces of information are needed in order to achieve the robustness of the watermarking from cropping attacks: the basis point, which is set as the center of a mass generally; scale information of the mesh; and a robust embedding region that can be acquired after a local deformation attack. Those three factors are determined in the watermarking process. In the template embedding, the determined factors are used.

In particular, the embedding region is defined on the basis of the basis point and the scale information. Therefore, the basis point and scale information are determined before the embedding region. In Sect. 2, the histogram of the vertex norm is simply divided by N to construct the bins. However, with that bin construction scheme, the watermark extraction is impossible to 5% of cropping since it changes the bin information. Figure 2 describes such a problem. Even with a small rate of cropping, the distribution of the histogram is altered. Figure 2a and b show the change of the bin information represented by the red dotted line.

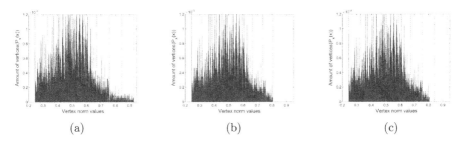

(a)   (b)   (c)

Fig. 2. The example of desynchronization by cropping attack. The red dotted lines means the boundary of bins. In the figures (b)–(c), the histograms are cropped about 3% of vertices. (a) original histogram, (b) bin construction of the previous method, (c) bin construction of the proposed method (Color figure online)

To solve such a problem, the proposed method constructs the bin in a new way. As mentioned before, we first construct the template sphere with a basis point and scale information. The center point of sphere S_c corresponds to the basis point, and the radius of sphere S_r corresponds to the scale information. The template sphere is constructed based on the distribution of vertex norm. The S_c is set by the center of mass of the mesh, and S_r is set as the $\lambda \cdot \rho_{max}$, which is λ times the maximum vertex norm ρ_{max}. In addition, the embedding region of the watermark is set as the region from $\xi \cdot \rho_{max}$ to ρ_{max}. Figure 3 represents that. Note that λ must always be set bigger than ξ. Figure 4 shows the template sphere of several models.

For the watermark embedding, the embedding region is divided by N. Here, the synchronization could be maintained even though some of the information is removed by cropping when the bin is constructed in the proposed way. Figure 2c describes that. It is clear that the remaining bin has the same data even if some of the histogram is altered.

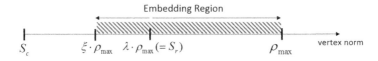

Fig. 3. The conceptual diagram of the embedding region. The embedding region is constructed based on maximum vertex norm value. Red dash region means embedding regions. (Color figure online)

(a)   (b)   (c)

Fig. 4. The example of the constructed sphere template on the models. ($\lambda = 0.4$) (a) *bunny*, (b) *elephant*, (c) *scorpion*

Alter the construction of the bins, we embed a 1-bit watermark into each bin. The watermark embedding process is the same as in Eqs. 3 and 6. The watermark bit is shuffled before embedding by secret key K.

3.2   Template Embedding

As we mentioned before, the vertices on the mesh that meet the template sphere S become the template vertex sample v_σ. Among those v_σ, the template is embedded in a way that modifies the ring information of the finally selected vertices. The template embedding process proceeds as the selection of the template vertex and the ring information modification for template embedding.

Selection of Template Vertex: In the first step, we assign the vertices to meet the pre-defined template sphere S as v_σ. We assign the vertices that are close within ϵ with S as the template vertex sample because the probability that two certain vertices meet is extremely low in a discrete domain. This can be represented as follows:

$$v_\sigma = \{v_i \big| |v_i - S| < \varepsilon\} \tag{8}$$

The proposed method selects the N_t vertices as template vertex v_t among v_σ. The standard of selection is the weighted residual error E of least-square circle fitting [19] using Gauss-Newton. We calculate E from the start ring r_s to the end ring r_e by accumulating errors. The circle shape has an advantage in invisibility because the shape of the ring is close to the circle. Equation 9 represents that.

$$E = \sum_i E_i \text{ , where } r_s < i < r_e \tag{9}$$

where E_i is weighted residual error of i-th ring.

A lower E value means that the shape of the target ring is similar to a circle. After this process, the proposed template method sets the least N_t as the template vertex because the target shape is also a circle. This helps the improvement in terms of invisibility. In addition, the selection based on the least residual error helps to drop the false positive rate in the extraction phase. Another factor that needs to be considered in selecting v_t is the distance among v_t. The overlapping of several markers that will be explained later may decrease the performance of the detection. Therefore, each template vertex must have at least δ distance.

Template Vertex Marking: The next process is embedding the marker by modifying the ring information of the template vertex. First, we move the N_t template vertex onto the sphere. The distance between S and v_t is at most ϵ. This process is done in a simple way that moves the v_t onto the S by a shortest way. We then modify the ring information of each v_t from r_s to r_e into a circle shape. The modification process is as follows:

- Step 1. Construct fitting circle c of the i-th ring r_i
- Step 2. Calculate the least distance of the fitting circle and vertex v_j on r_i
- Step 3. Displace the vertex v_j to the nearest points on fitting circle c

Figure 5 shows a comparison of the distribution of the original and modified vertices. The process of the template vertex marking is done by the displacement of all the v_t's rings.

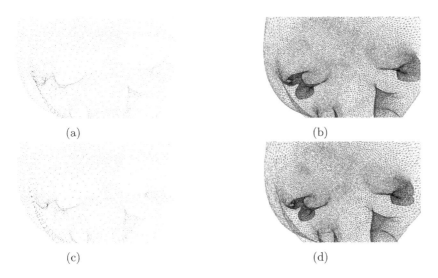

(a)   (b)

(c)   (d)

Fig. 5. The comparison of original and stero mesh (*elephant*) (a)–(b) original mesh, (c)–(d) stero mesh

3.3 Template Extraction

The entire extraction process of the template and watermark works in a blind way. In the extraction process, the watermark is extracted after the template because the watermark is embedded before the template in the embedding process. The extraction process includes the procedure that finds the candidate set v_τ using the marker and distinguishes the genuine template vertex among candidates.

Selection of the Candidate Vertex: The standard of selection of v_τ is the same as the way that selects the v_t as we described before. Therefore, the proposed method calculates the accumulated residual error E of the 3D circle fitting from r_s to r_e of all vertices v_i. Further, the N_τ with the least E is selected as the candidate for the template vertex. A strong attack increases the false positive rate by changing the circle shape of the template vertices. When N_τ is high, many of the muddling vertices are included as candidates, but it also creates an effect that includes the template vertex, which is not excluded from the candidates. In this study, we set the number of template vertices N_t as 15 and the candidates N_τ as 30.

Distinguishing Template Vertex from Candidates: Among the v_τ, the N_t template vertex is located on the same sphere. v_τ, which is not v_t, has a low probability to be located on the same sphere. The proposed method uses the fundamentals to distinguish the v_t from v_τ. Our method constructs the spheres using the four vertices combined from all v_τ. Since the sphere is uniquely determined by the four vertices, we able to construct a $_{N_\tau}C_4$ sphere. Among them, the sphere constructed by the only template vertex v_t had the same center point and radius, and the sphere constructed most of the time could be estimated as the template sphere S. Therefore, the sphere was determined by the maximum distribution of the radius and center point. Figure 6 represents the distribution of $_{N_\tau}C_4$ radius and center point (x-axis). In the middle of the graph, the flat regions are easily observed. Those flat regions represent identical spheres.

3.4 Watermark Extraction

The watermark extraction is done after the synchronization based on pre-determined template sphere S. Here, vertices V are translated and scaled by normalizing the template sphere into a unit sphere has a radius of 1 and a center point of O. According to this, new bins B_i' are constructed as follows:

$$B_i' = \{v_j | \xi/\lambda + i \cdot (1/\lambda - \xi/\lambda)/N \leq \\ \rho_j \leq \xi/\lambda + (i+1) \cdot (1/\lambda - \xi/\lambda)/N\}, \text{ for } 0 \leq i \leq N \tag{10}$$

The watermark extraction process from the range of the B_i' region is the same as the process in Eqs. 3–7. After the extraction of all the watermark bits, the final information is recovered by secret key K which was used in the embedding process.

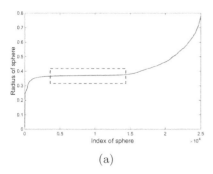
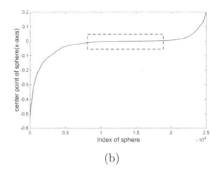

(a)   (b)

Fig. 6. The distribution of radius and center coordinate (x-axis) of the candidate spheres

4   Experimental Results

In this section, we provide the experimental results of the proposed method. In this experiments, we set the parameter of the proposed method as follows. The watermark bits N is set 64-bits. And λ, ξ, ϵ and δ are set as 0.4, 0.3, 0.005 and 0.1, respectively. In addition, N_t and N_τ are respectively set as 15, 30. Finally, we used from the third ring to the fifth ring as the marker. The Alface's [2] and Mun's [16] methods are compared with the proposed method to shows the performance objectively. Both comparison methods use the part of model since they are segmentation based method. For the reason, the methods do not show the enough performance with 64-bits watermark. Thus, we conduct the additional experiments with 16-bits watermark. For the Alface's method the watermark strength α is set as 0.2 and the smoothing ratio factor for *prong* detection is set as 0.85. For Mun's method, we set α as 0.1 and smoothing factor as 0.7 for coarser segmentation. Also, the number of lays and Gaussian for SDF calculation as 30, 4, respectively. In the robustness test for cropping attack, we combine the existing Cho's [17] method with our proposed template to show the effect of proposed watermarking method. For the Cho's method, N is set as 64 and α is set as 0.1.

4.1   Invisibility Test

We use maximum root mean square error (MRMS) [21] and mesh structural distortion measure (MSDM) [22] as the metric for the invisibility test. The MRMS metric reflects the geometric distortion while the MSDM metric reflects the human visual factors. Tables 1 and 2 shows the results of the invisibility test of the comparison and proposed methods. As mentioned before, the comparison methods use the part of mesh, not the entire mesh. For the reason, they have advantage in terms of the invisibility. However, the stero mesh have very small amount of geometric distortion when the MSDM value is less than 0.3 [1]. The results of the proposed method also corresponds that.

Table 1. The MRMS results of the various watermarked models of the proposed and comparison methods (10^{-3})

Models	Alface16	Alface64	Mun16	Mun64	Proposed
bunny	1.376	0.349	0.803	0.196	0.765
elephant	0.435	0.113	0.499	0.128	0.416
scorpion	54.560	13.835	40.190	10.777	42.376

Table 2. The MSDM results of the various watermarked models of the proposed and comparison methods

Models	Alface16	Alface64	Mun16	Mun64	Proposed
bunny	0.325	0.184	0.213	0.121	0.234
elephant	0.180	0.087	0.175	0.099	0.194
scorpion	0.289	0.166	0.207	0.144	0.233

4.2 Robustness Test

Here, we provide the result of the robustness test. In the robustness test, we could observed that the *prong* feature used in the Alface's method is changed by not only signal processing attack but also watermarking process. Therefore, that makes the performance drop for almost experiments. But, it show relatively better results when the model have sharp region.

The robustness test is conducted on the common signal processing and cropping attack. We use the metric for representing the robustness as bit error rate (BER). For the test for common signal processing, we conducted the experiment against the random additive noise, quantization, smoothing and simplification. At first, Table 3 shows the results about additive random noise. We use noise factor from 0.01% to 0.1%. The proposed method showed better results than comparison methods in terms of the stability and robustness.

Second results are about quantization process. We quantized the mesh into from 14-bits to 10-bits. Table 4 shows the proposed method robust to the quantization.

The third experiments were conducted to test smoothing. For the smoothing experiment, we use Taubin method [23] and smoothing factor is set as 0.4. We conducted the experiment from first iteration to the fifth iteration. Table 5 shows the result. The proposed method showed better results overall. In spite of that, the performance was dropped to the *scorpion* model since there were errors in the construction process of template sphere.

The last experiment of signal process attack is simplification. We conducted the results for the 2%–10% of the simplification. Table 6 show the results. The proposed method relatively vulnerable to the connectivity attack like simplification since it use ring information. Accordingly, the results show the drop of performance with *bunny* model.

Table 3. Robustness against random noise addition

Models	Amplitude	Alface16	Alface64	Mun16	Mun64	Proposed
bunny	0.02%	0.813	0.438	0.000	0.375	0.000
	0.04%	0.313	0.625	0.000	0.462	0.000
	0.06%	0.500	0.422	0.563	0.453	0.000
	0.08%	0.313	0.469	0.313	0.453	0.016
	0.1%	0.563	0.453	0.500	0.609	0.078
elephnat	0.02%	0.375	0.563	0.328	0.000	0.000
	0.04%	0.422	0.313	0.484	0.000	0.000
	0.06%	0.484	0.625	0.516	0.438	0.016
	0.08%	0.563	0.500	0.547	0.375	0.141
	0.1%	0.563	0.375	0.609	0.125	0.250
scorpion	0.02%	0.000	0.000	0.000	0.000	0.000
	0.04%	0.125	0.188	0.313	0.000	0.000
	0.06%	0.063	0.297	0.000	0.000	0.000
	0.08%	0.563	0.500	0.000	0.000	0.000
	0.1%	0.563	0.531	0.000	0.094	0.000

Table 4. Robustness against uniform quantization of the vertex coordinates

Models	Intensity	Alface16	Alface64	Mun16	Mun64	Proposed
bunny	14-bits	0.375	0.578	0.000	0.000	0.000
	13-bits	0.688	0.469	0.000	0.328	0.000
	12-bits	0.438	0.516	0.375	0.297	0.000
	11-bits	0.563	0.531	0.125	0.000	0.000
	10-bits	0.375	0.391	0.438	0.328	0.000
elephnat	14-bits	0.484	0.375	0.000	0.063	0.000
	13-bits	0.344	0.125	0.109	0.000	0.000
	12-bits	0.531	0.625	0.016	0.000	0.000
	11-bits	0.469	0.188	0.016	0.063	0.000
	10-bits	0.547	0.375	0.109	0.063	0.000
scorpion	14-bits	0.063	0.000	0.000	0.000	0.000
	13-bits	0.188	0.000	0.031	0.125	0.000
	12-bits	0.188	0.125	0.031	0.031	0.000
	11-bits	0.438	0.125	0.094	0.094	0.000
	10-bits	0.375	0.094	0.063	0.125	0.000

Table 5. Robustness against smoothing process

Models	Iteration	Alface16	Alface64	Mun16	Mun64	Proposed
bunny	1	0.500	0.547	0.000	0.406	0.000
	2	0.375	0.406	0.438	0.375	0.031
	3	0.313	0.422	0.125	0.438	0.031
	4	0.563	0.578	0.000	0.422	0.031
	5	0.438	0.344	0.125	0.391	0.516
elephnat	1	0.438	0.469	0.000	0.031	0.000
	2	0.063	0.000	0.000	0.078	0.016
	3	0.625	0.438	0.000	0.172	0.047
	4	0.500	0.391	0.000	0.094	0.047
	5	0.438	0.484	0.063	0.391	0.234
scorpion	1	0.000	0.000	0.000	0.000	0.000
	2	0.000	0.156	0.000	0.078	0.422
	3	0.000	0.297	0.000	0.141	0.016
	4	0.563	0.484	0.000	0.125	0.000
	5	0.688	0.484	0.500	0.141	0.000

Table 6. Robustness against surface simplification

Models	Ratio	Alface16	Alface64	Mun16	Mun64	Proposed
bunny	2%	0.500	0.688	0.141	0.000	0.000
	4%	0.469	0.625	0.547	0.125	0.469
	6%	0.547	0.375	0.375	0.000	0.609
	8%	0.656	0.313	0.547	0.313	0.484
	10%	0.563	0.563	0.516	0.438	0.484
elephnat	2%	0.516	0.500	0.422	0.000	0.016
	4%	0.484	0.500	0.516	0.000	0.000
	6%	0.500	0.063	0.578	0.000	0.000
	8%	0.438	0.500	0.484	0.375	0.000
	10%	0.484	0.500	0.484	0.438	0.578
scorpion	2%	0.000	0.000	0.172	0.000	0.000
	4%	0.000	0.000	0.328	0.000	0.000
	6%	0.125	0.188	0.219	0.063	0.000
	8%	0.531	0.375	0.328	0.563	0.000
	10%	0.641	0.500	0.313	0.063	0.000

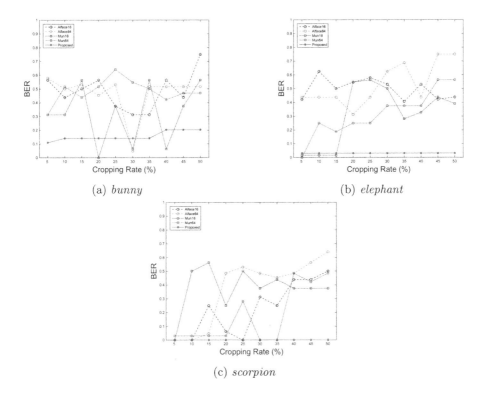

(a) *bunny*

(b) *elephant*

(c) *scorpion*

Fig. 7. Robustness against cropping attack

Next experiment is about the cropping attack. Figure 7 shows the results of the cropping attack. Here, we also shows the result of combination of the proposed template method and the existing method which is introduced in Sect. 2. We can easily observe that the BER is increased rapidly when the existing watermarking method is combined. On the other hands, the proposed methods show better performance. However, the proposed method shows the BER when certain bin information is removed by the cropping. Nevertheless, the proposed method enable to extract watermark information from the rest of bins by maintain the synchronization from the local deformation. Compared to the fact that the comparison methods shows drop of the performance to the more than 10% of cropping, the proposed method improved the performance significantly.

5   Conclusion

In this paper, we proposed a novel, blind and crop-resilient mesh watermarking scheme based on a template. The proposed method is capable of extracting a watermark even against a high rate of the cropping because the template maintains the synchronization against the local deformation, including cropping.

294	H.-Y. Choi et al.

With our design that considers cropping, it shows a low BER to a severe rate of cropping, which is a significant improvement over the previous methods.

The proposed scheme is robust not only against cropping attacks but also against signal processing attacks. In the proposed scheme, the template is extracted on the basis of the weighted residual error of the 3D circle fitting. In particular, the process of selecting a genuine template vertex from candidates significantly decreases the false positive error rate. Only if the attacks do not change the shape of the template entirely, the template can be extracted in a stable way.

The proposed method also has some limitations that should be overcome. First, the bit information cannot be extracted when a certain bin is completely removed by the cropping attack. The method is also vulnerable to a connectivity attack like simplification since it uses connectivity information. Finally, there was a decrease in the performance in terms of the invisibility because the proposed method embeds not only the watermark information but also template information. Those limitations could be overcome in the future studies.

Acknowledgments. This work was supported by the Institute for Information & communications Technology Promotion (IITP) grant funded by the Korean government (MSIP) (No. R0126-15-1024, Managerial Technology Development and Digital Contents Security of 3D Printing based on Micro Licensing Technology).

References

1. Wang, K., Lavoue, G., Denis, F., Baskurt, A., He, X.: A benchmark for 3D mesh watermarking. In: SMI 2010 - International Conference on Shape Modeling and Applications, Proceedings, pp. 231–235 (2010)
2. Alface, P.R., Macq, B.: Blind and robust watermarking of 3D models: how to withstand the cropping attack? In: Proceedings of the IEEE International Conference on Image Processing, pp. 465–468 (2007)
3. Wang, K., Lavoue, G., Denis, F., Baskurt, A.: A comprehensive survey on three-dimensional mesh watermarking. IEEE Trans. Multimedia **10**, 1513–1527 (2008)
4. Valette, S., Prost, R.: Wavelet-based multiresolution analysis of irregular surface meshes. IEEE Trans. Visual Comput. Graph. **10**, 113–122 (2004)
5. Wu, J., Kobbelt, L.: Efficient spectral watermarking of large meshes with orthogonal basis functions. Visual Comput. **21**, 848–857 (2005)
6. Li, L., Zhang, D., Pan, Z., Shi, J., Zhou, K., Ye, K.: Watermarking 3D mesh by spherical parameterization. Comput. Graph. **28**, 981–989 (2004)
7. Konstantinides, J.M., Mademlis, A., Daras, P., Mitkas, P.A., Strintzis, M.G.: Blind robust 3-D mesh watermarking based on oblate spheroidal harmonics. IEEE Trans. Multimedia **11**, 23–38 (2009)
8. Ohbuchi, R., Mukaiyama, A., Takahashi, S.: A frequency-domain approach to watermarking 3D shapes. Comput. Graph. Forum **21**, 373–382 (2002)
9. Kim, K.T., Barni, M., Tan, H.Z.: Roughness-adaptive 3-D watermarking based on masking effect of surface roughness. IEEE Trans. Inf. Forensics Secur. **5**, 721–733 (2010)

10. Rolland-Neviere, X., Doerr, G., Alliez, P.: Triangle surface mesh watermarking based on a constrained optimization framework. IEEE Trans. Inf. Forensics Secur. **9**, 1491–1501 (2014)

11. Bors, A.G.: Watermarking mesh-based representations of 3-D objects using local moments. IEEE Trans. Image Process. **15**, 687–701 (2006)

12. Bors, A.G., Luo, M.: Optimized 3D watermarking for minimal surface distortion. IEEE Trans. Image Process. **22**, 1822–1835 (2013)

13. Hou, J.U., Kim, D.G., Choi, S.H., Lee, H.K.: 3D print-scan resilient watermarking using a histogram-based circular shift coding structure. In: Proceedings of the 3rd ACM Workshop on Information Hiding and Multimedia Security - IH&MMSec 2015, pp. 115–121 (2015)

14. Wang, K., Lavoue, G., Denis, F., Baskurt, A.: Robust and blind mesh watermarking based on volume moments. Comput. Graph. **35**, 1–19 (2011)

15. Luo, M., Bors, A.G.: Surface-preserving robust watermarking of 3-D shapes. IEEE Trans. Image Process. **20**, 2813–2826 (2011)

16. Mun, S.M., Jang, H.U., Kim, D.G., Lee, H.K.: A robust 3D mesh watermarking scheme against cropping. In: International Conference on 3D Imaging (2015)

17. Cho, J.W., Prost, R., Jung, H.Y.: An oblivious watermarking for 3-D polygonal meshes using distribution of vertex norms. IEEE Trans. Sig. Process. **55**, 142–155 (2007)

18. Liu, Y., Prabhakaran, B., Guo, X.: Spectral watermarking for parameterized surfaces. IEEE Trans. Inf. Forensics Secur. **7**, 1459–1471 (2012)

19. Gander, W., Golub, G.H., Strebel, R.: Least-squares fitting of circles and ellipses. BIT Numer. Math. **34**, 558–578 (1994)

20. Zafeiriou, S., Tefas, A., Pitas, L.: Blind robust watermarking schemes for copyright protection of 3D mesh objects. IEEE Trans. Visual Comput. Graph. **11**, 596–607 (2005)

21. Cignoni, P., Rocchini, C., Scopigno, R.: Metro: measuring error on simplified surfaces. Comput. Graph. Forum **17**, 23–38 (2009)

22. Lavoue, G., Gelasca, E.D., Dupont, F., Baskurt, A., Ebrahimi, T.: Perceptually driven 3D distance metrics with application to watermarking. In: Proceedings of the SPIE 6312, Applications of Digital Image Processing XXIX, 6312 (2006)

23. Taubin, G.: A signal processing approach to fair surface design. In: Proceedings of the 22nd Annual Conference on Computer Graphics and Interactive Techniques, pp. 351–358 (1995)

Fragile Watermarking Based Proofs of Retrievability for Archival Cloud Data

Xin Tang[1,2]([✉]), Yining Qi[1,2], and Yongfeng Huang[1,2]

[1] Department of Electronic Engineering, Tsinghua University, Beijing 100084, China
[2] Tsinghua National Laboratory for Information Science and Technology,
Beijing 100084, China
xtang@tsinghua.edu.cn

Abstract. Cloud storage is widely used to ease the storage burden of clients. Meanwhile it raises a basic issue in the security of outsourced data: whether the corruption can be detected and recovered? Focusing on this problem, most existing proofs of retrievability (POR) schemes relies on precomputed tokens or tags as well as code redundancy to achieve integrity verification and corruption recovery, which, however, results in extra storage cost for cloud storage and high computational overhead for clients. Fragile watermarking provides a new way to implement the scheme without such drawbacks. In this paper, we propose a novel fragile watermarking based public auditable POR scheme for archival cloud data, which is able to not only improve the efficiency of audit process but also ensure both privacy-preserving and replay attack resistance simultaneously. The simulation results validate both the correctness of our scheme in detecting and recovering data corruption and the large improvement in performance compared to traditional POR schemes.

Keywords: Fragile watermarking · Proofs of retrievability · Cloud storage

1 Introduction

Cloud storage has been widely used to ease the burden of setting up and maintaining a local data center for clients. It provides nearly unlimited storage space for clients at relatively low price. However, since the client is fully deprived of the physical control for their outsourced data, the risk of data corruption in cloud storage is increased. To solve this problem, Proofs of Retrievability (POR) schemes are proposed, which enables the cloud to generate a proof that the client is able to retrieve the outsourced data. With the help of the POR scheme, the client is not only able to check whether its outsourced data is tampered or damaged, but also has the ability to recover the corrupted data.

Most previous POR schemes are designed indiscriminately for both archival data and hot data, relying on precomputed tokens or tags to check the data integrity and code redundancy to realize corruption recovery. This kind of design results in two main drawbacks, heavy extra storage cost and high computational

© Springer International Publishing AG 2017
Y.Q. Shi et al. (Eds.): IWDW 2016, LNCS 10082, pp. 296–311, 2017.
DOI: 10.1007/978-3-319-53465-7_22

overhead. Because of relying on encoding method, there must be a large proportion of storage space in clouds occupied by verification tokens or tags as well as code redundancy which is called the parity vectors in encoding-based POR scheme. The extra storage cost leads to extra financial cost upon the clients. On the other hand, due to the diversity of client devices, their computational abilities vary very differently. Unfortunately, the encoding preprocess and decoding-based recovery are both based on matrix manipulation and requests for a large amount of computing resources, which is quite a disadvantage to the clients with limited computational capacities.

To improve the performance of traditional POR schemes, we focus on archival data which occupies a larger proportion of cloud storage [1]. In this paper, we devise a novel fragile watermarking based POR scheme for archival cloud data and the main contributions are listed as follows:

1. We propose a fragile watermarking based public verifiable POR scheme for archival data which is able to decrease the computational overhead for clients as well as extra storage cost for cloud at the same time.
2. Take archival image storage for instance, we design a new watermark generating and embedding method to adapt to the public audit scenario. The method is effective to prevent the probable replay attack from cloud storage server. Besides, it ensures the privacy-preserving property during the public audit process.

2   Related Work

In order to achieve data integrity audit in cloud storage, many works are proposed as solutions. G. Ateniese et al. [2] propose the first provable data possession (PDP) scheme in 2007. It provides a way for the client to verify the intactness of outsourced data without downloading. Following their work, various schemes [3–7] are proposed. They aim at different research issues, such as property of privacy preserving [3], public auditability and data dynamics [4], extended scenarios [5,6] as well as enhanced security using identity-based cryptography [7].

However, the PDP scheme has a drawback that it cannot recover corrupted data blocks, thus proofs of retrievability (POR) schemes are raised to fill the gap. In 2007, Juels et al. [8] propose a POR scheme that combines sentinel-based spot-checking and erasure-correcting code together to ensure the retrievability of outsourced data. As a follow-up work, C. Wang et al. [9] enable incomplete dynamic data operations, modification, deletion and appendant. However, the sentinel-based method has a significant defect that the precomputed tokens or tags can only support limited times of audit. As an improvement, H. Shacham et al. [10] realize a POR scheme with unlimited audit times in the random oracle model. On the other hand, focusing on recovery cost, a series of works emerge. N. Cao et al. [11] replace RS code with LT code to improve the decoding speed during data retrieval and reduce data repair complexity at the same time. One step further, C.H. Chen et al. [12] introduce regenerating code which has the property of fault tolerance and requires less repair traffic in corruption recovery. Taking advantage of their works, K. Yang et al. [13] extend the application scenario of POR scheme to batch auditing for multi-user and multi-cloud. However, similar to the aforementioned work, most POR schemes are based on coding redundancy which accounts for extra storage space. Also, it brings in huge computational overhead to clients in the procedure of corruption recovery.

Besides traditional PDP and POR schemes, fragile watermark also provides an effective way to detect and recover data corruption. Often these watermarks are embedded in an imperceptible way so that they do not affect the use of data. Taking digital image for instance, P.W. Wong et al. [14] propose a public verifiable watermarking framework for corruption detection. This scheme encrypts watermarks with private key before embedding to prevent any unauthorized party from arbitrary forgery meanwhile the trusted verifiers can use public key to extract the watermark. To further improve security and accuracy of tamper localization, H.J. He et al. [15] hide the watermark of one block in another one according to a random permutation block-chain, which can decrease the probabilities of simultaneous corruption upon both content and watermark. Besides tampering detection based on verification watermark, some works [16–18] also focus on corruption recovery by recovery watermark. P.L. Lin et al. [16] present a hierarchical watermarking method to ensure high precision of tampering detection and implement corruption recovery by refilling each 2×2 block with the average intensity of its pixels. T.Y. Lee et al. [17] propose a dual watermarking scheme which embeds recovery watermark repeatedly to enhance the security. Z.X. Qian et al. [18] introduce a watermarking method with improved restoration capability via DCT coefficients and expanded reference bits.

However, although fragile watermarking has been used to detect and recover data corruption, it remains a challenge to implement a watermark based POR scheme since all these works have a common defect: the difficulty in achieving both privacy preservation and replay attack resistance at the same time. The privacy-preserving watermarks, such as those based on hash values of image content, can be precomputed and stored by the CSS to pass the verification at any time. This problem remains to be the biggest obstacle of realizing watermark-based POR scheme.

3   Problem Statement

3.1   The System and Threat Model

A system architecture for fragile watermarking based POR scheme is illustrated in Fig. 1. In the architecture, there are three different entities: Cloud Service Server (CSS), which has a massive storage capacity and provides storage service in the pay-as-you-go pricing model; Client, who has only limited local storage and computation abilities but a large amount of data to store on the cloud; Third Party Auditor (TPA), who has more expertise and ability than the client and is trusted by the client to verify the integrity of the outsourced data.

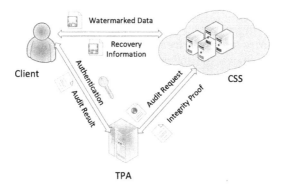

Fig. 1. System model

In this architecture, the whole protocol is divided into three phases: Setup Phase, Verification Phase and Recovery Phase. In Setup Phase, the client first generates public and private parameters, then produces verification watermark and recovery watermark which are used to detect and recover data corruption respectively. At last, both watermarks are embedded into the data in local storage before outsourcing to the CSS. In Verification Phase, the client checks the integrity of outsourced data by resorting to the TPA which does verification in a challenge-response way. In Recovery Phase, the client fixes the corrupted blocks through recovery watermarks retrieved from CSS.

Before we are convinced that the whole watermark-based mechanism is secure, some threats must be eliminated. First of all, we consider the CSS to be semi-trusted. That is to say, it provides normal storage service to clients in most of the time. However, once the outsourced data is corrupted in the cloud storage, the CSS may try its best to hide the corruption for its own sake. This characteristic of CSS leads to two kinds of misbehaviors: replay attack and watermark forgery. The so-called replay attack means, since the outsourced data is in physical control of the cloud, CSS is able to pass the verification with a pre-generated proof, instead of generating a new one based on the data in storage. On the other hand, watermark forgery is that CSS generates watermarks according to the features extracted from corrupted or tampered data, and embeds them to replace the original ones. If the verification watermarks are forged, CSS is able to deceive the TPA to pass integrity audit. Also, there exists risk that the recovery watermark can be tampered for inducing clients to recover content specified by CSS, which should be taken into consideration. The proposed scheme must be designed to prevent the aforementioned attacks. Secondly, during the process of public audit, clients also face the threats of data privacy disclosure. During the process of verification, any possible leakage of clients data toward the TPA should be prohibited.

3.2   Design Goals

To enable the security and effectiveness of the watermark-based POR scheme, our design should achieve the following security and performance guarantee: (1) Public auditability: to enable the TPA to audit the integrity of the client's data without retrieving the full copy; (2) Privacy-preserving: to prevent the privacy from leaking to the TPA during the process of integrity audit; (3) Security: to eliminate the replay attack as well as watermark forgery launched by CSS, and also to avoid the risk that the recovered content is specified by CSS; (4) Retrievability: to enable the client to retrieve the corrupted data once the result of the verification is false; (5) Lightweight: to ensure the storage, communication and computational overhead are lightweight for the verification and corruption recovery.

3.3   Preliminaries and Implementation Framework

Before describing the implementation framework to achieve our scheme, we first introduce the following two methods as preliminaries to construct our fragile watermarking based POR scheme that supports the design goals: public key watermarking and Diffie-Hellman protocol based information exchange.

- Public key watermarking
  The first method is designed based on Wong's public key watermarking scheme [14]. The main principle of this method is to introduce the public key encryption and decryption scheme into the watermark embedding and extracting process. That is to say, all the watermarks should be encrypted with private key before embedding and decrypted with public key after extracting. The application of public key encryption prevents CSS from forgery and is quite appropriate for public auditing, for that anyone with a public key is able to perform image verification. Also, it makes sure that recovery watermarks are under protection, which means the risk that the recovered content is arbitrarily specified by CSS is avoided.
- Diffie-Hellman protocol based message exchange
  This method is firstly proposed by Y. Deswarte et al. [19], which applies the principle of Diffie-Hellman key exchange to message exchange between clients and remote server for outsourced files. We find it effective to resist replay attack in cloud storage. Let p be a prime integer and g is a primitive root of $\mathbb{Z}_p$. M is outsourced data and $m = g^M \bmod N$ is the corresponding message digest pre-computed by the client. Now the client tries to verify M with m and wants to ensure that the received message digest is not a pre-computed one. To solve this problem, the client firstly chooses a random integer $r \in \mathbb{Z}_p$, and sends $A = g^r \bmod N$ to the cloud. Once receiving the request, the cloud returns $B = A^M \bmod N$. Finally, the client compares B with $m^r \bmod N$. If consistent, the verification is success; otherwise, failed. Due to the privacy-preserving property of the message digest, it is easy to extend this protocol to the three party scenario. That is to say, even if the client is replaced by TPA,

the method remains valid because the message digest m is privacy-preserving to original data M. So in our scheme, verification watermarks are generated from m, which is able to resist replay attack effectively.

Now we describe the implementation framework in the form of basic algorithms and a detailed description of our scheme will be introduced in next section.

$(pk, sk) \leftarrow GenKey(1^k)$. $GenKey$ is an algorithm to generate public and private parameters, which is run by clients. It takes security parameter 1^k as input, and returns public and private parameters (pk, sk), which are necessary to generate, embed and verify watermarks.

$(W_1, W_2) \leftarrow GenWatermark(I, ID, pk)$. Once the public parameters are generated, the client generates watermarks of file I, which is identified by identity code ID. This algorithm outputs the verification watermark W_1 and the recovery watermark W_2 of I respectively.

$(\widetilde{I}) \leftarrow Embed(I, W_1, W_2, pk, sk)$. $Embed$ is an algorithm run by the client to embed both types of watermark W_1 and W_2 into the original data I. Public and private parameters (pk, sk) are used to protect watermarks before embedding. Finally, the client outsources the watermarked data $\widetilde{I}$ to the cloud storage.

$(P) \leftarrow GenProof(\widetilde{I}, pk, chal)$. $Genproof$ is run by the CSS to generate the proof for challenge. The input of the algorithm consists of watermarked data $\widetilde{I}$, public parameters pk as well as challenge $chal$, and the output is proof P.

$(TRUE, FALSE) \leftarrow VerifyProof(P, pk, sk, chal)$. Once receiving the proof P for challenge $chal$ from the CSS, the TPA verifies the correctness of the proof. The algorithm returns $TRUE$ is the verification is passed, otherwise $FALSE$.

$(C_{k2}, b_{i'}) \leftarrow Retrieve(request)$. $Retrieve$ is an algorithm run by the CSS. It receives request from the client and returns encrypted recovery watermark C_{k2} as well as corresponding data block $b_{i'}$ whose recovery watermark was stored in the corrupted one before.

$(\widetilde{b_i}) \leftarrow Recover(C_{k2}, b_{i'}, sk, pk)$. Once received the recovery information from the CSS, this algorithm will be run by the client. It recovers the corrupted block to fixed ones $\widetilde{b_i}$ with the help of recovery watermarks C_{k2} and necessary parameters. Also the recovery watermark of $b_{i'}$ will be embedded into $\widetilde{b_i}$.

4   The Proposed Scheme for Archival Image Storage

In this section, we take archival image storage for instance, to show a concrete implementation of our fragile watermarking based POR scheme. Archival images are those images which are only kept in storage and will not be modified any more. That is to say, it is not necessary to consider data dynamics in this scenario. In the following, we divide the whole protocol into three parts and present their details respectively. Sequence diagram of the whole scheme is shown in Fig. 2.

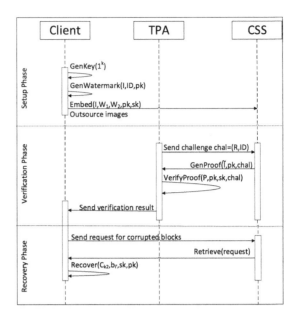

Fig. 2. Sequence diagram of proposed scheme for archival image storage

4.1 Setup

The client generates its public and private parameters by invoking $GenKey$. By running $GenWatermark$, the client produces the verification watermark and the recovery watermark for the archival image, which could be used to verify the integrity of data and recover the corrupted blocks respectively. Once obtaining watermarks, the client runs $Embed$ to embed both kinds of watermark into images. For simplicity, we just take grayscale images for instance, where the number of gray levels is 256.

$GenKey(1^k)$. The client generates public and private parameters (pk, sk). Choose a random prime number N, a primitive root g of $\mathbb{Z}_N$, and a secret key key_{PRP} for a pseudo random permutation function $f(\cdot)$. A key for symmetric encryption key_{sym} is also generated. Finally, $pk = (N, g)$ and $sk = (key_{PRP}, key_{sym})$.

$GenWatermark(I, ID, pk)$. Given an image I, the client sets the 2 least significant bits (LSB) to zero and divides it into non-overlapping blocks $(b_1, b_2, \cdots, b_n)$, where the size of each b_i is $w \times h$ and for simplicity we suppose both w and h are even numbers. Then the client calculates the verification watermark of each block as $W_{i1} = H(ID, i, g^{b_i} \bmod N), i \in [1, n]$, where ID is a unique identity code for distinguishing each image, i is the index of block and $H(\cdot)$ is a cryptographic hash function. Verification watermark $W_1 = (W_{11}, \cdots, W_{n1})$ reflects the feature of every blocks in the image. To improve the recovery accuracy, each block b_i is further divided into 2×2 sub-blocks $\{b_{ij}\}, j \in [1, \frac{wh}{4}]$. According to the order from top to bottom, from left to right, the four pixels of

b_{ij} are represented as $b_{ij1}, \cdots, b_{ij4}$. The recovery watermark of b_{ij} is generated as $W_{ij2} = \lfloor \frac{1}{4} \sum_{t=1}^{4} \lfloor \frac{b_{ijt}}{4} \rfloor \rfloor$, which equals to the mean value of the pixels in each sub-block removing two LSBs. The recovery watermark of block b_i is denoted as $W_{i2} = \{W_{ij2}, j \in [1, \frac{wh}{4}]\}$ and $W_2 = (W_{12}, \cdots, W_{n2})$.

$Embed(I, W_1, W_2, pk, sk)$. For each 2×2 sub-block, every pixel offers two LSBs to embed watermarks so that the capacity is 8 bits per sub-block. The first three pixels from upper left to lower right are used to store recovery watermark and the last pixel is for verification watermark. The embedding space for verification watermark is determined by the number of sub-blocks in one block. And 6 bits per sub-block is just the size of mean-value recovery watermark.

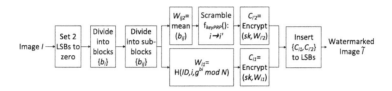

Fig. 3. Procedure of watermark generation and embedding

The whole procedure of watermark generation and embedding is shown in Fig. 3. Before inserting watermarks into LSBs, the client needs some extra processing to enhance the security. First of all, it must be noted that the recovery watermark $W_{i2} = \{W_{ij2}\}$ of each block b_i should be stored in another block b_k, to ensure its intactness when b_i is corrupted. So the client uses a secret key key_{PRP} and a pseudo random permutation function $f(\cdot)$, scrambling i to i'. That is to say, the recovery watermark stored in block b_i can be $W_{i'2}$, which is used to restore $b_{i'}$. Secondly, to prevent any other one except the client from inserting watermarks into images, W_1 and W_2 should be block-wise encrypted to C_1 and C_2 using symmetric key key_{sym} and inserted into LSBs. Finally, the client outsources all the watermarked images to clouds and the setup phase is finished.

4.2 Integrity Verification

In this phase, the TPA specified by the client would check the integrity of images by challenging the CSS with a message $chal$. To prevent replay attack, the TPA picks a random element $r \in \mathbb{Z}_N$ so that $gcd(N - 1, r) = 1$, and computes $R = g^r \bmod N$, which is necessary for DH information exchange. Furthermore, since $gcd(N - 1, r) = 1$, there must exist an s that satisfies $sr \equiv 1 \bmod (N - 1)$, which is used in proof verification later. Finally, a challenge $chal = (R, ID)$ is sent to the CSS.

$GenProof(\tilde{I}, pk, chal)$. Once receiving the challenge, the CSS takes the required watermarked images $\tilde{I}$ as input and generates the integrity proof by the following steps. It firstly extracts encrypted watermark C_1 from LSBs. Then,

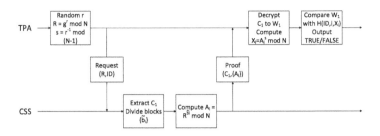

Fig. 4. Integrity verification process

following the same method in embedding process, the LSBs of every pixel are set to zero and the images are divided into blocks $\widetilde{b}_i$. Then the CSS computes $A_i = R^{\widetilde{b}_i} \, mod \, N$ and sends proof $P = (C_1, \{A_i\}), i \in [1, n]$ to the TPA. Since R is randomly decided by the TPA, the CSS cannot precompute any values to generate A_i. Thus the application of DH based information exchange is able to prevent replay attack.

$VerifyProof(P, pk, sk, chal)$. When the TPA starts to verify the proof from the CSS, it decrypts C_1 to W_1 with the symmetric key key_{sym} at first. In order to verify the integrity of archival images, the TPA should extract features from $\{A_i\}$ which are necessary for reconstructing watermarks. Since $sr \equiv 1 \, mod \, (N-1)$, there must exist an integer k so that $sr = k(N-1) + 1$. According to Fermat's little theorem, $g^{N-1} \equiv 1 \, mod \, N$, we can deduce that

$$X_i = A_i^s = (g^{\widetilde{b}_i})^{rs} = (g^{\widetilde{b}_i})^{k(N-1)+1} = g^{\widetilde{b}_i} \, mod \, N \tag{1}$$

That is to say, the features of image blocks $X_i = g^{\widetilde{b}_i} \, mod \, N$ can be extracted from $\{A_i\}$ by computing

$$X_i = A_i^s \, mod \, N \tag{2}$$

Finally, the TPA reconstructs verification watermarks as $\widetilde{W}_{i1} = H(ID, i, X_i), i \in [1, n]$ and compares them with the decrypted ones W_{i1}. More specifically, the verification is checking whether $H(ID, i, g^{\widetilde{b}_i} \, mod \, N)$ equals to $H(ID, i, g^{b_i} \, mod \, N)$. Once the block $\widetilde{b}_i$ is corrupted, the corresponding hash value will fail to match with W_{i1}. Thus if the result is consistent, it means $\widetilde{b}_i = b_i, i \in [1, n]$ and the TPA outputs $TRUE$; otherwise, it outputs $FALSE$ and informs the client which block or blocks are corrupted. The whole process of integrity verification is shown in Fig. 4.

By the end of this part we discuss the case of batch verification. According to the probabilistic proof in [2], if the corruption rate of all the data is 1%, the TPA is able to detect the corruption with probability of 99% by randomly choosing only 460 blocks from different archival images to be verified. So if the TPA needs to check a large amount of images, it can follow this method. Another issue in batch auditing is whether the aggregation of proofs similar to [2] is necessary since it seems to be able to decrease the communication overhead. However, it fails to provide a method to find out which block is corrupted and still has to check every block one by one again in the recovery phase [11].

4.3   Corruption Recovery

If the ith block is verified to be corrupted, the client firstly calculates the location of its recovery watermark and the index of data block corresponding to the recovery watermark stored in the ith block. Denote as $k = f^{-1}_{key_{PRP}}(i)$ and $i' = f_{key_{PRP}}(i)$ respectively. Then the $request = (ID, k, i')$ is sent to CSS to ask for the recovery watermark stored in block b_k and the block $b_{i'}$ whose 2 LSBs are set to zero. Once received the request, algorithm $Retrieve$ will be invoked by the CSS to generate a response. Then the client runs algorithm $Recover$ to restore the corrupted images.

$Retrieve(request)$. The CSS first finds out the image corresponding to ID in $request$, then extracts the recovery watermark from the kth block. At last, the extracted encrypted recovery watermark C_{k2} would be sent to the client together with the $i'th$ block $b_{i'}$.

$Recover(C_{k2}, b_{i'}, sk, pk)$. The client begins its restoration with decrypting C_{k2} to W_{k2} using key_{sym}. Then the corrupted block b_i is approximately recovered by refilling sub-blocks with mean value contained in watermarks and the recovered block is denoted as $\widetilde{b}_i$. The client revokes $GenWatermark()$ to generate verification watermark of $\widetilde{b}_i$ as well as recovery watermark of $b_{i'}$ and embeds them into $\widetilde{b}_i$ by $Embed()$.

5   Security Analysis

Theorem 1. Once a data block is corrupted, the corresponding verification watermark is able to detect the corruption.

Proof. First of all, we will prove that when a block b_i is corrupted to b'_i, its reconstructed verification watermark W'_{i1} must be inconsistent with the original one W_{i1}. Since $b'_i \neq b_i$, it is apparent that holds $g^{b'_i} \neq g^{b_i} \bmod N$. According to the property of cryptographic hash function $H(\cdot)$, even a tiny difference of $|g^{b'_i} - g^{b_i}| \bmod N$ will cause significant change in W'_{i1} compared to W_{i1}. So the reconstructed watermark based on corrupted block is sure to be inconsistent with the original one. Secondly, once a block is corrupted, the encrypted verification watermark embedded in its LSBs is quite likely to be damaged. It can be easily concluded that the decrypted watermark will also be changed. Finally, since apparently the probability that the reconstructed watermark of corrupted block equals to the changed decrypted watermark is negligible, we can deduce that the verification watermark must be able to detect the corruption.

Theorem 2. From the response of CSS, the TPA does not has ability to infer the content of the original image so that the proposed public auditable scheme is privacy-preserving.

Proof. According to our scheme, the proof sent from CSS to TPA consists of two parts, the encrypted watermark and the DH based exchanged information, which are denoted as $P = (C_1, \{A_i\}), i \in [1, n]$. Thus we prove the *Theorem* 2 in two steps. First, we show that no information of original block b_i can be learned from $C_{i1}, i \in [1, n]$. Once received the proof, W_{i1} can be decrypted from C_{i1} by TPA, where

$$W_{i1} = H(ID, i, g^{b_i} \bmod N) \tag{3}$$

It can be analyzed as the following process. Since W_{i1} is a cryptographic hash value, due to the one-way property of hash function, the TPA cannot derive $g^{b_i} \bmod N$ from $H(ID, i, g^{b_i} \bmod N)$. Thus no information of b_i can be learned.

Second, we show that no information of outsourced data block $\widetilde{b}_i$ in cloud storage can be learned from $A_i, i \in [1, n]$, where

$$A_i = R^{\widetilde{b}_i} = (g^{\widetilde{b}_i})^r \bmod N \tag{4}$$

As the TPA already has value of r, inferring $\widetilde{b}_i$ is equivalent to solving the Discrete Logarithm Problem (DLP): although given prime N, generator g and value $g^{r\widetilde{b}_i} \bmod N$, the computation of $r\widetilde{b}_i$ is still hard. So the TPA cannot learn $\widetilde{b}_i$ from A_i. This completes the proof of *Theorem* 2.

Theorem 3. The proof generated by CSS has the property of unforgeability and the proposed scheme is able to resist replay attack.

Proof. As already known, the proof generated by CSS is $P = (C_1, \{A_i\}), i \in [1, n]$, so the proof of unforgeability consists of two parts: the unforgeable property of C_{i1} and that of A_i. As C_1 is the ciphertext of verification watermark W_1 so that its unforgeability is ensured by the security of symmetric encryption. And according to (4), if the CSS tries to forge A_i to pass the verification, it must compute $g^{r b_i} \bmod N$. Even though the value of $g^{b_i} \bmod N$ can be precomputed and stored by the CSS, the forgery of A_i is equivalent to solving the computational Diffie-Hellman problem: given prime N, generator g and value $g^{b_i} \bmod N, g^r \bmod N$, it is still difficult to compute $g^{r b_i} \bmod N$. Thus A_i is unforgeable.

On the other hand, since the challenge $chal = (R, ID)$ is sent from TPA to CSS, where $R = g^r \bmod N$ is randomly chosen by the TPA, due to the complexity of solving the discrete logarithm problem, it is impossible for the CSS to derive r from R. Thus our scheme is ensured to resist replay attack based on random oracle model and difficulty of computing DLP.

6   Performance Analysis and Simulation Results

In this section, we demonstrate the performance of our proposed scheme in terms of correctness and efficiency respectively. The correctness of our scheme will be evaluated via watermark imperceptibility, corruption detection and data recovery. And the efficiency analysis will focus on storage cost as well as computational overhead. Experiments are conducted using C++ on a desktop computer with Intel Core i5-4590 CPU @ 3.30 GHz, 8 GB RAM and a 1 TB hard drive. We implement algorithms using the crypto library of OpenSSL version 1.0.2h.

6.1   Correctness

In this part, we choose an image Lena with size of 384×384 to show the correctness of the proposed scheme. The image is divided into 16×16 blocks so that the embedding space for verification watermark in each block is 128 bits. MD5 is selected as the cryptographic hash function to generate verification watermark, whose length of value is just 128 bits. The experiment results are as follows.

(a) Original Lena   (b) Watermarked Lena

Fig. 5. Comparison between original image and watermarked one

As shown in Fig. 5, (a) is the original image and (b) is the watermarked one. To quantize the imperceptibility of the watermark, we use the value of peak signal to noise ratio ($PSNR$) as the indicator for quality loss of image:

$$PSNR = 10 \times log_{10} \frac{255^2}{MSE} dB \qquad (5)$$

where MSE is the mean square error between the two images. For Fig. 5(b), $PSNR$ of the watermarked Lena is 44.1503 dB and thus the imperceptibility is ensured.

Then we modify the watermarked image to test the effectiveness of corruption detection and recovery. The watermarked image is tampered as shown in Fig. 6(a)

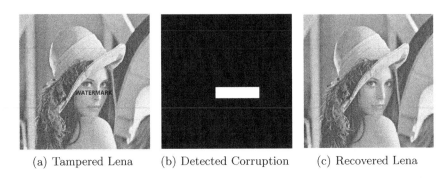

(a) Tampered Lena   (b) Detected Corruption   (c) Recovered Lena

Fig. 6. Tampered image and recovery

and the verification result is shown in Fig. 6(b), in which the white area means corruption while the black one refers to intactness. The recovered image is shown in Fig. 6(c) and the quality of restoration can also be evaluated by $PSNR$, which is 41.6426 dB.

6.2   Efficiency

In this part, we compare our proposed fragile watermarking based POR scheme with encoding-based ones in terms of both theoretical complexity and simulation results. We choose two typical scheme based on RS code [9] and LT Code [11] respectively.

The theoretical performance comparison is shown in Table 1, where $|F|$ is the size of original file, n is the total number of original data blocks, and $|B|$ is the size of corrupted block. For the encoding-based scheme, N represents the total number of servers and K represents the allowed minimum number of healthy servers to recover corruption. In the RS code scheme, t denotes number of the limited times for integrity verification and $|v|$ is the size of precomputed verification tag which is an element of $GF(2^p)$. In the LT code scheme, ϵ means any K original blocks can be recovered from $K(1 + \epsilon)$ encoded blocks, while s refers to the number of sectors divided from one block. The LT code scheme has three kinds of verification tag $|v|$ which belong to a cyclic group $\mathbb{G}, \mathbb{G} \times \mathbb{G} \to \mathbb{G}_T$ and supports pairing-based bilinear verification, as well as so-called coding vector $|\Delta|$ which has a length of n-bit.

From the table we can see that the theoretical complexity of our scheme is significantly lower than the encoding-based ones. The encoding-based schemes, no matter with or without limited audit times, suffer from not only complex computation of data encoding and tag precomputing, but also high additional storage cost of code redundancy and verification tags. Furthermore, in the case of retrieving data, because of the property of watermark and Vandermonde encoding matrix respectively, both our scheme and the RS code one need no decoding process, not so for the LT code scheme. Also our scheme requires the lowest communication overhead for data recovery among all the three schemes.

Table 1. Theoretical performance analysis

	RS code [9]	LT code [11]	Our scheme
Unlimited audit times	×	√	√
Total storage cost	$\frac{N}{F}|F| + tN|v|$	$\frac{N(1+\epsilon)}{K}|F| + [\frac{N}{K}(1+s)(1+\epsilon)n + N]|v| + n|\Delta|$	$|F|$
Encoding computation	$O(\frac{Nn^2}{K})$	$O(\frac{N}{K}(1+\epsilon)n\ln n)$	–
Tag precomputation/Watermark embedding	$O(tN)$	$O(\frac{N}{K}(1+s)(1+\epsilon)n + N)$	$O(n)$

Another reason for why we describe our scheme as light-weighted is the lower computational overhead for clients. There are two phases that need the client to do calculation with their local computational resources. One is the setup phase and the other one is the recovery phase. In setup, the client generates watermarks and embeds them into the images before outsourcing to the cloud. Equivalently, the preprocessing work in correcting code based POR schemes is encoding. In the following experiment, we compare the computational overhead in setup phase. We implement the encoding of Reed-Solomon code with two different parameters, $(255, 223)$ and $(255, 239)$. The experimental result in Fig. 7(a) shows that the computational overhead of our scheme is lower than that of encoding method.

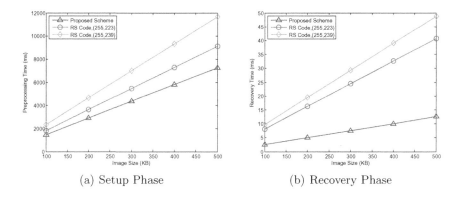

(a) Setup Phase   (b) Recovery Phase

Fig. 7. Computational overhead of the client

Now we consider the computational overhead for clients in recovery phase. To repair the corrupted block in our scheme, the client needs to decrypt the recovery watermark with symmetric key, refill all the sub-blocks with mean values and regenerate the verification watermark as well as the recovery watermark which has been stored in it before. All these computation only involves two blocks while the encoding method needs to do matrix computation with another m blocks, which is more complex. We compare the recovery time of our method with *RS*

code based scheme and the result is shown in Fig. 7(*b*), telling that our method
has lower overhead.

7   Conclusion

In this paper, we propose a fragile watermarking based POR scheme for archival
cloud data, which requires no extra storage cost and only lightweight computation for data verification and corruption recovery. In our scheme, we utilize the
public key watermarking and Diffie-Hellman protocol based message exchange to
prevent watermark forgery and replay attack. The effectiveness of our proposed
scheme is tested by experiments and the result shows that it is not only able to
detect and recover data corruption, but also effective to decrease storage cost
and computational overhead. Besides, the imperceptibility of both verification
watermark and recovery watermark is also ensured.

Acknowledgment. This work is supported by the National Natural Science Foundation of China under Grant No. U1405254, No. U1536201 and No. 61472092; The
National High Technology Research and Development Program of China (863 Program) under Grant No. 2015AA020101.

References

1. Zhang, Q.L., Dai, Y.F., Zhang, L.T.: UStore: a low cost cold and archival data storage system for data centers. In: 35th IEEE International Conference on Distributed
Computing Systems, Columbus, pp. 431–441. IEEE Press (2015)
2. Ateniese, G., Burns, R., Curtmola, R., Herring, J., Kissner, L., Peterson, Z., Song,
D.: Provable data possession at untrusted stores. In: 14th ACM Conference on
Computer and Communications Security, pp. 598–609. ACM, New York (2007)
3. Wang, C., Wang, Q., Ren, K., Lou, W.J.: Privacy-preserving public auditing for
data storage security in cloud computing. In: 30th IEEE International Conference
on Computer Communications, San Diego, pp. 1–9. IEEE Press (2010)
4. Wang, Q., Wang, C., Ren, K., Lou, W.J.: Enabling public auditability and data
dynamics for storage security in cloud computing. IEEE Trans. Parallel Distrib.
22, 847–859 (2010)
5. Liu, C., Ranjan, R., Yang, C., Zhang, X.Y., Wang, L.Z., Chen, J.J.: MuR-DPA:
top-down levelled multi-replica merkle hash tree based secure public auditing for
dynamic big data storage on cloud. IEEE Trans. Comput. **64**, 2609–2622 (2015)
6. Zhu, Y., Hu, H.X., Ahn, G.J., Yu, M.Y.: Cooperative provable data possession
for integrity verification in multi-cloud storage. IEEE Trans. Parallel Distrib. **23**,
2231–2244 (2012)
7. Wang, H.Q.: Identity-based distributed provable data possession in multicloud storage. IEEE Trans. Serv. Comput. **8**, 328–340 (2015)
8. Juels, A., Kaliski, B.S.: Pors: proofs of retrievability for large files. In: 14th
ACM Conference on Computer and Communications Security, pp. 584–597. ACM,
New York (2007)
9. Wang, C., Wang, Q., Ren, K., Lou, W.J.: Ensuring data storage security in cloud
computing. In: 17th International Workshop on Quality of Service, Charleston, pp.
1–9. IEEE Press (2009)

10. Shacham, H., Waters, B.: Compact proofs of retrievability. J. Cryptol. **26**, 442–483 (2013)
11. Cao, N., Yu, S.C., Yang, Z.Y., Lou, W.J., Hou, Y.T.: LT codes-based secure and reliable cloud storage service. In: 32th IEEE International Conference on Computer Communications, Orlando, pp. 693–701. IEEE Press (2012)
12. Chen, C.H., Lee, P.C.: Enabling data integrity protection in regenerating-coding-based cloud storage. In: IEEE Symposium on Reliable Distributed Systems, Irvine, pp. 51–60. IEEE Press (2012)
13. Yang, K., Jia, X.H.: An efficient and secure dynamic auditing protocol for data storage in cloud computing. IEEE Trans. Parallel Distrib. **24**, 1717–1726 (2013)
14. Wong, P.W.: A public key watermark for image verification and authentication. In: 5th International Conference on Image Processing, Chicago, pp. 455–459. IEEE Press (1998)
15. He, H.-J., Zhang, J.-S., Tai, H.-M.: Block-chain based fragile watermarking scheme with superior localization. In: Solanki, K., Sullivan, K., Madhow, U. (eds.) IH 2008. LNCS, vol. 5284, pp. 147–160. Springer, Heidelberg (2008). doi:10.1007/978-3-540-88961-8_11
16. Lin, P.L., Hsieh, C.K., Huang, P.W.: A hierarchical digital watermarking method for image tamper detection and recovery. Pattern Recogn. **38**, 2519–2529 (2005)
17. Lee, T.Y., Lin, S.F.: Dual watermark for image tamper detection and recovery. Pattern Recogn. **41**, 3497–3506 (2008)
18. Qian, Z.X., Feng, G.R., Zhang, X.P., Wang, S.Z.: Image self-embedding with high-quality restoration capability. Digit. Sig. Process. **21**, 278–286 (2011)
19. Deswarte, Y., Quisquater, J.-J., Saïdane, A.: Remote integrity checking. In: Jajodia, S., Strous, L. (eds.) Integrity and Internal Control in Information Systems VI. IIFIP, vol. 140, pp. 1–11. Springer, Heidelberg (2004). doi:10.1007/1-4020-7901-X_1

Multiple Watermarking Using Multilevel Quantization Index Modulation

Bingwen Feng[1], Jian Weng[1], Wei Lu[2], and Bei Pei[3]([✉])

[1] College of Information Science and Technology,
Jinan University, Guangzhou 510632, China
bingwfeng@gmail.com, cryptjweng@gmail.com
[2] Guangdong Key Laboratory of Information Security Technology,
School of Data and Computer Science,
Sun Yat-sen University, Guangzhou 510006, China
luwei3@mail.sysu.edu.cn
[3] Key Lab of Information Network Security,
Ministry of Public Security, Shanghai 200000, China
peibei@stars.org.cn

Abstract. In this paper, a type of multilevel Quantization Index Modulation (QIM) algorithms is proposed by adopting the concept of multilevel nested lattice coding. We first introduce the multilevel scalar-QIM and then extend it to the vector case by using lattice-QIM. The lattice definition and nested lattices construction are specified such that the constructed nested lattices is suitable for multilevel lattice-QIM. The proposed scheme embeds multiple watermark sequences into the same host signal via several embedding rounds. Each round of embedding uses quantizers of different radii, and thus provides different robustness. As a result, the embedded watermark sequences can be used for various purposes. Benefiting from the scalable robustness and adjustable embedding rate, the proposed multilevel QIM presents good performances and supports a wide range of applications.

Keywords: Multiple watermarking · Robustness · Quantization Index Modulation (QIM) · Multilevel nested lattices

1 Introduction

Digital watermarking is a technique related to multimedia security. Robustness and imperceptibility are necessary for effective watermarking algorithms. It can be used to copyright protection [1–4], content authentication [5], integrity verification [6], covered communication [7], and so on. Many watermarking schemes with different properties have been developed to address different issues. For example, robust watermarking is usually suggested for copyright protection while fragile watermarking can be used for integrity verification.

Multiple watermarking conveys multiple sets of watermark sequences simultaneously. These watermark sequences present different properties and are used

© Springer International Publishing AG 2017
Y.Q. Shi et al. (Eds.): IWDW 2016, LNCS 10082, pp. 312–326, 2017.
DOI: 10.1007/978-3-319-53465-7_23

for several goals. Multiple watermarking can be achieved by segmenting the host signal into several parts, within each of which one watermark sequence is allocated. Subbands of wavelet decomposition are frequently employed for this purpose [8,9]. Other transforms such as local binary pattern [6], discrete cosine transform [10], and singular value decomposition [11] are also reported to implement multiple watermarking. The properties of embedded watermarks in these schemes lie on the explored transformed domain. Therefore, it is difficult to extend these approaches to other watermarking applications. A better way is to develop multiple watermarking schemes independent of the host signal.

Quantization Index Modulation (QIM) [12,13] is an attractive alternative for implementing practical watermarking schemes. As a blind approach, it can reach the capacity bound with the aid of random binning coding [12]. QIM can be extended to high-dimensional cases by using sparse QIM or lattice QIM [13]. The former embeds one watermark bit in a spread transformed host vector of length n, reaching an embedding rate as $1/n$. The latter constructs nested lattices and maps watermarks to each coset leader of the nested lattices. The embedding rate of lattice QIM can be adjusted and is usually larger than 1. On the other hand, QIM-based algorithms with special properties have been proposed. For example, angle QIM [1] and rational dither modulation [2] are suggested to deal with the gain attack. The logarithmic quantization is introduced in [4] to feature perceptual advantages. Many QIM-based watermarking schemes are also proposed to handle the tradeoff between the perceptual quality and robustness according to human visual system characteristics [14,15]. This paper focuses on employing QIM for multiple watermarking.

Higher-dimensional quantization usually achieves better performance [16]. Therefore, we are devoted to studying high-dimensional multiple QIM. It should be noted that multilevel scalar-QIM is employed in [17] for steganography, and the multilevel nested bins has also been used in [18] to provide scalable security. However, their motivations are different from here. As a result, they cannot be straightforwardly employed for multiple watermarking. Another multiple embedding algorithm is the one based on the orthogonal projection [3]. It presents high robustness due to the optimality of sparse QIM. However, it cannot provide scalable robustness. Furthermore, its embedding rate is rather low, which limits the real application.

In this paper, a multilevel QIM-base embedding method is proposed for multiple watermarking. The proposed method is based on the perfect packing of the Voronoi regions [19] associated with different level lattices. We first introduce the concept of multilevel QIM by using scalar-QIM. It employs quantizers of different steps to embed watermark bits from different watermark sequences into one host sample. Then the method is extended to the vector case by resorting to lattice-QIM. We construct multilevel nested lattices that are suitable for embedding. The embedding is performed via several rounds by using quantizers whose radii decrease with increasing embedding rounds. Watermarks embedded in the first few embedding rounds present high robustness, while those embedded in the last round are fragile. Therefore, they can be used for different issues. The complexity of operations on the employed nested codes is low, which allows a arbitrarily high-dimensional embedding in practice.

2   Multilevel Scalar-QIM

Given a host signal sample $x \in \mathbb{R}$, scalar-Quantization Index Modulation (scalar-QIM) embeds one watermark bit $m \in \{0, 1\}$ by using the following encoder [13]

$$y = Q(x - d_m) + d_m, \ m \in \{0, 1\} \tag{1}$$

where $d_0 = -\Delta/4$ and $d_1 = \Delta/4$. $Q(x) \triangleq \Delta \lfloor x/\Delta \rfloor$ defines a uniform quantizer with step size Δ. It can be observed that the minimum distance between codewords is $\Delta/2$. Therefore, scalar-QIM creates a vacation of length $\Delta/2$ to tolerate potential distortions. We can use this vacation to embed more watermark bits.

The embedding procedure of multilevel scalar-QIM is implemented in several rounds. Let $y^{(\gamma)}$ denote the watermarked sample obtained in the (γ)-th round, and $y^{(0)} = x$. For the γ-th round, the watermark bit $m^{(\gamma)}$ is embedded by performing

$$y^{(\gamma)} = Q^{(\gamma)} \left(y^{(\gamma-1)} - d_{m^{(\gamma)}}^{(\gamma)} \right) + d_{m^{(\gamma)}}^{(\gamma)}, \ m^{(\gamma)} \in \{0, 1\} \tag{2}$$

where

$$d_0^{(\gamma)} = -\Delta/2^{\gamma+1}, \ d_1^{(\gamma)} = \Delta/2^{\gamma+1} \tag{3}$$

and the quantizer $Q^{(\gamma)}(x)$ is similar as that in Eq. (1) except that its step size is now of value $\Delta/2^{\gamma-1}$. Figure 1 demonstrates an example of a 3-level scalar-QIM, where three messages, $m^{(1)} = 0, m^{(2)} = 1$, and $m^{(3)} = 1$, are successively embedded into host sample x via three embedding rounds.

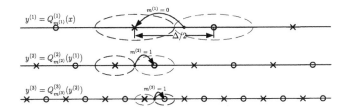

Fig. 1. Demonstration of the embedding procedure of multilevel scalar-QIM. Points corresponded to message bits 0 and 1 are represented by crosses and circles, respectively. The line segments surrounded by ellipses demonstrate the Voronoi regions of points.

The watermarked signal is then transmitted to the receiver via a noisy channel. Suppose the received signal sample is $\hat{y}$. The embedded watermark bit in the γ-th round can be extracted by a minimum-distance decoder

$$\hat{m}^{(\gamma)} = \arg \min_{i \in \{0, 1\}} \left\| Q^{(\gamma)} \left(\hat{y} - d_i^{(\gamma)} \right) + d_i^{(\gamma)} - \hat{y} \right\| \tag{4}$$

Figure 1 indicates that the quantization error on $y^{(\gamma)}$ incurred by the quantizer $Q_i^{(\gamma+1)}$ is in range $[-\Delta/2^{\gamma+1}, \Delta/2^{\gamma+1}]$, which is covered by the Voronoi region [19] of $y^{(\gamma)}$ with respect to quantizer $Q_i^{(\gamma)}$. Therefore, watermark bits embedded in each round can be extracted correctly by Eq. (4) when the magnitude of the noise is in an acceptable range.

3   Multilevel Lattice-QIM

Now we extend the multilevel QIM to the vector case. Broadly, there are two methods to achieve high-dimensional QIM: sparse-QIM and lattice-QIM. Sparse-QIM projects the host vector along a given direction and then embeds one watermark bit via an encoder similar to Eq. (1) [12,13]. Therefore, it is easy to apply multilevel QIM on this method. In view of this, we focus on applying multilevel QIM on lattice-QIM.

3.1   Construction of Nested Lattices

The fist step of lattice-QIM is to construct nested lattices. An n-dimensional lattice Λ is the set of the n-dimensional vectors that are in the form

$$\Lambda \triangleq \{\mathbf{p} = \mathbf{v}G, \mathbf{v} \in \mathbb{Z}^n\} \tag{5}$$

where row vectors $\mathbf{p}$ and $\mathbf{v}$ are of size $1 \times n$, and the $n \times n$ sized generator matrix G is comprised of the basic vectors of the lattice. Given specified lattice, the associated uniform quantizer Q_Λ quantizes a vector to its nearest lattice point, that is [20]

$$Q_\Lambda(\mathbf{x}) = \mathbf{p} \in \Lambda \text{ if } \|\mathbf{x} - \mathbf{p}\| \leq \|\mathbf{x} - \mathbf{p}'\|, \forall \mathbf{p}' \in \Lambda \tag{6}$$

A pair of lattices, $\Lambda^{(\gamma)}$ and $\Lambda^{(\gamma+1)}$, is nested if

$$G^{(\gamma)} = G^{(\gamma+1)} \cdot J \tag{7}$$

where $G^{(\gamma)}$ and $G^{(\gamma+1)}$ are the generator matrices associated with $\Lambda^{(\gamma)}$ and $\Lambda^{(\gamma+1)}$, respectively, and J is an $n \times n$ integer matrix with determinant greater than one.

Suppose $\mathbf{p} \in \Lambda^{(\gamma)}$ and $\mathbf{q} \in \Lambda^{(\gamma+1)}$. According to Fig. 1, the nested lattices suitable for multilevel embedding should satisfy

$$\bigcup_{\exists \mathbf{q}, Q_{\Lambda^{(\gamma)}}(\mathbf{q})=\mathbf{p}} \mathcal{V}^{(\gamma+1)}(\mathbf{q}) \subseteq \mathcal{V}^{(\gamma)}(\mathbf{p}) \tag{8}$$

where $\mathcal{V}^{(\gamma)}(\mathbf{p})$ denotes the Voronoi region of $\mathbf{p}$ with respect to lattice $\Lambda^{(\gamma)}$. It means that there are $\mathbf{q} \in \Lambda^{(\gamma+1)}$ whose Voronoi regions can pack the Voronoi region of one point, say $\mathbf{p}$, in the coarser lattice $\Lambda^{(\gamma)}$. Figure 2(a) demonstrates such an example, where the nested lattices are constructed from hexagonal lattice

"A2". In order to take full advantage of the points in $\Lambda^{(\gamma+1)}$, the Voronoi regions of $\Lambda^{(\gamma+1)}$ is desired to perfectly pack each Voronoi region of $\Lambda^{(\gamma)}$, that is

$$\bigcup_{\forall \mathbf{q}, Q_{\Lambda^{(\gamma)}}(\mathbf{q})=\mathbf{p}} \mathcal{V}^{(\gamma+1)}(\mathbf{q}) = \mathcal{V}^{(\gamma)}(\mathbf{p}) \tag{9}$$

Some lattices can not be used to construct nested lattices satisfying Eq. (9), such as lattice "A2" shown in Fig. 2(a). As a result, we only consider n-dimensional affine cubic lattice "Zn", whose generator matrix is

$$G = \frac{\Delta}{2} A \cdot \prod_{1 \le i,j \le n} V(i, j, \theta_{i,j}) \tag{10}$$

where $A \triangleq \mathrm{diag}(\alpha_1, \dots, \alpha_n), \sum_i \alpha_i = 1$, scales the lattice, and $V(i, j, \theta_{i,j})$ denotes the Givens rotation matrix [21], which rotates the lattice in the (i, j) plane of $\theta_{i,j}$ radius. It can be observed that the packing radius [19] of this lattice is $\left(\frac{\Delta}{4} \min \alpha_i\right)$. For the sake of simplicity, unless mentioned otherwise, we only consider $G = \frac{\Delta}{2} I$, I is the n-dimensional identity matrix, in the rest of this paper.

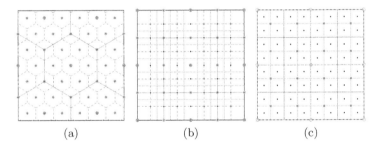

(a)   (b)   (c)

Fig. 2. (a) is an example of nested lattices constructed from "A2" lattice. (b) and (c) are examples of 3-level nested lattices constructed from "Z2" lattice with $\rho = 2$. (b) is obtained with the original origin while (c) with the dithered origin. $\Lambda^{(1)}$, $\Lambda^{(2)}$, and $\Lambda^{(3)}$ are represented by "o", "*", and ".", respectively. The boundaries of Voronoi regions are also illustrated.

The uniform quantizer defined in Eq. (6) constrains all the Voronoi regions of a lattice to be congruent. Therefore, Eq. 9 requires that the Voronoi regions of $\Lambda^{(\gamma)}$ should be as a scaled version of that of $\Lambda^{(\gamma+1)}$. This can be achieved by redefining Eq. (7) as

$$G^{(\gamma+1)} = \frac{1}{\rho} G^{(\gamma)} \tag{11}$$

where ρ is a positive integer. It can be observed that this construction is a special case of the self-similar construction [22]. Note that some points in $\Lambda^{(\gamma+1)}$, say $\mathbf{q}'$, will located at the boundaries of the Voronoi regions of $\mathbf{p} \in \Lambda^{(\gamma)}$ when ρ is even. Therefore, we must further shift $\Lambda^{(\gamma+1)}$ to guarantee the perfect packing of the Voronoi regions. A straightforward way is to move $\Lambda^{(\gamma+1)}$ a distance equal to the packing radius of its Voronoi region along the norm directions of the faces of the Voronoi regions of $\Lambda^{(\gamma)}$, such that the Voronoi regions of $\mathbf{q}'$ and $\mathbf{p}$ are internally tangent. In the case of "Z2" lattice, the multilevel nested lattices used for multilevel lattice-QIM can be formed as $\{\Lambda^{(1)}, \Lambda^{(2)}, \ldots\}$ where

$$\Lambda^{(\gamma)} \triangleq \left\{ \mathbf{p} = \frac{1}{\rho^{\gamma-1}} \mathbf{v} G + \mathbf{o}^{(\gamma)}, \mathbf{v} \in \mathbb{Z}^n \right\}, \gamma = 1, 2, \ldots \tag{12}$$

where G has been given in Eq. (10), and the $1 \times n$ sized row vector $\mathbf{o}^{(\gamma)}$ can be considered as the dithered origin, which is set as

$$\mathbf{o}^{(\gamma)} = \begin{cases} \mathbf{o}^{(\gamma-1)} + [1, \ldots, 1] \cdot 2^{-1} \rho^{1-\gamma} G & \text{if } \rho \text{ is even} \\ [0, \cdots, 0] & \text{if } \rho \text{ is odd} \end{cases} \tag{13}$$

Examples of 3-level nested lattices constructed from "Z2" lattice are shown in Fig. 2, where ρ is set with 2. The nested lattices in Fig. 2(b) is obtained without shifting. It can be observed that all the finer lattice points are located at the boundary of Voronoi regions. By the shifting operation, perfect packing of Voronoi regions is achieved, as shown in Fig. 2(c). It should be noted that the family of "Zn" lattices is not a good choice for quantization [19]. However, they are easy to be employed to construct multilevel nested lattices, because their basic vectors are orthogonal, which allows a simple solution for finding the dithered origin.

3.2 Multilevel Encoder and Decoder

The multilevel nested lattices $\{\Lambda^{(1)}, \Lambda^{(2)}, \ldots\}$ allow us to use each pair of consecutive lattices to embed one watermark sequence. The multilevel lattice-QIM is comprised of multiple round embedding. Nested lattices $\{\Lambda^{(\gamma)}, \Lambda^{(\gamma+1)}\}$ are used in the (γ)-th round to embed one watermark sequence. Suppose the $1 \times n$ sized host vector $\mathbf{x}$ is changed to $\mathbf{y}^{(\gamma-1)}$ after the $(\gamma-1)$-th round embedding. A watermark symbol $m^{(\gamma)} \in \{0, 1, \ldots, p-1\}$, where the number of codewords p is calculated by

$$p = \rho^n \tag{14}$$

can be embedded into $\mathbf{y}^{(\gamma-1)}$ by using

$$\mathbf{y}^{(\gamma)} = Q_{\Lambda^{(\gamma)}} \left(\mathbf{y}^{(\gamma-1)} - \mathbf{d}_{m^{(\gamma)}}^{(\gamma)} \right) + \mathbf{d}_{m^{(\gamma)}}^{(\gamma)} \tag{15}$$

where the coset leader $\mathbf{d}_{m^{(\gamma)}}^{(\gamma)}$ is selected from the set [20]

$$\mathcal{C}^{(\gamma)} \triangleq \left\{ \mathbf{d}_i^{(\gamma)} \middle| \mathbf{d}_i^{(\gamma)} \in \Lambda^{(\gamma+1)} \text{ and } Q_{\Lambda^{(\gamma)}} \left(\mathbf{d}_i^{(\gamma)} \right) = \mathbf{o}^{(\gamma)} \right\} \tag{16}$$

according to the codeword-coset leader mapping.

Assume the received vector is as $\hat{\mathbf{y}} = \mathbf{y}^{(\Gamma)}$ where $\mathbf{y}^{(\Gamma)}$ is the watermarked vector obtained after the last round embedding. Watermark symbol embedded in the (γ)-th round can be extracted from $\hat{\mathbf{y}}$ by

$$\hat{m}^{(\gamma)} = \underset{0 \le i \le p-1}{\arg\min} \left\| Q_{\Lambda^{(\gamma)}} \left(\hat{\mathbf{y}} - \mathbf{d}_i^{(\gamma)} \right) + \mathbf{d}_i^{(\gamma)} - \hat{\mathbf{y}} \right\| \tag{17}$$

Now we discuss the feasibility of the watermark extraction.

The watermarked vector obtained in the (γ)-th round embedding, $\mathbf{y}^{(\gamma)}$, is located at the point in $\Lambda^{(\gamma+1)}$. The subsequent round embedding moves the watermarked vector to the point in $\Lambda^{(\gamma+2)}$, which disturbs $\mathbf{y}^{(\gamma)}$ with

$$\mathbf{e}^{(\gamma+1)} \triangleq \mathbf{y}^{(\gamma+1)} - \mathbf{y}^{(\gamma)} = \mathbf{d}_i^{(\gamma+1)} - \mathbf{o}^{(\gamma+2)}, \ 0 \le i \le p-1 \tag{18}$$

Substituting Eq. (12) for the $\Lambda^{(\gamma+1)}$ in Eq. (16) and considering the definition of G in Eq. (10), the coset leader set can be calculated as

$$\left\{ \mathbf{d}_i^{(\gamma)} = \frac{\mathbf{v}^{(\gamma)} G}{\rho^{\gamma}} + \mathbf{o}^{(\gamma+1)}, \ \mathbf{v}^{(\gamma)} \in \left\{ -\left\lfloor \frac{\rho}{2} \right\rfloor, -\left\lfloor \frac{\rho}{2} \right\rfloor + 1, \dots, \left\lceil \frac{\rho}{2} \right\rceil - 1 \right\}^n \right\} \tag{19}$$

As a result, after the $(\gamma + \gamma')$-th round embedding, the watermarked vector satisfies

$$\mathbf{y}^{(\gamma+\gamma')} \in \left\{ \mathbf{y}^{(\gamma)} + \sum_{k=\gamma+1}^{\gamma+\gamma'} \mathbf{e}^{(k)} \right\} = \left\{ \mathbf{y}^{(\gamma)} + \left(\sum_{k=1}^{\gamma'} \frac{\mathbf{v}^{(k)}}{\rho^k} \right) \frac{1}{\rho^{\gamma}} G \right\} \tag{20}$$

$$\subset \mathbf{y}^{(\gamma)} + \frac{1}{\rho^{\gamma}(\rho-1)} \times \left[-\frac{\rho}{2}, \frac{\rho}{2} \right]^n \tag{21}$$

$$= \mathcal{V}^{(\gamma)} \left(\mathbf{y}^{(\gamma)} \right)$$

It means that Eq. (17) works well in the absent of noise.

4   Experimental Result

4.1   Theoretical Analysis

The proposed multilevel QIM embeds watermark sequences by using quantizers whose radii decrease with the increasing of the embedding rounds. A quantizer of larger radius allows greater distance between codewords. Thus, watermark sequences embedded in the first few rounds would present the best robustness. In this section we theoretically discuss the performance of multilevel QIM on artificial signals in the Additive White Gaussian Noisy (AWGN) channel. The robustness is measured by the error probability P_e, defined as

$$P_e = \frac{1}{p} \sum_{0 \le m \le p-1} \Pr\{\hat{m} \ne m \mid m \ \text{send}\} \tag{22}$$

Note that the multilevel scalar-QIM is identical to the multilevel lattice-QIM defined in "Z1" lattice. Therefore, we only consider the vector case here. Suppose the total number of embedding rounds is Γ. According Eq. (20), it follows that, for $1 \leq \forall \gamma \leq \Gamma$,

$$\mathbf{y}^{(\Gamma)} = \mathbf{d}_{m^{(\gamma)}}^{(\gamma)} + \sum_{k=\gamma+1}^{\Gamma} \left(\mathbf{d}_{m^{(k)}}^{(k)} - \mathbf{o}^{(k+1)} \right) \tag{23}$$

Suppose the received vector is corrupted by the attacker as $\hat{\mathbf{y}} = \mathbf{y}^{(\Gamma)} + \mathbf{n}$, where $\mathbf{n}$ represents the channel noise. The decoder for the (γ)-th watermark sequence first takes the modulus

$$\tilde{\mathbf{y}} = \hat{\mathbf{y}} \mod \Lambda^{(\gamma)}$$

$$= \left(\mathbf{d}_{m^{(\gamma)}}^{(\gamma)} + \left(\sum_{k=\gamma+1}^{\Gamma} \left(\mathbf{d}_{m^{(k)}}^{(k)} - \mathbf{o}^{(k+1)} \right) \right) + \mathbf{n} \right) \mod \Lambda^{(\gamma)}$$

$$\triangleq \left(\mathbf{d}_{m^{(\gamma)}}^{(\gamma)} + \mathbf{e} + \mathbf{n} \right) \mod \Lambda^{(\gamma)} \tag{24}$$

where $\left(\mathbf{x} \mod \Lambda^{(\gamma)} \right) \triangleq \left(\mathbf{x} - Q_{\Lambda^{(\gamma)}}(\mathbf{x}) \right) \in \mathcal{V}^{(\gamma)}(\mathbf{o}^{(\gamma)})$, and the self-noise $\mathbf{e} \triangleq \sum_{k=\gamma+1}^{\Gamma} \left(\mathbf{d}_{m^{(k)}}^{(k)} - \mathbf{o}^{(k+1)} \right)$ is caused by the subsequent rounds of embedding. Therefore, $\tilde{\mathbf{y}}$ can be viewed as the output of a Module Additive Noise Channel (MANC) [13] with input $\mathbf{d}_{m^{(\gamma)}}^{(\gamma)}$ and noise

$$\tilde{\mathbf{v}} = (\mathbf{e} + \mathbf{n}) \mod \Lambda^{(\gamma)}$$

$$= \left(\left(\mathbf{e} \mod \Lambda^{(\gamma)} \right) + \left(\mathbf{n} \mod \Lambda^{(\gamma)} \right) \right) \mod \Lambda^{(\gamma)}$$

$$\triangleq (\tilde{\mathbf{e}} + \tilde{\mathbf{n}}) \mod \Lambda^{(\gamma)} \tag{25}$$

It is reasonable to assume that the watermark sequence is i.i.d. and uniformly distributed in $\{0, 1, \ldots, p-1\}$. Consequently, the modular self-noise $\tilde{\mathbf{e}} \triangleq \left(\mathbf{e} \mod \Lambda^{(\gamma)} \right)$ is uniformly distributed in

$$\left\{ \mathbf{p} \,\middle|\, Q_{\Lambda^{(\gamma)}}(\mathbf{p}) = \mathbf{o}^{(\gamma)}, \mathbf{p} \in \Lambda^{(\Gamma+1)} \right\} \tag{26}$$

This yields the probability density function (pdf) of $\tilde{\mathbf{e}}$ as

$$p_{\tilde{\mathbf{E}}}(\tilde{\mathbf{e}}) = \begin{cases} 1/p^{\Gamma-\gamma} & \text{if } \mathbf{e} \text{ belongs to Eq. (26)} \\ 0 & \text{otherwise} \end{cases} \tag{27}$$

Suppose the channel noise follows $\mathbf{n} \sim N(0, \sigma_n^2 I)$. The pdf of the modular noise $\tilde{\mathbf{n}} \triangleq \left(\mathbf{n} \mod \Lambda^{(\gamma)} \right)$ takes the form

$$p_{\tilde{\mathbf{N}}}(\tilde{\mathbf{n}}) = \sum_{\mathbf{p} \in \Lambda^{(\gamma-1)}} p_{\mathbf{N}}(\mathbf{n} + \mathbf{p}) \tag{28}$$

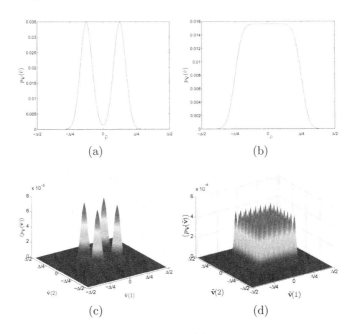

Fig. 3. Pdfs of modular self-noises $\tilde{\mathbf{v}}$ on (a) $y^{(1)}$ for 2-level scalar-QIM, (b) $y^{(1)}$ for 4-level scalar-QIM, (c) $\mathbf{y}^{(1)}$ for 2-level lattice-QIM, and (d) $\mathbf{y}^{(1)}$ for 4-level lattice-QIM. WNR = 20. The multilevel nested lattices are constructed from "Z2" lattice with $\rho = 2$ in the multilevel lattice-QIM.

Since $\tilde{\mathbf{e}}$ and $\tilde{\mathbf{n}}$ are statistically independent, the pdf of $\tilde{\mathbf{v}}$ is their circular convolution

$$p_{\tilde{\mathbf{V}}}(\tilde{\mathbf{v}}) = (p_{\tilde{\mathbf{E}}} \star p_{\tilde{\mathbf{N}}})(\tilde{\mathbf{v}}), \ \tilde{\mathbf{v}} \in \mathcal{V}^{(\gamma)}(\mathbf{o}^{(\gamma)}) \tag{29}$$

Figure 3 depicts the pdfs of $\tilde{\mathbf{v}}$ in the cases of multilevel scalar-QIM and multilevel lattice-QIM.

The receiver needs to decide among the rival hypotheses

$$H_i : \tilde{\mathbf{y}} \sim q_i(\tilde{\mathbf{y}}) = p_{\tilde{\mathbf{V}}}(\tilde{\mathbf{y}} - \mathbf{d}_i^{(\gamma)}), \quad 0 \le i < p \tag{30}$$

Based on this statistic model, error probability can be estimated by [13]

$$P_e = (p - 1)\exp(-\min_{i \neq j} B(q_i, q_j)) \tag{31}$$

where the Bhattacharyya distance $B(q_0, q_1)$ is calculated by

$$B(q_i, q_j) \triangleq -\ln \int_{\mathcal{V}^{(\gamma)}(\mathbf{o}^{(\gamma)})} \sqrt{q_i(\mathbf{y})q_j(\mathbf{y})} \, d\mathbf{y} \tag{32}$$

Note that a deeper theoretical analysis may be achieved by using the approaches in [23,24]. However, we employ the simple MANC suggested in [13] for a quick derivation. Let the host signal $\mathbf{X}$ consist of 500 host vectors

$\mathbf{x}$, $\mathbf{x} \sim N(0, 10^2 I)$. It is used to send 3 pseudorandom watermark sequences, $\{\mathbf{m}^{(1)}, \mathbf{m}^{(2)}, \mathbf{m}^{(3)}\}$, by using 3-level QIM, which gives the watermarked signal $\mathbf{Y} = \mathbf{Y}^{(3)}$. The error probability is evaluated under the sense of different Watermark to Noise Ratio (WNR), which is defined as

$$\text{WNR} = \frac{\text{var}(\mathbf{Y} - \mathbf{X})}{\sigma_n^2} \tag{33}$$

Figure 4 compares the theoretical error probability with the experimental case by using 3-level scalar-QIM. We further compare the theoretical and experimental BERs using 3-level lattice-QIM. Comparison results on "Z2" and "Z3" lattices are reported in Figs. 4(b) and (c), indicating that the theoretical and experimental results match well. Furthermore, it confirms that watermark sequences embedded in the earlier embedding rounds are more robust than those embedded in the later embedding rounds. It is because watermark sequences embedded in the earlier embedding rounds provides more vacation to tolerate attacks.

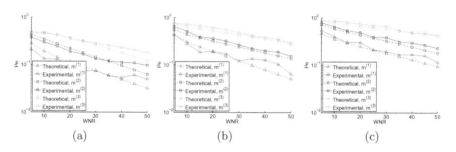

(a)   (b)   (c)

Fig. 4. Comparisons between theoretical and experimental error probabilities w.r.t. watermarks embedded in different rounds. 3-level scalar-QIM is used in (a) while 3-level lattice-QIM in (b) and (c). WNRs are in the range $[5, 50]$. The multilevel nested lattices are constructed from (b) "Z2" lattice and (c) "Z3" lattice with $\rho = 2$.

On the other hand, under the high-rate quantization model [13], the embedding distortion $(\mathbf{y}^\Gamma - \mathbf{x})$ is uniformly distributed in the Voronoi region $\mathcal{V}^{(1)}(\mathbf{o}^{(1)})$ for $\forall \Gamma \geq 1$. It means that performing multilevel embedding will not degrade the fidelity compared with only performing one level embedding. However, as shown in Fig. 3, more embedding rounds will introduce stronger self-noise and thus reduce the robustness of watermark sequences embedded earlier. Figure 5 demonstrates the changes on Signal-to-Noise Ratio (SNR), defined as

$$\text{SNR} = 10 \log_{10}\left(\frac{\text{var}(\mathbf{X})}{\text{var}(\mathbf{Y} - \mathbf{X})}\right) \tag{34}$$

and error probability with varying the total number of embedding rounds. It can be observed that the SNR scores is nearly constant, while P_e decreases dramatically when increasing the embedding rounds. P_e turns to rise slowly when $\Gamma > 3$.

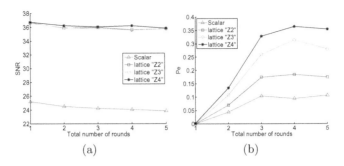

Fig. 5. Changes on (a) SNR and (b) error probability of detecting $\mathbf{m}^{(1)}$ in the case of WNR = 20. The total number of embedding rounds varies from 1 to 5. $\Delta = 2$ within all the multilevel QIM in this figure and $\rho = 2$ for the lattice cases.

This is because the extra embedding distortion, as given in Eq. (21), decreases exponentially as the embedding round increases. However, watermark sequences embedded in the relative large embedding rounds present poor robustness.

4.2   Application on Natural Images

Lastly, we apply 3-level lattice-QIM on real images for the purposes of copyright protection, host image recovery, and forgery detection. The embedding procedure is detailed as follows:

1. Apply first level DWT decomposition to the $n_1 \times n_2$ sized host image $\mathbf{X}$. Divide its LL subband into 4×4 blocks.
2. Consider the $\frac{n_1 \times n_2}{64}$-length copyright message as $\mathbf{m}^{(1)}$. Generate the halftone representation of the LL subband, and perform Arnold permutation to yield the recovery information, which is used as $\mathbf{m}^{(2)}$. Use a secret key to generate a pseudorandom binary matrix of size $\frac{n_1}{2} \times \frac{n_2}{2}$, which is used for forgery detection and considered as $\mathbf{m}^{(3)}$.
3. Construct 3-level nested lattices from "Z16" lattice with $\rho = 2$ and $\Delta = 30$.
4. For each coefficient block $\mathbf{x}$, use the mapping

$$\{0, 1\} \leftrightarrow \left\{ \mathbf{d}_0, \mathbf{d}_1 \,\middle|\, \mathbf{d}_0, \mathbf{d}_1 \in \mathcal{C}^{(\gamma)}, \mathbf{d}_0 + \mathbf{d}_1 = 2\mathbf{o}^{(\gamma)} \right\} \qquad (35)$$

to convert each copyright message bit to codewords, which is then embedded in the first embedding round.
5. Convert the coefficients in $\mathbf{m}^{(2)}$ and $\mathbf{m}^{(3)}$ which are located at the same location of $\mathbf{x}$ into hexadecimal digits. Then use the associated codewords to perform the second and third rounds of embedding.
6. Repeat from step 4 until all the message bits have been embedded.
7. Perform inverse DWT transform to obtain the watermarked image $\mathbf{Y}$.

The extraction procedure is similar and omitted here. It can be observed that the copyright information presents the highest robustness while the information

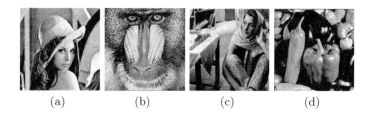

(a)   (b)   (c)   (d)

Fig. 6. Test images: (a) "Lena", (b) "Baboon", (c) "Barbara", and (d) "Peppers".

for forgery detection is most fragile. We evaluate the proposed scheme on four 512×512 grayscale images: "Lena", "Baboon", "Barbara", and "Peppers", as given in Fig. 6. Therefore, the watermark sequence $\mathbf{m}_1$ should be of length 4096, while $\mathbf{m}_2$ and $\mathbf{m}_3$ should be of sizes 256×256.

Two schemes in [6] (denoted by LBP) and [3] (denoted by MSTDM) are employed for comparison. LBP is developed for tamper detection. It extracts two host signals from a test image by dividing the local binary pattern into two parts. Therefore 2 watermark sequences can be embedded simultaneously. MSTDM projects each 8×8 DCT block to multiple orthogonal projection vectors, which embed different watermark sequences by using dither modulation. Watermarks at the same level in all the compared schemes are set with the same length.

Peak Signal-to-Noise Ratio (PSNR) and Mean Structural SIMilarity (MSSIM) [25] are employed as perceptual distortion measurements. Parameters in the compared are adjusted so that the watermarked images obtained by all the schemes are of the similar PSNR scores. Table 1 lists the perceptual comparison result.

Table 1. Comparison of PSNRs and MSSIMs

	Lena		Baboon		Barbara		Peppers	
	PSNR	MSSIM	PSNR	MSSIM	PSNR	MSSIM	PSNR	MSSIM
Proposed	41.51	0.9833	41.49	0.9894	41.55	0.9825	41.54	0.9835
LBP [6]	41.21	0.9912	37.13	0.9867	38.71	0.9891	41.38	0.9934
MSTDM [3]	41.59	0.9856	41.61	0.9945	41.62	0.9907	41.59	0.9859

The Robustness comparison in the present of JPEG and AWGN are reported in Fig. 7, where the results are averaged over 50 runs with 50 different pseudo-random sequences. It can be observed that the proposed scheme provides various robustness. All the watermarks in LBP are fragile while all those in MSTDM are robust. It should be noted that MSTDM is more robust against AWGN attack credited with the advantageous of sparse QIM at low WNR. Nevertheless, the multilevel robustness and changeable embedding rounds makes the proposed scheme more suitable for scalable authentication.

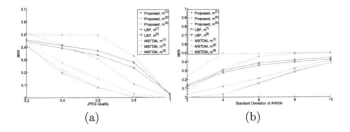

Fig. 7. Comparison of robustness against (a) JPEG compression and (b) AWGN.

The second and third watermark sequences in the proposed scheme is fragile, which fits the requirement of image recovery and integrity verification. Figure 8 tests the performance on forgery detection of the proposed scheme. The tampering operation is simulated in Fig. 8(b) and the copy-move operation is simulated in Fig. 8(c). It can be observed that the proposed scheme can accurately locate the forgery region. Moreover, the original image content in the forgery region can be partly recovered, as shown in Figs. 8(f) and (h).

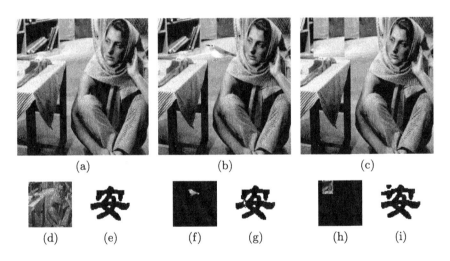

Fig. 8. (a) is the original watermarked image. (d) and (e) are the watermark sequences for image recovery and copyright protection, respectively. (b) is the forged image by adding a bird, while (f) and (g) are the forgery detection result and copyright message. (c) is obtained by copy-move operation. The corresponded forgery detection result and copyright message are shown in (h) and (i).

5 Conclusion

In this paper, a type of multilevel QIM algorithms is proposed for multiple watermarking. The construction of multilevel QIM on both scalar and high-dimensional

QIM is provided. It is suggested that, in order to guarantee a correct watermark extraction, there should be lattice points whose Voronoi regions perfectly pack the Voronoi region of a point in its coarse lattice in the multilevel lattice-QIM profile. For this purpose, we define a special family of lattices, i.e., affine "Zn" lattices, and develop a construction of multilevel nested lattices from the defined lattices. The embedding rate of the proposed scheme can be controlled by adjusting the density of finer lattices. With the increasing of the embedding round, the robustness of the watermark sequence embedded declines. Therefore, the proposed multilevel QIM provides various robustness levels simultaneously. It allows the embedded watermark sequences to be used for different goals. For example, the robust watermark sequence can be used for ownership protection while the fragile one can be used for integrity verification. Moreover, each watermark sequence can be encrypted with different secrete keys, and their extraction is separable. Therefore, it can be used in multiparty multilevel digital rights management. The proposed scheme can be combined with distortion compensation method to gain the robustness against known attacks. Secrete dithers can be also introduced for additional security. However, experimentally we find that the secret dither will break the packing of Voronoi regions when the total number of embedding rounds is larger than 2. Exploiting multilevel QIM with more properties is our future research.

Acknowledgements. This work is supported by the Natural Science Foundation of Guangdong (No. 2016A030313350), the Special Funds for Science and Technology Development of Guangdong (No. 2016KZ010103), the Fundamental Research Funds for the Central Universities (No. 16LGJC83), and the Key Lab of Information Network Security, Ministry of Public Security.

References

1. Ourique, F., Licks, V., Jordan, R., Pérez-González, F.: Angle QIM: a novel watermark embedding scheme robust against amplitude scaling distortions. In: Proceedings of IEEE International Conference on Acoustics, Speech, and Signal Processing (ICASSP 2005), vol. 2, p. ii-797. IEEE (2005)
2. Pérez-González, F., Mosquera, C., Barni, M., Abrardo, A.: Rational dither modulation: a high-rate data-hiding method invariant to gain attacks. IEEE Trans. Signal Process. **53**(10), 3960–3975 (2005)
3. Xiao, J., Wang, Y.: Multiple watermarking based on spread transform. In: 2006 8th International Conference on Signal Processing (2006)
4. Kalantari, N.K., Ahadi, S.M.: A logarithmic quantization index modulation for perceptually better data hiding. IEEE Trans. Image Process. **19**(6), 1504–1517 (2010)
5. Tong, L., Zheng-ding, Q.: The survey of digital watermarking-based image authentication techniques. In: 2002 6th International Conference on Signal Processing, vol. 2, pp. 1556–1559. IEEE (2002)
6. Wenyin, Z., Shih, F.Y.: Semi-fragile spatial watermarking based on local binary pattern operators. Opt. Commun. **284**(16), 3904–3912 (2011)
7. Cayre, F., Fontaine, C., Furon, T.: Watermarking security: theory and practice. IEEE Trans. Signal Process. **53**(10), 3976–3987 (2005)

8. Wheeler, G.E., Safavi-Naini, R., Sheppard, N.P.: Weighted segmented digital watermarking. In: Cox, I.J., Kalker, T., Lee, H.-K. (eds.) IWDW 2004. LNCS, vol. 3304, pp. 89–100. Springer, Heidelberg (2005). doi:10.1007/978-3-540-31805-7_8

9. Hana, O., Hela, M., Kamel, H.: A robust multiple watermarking scheme based on the DWT. In: International Multi-conference on Systems, Signals & Devices, pp. 1–6 (2013)

10. Liu, C.C., Chen, W.Y.: Multiple-watermarking scheme for still images using the discrete cosine transform and modified code division multiple-access techniques. Opt. Eng. **45**(7), 921–932 (2006)

11. Zhang, L., Xiao, J.W., Luo, J.Y., Zheng, H.M.: A robust multiple watermarking based on DWT and SVD. In: Proceedings of the 12th ACM International Conference on Multimedia, New York, 10–16 October 2004, pp. 424–427 (2004)

12. Chen, B., Wornell, G.W.: Quantization index modulation: a class of provably good methods for digital watermarking and information embedding. IEEE Trans. Inf. Theory **47**(4), 1423–1443 (2001)

13. Moulin, P., KoeTter, R.: Data-hiding codes. Proc. IEEE **93**(12), 2083–2126 (2005)

14. Li, Q., Cox, I.J.: Using perceptual models to improve fidelity and provide resistance to valumetric scaling for quantization index modulation watermarking. IEEE Trans. Inf. Forensics Secur. **2**(2), 127–139 (2007)

15. Feng, B., Lu, W., Sun, W., Liang, Z., Liu, J.: Blind watermarking based on adaptive lattice quantization index modulation. In: Shi, Y.-Q., Kim, H.J., Pérez-González, F., Echizen, I. (eds.) IWDW 2015. LNCS, vol. 9569, pp. 239–249. Springer, Heidelberg (2016). doi:10.1007/978-3-319-31960-5_20

16. Bardyn, D., Dooms, A., Dams, T., Schelkens, P.: Comparative study of wavelet based lattice QIM techniques and robustness against AWGN and JPEG attacks. In: Ho, A.T.S., Shi, Y.Q., Kim, H.J., Barni, M. (eds.) IWDW 2009. LNCS, vol. 5703, pp. 39–53. Springer, Heidelberg (2009). doi:10.1007/978-3-642-03688-0_7

17. Sarkar, A., Manjunath, B.S.: Double embedding in the quantization index modulation framework. In: IEEE International Conference on Image Processing, pp. 3653–3656 (2009)

18. Ly, H.D., Liu, T., Blankenship, Y.: Security embedding codes. IEEE Trans. Inf. Forensics Secur. **7**(1), 148–159 (2011)

19. Sloane, N.J., Conway, J., et al.: Sphere Packings, Lattices and Groups, vol. 290. Springer, New York (1999)

20. Zamir, R., Shamai, S., Erez, U.: Nested linear/lattice codes for structured multi-terminal binning. IEEE Trans. Inf. Theory **48**(6), 1250–1276 (2002)

21. Bindel, D., Demmel, J., Kahan, W., Marques, O.: On computing givens rotations reliably and efficiently. ACM Trans. Math. Softw. (TOMS) **28**(2), 206–238 (2002)

22. Forney, G.D.: Multidimensional constellations. II. Voronoi constellations. IEEE J. SEL. AREAS COMMUN. **7**(6), 941–958 (1989)

23. Eggers, J.J., Bäuml, R., Tzschoppe, R., Girod, B.: Scalar costa scheme for information embedding. IEEE Trans. Signal Process. **51**(4), 1003–1019 (2003)

24. Pérez-González, F., Balado, F., Martin, J.R.H.: Performance analysis of existing and new methods for data hiding with known-host information in additive channels. IEEE Trans. Signal Process. **51**(4), 960–980 (2003)

25. Wang, Z., Bovik, A.C.: Image quality assessment: from error visibility to structural similarity. IEEE Trans. Image Process. **13**(4), 1–14 (2004)

Increasing Secret Data Hiding Capacity in QR Code Using 3 × 3 Subcells

Wisdarmanto Erlangga[✉] and Ari Moesriami Barmawi

School of Computing, Telkom University,
Jl. Telekomunikasi 1, Bandung, West Java 40257, Indonesia
erlangga@telkom.co.id, mbarmawi@melsa.net.id

Abstract. Recently, the use of QR code is becoming increasingly popular such that the majority smart-phone devices nowadays are capable reading them. Based on the development of camera technology in latest smart-phone devices, Teraura et al. proposed a method for hiding an additional data into a fine subcell structure of a monochrome QR code. Based on 3×3 subcells configuration, the cover data is placed at the outer subcells while the embedded data is placed in a single center subcell. In general, QR code reader detects a cell color from its center pixel and such that it is difficult to extract the cover data of a 3 × 3 subcells QR code. This research proposes an alternative method by accommodating different approaches in recognizing a cell color. The subcell selection for embedded data was kept secret by applying pseudorandom to randomize the bit data position in each cell. Experimental results show that using the proposed method, 97% of 3 × 3 subcells QR code can be read by a general QR code reader. It uses 4 subcells to store 4 bits additional data and had embedded data capacity 4 times higher than the method of Teraura et al.

Keywords: QR code · Information hiding · Subcells

1 Introduction

Along with the development of the Internet, smartphone, and the growing use of Quick Response Code (QR code), there are conditions when we want to send a confidential message into a QR code to be read by particular parties. An information can be hidden by means superimposed or covered into a QR code symbol [2–5] in spatial domain or hiding a QR code itself into a cover media [6] in frequency domain. An image processing in spatial domain when compared with frequency domain based such as Discrete Cosine Transform (DCT) and Discrete Wavelet transform (DWT) is that the algorithm is simple so it does not take a long time to carry out the process and suitable to be implemented as a mobile application. Due to the improvement in camera resolution, as a higher-resolution camera is able to identify detailed information of a single cell in a

---

This work was supported by PT. Telekomunikasi Indonesia, Tbk.

Y.Q. Shi et al. (Eds.): IWDW 2016, LNCS 10082, pp. 327–342, 2017.
DOI: 10.1007/978-3-319-53465-7_24

QR code symbol, Teraura et al. [5] propose a method for hiding a confidential secret part using a fine subcell structure in a single cell of QR code. In a 3×3 subcells configuration, it stores a single bit cell data into 8 outer subcells and uses a single subcell in the center to store one bit of secret data. As a single subcell could be used to represent a single bit of data, then 8 outer subcells is considered improvidence as it is used to store only a single bit of data. There is still a room for improving the embedded data capacity in existing 3×3 subcells QR code. Further more, this subcell selection for data placement, is contrary to what it is believed by Teraura and Sakurai (2012, p.653) them self by stating:

> "Besides, as reader units of the existing cell-level 2D code often identify a pixel near the center of the cell, it seems appropriate to make this central subcell take the cell color in order that existing equipment can still read the code."

Thus, a general QR code reader that usually reads the center pixel, it reads the "unhidden" embedded data and unable to read the cover data in existing 3×3 subcells QR code.

In this work, the subcells selection strategy was proposed based on the existing cell detection methods used in [5,7] and they were used to determine which subcells that could be assigned to carry the hidden data, so that the embedded data capacity is greater than one bit per cell and a standard QR code reader is still able to extract the cover data from a 3×3 subcells QR code.

2 3×3 Subcells QR Code

Teraura et al. [5] proposed a 3×3 subcells QR code that can carry additional confidential secret information data that utilizes fine subcells structures. Each subcell is a square with the same size and ratio as seen in Fig. 1. When a QR code image is produced from a shaky camera condition, the pixel color at the outer edge of a cell will be superimposed with the pixel color form its neighbor cells. As for individual cell identification, this border area is considered as a pointer for distinguishing one cell to another. The outer subcells on the cell border are given the same color as the cover cell, and subcell in the center can have an opposite color. The example of 3×3 subcells is shown in Fig. 2. The center subcell is the peripheral part and the outer subcells carry the same color as its cover cells. As the center part express 1-bit of data, it can store a secret data of the same size

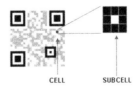

CELL   SUBCELL

Fig. 1. Relationship between a cell and its subcells in 3×3 subcells QR code

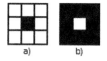

Fig. 2. Encoding pattern for a 3 × 3 subcells configuration. (a) White cell, contain binary "1" secret data, (b) Black cell, contain binary "0" secret data

3x3 subcell QR code

Fig. 3. Data layout in 3 × 3 subcells.

as its cover cell. The data layout concept for a 3 × 3 subcells QR code consists of two identical data size in the form of complete QR code symbol as seen in Fig. 3. Each QR code symbol has the same version, error level, format and masking pattern. When a code-blocks $U = (u_0, u_1)$ is obtained from every cells, u_0 is the data represented by the color of the outer subcells level (the cover data), and u_1 is the data represented by the color of the center subcell level (embedded data).

2.1 Encoding Process

The four-step encoding process of Teraura et al. [5] is shown in Fig. 4. The error-correction process in standard QR code was omitted as it is beyond the scope of this paper. First of all, the encoder recognize the input data as letters and/or numbers to be prepared as cover data (d_0) and the secret data (d_1). Then code-blocks$_0$ (u_0) generated from d_0 to create a cover QR code. The next process is generating code-blocks$_1$ (u_1) from d_1 and placed into a cover QR code.

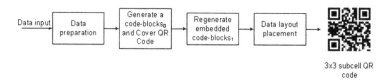

3x3 subcell QR code

Fig. 4. Encoding process in 3 × 3 subcells.

2.2   Decoding Process

The decoding action consists of four process as shown in Fig. 5. From the scanned symbol, code-blocks$_0$ (u_0) is determined from the majority color of all outer subcells and code-blocks$_1$ (u_1) is determined from the color of an inner subcell. Then decode (u_0) and (u_1) accordingly to recover the cover data and the secret data.

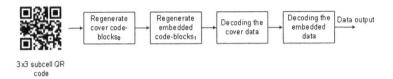

Fig. 5. Decoding process in 3×3 subcells.

3   Proposed Method

To address the main goals of this research, a 3×3 subcells QR code structure design in [5] was adopted and some adjustments was made in subcell selection to improve the embedded data capacity and maintain backward compatibility. The discussions of this chapter includes the subcell selection strategies, bit placement of the embedded data, and the procedure to encode and decode a 3×3 subcells QR code.

3.1   Subcell Selection

The subcell selection used to represent the hidden/embedded data, was based on consideration in cell color identification methods according to [5,7] namely: calculating all the pixel value of a cell, only calculate the center pixel value, and by sampling method which only consider some of the pixels that represent its parent cell. These three cell color identification methods can be explained in detail as follows:

1. *Calculate the intensity mean value of all pixels in a cell*
   Five subcells were the minimum number of subcells, which should have the same color as its cover cell to guarantee that a cell could be recognized correctly. The remaining 4 subcells considered only as a supplement and they could be used to store an additional color that represents an embedded data.
2. *Read the center pixel intensity value*
   The center pixel is chosen to determine the color of a cover cell. To comply with this condition, the center subcell should has the same color as its cover cell.

3. *By sampling method*

By drawing an imaginer "+" symbol at the center of cell then the color ratio in the pixel traversed by this symbol is calculated. The "+" symbol in a 3×3 subcells, clearly visible in Fig. 6 as a dotted "cross" sign in the middle cell marked with 5 grayed color of subcells: 2, 4, 5, 6, and 8.

To be considered as a representation of its covers cell color, the mean intensity value from this "+" subcells should match with its cell cover value. For M_c = "+" mean intensity and s_i = intensity of i_{th} subcell, G = Global Threshold, then:

$$M = \left\lceil \frac{s_2 + s_4 + s_5 + s_6 + s_8}{5} \right\rceil \tag{1}$$

$$Cellvalue = \begin{cases} 1 & \text{if } M_c \geq G \\ 0 & \text{if } M_c < G \end{cases} \tag{2}$$

From the median value off all the five "+" subcells, three "+" subcells were considered enough to represent its cover color cell, so there were 2 more supplement parts to be used as the peripheral parts except for the center subcells. If only 3 subcells were used as the the chosen "+" subcells, then there were 6 pieces of subcells that could be used as the peripheral parts.

Fig. 6. An imaginer symbol "+" (dotted line) in the middle of a cell.

To accommodate different approaches recognizing a cell's color in any standard QR code reader, the subcells selection should comply to all of the requirements and it was assumed that:

- Only 4 subcells could be used as the peripheral parts, because minimum 5 subcells were considered sufficient to represent cover cell color.
- The center subcells should has the same color as its cover cell.
- Two from five "+" subcells, could be used as the peripheral parts.

3.2   Bit Placement of Embedded Data

To secure the embedded data, permutation was used to hide the embedded data in each cell of the cover symbol. The other party which were not known the exact permutation, should not be able to read the exact location of the embedded data block codewords. In regard to the cost of computing and interval of a random number generated by the mechanism of the DRBG in SP 800-90A

[8–10], CTR_DRBG (AES) was selected to generate pseudo-random numbers in this research as it is validated in [10] as a cryptographic secure pseudorandom number generator. It has a maximum 2^{48} requests of 2^{19} bits number and considered secure as the largest QR code version 40 with 177×177 matrix in size, was only needed a random number as many as $177 \times 177 = 31,329$ (15 bits) numbers. Thus, CTR_DRBG was still able to serve a pseudo-random number request because the number of random numbers was below 48 bits. There were 53 patterns as seen in Fig. 7 that could be utilized to randomize the bit location of the embedded data in each cell. The goal of this process was to hide the extra data contained therein. Without knowing the permutation of these combinations then someone was only be able to decode the symbol as it was an ordinary QR code.

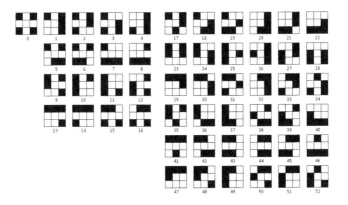

Fig. 7. A white cell considered in 3×3 subcells form, carry four peripheral parts in 53 different patterns which are comply with the subcells selection requirements.

If the number of embedded data $k = 4$, available patterns $C = 53$ and the number of peripheral parts $n = 4$, then the number of permutations that could be generated were as much as:

$$P_k^n * C = \frac{n!}{(n-k)!} * 53$$
$$= \frac{4!}{(4-4)!} * 53 \tag{3}$$
$$= 1,272 \; permutations$$

The embedded data bit placement in each cell was depend on its cells pattern and randomized using pseudo-random number generator CTR_DRBG where:

$$Cell_i Pattern = pseudorandom[i] \mod 1,272 \tag{4}$$

for i = total number of cells in the cover QR code. Thus, without knowing the sequence of random numbers were used, the user could not able to read the embedded data on a 3×3 subcells QR code.

3.3   Procedure to Generate 3 × 3 Subcells QR Code

To generate a 3 × 3 subcells QR code there were two main processes namely: *QR code standard process* where a template cover symbol was produced and 3 × 3 *subcells process* where the output was a 3 × 3 subcells QR code with hidden embedded data. This generation process could be seen in Fig. 8.

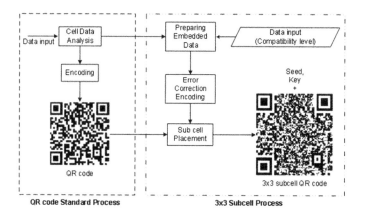

Fig. 8. Proposed 3 × 3 subcells generating process

1. **QR code Standard Process.** This is the standard procedure to generate a QR code symbol as seen in Fig. 8 and was simplified into two main processes which are:
   (a) *Cell Data Analysis.* Data input preparation for cover data d_0 was performed at this process. UTF-8 in byte mode was used in this research to handle 8-bit Latin character set and encoded at a density of 8 bits/character. Then the QR code symbol size and error correction level were determined based on the length of data input character.
   (b) *Encoding.* This process consists of several processes carried from the standard QR code encoding which are:
      – **Error Correction Coding and Interleaving.** The bit stream produced from previous process, was encoded into Reed Solomon codewords and constructed into final message codeword sequence.
      – **Codewords Placement in Matrix.** Codeword sequence from previous process was placed in the symbol matrix along with the function pattern.
      – **Masking** At this process the masking pattern was selected based on the lowest penalty score points.
      – **Format & Version Information.** The Format & Version Information codewords were generated after masking pattern had been selected.

– *Final Symbol Construction.* The selected masking pattern then applied to the encoding region of the symbol and then the Format & Version Information modules were placed in its positions.

As the output symbol was used as a cover template, the module/cell structure in the output symbol was in the form of 3×3 subcells to prepare the subcell level data insertion as seen in Fig. 9.

2. **3×3 SubCells Process.** After the cover QR code symbol had been obtained, the variable of data type, the maximum data length and error correction level were passed to the next process to produce a 3×3 subcells QR code. This process was divided into three main processes which are:

(a) *Preparing Embedded Data.* In this process, the four embedded data d_1, d_2, d_3, and d_4 were prepared to match with the cover symbol. There were three requirements and variables which had to be fulfilled. The first one was that the *maximum data length* for each embedded data should not exceed the QR code data capacity. The second and third one were the *data type* and *error correction level* which should match exactly with the cover QR code. These three variable were obtained from cell data analysis in QR code standard process.

(b) *Error Correction Encoding.* After the data preparation process had been done, the next step was to encode each of the embedded data set into Reed Solomon Codewords and then constructed into a sequence of final message codeword. This encoding process was similar with the existing error correction encoding used in QR code Standard Process (encoded with the same Reed Solomon error correction code). The resulted outputs were interleaved data block codewords u_1, u_2, u_3, and u_4 as a final messages for each embedded data set that were ready to be embedded into cover QR code.

(c) *Subcell Placement.* The hiding process of the embedded data final message datablock on subcell area, was relied heavily on CTR_DRBG Pseudorandom number. The two keys (key and seed) were used to reproduce a pseudo-random number. Without these keys, the embedded data in 3×3 subcells QR code could not be extracted, due to the random number sequence was unknown. The key and seed were 256 bits long, and stored outside of the QR code symbol. Keys distribution should be secure, because if not, then 3rd party who obtained these keys, would be able to read the content of the embedded data on subcells QR code. The size

Fig. 9. Standard QR code with 3×3 subcells fine structure. Each cell contains 9 smaller subcells.

of random number was as many as the bit length of the cell data code-blocks C_0. Key, seed and random number sequence were produced at this process in the form of a file. Since the key and seed files were the main variable for generating this random number, then it should be kept secret by the intended parties such that the embedded data in 3×3 subcells QR code could be extracted.

3.4   Decoding Procedure

The decoding process of a 3×3 subcells QR code as seen in Fig. 10, was the inverse of the encoding process. It consists of the following processes:

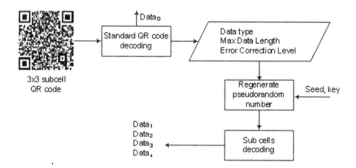

Fig. 10. Reading 3×3 subcells QR code process design.

- *Standard QR Code Decoding*
  A standard QR code decoding procedure was used to read the contents of $Data_0$ at the cell level. The variables required for the next process were obtained in here. For better symbol detecting accuracy, the Finder Pattern of a 3×3 subcells symbol was considered having a minimum 3:3:9:3:3 ratio of black and white module as illustrated in Fig. 11a. This was to assured that the subcell had minimum size of 1 pixel wide. The Alignment pattern also readjusted as supposed to have a ratio of 3:3:3:3:3 module width as describe in Fig. 11b.
- *Regenerate Pseudorandom Number*
  To be able to read the embedded data at a subcell level, the keys at the previous encoding process were required to generate the same random number. Using Eq. 4, each random number determined the placement order of a bit codewords in each subcell.
- *Subcells Decoding*
  Decoding process could begin after obtaining a series of random sequence related to a bit permutations in each cell. Then the data block codewords u_1, u_2, u_3, and u_4 could be extracted to get the embedded data: $Data_1$, $Data_2$, $Data_3$, and $Data_4$.

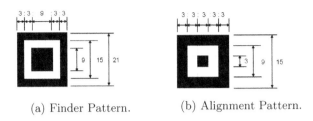

(a) Finder Pattern.   (b) Alignment Pattern.

Fig. 11. Structure of Finder and Alignment pattern in 3×3 subcells symbol.

4   Experimental Result and Analysis

The research experiment was conducted to ensure that the proposed method could fulfill the objectives of this research. The experiments were divided into three categories namely:

(A) **Backward compatibility testing.** This experiment was conducted to make sure that the proposed method had a backward compatibility. The decoder software were top 5 most downloaded QR code reader application picked from Android playstore. They were used to extract the cell data in the 3×3 subcells QR code.

(B) **Embedded data capacity measurement.** This experiment compared the capacity of the embedded data held on the previous method versus the proposed method. This was the main objective of the research.

(C) **Error correction capability (ECC) testing.** This experiment was conducted to prove that the proposed method had the same error correction capability as in the previous method. The cover QR code and the embedded data were extracted from a wounded 3×3 subcells symbol with four different level of error corrections L, M, Q and H.

The QR code symbol to be decoded was printed and scanned with the following specification:

– Using QR code symbol version 1 up to version 40 with different error correction level from L to H.
– Text string length for cover QR code data was 3,494 characters and 23,650 characters of text string was used for embedded data.
– All symbols carried text data, which was encoded in UTF-8 byte mode, at maximum capacity for each symbol.
– Printed on 80 gr A4 white paper.
– Using Kyocera printer FS-1030D, 300 dpi.
– Subcell size was one pixel wide represented as 4 printer dots = 0.34 mm (round up).
– Cell size in standard QR code symbol was at one pixel represented as four printer dots = 0.34 mm (round up).

- Scan distances were 13 cm and 16 cm, with environment light source about 4000 lux measured from the handset light sensor.
- Each symbol was scanned 10 times in a row.

For online scanning, the symbol was captured using android video camera frame with Full HD resolution. At 13 cm scanning distance the subcell size could be detected at 4 pixels wide and for 16 cm scanned distance, the subcell could be retrieved at 3 pixels wide.

4.1 Backward Compatibility Testing and Analysis

Since the general QR code reader had difficulties to extract the cover QR code data held in the previous 3 × 3 subcells symbol, this experiment was conducted to make sure that the proposed method did not suffer from such an issues. First of all, the size difference between a standard and a 3 × 3 subcells QR code symbol was analyzed. As shown in Fig. 12, for the same symbol version, a 3 × 3 subcells QR code symbols has a size three times larger than the standard one. This size difference is due to the matrix size of the symbol which is previously designed in [5] and as recommended by Denso [11] for stable reading, the smallest part of a symbol is printed at a minimum 4 printer dots. As each tested application had different viewfinder, based on the maximum symbol version fit into each scanner viewfinder application, Table 1 shown the average percentage of correctly decoded cover data in QR code symbol. A 3 × 3 subcells QR code which used the proposed method, had 97% success rate which was higher then 3 × 3 subcells QR code [5] which only had 53% success rate. This happened because all of the general QR code reader tested, they were detecting the center pixel of a cell to determine the cell color. Thus, they were having difficulties to extract the cell level data at existing 3 × 3 subcells QR code which is stored at the outer subcells.

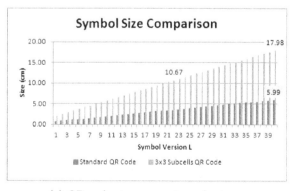

(a) QR code size comparison chart

(b) Symbol version 2 size different. Left is a standard QR code and right is a 3x3 subcells QR code.

Fig. 12. A 3 × 3 subcells has a size 3 times bigger than a standard QR code symbol.

Table 1. Success rate comparison in decoding cover data using various QR code reader

QR code reader	Max symbol version	Success decoding rate		
		Standard QR code	3 × 3 Sub cells [5]	Proposed method
QR code scan	16	100%	9%	100%
Zxing	13	100%	8%	100%
QR barcode scanner	14	100%	100%	100%
QR code reader	14	100%	49%	86%
QR & barcode scanner	14	100%	100%	100%
Average	14.2	100%	53%	97%

4.2   Embedded Data Capacity Measurement and Analysis

This experiment was conducted to compare the embedded data capacity in existing 3 × 3 subcells QR code versus the proposed method. Figure 13 shown the maximum 3 × 3 symbol version that can be decoded both the cover and the embedded data. At 13 cm scanning distance, the reader detected a single subcell size approximately 4 pixels wide and the proposed method was only able to be decoded at maximum symbol version 17L as version 18L actually did not fit into reader viewfinder display. For 16 cm scanning distance, the reader detected a single subcell size approximately 3 bits wide and it could be decoded at maximum version 21L as version 22L was not fit into application viewfinder. Based on the maximum readable symbol size, Fig. 14 shown the embedded data capacity for the proposed method up to version 21L. The proposed method had embedded data capacity 4 times larger than the previous method as it stored 4 bit hidden data into the outer subcells. The special reader was able to read the additional 4 bit random hidden data in each cell by using the same keys that was previously produced at the generating process of 3 × 3 subcell QR code.

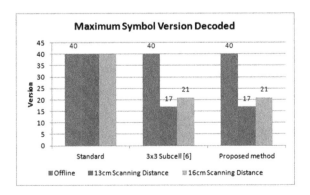

Fig. 13. Maximum decoded 3 × 3 subcells QR code symbol version.

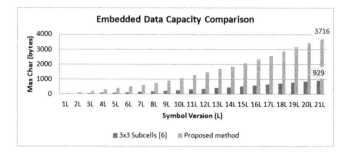

Fig. 14. Embedded data capacity comparison between existing and proposed 3×3 subcells QR code.

4.3 Error Correction Capability Testing

This experiment was conducted to prove that the proposed method had the same error correction capability as the previous method. It was previously design in [5] to have the same error correction capability at the same level as its cover symbol which were: level L (able to recover 7% of broken codewords); level M (able to recover 15% of broken codewords); level Q (able to recover 25% of broken codewords) and level H (able to recover 30% of broken codewords) according to standard QR code specification [1]. Without introducing an error pattern into a symbol, a series of codeword error already raised when reading the proposed method as seen in Fig. 15. Under version 11L, the proposed method was stable enough as it could have 8 times 0 codewords error from 10x scanned attempt. On particular concern, the 80 gr A4 paper that was used as the print media, its condition after came out from printer machine was not controllable. It shape could be deformed after being printed. Any slightly wavy paper where a QR code was printed on, it would yield codeword error when scanned. The larger the printed symbol, the more likely the paper would become deformed thus, the greater the codeword error would occur. As seen in Fig. 15c and d, from version 13L and up the error generated looks random and getting higher as the result of slightly deformed printed media. Based on the limitations of the existing conditions: the maximum preview size; and printed media deformation, a 3×3 subcells symbol version 15 was the maximum recommended symbol version that could be used for online decoding. It was stable to be decoded at a maximum one codeword error in extracting embedded data at 13 cm scanning distance despite there was exist deformation in printed media. A standard QR code version 15L, has a maximum 110 codewords per block that consist of 11 error correction codewords. It has error correction capability of $11/110 = 10\%$. The proposed method reduced the error correcting capability up to: $(11 - 1)/110 = 9.1\%$, decreasing with only a 0.9% error correction capability losses.

Furthermore, the error correction capability was tested by using six different error patterns as seen in Fig. 16. There were four cropped patterns a, b, c and d. Each of it had a pattern of 7%, 13%, 20% and 24% cropped area. They were

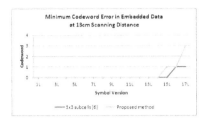

(a) Minimum codeword error comparison in extracting embedded data at 13 cm scanning distance.

(b) Minimum codeword error comparison in extracting embedded data at 16 cm scanning distance.

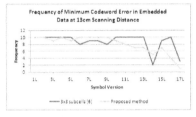

(c) Frequent of minimum codeword error occurrences in extracting embedded data at 13 cm scanning distance.

(d) Frequent of minimum codeword error occurrences in extracting embedded data at 16 cm scanning distance.

Fig. 15. Minimum codeword error in various QR code type from two different scanning distances.

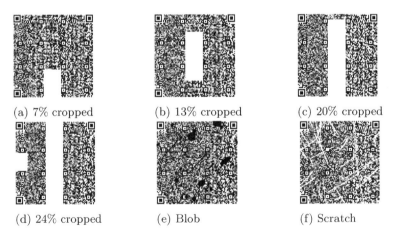

(a) 7% cropped   (b) 13% cropped   (c) 20% cropped

(d) 24% cropped   (e) Blob   (f) Scratch

Fig. 16. Different type of error pattern.

Table 2. The result of adding error patterns experiments

Version	Extraction success based on cropping type					
	Type a	Type b	Type c	Type d	Type e	Type f
15-L	✓	x	x	x	x	x
15-M	✓	✓	x	x	x	x
15-Q	✓	✓	✓	x	∂	x
15-H	✓	✓	✓	✓	✓	✓

applied to symbol version 15-L, 15-M, 15-Q and 15-H accordingly and all the wounded symbol were able to be extracted both the cover and embedded data as seen in Table 2. This data recovery was possible because each embedded data virtually was a QR code, which has the same error correction capability as its cover QR code. Whereas blob and scratch patterns in Fig. 16e and f that were applied to all symbols version 15 conceded another different result. Only symbol version 15-Q and 15-H that were suffered from blob pattern were able to be decoded. A wounded symbol 15-Q from blob error pattern, its embedded data was partially decoded. This occurrence was predicted as the result of 0.9% loss of error correction capability in symbol version 15 as discussed earlier, that one of the embedded data already reach its reduced ECC (maximum codewords error ∗ 0.9%). For scratch pattern, a symbol could be decoded if using error correction level H which capable to recover 30% of broken codewords as this type of error was damaging a lot of codewords so it needs a larger error correction capability.

5   Conclusion

This research was set out to increase the secret data hiding capacity in 3 × 3 monochrome subcells QR code. As the size of 3 × 3 subcells QR code is 3 times bigger then a standard QR code symbol, the maximum symbol version that could be scanned was depend on each reader device which had its own camera and display limitation. Symbol version 21 was the maximum readable 3 × 3 subcells QR code that could be scanned in real time using Android device with Full HD resolution display. Symbol version 15 was the maximum recommended version that could be used as it was stable to be decoded despite it had loss 0.9% of error correction capability. Using proposed method, a 3 × 3 subcells QR code was 97% compatible to be read by a general QR code reader. It used 4 subcells to store 4 bits additional data and has embedded data capacity 4 times higher than the previous method in [5].

By complying cell color detection approaches in [5,7], the proposed method could maintain backward compatibility, having error correction capability and had higher secret data capacity than the previous method. With a larger secret data hiding capacity and reliable backward compatibility, opens up an opportunity to hide various data types of content authentication or legal ownership for digital multimedia data. By using a better video device and non deformed printed media, the maximum 3×3 subcells QR code symbol version that could be decoded in a real time might be improved.

References

1. Wave, D.: Information technology automatic identification and data capture techniques QR code bar code symbology specification. International Organization for Standardization, ISO/IEC:18004, February 2015
2. Lin, P.-Y., Chen, Y.-H., Lu, E.J.-L., Chen, P.-J.: Secret hiding mechanism using QR barcode. In: 2013 International Conference on Signal-Image Technology and Internet-Based Systems (SITIS), pp. 22–25. IEEE (2013)
3. Bui, T.V., Vu, N.K., Nguyen, T.T., Echizen, I., Nguyen, T.D.: Robust message hiding for QR code. In: 2014 Tenth International Conference on Intelligent Information Hiding and Multimedia Signal Processing (IIH-MSP), pp. 520–523. IEEE (2014)
4. Barmawi, A.M., Yulianto, F.A.: Watermarking QR code. In: 2015 2nd International Conference on Information Science and Security (ICISS), pp. 1–4. IEEE (2015)
5. Teraura, N., Sakurai, K.: Information hiding in subcells of a two-dimensional code. In: The 1st IEEE Global Conference on Consumer Electronics 2012, pp. 652–656, October 2012
6. Kor Ashwini N, Kazi, N.M.: A survey of water mark technique. Int. J. Adv. Res. Electr. Electron. Instrum. Eng. **3**(2) (2014)
7. Chen, W., Yang, G., Zhang, G.: A simple and efficient image pre-processing for QR decoder. In: 2nd International Conference on Electronic and Mechanical Engineering and Information Technology. Atlantis Press (2012)
8. Barker, E.B., Kelsey, J.M.: Recommendation for random number generation using deterministic random bit generators (revised). Information Technology Laboratory, Computer Security Division, National Institute of Standards and Technology, US Department of Commerce, Technology Administration (2007)
9. Fips, P.: 140-2. Security Requirements for Cryptographic Modules, vol. 25 (2001)
10. Easter, R.J., French, C., Gallagher, P.: Annex c: approved random number generators for FIPS PUB 140–2, security requirements for cryptographic modules. NIST, February 2012
11. Wave, D.: Point for setting the module size. qrcode.com—denso wave (2016). http://www.qrcode.com/en/howto/cell.html

Databases Traceability by Means of Watermarking with Optimized Detection

Javier Franco-Contreras[1(✉)] and Gouenou Coatrieux[2,3]

[1] WaToo, 135 rue Claude Chappe, 29280 Plouzané, France
javier.francocontreras@telecom-bretagne.eu
[2] Institut Mines-Télécom, Télécom Bretagne, Inserm U1101 LaTIM,
Technopôle Brest Iroise CS 83818, 29238 Brest Cedex 3, France
gouenou.coatrieux@telecom-bretagne.eu
[3] Université Européenne de Bretagne, Rennes, France

Abstract. In this paper, we propose a robust lossless database watermarking scheme the detection of which is optimized for the traceability of databases merged into, for example, shared data warehouses. We basically aim at identifying a database merged with different other watermarked databases. Based on the modulation of attribute circular histogram's center of mass, we theoretically prove that the impact of the database mixture on the embedded identifier is equivalent to the addition of a Gaussian noise, the parameters of which can be estimated. From these theoretical results, an optimized watermark detector is proposed. This one offers higher discriminative performance than the classic correlation-based detector. Depending on the modulated attribute, it allows us to detect a database representing at least 4% of the databases mixture with a detection rate close to 100%. These results have been experimentally verified within the framework of a set of medical databases containing inpatient hospital stay records.

Keywords: Traceability · Watermarking · Relational database · Information security

1 Introduction

Nowadays, data gathering and management into data warehouses or simple databases represent important economic and strategic concerns for both enterprises and public institutions, related in part to the progress of data-mining and assisted decision tools [9]. Cloud computing boosts such an evolution allowing different entities to cooperate and reduce expenses, with remote access and storage-resource pools being now a reality [2]. However, these new access capabilities induce at the same time an increase of the security needs. Among them, data traceability takes a particular importance. Indeed, databases can be rerouted or redistributed without permission, as illustrated by information leaks revealed each year, even in sensitive areas like defense or health care [15].

© Springer International Publishing AG 2017
Y.Q. Shi et al. (Eds.): IWDW 2016, LNCS 10082, pp. 343–357, 2017.
DOI: 10.1007/978-3-319-53465-7_25

In this context, being able to trace data sets merged into one unique database presents interesting perspectives. To do so, watermarking has a great interest. Basically, it is an *a posteriori* protection that leaves access to data while maintaining them secured. Watermarking lies in the insertion of a message (some security attributes) or a watermark into a host document (e.g., image or database) by slightly modifying host data based on the principle of controlled distortion. Thus, one may want to embed a sequence identifying the owner or the recipient of one database; identifier used by next for verifying its presence in a mixture. This may serve to identify the different contributors in a collaborative database or to localize the origin of a data leak as examples. Database watermarking was introduced in 2002 by Agrawal and Kiernan [1]. Since then, several methods have been proposed with as main applications in copyright protection [19,20] or integrity and authenticity control [5,13]. However, little attention has been paid to the traceability of outsourced databases.

This scenario is not far from the multimedia content traitor tracing problem. A well-known example corresponds to the video on demand framework, where one multimedia content is distributed to several users. One common traitor tracing solution stands on the use of fingerprinting codes, or more precisely anti-collusion codes inserted into the document to share. Each user is uniquely identified by means of sequence of m symbols embedded into the host content. This results in a set of different, but perceptually similar watermarked video copies. In this framework, a collusion attack consists of c users who cooperate by mixing their copies and consequently their identifiers. More clearly, at the detection or verification stage, one will not extract an individual identifier but a mixture of them. The concept of anti-collusion codes is based upon the marking assumption that is considered when constructing the pirate copy [4]. This assumption is intimately linked to the kind of data to protect, that is to say videos or images which are divided into pixel blocks, a block into which one symbol of the message, i.e., of the anti-collusion code, is embedded. The marking assumption states the following: *for one block b containing the same symbol S_b in all the merged copies, the resulting symbol in the pirate version of b is necessarily equal to S_b.*

Several anti-collusion codes have been proposed so far. Among them, one can cite anti-collusion codes by concatenation of error correcting codes [4,18]. Even though they are difficult to apply in practice due to the length of their codewords [11], they have been considered for relational database fingerprinting in [14]. Probabilistic anti-collusion codes seminally introduced by Tardos [21] provide a better performance for a shorter codeword length. Lafaye *et al.* consider them for database fingerprinting in [12].

Although these database fingerprinting schemes represent a notable contribution, anti-collusion codes are not really appropriated for most database watermarking schemes in which the message is embedded into groups of tuples. As we will explain in Sect. 2.2, this is due to the fact that the marking assumption is not valid in that case. Another difference between fingerprinting and our scenario is that we want to identify one database at a time contrarily to the classical traitor tracing scenario where several colluders can be simultaneously identified.

In this paper, we propose to apply the robust lossless database watermarking scheme introduced in [8] so as to insert an identifier into groups of tuples. This scheme is based on the modulation of circular histograms centers of mass originally proposed by De Vleeschouwer *et al.* for images [6]. The detector of the proposed scheme has been optimized for database traceability in the context of database mixtures. The theoretical analysis of the impact of the database mixture on the watermark detection process constitutes the first contribution of this paper. As we will see, it is equivalent to the addition of a Gaussian noise the parameters of which can be estimated. Based on this knowledge, an optimized score based detector can be derived, as shown in [3,16], providing a higher detection performance than the correlation based detector. This detector constitutes the second main contribution of this paper.

The rest of this paper is organized as follows. Section 2 presents the main steps of a common database watermarking chain and explains why the marking assumption of anti-collusion codes is not respected. We next introduce our robust lossless watermarking scheme and its application for identifier embedding into databases. The decoder optimization based on these theoretical results is given in Sect. 3. This one is experimentally verified in Sect. 4 in the case of one real medical database of patient stay records. The proposed scheme is also compared to a common correlation based detector so as to show the gain of performance. Section 5 concludes this paper.

2   Database Traceability by Means of Watermarking

2.1   A General Database Watermarking Chain

A database can be defined as a collection of data organized into a finite set of relations $\{R_i\}_{i=1,...,N_R}$. For sake of simplicity, we will consider one database composed of one single relation composed of N unordered tuples $\{t_u\}_{u=1,...,N}$ associating M attributes $\{A_1,...,A_M\}$, where $t_u.A_n$ refers to the value of the nth attribute of the uth tuple. The values of the attribute A_n are issued from a set called attribute domain. Furthermore, each tuple is uniquely identified by means of either one attribute or a set of attributes we call its primary key $t_u.PK$.

Most of the existing database watermarking schemes follow the stages illustrated in Fig. 1. For message embedding, tuples are first preprocessed so as to make the watermark insertion/extraction independent from the database storage structure. This stage consists essentially in the construction of a set of N_g non-intersecting groups of tuples $\{G^i\}_{i=1,...,N_g}$.

The group number of one tuple is usually calculated by means of a cryptographic hash function applied to the concatenation of its primary key $t_u.PK$ with a secret watermarking key K_S as exposed in (1) where '|' represents the concatenation operator [19,20]. The use of a cryptographic hash function, e.g. Secure Hash Algorithm (SHA), ensures the secure and uniform repartition of tuples into groups.

$$n_u = H(K_S|H(K_S|t_u.PK)) \bmod N_g \tag{1}$$

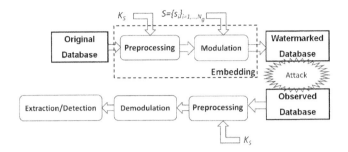

Fig. 1. A common database watermarking chain.

Thus, for a total number of tuples in the database N, each group roughly contains $\frac{N}{N_g}$ tuples. Then, one symbol of the message is embedded per group. To do so, the values of one or several attributes are modified accordingly to a watermarking modulation. Thus, one may expect to embed a message corresponding to a sequence of N_g symbols $S = \{s_i\}_{i=1,...,N_g}$.

Watermark extraction works in a similar way. First, tuples are distributed into N_g groups. Depending on the watermarking modulation, one symbol is extracted from each of these groups. The knowledge of the primary keys and the watermarking key ensures synchronization between watermark embedding and extraction stages.

These same steps are considered in our system, whose purpose is the traceability of a database in a mixture. Such a scheme could if necessary take into account distortion constraints, preserving the database statistics [10,19] as well as the semantic meaning of tuples, based for instance on an ontology [7]. However, this is beyond the scope of this paper.

2.2   Identification of a Database in a Mixture

As exposed in Sect. 1, we are interested in embedding an identifier into a database for traceability purposes, i.e., to be able to verify the presence of a database in a mixture. To do so and as illustrated in Fig. 2, for a database j, a set of N_g groups of tuples is constructed by means of a secret key K_S^j as described in the previous section. Then, each symbol of an identification sequence $S^j = \{s_1^j, ..., s_{N_g}^j\}$, with $s_i^j \in \{-1, 1\}$, is embedded into one group of tuples. Once these databases are uploaded to a warehouse, their tuples are mixed.

At the detection, in order to determine if the database j is present in the data warehouse, we seek to detect the sequence S^j. That is to say, we aim at detecting the sequence S^j into the groups of tuples reconstructed over the whole mixed database by means of the secret key K_S^j.

Due to the grouping operation based on a cryptographic hash function, symbols inserted into different protected databases do not superpose in a single group of tuples, i.e., they do not respect the marking assumption. More clearly,

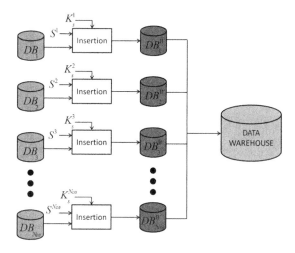

Fig. 2. Embedding stage for the proposed solution. Each database is identified by means of a sequence S^j, the embedding of which is performed by means of a secret key K^j_s.

tuples that encode one symbol of the identifier of one protected database, e.g., DB^W_2, will be uniformly distributed into the groups of DB^W_1. This means that one symbol embedded into DB^W_2 will be spread over all the symbols of DB^W_1. In that context, anti-collusion codes are not effective. As a consequence, the identifiers considered in the sequel are constructed of uniformly distributed symbols, i.e., $Pr(s^j_i = -1) = Pr(s^j_i = 1) = \frac{1}{2}$.

The embedding of these uniformly distributed sequences S^j into each database j is performed by means of the robust lossless scheme presented in [8] which makes use of the circular histograms center of mass modulation originally proposed in [6] for image watermarking. This modulation offers an important robustness to tuple addition attacks, granting the detection of the embedded sequence when more than 100% of new tuples are added to the database. Even though reversibility is only ensured at a local level, i.e., original non-watermarked data can not be obtained from the data warehouse, this property is useful for the owner, who can locally store his or her watermarked database so as to protect it from internal leaks and retrieve the original data when needed. The basic principles of this modulation are recalled in the next section.

2.3 Lossless Circular Histogram Center of Mass Modulation

This scheme embeds one symbol of the sequence $S = \{s_1, ..., s_{N_g}\}$ per group of tuples. To do so, it modulates the relative angular position of the circular histogram center of mass of one numerical attribute. Due to space limitation, we just sum-up its basic principles. We invite the reader to consult [8] for more details. Anyway, let us assume the attribute A_t, the domain of which corresponds to the integer range $[0, L-1]$, is considered for message embedding. Let us also

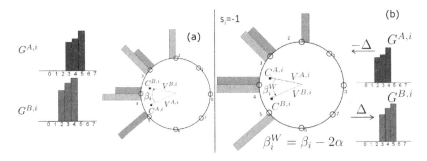

Fig. 3. (a) Histogram mapping of each sub-group $G^{A,i}$ and $G^{B,i}$ onto a circle. The angle between the vectors pointing the centers of mass is modulated in order to embed one symbol of the message. (b) The embedding of a symbol $s_i = -1$ corresponds to a rotation of the circular histograms of $G^{A,i}$ and $G^{B,i}$ in opposite directions with an angle step α in order to modify the sign of β_i. This is equivalent to the addition of Δ to the attribute values in $G^{B,i}$ and $-\Delta$ to those of $G^{A,i}$.

consider the group of tuples G^i in which we are going to embed one symbol $s_i = \{-1, 1\}$. This task is conducted by equally dividing G^i into two sub-groups $G^{A,i}$ and $G^{B,i}$ following the same strategy as exposed in (1) (see Sect. 2.1).

Then, as illustrated in Fig. 3a, the histograms of A_t in each subgroup are calculated and mapped onto the unit circle. In order to embed s_i, the relative angle $\beta_i = (\widehat{V^{A,i}, V^{B,i}}) \simeq 0$ between the vectors $V^{A,i}$ and $V^{B,i}$ associated to the histograms' centers of mass is modulated. Depending on the value of s_i, the circular histograms of $G^{A,i}$ and $G^{B,i}$ are rotated in opposite directions with an angle step $\alpha = \frac{2\pi\Delta}{L}$, where Δ corresponds to the shift amplitude of the histogram. More precisely, modifying the angle β_i of $2\alpha(s_i)$ results in adding $(s_i)\Delta$ to the values of A_t in $G^{A,i}$ and $(-s_i)\Delta$ to those in $G^{B,i}$ (see Fig. 3b). At the reading stage, the groups and subgroups of tuples are reconstructed and the histograms calculated and projected again into the unit circle. Then, the sign of the watermarked angle β_i^w indicates the embedded symbol in G^i as well as the direction of rotation to follow so as to invert the insertion process. Due to the fact α is a fixed value, not all of the groups of tuples can convey one symbol of message, in particular those for which $|\beta_i| > 2\alpha$. We call this groups non-carriers. In order to allow their identification by the reader and ensure reversibility, these groups are also modified of a fixed value $\pm 2\alpha$ depending on the original sign of β_i in the group. Thus, the reader will identify groups for which $|\beta_i^w| > 4\alpha$ as non-carriers. This can be summarized as:

$$\beta_i^w = \begin{cases} \beta_i + s_i \cdot 2\alpha & \text{if } |\beta_i| > 2\alpha \\ \beta_i + \text{sign}(\beta_i) \cdot 2\alpha & \text{if } \pi - 2\alpha > |\beta_i| \geq 2\alpha \end{cases} \tag{2}$$

One last class to consider includes what we call "overflow" groups, i.e., groups for which $|\beta_i| \geq \pi - 2\alpha$. These groups are quite rare, but they can appear. They correspond to non-carriers the angle β_i of which will change of sign when adding 2α or -2α. This implies that, if modified, they will not be correctly restored by the reader when inverting the embedding rules. Thus, these groups are left unchanged at the embedding stage and a message overhead, a reconstruction sequence or message, is embedded along with the owner identifier. We invite the reader to consult [8] for more details in how this message is constituted.

In the case this scheme is used in order to identify the owner or the recipient of the database, the detection will have to verify that the sequence S (the user identifier) is present in the database even if this one has been be "attacked" (e.g. tuple addition/suppression). This can be commonly achieved by means of a correlation based detector, e.g., $C_S = <S, \hat{S}>$, where $\hat{S}$ is the extracted sequence. If C_S is greater than a decision threshold Tr_S then S is said to be present in the database.

As we will see by next, this detector is not the most appropriate when focusing on the detection of a protected database in a mixture of watermarked databases. On the contrary, after having modeled the impact of the mixture on the embedded message, an optimized detector can be proposed.

3   Decoder Optimization

In this section, we first present some theoretical results related to the impact the mixture of databases has on the detection of the sequence embedded into one of them. These preliminary results will then be used so to optimize the message decoder in terms of detection.

3.1   Preliminary Results

As proved in [8], for a given database DB and a given numerical attribute A_t, whatever the distribution of this latter, the angle β_i, i.e., $\widehat{V^{A,i}, V^{B,i}}$, follows a centered normal distribution $\mathcal{N}(0, \sigma_{\beta_i}^2)$ of variance $\sigma_{\beta_i}^2$; a variance which can be estimated from the attribute values. Moreover, the resulting distribution of the watermarked angles, i.e., of the random variable β_i^W, over the whole database can also be modeled.

Once the distribution of β_i^W is known for one database, it is possible to evaluate the impact the addition of the watermarked tuples from the other databases of the mixture will have on it. Let us consider we want to identify DB_1^W in a databases mixture. Because of the cryptographic hash function parameterized with the watermarking key K_S^1 (K_S^1 is different from the watermarking keys of the other databases $\{K_S^u\}_{u=2,...,N_{DB}}$) used so as to distribute tuples into groups and sub-groups (see (1) in Sect. 2.1), we can consider that the tuples of the different databases $\{DB_u^W\}_{u=2,...,N_{DB}}$ are uniformly distributed among the groups $\{G^i\}_{i=1,...,N_g}$ as well as in the sub-groups of tuples $G^{A,i}$ and $G^{B,i}$ of DB_1^W. From here on, it is possible to possible to estimate the probability of β_i^W after the inclusion of DB_1^W in the mixture.

Let us consider that DB_1^W is merged with a set of U different databases, constituting a new set U'. Each of these databases contains $\{N_u\}_{i=2,...,|U|+1}$ tuples, where $|U|$ represents the cardinality of U, with the same attribute set

$\{A_1, ..., A_M\}$ and is watermarked with a different secret key. From the "point of view" of DB_1^W, we can consider that the merging of this set of bases results in the mixture of populations of tuples. The mixture proportions can be easily calculated as:

$$P_{DB_u} = \frac{N_u}{\sum\limits_{k=2}^{|U|+1} N_k}, \quad \forall u \in [2, |U| + 1] \tag{3}$$

In terms of the angles β_i^W, this mixture can be modeled as a weighted sum between β_i^W and a random variable β_i^{mix} associated to the tuples of $\{DB_u^W\}_{u=1,...,N_{DB}}$. β_i^{mix} follows a centered normal distribution $\mathcal{N}(0, \sigma_{\beta_i^{mix}}^2)$ of variance $\sigma_{\beta_i^{mix}}^2$ obtained such as:

$$\sigma_{\beta_i^{mix}}^2 = 2\frac{\sigma_{s,mix}^2}{\frac{\sum\limits_{k=2}^{|U|+1} N_k}{2N_g} R_{mix}^2} \tag{4}$$

where:

$$R_{mix}^2 = \left[P_{ov} + (1 - P_{ov}) \cos\left(\frac{2\pi\Delta}{L}\right) \right]^2 \cdot R^2 \tag{5}$$

and

$$\sigma_{s,mix}^2 = \sum_{k=2}^{|U|+1} P_{DB_k} \left(\sigma_{s,k}^2 P_{ov} + (1 - P_{ov}) \left[\sigma_{s,k}^2 \cos\left(\frac{4\pi\Delta}{L}\right) + \sin^2\left(\frac{2\pi\Delta}{L}\right) \right] \right) \tag{6}$$

The calculation of R (module of the center of mass vector), σ_s^2 (squared-sinus variance, as proposed in [17]) and P_{ov} (overflow group probability) is given in [8].

The distribution of β_i^W in the final database, or more precisely into the groups of tuples based on the secret key used to watermark DB_1^W is perturbed by the noise induced by the watermarked tuples of the set U. In fact, the conditional density functions of the resulting β_i^{merge}, i.e., the weighted sum of β_i^W and β_i^{mix}, remain normal. If we define the mixture proportions for DB_1 and for the databases in the set U such as $P_{DB_1} = N_1 / \left(N_1 + \sum_{k=2}^{|U|+1} N_k \right)$ and $P_{mix} = 1 - P_{DB_1}$ respectively, then the mean and variance of β_i^{merge} are such as:

$$\mathrm{E}[\beta_i^{merge} | s_i = -1] = P_{DB_1} \mathrm{E}[\beta_i^W | s_i = -1] + P_{mix} \mathrm{E}[\beta_i^{mix}]$$
$$= P_{DB_1} \cdot \left(-\frac{4\pi\Delta}{L}\right) \tag{7}$$

$$\mathrm{E}[\beta_i^{merge} | s_i = +1] = P_{DB_1} \mathrm{E}[\beta_i^W | s_i = +1] + P_{mix} \mathrm{E}[\beta_i^{mix}]$$
$$= P_{DB_1} \cdot \left(\frac{4\pi\Delta}{L}\right) \tag{8}$$

and

$$\sigma_{\beta_i^{merge}}^2 = P_{DB_1}^2 \sigma_{\beta_i}^2 + P_{mix}^2 \sigma_{\beta_i^{mix}}^2 \tag{9}$$

3.2 Informed Decoder

The knowledge about the impact of the database mixture on the embedded sequence allows us to search for an optimized detector compared to the classic correlation based detection. The optimization we propose is based on an informed decoder [3,16] that takes into account that databases merged with the one we want to detect appear as a centered Gaussian noise added to the watermarked angle random variable β_i^W. Our detection problem can be then described by means of hypothesis testing between the following hypothesis:

- H0: Database j is not part of the database mixture, which means that K_s^j has not been used for group creation at the embedding stage and its identification sequence S^j is independent of $\hat{S}$.
- H1: Database j is part of the database mixture, which means that K_s^j has been used for group creation at the embedding stage and $\hat{S}$ has been created from its identification sequence S^j.

In practice, each element of the sequence $\hat{S}$ extracted from a group of tuples i corresponds to the value of the extracted angle $\hat{\beta}_i$, i.e., a real value, instead of a symbol in $\{-1, 1\}$. In that context, detection theory tells us that the score given by the log-likelihood ratio (LLR) is optimally discriminative in the Neyman-Pearson sense. Considering K_s^{emb} the secret watermarking key used at the embedding stage, this score is calculated as:

$$Sc^j = \sum_{i=1}^{N_g} Sc_i^j = \sum_{i=1}^{N_g} \log \frac{p(\hat{s}_i | K_s^{emb} = K_s^j, s_i^j)}{p(\hat{s}_i | K_s^{emb} \neq K_s^j)} \tag{10}$$

where $p(\hat{s}_i | K_s^{emb} \neq K_s^j)$ is the probability density function of the ith symbol $\hat{s}_i$ of the extracted sequence $\hat{S}$ when the secret key K_s^j has not been used for the construction of groups in the embedding stage, i.e., the probability $p(\hat{\beta}_i | K_s^{emb} \neq K_s^j)$.

As previously exposed, due to the uniform distribution of tuples into groups, the p.d.f $p(\hat{s}_i | K_s^{emb} \neq K_s^j)$ is a centered normal $\mathcal{N}(0, \sigma_{\beta_i^{mix}}^2)$, where $\sigma_{\beta_i^{mix}}^2$ corresponds to the variance of the angle β_i of a mixture of $|U|$ databases. Figure 4 illustrates these different distributions.

Thus knowing both p.d.f. $p(\hat{s}_i | K_s^{emb} = K_s^j, s_i^j)$ and $p(\hat{s}_i | K_s^{emb} \neq K_s^j)$, the complete expression for the detection score is:

$$Sc_i^j = \log \left(\frac{\sigma_{\beta_i^{mix}}}{\sigma_{\beta_i^{merge}}} \right) + \frac{\beta_i^2 (\sigma_{\beta_i^{merge}}^2 - \sigma_{\beta_i^{mix}}^2)}{2 \sigma_{\beta_i^{mix}}^2 \sigma_{\beta_i^{merge}}^2}$$

$$+ \frac{2 s_i^j \beta_i \sigma_{\beta_i^{mix}}^2 P_{DB_j} \frac{4\pi\Delta}{L} - \sigma_{\beta_i^{mix}}^2 (P_{DB_j} \frac{4\pi\Delta}{L})^2}{2 \sigma_{\beta_i^{mix}}^2 \sigma_{\beta_i^{merge}}^2} \tag{11}$$

Due to the central limit theorem, the detection score of a database that has not been uploaded to the data warehouse is normally distributed. Thus, one can

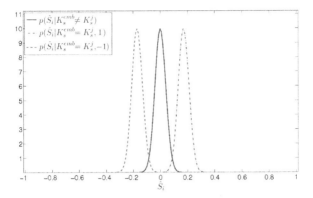

Fig. 4. Probability density functions $p(\hat{S}_i | K_s^{emb} = K_s^j, s_i^j)$ and $p(\hat{S}_i | K_s^{emb} \neq K_s^j)$ considered in this section. In this particular example, the length of the attribute integer range is $L = 110$. This attribute was watermarked considering $N_g = 100$ groups and $\Delta = 3$. In the example, $\sigma^2_{\beta_i^{merge}} \approx \sigma^2_{\beta_i^{mix}} = 0.0016$.

compute an optimal detection threshold Z for a given false alarm probability such as [16]:

$$Z = \sqrt{2\sigma^2_{SC}} \cdot \text{erfc}^{-1}(2P_{FA}/n) + m_{SC} \tag{12}$$

where n corresponds to number of users who may upload their database to the warehouse, i.e., the number of identification sequences.

Notice that in this case, additionally to the calculation of σ^2_{SC}, a term m_{SC} has to be calculated in order to obtain Z. This is due to the fact that the mean of the detection scores is not zero (see 11). However, m_{SC} can be calculated as:

$$m_{SC} = N_g \left[\log\left(\frac{\sigma_{\beta_i^{mix}}}{\sigma_{\beta_i^{merge}}}\right) - \frac{(P_{DB_j}\frac{4\pi\Delta}{L})^2}{2\sigma^2_{\beta_i^{merge}}} + \frac{\sigma^2_{\beta_i^{merge}} - \sigma^2_{\beta_i^{mix}}}{2\sigma^2_{\beta_i^{merge}}} \right] \tag{13}$$

The variance σ^2_{SC} is calculated as:

$$\sigma^2_{SC} = N_g \sigma^2_{\beta_i^{mix}} \left[\left(\frac{4\pi\Delta P_{DB_j}}{L\sigma^2_{\beta_i^{merge}}}\right)^2 + 2\sigma^2_{\beta_i^{mix}} \left(\frac{\sigma^2_{\beta_i^{merge}} - \sigma^2_{\beta_i^{mix}}}{2\sigma^2_{\beta_i^{mix}}\sigma^2_{\beta_i^{merge}}}\right)^2 \right] \tag{14}$$

4   Experimental Results

In this section we experimentally verify the above theoretical results in the following way. We recall that our basic idea is to identify one database merged with several others in a data warehouse. To do so, each database is watermarked by means of the robust lossless scheme presented above so as to insert its unique identifier, i.e., the binary sequence S^j, for the database j. Each database is watermarked using a distinct secret key K_s^j, key which is the base of tuple group construction.

4.1   Considered Database and Experimental Framework

Following experiments have been conducted on a test database constituted of more than ten million tuples of 15 attributes each; attributes that describe inpatient stays in French hospitals like the hospital identifier (*id_hospital*), the patient stay identifier (*id_stay*), the patient age (*age*), the stay duration (*dur_stay*), the attribute GHM (patient homogeneous group, French equivalent of the the Diagnosis-Related Groups or DRG of the US Medicare system), the attribute ICD10 principal diagnosis and several other data useful for statistical analysis of hospital activities. $N = 1048000$ tuples were extracted from this database for our test purposes.

In order to constitute the groups of tuples (see Sect. 2), the attributes *id_stay* and *id_hospital* were considered as the primary key. Two numerical attributes were considered for message embedding and watermarked independently: patient age (*age*) and stay duration (*dur_stay*). These attributes were chosen because of the specificity of their distributions. The attribute *age* is slightly uniformly distributed, while the attribute *dur_stay* presents an exponential distribution concentrated over the lower values of its domain. In order to compare the detection performance of the different approaches exposed above, the following experience plan was applied:

1. Creation of nine databases from the considered extract.
2. Watermarking of each database with its unique identifier S^j, based on a secret key K_s^j.
3. Databases merging under the constraint that DB_1 represents a $D\%$ of the total number of tuples.
4. Detection of the database of interest DB_1 considering its secret key K_s^1.

The plan of experimentation was conducted with various: watermark distortion amplitude (Δ); number of groups (N_g), which represents the length of the embedded identifier; percentage D of tuples DB_1 represents into the total database; false detection probability P_{FA}. Notice that for sake of simplicity, all nine databases were watermarked in the same way. The number of identification sequences was fixed to $n = 50$. Furthermore, the detection probability results are given after 50 random simulations with the same parameterization but with different groups configuration.

4.2   Proposed Detector Performance

In a first time, we were interested in comparing the discriminative performance of the proposed informed detector with the classic correlation-based detection in the database traceability framework. To do so, we evaluate the receiver operating characteristic (ROC) curves of both detectors for different watermarking parameterizations. The ROC curve plots the true positive rate, i.e., a database present in the warehouse is correctly detected, against the false positive rate, i.e., a database non-present in the warehouse is detected as present, for different detection thresholds. Figure 5a illustrates the ROC curves for both detectors when the attribute *age* was watermarked considering values $\Delta = 2$, $N_g = 130$ and $D = [5, 7, 9]\%$. The discriminative performance improves as the proportion D of tuples increases. As it can be seen, the proposed detector outperforms the correlation-based detector for all the considered values of D. This is the same for all the considered parameterizations. As depicted in Fig. 5b, a better performance is obtained for higher values of Δ, with again the proposed detector offering the best results. The number of groups, i.e., the length of the embedded sequence, has also an impact on performance as reflected in Fig. 5c. A lower number of groups, e.g., $N_g = 70$ in the figure, provides better results. Notice that a longer sequence will be more discriminative but more fragile. It is then necessary to find an identifier length so as to obtain a good a trade-off between good detection (shorter sequences are more robust to the mixture) and false detection (longer sequences allow better discrimination).

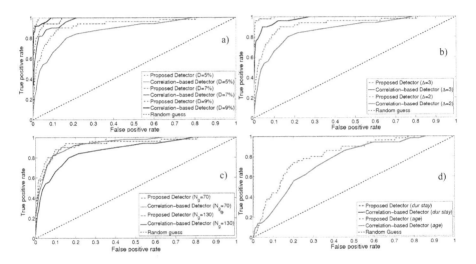

Fig. 5. Receiver operating characteristic curves for the proposed and the correlation-based detectors considering the attribute *age* with: (a) $\Delta = 2$, $N_g = 130$ and different values of $D = [5, 7, 9]\%$; (b) $\Delta = 2$ and $\Delta = 3$ with $N_g = 130$ and $D = 5\%$; (c) $\Delta = 2$ with $N_g = 70$ and $N_g = 130$ and $D = 5\%$; (d) $\Delta = 2$, $N_g = 130$ and $D = 3\%$ for different modulated attributes *dur_stay* and *age*. Proposed detector performances are depicted in dash-dot lines while the correlation-based detector performances are given in solid lines.

Finally, the influence of the attribute distribution in the discriminative performance was analyzed. As depicted in Fig. 5d, for a same value of $\Delta = 2$ and $N_g = 130$, obtained performances when the identifier was embedded in the attribute *dur_stay*, i.e., an attribute with a more concentrated distribution, are better than those obtained when the attribute *age*, i.e., a more uniform attribute, was modulated. This is due to the fact that the considered watermarking modulation presents a higher robustness for more concentrated attributes (see [8] for

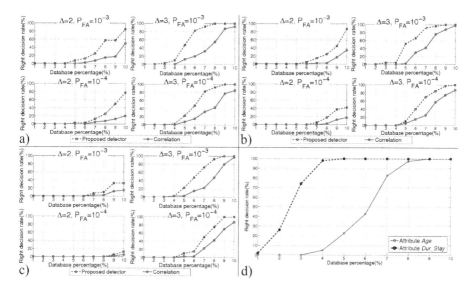

Fig. 6. Detection performance obtained by the proposed detection strategy versus the correlation-based detector for: (a) $N_g = 70$; (b) $N_g = 130$; (c) $N_g = 250$; (d) $N_g = 130$ considering the attribute dur_stay with $\Delta = 1$ and age with $\Delta = 3$ for values of $D = [1\%, 10\%]$ and $P_{FA} = 10^{-3}$. Proposed detector performances are depicted in dashed lines while the correlation-based detector performances are given in solid lines, except for (d) in which solid line represents the performance for attribute age while the dashed line refers to attribute dur_stay.

more details). In case all the attributes in the database are completely uniform, the watermark embedding becomes impossible (as it occurs in the case of image watermarking for example) and some strategy has to be found in order to embed the identifier. However, the analysis of possible strategies is beyond the scope of this paper.

In a second experiment we searched to compare the detection performance of both detectors for a fixed optimal detection threshold. The attribute age was used for identifier embedding, with DB_1 representing $D = [1\%, 10\%]$ of the data warehouse. Two values of the distortion amplitude $\Delta = [2, 3]$, as well as three number of groups values $N_g = [70, 130, 250]$, i.e., sequence lengths, and two values of $P_{FA} = [10^{-3}, 10^{-4}]$ were considered. In the case of the correlation-based detector, the optimal threshold can be calculated as $Z_{corr} = \sqrt{2/N_g} \cdot \text{erfc}^{-1}(2P_{FA}/n)$. For the proposed detector, this threshold is calculated as exposed in Sect. 2.2. Results for the different parameters' combinations are illustrated in Figs. 6a, b and c. The proposed detector outperforms the results achieved by the correlation-based detector in all the cases. Notice also that, in the best case, we obtain a detection rate of 100% even if DB_1 represents only 8% of the data warehouse. This detection performance increases if we consider the embedding of the identifiers in the attribute dur_stay, when a DB_1 representing only 4% can be detected. As illustrated in Fig. 6d, where results were obtained for $N_g = 130$ considering the attributes *dur_stay* with $\Delta = 1$ and *age* with $\Delta = 3$ for values of $D = [1\%, 10\%]$ and $P_{FA} = 10^{-3}$.

Finally, we searched to measure the performance of the proposed detector in terms of false detection rate when a different secret key is used at the detection, e.g., when an attacker tries to detect with a self-generated key his or her identifier. Obtained results show 0% of false detections in this case. This is logic due to the random and uniform repartition of tuples into groups obtained by means of the cryptographic hash function (see Sect. 2).

5   Conclusion

In this paper, we addressed the traceability of databases in the case when they are merged in a data repository or even in a data warehouse. This is an issue of rising interest as there is a trend to the creation of inter-institutional shared data warehouses giving access to big amounts of data.

Our final database traceability system is based on two main aspects: first, the robust lossless watermarking scheme presented in [8], which allows to embed a message that will resist an important degree of attacks to the database; second, the theoretical modeling of the impact of database aggregation onto the detection process of one single database. Both allow us to search the more optimal detector based on a soft-decision decoding.

In order to prove the benefits of the proposed detection improvements, our solution has been tested on the mixture of several real medical databases, with different mixture proportions and watermarking parameterization. As exposed, the proposed detector improves the performance obtained by the correlation based detection. Indeed, it allows identifying a database representing a low percentage of the total of tuples (e.g., around 8% for an insertion in the attribute *age* and 4% for the attribute *dur_stay*) in nearly a 100% of the cases.

Acknowledgment. The authors are very grateful to the Department of Medical Information and Archives, CHU Lille; UDSL EA 2694; Univ. Lille Nord de France; F-59000 Lille, France, for the experimental data used in this study.

References

1. Agrawal, R., Kiernan, J.: Chapter 15 - watermarking relational databases. In: VLDB 2002: Proceedings of the 28th International Conference on Very Large Databases, pp. 155–166 (2002)
2. Armbrust, M., Fox, A., Griffith, R., Joseph, A.D., Katz, R., Konwinski, A., Lee, G., Patterson, D., Rabkin, A., Stoica, I., Zaharia, M.: A view of cloud computing. Commun. ACM **53**(4), 50–58 (2010)
3. Barni, M., Bartolini, F., De Rosa, A., Piva, A.: Optimum decoding and detection of multiplicative watermarks. IEEE. Trans. Signal Process. **51**(4), 1118–1123 (2003)
4. Boneh, D., Shaw, J.: Collusion-secure fingerprinting for digital data. IEEE Trans. Inf. Theory **44**(5), 452–465 (1996)

5. Coatrieux, G., Chazard, E., Beuscart, R., Roux, C.: Lossless watermarking of categorical attributes for verifying medical data base integrity. In: Proceedings of the IEEE EMBC, pp. 8195–8198. IEEE (2011)
6. De Vleeschouwer, C., Delaigle, J.F., Macq, B.: Circular interpretation of bijective transformations in lossless watermarking for media asset management. IEEE Trans. Multimed. **5**(1), 97–105 (2003)
7. Franco-Contreras, J., Coatrieux, G.: Robust watermarking of relational databases with ontology-guided distortion control. IEEE Trans. Inf. Forensics Secur. **10**(9), 1939–1952 (2015)
8. Franco-Contreras, J., Coatrieux, G., Cuppens-Boulahia, N., Cuppens, F., Roux, C.: Robust lossless watermarking of relational databases based on circular histogram modulation. IEEE Trans. Inf. Forensics Secur. **9**(3), 397–410 (2014)
9. Harvard Business Review Analytic Services: The evolution of decision making: How leading organizations are adopting a data-driven culture (2012)
10. Kamran, M., Suhail, S., Farooq, M.: A robust, distortion minimizing technique for watermarking relational databases using once-for-all usability constraints. IEEE Trans. Knowl. Data Eng. **25**(12), 2694–2707 (2013)
11. Kuribayashi, M.: A simple tracing algorithm for binary fingerprinting code under averaging attack. In: Proceedings of the First ACM Workshop on Information Hiding and Multimedia Security, (IH&MMSec 2013), NY, USA, pp. 3–12. ACM, New York (2013)
12. Lafaye, J., Gross-Amblard, D., Constantin, C., Guerrouani, M.: Watermill: an optimized fingerprinting system for databases under constraints. IEEE Trans. Knowl. Data Eng. **20**, 532–546 (2008)
13. Li, Y., Guo, H., Jajodia, S.: Tamper detection and localization for categorical data using fragile watermarks. In: Proceedings of ACM Workshop on Digital Rights Management (DRM 2004), pp. 73–82 (2004)
14. Li, Y., Swarup, V., Jajodia, S.: Fingerprinting relational databases: schemes and specialties. IEEE Trans. Dependable Secure Comput. **2**(1), 34–45 (2005)
15. McNickle, M.: Top. 10 data security breaches in 2012. http://www.healthcarefinancenews.com/news/top-10-data-security-breaches-2012 in Healthcare Finance News. Accessed 21 July 2016
16. Ng, T., Garg, H.: Maximum-likelihood detection in DWT domain image watermarking using Laplacian modeling. IEEE Signal Process. Lett. **12**(4), 285–288 (2005)
17. Quinn, B.: Phase-only information loss. In: 2010 IEEE International Conference on Acoustics Speech and Signal Processing (ICASSP), pp. 3982–3985, March 2010
18. Schaathun, H.: On error-correcting fingerprinting codes for use with watermarking. Multimed. Syst. **13**(5–6), 331–344 (2008)
19. Shehab, M., Bertino, E., Ghafoor, A.: Watermarking relational databases using optimization-based techniques. IEEE Trans. Knowl. Data Eng. **20**, 116–129 (2008)
20. Sion, R., Atallah, M., Prabhakar, S.: Rights protection for relational data. IEEE Trans. Knowl. Data Eng. **16**(12), 509–1525 (2004)
21. Tardos, G.: Optimal probabilistic fingerprint codes. In: Proceedings of the Thirty-Fifth Annual ACM Symposium on Theory of Computing (STOC 2003), pp. 116–125 (2003)

A New Card Authentication Scheme Based on Image Watermarking and Encryption

Xinxin Peng[1], Jianfeng Lu[1], Li Li[1], Chin-Chen Chang[2], and Qili Zhou[1(✉)]

[1] Institute of Graphics and Image, Hangzhou Dianzi University, Zhejiang, China
zql@hdu.edu.cn
[2] Department of Information Engineering and Computer Science,
Feng Chia University, No. 100, Wenhwa Road, Seatwen, Taichung 40724, Taiwan

Abstract. With smart card's vast use, the security is becoming more and more important. Traditional password authentication can't meet user requirements. Many user's authentication schemes have been proposed, especially, based on image encryption. However, most existing schemes have problems of single authentication mode, low encryption intensity and poor quality of restored image. In this paper, we propose a dual authentication scheme using fingerprint biometric modality and digital watermarking techniques. Experimental results show that our dual authentication scheme is of more security, efficiency and low storage cost.

Keywords: Image encryption · Authentication · Smart card · Fingerprint · Biological mode

1 Introduction

With the popularity of smart card, it brings convenience to our daily lives, but also results in losses to our economy if illegal used. In order to verify the legitimacy of smart card user, many smart card based authentication schemes have been proposed [1–7]. But, many researchers believe that a single authentication scheme is less secure. In order to prevent malicious third party stealing the card and posing as the real users, more complicated schemes were proposed [8–10]. In terms of image encryption, a few schemes have been proposed using various approaches, such as multi-frame image encryption [11–13], chaotic cat maps [14–17], and chaotic dynamical systems [18–20].

In terms of smart card authentication, image encryption methods generally have much better performance. Therefore, Zhao et al. proposed a scheme based on generalized image morphing [21]. The basic idea is to hide the user's face image into a public image through morphing technology, and restore the user's face by de-morphing technology. However, the quality of the recovered image is relatively poor, due to the limitations of morphing technology. Chang et al. proposed a card authentication scheme based on image encryption [22]. They use DCT transform, scrambling and cryptography technology to process the user's face image. The keys and the data information are generated by the above process

Y.Q. Shi et al. (Eds.): IWDW 2016, LNCS 10082, pp. 358–369, 2017.
DOI: 10.1007/978-3-319-53465-7_26

and stored in the bank and smart card. Therefore, the authentic holder's face image of the card is restored when the card is used. Although this scheme is quite good, but it is not good to resist attack and have a better quality of the restored image.

We propose a dual authentication scheme based on image watermarking and encryption, to overcome the above shortcomings. First, we use biometric authentication methods, to collect the user's fingerprint. Second, we hide the user's fingerprint in the user image data. Finally, we use the DCT transform and compression technology to complete the image encryption process. The experimental results show that our scheme can resist the simulated attacks, and have a better quality of user face image, and have low storage cost.

The rest of the paper is organized as follows. In Sect. 2, we introduce the basic algorithms used in this paper and review Chang et al.'s method. In Sect. 3, we propose the image watermarking and encryption scheme. Then Sect. 4 provides the experimental results and analysis. The summary is presented in Sect. 5.

2   Preliminaries

The basic theories used in our paper are reviewed. Then, the Arnold algorithm and the diffusion algorithm are introduced. This part includes a review of Chang et al.'s scheme as well.

2.1   Diffusion Algorithm

In this study, we use the basic diffusion algorithm, which is good to change the real image pixel value, and to prevent the plaintext attack.

$$A_1(i,j) = A(i,j) * ((i+j) \bmod L). \tag{1}$$

When we need to restore the original matrix, it is necessary to use the inverse transform.

$$A(i,j) = A_1(i,j) / (i+j) \bmod L. \tag{2}$$

2.2   Image Scrambling Based on Arnold Transform

Arnold algorithm is a classic scrambling algorithm, where a, b and N are the basic parameter. In this study, (x_n, y_n) is the original pixel coordinates, and (x_{n+1}, y_{n+1}) is the new coordinates after scrambling.

$$\begin{pmatrix} x_{n+1} \\ y_{n+1} \end{pmatrix} = C \begin{pmatrix} x_n \\ y_n \end{pmatrix} \bmod N, \quad C = \begin{pmatrix} 1 & a \\ b & ab+1 \end{pmatrix}. \tag{3}$$

When we need to restore the original matrix, it is necessary to use the inverse transform.

$$\begin{pmatrix} x_{n+1} \\ y_{n+1} \end{pmatrix} = \begin{pmatrix} ab+1 & -a \\ -b & 1 \end{pmatrix} \begin{pmatrix} x_n \\ y_n \end{pmatrix} \bmod N. \tag{4}$$

2.3 Chang et al.'s Authentication Scheme Based on Frequency Domain

When a user goes to the bank to register the card, Chang et al. will record an image of his face. First, the user needs to provide five initial values a, b, t, λ, L_d. Then the image is transformed by DCT, and the coefficient matrix does the compression, scrambling and diffusion by using the above five values. Finally, the values of a, b, t, λ, L_d are to share the five shares, (x_1, y_1), (x_2, y_2), (x_3, y_3), (x_4, y_4), (x_5, y_5) by the second-degree polynomial function $f(x)$. So, When the user uses the card in a shop, he will use the five shares to restore the five values a, b, t, λ, L_d and use the five values to restore the face image P. When the restored image P looks the same as the original face image, the authentication is successful; otherwise, the authentication is fails.

3 Fingerprint Watermarking Based Card User Authentication

In the section, we put forward a new image encryption scheme based on fingerprint watermarking. Our algorithm is to extract the user fingerprint information as the watermark, and perform DCT transform, Arnold transform, compression to the user face image. Then the watermark information is embedded into the image frequency domain matrix. Meantime, the watermark and the face image can be extracted when we use the card in a shop. Therefore, our scheme includes two phases: the registration phase and the authentication phase. All the details will be described in the following sections. The overall flowchart is shown in Fig. 1.

3.1 Registration Phase

When a user registers a card in a bank, he will provide an image of his face and the thumb fingerprint information will be collected by a professional device. The photo provided by the user is a gray scale image of $M \times M$, and the image depth is 256. Next, the bank will do the following steps to make a smart card.

Step 1: (fingerprint collection)
First, the bank will collect the user's fingerprint information, and convert them to digital images. But the image quality is not good due to lots of noise. In order to extract and compare the fingerprint information more clearly, we will be preprocessing this image. Only after which, a clear outline of the binary image is generated.

Step 2: (face image processing)
The original face image P is split into 8×8 blocks and each block is manipulated by DCT. Then, the quantization table (Fig. 2) is applied to quantify each block. In each DCT block, the upper left corner is the largest coefficient and still the largest after quantization. Therefore, zigzag scan of the matrix, and extraction of the first nine elements will produce a 3×3 sub-block. Finally, the compressed DCT matrix M_1 is generated. Figure 3 shows the compressing process.

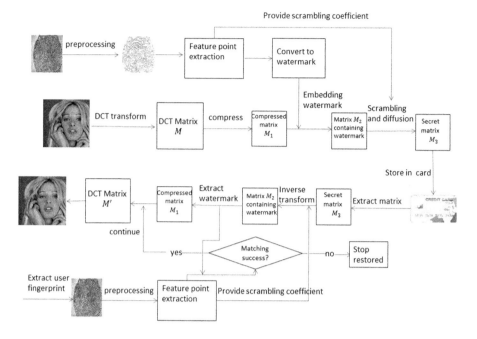

Fig. 1. Overall flowchart.

11	11	12	16	24	40	51	61
12	12	14	19	26	58	60	55
14	13	16	24	40	57	69	56
14	17	22	29	51	87	80	62
18	22	37	56	68	109	103	77
24	35	55	64	81	104	113	92
49	64	78	87	103	121	120	101
72	92	95	98	112	100	103	99

Fig. 2. Quantization table.

Step 3: (embedding watermark and encryption)
Fingerprint image is extracted from feature points and false feature points be removed [23]. Select a feature point as the reference point, and calculate all other feature points polar coordinates and angles. Polar coordinates and angles of all points are converted into binary sequences, and stored in the array s []. Then, scan the eight neighbors of each feature point, if the field has a

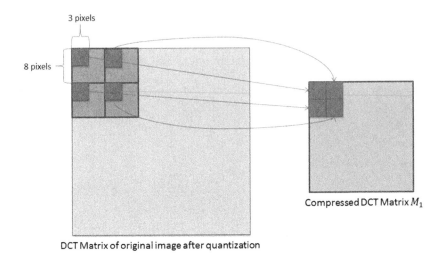

Fig. 3. Compression of the DCT matrix.

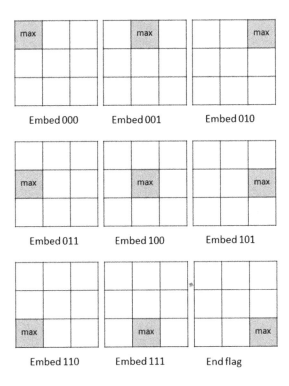

Fig. 4. Watermark embedding rules.

value equal to 1, then, count plus 1. Until all feature points are scanned, the resulting value is given to value a. The upper left corner of each 3×3 block is the largest coefficient in the compression matrix M_1. Therefore, we can exchange the position of the maximum coefficient and other coefficients in the 3×3 block to achieve the purpose of embedding the watermark information. The embedding process is as follows: (1) in the array s [], three values are put into a group, and if at the end, the sequence is less than three, 0 is added to complete. (2) The position of the maximum coefficient is used to represent the embedded watermark information (Fig. 4). (3) When the maximum coefficient is in the lower right corner, it is the representative of the end of the watermark. Then, we get the matrix M_2, after embedding the watermark into M_1.

Then the user will provide three parameters b, t and L. The value N of Arnold transformation is equal to size of matrix M_2. The matrix M_2 is scrambled t times by the Arnold transformation shown as Eq. (3), therefore, the matrix M_3 is generated. Then, the matrix M_3 is diffused calculation processing using Eq. (1), and the secret matrix S be obtained. Therefore, matrix S and parameters b, t and L are stored together in the card. In addition, the user's face image will be printed on the card.

3.2   Authentication Phase

When the user uses a smart card in a store, the store must authenticate if the user is the true holder or not.

Step 1: (fingerprint acquisition)
The store will collect the user's fingerprint, and turn it into a digital image. Then the image is preprocessed according to the requirement of matching, including noise correcting, image enhancement, and image thinning. The system will extract all the real image feature points, and scan the eight neighbors of each feature point, if the field has a value equal to 1, then, count plus 1. Until all feature points are scanned, the value a will be restored. Then the user provides three parameters b, t and L. The store reads the secret matrix S from the card, and he restored the matrix M_3 based on Eq. (2) of Sect. 2.1. Then the store extracts the size of M_3 to N, and recovers the matrix M_2 by Eq. (4). After that, the watermark information is extracted from the matrix M_2, and the maximum coefficient put back to the upper left corner.

Step 2: (fingerprint matching)
The store terminal converts the watermark information into the original polar coordinates, and stores into $O(5)$. A set of polar coordinates are obtained by using each of the points in the user's fingerprint as a reference point. Then, a set of polar coordinates $Q(6)$ is obtained. To match the two sets of polar coordinates O and Q, if the matching is successful, continue to Step 3, otherwise, the authentication fails.

$$O = \left((r_1^O, \theta_1^O)^T, \ldots, (r_M^O, \theta_M^O)^T \right). \qquad (5)$$

User's fingerprint polar coordinates.

$$Q = ((r_1^q, \theta_1^q)^T, \ldots, (r_M^q, \theta_M^q)^T). \tag{6}$$

The acquisition of the fingerprint polar coordinates

Step 3: (face comparison)
In matrix M_2, each 3×3 sub-block is return to the upper left corner in each 8×8 DCT block, and the remaining coefficients are filled as 0. Then, inverse quantization matrix M_1, using the quantization table (Fig. 2). Then, the inverse DCT transformation is processed on matrix M_1, and the restored image P_0 is generated. The store compares the restored image P_0 with the original image P. If the two image looks the same, authentication is successful; or else, the authentication fails.

4   Experiment Results

In this section, we will show the experimental results and security analysis. Then, we will compare the image quality with changes paper.

4.1   Watermarking Matching, Encryption and Decryption Results

Our approach combines both the fingerprint recognition and digital watermarking. The watermark signal is generated by fingerprint feature information, and hidden in the host image. Our fingerprint image size is 300×300, from the FCV2004 database. We have studied preprocessed fingerprint images with experiments, including fingerprint image filter enhancement, fingerprint image binary, and thinning of fingerprint ridges. Each image in the fingerprint database matches all the other images in library. Based on the FCV2004 database, the fingerprint matching recognition rate is 99.5%.

The image "Tiffany" with the size of 512×512 pixels was used for encryption. For each DCT block, only nine, low-frequency coefficients were used. We set the parameters $a = 102$, $b = 8$, and $N = 128$ and the values $L = 5$. Then, Fig. 5(a) shows the original image. Figure 5(b) shows the compressed image. The encrypted image is shown in Figs. 5(c)–(e), where Figs. 5(c), (d), and (e) are iterated 1, 36, and 108 times, respectively. After the Arnold transformation and diffusion, the images (c), (d), and (e) can be decrypted as (f). Compare with (b), the PSNR of (f) is infinite.

4.2   Security Analysis

In this paper, a dual authentication scheme using fingerprint biological modality and digital watermarking technique was proposed. We assumed that Dave masquerading as legitimate users. He steals smart card from authentic holder's Abel. To evaluate the security of smart card based on fingerprint watermarking and image encryption schemes, we assume that Dave can achieve the following things:

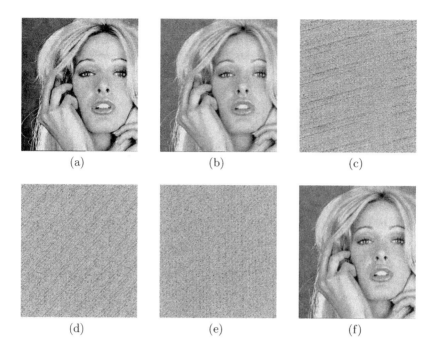

(a)　　　　　　　(b)　　　　　　　(c)

(d)　　　　　　　(e)　　　　　　　(f)

Fig. 5. Result of image scrambling in the DCT domain.

(1) Dave can replace the Abel's photo on the smart card with herself face photo.
(2) Dave can steal the key information of b, N, L.
(3) Dave can replace the matrix information stored in the smart card.

According to the above mentioned possibilities, we will discuss the following cases.

Case 1. Dave achieves (1) and (2) at the same time. He has to acquire the finger-prints information and extract the value a. Because of the uniqueness of the fingerprint, the value a will not be the same. So, his fingerprints can't match Abel's, and the restored image with a, b, N and L also can't be the same as Abel's. Therefore, he disguised as a legitimate user that fails.

Case 2. If Dave gets the matrix information from the smart card, and he can also obtain the secret key information. Then, he can get his own matrix information through the bank's legal process. So, he uses his matrix information to replace Abel's matrix which stored in Abel's smart card. However, when the store authenticates, his fingerprint can't match the success, and the image restored becomes meaningless because of the value a extracted by Dave's fingerprint is not the real value a.

Therefore, our scheme is tested to be very secure.

4.3   Performance Comparison

In this section, we conduct experiments with several different images, and evaluate the image quality with PSNR. The quality of the restoration image is excellent, as seen from the Table 1.

Table 1. The results of several different images

Original image	Restored image	PSNR
		37.2
		41.4
		34.5

We compare the performances of Chang et al.'s scheme [22] with our scheme. In order to compare the performance, we used the image "Tiffany" as also in Chang's paper. The "Tiffany" image is size of 512×512, the depth is 256. We used different storages, such as $8 \times (512)^2$ bits, $4 \times (512)^2$ bits, $3 \times (512)^2$ bits, $2 \times (512)^2$ bits, and $(512)^2$ bits. Table 2 shows the comparison results.

Table 2 shows that our image quality is much better than Chang et al.'s scheme in any storage space. From Table 2, we can see in the storage between $8 \times (512)^2$ bits and $2 \times (512)^2$ bits, our PSNR values have been maintained at 34.5. This is because our image DCT matrix after quantization and compression is still less than $2 \times (512)^2$ bits. When we use the $(512)^2$ bits storage, we will have to extract the first 8 elements from the 3×3 sub-blocks. So, our PSNR value is reduced to 34.3. However, our watermarking information is complete in any storage space, so our fingerprint matching will not be affected by the storage space. The low memory storage is very important, because of the limitation of the smart card memory space. Therefore, our scheme is more suitable for smart card authentication, and also more secure.

Table 2. The comparison of Chang et al.'s scheme and our scheme

Scheme	Storage bits/rate	PSNR (dB)	Recovered Image	Watermark extraction accuracy	Fingerprint Matching rate
Chang et al.'s	$8 \times (512)^2/100\%$	29.1		–	–
Our Scheme		34.5		100%	99.5%
Chang et al.'s	$4 \times (512)^2/50\%$	27.5		–	–
Our Scheme		34.5		100%	99.5%
Chang et al.'s	$3 \times (512)^2/37.5\%$	26.1		–	–
Our Scheme		34.5		100%	99.5%
Chang et al.'s	$2 \times (512)^2/25\%$	24.1		–	–
Our Scheme		34.5		100%	99.5%
Chang et al.'s	$(512)^2/12.5\%$	21.2		–	–
Our Scheme		34.3		100%	99.5%

5   Conclusions

In this paper, we propose a dual authentication scheme using fingerprint biometric modality and digital watermarking technique. First, we perform the DCT transform and compression of the user face image. Secondly, we use the fingerprint as the watermark information embedded in the frequency domain. Through the experimental results, we can see that our scheme is robust significantly and the image quality is good significantly. Therefore, our scheme is more suitable for smart card authentication.

Acknowledgement. This work was mainly supported by National Natural Science Foundation of China (No. 61370218).

References

1. Juang, W.S., Chen, S.T., Liaw, H.T.: Robust and efficient password-authenticated key agreement using smart cards. IEEE Trans. Ind. Electron. **55**, 2551–2556 (2008)
2. Guo, C., Chang, C.C., Sun, C.Y.: Chaotic maps-based mutual authentication and key agreement using smart cards for wireless communications. J. Inf. Hiding Multimedia Sig. Process. **4**, 99–109 (2013)
3. Chang, C.C., Wu, L.H.: A password authentication scheme based upon Rabin's public-key cryptosystem. In: Proceedings of International Conference on Systems Management, pp. 425–429 (1990)
4. Li, X., Qiu, W., Zheng, D., Chen, K., Li, J.: Anonymity enhancement on robust and efficient password-authenticated key agreement using smart cards. IEEE Trans. Ind. Electron. **57**, 793–800 (2010)
5. Hwang, M.S., Li, L.H.: A new remote user authentication scheme using smart cards. IEEE Trans. Consum. Electron. **46**, 28–30 (2000)
6. Rankl, W., Effing, W.: Smart Card Handbook. Wiley, New York
7. Zhao, Q.F., Hsieh, C.H.: Card user authentication based on generalized image morphing. In: Proceedings of the 3rd International Conference on Awareness Science and Technology, pp. 117–122 (2011)
8. Thongkor, K., Amornraksa, T.: Digital image watermarking for photo authentication in Thai national ID card. In: Proceedings of the 9th International Conference on Electrical Engineering/Electronics, Computer, Telecommunications and Information Technology, pp. 1–4 (2012)
9. Shankar, T.N., Sahoo, G., Niranjan, S.: Image encryption for mobile devices. In: Proceedings of IEEE International Conference on Communication Control and Computing Technologies, pp. 612–616 (2010)
10. Chang, C.C., Hwang, M.S., Chen, T.S.: A new encryption algorithm for image cryptosystems. J. Syst. Softw. **58**, 83–91 (2001)
11. Zhao, G., Yang, X., Zhou, B., Wei, W.: RSA-based digital image encryption algorithm in wireless sensor networks. In: Proceedings of the 2nd International Conference on Signal Processing Systems, pp. V2-640–V2-643 (2010)
12. Zhao, Z., Zhang, X.: ECC-based image encryption using code computing. In: Yang, G. (ed.) Proceedings of the ICCEAE 2012. AISC, vol. 181, pp. 859–865. Springer, Heidelberg (2013). doi:10.1007/978-3-642-31698-2_121
13. Li, L., Abd El-Latif, A.A., Niu, X.: Elliptic curve ElGamal based homomorphic image encryption scheme for sharing secret. Sig. Process. **92**, 1069–1078 (2012)

14. Wang, Y., Wong, K.W., Liao, X., Chen, G.: A new chaos-based fast image encryption algorithm. Appl. Soft Comput. **11**, 514–522 (2011)
15. Seyedzadeh, S.M., Mirzakuchaki, S.: A fast color image encryption algorithm based on coupled two-dimensional piecewise chaotic map. Sig. Process. **92**, 1202–1215 (2012)
16. Francois, M., Grosges, T., Barchiesi, D., Erra, R.: A new image encryption scheme based on a chaotic function. Sig. Process. Image Commun. **27**, 249–259 (2012)
17. Rajput, A.S., Sharma, M.: A novel image encryption and authentication scheme using chaotic maps. Adv. Intell. Inform. **320**, 277–286 (2015)
18. Chen, G., Mao, Y., Chui, C.K.: A symmetric image encryption scheme based on 3D chaotic cat maps. Chaos Solitons Fractals **21**, 749–761 (2004)
19. Singhpippal, R., Gupta, P., Singh, R.: A novel smart card authentication scheme using image encryption. Int. J. Comput. Appl. **72**(9), 8–14 (2013)
20. Mao, Q., Chang, C.C., Wu, H.L.: An image encryption scheme based on concatenated torus automorphisms. KSII Trans. Internet Inf. Syst. **7**, 1492–1511 (2013)
21. Zhao, Q., Hsieh, C.: Card user authentication based on generalized image morphing. In: International Conference on Awareness Science & Technology, pp. 117–122 (2011)
22. Chang, C.C., Wu, H.L., Wang, Z.H., Mao, Q.: An efficient smart card based authentication scheme using image encryption. J. Inf. Sci. Eng. **29**, 1135–1150 (2013)
23. Singh, P., Kaur, L.: Fingerprint feature extraction using morphological operations. In: Computer Engineering & Applications, pp. 764–767 (2015)

Copyright Protection for 3D Printing by Embedding Information Inside 3D-Printed Objects

Kazutake Uehira[1], Masahiro Suzuki[1(✉)],
Piyarat Silapasuphakornwong[1], Hideyuki Torii[1],
and Youichi Takashima[2]

[1] Department of Information Network and Communication,
Kanagawa Institute of Technology, Atsugi, Kanagawa, Japan
msuzuki@ctr.kanagawa-it.ac.jp
[2] NTT Service Evolution Laboratories,
Nippon Telegraph and Telephone Corporation,
Yokosuka, Kanagawa, Japan

Abstract. This paper proposes a technique that can protect the copyrights of digital content for 3D printers. It embeds the copyright information inside 3D-printed objects by forming a fine structure inside the objects as a watermark. Information on copyrights is included in the digital data for a real object before data are input into the 3D printer. This paper also presents a technique that can non-destructively read out information from inside real objects from a transparent image of the object using near infrared light. We conducted experiments using polylactide resin where we structured fine domains inside the objects. The domains have higher density than other regions. The disposition of the fine domains expressed binary code depending on whether or not they were at a designated position. The results obtained from the experiments demonstrated that the image of the fine domain inside the object can be captured by the near infrared camera and binary code could be read out successfully. These results demonstrated the feasibility of our technique showing that enough information can be embedded for copyright protection.

Keywords: Digital fabrication · 3D printer · Copyright protection · Near infrared light

1 Introduction

3D printers have been attracting a great deal of attention because they are expected to enable the systems of manufacturing and logistics to be changed [1, 2]. This is because they can produce hardware products not only in factories of manufacturers but also in user's offices or home by just obtaining the digital data through the Internet.

In this case, the digital data, not the 3D-printed objects, have value, although 3D-printed objects are the final products that consumers obtain. Therefore, a consumer pays for digital data and not real objects. As businesses that sell consumers digital data for 3D printers to produce real objects at home become more widespread, the copyright

© Springer International Publishing AG 2017
Y.Q. Shi et al. (Eds.): IWDW 2016, LNCS 10082, pp. 370–378, 2017.
DOI: 10.1007/978-3-319-53465-7_27

of the digital data for producing the real object using 3D printer is also becoming important because once consumers obtain digital data, they can easily produce any number of final products themselves.

To protect copyrights for digital content such as music and image, some techniques such as digital watermarking have been developed [3–5]. Moreover, digital watermarking for 3D content has also been developed [6, 7]. However, copyright protecting techniques developed so far cannot be applied to cases where real objects are produced from digital content by consumers because digital watermarking is only read out from digital content and cannot be read out after real objects are produced.

We proposed a technique that can protect the copyrights of digital data for homemade products using digital fabrication technologies such as those in 3D printers [8–11]. It embeds information on copyrights inside real objects produced by 3D printers by forming fine structures inside the objects that cannot be observed from the outside.

Some previous studies also proposed a technique of embedding information into real objects fabricated with 3D printer, however, in that study, the part that includes information was produced separately from the body part and after producing, they were combined [12]. In contrast, in our technique, fine structures are integrally formed with the body, therefore, it does not need additional process.

We also proposed a technique that can non-destructively read out information from inside real objects using thermography [8–11]. We conducted experiments to confirm its feasibility.

Although we demonstrated the feasibility of the technique we developed for copyright protection for 3D printing, we need some alternative non-destructive readout techniques. This is because many kinds of methods of fabrication are expected to be used for 3D printing and internal states such as density differ depending on the method of fabrication and the technique we proposed will probably not be effective for all kinds of fabrication methods.

This paper presents a new non-destructive readout technique that uses a near infrared camera. It also describes the experiment we conducted to demonstrate its feasibility.

2 Embedding Information Inside Real Fabricated Objects and Reading It Using a Near Infrared Camera

2.1 Embedding Information

Figure 1 outlines the basic concept underlying the technique we proposed [8]. The content creator or provider produces the digital data of the object for 3D printing using 3D-CAD or 3D-CG tools. The copyright information for the digital data is then integrated into the content data by providers.

When a customer purchases digital data through the Internet and 3D-prints an object at home, fine structures are simultaneously formed inside the physical 3D object in accordance with the copyright information that is integrated with digital data of the object by the provider. If content providers can analyze these structures inside the

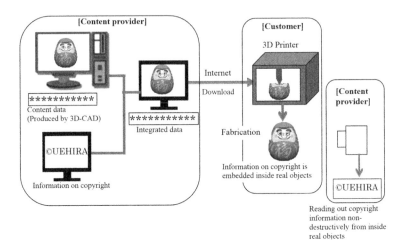

Fig. 1. Basic concept underlying proposed technique

object from the outside, they can find out the information embedded by providers. Therefore, these structures work as watermarking hidden inside the physical object, that is, this has an effect of restraining illegal copies or production.

The easiest and simplest way of expressing information is by using fine structures inside objects to form character shaped structures. However, this can also be easily observed by people who are trying to illegally produce objects. Another way is to form code that is encoded from character information. Figure 2 shows a simple example of this method. A 3D-printed object contains fine domains whose physical characteristics such as optical, acoustic, or heat conduction differ from the body of the object. For example, 3-D printers using fused deposition modeling can fabricate fine cavities inside 100% filled objects, and the cavities and bodies of the objects differ in heat conduction. The disposition of the fine domain expresses this information. Although there are various ways of expressing information due to the disposition of the fine domain, one example is where binary data, "1" or "0", are expressed due the fine domain existing or not in a designated position, as shown in Fig. 2. Therefore, we can expect to read out these embedded binary data using some measures utilizing the difference in physical characteristics between the fine domain and the body material of the object.

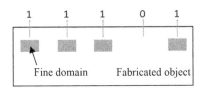

Fig. 2. Example of expressing information. Binary data, "1" or "0", are expressed due to the fine domain existing or not in a designated position inside a fabricated object.

2.2   Reading Embedded Information Using a Near Infrared Camera

There are various methods for analyzing the structures inside fabricated object from the outside non-destructively depending on the characteristics of the fine domains. In this study, we studied the method that uses transparent images.

We presuppose the use of plastic resin as material in this study because many conventional widespread 3D printers use it. Plastic transmutes light although a part of the light is scattered. Usually, plastic resin of a 3D-printed object has very low density because minimal materials are used and the fabrication time is shortened, and little light is scattered in low density material. Therefore, if we form high-density regions inside a low-density object as fine domains and illuminate this object from one side by strong light and capture a transparent image of it from the other side with a camera as shown in Fig. 3, fine domains in the image can be expected to be captured as regions darker than the other region since little light passes through them because most light is scattered there.

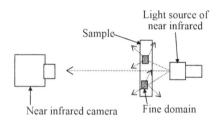

Fig. 3.   Reading embedded information using a near infrared camera

We cannot see inside in usual ambient light because the surface shell of the object has high density and most light is scattered there. Therefore, we can hide the information inside the object. Then, we can see the fine domain inside the object only when illuminating it using strong light.

However, since a large part of light is scattered in the shell, the transparent image will be unclear. Therefore, we used near infrared light because it has a longer wavelength than visible light, and the longer the wavelength of the light, the less light is scattered. Therefore, using near infrared light is expected to make the transparent image clearer than using visible light.

3   Experiments

We conducted experiments to evaluate the feasibility of the method we proposed. We produced samples with a stereolithographic 3D printer and polylactide (PLA) resin was used as their material. Figure 4 shows the layout of the sample we used in an experiment, which was $50 \times 50 \times 10$ mm. The domains were $1 \times 1 \times 8$ mm and $2 \times 2 \times 8$ mm. The spaces between the domains were 1 mm and 2 mm. Therefore, by combining two sizes and two spaces, there were four domain groups as shown in Fig. 4 and Table 1. The domains extended from bottom to top shells.

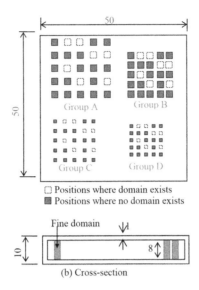

Fig. 4. Layout of the fine domains in sample used in experiment (numeric values are in mm)

Table 1. Layout parameters of domains in sample

	W	S
Group A	2	2
B	2	1
C	1	2
D	1	1

(mm)

W: Size of domain
S: Space between domains

Figure 5 shows the inside of the object. It contains walls that sustain the structure, and no material is inside the shell except for these walls and fine domains.

We used different colored PLAs because transmissivity of the PLA for near infrared light was expected to strongly depend on the color of PLA raisin.

Figure 6 shows the experimental setup. We used a near infrared camera with a InGaAs sensor that had 128 × 128 pixels. The sensor was sensitive to near infrared light with a wavelength ranging from 800 nm to 1700 nm.

The light source with LEDs that emitted near infrared light with a 840 nm wavelength was used to illuminate the samples. The spot of the light beam of the light source was about 30 mm, so we took an image of each group of the domains since we could not capture an image of the whole area of image of the sample.

For reference, we took a transparent image of the orange sample by using visible light. The experimental setup was the same as that shown in Fig. 6. We used a white

Fine domain

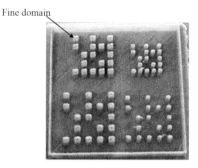

Fig. 5. Photograph of the inside sample

Sample   Light source

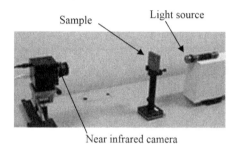

Near infrared camera

Fig. 6. Photograph of experimental setup

light that had almost the same size and shape as the near infrared light shown in Fig. 6. We used a digital camera with 4608 × 3456 pixels.

4 Results and Discussion

Figure 7 shows images of the samples captured with the near infrared light camera. These are for domain groups C and D, where domain size is 1 × 1 mm. Figure 7(a) shows the original images of Sample 1, which was blue, and Fig. 7(b) shows the image with enhanced contrast. Figure 7(b)–(e) show the images for Samples 2–4, each of which has a different color. It can be seen from Fig. 7 that the clarity of the domain image depends on the color of the sample as we expected, and we can see clear domain images for blue and green samples. We can see the existence or non-existence of the domains at designated positions clearly in those images. On the other hand, those for red and orange samples are less clear than those for blue and green samples. Even so, we can still see the existence or non-existence of the domains at designated positions, however.

These results suggest that information of a few tens of bits per square centimeter can be embedded, and if objects are several centimeters in size, enough information for copyright protection can be embedded.

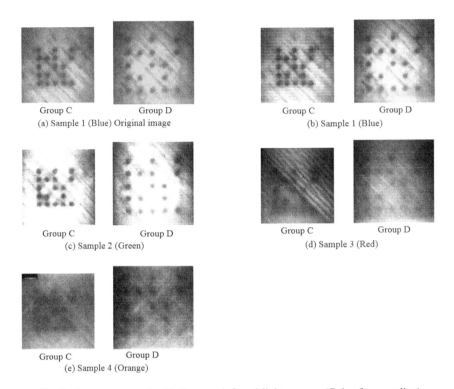

Group C   Group D
(a) Sample 1 (Blue) Original image

Group C   Group D
(b) Sample 1 (Blue)

Group C   Group D
(c) Sample 2 (Green)

Group C   Group D
(d) Sample 3 (Red)

Group C   Group D
(e) Sample 4 (Orange)

Fig. 7. Images captured with the near infrared light camera (Color figure online)

Figure 8 shows images captured with the digital camera using white light. We can barely see the pattern of domains in these images shown. The reason for this is thought to be that visible light is scattered more than near infrared light.

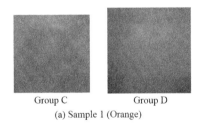

Group C   Group D
(a) Sample 1 (Orange)

Fig. 8. Images captured with digital camera using visible white light source (Color figure online)

In future work, we have to study from the point of view of exact spectral transmission characteristics of the material and investigate the dependence of image clarity on the wavelength of near infrared light because we used only light with a 840 nm wavelength. Moreover, optimum layout and some other conditions including the size of the domain have to be clarified in future work because the layout in Fig. 4 is only one example.

5 Conclusions

We previously proposed a technique that can protect the copyright of digital data for 3D-printed products. It embeds copyright information inside 3D-printed objects by using fine structures inside objects. In this paper, we proposed a technique that can non-destructively read out information from inside real objects from transparent images of the object using near infrared light. We conducted experiments where we formed fine domains as fine structures inside objects to express binary information depending on whether the domains existed or not at designated positions. The experimental results demonstrated that existence or non-existence of the domains at designated positions can be observed for 1×1 mm domains, and we could confirm that enough information can be embedded to protect copyrights for the original 3D data of the fabricated object. These results demonstrate the feasibility of our proposed technique.

We intend to clarify the optimum conditions for this technique in future work.

Acknowledgments. This work was supported by JSPS KAKENHI Grant Number 15H02707.

References

1. Berman, B.: 3-D printing: the new industrial revolution. Bus. Horiz. **55**(2), 155–162 (2012)
2. Garrett, B.: 3D printing, "New Economic Paradigms and Strategic Shifts". Glob. Policy **5**(1), 70–75 (2014)
3. Cox, I.J., Kilian, J., Leighton, F.T., Shamoon, T.: Secure spread spectrum watermarking for multimedia. IEEE Trans. Image Process. **6**(12), 1673–1687 (1997)
4. Swanson, M.D., Swanson, M.D., Kobayashi, M., Tewfik, A.H.: Multimedia data-embedding and watermarking technologies. Proc. IEEE **86**(6), 1064–1087 (1998)
5. Hartung, M., Kutter, M.: Multimedia watermarking techniques. Proc. IEEE **87**(7), 1079–1107 (1999)
6. Alface, P.R., Macq, B.: From 3D mesh data hiding to 3D shape blind and robust watermarking: a survey. In: Shi, Y.Q. (ed.) Transactions on Data Hiding and Multimedia Security II. LNCS, vol. 4499, pp. 91–115. Springer, Heidelberg (2007). doi:10.1007/978-3-540-73092-7_5
7. Ai, Q.S., Liu, Q., Zhou, Z.D., Yang, L., Xie, S.Q.: A new digital watermarking scheme for 3D triangular mesh models. Signal Process. **89**(11), 2159–2170 (2009)
8. Suzuki, M., Silapasuphakornwong, P., Unno, H., Uehira, K., Takashima, Y.: Copyright protection for 3D printing by embedding information inside real fabricated objects. In: The International Conference on Computer Vision Theory and Application, pp. 180–185 (2015)
9. Okada, A., Silapasuphakornwong, P., Suzuki, M., Torii, H., Takashima, Y., Uehira, K.: Non-destructively reading out information embedded inside real objects by using far-infrared light. In: Proceedings of SPIE 9599: Applications of Digital Image Processing XXXVIII, vol. 9599, pp. 95992V-1–95992V-7 (2015)
10. Silapasuphakornwong, P., Suzuki, M., Unno, H., Torii, H., Uehira, K., Takashima, Y.: Nondestructive readout of copyright information embedded in objects fabricated with 3-D printers. In: Shi, Y.-Q., Kim, H.J., Pérez-González, F., Echizen, I. (eds.) IWDW 2015. LNCS, vol. 9569, pp. 232–238. Springer, Heidelberg (2016). doi:10.1007/978-3-319-31960-5_19

11. Suzuki, M., Silapasuphakornwong, P., Takashima, Y., Torii, H., Unno, H., Uehira, K.: Technique for protecting copyrights of digital data for 3-D printing, and its application to low infill density objects. In: The Eighth International Conferences on Advances in Multimedia, pp. 56–59 (2016)
12. Willis, K.D., Wilson, A.D.: InfraStructs: fabricating information inside physical objects for imaging in the terahertz region. ACM Trans. Graph. 32(4), 138-1–13810 (2013)

Watermarking with Fixed Decoder for Aesthetic 2D Barcode

Minoru Kuribayashi[1]([✉]), Ee-Chien Chang[2], and Nobuo Funabiki[1]

[1] Graduate School of Natural Science and Technology, Okayama University,
3-1-1 Tsushima-naka, Kita-ku, Okayama 700-8530, Japan
{kminoru,funabiki}@okayama-u.ac.jp
[2] School of Computing, National University of Singapore,
13 Computing Drive, Singapore S117417, Republic of Singapore
changec@comp.nus.edu.sg

Abstract. An aesthetic 2D-barcode, e.g. QR code, carries a given message in the payload and yet its visual appearance resembles another given logo image. The requirement of embedding a message in a "cover" image is similar to digital watermarking but with a crucial difference that, for the aesthetic 2D-barcode, the decoder is predetermined and fixed. Hence the designs and performances of the aesthetic 2D-barcode heavily rely on the predetermined decoder. In this paper, we focus on the underlying systematic encoding function in QR code. We first formulate a framework that optimizes the visual appearance of the codeword and yet meets the coding requirement. Since finding such an optimal codeword is computationally expensive, we next propose a heuristic to search for a feasible solution, and incorporate image processing operations to enhance the visual appearance. Although our method is designed for QR code, our approach can be applied to other 2D-barcodes that employ similar coding mechanisms of error correction code.

1 Introduction

QR code is a machine-readable optical 2D barcode which can be a carrier in conveying information to mobile devices equipped with camera. Although the effectiveness of such visual channel rely on hardware that are not widely available for consumers a few years ago, recent enhancement of camera quality and processing power on consumer mobile phones has improved reliability and responsiveness in decoding QR code. Together with the freely available QR code decoder, and awareness of QR code among consumers, QR code is gaining wide adoption in marketing industry.

Visually, a QR code is an arrangement of seemingly random white and black squares (a square corresponds to a module in QR code) that makes no sense to human viewers. Nevertheless, it is possible to make a QR code visually appealing without significantly degrade machine-readability. Such a QR code is called *aesthetic QR code* or *artistic QR code.*

© Springer International Publishing AG 2017
Y.Q. Shi et al. (Eds.): IWDW 2016, LNCS 10082, pp. 379–392, 2017.
DOI: 10.1007/978-3-319-53465-7_28

1.1   Background

There are a few basic mechanisms to embed an image onto a QR code. (1) The first mechanism exploits the error correcting capability of QR code by flipping a few modules, so that the resulting QR code resembles the intended logo image [6,7,10]. (2) The second mechanism modifies the square modules according to the pixel of the logo image, without significantly degrading the readability of each module. For instance, Visualead [11] and LogoQ [5] keep a concentric region of modules untouched and uniformly blend the neighboring regions with pixels of an image preserving the original contrast. (3) The third mechanism utilizes the padding modules, which corresponds to unused payload, to embed the logo image [12,13]. A software QR-JAM MAKER [8] that employs this mechanism is publicly available. (4) The forth mechanism extends the third mechanism by modifying the encoding function of Reed-Solomon (RS) code, such that the logo image are not restricted to the padding modules [3,4].

Some other works studied combination of the above mechanisms. Chu et al. [1] applied the half-toning technique for displaying image to produce an aesthetic QR code. Fang et al. [2] proposed a framework that considers the sampling process and error correction of the decoder, and formulated aesthetic QR code generation as watermark embedding with fixed decoder. Zhang et al. [14] proposed two-stage approach that is a combination of module-based and pixel-based embedding. Even though these methods can enhance the visual appearance, they reduce the noise-like appearance at the center of image by using error correcting capability or shape of modules. If the number of modules which pixel values are different from a given logo image are small, the visual appearance is good in general. The essential solution should be the reduction of the number of such modules.

1.2   Our Contribution

In this paper, we focus on the underlying RS error correction code in QR code, and attempt to modify the RS encoding process so as to minimize the visual distance from the logo image. We adopt the watermarking-based formulation [2] to generalize the above-mentioned third and forth mechanism. Specifically, given a message d, a logo image I, and a distance function, we seek for a codeword c, such that the distance of c from the logo image is minimized, and c carries the message d. This can be viewed as a digital watermarking process, whereby the host image is the logo image I, the watermarking message is d, the watermarked image is the output c, and the distance function gives the visual distance between I and c.

We consider cases where the message d is shorter than the capacity of the RS code. Hence there is a one to many mapping from the messages to the RS codewords. For instance, version 10 of QR code can embed up to 174 characters at H level. Nevertheless, the actual message d could be less than that, for example, d can be

"en.wikipedia.org/wiki/QR_code"

which consists of only 30 characters (including the end-of-line character), and the remaining 144 characters would be discarded after decoding and thus can be arbitrary values. As a result, there are many possible codewords being mapped to a message. Certainly, in cases where the length of d is largest possible, then there is only a single codeword correspond to the message, and this codeword can be found using the typical RS encoding. For short d, we can search for the visually best codeword (i.e. the codeword with the minimum visual distance from the logo image) in the subspace of codewords that maps to d. Unfortunately, the space can be large and it is not clear how to efficiently find the optimal with respect to the visual distance function. In view of the difficulty, we give a heuristic to search for a good feasible solution. Our heuristic employs technique in systematic code and search for codewords with certain symbols fixed.

Note that in our formulation, since the output c is a codeword, there is no lost of error correcting capability. In other words, the robustness is equivalent to the unmodified QR code. Also note that the RS codebook is fixed and cannot be modified for better performance. This restriction is due to the constrain that QR code is a standard, and thus the QR code readers are fixed and cannot be modified. This is in contrast to watermarking problem where both the encoder and decoder can be part of the solution.

We take weighted distance as the visual distance between the logo image I and the output c. While the weights of this function can be specified by the user, we give an image processing-based methods to automatically find the region of interest (ROI) and derive a good choice of the weights.

To further improve the visual appearance of the final QR code, we also modify the shape and pixel values of the individual module. However, note that the modification of the module could degrade the readability of the module. Hence, unlike previous steps that do not lower the robustness of the aesthetic QR code compare to the original QR code, this last step could lower the robustness.

2 Preliminaries

2.1 QR Code

A standard QR code is composed of square modules which are black and white patterns representing 1 bit information. The module is the smallest component of a QR code. The size of a QR code is controlled by the version number v. The number of modules for a version v is $(17 + 4v) \times (17 + 4v)$. For the synchronization of position at the detection, the QR code has function patterns (i.e. finder pattern, alignment pattern, and timing pattern).

The QR code uses the RS code with 4 levels of error correction capability: L, M, Q, and H in the increasing order. Each error correction level can correct symbols up to about 7%, 15%, 25% and 30% to all symbols of the QR code. Because of the standardization, the number of codewords and their constructions expressed by (n, k, d) are uniquely determined for the version number and the error correction level, where n, k, and d stand for the code length, the number of information symbols, and the minimum distance satisfying $d = n - k + 1$. The code length n is increased with the version number, while k is decreased with the error correction level.

Considering the readability by optical camera devices, the number of black and white modules should be balanced in the QR code. There are eight mask patterns that changes the bits according to their coordinates in order to make the QR code easier to read. At the encoding, each element of a selected mask pattern is XORed with a current module.

2.2   Modified RS Encoding Function

The QR code standard adopts systematic RS error correction codes. Hence, for the (n, k, d)-RS code, the k information symbols appear in the leading symbols of the codeword. In addition, in the QR code adoption, the length of the message can be shorter than k, even if the (n, k, d) code is adopted. In such cases, the short message is to be padded with *padding symbols*. Such padding symbols can be arbitrary and is typically randomly chosen.

Specifically, consider the (n, k, d)-code, and let $\boldsymbol{d} = (d_1, d_2, \ldots, d_k)$ be information symbols, and $\boldsymbol{p} = (p_1, p_2, \ldots, p_{n-k})$ the encoded parity symbols. In other words, the codeword $\boldsymbol{c}$ for $\boldsymbol{d}$ is

$$\boldsymbol{c} = (c_1, c_2, \ldots, c_n) = (d_1, d_2, \ldots, d_k, p_1, p_2, \ldots p_{n-k}). \tag{1}$$

As mentioned above, QR code allows shorter message. When a message contains $\hat{k}(< k)$ symbols, the remaining $k - \hat{k}$ are to be padded. The length $\hat{k}$ is implicitly indicated by the present of the EOF (end-of-file) special symbol, which is called *terminator* in the specification of QR code. For convenience, we assume that the $\hat{k}$-symbol message includes the EOF symbol. If no error is occurred, the leading k symbols are output by the decoder. If the number of errors is within the error correcting capability, the k-symbol message (including the padding) will be correctly decoded from the corrupted codeword.

By employing systematic coding, we can choose k positions and decide the corresponding symbols in the codeword $\boldsymbol{c}$, while the RS encoder decides the remaining $(n - k)$ parity symbols. Since a standard QR code decoder would output the leading k symbols, for correct decoding, the codeword must be of the form:

$$\boldsymbol{c} = (d_1, d_2, \ldots, d_{\hat{k}}, c_{\hat{k}+1}, \ldots, c_n). \tag{2}$$

Now, since we can choose k positions, and $\hat{k}$ of them are already occupied, we still have $k - \hat{k}$ positions that we can arbitrary decide their corresponding symbols. This flexibility can be exploited to improve the visual quality of the QR code. This observations is essentially the basis of the third and forth mechanisms mentioned in Sect. 1.

3   Proposed Framework on Error Correction Code

3.1   Definitions and Notations

Logo image and modules.   Let us call the image to be embedded to the barcode the *logo image* and denote it as $\boldsymbol{I}$. We represent the two dimensional image as an one-dimensional sequence of sub-images $I = (I_1, I_2, \ldots, I_{8n})$, such that each sub-image corresponds to a square region in the image, which is also the region occupied by a module in the QR code. Let us call $b = (b_1, b_2, \ldots, b_{8n})$ the binarised logo image, where each b_j is a binary value that is derived from I_j using some functions. We can viewed b as a lower resolution binary image of the logo image. For a QR code with $8n$ modules, let us denote the modules as $m = (m_1, m_2, \ldots, m_{8n})$ where each M_i is a binary value, with 0 represents a black module, and 1 represents a white module. Ideally, we would want to generate a QR code where the m is visually as close as possible to the binarised image b.

Unless otherwise specified, we consider a (n, k, d)-RS code with 8-bit symbols. In QR code adoption, the modules in m are grouped, so that 8 modules are grouped into a 8-bit symbol in the RS codeword. The QR code standard specifies the grouping and we omit the details in this discussion. Let $c = (c_1, c_2, \ldots, c_n)$ be the generated RS codeword, which in turn determines the modules in m. Let us similarly group the bits in a binarised logo image using the same grouping, and call $B = (B_1, B_2, \ldots, B_N)$ the image symbols, where each B_j is an 8-bit symbol.

Reed-Solomon (RS) code. Although the RS error-correcting capacity can encode k symbols, QR code adoption allows message $d = (d_1, d_2, \ldots, d_{\hat{k}})$ with length $\hat{k}$ shorter than k. This is achieved by, after successfully decoded the k symbols, the decoder only outputs the leading $\hat{k}$ symbols, in which the last symbol represents End-Of-File that terminates the string. During encoding, a standard encoder will pad the message with $n - \hat{k}$ padding symbols, and from the padded information symbols (a total of k symbols), the encoder generates the unique $n - k$ parity symbols. Figure 1 depicts the arrangement of these components.

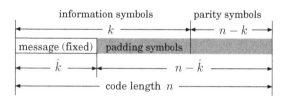

Fig. 1. A systematically encoded RS codeword, where the first $\hat{k}$ symbols are message to be encoded in a QR code.

As highlighted before, padding provides redundancy for us to find a QR code that visually resembles the logo image. Although the decoder is fixed, the encoder has the freedom to set arbitrary values for the $k - \hat{k}$ padding symbols. This flexibility is exploited by the third mechanism described in Sect. 1.

Moreover, instead of restricting to positions at the $(k - \hat{k})$ padding symbols, it is also possible to set arbitrary values for *any* $(k - \hat{k})$ symbols other than the message, as illustrated in Fig. 2. In other words, when given a $\hat{k}$-symbol message,

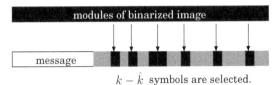

Fig. 2. Composition of information symbols in RS codeword, where $k - \hat{k}$ symbols are fixed and the shaded symbols are calculated by a modified encoding method.

the encoder can choose any $(n - \hat{k})$ positions, other than the first $\hat{k}$ positions occupied by the message, and set them to arbitrary values of the encoder's choice. Note that in total, symbols in k positions are fixed: $\hat{k}$ positions from the message, and $(k - \hat{k})$ chosen by the encoder. Now, there is an unique RS codeword with the values at this k positions and it can be efficiently found using systematic RS encoding. This observation is exploited in [4] and is classified as the forth mechanism in Sect. 1.

We highlight that, for optimal visual quality, it is not straightforward in choosing these $(k - \hat{k})$ positions. One may attempt to employ a greedy approach to select the $(k - \hat{k})$ most visually important positions, however, this does not guarantee optimality since the parity symbols also contributed to the visual quality.

Visual distance. We measure the visual quality of a QR code by a distant function from the logo image. Given a codeword c, and the corresponding modules $m = (m_1, m_2, \ldots, m_{8n})$ we measure its distant from the logo image $I = (I_1, I_2, \ldots, I_{8n})$. In this paper, we consider a form of weighted Euclidean distance. The distant is

$$D_w(m, I) = \sum_{i=1}^{8n} w_i \hat{D}(m_i, l_i) \tag{3}$$

where $w = (w_1, w_2, \ldots, w_{8n})$ is a sequence of weights, and $\hat{D}(\cdot, \cdot)$ is another distant function that measures the visual distant between a square module and a square sub-image. Any such distant function can be adopted and thus its choice is omitted in this section. The weight of an module indicates its weightage in visual appearance, and is to be specified by the application. Hence, they are considered as input in our coding problem. In the next section, we also propose automated methods to determine such weights from the logo image. Note that our formulation can also be extended to other form of distance function, as long as, given a codeword, the distance can be efficiently computed.

3.2 Proposed Formulation

In this section, we present a proposed method for the generation of aesthetic QR code. As explained in Sect. 3.1, for the binarized image $b = (b_1, b_2, \ldots, b_{8n})$, our objective is to efficiently find the similar RS codeword c in a sense such that the visual distance is minimum. This can be interpreted as the watermarking process. For a given logo image I, the message d is embedded in the first $\hat{k}$ symbols using a secret parameter and output c as a watermarked image which is visually similar to I.

In general, some parts of an image are less important than the others. If we give each weight for the purpose of classification at each module, we will be able to find the most beautiful aesthetic QR code. Recall that each symbol is composed of 8 modules. An example of the layout is illustrated in Fig. 3. The white modules represent the message to be encoded in a QR code. The black modules are the selected $(k - \hat{k})$ symbols, namely the number of selected pixels are $8(k - \hat{k})$ in total. The shaded modules can be uniquely calculated from the white and black modules using a modified encoding function. In the proposed method, the weights $w_{i,j}$ are measured at module by modules. The sum of the weights $w_{i,j}$ of 8 modules, which is denoted by W_i, should be considered for the selection of $k - \hat{k}$ symbols at the encoding.

The weights W_i indicate priorities for generating candidates of aesthetic QR codes. Notice that even if $k - \hat{k}$ symbols which have highest $k - \hat{k}$ symbols are selected and its codeword is generated, the other symbols are not always close to the binarized image. In order to find the closest one which weighted Euclidean distance becomes minimum, we still need to generate some candidates. The proposed method is composed of the following steps to find the best one among a restricted number of candidates.

1. Calculate weights W_i for symbols at the position $i \in [\hat{k} + 1, n]$.
2. Find the top $(k - \hat{k} + t)$ of the weights, where t is a control parameter.
3. Select the symbols positions which symbols have the top $(k - \hat{k} + t)$ weights. The set of positions is denoted by $\mathcal{P}$.
4. Among the combination of $k - \hat{k}$ out of $k - \hat{k} + t$ selected from $\mathcal{P}$, find the codeword which weighted Euclidean distance becomes minimum.

For instance, when the version is $v = 5$ and the error correction level is L, the number of information symbols is $k = 106$. In case of $\hat{k} = 50$, the number of candidates is 56 if $t = 1$ and it is 1540 if $t = 2$. For a fixed parameter t, it is possible to use a deterministic algorithm such that the weighted Euclidean distance are checked for all candidates of codewords generated by the above strategy. If one wants to control the computational costs, a probabilistic algorithm should be employed to select some candidates among them. For a given parameter t, the candidates are randomly generated among the possible combinations of symbols whose have top $(k - \hat{k} + t)$-th weights.

The difficulty in the proposed method is how to calculate the weights W_i. There are several measurements for calculating weights under the consideration

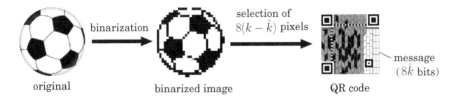

original   binarized image   QR code

Fig. 3. Examples of layout of modules in a QR code version 5, where black modules are the selected $8(k - \hat{k})$ pixels of binarized image and the shaded modules are calculated by a modified encoding function.

of visual appearance. In the next section, we show some image processing operations for calculating the weights. It is noted that the proposed method is a heuristic and the solution find may not be optimal.

4   Enhancement Using Image Processing Techniques

Considering the characteristics of the image, some signal processing operations are performed to preserve the visual quality of aesthetic QR code. For the beautification, each module of QR code should be represented by more than a single pixel. In order to reflect the pixels of original image, the resolution of the module should be considered.

4.1   Module Shape

Because a high quality camera device is equipped on smart phones, the accuracy of the QR code reader is improved. With the increase of pixels in one module, the binarization can be flexibly performed considering the effects of noise. Typical QR code readers use a sampling function to obtain the intensity of a module. One way is to average a few pixels surrounding the center of module, and to judge black or white using a certain predefined threshold. In the proposed method, a Gaussian-like sampling function is employed.

Suppose that a module is composed of $\gamma \times \gamma$ pixels. For convenience, we assume that γ is an odd number. The pixel intensity to be displayed at the module is $f(x, y)$, $-\lfloor \gamma/2 \rfloor \leq x, y \leq \lfloor \gamma/2 \rfloor$, namely $f(0, 0)$ is the center of a module. Let α be an intensity and σ^2 be a variance. Then, the Gaussian value $g(x, y)$ is given as follows.

$$g(x, y) = \alpha \exp \left\{ \frac{-(x^2 + y^2)}{2\sigma^2} \right\}, \tag{4}$$

where $\alpha \in [0, 127]$. The pixel intensity is modified based on the black/white modules in the following rule.

$$f'(x, y) = \begin{cases} \min \{ f(x, y), \theta - g(x, y) \} & \text{(black)} \\ \max \{ f(x, y), \theta + g(x, y) + 1 \} & \text{(white)} \end{cases}, \tag{5}$$

where θ is a threshold for classifying black and white. Typically $\theta = 127$. It is noticed that if $\alpha = 127$, $\sigma = \infty$, and $\theta = 127$, the pixel intensity in a module becomes 0 or 255.

With the increase of γ, the resolution of aesthetic QR code becomes high, and hence, the visual appearance can be improved. However, if a QR code is displayed or printed in a small size, the improvement of the appearance is limited. In order to display an image beautifully, the resolution of the image should be changed according to the actual size of generating QR code. For instance, when the version of QR code is $v = 5$ and $\gamma = 9$, the actual size is 333×333 pixels because $(17 + 4 \cdot 5) \cdot 9 = 333$.

The center region of each module is important to guarantee the readability of QR code. With the increase of γ, the outer region of each module becomes less important. By introducing a parameter T, the modification of pixel intensity is controlled at the outer region of module to improve the visual appearance.

$$f^{\star}(x,y) = \begin{cases} f'(x,y) & \text{if } g(x,y) > T \\ f(x,y) & \text{otherwise} \end{cases} \tag{6}$$

It is noticed that $g(x,y) > 0$ from Eq. (5). Therefore, if $T = 0$, then $f^{\star}(x,y) = f'(x,y)$.

4.2   Region of Interest

It is reasonable to assume that an image to be displayed has an ROI. Because the ROIs are more important than the other regions, we manage to separate ROIs from an image and to give high weights under the following encoding policy. If a module has a high weight, it should be selected as the information symbol of RS code at the modified encoding method.

There are some approaches to classify the ROIs from an still image. In this study, we employ the foreground and face detection algorithms included in the OpenCV library[1]. One famous algorithm to detect foreground is known as GrabCut [9]. The GrabCut is interactive algorithm to extract the foreground. Even though the requirements of interaction are small, the interactive setting of parameters becomes the barrier of automatic generation of aesthetic QR codes. Hence, in this study, we fix parameters allowing some detection errors.

The well-known method to detect a face is the Haar-cascade detection in OpenCV. Because the face detection algorithm only outputs a rectangle region, some modules in the region are not the face. For simplicity, we give high weights to the modules inside of the rectangle.

The outer edge region of an image is also less important than the center region. Thus, high weights are given to the center and the weight becomes lower accordingly. The illustration of the weighting strategy is shown in Fig. 4.

---

[1] http://opencv.org [Online; accessed 17-August-2016].

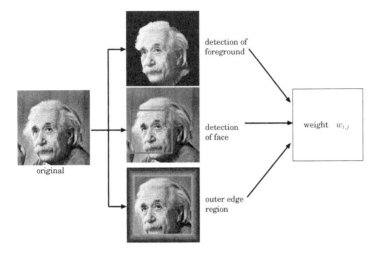

Fig. 4. Weighting strategy in the proposed method.

4.3 Variance of Pixels in Single Module

In [4], the Laplacian filter detects noisy regions, which are mainly edge regions of an image. However, the filter is performed on the binarized image, and the edge regions sometimes retain important features of an image. Therefore, in this study, we measure the variance of pixels in a single module. As explained in Sect. 4.1, when the number of pixels in a module is γ^2, some modules may be modified to black/white which intensity is determined by the Eq. (5). If the variance in a module is large, the changes of intensities do not seriously degrade the visual quality. Therefore, we calculate the weight according to the variance.

5 Examples

In this section, we show some examples of generated aesthetic QR codes. For convenience of comparison, some parameters are fixed in the generated examples in this section. $\theta = 96$, $\sigma^2 = 0.6$, and the message to be encoded is "http://www.iwdw.net". We implemented a probabilistic method that selects 100 codewords from the candidates under the constraints explained in Sect. 3.2. For its simplicity, we use the Hamming distance as the distance function in this experiment.

5.1 Weighting Parameter

As mentioned above, there are four parameters to calculate the weight $w_{i,j}$ for each module. The weights $w_{i,j}^{FG}$ for foreground/background are given by

$$w_{i,j}^{FG} = \begin{cases} 128 & \text{(foreground)} \\ 0 & \text{(background)} \end{cases}, \tag{7}$$

and the weights $w_{i,j}^{face}$ for face detection are given by

$$w_{i,j}^{face} = \begin{cases} 128 & \text{(faceregion)} \\ 0 & \text{(others)} \end{cases}. \tag{8}$$

For the δ-th outer edge region, the weights $w_{i,j}^{out}$ are given by

$$w_{i,j}^{out} = \begin{cases} 128 - 16\delta & (\delta \leq 8) \\ 128 & \text{(others)} \end{cases}. \tag{9}$$

The variance $\sigma_{i,j}^2$ of pixels at the (i,j)-th module is calculated by

$$\sigma_{i,j}^2 = \frac{1}{\gamma^2} \sum \left(f(x,y) - \bar{f}(x,y) \right)^2, \tag{10}$$

where $\bar{f}(x,y)$ is the average of pixel intensity $f(x,y)$ in the module. The weights $w_{i,j}^{var}$ are calculated from the standard derivation $\sigma_{i,j}$.

$$w_{i,j}^{var} = \min\{\sigma_{i,j}, 128\} \tag{11}$$

Using these parameters, the weight $w_{i,j}$ is obtained.

$$w_{i,j} = w_{i,j}^{FG} + w_{i,j}^{face} + w_{i,j}^{out} + w_{i,j}^{var} \tag{12}$$

5.2   Generated QR Code

Figure 5 shows the examples by changing the size of modules γ, where D_H stands for the Hamming distance and the version is $v = 5$. For a fair comparison, the scale of image is adjusted to display in this figure. It is observed that the appearance is almost similar when $\gamma \geq 9$. Generally, the displayed size of QR code is not large. So we can say that $\gamma = 9$ shows sufficient resolution for aesthetic QR code.

Figure 6 shows the visual appearance for different threshold T, where $\gamma = 9$. It is observed that some module shapes in Fig. 6(a) are square. It means all pixels in a module is replaced by the Gaussian-like pattern, which degrade the visual quality much worse than the other two cases (b) and (c). On the other hand, when $T = 16$, only small center region of a module is replaced by the Gaussian-like pattern. In this case, the readability is dropped seriously. Hence, under this experimental condition, the threshold $T = 8$ shows a good trade-off.

The results of other images are shown in Figs. 7 and 8. Because the image in Fig. 7(a) shows a temple, no face is detected. Even in such a case, the ROI is roughly classified by the detection of foreground. Therefore, most of the modules which color is different from the original pixels are appeared at the outer edge region of an image. It is interesting to show that the face part of a logo image is also detected in Fig. 8. In addition, the Gaussian-like module shape helps to draw the curve lines in the logo image.

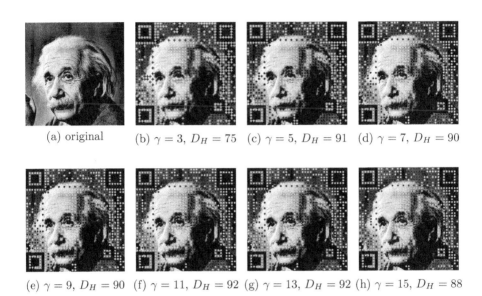

(a) original   (b) $\gamma = 3$, $D_H = 75$ (c) $\gamma = 5$, $D_H = 91$ (d) $\gamma = 7$, $D_H = 90$

(e) $\gamma = 9$, $D_H = 90$ (f) $\gamma = 11$, $D_H = 92$ (g) $\gamma = 13$, $D_H = 92$ (h) $\gamma = 15$, $D_H = 88$

Fig. 5. Examples of generated aesthetic QR code of version $5L$, where $T = 8$.

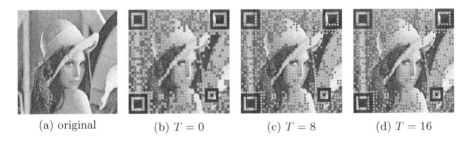

(a) original   (b) $T = 0$ (c) $T = 8$ (d) $T = 16$

Fig. 6. Comparison of visual appearance for the threshold T, where the version is $5M$, $\gamma = 9$, and $D_H = 164$.

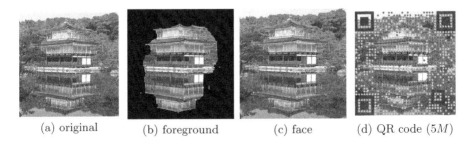

(a) original   (b) foreground   (c) face   (d) QR code ($5M$)

Fig. 7. Detection of ROI and the generated aesthetic QR code for an image "temple", where $T = 8$, $\gamma = 9$, and $D_H = 166$.

(a) original   (b) foreground   (c) face   (d) QR code ($5M$)

Fig. 8. Detection of ROI and the generated aesthetic QR code for an image "starbucks", where $T = 8$, $\gamma = 9$, and $D_H = 158$.

6 Conclusion Remarks

In this paper, we proposed a framework for generating beautiful aesthetic QR codes considering the characteristics of image to be displayed. In this framework, the basic method is the modification of systematic encoding function of RS code. Different from the Hamming distance, the visual distance should be introduced for the measurement. In order to find a best RS codeword for a given message and image, the proposed method requires weights to measure the visual distance under a certain criteria for evaluating the visual appearance.

We introduced two image processing operations to classify ROIs. (1) detection of foreground and (2) detection of face. In addition, the weights at the outer edge region are decreased considering the tendency such that such a region is less important than the centers. Considering the size of displayed/printed QR code, the resolution of each module is measured by experiment. Even though the readability is strongly dependent on the QR code reader and the environment of displayed/printed media, the Gaussian-like shape of module is suitable to represent black/white.

Acknowledgments. This research was partially supported by JSPS KAKENHI Grant Number JP16K00185.

References

1. Chu, H.K., Chang, C.S., Lee, R.R., Mitra, N.J.: Halftone QR codes. ACM Trans. Graph. **32**(6), 2171–2178 (2013)
2. Fang, C., Zhang, C., Chang, E.-C.: An optimization model for aesthetic two-dimensional barcodes. In: Gurrin, C., Hopfgartner, F., Hurst, W., Johansen, H., Lee, H., O'Connor, N. (eds.) MMM 2014. LNCS, vol. 8325, pp. 278–290. Springer, Heidelberg (2014). doi:10.1007/978-3-319-04114-8_24
3. Fujita, K., Kuribayashi, M., Morii, M.: Expansion of image displayable area in design QR code and its applications. In: Proceedings FIT 2011, pp. 517–5520 (2011)

4. Kuribayashi, M., Morii, M.: Enrichment of visual appearance of aesthetic QR code. In: Shi, Y.-Q., Kim, H.J., Pérez-González, F., Echizen, I. (eds.) IWDW 2015. LNCS, vol. 9569, pp. 220–231. Springer, Heidelberg (2016). doi:10.1007/978-3-319-31960-5_18

5. logoQ. http://logoq.net. Accessed 17 Aug 2016

6. Ono, S., Morinaga, K., Nakayama, S.: Two-dimensional barcode decoration based on real-coded genetic algorithm. In: Proceedings CEC 2008, pp. 1068–1073 (2008)

7. Ono, S., Nakayama, S.: A system for decorating QR code with facial image based on interactive evolutionary computation and case-based reasoning. In: Proceedings NaBIC 2010, pp. 401–406 (2010)

8. QR-JAM. https://www.risec.aist.go.jp/project/qrjam. Accessed 17 Aug 2016

9. Rother, C., Kolmogorov, V., Blake, A.: "GrabCut": Interactive foreground extraction using iterated graph cuts. ACM Trans. Graph. **23**(3), 309–314 (2004)

10. Samretwit, D., Wakahara, T.: Measurement of reading charactristics of multiplexed image in QR code. In: Proceedings INCoS 2011, pp. 552–557 (2011)

11. Visualead. http://www.visualead.com. Accessed 17 Aug 2016

12. Wakahara, T., Yamamoto, T.: Image processing of 2-dimensional barcode. In: Proceedings NBiS 2011, pp. 484–490 (2011)

13. Wakahara, T., Yamamoto, T., Ochi, H.: Image processing of dotted picture in the QR code of cellular phone. In: Proceedings 3PGCIC 2010, pp. 454–458 (2010)

14. Zhang, Y., Deng, S., Liu, Z., Wang, Y.: Aesthetic QR codes based on two-stage image blending. In: He, X., Luo, S., Tao, D., Xu, C., Yang, J., Hasan, M.A. (eds.) MMM 2015. LNCS, vol. 8936, pp. 183–194. Springer, Heidelberg (2015). doi:10.1007/978-3-319-14442-9_16

Two-Dimensional Histogram Modification for Reversible Data Hiding in Partially Encrypted H.264/AVC Videos

Dawen Xu[1(✉)], Yani Zhu[2], Rangding Wang[3], Jianjing Fu[4], and Kai Chen[1]

[1] School of Electronics and Information Engineering,
Ningbo University of Technology, Ningbo 315016, China
xdw@nbut.edu.cn
[2] College of Information Engineering, Zhejiang University of Technology,
Hangzhou, China
[3] CKC Software Lab, Ningbo University, Ningbo 315211, China
[4] College of New Media, Zhejiang University of Media and Communications,
Hangzhou 310018, China

Abstract. Due to the security and privacy-preserving requirements from cloud computing platforms, it is sometimes desired that the video content is accessible in encrypted form. Reversible data hiding in the encrypted domain has gained increasing attention, as it can perform data hiding in encrypted medias without decryption which preserves the confidentiality of the content. In this paper, an efficient reversible data hiding scheme for encrypted H.264/AVC videos is proposed. During H.264/AVC encoding, the intra-prediction mode (IPM), motion vector difference (MVD), and the sign bits of residue coefficients are encrypted using a standard stream cipher. Then, every two adjacent coefficients are grouped into coefficient pairs. Based on the resulting coefficient pairs, the data-hider may reversibly embed secret data into the encrypted H.264/AVC video by using two-dimensional histogram modification. In addition, dynamic threshold is utilized to determine the embedding region. With an encrypted video containing hidden data, data extraction can be carried out either in encrypted or decrypted domain. Experimental results demonstrate the superiority of the proposed scheme.

Keywords: Video encryption · Reversible data hiding · Two-dimensional histogram modification · H.264/AVC

1 Introduction

With the rapid developments occurring in cloud computing and mobile Internet, security and privacy protection become one of the most important issues that have to be addressed. Given that cloud services may attract more attacks and are vulnerable to untrustworthy system administrators, some sensitive information is preferable to be encrypted before being forwarded to the third party for further processing. Consequently, the data manager (e.g., the cloud provider) is authorized to access the

© Springer International Publishing AG 2017
Y.Q. Shi et al. (Eds.): IWDW 2016, LNCS 10082, pp. 393–406, 2017.
DOI: 10.1007/978-3-319-53465-7_29

encrypted version of video signal (i.e., ciphertext) instead of the original content. Signal processing in the encrypted domain is a new field of research aiming at developing a set of specific tools for processing encrypted data. For example, in some application scenarios, it is more promising to directly embed some additional information (e.g., authentication data or owner identity information) into the encrypted video for tampering detection or ownership declaration. To address this problem, researchers have been studying the possibility of performing data hiding directly in the encrypted domain.

In general, the cloud service provider has no right to introduce permanent distortion during data embedding in encrypted data. This implies that, for a legal receiver, the original plaintext content should be recovered without any error after image decryption and data extraction. To solve this problem, reversible data hiding (RDH) in encrypted domain is preferred. Although RDH techniques have been studied extensively [1–3], these techniques are suitable for unencrypted covers rather than encrypted covers. Nowadays, there is a considerable amount of scientific literature on data hiding into encrypted images, which can be divided into two categories, The first one is to VRAE (vacating room after encryption) [4–7], and the second one is to RRBE (reserving room before encryption) [8–11]. Although these works are very innovative, they cannot be directly applied to video because of video coding having its different structure.

The literature on data hiding into encrypted H.264/AVC streams is far less extensive, only a few specific methods have been published. Lian et al. [12] proposed a commutative video watermarking and encryption scheme. During H.264/AVC compression, the intra-prediction mode (IPM), motion vector difference (MVD) and DCT coefficients' signs are encrypted, while DCT coefficients' amplitudes are used for watermarking adaptively. Xu et al. [13] proposed a novel scheme of data hiding directly in the encrypted version of H.264/AVC stream by using *code-word* substitution. The *code-words* of intra-prediction modes, the *code-words* of motion vector differences, and the *code-words* of residual coefficients are encrypted by applying the bitwise XOR operation with stream ciphers. A data-hider, without knowing the original video content, can embed the additional data in the encrypted domain via *code-word* substitution. Later, Xu and Wang [14] proposed a scheme of data hiding directly in a partially encrypted version of H.264/AVC videos by using Context Adaptive Binary Arithmetic Coding (CABAC) bin-string substitution. Although the aforementioned schemes [12–14] have provided promising performance in encrypted domains, they are insufficient for some sensitive scenarios, e.g., military and remote sensing, law forensics, and medical image sharing. In these scenarios, the media content should be not only kept secret strictly, but also be losslessly recovered after data extraction.

The majority of the existing RDH algorithms are designed over the plaintext domain. In our previous paper [15], an efficient reversible data hiding scheme for encrypted H.264/AVC videos is presented. This scheme can achieve reversibility and scalable embedding capacity. First, the encrypted H.264/AVC stream is obtained by encrypting the IPM, MVD, and DCT coefficients' signs with a stream cipher. Then, reversible data hiding in encrypted domain is performed based on histogram-shifting of residue coefficients. In this paper, a novel embedding mechanism based on two-dimensional (2D) histogram modification is proposed. In contrast to the prior RDH methods, every two adjacent coefficients are taken as a unit to generate coefficient pairs, then a 2D coefficient histogram is obtained. Data embedding in encrypted domain is accomplished by using pairwise coefficient modification, i.e., by expanding or shifting the 2D coefficient histogram bins. Experimental results verify that the proposed 2D RDH-based method can achieve an improved performance.

The rest of the paper is organized as follows. In Sect. 2, we describe the proposed scheme, which includes three parts, i.e., H.264/AVC video encryption, data embedding in encrypted video, data extraction and original video recovery. In Sect. 3, experimental results and analysis are presented. Finally, conclusion and future work are drawn in Sect. 4.

2 Proposed Scheme

Similar to our previous scheme [15], the proposed method is also made up of three parts, i.e., H.264/AVC video encryption, data embedding, data extraction and video recovery. The content owner encrypts the original H.264/AVC video using standard stream ciphers to produce an encrypted video. Then, the data-hider (e.g., a database manager, or a cloud provider) can embed some additional data into the encrypted video. At the receiver end, maybe the content owner himself or an authorized third party can extract the embedded data either in encrypted or decrypted video.

2.1 H.264/AVC Video Encryption

H.264/AVC is a hybrid video encoding standard which consists of several crucial processes, including prediction, transformation, quantization, and entropy coding. Generally, the encrypted stream will be not recognizable but decodable. Over the years, various encryption techniques [16] have been proposed to address some of the video-specific issues. Essentially, encryption is applied either in bitstream, i.e., the final compressed codestream or in the compression pipeline itself, i.e., spatial or transform steps. In this paper, the selective encryption method in [15] is directly utilized to encrypt H.264/AVC video, since it has good performance in terms of security, efficiency, and format compliance. Therefore, the improvement in this work is particularly focus on providing a more efficient mechanism for data embedding. In this section, we briefly introduce video encryption scheme proposed in [15].

IPM (intra-prediction mode) Encryption: For Intra_16 × 16 block, the IPM encryption can be performed by XORing the last bit of the *codewords* with pseudo-random bits to keep the value of *CBP* and the length of *codeword* unchanged. For Intra_4 × 4 block, there are 9 prediction modes for selection. When the current *IPM* is equal to the best *IPM*, the *codeword* is composed of a bit "1". Otherwise, the *codeword* is composed of one sign bit "0" and three bits fixed-length code. *IPM* encryption is performed by XORing three bits fixed-length *codeword* with pseudo-random bits. The resulting ciphertexts are still valid *codewords*.

MVD (motion vector difference) Encryption: The motion vector data are subject to further processing before entropy coding, i.e., motion vector prediction, which yields

MVDs. In H.264/AVC baseline profile, Exp-Golomb entropy coding is used to encode *MVD*. In order to avoid the bit-overhead and satisfy the format compliance, only sign bits of *MVDs* are encrypted using a standard stream cipher.

Residue Encryption: In H.264/AVC baseline profile, Context-Adaptive Variable Length Coding (*CAVLC*) is used to encode the quantized transform coefficients of a residual block. The signs ("0"—positive, "1"—negative) of non-zero coefficients are encrypted using a standard stream cipher.

2.2 Embedding Zone Selection

Since changing zero-quantized residuals to nonzero values would significantly increase the video bit rate when coefficients are encoded using run-length codes, our proposed algorithm only embeds the information in nonzero residuals in P-frames.

All of the transform coefficients within 4×4 blocks are generally scanned in a zig-zag fashion and can be marked in a sequential order, from 0, 1, ..., up to 15. Suppose the embedding region is $R = [T_1, T_2]$, where T_1 and T_2 are two sequential numbers along the zig-zag scan order, i.e., $0 \leq T_1 < T_2 \leq 15$. That is, the transform coefficients lying in $[T_1, T_2]$ are modified to embed data while those outside the range are left unchanged. In this paper, T_2 is set as 15, while T_1 is set as follows.

$$T_1 = \begin{cases} Loc_1 & if \ \left(\sum_{k=1}^{15} Ac\_count[k] \right) \leq 2 \\ Loc_2 & if \ \left(\sum_{k=1}^{15} Ac\_count[k] \right) > 2 \end{cases} \tag{1}$$

$$Ac\_count[k] = \begin{cases} 1 & if \ Ac\_coef[k] \neq 0 \\ 0 & if \ Ac\_coef[k] = 0 \end{cases}$$

where $Ac\_coef[k]$ represents the k-th AC coefficients, while Loc_1 and Loc_2 denotes the position of the first and second non-zero AC coefficients, respectively. As can be seen, the parameter T_1 is not fixed, but dynamic.

2.3 Data Embedding in the Encrypted Domain

The method in [15] mainly focus on exploiting one-dimensional (1D) coefficient histogram for RDH. The 1D coefficient histogram is usually defined as

$$h(r) = \#\{f_{i,j}(k)|f_{i,j}(k) = r\} \tag{2}$$

where $\#$ denotes the cardinal number of a set, r is an integer, $f_{i,j}(k)$ denotes the nonzero quantized DCT coefficients in the j-th block of the i-th macroblock. Examples on how to embed data by histogram shifting with $\beta = 0$ and $\beta = 1$ is illustrated in Fig. 1. The embedding capacity denoted as EC_1 is

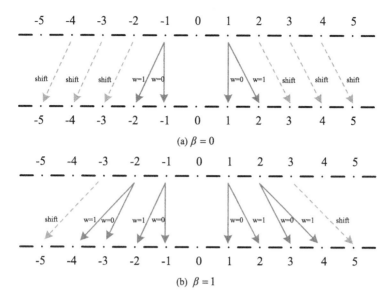

Fig. 1. Illustration of the conventional 1D histogram modification

$$EC_1 = \sum_{\tau=0}^{\beta} (h(-1-\tau) + h(1+\tau)) \tag{3}$$

More details can refer to Ref. [5]. Specifically, the conventional 1D RDH can also be implemented in an equivalent way by modifying the 2D coefficient histogram [17]. By considering every two adjacent residual coefficients together, the associated 2D histogram can be defined as

$$h(r_1, r_2) = \#\left\{ \left(f_{i,j}(2m), f_{i,j}(2m+1)\right) \middle| f_{i,j}(2m) = r_1, f_{i,j}(2m+1) = r_2 \right\} \tag{4}$$

In particular, various histogram modification strategies can be designed based on 2D histogram. A reasonable histogram modification strategy directly contributes to the superior performance. The intention of our improvement is to expand and shift histogram in a less distorted direction. For this purpose, a modified 2D RDH technology is proposed as shown in Fig. 2, in which the mapping direction with large distortion is discarded, and thus an improved embedding performance can be achieved.

Suppose the to-be-embedded message is a binary signal denoted as $W = \{w_l | l = 1, 2, \ldots, M, \ w_l \in \{0, 1\}\}$. The transform coefficients lying in $[T_1, T_2]$ are divided into pairs by taking $\left(f_{i,j}(2m), f_{i,j}(2m+1)\right)$. If the number of non-zero coefficients is odd, the 1D histogram modification strategy in [15] is performed on the first non-zero coefficient, and the 2D histogram modification is performed on the remaining non-zero coefficients. If the number of non-zero coefficients is even, the 2D histogram modification is directly executed. The 2D histogram modification in the encrypted

398   D. Xu et al.

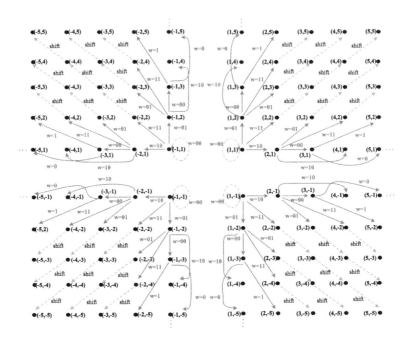

Fig. 2. Illustration of the proposed 2D histogram modification

domain can be described as follows. According to the symmetry in Fig. 2, only the modification in the upper-right quadrant is described for simplicity.

(1) If $\left(f_{i,j}(2m), f_{i,j}(2m+1)\right) = (1,1)$, it has four candidate directions for modification. In this case, two bits can be embedded. Specifically, the marked coefficient pair $\left(f'_{i,j}(2m), f'_{i,j}(2m+1)\right)$ is determined as follows.

$$\left(f'_{i,j}(2m), f'_{i,j}(2m+1)\right) = \begin{cases} (1,1) & \text{if } w_l = 00 \\ (1,2) & \text{if } w_l = 01 \\ (2,1) & \text{if } w_l = 10 \\ (2,2) & \text{if } w_l = 11 \end{cases} \tag{5}$$

(2) If $\left(f_{i,j}(2m), f_{i,j}(2m+1)\right) = (2,1)$, it can be embedded with 2 bits. The marked coefficient pair $\left(f'_{i,j}(2m), f'_{i,j}(2m+1)\right)$ is determined as follows.

$$\left(f'_{i,j}(2m), f'_{i,j}(2m+1)\right) = \begin{cases} (3,1) & \text{if } w_l = 00 \\ (3,2) & \text{if } w_l = 01 \\ (4,1) & \text{if } w_l = 10 \\ (4,2) & \text{if } w_l = 11 \end{cases} \tag{6}$$

(3) If $\left(f_{i,j}(2m), f_{i,j}(2m+1)\right) = (1, 2)$, it can also be embedded with 2 bits. The marked coefficient pair $\left(f'_{i,j}(2m), f'_{i,j}(2m+1)\right)$ is determined as follows.

$$\left(f'_{i,j}(2m), f'_{i,j}(2m+1)\right) = \begin{cases} (1,3) & \text{if } w_l = 00 \\ (2,3) & \text{if } w_l = 01 \\ (1,4) & \text{if } w_l = 10 \\ (2,4) & \text{if } w_l = 11 \end{cases} \quad (7)$$

(4) If $\left(f_{i,j}(2m), f_{i,j}(2m+1)\right) = (y, 1)$, 1 bit can be embedded in each coefficient pair. Then, the marked coefficient pair $\left(f'_{i,j}(2m), f'_{i,j}(2m+1)\right)$ is determined as follows.

$$\left(f'_{i,j}(2m), f'_{i,j}(2m+1)\right) = \begin{cases} \left(f_{i,j}(2m) + 2, f_{i,j}(2m+1)\right) & \text{if } w_l = 0 \\ \left(f_{i,j}(2m) + 2, f_{i,j}(2m+1) + 1\right) & \text{if } w_l = 1 \end{cases} \quad (8)$$

where y is an integer greater than 2.

(5) If $\left(f_{i,j}(2m), f_{i,j}(2m+1)\right) = (1, z)$, the marked coefficient pair $\left(f'_{i,j}(2m), f'_{i,j}(2m+1)\right)$ is determined as follows.

$$\left(f'_{i,j}(2m), f'_{i,j}(2m+1)\right) = \begin{cases} \left(f_{i,j}(2m), f_{i,j}(2m+1) + 2\right) & \text{if } w_l = 0 \\ \left(f_{i,j}(2m) + 1, f_{i,j}(2m+1) + 2\right) & \text{if } w_l = 1 \end{cases} \quad (9)$$

where z is an integer greater than 2.

(6) If $f_{i,j}(2m) \geq 2$ and $f_{i,j}(2m+1) \geq 2$, the coefficient pair $\left(f_{i,j}(2m), f_{i,j}(2m+1)\right)$ is shifted to $\left(f'_{i,j}(2m), f'_{i,j}(2m+1)\right)$ as follows.

$$\left(f'_{i,j}(2m), f'_{i,j}(2m+1)\right) = \left(f_{i,j}(2m) + 1, f_{i,j}(2m+1) + 1\right) \quad (10)$$

According to the above-described step, the embedding capacity of the proposed 2D RDH method denoted as EC_2 can be computed by

$$EC_2 = 2 \cdot h(1, 1) + 2 \cdot h(2, 1) + 2 \cdot h(1, 2) + \sum_{y>2} h(y, 1) + \sum_{z>2} h(1, z) \quad (11)$$

2.4   Data Extraction and Original Video Recovery

In this scheme, data extraction and video encryption are separable, i.e., the hidden data can be extracted either in encrypted or decrypted domain. In addition, our method is also reversible, where the hidden data could be removed to obtain the original video.

A. Scheme I: Data Extraction in the Encrypted Domain

In order to protect the users' privacy, the database manager does not have sufficient permissions to access original video content due to the absence of encryption key. But the manager sometimes need to note and mark the personal information in corresponding encrypted videos as well as to verify videos' integrity. In this case, both data embedding and extraction should be manipulated in encrypted domain.

It should be noted that the hidden data is extracted previously to the de-quantization process. As a consequence, the host block is decoded without extra distortion. According to this characteristic, the complete reversibility can be achieved, which is capable of recovering the original block generated at the decoder side. From the marked encrypted video, the hidden message $\overline{w}_l$ can be extracted in the zones $[T_1, T_2]$. If the number of non-zero coefficients is odd, the hidden data in the first non-zero coefficient can be extracted using the scheme in [15], and the hidden data in the remaining non-zero coefficients can be extracted using Eq. (12). If the number of non-zero coefficients is even, all hidden data in the non-zero coefficients can be extracted using Eq. (12).

$$
\overline{w} = \begin{cases}
00 & if \left(f'_{i,j}(2m), f'_{i,j}(2m+1)\right) \in \{(1,1), (3,1), (1,3)\} \\
01 & if \left(f'_{i,j}(2m), f'_{i,j}(2m+1)\right) \in \{(1,2), (3,2), (2,3)\} \\
10 & if \left(f'_{i,j}(2m), f'_{i,j}(2m+1)\right) \in \{(2,1), (4,1), (1,4)\} \\
11 & if \left(f'_{i,j}(2m), f'_{i,j}(2m+1)\right) \in \{(2,2), (4,2), (2,4)\} \\
0 & if \left(f'_{i,j}(2m), f'_{i,j}(2m+1)\right) \in \{(y+2,1), (1,z+2)\} \\
1 & if \left(f'_{i,j}(2m), f'_{i,j}(2m+1)\right) \in \{(y+2,2), (2,z+2)\}
\end{cases} \tag{12}
$$

where $\overline{w}$ denotes the extracted message bits.

After the hidden bits are extracted, the original coefficient pair $\left(f_{i,j}(2m), f_{i,j}(2m+1)\right)$ can be further recovered by

$$
\left(f_{i,j}(2m), f_{i,j}(2m+1)\right) = \begin{cases}
(1,1) & if \left(f'_{i,j}(2m), f'_{i,j}(2m+1)\right) \in \{(1,1,), (1,2), (2,1), (2,2)\} \\
(2,1) & if \left(f'_{i,j}(2m), f'_{i,j}(2m+1)\right) \in \{(3,1), (3,2), (4,1), (4,2)\} \\
(1,2) & if \left(f'_{i,j}(2m), f'_{i,j}(2m+1)\right) \in \{(1,3), (2,3), (1,4), (2,4)\} \\
(y,1) & if \left(f'_{i,j}(2m), f'_{i,j}(2m+1)\right) \in \{(y+2,1), (y+2,2)\} \\
(1,z) & if \left(f'_{i,j}(2m), f'_{i,j}(2m+1)\right) \in \{(1,z+2), (2,z+2)\} \\
\left(f'_{i,j}(2m)-1, f'_{i,j}(2m+1)-1\right) & if\ f'_{i,j}(2m) > 2\ \&\ f'_{i,j}(2m+1) > 2
\end{cases} \tag{13}
$$

Since the whole process is entirely performed in the encrypted domain, it avoids the leakage of the original content. Furthermore, because the embedding and extraction rules are reversible, both the host encrypted videos and the hidden messages can be recovered losslessly when the stego videos are not attacked. With the encryption keys, the content owner can further decrypt the video to get the original cover video.

B. Scheme II: Data Extraction in the Decrypted Domain

In scheme I, both data embedding and extraction are performed in encrypted domain. However, in some cases, users want to decrypt the video first and then extract the hidden data from the decrypted video when it is needed. For example, with the encryption key, an authorized user wants to achieve the decrypted video containing the hidden data, which can be used to trace the source of the data. In this case, data extraction after video decryption is suitable. The marked encrypted video is first passed through the decryption module. The entire process is comprised of the following steps.

Step1: Generating the marked decrypted video with the encryption keys. Because of the symmetry of the XOR operation, the decryption operation is symmetric to the encryption operation. That is, the encrypted data can be decrypted by performing XOR operation with generated pseudorandom bits, and then two XOR operations cancel each other out, which renders the original plain text. Since the pseudorandom bits depend on the encryption keys, the decryption is possible only for the authorized users. As an efficient scheme, the marked decrypted video should keep perceptual transparency compared with original video. This will be verified in the subsequent experiments.

Step2: Data extraction. After generating the marked decrypted video, the content owner can further extract the hidden data and recover the original video. The process is essentially similar to that of scheme I. The embedded data bit w_l can also be extracted from the marked decrypted video using Eq. (12), since encryption simply changes the sign of the coefficient while data-hiding causes coefficient expansion that is symmetric about zero, without introducing sign changes. For example, the paired coefficients (1, 1) may be changed to (1, 1), (1, −1), (−1, 1) or (−1, −1) during the encryption process. But according to Fig. 2, coefficient pairs (1, 1), (1, −1), (−1, 1) and (−1, −1) are all correspond to the hidden bit "00". Similarly, coefficient pairs (2, 2), (2, −2), (−2, 2) and (−2, −2) correspond to the hidden bit "11". The difference is that $\left(f'_{i,j}(2m), \right.$ $\left. f'_{i,j}(2m+1) \right)$ should be the decrypted coefficients.

Step3: Video recovery. The original video can be further recovered via Eq. (13). Similarly, $\left(f'_{i,j}(2m), f'_{i,j}(2m+1) \right)$ should be the decrypted coefficients.

3   Experimental Results and Analysis

The proposed data hiding scheme has been implemented in the H.264/AVC JM-12.2 reference software [18]. Similarly, eight well-known standard video sequences (i.e., *Carphone, News, Foreman, Hall, Mobile, Tempete, Table,* and *Stefan*) in QCIF format (176 × 144) at the frame rate 30 frames/s are used for our simulation. The first 100 frames in each video sequence are used in the experiments. The GOP (Group of Pictures) structure is "IPPPP: one I frame followed four P frames (QP: I 28, P 28)". Obviously, the method can also be applied to any other format, e.g., CIF.

Since the encryption method in [15] is directly utilized in our proposed framework, the security analysis can refer to Ref. [15]. The subjective results are also shown in Figs. 3 and 4. Thus, in the following analysis will focus on the improvement of visual quality and embedding capacity.

Fig. 3. Original video frames

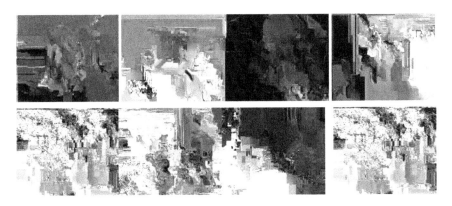

Fig. 4. The corresponding encrypted frames

3.1 Embedding Capacity

The maximum embedding capacity in each video encoded with different *QP* (quantization parameter) values is given in Table 1. It is clear that the overall embedding capacity varies greatly and strongly depends on video content and the *QP* values. The reason for this is that each video stream has a different number of qualified coefficients. As shown in Table 1, the sequences *Mobile, Tempete, Table, and Stefan* provide larger embedding capacity than other sequences. The sequences *Table and Stefan* have considerable motion, whereas the sequences *Mobile* and *Tempete* are highly textured. The number of nonzero coefficients in P-frames of these video sequences is very large compared to the sequences *Carphone, News, Foreman*, and *Hall* which are mostly static with limited motion in some frames.

In addition to the difference in video content, the quantization parameter (QP) has a great impact on the embedding capacity. Capacity reduces with increase in QP values. For example, when *QP* value equals to 24, a large number of quantized coefficients can be

Table 1. Maximum capacity comparison between the proposed method and the method in [15]

Sequence	QP	Method in [15]	Proposed method	Rate of increase (%)	Sequence	QP	Method in [15]	Proposed method	Rate of increase (%)
Carphone	24	20860	25150	+20.57	Stefan	24	276285	261668	−5.29
	28	6523	9137	+40.07		28	149033	145557	−2.33
	32	1630	2814	+72.64		32	52353	54394	+3.90
Foreman	24	22162	26206	+18.25	Mobile	24	160898	163145	+1.40
	28	5646	8088	+43.25		28	54267	59268	+9.22
	32	1330	2287	+71.95		32	12852	15444	+20.17
Tempete	24	235728	230516	−2.21	Hall	24	14728	16627	+12.89
	28	112343	115262	+2.60		28	6263	7382	+17.87
	32	34767	38628	+11.11		32	2554	3374	+32.11
News	24	13764	15568	13.11	Table	24	115241	115405	+0.14
	28	5854	7245	23.76		28	49045	51078	+4.15
	32	2091	2934	40.32		32	19804	21148	+6.79

used for data hiding and hence payload is high. While QP value equals to 32, the payload is lower, since quantized coefficients which can be used for data hiding are fewer.

Compared with Xu et al.'s work [15], the proposed scheme can provide higher maximum capacity. Simulation results show that the statistical average increase in the embedding capacity is about 7.36%, 17.32% and 32.37% with different QP values of 24, 28, and 32, respectively. To summarize, a higher embedding capacity can be achieved by using our proposed scheme, which is helpful to make a tradeoff between the capacity and the visual quality according to the different practical requirements. In fact, pairwise coefficient modification has a lot of freedom in design, and various mappings based on 2D histogram can be obtained. How to select the optimal 2D mapping for specific application would be a valuable work, and this can be done in the future work.

3.2 Marked Video Quality

Since the embedding scheme is reversible, the original cover content can be perfectly recovered after extraction of the hidden data. To ensure video playback at certain quality, the decrypted video containing the hidden data should also be readily decodable by standard decoders with acceptable perceptual quality. To verify this, quality of the marked-decrypted video is investigated. Some corresponding decrypted versions containing the hidden data are shown in Fig. 5. From our subjective examination, it can be seen that the marked content cannot be visually distinguished from non-marked content. Other frames have a similar effect on visual quality. Due to space limitations, we do not list the visual results of all frames.

Furthermore, average *PSNR* (Peak Signal to Noise Ratio) of the luminance component is utilized as the objective metric to evaluate the visual quality. Generally, the PSNR value decreases with any increase in the QP value, for both original and marked videos. When the embedding capacity is set to the lesser of the maximum capacity, *PSNR* comparison between the proposed method and the method in [15] is given in

Fig. 5. The corresponding decrypted frames containing the hidden data

Table 2. *PSNR* comparison between the proposed method and the method in [15]

Sequence	QP	Method in [15] (dB)	Proposed method (dB)	Δ-*PSNR* (dB)	Sequence	QP	Method in [15] (dB)	Proposed method (dB)	Δ-*PSNR* (dB)
Carphone	24	40.04	40.09	+0.05	*Stefan*	24	33.53	34.09	+0.56
	28	37.64	37.65	+0.01		28	32.17	32.44	+0.27
	32	34.98	34.96	−0.02		32	30.22	30.26	+0.04
Foreman	24	38.52	38.57	+0.05	*Mobile*	24	35.31	35.47	+0.16
	28	36.14	36.15	+0.01		28	33.39	33.44	+0.05
	32	33.59	33.59	0		32	30.38	30.38	0
Tempete	24	33.91	34.28	+0.37	*Hall*	24	39.47	39.59	+0.12
	28	32.41	32.49	+0.08		28	37.45	37.52	+0.07
	32	30.12	30.09	−0.03		32	34.79	34.80	+0.01
News	24	39.97	40.07	+0.10	*Table*	24	35.49	35.79	+0.30
	28	37.40	37.44	+0.04		28	33.46	33.66	+0.20
	32	34.43	34.44	+0.01		32	31.37	31.44	+0.07

Table 2. As can be observed, in the case of the same capacity, the proposed method can derive a better *PSNR* in most cases.

3.3   Bit Rate Variation

In addition, bit-rate variation (*BR_var*) is introduced to further evaluate the performance, which is defined as

$$BR\_var = \frac{BR\_prop - BR\_prev}{BR\_prev} \times 100\% \tag{14}$$

where *BR_prop* is the bit rate generated by the proposed data embedding encoder, and *BR_prev* is the bit rate generated by the encoder of [15]. When the embedding capacity is set to the lesser of the maximum capacity, bit-rate comparison between the proposed

Table 3. *Bit-rate* comparison between the proposed method and the method in [15]

Sequence	QP	Method in [15] (kbit/s)	Proposed method (kbit/s)	BR_var (%)	Sequence	QP	Method in [15] (kbit/s)	Proposed method (kbit/s)	BR_var (%)
Carphone	24	345.14	345.400	0.075	Stefan	24	1428.92	1425.38	−0.248
	28	206.05	206.04	−0.005		28	981.35	980.99	−0.037
	32	123.14	123.13	−0.008		32	589.06	589.08	0.003
Foreman	24	424.10	424.33	0.054	Mobile	24	1365.89	1366.06	0.012
	28	239.65	239.66	0.004		28	839.71	839.45	−0.031
	32	142.42	142.41	−0.007		32	460.49	460.32	−0.037
Tempete	24	1376.29	1375.96	−0.024	Hall	24	286.42	286.62	0.070
	28	890.06	890.58	0.058		28	186.32	186.37	0.027
	32	492.31	492.48	0.035		32	125.20	125.19	−0.008
News	24	317.68	317.92	0.076	Table	24	919.22	919.82	0.065
	28	217.20	217.21	0.005		28	518.70	519.43	0.141
	32	146.42	146.44	0.014		32	270.92	271.32	0.148

method and the method in [15] is given in Table 3. Basically, after encrypting and data hiding, the bit-rate of our proposed method is very close to the method in [15].

4 Conclusions and Future Work

Although reversible data hiding and cryptography have been studied extensively and many techniques are available, but reversible data hiding in encrypted domain is a highly interdisciplinary area of research. Technical research in this field has only just begun, and there is still an open space for research in this interdisciplinary research area. In this paper, an algorithm to reversibly embed secret data in encrypted H.264/AVC streams is presented, which consists of video encryption, data embedding and data extraction three phases. The IPM, MVD, and the sign bits of residue coefficients are encrypted using a standard stream cipher without violating format compliance. The data-hider can embed the secret data into the encrypted video using 2D histogram modification method. Since the embedding is done on the encrypted data directly without knowing the decryption key, which avoids the leakage of media content. The additional data can be extracted either in encrypted domain or decrypted domain. Furthermore, this algorithm can achieve real reversibility, and high quality of marked decrypted videos. One of the possible applications of this method is video annotation in cloud computing where high video quality and reversibility are greatly desired.

Obviously, the proposed two-dimensional histogram modification strategy is certainly not optimal. In fact, some other histogram modifications could also be explored. How to explore the optimal modification by combining the characteristics of H.264/AVC coefficients is valuable to investigate in the further work.

Acknowledgements. This work is supported by the National Natural Science Foundation of China (61301247, 61672302), Zhejiang Provincial Natural Science Foundation of China (LY17F020013, LZ15F020002), Public Welfare Technology Application Research Project of Zhejiang Province (2015C33237, 2015C31110), National undergraduate innovation and entrepreneurship training programs (201611058002).

References

1. Ni, Z.C., Shi, Y.Q., Ansari, N., Su, W.: Reversible data hiding. IEEE Trans. Circ. Syst. Video Technol. **16**(3), 354–362 (2006)
2. Tian, J.: Reversible data embedding using a difference expansion. IEEE Trans. Circ. Syst. Video Technol. **13**(8), 890–896 (2003)
3. Khan, A., Siddiqa, A., Mubib, S., Malik, S.A.: A recent survey of reversible watermarking techniques. Inf. Sci. **279**, 251–272 (2014)
4. Zhang, X.P.: Reversible data hiding in encrypted image. IEEE Signal Process. Lett. **18**(4), 255–258 (2011)
5. Zhang, X.P.: Separable reversible data hiding in encrypted image. IEEE Trans. Inf. Forensics Secur. **7**(2), 826–832 (2012)
6. Qian, Z.X., Zhang, X.P.: Reversible data hiding in encrypted images with distributed source encoding. IEEE Trans. Circ. Syst. Video Technol. **26**(4), 636–646 (2016)
7. Wu, X.T., Sun, W.: High-capacity reversible data hiding in encrypted images by prediction error. Sig. Process. **104**, 387–400 (2014)
8. Ma, K.D., Zhang, W.M., Zhao, X.F., et al.: Reversible data hiding in encrypted images by reserving room before encryption. IEEE Trans. Inf. Forensics Secur. **8**(3), 553–562 (2013)
9. Zhang, W.M., Ma, K.D., Yu, N.H.: Reversibility improved data hiding in encrypted images. Sig. Process. **94**, 118–127 (2014)
10. Cao, X.C., Du, L., Wei, X.X., et al.: High capacity reversible data hiding in encrypted images by patch-level sparse representation. IEEE Trans. Cybern. **46**(5), 2168–2267 (2016)
11. Xu, D.W., Wang, R.D.: Separable and error-free reversible data hiding in encrypted images. Sig. Process. **123**, 9–21 (2016)
12. Lian, S.G., Liu, Z.X., Ren, Z.: Commutative encryption and watermarking in video compression. IEEE Trans. Circ. Syst. Video Technol. **17**(6), 774–778 (2007)
13. Xu, D.W., Wang, R.D., Shi, Y.Q.: Data Hiding in encrypted H.264/AVC video streams by codeword substitution. IEEE Trans. Inf. Forensics Secur. **9**(4), 596–606 (2014)
14. Xu, D.W., Wang, R.D.: Context adaptive binary arithmetic coding-based data hiding in partially encrypted H.264/AVC videos. J. Electron. Imaging **24**(3), 1–13 (2015)
15. Xu, D.W., Wang, R.D.: Efficient reversible data hiding in encrypted H.264/AVC videos. J. Electron. Imaging **23**, 1–14 (2014)
16. Stütz, T., Uhl, A.: A survey of H.264 AVC/SVC encryption. IEEE Trans. Circ. Syst. Video Technol. **22**(3), 325–339 (2012)
17. Ou, B., Li, X.L., Zhao, Y., et al.: Pairwise prediction-error expansion for efficient reversible data hiding. IEEE Trans. Image Process. **22**(12), 5010–5021 (2013)
18. H.264/AVC Reference Software JM 12.2. http://iphome.hhi.de/suehring/tml/

Second Order Perdicting-Error Sorting for Reversible Data Hiding

Jiajia Xu, Hang Zhou, Weiming Zhang$^{(\boxtimes)}$, Ruiqi Jiang, Guoli Ma, and Nenghai Yu

University of Science and Technology of China, No. 96, Baohe District, Hefei 230026, People's Republic of China
{xujiajia,jrq123}@mail.ustc.edu.cn, hangzhou_ryan@163.com, {zhangwm,ynh}@ustc.edu.cn

Abstract. Reversible data hiding (RDH) schemes compete against each other for a sharply distributed prediction error histogram, which is often realized by utilizing prediction strategies together with sorting techniques. The sorting technique aims to estimate the local context complexity for each pixel to optimize the embedding order. In this paper, we propose a novel second order perdicting and sorting technique for reversible data hiding. Firstly, the prediction error is obtained by an interchannel secondary prediction using the prediction errors of current channel and reference channel. Experiments show that this prediction method can produce a shaper second order prediction-error histogram. Then, we will introduce a novel second order perdicting-error sorting (SOPS) algorithm, which make full use of the feature of the edge information obtained from another color channel and high correlation between adjacent pixels. So it will reflect the texture complexity of current pixel better. Experimental results demonstrate that our proposed method outperforms the previous state-of-arts counterparts significantly in terms of both the prediction accuracy and the overall embedding performance.

Keywords: Reversible data hiding · Channel correlation · Second order perdicting-error

1 Introduction

Reversible data hiding (RDH) [1], as being a special branch of information hiding, has received a lot of attention in the past few years. It is not only concerned about the user's embedding data, but also pays attention to the carriers themselves. RDH ensures that the cover data and the embedded message can be extracted from the marked content precisely and losslessly. This important data hiding technique provides valuable functions in many fields, such as medical image

This work was supported in part by the Natural Science Foundation of China under Grants 61170234 and 60803155, and by the Strategic Priority Research Program of the Chinese Academy of Sciences under Grant XDA06030601.

© Springer International Publishing AG 2017
Y.Q. Shi et al. (Eds.): IWDW 2016, LNCS 10082, pp. 407–420, 2017.
DOI: 10.1007/978-3-319-53465-7_30

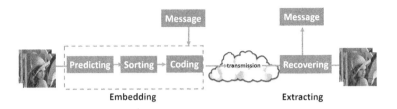

Fig. 1. Framework of RDH embedding/extraction.

protection, authentication and tamper carrier recovery, digital media copyright protection, military imagery and legal, where the cover can not be damaged during data extraction. A framework of RDH for digital images is illustrated in Fig. 1.

In order to improve the efficiency of RDH, researchers have proposed many methods in the past decades. Generally speaking, prediction and sorting play an important role in the process of reversible information hiding. The prediction focuses on how to better exploit inter-pixel correlations to derive a sharply distributed one. And the emphasis of sorting technique is exploiting the correlation between neighboring pixels for optimizing embedding order.

The improvement of the prediction is important for both histogram shifting and difference expansion based on RDH schemes. Some predictors [4] have proposed such as median edge detection (MED), gradient adjusted prediction (GAP), and differential adaptive run coding (DARC). The MED predictor tends to select the lower vertical neighbor in the cases where a vertical edge exists right to the current location, the right neighbor in cases of a horizontal edge below it, or a linear combination of the context pixels if no edge is detected. The GAP algorithm weighs the neighboring pixels according to local gradient and classifies the edges to three classes namely, sharp, normal, and weak, which uses seven neighboring pixels to estimate unknown pixel value. The DARC is a non-linear adaptive predictor that uses three neighboring pixels to estimate the unknown pixels. Dragoi and Coltuc [3] have proposed extended gradient-based selection and weighting (EGBSW) for RDH. EGBSW [3] algorithm uses four linear predictors, computing the output value as a weighted sum between the predicted values corresponding to the selected gradients, then predicted value is obtained.

Sorting [5,6] is a fundamental step to exploit the correlation between neighboring pixels for optimizing embedding order, hence sorting is a fundamental step to enhance the embedding capacity and visual quality. Kamstra and Heijmans' [7] use of sorting introduced a significant performance advantage over previous methods. They reduced the location map size through arranging the pairs of pixels in order. Sachnev et al. [5] used local variance values to sort the predicted errors. They sort the cells in ascending order of the local variance values, which first embeds the smoother cells with lower local variance values. But in some cases, it does not work directly accurate. For example, Afsharizadeh [6] extended Sachnev et al.'s work [5] by using a new proposed efficient sorting technique, which is a new sorting measure resulted from more accurate sorting procedures. Ou [8] proposed a simple and efficient sorting method by calculating its local complexity, which is the sum of absolute differences between diagonal blank pixels in the 4×4 sized neighborhood. A small local complexity indicates that the pair is located in a smooth image region and should be used preferentially for data embedding. However, the above algorithms did not consider the characteristic of prediction-error distribution.

However, we notice that the existing research about RDH is commonly focused on gray-scale images. In real life, it is the color images that are widely used. In recent days, reversible data hiding for color images is a rarely studied topic in [9,10]. Considering that the color channels correlate with each other, Li et al. [11] propose a RDH algorithm based on prediction-error expansion that can enhance the prediction accuracy in one color channel through exploiting the edge information from another channel. By doing so, the entropy of the prediction-error is decreased statistically. Based on the inter-channel correlation of color image Li et al.[11], a novel inter-channel prediction method is examined and a corresponding reversible data hiding algorithm is proposed.

In our proposed method, the prediction error is obtained by an interchannel secondary prediction using the prediction errors of current channel and reference channel. Experiments show that this prediction method can produce a shaper second order prediction-error histogram. Then, we will introduce a novel second order perdicting-error sorting (SOPS) algorithm, which make full use of the feature of the edge information obtained from another color channel and high correlation between adjacent pixels. So it will reflect the texture complexity of current pixel better. Experimental results demonstrate that our proposed method outperforms the previous state-of-arts counterparts significantly in terms of both the prediction accuracy and the overall embedding performance.

The paper is organized as follows. Section 2 describes the proposed second order perdicting-error sorting algorithm for reversible data hiding. The simulations done using the proposed technique and the obtained results are presented in Sect. 3. In Sect. 4, conclusions are briefly drawn based on the results.

2 Second Order Perdicting-Error Sorting (SOPS) for Color Image

2.1 Second Order Perdicting-Error Based on Correlation Among Color Channels

Naturally, the edges of images play a critical role in human visual system (HVS), which is revealing with jump in intensity. How to use the property to predict pixel is very important. Some predictors have proposed for RDH such as median edge detection (MED) and gradient adjusted prediction (GAP) [2] may be ineffective for the rough region. The perdicting-error in this situation usually differs greatly from the pixel because of the large difference between the pixels along the gradient direction in rough region. However, more precise perdicting-error can

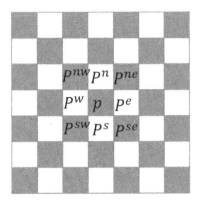

Fig. 2. The current pixel and its neighboring pixels

be obtained by the pixels, which is along the edge direction. Especially for color image, we can make full use of the feature of the edge information obtained from another color channel and high correlation between adjacent pixels. In [11], Li *et al.* pointed out that the edge information drawn from different color channels is similar to each other. Hence, if an edge is detected in one color channel, there would be an identical edge in the same position in the other channels.

In each channel, we use double-layered embedding method proposed by Sachnev *et al.* [13], with all pixels divided into the shadow pixel set and the blank set (see Fig. 2). In the first round, the shadow set is used for embedding data and blank set for computing predictions. While in the second round, the blank set is used for embedding and shadow set for computing predictions. Since the two layers embedding processes are similar in nature, we only take the shadow layer for illustration.

Let p_c and p_r denote the sample of a pixel p in the current channel and reference channel. In order to determine whether the pixel is located on the edge of the image, we need to calculate the two parameters. The average distance D_{avg} and direction distance D_{dir} can be given by

$$D_{avg} = \left| \sum_{k=1}^{8} \alpha_{avg}^k p_r^k - p_r \right| \tag{1}$$

where α_{avg}^k (k = 1, 2, ... 8) are coefficients of eight neighbors $p_r^1 = p_r^{nw}$, $p_r^2 = p_r^n$, $p_r^3 = p_r^{ne}$, $p_r^4 = p_r^w$, $p_r^5 = p_r^e$, $p_r^6 = p_r^{sw}$, $p_r^7 = p_r^s$ and $p_r^8 = p_r^{se}$. If p_r locate at smooth region, the average distance D_{avg} should be small. On the contrary, if p_r locate at rough region, the D_{avg} is very large. However, how to determine the direction of the edge in the image. Next, we determine the direction by calculating the direction distance D_{dir} as follow

$$D_{dir} = min\left\{ \left| \frac{p_r^w + p_r^e}{2} - p_r \right|, \left| \frac{p_r^n + p_r^s}{2} - p_r \right|, \right. \tag{2}$$
$$\left. \left| \frac{p_r^{nw} + p_r^{se}}{2} - p_r \right|, \left| \frac{p_r^{ne} + p_r^{sw}}{2} - p_r \right| \right\}$$

where $|(p_r^w + p_r^e)/2 - p_r|$, $|(p_r^n + p_r^s)/2 - p_r|$, $|(p_r^{nw} + p_r^{se})/2 - p_r|$, and $|(p_r^{ne} + p_r^{sw})/2 - p_r|$ represent the four edge directions, which are horizontal, vertical, diagonal and antidiagonal. Taking the smallest one as D_{dir}. Edges are revealing with jump in intensity, for instance, the smallest means the pixels are locate on the edges of image.

The $|D_{avg} - D_{dir}|$ can be used to indicate whether the reference sample is located on an edge region. Considering that all the color channels have similar edge distribution in [11], the prediction of the pixels should be taken into account the edge information obtained from another channel. Therefore, we can employ $|D_{avg} - D_{dir}|$ to classify the location of the current sample p_c. If the $|D_{avg} - D_{dir}|$ is close to zero or very small, which means the current sample p_c locate on the smooth region of image. In this case, the edge information obtained from another channel is useless, we can make full use of the eight neighbors of p_c. On the other hand, if $|D_{avg} - D_{dir}|$ is larger than a predefined threshold ρ, we think that p_c is located at or near to an image edge area at a high possibility. Under the circumstances, the edge information obtained from another channel should be taken into account. So, we can get

$$\hat{p}_c = \begin{cases} \lfloor (p_c^w + p_c^e + p_c^n + p_c^s)/4 + 0.5 \rfloor & |D_{avg} - D_{dir}| \le \rho, \\ \lfloor P(p_c^k | D_{dir}) + 0.5 \rfloor & |D_{avg} - D_{dir}| > \rho. \end{cases}$$

where $P(p_c^k | D_{dir})$ according to D_{dir}. For instance, when $D_{dir} = |(p_r^w + p_r^e)/2 - p_r|$, then $P(p_c^k | D_{dir}) = (p_r^w + p_r^e)/2$. When $D_{dir} = |(p_r^n + p_r^s)/2 - p_r|$, then $P(p_c^k | D_{dir}) = (p_r^n + p_r^s)/2$. When $D_{dir} = |(p_r^{nw} + p_r^{se})/2 - p_r|$, then $P(p_c^k | D_{dir}) = (p_r^{nw} + p_r^{se})/2$. When $D_{dir} = |(p_r^{ne} + p_r^{sw})/2 - p_r|$, then $P(p_c^k | D_{dir}) = (p_r^{ne} + p_r^{sw})/2$.

Then we can get the first order perdicting-error based on correlation among color channels as follow

$$\Delta e_c = p_c - \hat{p}_c \tag{3}$$

$$\Delta e_r = p_r - \hat{p}_r \tag{4}$$

where Δe_c is first order perdicting-error in the current channel and Δe_r is first order perdicting-error reference channel. Next, the second order prediction-error is computed by

$$\Delta^2 e = \Delta e_c - \Delta e_r \tag{5}$$

when the pixels in the smooth region of image, the pixels are similar to each other and the first order perdicting-errors Δe_c and Δe_r are close to zero. Therefore, the second order prediction-errors are also close to zero. On the other hand, when the pixels are located at rough region, the first order perdicting-errors Δe_c and Δe_r relatively large. However, considering that all the color channels have similar edge distribution and take into account the edge information obtained from another channel. the second order prediction-errors become smaller. So, the second order prediction-error sequence $\Delta^2 e = (\Delta^2 e_1, \cdots, \Delta^2 e_N)$ is derived.

How to evaluate the prediction method? The entropy value of the prediction-error can be used to evaluate the performance of the proposed prediction method. If the entropy is smaller, the performance of prediction is better. On the contrary,

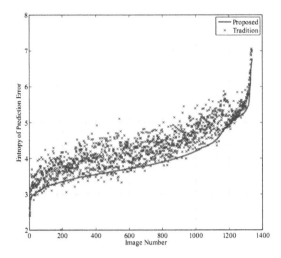

Fig. 3. The entropy value of the prediction-error obtained by our proposed prediction method and other tradition methods

if the entropy is larger, the performance of prediction is worse. In this paper, the UCID (Uncompressed color image database) is employed in our experiment, which has over 1300 uncompressed color images. In the Fig. 3, we can observe that the entropy value of our proposed method is smaller than that corresponding to other tradition methods such as MED, rhombus and first order perdicting-error based on correlation among color channels.

2.2 Second Order Perdicting-Error Sorting Based on Generalized Normal Distribution

The generalized "error" distribution is a generalized form of the normal, it possesses a natural multivariate form, and has a parametric kurtosis that is unbounded above and possesses special cases that are identical to the Normal and the double exponential distributions [21]. Given that the probability density function (PDF) of prediction-error follows generalized normal distribution or gaussian distribution, we consider using this model to describe the prediction-error in Fig. 3. Generalized normal distribution density function is defined by Nadarajah [9].

$$f(\Delta e|u, \alpha, \beta) = \frac{\beta}{2\alpha\Gamma(\frac{1}{\beta})} exp\left\{-\left|\frac{(\Delta e - u)}{\alpha}\right|^{\beta}\right\},\tag{6}$$

where Δe is prediction-error with mean u and variance σ^2. $\alpha = \sqrt{\sigma^2\Gamma(1/\beta)/\Gamma(3/\beta)}$ is a scale parameter, playing the role of a variance that determines the width of the PDF, while $\beta > 0$, called the shape parameter, controls the fall-off rate in the vicinity of the mode (the higher β, the lower the fall-off rate). $\Gamma(.)$ denotes the Gamma function such that $\Gamma(t) = \int_0^\infty x^{t-1} exp(-x)dx$. It is easy to see that the Eq. (6) reduces to the normal distribution for $\beta = 2$, and Laplacian distribution for $\beta = 1$.

Based on Eq. (6), we can easily get $\Delta e_c \sim GND(u_c, \alpha_c, \beta_c)$ and $\Delta e_r \sim GND(u_r, \alpha_r, \beta_r)$. Then $\Delta^2 e = \Delta e_c - \Delta e_r$ can be given by

$$
\begin{aligned}
f(\Delta^2 e) &= -\int_{-\infty}^{+\infty} f_{\Delta e_c - \Delta e_r}(\Delta e_c, \Delta^2 e - \Delta e_c)d\Delta e_c \\
&= -\int_{-\infty}^{+\infty} \frac{\beta_c \beta_r}{4\alpha_c \alpha_r \Gamma(1/\beta_c)\Gamma(1/\beta_r)} \\
&\quad \times exp\left(-\left|\frac{\Delta e_c - u_c}{\alpha_c}\right|^{\beta_c} - \left|\frac{\Delta^2 e - \Delta e_c - u_r}{\alpha_r}\right|^{\beta_r}\right)d\Delta e_c
\end{aligned}
$$

(7)

According to Eq. (7), there does not appear to exist a closed form expression. However, in order to simplify and reduce the complexity of the problem, we take $\beta = 1$ as a particular case of generalized normal. When $\beta = 1$ is corresponding to the Laplace distribution as follows

$$
\begin{aligned}
f(\Delta^2 e) &= -\int_{-\infty}^{+\infty} f_c(\Delta e_c) f_r(\Delta^2 e - \Delta e_c)d\Delta e_c \\
&= \frac{\alpha_c}{2(\alpha_c^2 - \alpha_r^2)} exp\left(-\frac{|\Delta^2 e - (u_c - u_r)|}{\alpha_c}\right) \\
&\quad - \frac{\alpha_r}{2(\alpha_c^2 - \alpha_r^2)} exp\left(-\frac{|\Delta^2 e - (u_c - u_r)|}{\alpha_r}\right)
\end{aligned}
$$

(8)

It can easily be seen that the $f(\Delta^2 e)$ is the difference between the two Laplace distributions with the same mean $u_c - u_r$ under different weights. The probability density function (PDF) of second order prediction-error can be seen in Fig. 4. As shown in Fig. 4, the distance from $u_c - u_r$ to y axis can be used to reflect the

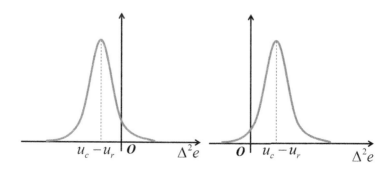

Fig. 4. The distribution of $f(\Delta^2 e)$

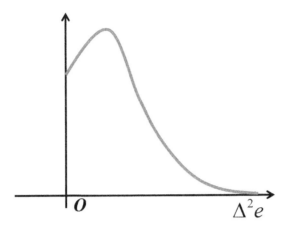

Fig. 5. The distribution of $\Phi(\Delta^2 e)$

accuracy of the second order prediction error. The smaller the distance is, the
better the accuracy of prediction is. Since the distance is used to measure the
accuracy of the prediction error, we can get a new function $\Phi(\Delta^2 e) = |f(\Delta^2 e)|$
(Fig. 5). The distribution of $\Phi(\Delta^2 e)$ can be given by It can easily be seen that
the expectation of function $E[\Phi(\Delta^2 e)]$ has positive correlation to $u_c - u_r$. So it
can be used to characterize the accuracy of the second order prediction error.
For example, if the $E[\Phi(\Delta^2 e)]$ is higher, which means the pixels in image region
are more random or unpredictable. Consequently, the pixels are hard to predict
accurately in this region. Thus, the prediction-errors can be rearranged by sorting
according to $E[\Phi(\Delta^2 e)]$. Let $u = u_c - u_r$, $a = \frac{\alpha_c}{2(\alpha_c^2 - \alpha_r^2)}$ and $b = \frac{\alpha_r}{2(\alpha_c^2 - \alpha_r^2)}$. The
$\Phi(\Delta^2 e)$ can be given by

$$
\begin{aligned}
\Phi(\Delta^2 e) &= \frac{a}{2\alpha_c}(exp(-\frac{|u - \Delta^2 e|}{\alpha_c}) + exp(-\frac{u + \Delta^2 e}{\alpha_c})) \\
&\quad - \frac{b}{2\alpha_r}(exp(-\frac{|u - \Delta^2 e|}{\alpha_r}) + exp(-\frac{u + \Delta^2 e}{\alpha_r}))
\end{aligned}
\tag{9}
$$

where $\Delta^2 e, u \geq 0$. Then we can get the $E[\Phi(\Delta^2 e)]$ as follow

$$
\begin{aligned}
E(\Phi(\Delta^2 e)) &= -\int_0^{+\infty} \Delta^2 e \Phi(\Delta^2 e) d\Delta^2 e \\
&= a \times exp(-\frac{u}{\alpha_c}) - b \times exp(-\frac{u}{\alpha_r}) + u
\end{aligned}
\tag{10}
$$

As shown in Fig. 2, the the parameters u and α can be estimated by

$$
u_c = min\{(d_1 + d_3)/2, (d_2 + d_4)/2\}
\tag{11}
$$

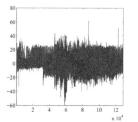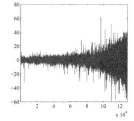

Fig. 6. The prediction-error of lena

$$\alpha_c = \sqrt{\frac{1}{4 \times 2} \sum_{4}^{k=1}(d_k - u_c)^2} \tag{12}$$

where $d_1 = p_c^w - p_c^n$, $d_2 = p_c^n - p_c^e$, $d_3 = p_c^e - p_c^s$ and $d_4 = p_c^s - p_c^w$.

Observed form above, $E[\Phi(\Delta^2 e)]$ is an increasing function of u_c, u_r, and α_c, α_r. The smaller u_c, u_r, and α_c, α_r is, the better the accuracy of prediction is. So, the $E[\Phi(\Delta^2 e)]$ can well characterize local context complexity for pixel and prediction accuracy of prediction-error.

By setting a threshold λ, the entropy satisfying $E[\Phi(\Delta^2 e)] \leq \lambda$ are utilized in data embedding while the others are skipped. For a specific payload R, λ is determined as the smallest value such that it can ensure the enough payload. Thus, the embedding process starts from the prediction-error with the smallest $E[\Phi(\Delta^2 e)]$ value in the sorted row, and moves on to the next prediction-error until the last bit of data is embedded. As shown in Fig. 6, the left is the prediction-error of the lena image before sorting and the error margin is very high. The right is sorted by our method and the results can be clearly seen that both error and entropy are small being sorted in front. The image quality can be improved significantly, because the message is embedded in the appropriate prediction-error.

3   Application, Experiment and Analysis

In this section, we apply second order prediction-error sorting (SOPS) algorithms to the Li *et al.* [11] method. It is stressed that the embedding and extraction procedures are the same with the algorithms in [11]. We just replace or add the prediction and sorting algorithm in experiments. Then frameworks of the proposed SOPS for RDH scheme are presented in Fig. 7. As shown in Fig. 7, we first hide data into the red and red channels by taking the green one as the reference channel. When hiding data into the green one itself, the reference channel is the marked red one. The embedding procedures and extracting procedures of second order perdicting-error sorting for color image are as follows:

We implemented these methods on the computer with Intel core i3 and 4GB RAM. The program developing environment is MATLAB R2011b based on Microsoft Windows 7 operating system. In the experiment, we employ four

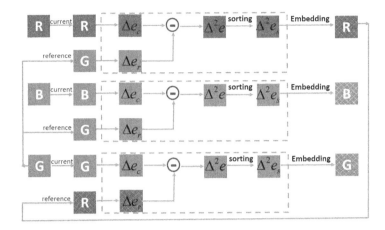

Fig. 7. The framework of data hiding for the three channels.

Fig. 8. Test image Lena, Barbara, Kodak-01 and Kodak-24.

color images (refer to Fig. 8) to test the performance of our proposed RDH algorithm via embedding capacity distortion curves. In the Fig. 8, the first two standard images are saved in TIFF format, with size 512×512. And the two Kodak images are the first and the last ones saved in the database (http://r0k. us/graphics/kodak/), with PNG format and 512×768 in size. Our method is evaluated by comparing with the other six recent works of Li et al. [11], Li et al. [12], Sachnev et al. [13], Alattar [14], Hu et al. [15], Yang and Huang [16]. For our method, we vary the embedding from 100,000 bits to 300,000 bits or 600,000 bits with step size 50,000 bits.

Algorithm 1. The Embedding Procedures of Second Order Perdicting-error Sorting for Color Image RDH.

Input:

The first order perdicting-error in current channel Δe_c.

The first order perdicting-error in reference channel Δe_r.

The embedding rate R.

Output:

1: Calculate the second order prediction-error by $\Delta^2 e = \Delta e_c - \Delta e_r$.

2: Sort the second order prediction-errors in ascending order according to their corresponding $E[\Phi(\Delta^2 e)]$. Process the prediction-errors satisfying $E[\Phi(\Delta^2 e)] \leq \lambda$ to embed the payload.

3: Hide the input data into the sorted sequence by the proposed method in J. Li *et al.* [11]. Using LSB replacement, embed the values of λ, the compressed location map size and the message size into LSBs of some first-line pixels.

4: **return**   After this step, the shadow layer embedding is completed. The marked second order prediction-error sequence $\Delta^2 e' = (\Delta^2 e'_1, \cdots, \Delta^2 e'_N)$.

Algorithm 2. The Extracting Procedures of Second Order Perdicting-error Sorting for Color Image RDH.

Input:

The marked second order prediction-error by $\Delta^2 e$.

The first order perdicting-error in reference channel Δe_r.

Output:

1: By reading LSBs of some first-line pixels, determine the values of the values of λ, the compressed location map size and the message size.

2: Use the same prediction and scan order to obtain the marked second order prediction-error sequence $\Delta^2 e' = (\Delta^2 e'_1, \cdots, \Delta^2 e'_N)$.

3: The recovery of these perdicting-errors are implemented by the inverse mapping of the proposed method in J. Li *et al.* [11].

4: **return**   Recover the original second order prediction-error sequence $\Delta^2 e = (\Delta^2 e_1, \cdots, \Delta^2 e_N)$. Then, the original shadow pixels are recovered.

Observing form Fig. 9, Our method is evaluated by comparing with the other six recent works. The comparison results are shown in Fig. 9(a)–(d). According to the experimental results, one can see that the proposed method outperforms these state-of-the-art works. Our method can provide a larger PSNR whatever the test image or capacity is. Comparing with Li *et al.* [11], experimental results show that our method provides an average increase in PSNR of 0.65dB for Lena, 3.63dB for Barbara, 2.66dB for Kodak-01 and 0.91dB for Kodak-24. our method, an average 1.96dB PSNR gains is earned compared with the Li *et al.* [11] method, and compared with Sachnev *et al.* [5], the gains of PSNR is much more higher (Fig. 10).

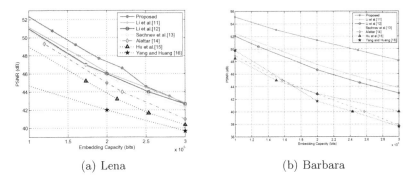

(a) Lena   (b) Barbara

Fig. 9. (a) and (b) is performance comparison between our method and six methods of Li et al. [11], Li et al. [12], Sachnev et al. [13], Alattar [14], Hu et al. [15], Yang and Huang [16].

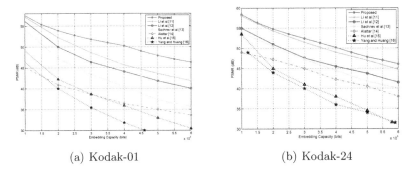

(a) Kodak-01   (b) Kodak-24

Fig. 10. (a) and (b) is performance comparison between our method and six methods of Li et al. [11], Li et al. [12], Sachnev et al. [13], Alattar [14], Hu et al. [15], Yang and Huang [16].

4   Conclusion

In this paper, we propose a novel second order perdicting and sorting technique for reversible data hiding. Firstly, the prediction error is obtained by an inter-channel secondary prediction using the prediction errors of current channel and reference channel. When the pixels in the smooth region of image, the pixels are similar to each other and the first order perdicting-errors are close to zero. Therefore, the second order prediction-errors are also close to zero. On the other hand, when the pixels are located at rough region, the first order perdicting-errors relatively large. However, considering that all the color channels have similar edge distribution and take into account the edge information obtained from another channel. the second order prediction-errors become smaller. Experiments show that this prediction method can produce shaper second order prediction-error histogram. Then, we will introduce a novel second order perdicting-error sorting

(SOPS) algorithm, which make full use of the feature of the edge information obtained from another color channel and high correlation between adjacent pixels. So it will reflect the local context complexity for pixel and prediction accuracy of prediction-error. Experimental results show that the proposed method has better results compared to the other six recent works of Li *et al.* [11], Li *et al.* [12], Sachnev *et al.* [13], Alattar [14], Hu *et al.* [15], Yang and Huang [16].

References

1. Tian, J.: Reversible data embedding using a difference expansion. IEEE Trans. Circ. Syst. Video Technol. **13**(8), 890–896 (2003)
2. Fridrich, J., Goljan, M.: Lossless data embedding for all image formats. Proc. SPIE **4675**, 572–583 (2002)
3. Dragoi, C., Coltuc, D.: Gradient based prediction for reversible watermarking by difference expansion. In: IH&MMSec 2014, pp. 35–41, June 2014
4. Rad, R.M., Attar, A.: A predictive algorithm for multimedia data compression. Multimedia Syst. **19**(2), 103–115 (2013)
5. Ni, Z., Shi, Y., Ansari, N., Wei, S.: Reversible data hiding. IEEE Trans. Circ. Syst. Video Technol. **16**(3), 354–362 (2006)
6. Afsharizadeh, M., Mohammadi, M.: A reversible watermarking prediction based scheme using a new sorting and technique. In: 10th International Conference on Information Security and Cryptology (ISC), pp. 98–104 (2013)
7. Kamstra, L.H.J., Heijmans, A.M.: Reversible data embedding into images using wavelet techniques and sorting. IEEE Trans. Image Process. **14**(12), 2082–2090 (2005)
8. Zhang, W., Chen, B., Yu, N.: Improving various reversible data hiding schemes via optimal codes for binary covers. IEEE Trans. Image Process. **21**(6), 2991–3003 (2012)
9. Nikolaidis, A.: Low overhead reversible data hiding for color JPEG images. Multimedia Tools Appl. **75**(4), 1869–1881 (2016)
10. Tseng, Y., Pan, H.: Data hiding in 2-color images. IEEE Trans. Comput. **51**(7), 873–880 (2002)
11. Li, J., Li, X., Yang, B.: Reversible data hiding scheme for color image based on prediction-error expansion and cross-channel correlation. Sig. Process. **93**(9), 2748–2758 (2013)
12. Li, J., Li, X., Yang, B.: PEE-based reversible watermarking for color image. In: International Conference on Image Processing (2012)
13. Sachnev, V., Kim, H.J., Nam, J., Suresh, S., Shi, Y.: Reversible watermarking algorithm using sorting and prediction. IEEE Trans. Circ. Syst. Video Technol. **19**(7), 989–999 (2009)
14. Alattar, A.M.: Reversible watermark using the difference expansion of a generalized integer transform. IEEE Trans. Image Process. **13**(8), 1147–1156 (2004)
15. Hu, Y., Lee, H., Li, J.: DE-based reversible data hiding with improved overflow location map. IEEE Trans. Circ. Syst. Video Technol. **19**(2), 250–260 (2009)
16. Yang, H., Hwang, K.: Reversible data hiding for color BMP image based on block difference histogram. In: Proceedings of the Fourth International Conference on UBI-Media Computing (U-Media), pp. 257–260 (2011)
17. Lee, S., Yoo, C.D., Kalker, T.: Reversible image watermarking based on integer-to-integer wavelet transform. IEEE Trans. Inf. Forensics Secur. **2**(3), 321–330 (2007)

18. Thodi, D.M., Rodriguez, J.J.: Expansion embedding techniques for reversible watermarking. IEEE Trans. Image Process. **16**(3), 721–730 (2007)

19. Li, X., Yang, B., Zeng, T.: Efficient reversible watermarking based on adaptive prediction-error expansion and pixel selection. IEEE Trans. Image Process. **20**(12), 3524–3533 (2011)

20. Coltuc, D.: Low distortion transform for reversible watermarking. IEEE Trans. Image Process. **21**(1), 412–417 (2012)

21. Giller, G.: A generalized error distribution. SSRN, 16 August 2005. http://dx.doi.org/10.2139/ssrn.2265027

22. Dragoi, C., Coltuc, D.: Improved rhombus interpolation for reversible watermarking by difference expansion. In: Proceedings of EUSIPCO, pp. 1688–1692 (2012)

23. Wu, H.-T., Huang, J.: Reversible image watermarking on prediction errors by efficient histogram modification. Sig. Process. **92**(12), 3000–3009 (2012)

24. Qin, C., Chang, C.-C., Huang, Y.-H., Liao, L.-T.: An inpaintingassisted reversible steganographic scheme using histogram shifting mechanism. IEEE Trans. Circ. Syst. Video Technol. **23**(7), 1109–1118 (2013)

25. Zhang, W., Hu, X., Li, X., Yu, N.: Recursive histogram modification: establishing equivalency between reversible data hiding and lossless data compression. IEEE Trans. Image Process. **22**(7), 2775–2785 (2013)

26. Zhang, W., Chen, B., Yu, N.: Capacity-approaching codes for reversible data hiding. In: Filler, T., Pevný, T., Craver, S., Ker, A. (eds.) IH 2011. LNCS, vol. 6958, pp. 255–269. Springer, Heidelberg (2011). doi:10.1007/978-3-642-24178-9_18

27. Schaefer, G., Stich, M.: UCID: an uncompressed colour image database. In: Proceedings of the SPIE Storage and Retrieval Methods and Applications for Multimedia, San Jose, CA, USA, pp. 472–480 (2004)

Reversible Data Hiding for Texture Videos and Depth Maps Coding with Quality Scalability

Yuanzhi Yao$^{(\boxtimes)}$, Weiming Zhang, and Nenghai Yu

Department of Electronic Engineering and Information Science,
University of Science and Technology of China, Hefei 230027, China
yaoyz@mail.ustc.edu.cn, {zhangwm,ynh}@ustc.edu.cn

Abstract. To support 3-D video and free-viewpoint video applications, efficient texture videos and depth maps coding should be addressed. In this paper, a novel reversible data hiding scheme is proposed to integrate depth maps into corresponding texture video bitstreams. At the sender end, the depth video bitstream obtained by depth down-sampling and compression is embedded in residual coefficients of corresponding texture video. The data embedding is implemented by the histogram shifting technique. At the receiver end, the depth maps can be retrieved with scalable quality after data extraction, video decoding and texture-based depth reconstruction. Due to the attractive property of reversible data hiding, the texture video bitstream can be perfectly recovered. Experimental results demonstrate that the proposed scheme can achieve better video rendering quality and coding efficiency compared with existing related schemes.

Keywords: Reversible data hiding · Depth map · Depth down-sampling · Histogram shifting · Texture-based depth reconstruction

1 Introduction

Differing from traditional 2-D imaging, the emerging stereoscopic imaging can provide arbitrary views of real 3-D scenes. Due to the increasing demand for 3-D video and free-viewpoint video applications, the stereoscopic imaging has been regarded as the next generation visual technology. One of the key problems for stereoscopic imaging is how to efficiently represent real 3-D scenes. Among many 3-D scene representation technologies [1], the texture-plus-depth representation has been extensively studied because of its low computing cost and high rendering quality. In the texture-plus-depth representation [2], virtual views can be synthesized from the acquired texture videos and their corresponding depth maps. The depth map records the relative distance between the observed object and the camera. Therefore, texture-plus-depth video coding and transmission have attracted considerable research effort [3–5]. In 3-D video coding, texture videos and depth maps should be jointly considered for obtaining the synthesized virtual views with high quality. Either the distortion of texture videos or the distortion of depth maps can degrade

© Springer International Publishing AG 2017
Y.Q. Shi et al. (Eds.): IWDW 2016, LNCS 10082, pp. 421–435, 2017.
DOI: 10.1007/978-3-319-53465-7_31

the quality of synthesized virtual views. Furthermore, the stereoscopic visual effect will no longer exist without depth maps in the texture-plus-depth representation.

With regard to the importance of depth maps, the transmission of depth maps can be achieved using the covert communication [6]. Hence, many schemes have been proposed to integrate the depth map into corresponding texture image/video using data hiding to address the security concern. Khan et al. [7] proposed to embed the depth map in its corresponding 2-D image to secure the transmission of the depth map. In [8], Tong et al. embedded the disparity of two stereo images in one of them for reducing storage space. In Wang et al.'s scheme [9], the depth map is embedded in quantized DCT coefficients of the JPEG image using the difference expansion technique [10]. Jung [11] proposed to embed the depth map in the JPEG compressed bitstream of corresponding texture image using super-pixel image segmentation and depth value clustering. Due to the spatial and temporal correlation of depth maps, the texture-plus-depth representation format can also be compressed using the efficient video coding technologies, such as H.264/AVC [12]. In [13,14], Wang et al. extended their watermarking scheme of coding depth maps from JPEG image to H.264/AVC video. They embedded the depth video bitstream obtained by compressing depth maps in quantized DCT coefficients of corresponding texture video.

The major concern of embedding depth maps in corresponding texture video is that the embedding capacity of texture video is limited due to high-efficiency video coding. Therefore, the difference expansion technique [10] is utilized in the schemes [13,14] to obtain relatively higher embedding capacity. However, data embedding in quantized DCT coefficients using the difference expansion technique can induce severe distortion in texture videos. As an alternative to the schemes [13,14], Shahid et al. [15] proposed to embed the depth video bitstream obtained by depth down-sampling and compression in quantized DCT coefficients of corresponding texture video using LSB replacement. Then, the depth maps can be reconstructed after data extraction, video decoding and depth up-sampling. The depth down-sampling is effective on reducing the size of depth video bitstream. Moreover, the depth maps can be reconstructed with scalable quality by adjusting the scaling factor. Unfortunately, the texture video cannot be losslessly recovered without reversible data hiding in [15]. Due to the motion compensation, the distribution of quantized DCT coefficients in videos can be modeled as the Laplacian probability distribution [16,17], which provides enough embedding capacity for the histogram shifting technique [18,19]. To obtain a tradeoff between the embedding capacity and the stego texture video quality, the histogram shifting and the depth down-sampling should be jointly used. In the depth down-sampling-based scheme, we should reconstruct the depth map where missing depth samples need to be estimated after data extraction and video decoding. According to the grouping principle in [20], the correlation of depth samples is associated with the similarity and the proximity of corresponding texture samples. It means that we can reconstruct the depth map with high quality based on the texture video. However, Shahid et al.'s scheme [15] does not utilize corresponding texture videos for reconstructing depth maps. Hence, new texture videos and depth maps coding schemes which support reversible depth embedding and texture-based depth reconstruction should be sought.

We propose a novel reversible data hiding scheme of integrating depth maps into corresponding texture video bitstreams for addressing the secure 3-D video coding in this paper. At the sender end, the depth video bitstream obtained by depth down-sampling and compression is embedded in residual coefficients of corresponding texture video. The data embedding is implemented by the histogram shifting technique. At the receiver end, the depth maps can be retrieved with scalable quality after data extraction, video decoding and texture-based depth reconstruction. The reversibility guarantees that the texture video bitstream can be losslessly recovered after data extraction. In conclusion, the highlights of this paper can be summarized as follows.

- The proposed scheme can embed the depth video bitstream in corresponding texture video with low distortion.
- The texture video bitstream can be losslessly recovered after data extraction.
- The depth maps can be reconstructed with scalable quality by adjusting the scaling factor.
- Texture-based depth reconstruction is used to obtain the depth maps with high quality.

The remainder of the paper is organized as follows. In Sect. 2, the proposed reversible data hiding scheme for texture videos and depth maps coding is elaborated. The experimental results are presented in Sect. 3. Section 4 finally concludes this paper.

2   Proposed Reversible Data Hiding Scheme for Texture Videos and Depth Maps Coding

In this section, the proposed reversible data hiding scheme for texture videos and depth maps coding is discussed in detail. Figure 1 illustrates the framework of the proposed scheme. The proposed scheme contains three components which are depth down-sampling and compression, depth video bitstream embedding and extraction, and texture-based depth reconstruction.

2.1   Depth Down-Sampling and Compression

In the 3-D video system, texture video sequences are captured by the camera array which is composed of several cameras with a certain interval. The depth maps can be acquired by depth estimation from adjacent-view texture video sequences. The real depth value is in floating-point type generally. To compress depth data using existing video coding technologies, real depth values should be quantized to the depth map in which sample values range from 0 to 255 [2]. Like the texture video sequence, the depth maps are also a series of images with spatial and temporal correlation. Afterwards, texture video sequences and depth maps can be compressed using existing video coding technologies, such as H.264/AVC [12].

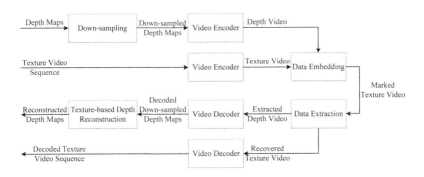

Fig. 1. Framework of the proposed reversible data hiding scheme.

To reduce the size of depth video bitstream, depth down-sampling is performed before compressing the depth maps. Differing from the texture image, the depth map usually has a well-defined object boundary. Therefore, it is important to maintain the object boundaries of the depth map for high-quality rendering at the receiver end. Considering that object boundaries are sensitive to coding errors, the edge-preserving filters [21,22] can be used to eliminate coding errors and refine object boundaries. Without loss of generality, the depth maps are down-sampled by dropping samples as follows.

$$Depth_{down}(i,j) = Depth(i \cdot step, j \cdot step) \qquad (1)$$

where *step* is the scaling factor. Then, the down-sampled depth maps are compressed by the video encoder to generate the depth video bitstream.

2.2 Depth Video Bitstream Embedding and Extraction

To address the secure transmission of depth maps, embedding the depth video bitstream obtained by depth down-sampling and compression in the texture video is a feasible solution. Reversible data hiding should be used to losslessly recover the texture video after data extraction. In video data hiding, when we embed data in the current frame, the embedding distortion in the current frame will propagate to subsequent frames. This is called the inter-frame distortion drift. Therefore, how to decrease the inter-frame distortion drift caused by data embedding deserves investigation.

We only focus on the distortion drift of P-frames, because B-frames do not cause distortion drift and I-frames are not used for data embedding. We suppose that the total frame number of the texture video is N and the GOP (Group of Pictures) structure of the texture video is IPPP, in which only the first frame is encoded as an I-frame and the remaining frames are encoded as P-frames.

According to the inter-frame distortion drift analysis in [23], the overall distortion $D(n)$ of the nth video frame at the receiver end is given by

$$D(n) = D_s(n) + D_e(n) \tag{2}$$

where $D_s(n)$ is the source distortion caused by lossy compression and $D_e(n)$ is the embedding distortion caused by embedding data in quantized DCT coefficients of the nth video frame. When the texture video bitstream is given, $D_s(n)$ is constant. Therefore, to decrease the overall distortion $D(n)$ and improve the decoded texture video quality, the left problem is to decrease $D_e(n)$ during data embedding [23]. We can rewrite Eq. (2) as follows.

$$\begin{aligned} D(n) &= D_s(n) + D_e(n) \\ &= D_s(n) + \alpha \cdot D_e(n-1) + p \cdot \mathrm{E}\{[\tilde{r}(n,i) - \hat{r}(n,i)]^2\} \end{aligned} \tag{3}$$

where α is a constant relating to the video content, p is the probability of embedding data in the nth frame ($n \geq 2$), and $E\{x(n,i)\}$ is denoted as the average (over all pixels) expected value of the random variable $x(n,i)$. In Eq. (3), $\tilde{r}(n,i)$ and $\hat{r}(n,i)$ represent the ith reconstructed residues of the nth video frame with embedded data and without embedded data respectively. It can be implied from Eq. (3) that we should decrease $\mathrm{E}\{[\tilde{r}(n,i) - \hat{r}(n,i)]^2\}$ to decrease the embedding distortion in the nth frame and the embedding distortion of each frame can accumulate as the frame index increases.

According to the property of integer 4×4 transform in H.264/AVC [24], the (i,j)th quantized DCT coefficient in the 4×4 block can be classified according to its induced independent embedding distortion[1] as follows.

$$\begin{cases} C_1 = \{(2,2),(4,2),(2,4),(4,4)\} \\ C_2 = \{(1,2),(2,1),(1,4),(2,3),(3,2),(4,1),(3,4),(4,3)\} \\ C_3 = \{(1,1),(3,1),(1,3),(3,3)\} \end{cases} \tag{4}$$

In Eq. (4), C_1, C_2 and C_3 represent the coefficient classification sets, in which modifying the coefficients in the given set can induce approximately equal embedding distortions. It has been verified that embedding data into coefficients in C_1 can induce the minimum distortion and embedding data into coefficients in C_3 can induce the maximum distortion [23]. Therefore, it is necessary to embed data using coefficient selection, which means that data should be embedded in the coefficients in C_1 with highest priority, the coefficients in C_2 with medium priority and the coefficients in C_3 with lowest priority.

The depth video bitstream is the to-be-embedded message sequence $\mathbf{b} = (b_1, b_2, \cdots, b_m)$ with length m. The Laplacian probability distribution of quantized DCT coefficients in videos [16,17] provides enough embedding capacity for the histogram shifting technique [18]. Therefore, we denote $T_p = 1$ and $T_n = -1$

---

[1] The independent embedding distortion is calculated by adding an error δ to the (i,j)th quantized DCT coefficient in the 4×4 block using the MSE (Mean Squared Error) measure.

as the two highest bins in the histogram of quantized luma DCT coefficients in the texture video. (Zero coefficients are not used for data embedding.) The embedding capacity is the sum of the number of bin T_p and the number of bin T_n. We describe the data embedding algorithm as follows.

- Case 1: If $|z_{ij}| > 1$, shift z_{ij} by 1 unit to the right or the left respectively.

$$z'_{ij} = \begin{cases} z_{ij} + 1 & \text{if } z_{ij} > 1 \\ z_{ij} - 1 & \text{if } z_{ij} < -1 \end{cases} \tag{5}$$

where z_{ij} is the (i,j)th original quantized DCT coefficient in the 4×4 block and z'_{ij} is the corresponding stego coefficient.

- Case 2: If $|z_{ij}| = 1$, modify z_{ij} according to the to-be-embedded message bit b_k.

$$z'_{ij} = \begin{cases} z_{ij} & \text{if } |z_{ij}| = 1 \text{ and } b_k = 0 \\ z_{ij} + 1 & \text{if } z_{ij} = 1 \text{ and } b_k = 1 \\ z_{ij} - 1 & \text{if } z_{ij} = -1 \text{ and } b_k = 1 \end{cases} \tag{6}$$

- Case 3: If $z_{ij} = 0$, z_{ij} remains unchanged.

$$z'_{ij} = z_{ij} \tag{7}$$

Using the above data embedding algorithm, the following steps should be conducted to complete embedding the depth video bitstream in the corresponding texture video.

- Step 1: Partial decoding is performed on the texture video bitstream to obtain the quantized luma DCT coefficients. The data embedding starts in the Nth frame.
- Step 2: Embed message bits in inter-coded macroblocks (excluding P_Skip mode coded macroblocks) within the current frame using coefficient selection. It means that data should be embedded into the coefficients in C_1 with highest priority, the coefficients in C_2 with medium priority and the coefficients in C_3 with lowest priority [23]. During data embedding process, record the number of embedded message bits k.
- Step 3: If $k < m$, return to Step 2 to embed data in previous frames one by one until all message bits have been embedded.
- Step 4: Partial encoding is performed on the quantized luma DCT coefficients to generate the stego texture video bitstream.

The number of embedded message bits m in the stego texture video bitstream should be synchronized between the sender end and the receiver end. Before data extraction, partial decoding is performed on the stego texture video bitstream to obtain the quantized luma DCT coefficients. The data extraction is the inverse process of data embedding. We can extract the embedded depth video bitstream $\mathbf{b} = (b_1, b_2, \cdots, b_m)$ as depicted in Eq. (8).

$$b_k = \begin{cases} 0 & \text{if } |z'_{ij}| = 1 \\ 1 & \text{if } |z'_{ij}| = 2 \end{cases} \tag{8}$$

where z'_{ij} is the (i,j)th stego quantized DCT coefficient in the 4×4 block.

The original quantized DCT coefficient recovery is described as follows.

$$z_{ij} = \begin{cases} z'_{ij} & \text{if } z'_{ij} \in \{-1, 0, 1\} \\ z'_{ij} - 1 & \text{if } z'_{ij} \geq 2 \\ z'_{ij} + 1 & \text{if } z'_{ij} \leq -2 \end{cases} \tag{9}$$

Since the data embedding process is reversible, the texture video can be losslessly recovered after data extraction.

2.3 Texture-Based Depth Reconstruction

After extracting the embedded depth video bitstream and decoding it, we can only obtain the decoded down-sampled depth maps. To reconstruct the depth map, the missing samples whose horizontal or vertical coordinates are multiples of the scaling factor need to be estimated. According to the analysis in [20], the correlation of depth samples is associated with the similarity and the proximity of corresponding texture samples. It is an effective way to reconstruct the depth map to its original resolution with high quality based on the texture video.

In the texture-based depth reconstruction, each existing depth sample has different weight on estimating missing depth samples based on the similarity and the proximity of corresponding texture samples. Moreover, the similarity and the proximity of texture samples can be measured separately. Therefore, the weight of existing depth sample can be calculated by

$$\omega(p, q) = \exp[-(\frac{\triangle c_{pq}}{\lambda_c} + \frac{\triangle g_{pq}}{\lambda_g})] \tag{10}$$

where $\triangle c_{pq}$ and $\triangle g_{pq}$ represent the distance between the colors of texture samples p and q, and the distance between texture samples p and q respectively [20]. λ_c and λ_g are two parameters to control the strength of similarity and the strength of proximity respectively. In Eq. (10), the $\triangle c_{pq}$ is calculated from the corresponding texture video using RGB color space in the ℓ_2-norm as follows.

$$\triangle c_{pq} = \sqrt{\sum_{C \in \{R, G, B\}} (C_p - C_q)^2} \tag{11}$$

where C_p and C_q are the color component values of texture samples p and q respectively. In Eq. (10), the $\triangle g_{pq}$ is calculated in the ℓ_1-norm[2] as follows.

$$\triangle g_{pq} = |i_p - i_q| + |j_p - j_q| \tag{12}$$

where (i_p, j_p) and (i_q, j_q) are the coordinates of texture samples p and q respectively.

---

[2] In [20], it is suggested that $\triangle g_{pq}$ should be calculated in the ℓ_2-norm. Actually, the better reconstructed depth map quality can be obtained if $\triangle g_{pq}$ is calculated in the ℓ_1-norm according to our experiments.

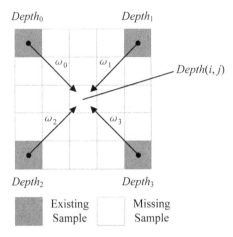

Fig. 2. Illustration of texture-based depth reconstruction.

The texture-based depth reconstruction algorithm can be illustrated in Fig. 2, in which the scaling factor is set as 4. To estimate the missing depth sample $Depth(i, j)$, we can locate four nearest existing depth samples which are $Depth_0$, $Depth_1$, $Depth_2$ and $Depth_3$ respectively. Using texture-based depth reconstruction, we can calculate the weight ω_k for the missing depth sample $Depth(i, j)$ and the nearest existing depth sample $Depth_k$ where $k \in \{0, 1, 2, 3\}$ as depicted in Eq. (10). When we have four weights, we can estimate the missing depth sample $Depth(i, j)$ using texture-based depth reconstruction as depicted in Eq. (13).

$$Depth(i, j) = \frac{\omega_0 \cdot Depth_0 + \omega_1 \cdot Depth_1 + \omega_2 \cdot Depth_2 + \omega_3 \cdot Depth_3}{\omega_0 + \omega_1 + \omega_2 + \omega_3} \quad (13)$$

Using the above texture-based depth reconstruction algorithm, the downsampled depth map can be reconstructed to its original resolution with high quality.

3   Experimental Results

The proposed reversible data hiding scheme for texture videos and depth maps coding has been implemented in the H.264/AVC reference software JM 10.2 [25]. Besides, the schemes proposed by Wang et al. [14] and Shahid et al. [15] are also implemented for performance comparison. As shown in Fig. 3, two free-viewpoint video sequences [26] which are Akko&Kayo with resolution 640×480 and Kendo with resolution 1024×768 respectively are used in the experiments. We use commonly adopted measurements PSNR and SSIM [27] to evaluate the objective visual quality of texture videos and depth maps. The PSNR (dB) and the SSIM are calculated by comparing the decoded reconstructed video sequence with the original video sequence. Texture video sequences are encoded using QP

(a)   (b)   (c)   (d)

Fig. 3. Free-viewpoint video sequences used in the experiments. (a) Akko&Kayo, (b) Depth map of Akko&Kayo, (c) Kendo, and (d) Depth map of Kendo.

16 and depth maps are encoded using QP 28. (QP is the quantization parameter.) The first 100 frames of each texture video sequence and depth maps are encoded at frame rate 30 fps. In the texture-based depth reconstruction in Eqs. (10) and (13), the parameter λ_c is set as the maximum value of color distances in the texture video[3] and the parameter λ_g is set as the scaling factor.

3.1 Visual Quality of the Stego Texture Video

In the experiments, video sequences Akko&Kayo in view 27 and Kendo in view 1 are used for comparing the visual quality of stego texture videos. The corresponding depth maps of each texture video sequence are down-sampled with different scaling factors respectively. Afterwards, the depth video bitstreams are embedded in the corresponding texture videos using Wang et al.'s scheme [14], Shahid et al.'s scheme [15] and our proposed scheme respectively.

The comparison of average luma PSNR (dB) of stego texture videos is listed in Table 1. The visual quality of cover texture videos without embedded data is also presented in Table 1. The bold digits in Table 1 mean that the corresponding scheme can achieve the best visual quality of stego texture videos. Our proposed scheme focuses on decreasing the inter-frame distortion drift so that it outperforms Wang et al.'s scheme and Shahid et al.'s scheme in the measurement of average luma PSNR. The notation "–" in Table 1 means that the stego texture video cannot contain the corresponding depth video bitstream. In Wang et al.'s scheme, the difference expansion technique is used to embed data so that the highest embedding capacity can be guaranteed. However, severe distortions are induced in stego texture videos.

Figure 4 shows the subjective results of the 16th frame, 31st frame, 46th frame, 61st frame and 76th frame of decoded texture video sequence Akko&Kayo in view 27 with scaling factor 4. Obvious visual distortion can be seen using Wang et al.'s scheme. Shahid et al.'s scheme and our proposed scheme can achieve better subjective visual quality.

---

[3] The color distance in the texture video is calculated between two texture samples which correspond to the missing depth sample and the nearest existing depth sample respectively.

Table 1. Comparison of average luma PSNR (dB) of stego texture videos.

Video sequence	Scaling factor	PSNR (dB)			
		Cover	Wang et al. [14]	Shahid et al. [15]	Proposed
Akko&Kayo	2	46.54	21.21	–	–
	4	46.54	21.20	31.70	**40.49**
	8	46.54	20.73	36.61	**44.64**
	16	46.54	21.60	38.54	**45.93**
Kendo	2	47.43	25.63	34.75	**38.23**
	4	47.43	25.34	36.01	**44.67**
	8	47.43	25.03	40.14	**46.46**
	16	47.43	24.95	42.79	**47.18**

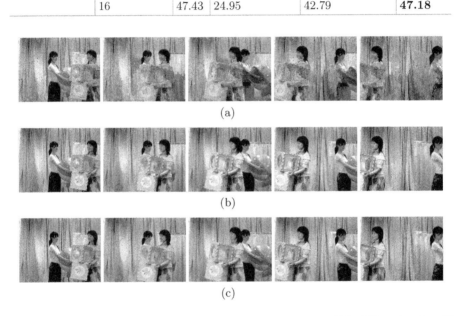

(a)

(b)

(c)

Fig. 4. Subjective results of decoded texture video sequence Akko&Kayo in view 27 with scaling factor 4. (a) Wang et al. [14], (b) Shahid et al. [15], and (c) Proposed.

3.2 Impacts on the Coding Efficiency

We measure the coding efficiency using the video bit rate increment BR_{inc} as follows.

$$BR_{inc} = \frac{BR_{texture+depth} - BR_{texture}}{BR_{texture}} \times 100\% \tag{14}$$

where $BR_{texture+depth}$ is the video bit rate used for coding both texture videos and depth maps and $BR_{texture}$ is the video bit rate used for coding texture videos. In data hiding-based schemes, $BR_{texture+depth}$ is equal to the bit rate of stego texture video. In the experiments, video sequences Akko&Kayo in view

Table 2. Comparison of video bit rate increments.

Video sequence	Scaling factor	$BR_{inc}(\%)$			
		Separate coding	Wang et al. [14]	Shahid et al. [15]	Proposed
Akko&Kayo	2	17.07	**13.20**	–	–
	4	17.07	5.41	6.93	**5.07**
	8	17.07	2.28	2.61	**1.92**
	16	17.07	1.29	1.20	**0.87**
Kendo	2	10.69	**8.86**	12.35	9.02
	4	10.69	3.76	5.00	**3.59**
	8	10.69	1.81	2.19	**1.55**
	16	10.69	1.00	0.97	**0.65**

27 and Kendo in view 1 are used. The comparison of video bit rate increments among Wang et al.'s scheme [14], Shahid et al.'s scheme [15] and our proposed scheme is listed in Table 2, in which bold digits mean that the corresponding scheme can achieve the smallest video bit rate increment. The notation "–" in Table 2 means that the stego texture video cannot contain the corresponding depth video bitstream. Separate coding denotes coding texture videos and depth maps independently without depth down-sampling and data hiding. Data hiding-based schemes can obtain smaller BR_{inc} and have higher coding efficiency compared with separate coding.

3.3 Visual Quality of the Reconstructed Depth Maps

To compare the visual quality of reconstructed depth maps, original depth maps of video sequences Akko&Kayo in view 27 and Kendo in view 1 are used. Without down-sampling depth maps, the average luma PSNR values of depth videos obtained by compressing depth maps of video sequences Akko&Kayo and Kendo are 41.03 dB and 47.23 dB respectively. Because the depth reconstruction algorithm is not explicit in Shahid et al.'s scheme [15], the decoded down-sampled depth maps are reconstructed using nearest-neighbor interpolation, bilinear interpolation, Wildeboer et al.'s scheme [28] and our proposed scheme respectively in the experiments. Nearest-neighbor interpolation and bilinear interpolation are implemented using OpenCV 2.4.9 [29]. A variant of nearest-neighbor interpolation which considers the texture sample distance and the color distance of texture samples is utilized in Wildeboer et al.'s scheme.

The comparison of average luma PSNR (dB) and average luma SSIM of reconstructed depth maps is listed in Table 3, in which bold digits mean that the corresponding scheme can achieve the best visual quality of reconstructed depth maps. Moreover, the subjective quality of the 51st reconstructed depth maps of video sequences Akko&Kayo in view 27 and Kendo in view 1 with scaling

432   Y. Yao et al.

Table 3. Comparison of average luma PSNR (dB) and average luma SSIM of reconstructed depth maps.

Video sequence	Scaling factor	PSNR (dB)				SSIM			
		Nearest-neighbor	Bilinear	Wildeboer et al. [28]	Proposed	Nearest-neighbor	Bilinear	Wildeboer et al. [28]	Proposed
Akko & Kayo	2	34.39	35.30	34.38	**36.07**	0.9196	0.9254	0.9188	**0.9297**
	4	29.99	31.17	30.04	**32.82**	0.8589	0.8774	0.8604	**0.8921**
	8	26.20	27.45	26.08	**29.54**	0.8143	0.8305	0.8156	**0.8572**
	16	22.76	24.04	22.56	**26.28**	0.8047	0.7891	0.8043	**0.8241**
Kendo	2	42.10	42.69	42.03	**43.17**	0.9798	0.9815	0.9795	**0.9822**
	4	37.83	38.68	37.85	**39.94**	0.9646	0.9701	0.9646	**0.9731**
	8	33.95	34.96	33.96	**36.90**	0.9495	0.9575	0.9495	**0.9634**
	16	30.42	31.58	30.43	**33.76**	0.9481	0.9451	0.9481	**0.9558**

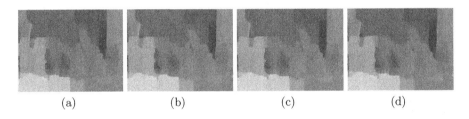

(a)   (b)   (c)   (d)

Fig. 5. Reconstructed depth maps of video sequence Akko&Kayo in view 27 with scaling factor 4. (a) Nearest-neighbor interpolation with PSNR = 27.940 dB and SSIM = 0.8380, (b) Bilinear interpolation with PSNR = 29.164 dB and SSIM = 0.8555, (c) Wildeboer et al.'s scheme [28] with PSNR = 27.962 dB and SSIM = 0.8395, and (d) Proposed scheme with PSNR = 30.999 dB and SSIM = 0.8781.

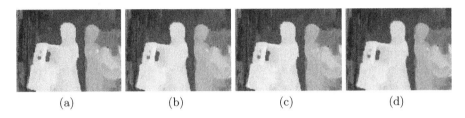

(a)   (b)   (c)   (d)

Fig. 6. Reconstructed depth maps of video sequence Kendo in view 1 with scaling factor 4. (a) Nearest-neighbor interpolation with PSNR = 38.442 dB and SSIM = 0.9674, (b) Bilinear interpolation with PSNR = 39.266 dB and SSIM = 0.9717, (c) Wildeboer et al.'s scheme [28] with PSNR = 38.497 dB and SSIM = 0.9676, and (d) Proposed scheme with PSNR = 40.592 dB and SSIM = 0.9757.

factor 4 can be seen in Figs. 5 and 6 respectively, in which the luma PSNR value and the luma SSIM value of each frame are presented. Through comparisons, it can be observed that our proposed scheme can achieve the best visual quality of reconstructed depth maps. By adjusting the scaling factor, the depth maps can be reconstructed with scalable quality.

3.4   Visual Quality of the Synthesized View

Before view synthesis, we firstly down-sample original depth maps of video sequences Akko&Kayo in view 27 and view 29 with scaling factor 4 and compress them. Then, the depth video bitstreams are embedded in corresponding texture videos. After data extraction, video decoding and depth reconstruction, the reconstructed depth maps in view 27 and view 29 can be obtained. The texture video sequence Akko&Kayo in view 28 is synthesized from adjacent view 27 and view 29 using the depth estimation and view synthesis software [30].

The comparison of visual quality of the 51st synthesized frames in view 28 is given in Fig. 7, in which the luma PSNR value and the luma SSIM value of each synthesized frame are presented. The visual quality of synthesized frames depends on the decoded texture video sequence and the reconstructed depth maps. The 51st original frame in view 28 captured by the camera array is presented as the ground truth. We set two comparison targets as follows. In comparison target Tar1, Shahid et al.'s scheme [15] is used for data embedding and bilinear interpolation is used for depth reconstruction. In comparison target Tar2, our proposed data embedding algorithm and Wildeboer et al.'s depth reconstruction algorithm [28] are used. The average luma PSNR values of all synthesized frames in view 28 using Tar1, Tar2 and our proposed scheme are 27.49 dB, 30.03 dB and 30.05 dB respectively. The average luma SSIM values of all synthesized frames in view 28 using Tar1, Tar2 and our proposed scheme are 0.8692, 0.8945 and 0.8970 respectively. In Tar1, the decoded texture video sequence cannot be losslessly recovered after data extraction, which is permanently distorted due to data embedding. In Tar2, the visual quality of reconstructed depth maps is lower than that in our proposed scheme. Due to the superiority of data embedding and depth reconstruction in our proposed scheme, the best visual quality of synthesized view 28 can be obtained as shown in Fig. 7.

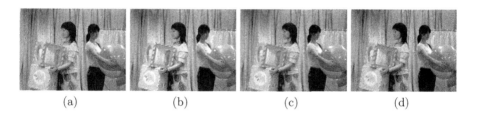

(a)   (b)   (c)   (d)

Fig. 7. Synthesized view rendering of video sequence Akko&Kayo in view 28 with scaling factor 4. (a) Original frame, (b) Tar1 with PSNR = 26.488 dB and SSIM = 0.8545, (c) Tar2 with PSNR = 29.650 dB and SSIM = 0.8875, and (d) Proposed scheme with PSNR = 29.702 dB and SSIM = 0.8913.

4   Conclusion and Future Work

In this paper, a novel reversible data hiding scheme for texture videos and depth maps coding is proposed. At the sender end, the depth video bitstream obtained by depth down-sampling and compression is embedded in residual coefficients of corresponding texture video. At the receiver end, the depth maps can be retrieved with scalable quality after data extraction, video decoding and texture-based depth reconstruction. The experimental results demonstrate the effectiveness of our proposed scheme. Our future work is to design the rate-distortion optimization criterion for texture videos and depth maps coding using reversible data hiding.

Acknowledgments. This work was supported in part by the National Natural Science Foundation of China under Grant 61572452, in part by the Strategic Priority Research Program of the Chinese Academy of Sciences under Grant XDA06030601, and in part by the China Scholarship Council Program under Grant 201506340006.

References

1. Alatan, A.A., Yemez, Y., Gudukbay, U., Zabulis, X., Muller, K., Erdem, C.E., Weigel, C., Smolic, A.: Scene representation technologies for 3DTV-a survey. IEEE Trans. Circ. Syst. Video Technol. **17**(11), 1587–1605 (2007)
2. Fehn, C.: Depth-image-based rendering (DIBR), compression and transmission for a new approach on 3D-TV. In: Proceedings of SPIE Stereoscopic Displays and Virtual Reality Systems XI, pp. 93–104 (2004)
3. Yuan, H., Chang, Y., Huo, J., Yang, F., Lu, Z.: Model-based joint bit allocation between texture videos and depth maps for 3-D video coding. IEEE Trans. Circ. Syst. Video Technol. **21**(4), 485–497 (2011)
4. Kim, W.-S., Ortega, A., Lai, P., Tian, D.: Depth map coding optimization using rendered view distortion for 3D video coding. IEEE Trans. Image Process. **24**(11), 3534–3545 (2015)
5. Shao, F., Lin, W., Jiang, G., Yu, M.: Low-complexity depth coding by depth sensitivity aware rate-distortion optimization. IEEE Trans. Broadcast. **62**(1), 94–102 (2016)
6. Cao, Y., Zhang, H., Zhao, X., Yu, H.: Covert communication by compressed videos exploiting the uncertainty of motion estimation. IEEE Commun. Lett. **19**(2), 203–206 (2015)
7. Khan, A., Mahmood, M.T., Ali, A., Usman, I., Choi, T.-S.: Hiding depth map of an object in its 2D image: reversible watermarking for 3D cameras. In: Proceedings of International Conference on Consumer Electronics, pp. 1–2 (2009)
8. Tong, X., Shen, G., Xuan, G., Li, S., Yang, Z., Li, J., Shi, Y.Q.: Stereo image coding with histogram-pair based reversible data hiding. In: Proceedings of International Workshop on Digital-Forensics and Watermarking, pp. 201–214 (2014)
9. Wang, W., Zhao, J., Tam, W.J., Speranza, F., Wang, Z.: Hiding depth map into stereo image in JPEG format using reversible watermarking. In: Proceedings of International Conference on Internet Multimedia Computing and Service, pp. 82–85 (2011)
10. Tian, J.: Reversible data embedding using a difference expansion. IEEE Trans. Circ. Syst. Video Technol. **13**(8), 890–896 (2003)
11. Jung, S.-W.: Lossless embedding of depth hints in JPEG compressed color images. Sig. Process. **122**, 39–51 (2016)

12. Wiegand, T., Sullivan, G.J., Bjontegaard, G., Luthra, A.: Overview of the H.264/AVC video coding standard. IEEE Trans. Circ. Syst. Video Technol. **13**(7), 560–576 (2003)
13. Wang, W., Zhao, J., Tam, W.J., Speranza, F.: Hiding depth information into H.264 compressed video using reversible watermarking. In: Proceedings of ACM Multimedia International Workshop on Cloud-based Multimedia Applications and Services for E-health, pp. 27–31 (2012)
14. Wang, W., Zhao, J.: Hiding depth information in compressed 2D image/video using reversible watermarking. Multimed. Tools Appl. **75**(8), 4285–4303 (2016)
15. Shahid, Z., Puech, W.: Synchronization of texture and depth map by data hiding for 3D H.264 video. In: Proceedings of International Conference on Image Processing, pp. 2773–2776 (2011)
16. Bellifemine, F., Capellino, A., Chimienti, A., Picco, R., Ponti, R.: Statistical analysis of the 2D-DCT coefficients of the differential signal for images. Sig. Process: Image Commun. **4**(6), 477–488 (1992)
17. Gormish, M.J., Gill, J.T.: Computation-rate-distortion in transform coders for image compression. In: Proceedings of SPIE Image and Video Processing, pp. 146–152 (1993)
18. Ni, Z., Shi, Y.-Q., Ansari, N., Su, W.: Reversible data hiding. IEEE Trans. Circ. Syst. Video Technol. **16**(3), 354–362 (2006)
19. Xu, D., Wang, R.: Efficient reversible data hiding in encrypted H.264/AVC videos. J. Electron. Imaging **23**(5), 053022-1–053022-14 (2014)
20. Yoon, K.-J., Kweon, I.S.: Adaptive support-weight approach for correspondence search. IEEE Trans. Pattern Anal. Mach. Intell. **28**(4), 650–656 (2006)
21. Tomasi, C., Manduchi, R.: Bilateral filtering for gray and color images. In: Proceedings of International Conference on Computer Vision, pp. 839–846 (1998)
22. Oh, K.-J., Vetro, A., Ho, Y.-S.: Depth coding using a boundary reconstruction filter for 3-D video systems. IEEE Trans. Circ. Syst. Video Technol. **21**(3), 350–359 (2011)
23. Yao, Y., Zhang, W., Yu, N.: Inter-frame distortion drift analysis for reversible data hiding in encrypted H.264/AVC video bitstreams. Sig. Process. **128**, 531–545 (2016)
24. ITU-T Recommendation: Advanced video coding for generic audiovisual services. ISO/IEC (2012)
25. The H.264/AVC joint model (JM), ver. 10.2. http://iphome.hhi.de/suehring/tml/download/old_jm/
26. Free-viewpoint video sequences. http://www.tanimoto.nuee.nagoya-u.ac.jp/mpeg/mpeg_ftv.html
27. Wang, Z., Bovik, A.C., Sheikh, H.R., Simoncelli, E.P.: Image quality assessment: from error visibility to structural similarity. IEEE Trans. Image Process. **13**(4), 600–612 (2004)
28. Wildeboer, M.O., Yendo, T., Tehrani, M.P., Fujii, T., Tanimoto, M.: Color based depth up-sampling for depth compression. In: Proceedings of Picture Coding Symposium, pp. 170–173 (2010)
29. OpenCV, ver. 2.4.9. http://opencv.org/
30. Depth estimation view synthesis software. http://www.tanimoto.nuee.nagoya-u.ac.jp/mpeg/mpeg_ftv.html

Reversible Data Hiding in Encrypted AMBTC Compressed Images

Xuejing Niu[1], Zhaoxia Yin[1,2(✉)], Xinpeng Zhang[2], Jin Tang[1], and Bin Luo[1]

[1] Key Laboratory of Intelligent Computing and Signal Processing, Ministry of Education, Anhui University, Hefei 230601 People's Republic of China
yinzhaoxia@ahu.edu.cn
[2] School of Communication and Information Engineering, Shanghai University, Shanghai 200072, People's Republic of China

Abstract. Signal processing in encrypted domain has attracted high attention during the needs of content security and privacy protection. Reversible data hiding in encrypted images (RDH-EI) also becomes a hot topic. However, most of the published techniques are designed for uncompressed images rather than JPEG-, VQ- and BTC-compressed images. In this paper, for the first time, a RDH-EI method for AMBTC images is proposed. In this method, the higher mean and lower mean of a triple in AMBTC compressed image is encrypted by using stream cipher with the same random bits. Therefore, the spatial correlation of a nature image is preserved and redundant space can be exploited by using the histogram of prediction error. Experimental results demonstrate that the proposed method can embed considerable bits while leave little distortion.

Keywords: Signal processing in encrypted domain · Privacy protection · Block Truncation Coding · Reversible Data Hiding in Encrypted Images

1 Introduction

By taking full advantage of the coding redundancy of multimedia and the insensitivity of human vision, data hiding, as one of the most significant research area of information security, embeds additional data into a host signal, and can be classified as non-reversible [1, 2] and reversible categories [3–5]. The original signal can be recovered inerrably with reversible data hiding which can be achieved mainly based on difference expansion (DE) [3, 4] and histogram shifting (HS) [5]. For plaintext images, all these methods have good efficiency. But the original cover images have to be accessible to or seen by the data hider during embedding process.

The needs of content security and privacy protection contribute to the emergence of signal processing in the encrypted domain (SPED) [6]. RDH-EI, as a typical SPED topic, enable additional data to be embedded into cipher-image without revealing the original content and original content to be recovered inerrably at receiver side. As a kind of emerging technology [7–13], RDH-EI is widely used. Take telemedicine system as an example, medical images are often encrypted to protect patients' privacy,

© Springer International Publishing AG 2017
Y.Q. Shi et al. (Eds.): IWDW 2016, LNCS 10082, pp. 436–445, 2017.
DOI: 10.1007/978-3-319-53465-7_32

while medical records etc. should be allowed to be embedded into encrypted images by database administrator. Meanwhile, after decryption of encrypted image and retrieval of hidden message, doctor can inerrably recover original medical images for diagnosis. RDH-EI is required.

The first RDH-EI method was proposed in Ref. [7]. In this method, original image is encrypted with Advanced Encryption Standard, and one bit can be embedded into a block consisting of n pixels. On receiver side, after decryption of the marked cipher-image, the analysis of the local standard deviation is indispensable for data extraction and image recovery. This is a great idea. But the quality of the decrypted image is rather poor and far from the human vision requirements if the receiver decrypt marked encrypted image directly.

In 2011, an entirely new idea was proposed [8], in which image owner can encrypt the original image by using stream cipher and one bit data can be embedded into cipher-image by flipping the three least significant bits (LSB) of pixels in each blocks. On receiver side, the marked cipher-image is decrypted to obtain an image which is approximate to original image. To form a new block, three LSBs of pixels in each block are flipped by receiver and a function is used to estimate each block's image-texture. Interfered block is assumed to be more rough than original block due to spatial correlation of natural images. Therefore, receiver can extract embedded bits and recover original image jointly. This well-known method has been paid great attention [9–13]. Hong et al. improve the performance by unbalanced bit flipping [9] and utilizing a side-match method to enhance embedding rate while leave lower error rates [10]. In 2015, Liao and Sun [11] evaluate the image-texture of each image block with a more precise function, which reduces the error rates of data extraction and image recovery. Furthermore, during data embedding in Qin and Zhang's method [12], rather than flipping the LSBs of half pixels, they flip the LSBs of fewer pixels leading to significant visual improvement of approximate image. To estimate the image-texture of each block, they utilize a new adaptive judging function, which is based on the distribution characteristic of local image contents, to some extent, decreasing errors of extracted bits and recovered image.

However, all methods introduced above are focusing on uncompressed images. There are few RDH-EI methods designed for JPEG (Joint Photographic Experts Group), BTC (Block Truncation Coding) and VQ (Vector Quantization). For JPEG images, Qian et al. proposed a method 2014 [14], in which additional data are embedded into the encrypted JPEG bit-stream and original bit-stream can be recovered by means of analyzing blocking artifacts induced by data hiding. In this paper, for the first time, a RDH-EI method designed for AMBTC compressed images is proposed. Compared with VQ and JPEG, AMBTC is more specifically suited to real-time application. It has been the subject of more development in the real-time image transmission field, such as CellB video encoding and Xmovie.

The proposed AMBTC RDH-EI method consists of three phases: image encryption, data embedding, and data extraction and image recovery. The higher mean and lower mean of a triple in AMBTC compressed image is encrypted by stream cipher with the same random bits. Therefore, the spatial correlation of a nature image is preserved and redundant space can be exploited by using the histogram of prediction error. Besides, the proposed method is applicable to real-time transmission due to the simple algorithm and low computational complexity.

2 Proposed Method

In the proposed method, image owner encrypt AMBTC compressed image with image encryption key. With data-hiding key, data owner embed additional data into encrypted AMBTC image in the absence of original image. In receiver side, with the marked cipher AMBTC image containing additional data, receiver is able to extract embedded data using data-hiding key, or decrypt it directly using image encryption key, or extract data and recover the original image inerrably using both keys.

2.1 Image Encryption

Lema and Mitchell proposed AMBTC [15]. To compress image I sized $H \times W$, I is subdivided into non-overlapping $m \times n$ blocks. Totally $N = \lfloor H/m \rfloor \times \lfloor W/n \rfloor$ blocks can be obtained. Denote $m \times n$ pixels in the i-th block as $P_i = \{p_{i,1}, p_{i,2}, \cdots, p_{i,m \times n}\}$ and the mean of P_i is $\bar{P}_i$. For the i-th block, lower mean l_i is the average of pixels whose value is smaller than $\bar{P}_i$. Similarly, higher mean h_i is the average of pixels whose value is not smaller than $\bar{P}_i$. Bit plane $b_i = \{b_{i,1}, b_{i,2}, \cdots, b_{i,m \times n}\}$ is generated to record the comparative result between $p_{i,j}$ and $\bar{P}_i$. If $p_{i,j}$ is smaller than $\bar{P}_i$, $b_{i,j}$ is 0, else $b_{i,j}$ is 1. Therefore, the i-th block in I can be compressed as triple (l_i, h_i, b_i), and compressed image $\tilde{I}$ can be represented as $\{(l_i, h_i, b_i)\}_{i=1}^{N}$.

It's obvious that l_i and h_i fall into $[0, 255]$. Encrypt l_i and h_i as follows:

$$H_i = h_i \oplus r_i \tag{1}$$

$$L_i = l_i \oplus r_i \tag{2}$$

Here $r_i \in [0, 255]$ is pseudo-random binary numbers determined by image encryption key. The correlation between l_i and h_i still exists for the existence of tradeoff between encryption and data embedding. Fully encrypted image, theoretically, has reached maximum information entropy, so embedding data in it is impractical.

Then to encrypt b_i, pseudo-random binary numbers $s_{i,k} \in \{0, 1\}$, which is also generated by image encryption key, are adopted. Here

$$B_{i,k} = b_{i,k} \oplus s_{i,k}, k = 0, 1, \cdots, m \times n \tag{3}$$

The encrypted b_i is $B_i = \{B_{i,1}, B_{i,2}, \cdots, B_{i,m \times n}\}$. Accordingly, the i-th encrypted triple is represented as (H_i, L_i, B_i). Both H_i, L_i together with B_i are encrypted with random binary numbers, therefore, for attacker without encryption key, it's impractical to reveal the content of plain image. $\tilde{I}$, consisting of N triples, is encrypted triple by triple, hence, the time complexity of image encryption is $O(N)$.

2.2   Data Embedding

When the AMBTC image is encrypted, the data hider has to embed additional data into the cipher image. Define prediction error as

$$PE_i = H_i - L_i, \ PE_i \in [-255, 255] \tag{4}$$

Calculate all triples, a histogram of PE can be obtained. Supposing two peak points are P_1 and P_2, and two zero points are Z_1 and Z_2 respectively. Here $Z_1 < P_1 < P_2 < Z_2$. If $PE_i = 0$, replace bit plane with binary additional data directly and set $flag_i = 1$, otherwise, set $flag_i = 0$. Then modify L_i as follows:

$$L_i' = \begin{cases} L_i + 1, & Z_1 < PE_i < P_1 \\ L_i + d, & PE_i = P_1 \ and \ flag_i \neq 1 \\ L_i - d, & PE_i = P_2 \ and \ flag_i \neq 1 \\ L_i - 1, & P_2 < PE_i < Z_2 \end{cases} \tag{5}$$

Here $d \in \{0, 1\}$ is one bit additional data. $flag_i$ is merely used for recording whether bit plane in i-th triple is replaced by additional data.

Note that overflow and underflow problems are likely to happen for L_i. To solve this problem, location map (LM) is adopted here. We label those pixel whose value is 255 or 0 with 1, and modify them into 254 or 1; label those whose value is 254 or 1 with 0. Embedding technique should be carried out after overflow and underflow processing so that LM can be embedded into host image. Get back to data embedding. After LM is obtained, 3 cases are considered in data embedding of i-th triple now:

Case 1: $PE_i = 1$, $L_i = 254$ and corresponding LM is 1;
Case 2: $PE_i = -1$, $L_i = 1$ and corresponding LM is 1;
Case 3: $PE_i = 0$, $L_i \neq 1$ and $L_i \neq 254$ or corresponding LM is 0;

In above 3 cases, the bit plane should be replaced by binary additional data and $flag_i = 1$; otherwise $flag_i = 0$. Then modify L_i according to Eq. (5).

So far, how to embed auxiliary information (AI) so that it need not sent to receiver via separate channel is a notable problem. AI consists of Z_1, P_1, P_2, Z_2 (32 bits), the length of LM ($\lceil \log_2 N \rceil$ bits), and LM. AI should be compressed and encrypted, and replace bit plane of first several triples. Those triples will be skipped in data embedding. The original bit planes are embedded into remaining triples together with additional data. By now all problems in data embedding phase are solved. Obviously, AMBTC image $\tilde{I}$, consisting of N triples, is processed triple by triple in additional data embedding, hence, the complexity of data embedding process is $O(N)$.

2.3   Data Extraction and Image Recovery

When the receiver only have data-hiding key, he can decrypt the AI. According to AI, data can be extracted. The detail of extracting phase in the i-th triple is:

Step 1: calculate PE_i according to Eq. (4), set $flag_i = 0$;

Step 2: recover L_i and extract additional data, 6 cases are considered:

Case1: if $Z_1 \leq PE_i < P_1 - 1$, then set $L_i = L'_i - 1$;

Case2: if $PE_i = P_1 - 1$, then set $d = 1$, and $L_i = L'_i - 1$;

Case3: if $PE_i = P_1$, then set $d = 0$, $L_i = L'_i$, and set $flag_i = 1$;

Case4: if $PE_i = P_2$, then set $d = 0$, $L_i = L'_i$, and set $flag_i = 1$;

Case5: if $PE_i = P_2 + 1$, then set $d = 1$, and $L_i = L'_i + 1$;

Case6: if $P_2 + 1 < PE_i \leq Z_2$, then set $L_i = L'_i + 1$;

Where d is the extracted data, and $flag_i$ is merely used for recording whether $PE_i = P_1$ or $PE_i = P_2$;

Step 3: to extract additional data in bit plane, 3 cases are considered:

Case 1: $PE_i = 1, L_i = 254$, and corresponding LM is 1;

Case 2: $PE_i = -1, L_i = 1$, and corresponding LM is 1;

Case 3: $PE_i = 0, L_i \neq 1$ and $L_i \neq 254$ or corresponding LM is 0;

In above 3 cases, the bits in bit plane are additional data. One bit data d extracted in step 2 should be abandoned if $flag_i = 1$.

Note that, first several triples into which AI has been embedded should be skipped here. After additional data is extracted, recover encrypted AMBTC image according to LM and recover bit plane of first several triples.

When receiver only have image encryption key, he can generate pseudo-random numbers r_i and $s_{i,k}$, then decrypt L_i, H_i, and B_i according to Eqs. (1), (2), and (3). Here, median filtering is adopted here to ensure the quality of decrypted image. When receiver have both data-hiding key and image encryption key, additional data can be extracted and encrypted image can be recovered first, after that, decrypt AMBTC image exactly. As for the efficiency, no matter which option is chosen, each triple in AMBTC image is visited once, so its time complexity is $O(N)$, too.

3 Experimental Results

All experimental results are performed with MATLAB. Standard images Lena, Peppers, Sailboat, Tiffany, Plane, Boat, Baboon, Splash and Man are adopted here.

Figure 1(a) gives the original AMBTC image with compression ratio 0.625. After encryption, original content is invisible shown in Fig. 1(b). And the marked cipher-image is shown in Fig. 1(c), which is the same as Fig. 1(b) observed by naked eye. If receiver has both data-hiding key and image encryption key, additional data can be extracted and Fig. 1(c) can be recovered error free, to get Fig. 1(d). However, if receiver only have image-encryption key, he can generate Fig. 1(e) by decrypting Fig. 1(c) directly and filter noise by using median filtering to get Fig. 1(f). The PSNR of directly decrypted image is 34.00 dB, which means directly decrypted image is similar to original AMBTC image.

Figure 2 gives the embedding payload of different AMBTC images under different compression rate. The horizontal axis shows compression rate, and the vertical axis shows all bits including AI and additional data embedded in AMBTC images. It can be observed that more additional data are embedded into those images with higher

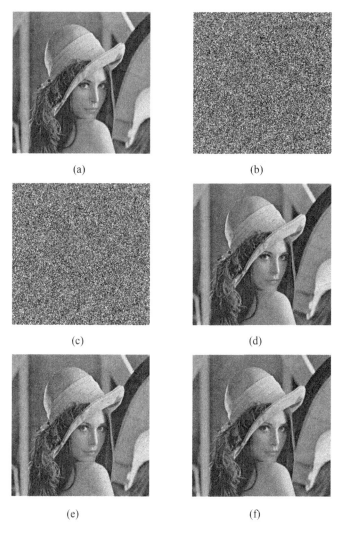

(a)   (b)

(c)   (d)

(e)   (f)

Fig. 1. (a) original AMBTC image Lena with compression ratio 0.625, (b) encrypted image, (c) cipher-image containing 5963 bits additional data, (d) recovered image, (e) directly decrypted image, (f) filtered version of (e) with PSNR 34.00 dB.

compression rate. The correlation between pure payload and compression rate are shown in Fig. 3. The vertical axis shows additional bits embedded in AMBTC images under different compression rate. The result is in accord with Fig. 2. But the payload in Fig. 2 is slightly higher than Fig. 3, because auxiliary information is included in Fig. 2. For example, under compression rate 0.625, the embedding payload of Lena is 6748 bits and the pure payload is 5963 bits.

The results of encryption of AMBTC image Lena under different compression rate are shown in Fig. 4. The higher compression rate is, the better encryption result is. Low

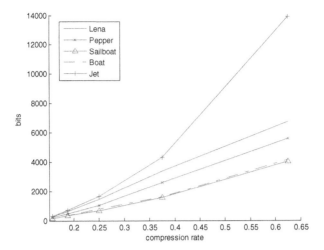

Fig. 2. The embedding payload of AMBTC image Lena, Pepper, Sailboat, Boat and Jet under different compression rate

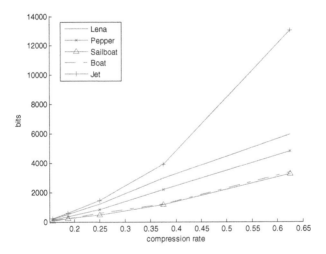

Fig. 3. The pure payload of AMBTC image Lena, Pepper, Sailboat, Boat and Jet under different compression rate

compression rate implies that the block size adopted in compression procedure is large, so the encryption results of those AMBTC image with low compression rate are not as good as high ones.

Table 1 lists payload, PSNR of directly decrypted images and PSNR of recovered image for different AMBTC image when the block size in compression procedure is 2×2 and 4×4 respectively. The PSNR of directly decrypted image are above 27 dB in most cases. And the image quality is better when the block size in compression procedure is 2×2 than 4×4. The PSNR of recovered image is infinite because the

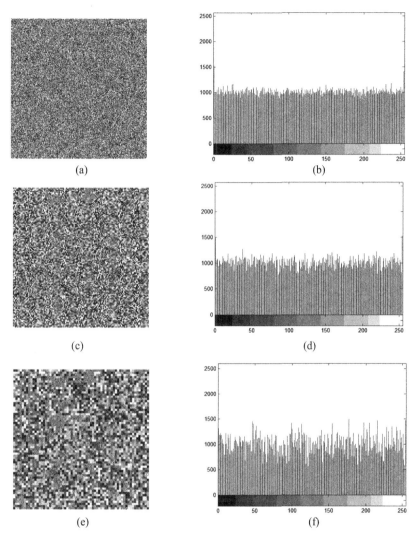

Fig. 4. The encrypted AMBTC image Lena under compression rate (a) 0.625, (c) 0.25, (e) 0.156, and corresponding image histogram (b), (d), (f)

proposed method can recover marked cipher-image without error when the receiver has both data-hiding key and image encryption key.

Table 2 and 3 give embedding payload and pure payload, and the length of AI with different block size for Lena and Jet respectively. Different images with the same block size produce similar amount of auxiliary information. For example, the length of auxiliary information hover around 800 bits, with Lena 785 bits and Jet 854 bits, when block size is 2×2. Therefore, the payload of encrypted image greatly depends on the space of AMBTC image itself, rather than the amount of auxiliary information.

Table 1. Payload (bits), PSNR of directly decrypted images (dB) and PSNR of recovered image (dB) with different block size for different AMBTC image

	2×2			4×4		
Lena	5963	34.00	$+\infty$	1213	30.04	$+\infty$
Pepper	4807	33.79	$+\infty$	819	29.24	$+\infty$
Tiffany	8259	33.18	$+\infty$	1687	27.46	$+\infty$
Jet	13028	32.40	$+\infty$	1458	27.66	$+\infty$
Baboon	1047	23.66	$+\infty$	141	23.40	$+\infty$
Splash	11043	34.83	$+\infty$	1666	30.16	$+\infty$
Man	6032	30.51	$+\infty$	556	27.68	$+\infty$

Table 2. The embedding payload and pure payload, and the length of auxiliary information under different block size for Lena

	2×2	4×2	8×2	2×4	4×4	8×4	8×2	8×4	8×8
Embedding payload	6748	3381	1420	2984	1433	638	1193	544	257
Pure payload	5963	2978	1196	2567	1213	497	953	429	203
Auxiliary information	785	403	224	417	220	141	240	115	54

Table 3. The embedding payload and pure payload, and the length of auxiliary information under different block size for Jet

	2×2	4×2	8×2	2×4	4×4	8×4	8×2	8×4	8×8
Embedding payload	13882	4288	1414	4314	1667	651	1564	720	302
Pure payload	13028	3882	1197	3915	1458	566	1341	587	216
Auxiliary information	854	406	217	399	209	85	223	133	86

4 Conclusion

In this paper, a reversible data hiding for encrypted AMBTC compressed image is presented, which is divide into three phases: image encryption, data embedding, and data extraction and image recovery. In image encryption phase, we encrypt the higher mean and lower mean of a triple in AMBTC compressed image with the same random numbers, therefore, the correlation of higher mean and lower mean of nature image is preserved. Then the redundant space of encrypted AMBTC compressed image can be exploited by using the histogram of prediction error in data embedding phase. Experimental results demonstrate that the proposed method can embed considerable bits while leave little distortion. Besides, the proposed method is very simple and its computational complexity is low so that it can be applied to real-time transmission.

Acknowledgement. This research work is partly supported by National Natural Science Foundation of China (61502009, 61525203, 61472235), China Postdoctoral Science Foundation (2016M591650), "Shu Guang" project supported by Shanghai Municipal Education Commission and Shanghai Education Development Foundation, Anhui Provincial Natural Science Foundation (1508085SQF216), Key Program for Excellent Young Talents in Colleges and Universities of Anhui Province (gxyqZD2016011), Quality Engineering Program for Colleges and Universities in Anhui Province (2015jyxm042) and Undergraduates Training Foundation of Anhui University (J10118511269).

References

1. Hong, W., Chen, T.S.: A novel data embedding method using adaptive pixel pair matching. IEEE Trans. Inf. Forensics Secur. **7**(1), 176–184 (2012)
2. Zhang, X., Wang, S.: Efficient steganographic embedding by exploiting modification direction. IEEE Commun. Lett. **10**(11), 781–783 (2006)
3. Hu, Y., Lee, H.K., Li, J.: DE-based reversible data hiding with improved overflow location map. IEEE Trans. Circ. Syst. Video Technol. **19**(2), 250–260 (2009)
4. Kim, H.J., Sachnev, V., Shi, Y.Q., Nam, J., Choo, H.G.: A novel difference expansion transform for reversible data embedding. IEEE Trans. Inf. Forensics Secur. **3**(3), 456–465 (2008)
5. Gao, X., An, L., Yuan, Y., Tao, D., Li, X.: Lossless data embedding using generalized statistical quantity histogram. IEEE Trans. Circ. Syst. Video Technol. **21**(8), 1061–1070 (2011)
6. Erkin, Z., Piva, A., Katzenbeisser, S., Lagendijk, R.L., Shokrollahi, J., Neven, G., Barni, M.: Protection and retrieval of encrypted multimedia content: when cryptography meets signal processing. EURASIP J. Inf. Secur. **2007**, 1–20 (2007)
7. Puech, W., Chaumont, M., Strauss, O.: A reversible data hiding method for encrypted images. In: Proceedings of SPIE, Electronic Imaging, Security, Forensics, Steganography, and Watermarking of Multimedia Contents X, vol. 6819. San Jose, CA, USA (2008)
8. Zhang, X.: Reversible data hiding in encrypted image. IEEE Sig. Process. Lett **18**(4), 255–258 (2011)
9. Hong, W., Chen, T.-S., Chen, J., Kao, Y.-H., Wu, H.-Y., Wu, M.-C.: Reversible data embedment for encrypted cartoon images using unbalanced bit flipping. In: Tan, Y., Shi, Y., Mo, H. (eds.) ICSI 2013. LNCS, vol. 7929, pp. 208–214. Springer, Heidelberg (2013). doi:10.1007/978-3-642-38715-9_25
10. Hong, W., Chen, T.S., Wu, H.Y.: An improved reversible data hiding in encrypted images using side match. IEEE Sig. Process. Lett. **19**(4), 199–202 (2012)
11. Liao, X., Shu, C.: Reversible data hiding in encrypted images based on absolute mean difference of multiple neighboring pixels. J. Vis. Commun. Image Represent. **28**, 21–27 (2015)
12. Qin, C., Zhang, X.: Effective reversible data hiding in encrypted image with privacy protection for image content. J. Vis. Commun. Image Represent. **31**, 154–164 (2015)
13. Zhang, W., Ma, K., Yu, N.: Reversibility improved data hiding in encrypted images. Sig. Process. **94**, 118–127 (2013)
14. Qian, Z., Zhang, X., Wang, S.: Reversible data hiding in encrypted JPEG bitstream. IEEE Trans. Multimedia **16**(5), 1486–1491 (2014)
15. Lema, M.D., Mitchell, O.R.: Absolute moment block truncation coding and its application to color image. IEEE Trans. Commun. **32**(10), 1148–1157 (1984)

Reversible 3D Image Data Hiding with Quality Enhancement

Wengai Liu, Rongrong Ni$^{(\boxtimes)}$, and Yao Zhao

Institute of Information Science and Beijing Key Laboratory of Advanced
Information Science and Network Technology, Beijing Jiaotong University,
Beijing 100044, China
{14120329,rrni,yzhao}@bjtu.edu.cn

Abstract. The 3D image constructed by a texture image plus a depth map is popular for stereo representation. When embedding data in the depth map, conventional reversible data hiding algorithms, which are designed for gray and color images, are not suitable. In this paper, we propose a novel reversible data hiding method in the depth map for quality enhancement. By optimizing the selection of prediction error and embedding data with the help of depth no-synthesis-error model (D-NOSE), the proposed scheme can embed more data with less distortion. The hidden data are the compressed residual error between the actual view and the virtual view. The watermarked depth map can directly be used to synthesis a same virtual view as in depth-image-based rendering (DIBR). After extracting the hidden data, a higher quality virtual view can be obtained by adding the residual error to the synthesized virtual view. Experimental results show that the virtual view with higher quality is obtained, and higher embedding capacity is achieved as well.

Keywords: Reversible data hiding · Depth map · D-NOSE model · Optimal selection · Quality enhancement

1   Introduction

Nowadays high capacity reversible data hiding methods are mainly based on difference expansion (DE) [1–5], histogram shifting (HS) [6–8] and prediction error expansion (PEE) [9–12]. Reversible data hiding based on difference expansion was first proposed by Tian [1]. An image is divided into pairs of pixels, and the hidden data are embedded into the differences of the pixel pairs that meet certain requirements. Reversible data hiding based on histogram shifting (HS) was first proposed by Ni et al. [6]. The pixels with the peak value in histogram are selected for embedding data, and other pixels are subtracted or added by 1. Thodi et al. [9] first proposed prediction error expansion technique by integrating DE with HS. Thereafter, many prediction approaches were proposed. Sachnev et al. [10] proposed a method combining sorting with two-pass-testing strategy to achieve high capacity and good quality. In [12], a new reversible data hiding

© Springer International Publishing AG 2017
Y.Q. Shi et al. (Eds.): IWDW 2016, LNCS 10082, pp. 446–455, 2017.
DOI: 10.1007/978-3-319-53465-7_33

method based on PEE for multiple histograms was proposed. It outperforms the previous PEE techniques by improving the marked image quality.

Besides lossless data hiding algorithms for 2D images, there are several studies on lossless data hiding for 3D images [13–19] for different purposes. Some methods focus on reducing the storage size and transmission bandwidth [13–17] by embedding information needed to recover the right view frames into the left view frames. Khan et al. [18] embedded the corresponding depth map into its 2D image to forbid illegal customers from accessing the depth map for security concerns. In [19], reversible data hiding is applied to depth maps for maximizing the embedding capacity. This scheme considers the D-NOSE model to preserve the virtual view after data hiding.

Due to the property of saving storage space, the 3D image containing a texture image and a depth map becomes popular for stereo images. The efficient 3D format can reduce the data because it is able to generate virtual views by DIBR principle. In the view synthesis, pixels in an original view are warped into a virtual view based on depth information. When embedding data in the depth map, distortions in depth data may cause some pixels being warped to different positions in the virtual view, which leads to synthesis errors in the virtual view. So directly applying conventional reversible data hiding methods to the depth maps is not reasonable for leading to visual artifacts in the rendered virtual view. This motivates us to design a reversible data hiding algorithm for depth map, which can achieve high embedding capacity without causing any synthesis errors after embedding.

The synthesized virtual view generated based on DIBR doesn't equal to the actual view. Some applications for super realistic representation require high quality rendering, such as medical images and cultural heritage images. We aim to embed the differences between the virtual view and the actual view into the 3D images based on the reversible data hiding. In this paper, a novel reversible data hiding framework for 3D images is proposed. The residual error between the virtual view and the actual view is generated and embedded in the depth map. An optimal prediction error selection method and a less distortion embedding method are designed. Besides, an effective and low complexity overhead embedding method is proposed. The experiments show that the embedding algorithm has higher capacity, and the generated virtual view with higher quality can be achieved as well.

The rest of this paper is organized as follows. The D-NOSE model is briefly reviewed in Sect. 2. The reversible data hiding method for quality enhancement is presented in Sect. 3. Experimental results are discussed in Sect. 4 and conclusions are drawn in Sect. 5.

2   The D-NOSE Model

The DIBR technique [21] is adopted for view synthesis. The virtual image is achieved by shifting the original 2D image horizontally. The horizontal disparity can be obtained from the real-world depth value by

$$d = D(z_q) = f \cdot l \cdot \frac{z_q}{255} \cdot \left(\frac{1}{z_n} - \frac{1}{z_f} \right) + \frac{1}{z_f} \tag{1}$$

where, f is the focal length and l is the spatial distance between two identical cameras. z_f and z_n mean the farthest and nearest depth value. z_q is the quantized depth value. In most cases the disparity obtained in (1) is a non-integer. In view synthesis algorithms, d is rounded to the neighbor integer position. For a more general analysis, λ-rounding with $1/N$ sub-pixel precision is as follows:

$$R(d) = \frac{\lceil (d - \lambda) \cdot N \rceil}{N} \tag{2}$$

After rounding the disparity, it can be noticed that some quantized depth values may correspond to the same integer disparity and depth variations within a certain range will not induce errors in pixel mapping. In [20], the allowable range is defined as follows:

$$\left\lceil D^{-1} \left(R(D(z_q)) - \frac{1}{N} + \lambda \right) \right\rceil \leq v + \Delta v \leq \lfloor D^{-1}(R(D(z_q)) + \lambda) \rfloor \tag{3}$$

Hence, by modifying the depth value with the allowable range $[z_l, z_h]$, data can be embedded into depth maps without changing the virtual views.

3   Reversible Data Hiding Method

The proposed reversible data hiding method for high quality 3D representation is divided into four parts, i.e. generating the hidden data, embedding the hidden data, extracting the hidden data and getting the high quality virtual view. The block diagram of the proposed algorithm in depth map is illustrated in Fig. 1.

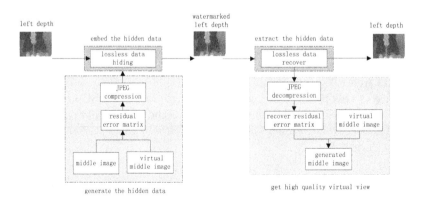

Fig. 1. The block diagram of the proposed method.

3.1 Generate the Hidden Data

The virtual middle views are first synthesized by the 2D images and the depth images from both left and right views. Then the residual matrix is obtained by computing the difference between the real middle view and the synthesized middle view. The residual error matrix lies in $[-255, 255]$. Because the original image and the synthesized image are very similar, most of the differences are close to 0. For reducing the data size, the residual error matrix is compressed by JPEG compression.

3.2 Embed the Hidden Data

(1) Hidden Data Embedding
Suppose that the host image I is a $M \times N$ depth map and all pixels are divided into two sets: the black set and the white set (as Fig. 2).
    The prediction of depth value $\hat{z}_q$ can be expressed as,

$$
\hat{z}_q = \begin{cases} \left\lfloor \dfrac{u+d}{2} \right\rfloor, & if \quad \dfrac{|u-d|}{|l-r|} < 0.5 \\[2ex] \left\lfloor \dfrac{l+r}{2} \right\rfloor, & if \quad \dfrac{|l-r|}{|u-d|} < 0.5 \\[2ex] \left\lfloor \dfrac{u+d+l+r}{4} \right\rfloor, & otherwise \end{cases} \tag{4}
$$

Then, the prediction error e is calculated by the following equation.

$$
e = z_q - \hat{z}_q \tag{5}
$$

    In the previous method [19], besides the prediction errors with value 0, the two prediction errors 1 or -1 with the higher frequency are selected. In fact, it is not reasonable since the actual capacity is not only determined by the numbers of prediction errors. The capacity is also related with distance between the prediction value and range bounds. If the prediction errors -1 are selected, the pixels with prediction errors -1 left shift and the pixels with prediction

Fig. 2. The black and white sets.

errors 0 right shift. If the prediction errors 1 are selected, the pixels shifting directions are opposite.

Therefore, we propose an optimal prediction error selection method according to the capacity. For convenience, we only consider that the prediction errors -1 are selected. The number of the embedding bits n is determined by

$$
n = \begin{cases} \lfloor log_2(\hat{z}_q - z_l) \rfloor, & if \quad e = -1 \\ \lfloor log_2(z_h - \hat{z}_q + 1) \rfloor, & if \quad e = 0 \\ 0, & otherwise \end{cases} \tag{6}
$$

From the above formula, we can see that the embedding capacity is related to the numbers of -1 and 0 and the distance between the prediction value and range bounds. Therefore, the prediction errors selection method according to the capacity is more reasonable than that in [19]. Furthermore, compared our capacity calculation method with that in [19], it is obvious that our capacity is higher in the case $e = -1$.

The prediction depth value is increased or decreased to embed the hidden data in the following way:

$$
e' = \begin{cases} -h - 1, & if \quad e = -1 \\ h, & if \quad e = 0 \end{cases} \tag{7}
$$

Where $h \in \{0, 1, ..., 2^n - 1\}$ is the hidden data.
Finally, the watermarked depth value z'_q can be obtained by

$$
z'_q = \hat{z}_q + e' \tag{8}
$$

Obviously, the watermarked depth value is still in the allowable range $[z_l, z_h]$.

To assure that the hidden data can be exactly extracted, we need to record if one pixel embeds the hidden data. When embedding data, the corresponding value in the location map M is set to 1. Otherwise, the value in the location map is 0. Then the location map is compressed using arithmetic coding and embedded in the first H pixels.

Compared to [19], the proposed method can obtain higher capacity with less distortion. For example, $z_l = 74$, $z_h = 83$, $z_q = 80$ and $\hat{z}_q = 81$, the prediction error is -1 and embedding capacity is 2 according to (5) and (6). Suppose that the hidden data $h = 011_2 = 3$, the watermarked depth value is 77. While using the method in [19], the watermarked depth value is 74. Thus the pixel modification of our method is smaller with the same capacity. So our method is better than the previous method in capacity and distortion.

(2) Overhead Embedding
Conventional methods usually embed the overheads in the first H pixels by the least significant bits (LSBs) replacement. But directly replacing the LSBs may introduce synthesis errors in the virtual view for the watermarked depth values exceeding the allow range. To avoid synthesis errors, a new overhead hiding

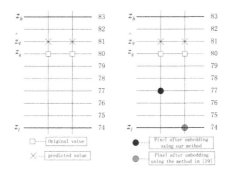

Fig. 3. The embedding method comparison.

method is proposed. The overheads include the compressed location map size, the hidden data size and the compressed location map. Since the first H pixels of the depth map is preserved to embed the overheads, the embedding for hidden data starts from the $(H + 1)$ pixel (Fig. 3).

In [19], a novel overhead embedding strategy is proposed based on the D-NOSE model. The allow range is first divided into disjoint subranges and each subrange only has two depth values: the upper and the lower bound. The quantized depth value will fall into a specific subrange. If the embedded data is 1, the depth value will change to the upper bound. Otherwise the depth value changes to the lower bound. To recover the original depth value in the extraction side, a correction bit is required to record if the depth value equals the upper or lower bound.

Note that the pixel with $z_q = z_h$ and $z_h - z_l$ occurring as even will not be used for embedding the overheads. For the depth map of balloons, suppose that H is 50000, the number of pixels which can't be used to embed data is 5855. Thus, the overhead embedding method is complex and ineffective. Therefore, we proposed a novel LSBs replacement for overhead embedding.

For LSBs replacement, the pixels are modified one at most when data embedding. So only the pixels $z_q = z_h$ and $z_q = z_l$ may exceed the allowable range $[z_l, z_h]$ and lead to synthesis errors in the virtual view. In order to avoid this problem, the pixels $z_q = z_l$ and $z_q = z_h$ should be changed to $(z_l + 1)$ and $(z_h - 1)$, respectively, and the others are kept unchanged. Then, if the pixel is modified, the flag is set to 1, and others are set to 0. The flags and the original LSBs are compressed by arithmetic coding and embedded as the hidden data.

The proposed overhead embedding method with low complexity is effective. Fewer pixels are used to embed the overhead, which can improve the embedding capacity.

3.3   Extract the Hidden Data

To extract the hidden data, we first extract the overheads by LSBs replacement. Then we can obtain the capacity and the location map M. Since the pixels with $M = 1$ can be used for embedding the hidden data, we only consider the extraction from the pixels with $M = 1$. According to the D-NOSE model, the watermarked depth value and the original depth value are utilized to calculate the same allowable range. Therefore, the allowable range is obtained by the watermarked depth value. The prediction value is calculated by (1), and the modified prediction error can be obtained. According to the sign of the modified prediction error, the prediction error can be obtained by (7). If the modified prediction error is negative, the prediction error is -1. Otherwise, the prediction error is 0. Associated with the allowable range, the prediction error can be used to calculate the embedding bits of each pixel by (6).

Finally, the hidden data can be extracted as follows:

$$
h = \begin{cases} e' - 1, & if \quad e = 1 \\ -e', & if \quad e = 0 \end{cases} \tag{9}
$$

After extracting the hidden data, the original quantized pixels z_q can be recovered by

$$
z_q = \hat{z}_q + e \tag{10}
$$

When the hidden data are extracted, the LSBs of the first H pixels are obtained. Then the original depth values can be recovered by LSBs replacement.

3.4   Generate the High Quality Virtual View

When the hidden data are extracted, the compressed residual error matrix is obtained. We can get the residual error matrix by JPEG decompression. Because of the lossy compression and decompression, the recover residual error matrix has some differences from the original residual error matrix. Even if we can compensate the difference by adding the residual error matrix, the compensated virtual view and the original view are not exactly the same but more similar.

If we need a high definition (HD) virtual view, we can compensate the virtual view by adding the residual error matrix. In this way, we can also enforce the quality grading management. Different users get the virtual views of different quality. If you are an ordinary user, you can only get the general quality virtual views. If you are an advanced user, such as a very important person (VIP) or a paid member, you can see the virtual views of HD.

4   Experimental Results

The proposed scheme is compared with the reversible data hiding method of Chung [19]. Since the depth map does not directly display, we compare the embedding capacity and the quality of the synthesized virtual view. Since this lossless data hiding method considers the D-NOSE model, directly using the watermarked depth map to synthesis virtual image will not cause variations. If a higher quality virtual image is needed, the residual error image can be extracted

Table 1. The comparison of capacity

Image	Chuang capacity	Proposed capacity	Increased capacity
Mobile	333688	335303	1615
Book arrival	779651	927827	148176
Kendo	789184	789346	162
Balloons	733118	733506	388
Dancer	2321975	2327433	5458

Table 2. The comparison of PSNR

Image	Synthesis PSNR	Compensated PSNR
Mobile	37.58	53.29
Book arrival	36.10	42.08
Kendo	35.88	46.23
Balloons	35.42	45.81
Dancer	39.68	45.77

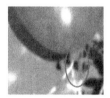

Fig. 4. The comparison of virtual image and the compensated virtual image.

to compensate the virtual view. The virtual view quality after compensating is greatly improved. It outperforms the virtual view in terms of PSNR and visual qualities. Table 1 shows the capacity of the proposed algorithm and the original. The comparison of PSNR is shown in Table 2. In Fig. 4, the left picture is the actual image, the middle is the directly synthesized image, and the right is the compensated image. It can be seen that some contents are lost in the synthesized image, i.e. some leaves. By adding the residual error, the contents can be found in the compensated virtual image. Experiments show that the compensated virtual image with higher quality is much closer to the actual image.

5   Conclusions

In this paper, we propose a novel reversible data hiding method in the depth map for quality enhancement. The proposed scheme can embed more data with less distortion by optimizing the selection of prediction error and the embedding method. The hidden data are the compressed residual error between the actual view and the virtual view. The watermarked depth map can directly be used to synthesis a same virtual view as in depth-image-based rendering (DIBR). After extracting the hidden data, a higher quality virtual view can be obtained by adding the residual error to the synthesized virtual view.

Acknowledgments. This work was supported in part by National NSF of China (61332012, 61272355, 61672090), Fundamental Research Funds for the Central Universities (2015JBZ002), the PAPD, the CICAEET.

References

1. Tian, J.: Reversible data embedding using a difference expansion. IEEE Trans. Circuits Syst. Video Technol. **13**(8), 890–896 (2003)
2. Alattar, A.M.: Reversible watermark using difference expansion of a generalized integer transform. IEEE Trans. Image Process **13**(8), 1147–1156 (2004)
3. Chang, C.C., Lu, T.C.: A difference expansion oriented data hiding scheme for restoring the original host images. J. Syst. Softw. **79**(12), 1754–1766 (2006)
4. Tai, W.L., Yeh, C.M., Chang, C.C.: Reversible data hiding based on histogram modification of pixel differences. IEEE Trans. Circuits Syst. Video Technol. **19**(6), 906–910 (2009)
5. Li, X., Zhang, W., Gui, X., Yang, B.: A novel reversible data hiding scheme based on two-dimensional difference-histogram modification. IEEE Trans. Inf. Forensics Secur. **8**(7), 1091–1100 (2013)
6. Ni, Z., Shi, Y.Q., Ansari, N., Su, W.: Reversible data hiding. IEEE Trans. Circuits Syst. Video Technol. **16**(3), 354–362 (2006)
7. Luo, L., Chen, Z., Chen, M., Zeng, X., Xiong, Z.: Reversible image watermarking using interpolation technique. IEEE Trans. Inf. Forensics Secur. **5**(1), 187–193 (2010)
8. Li, X., Li, B., Yang, B., Zeng, T.: General framework to histogram-shifting-based reversible data hiding. IEEE Trans. Image Process. **22**(6), 2181–2191 (2013)
9. Thodi, D.M., Rodriguez, J.J.: Expansion embedding techniques for reversible watermarking. IEEE Trans. Image Process. **16**(3), 721–730 (2007)
10. Sachnev, V., Kim, H.J., Nam, J., Suresh, S., Shi, Y.Q.: Reversible watermarking algorithm using sorting and prediction. IEEE Trans. Circuits Syst. Video Technol. **19**(7), 989–999 (2009)
11. Ou, B., Li, X., Zhao, Y., Ni, R., Shi, Y.Q.: Pairwise prediction-error expansion for efficient reversible data hiding. IEEE Trans. Image Process. **22**(12), 5010–5021 (2013)
12. Li, X., Zhang, W., Gui, X., Yang, B.: Efficient reversible data hiding based on multiple histograms modification. IEEE Trans. Inf. Forensics Secur. **10**(9), 2016–2027 (2015)
13. Coltuc, D.: On stereo embedding by reversible watermarking. In: Proceedings International Symposium on Signals, Circuits and Systems, pp. 93–96 (2007)
14. Coltuc, D., Caciula, I.: Stereo embedding by reversible watermarking: further results. In: Proceedings International Symposium on Signals, Circuits and Systems, pp. 1–4 (2009)
15. Ellinas, J.N.: Reversible watermarking on stereo image sequences. Int. J. Sig. Process. **5**(3), 210–215 (2009)

16. Chen, H., Zhu, Y.: An effective stereo image coding method with reversible water-marking. J. Comput. Inf. Syst. **8**(7), 2761–2768 (2012)
17. Tong, X., Shen, G., Xuan, G., Li, S., Yang, Z., Li, J., Shi, Y.-Q.: Stereo image coding with histogram-pair based reversible data hiding. In: Shi, Y.-Q., Kim, H.J., Pérez-González, F., Yang, C.-N. (eds.) IWDW 2014. LNCS, vol. 9023, pp. 201–214. Springer, Heidelberg (2015). doi:10.1007/978-3-319-19321-2_15
18. Khan, A., Malik, S.A., Ali, A.: Intelligent reversible watermarking and authentication: hiding depth map information for 3D cameras. Inf. Sci. **216**, 155–175 (2012)
19. Chung, K.L., Yang, W.J., Yang, W.N.: Reversible data hiding for depth maps using the depth no-synthesis-error model. Inf. Sci. **269**, 159–175 (2014)
20. Zhao, Y., Zhu, C., Chen, Z., Yu, I.: Depth no-synthesis-error model for view synthesis in 3-D video. IEEE Trans. Image Process. **20**(8), 2221–2228 (2011)
21. Fehn, C.: Depth-Image-Based Rendering (DIBR), compression, and transmission for a new approach on 3D-TV. In: International Society for Optics and Photonics, pp. 93–104 (2004)

An Adaptive Reversible Data Hiding Scheme for JPEG Images

Jiaxin Yin[1,3], Rui Wang[1], Yuanfang Guo[1(✉)], and Feng Liu[1,2]

[1] State Key Laboratory of Information Security,
Institute of Information Engineering, Chinese Academy of Sciences, Beijing, China
{yinjiaxin,wangrui,guoyuanfang,liufeng}@iie.ac.cn
[2] School of Cyber Security,
University of Chinese Academy of Sciences, Beijing, China
[3] School of Computer and Control Engineering,
University of Chinese Academy of Sciences, Beijing, China

Abstract. Currently JPEG is the most popular image file format and the majority of images are stored in JPEG format due to storage constraint. Recently, reversible data hiding (RDH) for JPEG images draws researchers attention and has been developed rapidly. Due to the compression, performing RDH on a typical JPEG image is much more difficult than that on an uncompressed image. In this paper, we propose an adaptive reversible data hiding method for JPEG images, which is based on histogram shifting. We propose to select the optimal expandable bins-pair at image level by adopting a k-th nearest neighbors (KNN) algorithm. By developing a new block selection strategy, we can adaptively select the to-be-embedded blocks. Then, the message bits are embedded into the selected blocks at a specific bins-pair via the histogram shifting algorithm. Experimental results demonstrate that our proposed method can achieve a higher image quality and a less increased file size compared to the current state-of-the-art RDH method for JPEG images.

Keywords: Reversible data hiding · JPEG image · KNN · Histogram shifting

1 Introduction

In the past two decades, digital image data embedding technologies, which usually embed a data stream into image(s), has been developed rapidly due to the large demand of image data embedding applications. According to different application scenes, it evolves many technologies. For example, steganography [11] technology is applied to secret communication, and watermarking [13] is used in authentication, broadcast, copyright protection and copy control. However, both kind of methods did not consider to restore the original cover object. In reality, some special areas such as medical, art, military and etc., usually value data integrity and cannot tolerate any extra modifications on the original data. Under these circumstances, reversible data hiding (RDH) has been developed

© Springer International Publishing AG 2017
Y.Q. Shi et al. (Eds.): IWDW 2016, LNCS 10082, pp. 456–469, 2017.
DOI: 10.1007/978-3-319-53465-7_34

for hiding data into a cover object, such that the hidden information can be extracted and the original cover object can also be reconstructed.

Ordinary RDH algorithms, such as histogram shifting [9], difference expansion [6,14], pixel groups' geometric structure [18], DNA XNOR [15] etc., are usually applied to uncompressed images. However, due to the characteristics of compression, most of the ordinary RDH methods cannot be directly applied to compressed images such as JPEG [16] images. Therefore, RDH for compressed images demands a special design. In this paper, we focus on the RDH schemes for JPEG images. As it summarized in [5], designing a RDH method for JPEG images usually have three difficulties. Firstly, the redundancies, which is usually being utilized by the RDH method to achieve embedding, in JPEG images are usually less than uncompressed images. Secondly, the JPEG quantization process usually prevent RDH methods to embed before quantization while the embedding after quantization may introduces large distortions. Thirdly, since JPEG images usually have small file size, which is also the advantage of compressed images, the file size increasement after embedding should be constrained to be small.

Despite the difficulties when designing the RDH schemes for JPEG images, recently, RDH for JPEG images has been developed rapidly by many researchers due to the popularity of JPEG file format. [3] compresses the sequence of LSB values of the cover image coefficients, such that the watermark can be embedded into the empty space. Unfortunately, this method has low embedding capacity and large increasement of the file size. [17] manipulates the content of the quantization table such that the LSBs of the newly quantized coefficients at some locations, which corresponds to the manipulated locations in the quantization table, can load the secret message. Experimental results of this method indicate that it owns a large embedding capacity and a good image quality of the embedded image accompanied by a large increasement of file size. The methods in [8] and [4] embed information by modifying the Huffman table, which yields a good embedded image quality but a small embedding capacity. In [10], Nikoladis et al. propose a different method which modifies the zero value coefficients behind the last non-zero coefficient of each block, and achieves an excellent performance in terms of the visual quality which fails in preserving the file size.

Besides of the above mentioned methods, recently, the histogram shifting (HS) based RDH methods has been developed quickly for JPEG images. In Xuan et al.'s paper [19], a RDH method, the which only gives limited performance, has been proposed by simply applying the HS algorithm to the quantized DCT coefficients. Sakai et al. in [12] improved Xuan et al.'s method by an adaptive embedding method. It chooses smooth region of the image to embed message, and gives superior performance compared to Xuan et al.'s method. In [7], the proposed method selects the JPEG coefficients at certain frequencies, and only embeds the data at these selected coefficients by a HS algorithm. Recently, Huang et al. in [5] also proposed a HS based RDH method for JPEG images by selecting the to-be-embedded blocks adaptively according to the number of zero AC coefficients of the block. Only AC coefficients whose value is 1 or -1 are expanded to carry message bits. Although this method introduces the current state-of-the-art performance, the embedding bins-pair $(-1, 1)$ may not be optimal for different image contents and embedding messages. Both of the visual quality and image's file size it achieves advantage than the formal level of this kind method.

To inherent the strength of HS based RDH method for JPEG images while further improve the performance, in this paper, we propose a new reversible data hiding method, RDH for JPEG image via Adaptive Bins-pair and Block Selection (ABBS), for JPEG images based on Huang et al.'s method [5]. To achieve a higher payload and protect the marked JPEG image's quality. The proposed method propose an algorithm to adaptively select the optimal expandable bins-pair for each cover image by adopting a KNN algorithm. Then ABBS chooses the to-be-embedded blocks via a new block selection strategy. With the embedding blocks and bins-pair selected, the embedding can be achieved. Experiments demonstrate that the proposed method achieves better performance compared to the current state-of-the-art Huang et al.'s method.

The rest of the paper is organized as follows. In Sect. 2, backgrounds of JPEG compression and Huang et al.'s method are introduced. Section 3 describes the proposed method. Section 4 presents the experimental results. The conclusion is drawn in Sect. 5.

2   Backgrounds

In this section, a brief introduction of JPEG compression is given. Then, an interpretation of Huang et al. [5]'s method is explained.

2.1   JPEG Compression

JPEG compression is a common lossy compression standard for digital images. As a parameter of JPEG compression process, the quality factor (QF) corresponds to the compression ratio and image quality after the compression, QF is from 1 to 100 (100 is near lossless).

Figure 1 shows the main procedures of JPEG compression. The system firstly divides the raw image into the non-overlapped 8×8 blocks. Then, DCT (Discrete Cosine Transform) is applied to each block. According to the JPEG quality factor, a corresponding quantization table is selected and the DCT transformed blocks are quantized accordingly. Figure 2 shows an example of a quantization table for $QF = 50$. After quantization, the quantized coefficients will be pre-compressed. The direct current (DC) coefficients will be encoded by the differential pulse code modulation (DPCM), while the alternating current (AC) coefficients will be arranged in a zigzag order and encoded with the run length encoding (RLE). Finally, Huffman coding is applied to the symbol string. A complete JPEG compression file is consist of the head information and the encoded data.

Fig. 1. JPEG compression process.

16	11	10	16	24	40	51	61
12	12	14	19	26	58	60	55
14	13	16	24	40	57	69	56
14	17	22	29	51	87	80	62
18	22	37	56	68	109	103	77
24	35	55	64	81	104	113	92
49	64	78	87	103	121	120	101
72	92	95	98	112	100	103	99

Fig. 2. Quantization table (QF = 50).

2.2 RDH Method in [5]

As we mentioned in Sect. 1, Huang et al. [5] proposed a HS based RDH method for JPEG images. The procedures of Huang et al.'s method is given in Fig. 3. The method generates a histogram of quantized DCT coefficients firstly. Then they perform a block selection strategy which can adaptively choose the to-be-embedded blocks. At last, the bins-pair $(-1, 1)$ of the selected blocks are expanded for embedding the message bits. However, the method only exploits the $(-1, 1)$ pair as the expandable bins-pair for every image. Without considering the different features of different images, employing a fixed bins-pair for all images might not be the best approach. For example, when the cover image contains many quantized DCT coefficients whose absolute value is larger than 1 and the to-be-embedded message length is relatively short, the $(-1, 1)$ may not be the best expandable bins-pair, because more coefficients may be changed in the progress of the histogram shifting embedding at $(-1, 1)$. This may introduce more distortions than employing other bins-pair. Thus, we proposes an adaptively bins-pair selection method which is explained in next section.

3 Proposed Method

In this section, we present our method, RDH for JPEG image via Adaptive Bins-pair and Block Selection (ABBS) in details. At first, a histogram of the quantized DCT coefficients is generated and the expandable bins-pair is calculated. Then ABBS chooses a set of blocks from the cover image. Only these blocks will be embedded. At last, we embed the message bits in the bins-pair of the selected

The steps of the embedding :
- generate histogram about the JPEG coefficients of the image, set the (-1,1) as the bins-pair which used to hide message bits;
- Let *t* be the number of zero JPEG coefficients of a block. Find the biggest *t* so that the embedding capacity of those blocks ,that have a zero JPEG coefficients no more than *t*, is more than serect message length. Note the biggest *t* as *Tz* ;
- visit every blocks . If its *t* is small than *Tz* then skip, else use histogram-shifting method to expand the 1 or -1 coefficient to embed message bits.

The steps of the extraction:
- get the information of *Tz*;
- visit every blocks. If its *t* is small than *Tz* then skip, else extact data and backfill the bins with value 1 and -1.

Fig. 3. Summary of Huang et al.'s method.

blocks. Therefore, in this section, we first introduce our expandable bins-pair and block selection strategy and then summarize the framework.

Note that, in this method, we only consider amending the AC coefficients, because DC coefficients can only offer a small embedding capacity while introduce large distortions. As mentioned in Sect. 2.1, the AC coefficients are encoded with RLE. Since changing the coefficients after the position of last nonzero coefficients, may significantly increases the JPEG file size and introduces large distortion, the proposed method only considers to amend the AC coefficients on and before the position of last nonzero coefficients. For simplicity, the DCT coefficients in the following sections represents the AC coefficients on and before the position of last nonzero coefficients.

3.1 Expandable Bins-Pair in Histogram and Block Selection

Huang et al.'s method exploits $(-1,1)$ as the expandable bins-pair, which is not an adaptive pattern, and there often exists other bins-pair which gives better performance. According to the HS mechanism, the expandable bins-pair directly corresponds to the embedded image quality and the increased file size. Thus it is important to select a good bins-pair for each image. ABBS proposes to find the different bins-pairs for different images by adopting a KNN (k-nearest neighbors) algorithm [1]. The embedding block selection method is also different from the Huang et al.'s.

KNN for Choosing Bins-Pair. Since different bins-pair results different modified histogram, a good bins-pair must satisfies certain criteria. Firstly, the bins-pair can offer enough payload. Secondly, the embedding distortions is low. Thirdly, the file size is preserved.

With the three criteria, we can try to find the optimal bins-pair for any histogram. Here, the histogram is derived from the quantized DCT coefficients. As we mentioned in Sect. 2.1, changing the quantized DCT coefficients will affect the file size and image's visual quality. In our method, we adopts the KNN algorithm to find the optimal bins-pair from the quantized DCT coefficients histogram.

We first prepare an image database and find the optimal bins-pair of each image according the three criteria. In this case, the bins-pair is the class label, images which own identical bins-pairs are in the same class. Then we extract features of each image. These features and corresponding labels serve as training set.

The key point is feature. To better illustrate the feature, suppose an image named $I(512 \times 512)$ is going to be processed. We firstly transform I to $I^{'}(64 \times 4096)$. Each column of $I^{'}$ is a block of I with the zigzag scanning order. Discard the first row of $I^{'}$ to get I_a because DC coefficients are unchanged in our method. Then the algorithm calculates the threshold M, where the histogram of first M rows of I_a can support at least one bins-pair. Let S_M be the set consists of all the elements in the first M rows of I_a. We denote $(x_1, x_2, ..., x_n)$ as a feature of I.

$$x_i = \frac{h(i)}{messagelength}, 1 \leq i \leq n. \tag{1}$$

where $h(1)$ is the number of $0s$ in S_M, $h(2)$ is the number of $1s$ in S_M, $h(3)$ is the number of $-1s$ in S_M, $h(4)$ is the number of $2s$ in S_M, $h(5)$ is the number of $-2s$ in S_M, etc.

After collecting the features and optimal bins-pairs of the images, the training set is constructed. Note that the paper adopt Euclidean distance to calculate the distance between two features.

After the training is finished, the optimal bins-pair selection can be performed as follow. Given an image which is going to be embedded, we extract its feature. Then we search for the nearest k neighbors of the feature in the training set. The most common label of the k neighbors is the current optimal label for this to-be-embedded image. As we explained above, the label represent optimal bins-pair.

According to the quantization tables in JPEG compression (for example as Fig. 2), lower frequency components are usually being quantized with smaller quantization step than the high frequency components. This indicates that the modifications on low frequency components are usually smaller than modifying the high frequency components. Then, if the quantized coefficients must be amended for embedding, it will cause less image quality distortions to change the low frequency values. Thus we only consider first M rows of I_a.

In our experiments, the dimension of the feature n is set to be 17, because the dimension of the features must be fixed for latter distance calculations and fact is that there only exist a few candidate bins-pair which possesses the potential to be the optimal bins-pair. As the empirical results in Fig. 4 indicate, most coefficients usually contributes little.

Figure 4 includes four histograms of quantized DCT coefficient at four QF levels. The coefficients are from S_M where $M = 10$. As we can observe, the bins which are far away from the peak bin usually gives near zero count number, thus they can only provide a near zero embedding capacity. Moreover, these

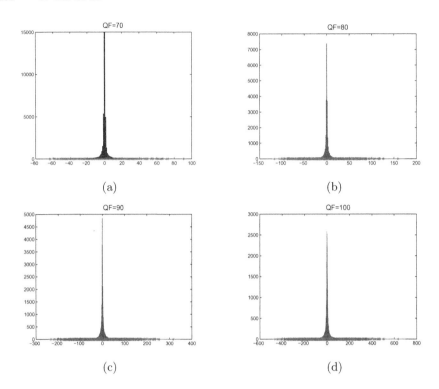

Fig. 4. Histogram of quantized DCT coefficients of S_{10} from lena.jpg: (a) QF = 70, (b) QF = 80, (c) QF = 90, (d) QF = 100.

coefficients are more likely to be in the high frequency locations. Therefore, in general, these bins have a very small possibility to be the optimal bins-pair.

Block Selection Strategy. Since the proposed method only modifies the AC coefficients on and before the position of the last nonzero coefficient, we denote these coefficients as changeable-coefficients. Unfortunately, not all the blocks are suitable for HS embedding. The blocks with lots of changeable-coefficients will introduce more distortions than others when performing the embedding. Hence, those blocks are unappropriate to embed the information. ABBS selects suitable blocks for carrying out embedding. The details are explained as following.

Blocks with different number of changeable-coefficients own different characteristics. The Empirical results indicate that in the low frequency part, the coefficients of block with a large number of changeable-coefficients are usually more divergent than that of the blocks with a small number of changeable-coefficients.

Figure 5 employs the test image Baboon and different JPEG quality factors. The horizontal axis represents 63 block sets, each of which contains a corresponding number of changeable-coefficients. For example, 1 in the horizontal axis represent the block set which consists of blocks only have one changeable-coefficients.

The vertical axis shows the entropy of different sets (in their low frequency part). Similarly, Fig. 6 employs the test image Lena and different JPEG quality factors.

According to the Figs. 5 and 6, the blocks which contains less coefficients own a smaller entropy, i.e., those blocks with less changeable-coefficients will have a smaller entropy.

Since when a data set has a higher entropy, the histogram will be more flat and vice versa, and a flat histogram yields more distortions during the embedding, in the proposed method, only the blocks with small number of changeable-coefficients are select to embed the message bits. We search for the threshold C, select those blocks, whose number of changeable-coefficients is smaller than C, to form a block set S_C. C should satisfy a condition that S_C can offer enough payload. After C is calculated, only the block in S_C will be embedded.

3.2   Embedding Procedure of ABBS

The embedding procedure can be summarized as follows.

- **step 1:** Calculate the optimal bins-pair $(bin1, bin2)$.
- **step 2:** Calculate the threshold C.
- **step 3:** Generate a block set S_C according to C.

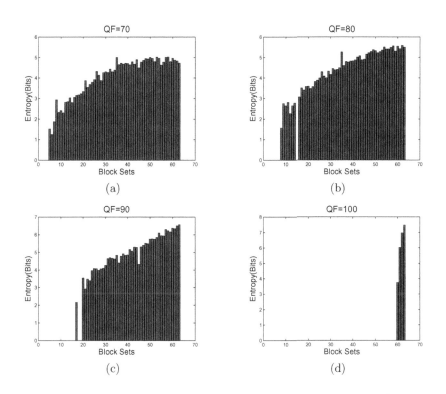

Fig. 5. Statistic Entropy Information of the image Baboon at different QF levels.

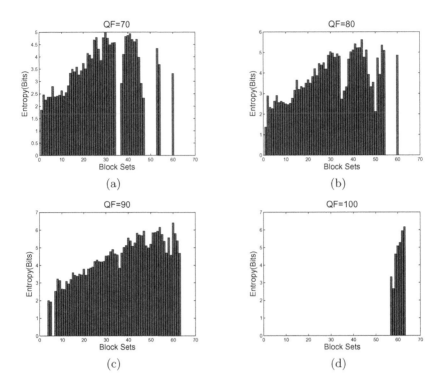

Fig. 6. Statistic Entropy Information of the image Lena at different QF levels.

- **step 4:** Histogram shifting in S_C according to message bits.
- **step 5:** Add the side information$((bin1, bin2), C)$ into the image.

Suppose a message with M bits is required to be embedded into an image I. The feature f will firstly be extracted. The optimal bins-pair $(bin1, bin2)$ can be obtained via the proposed bins-pair selection approach. Then, according to the $(bin1, bin2)$ and embedding capacity, ABBS calculates the C, and thus obtain the embedding block set. S_C, in which each block possesses a number of changeable-coefficients smaller than C. Note that C must satisfy that S_C provides enough capacity to embed M bits. Then, ABBS embeds data in the blocks belongs to S_C as Eqs. 2 and 3.

$$\widetilde{X_i} = \begin{cases} X_i + sign(X_i) * m & X_i = bin1 \text{ or } X_i = bin2, \\ X_i + sign(X_i) & X_i < bin1 \text{ or } X_i > bin2. \end{cases} \quad (2)$$

$$sign(x) = \begin{cases} 1 & x > 0, \\ 0 & x = 0, \\ -1 & x < 0. \end{cases} \quad (3)$$

In the Eq. 2, we suppose $bin1 < bin2$. The symbol X_i is a changeable quantized AC coefficient in a block which belongs to S_C. m is the current to be embedded message bit of M. Besides of M, note that the values of $(bin1, bin2)$ and C are treated as side information which is going to be embedded into the pre-determined blocks.

The data extraction and cover image reconstruction is quite simple. First, the proposed method accesses the pre-determined blocks and retrieves the information about $(bin1, bin2)$ and C. Then, ABBS generates the S_C with respect to the side information. After located all the changeable coefficients($\widetilde{X}$) in the blocks in S_C, data extraction and cover image reconstruction is conducted as Eqs. 4 and 5, respectively.

$$m' = \begin{cases} 0 & \widetilde{X}_i = bin1 \text{ or } \widetilde{X}_i = bin2, \\ 1 & \widetilde{X}_i = bin1 - 1 \text{ or } \widetilde{X}_i = bin2 + 1. \end{cases} \tag{4}$$

$$X_i' = \begin{cases} \widetilde{X}_i - sign(\widetilde{X}_i) & \widetilde{X}_i \leq bin1 - 1 \text{ or } \widetilde{X}_i \geq bin2 + 1, \\ \widetilde{X}_i & otherwise. \end{cases} \tag{5}$$

Where m' in Eq. 5 is the extracted message bits and X_i' is the reconstructed coefficients.

4   Experimental Results

In the experiments, two image sets are constructed where the images are from the BOSSbase 1.01 image library [2]. One is the training image set, which is employed to generate the training samples of KNN algorithm. The other one is the testing image set, whose elements are randomly selected from the BOSSbase. The two image sets are non-overlapped.

Note that the images in BOSSbase are raw files. Thus, these images should be compressed with JPEG standard. In this paper, we employed the JPEG library "Libjpeg" to compress images. It was developed by Tom Lane and the Independent JPEG Group (IJG), and Libjpeg is a wildly adopted library for processing JPEG images. To test the results in different payloads and different QFs, the training image set and testing image set is compressed with four different quality factors (QF = 70,80,90,100) respectively. For each QF level, 4 levels of payloads, 4k, 10k, 15k and 20k, are embedded into these images. In this case, we select 1000 images in BOSSbase randomly, and then, generated four image set by compressed them in the four QF levels respectively. 4 levels of payload will be tested at each QF level. These 16 image sets constitute the testing samples. On the other hand, according to the criteria of selecting a bins-pair which is introduced in Sect. 3.1, we elaborately select images of the remaining images of BOSSbase into 16 image sets. Obviously, each image set corresponds to a certain QF level and a payload level. These 16 image sets form the training samples of the KNN algorithm. The size of each training image set is influenced by the QF and payload level. For example, the possible bins-pairs of a 20k bits payload is smaller than the possible bins-pairs of a 4k bits payload, so the image sets corresponding to the two payloads have different number of images. In this paper, the average size of the 16 training image sets is 200.

In this paper, the performance of the proposed method is evaluated with respect to the stego image quality and the file size preservation. As we mentioned above, the proposed method is based on [5]. Thus, for fair comparison, the proposed method is compared with Huang et al.'s method, where the two methods belong to the same category of RDH methods for JPEG images.

4.1 Image Quality Comparisons

In the experiments, the peak signal-to-noise ratio(PSNR) is employed as the measurement of the stego image's visual quality, which is defined in Eq. 7.

$$MSE = \frac{1}{mn} \sum_{i,j} (X_{i,j} - \widetilde{X_{i,j}})^2. \tag{6}$$

$$PSNR = 10 \log \frac{Max((X_{i,j})^2)}{MSE}. \tag{7}$$

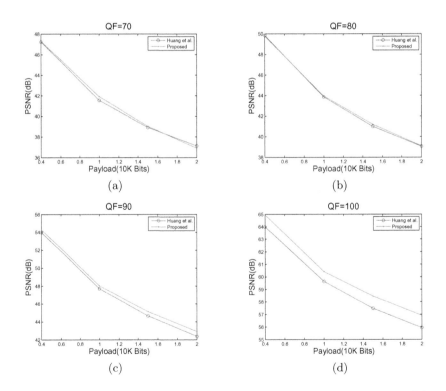

Fig. 7. Average PSNR values with different embedding payloads: (a) QF = 70, (b) QF = 80, (c) QF = 90, (d) QF = 100.

The comparison results are shown in Fig. 7. The four sub-figure (a)–(d) corresponds to different quality factors when performing JPEG compression to the test images. The horizontal axis is the embedding payload while the vertical axis is the average PSNR of the tested 1000 images.

Figure 7 indicates that both of methods achieves a decent PSNR value. Comparing with Huang et al.'s method, with the increasing QF level, the PSNR gain of our method is also increasing. When $QF = 100$ the proposed method gives at least 1 dB gain. Note that the results of the proposed method at certain QF levels similar to Huang et al.'s, especially when the payload is small, as shown in Fig. 7 (a) and (b). One possible reason is that the bins-pairs of the two method may be identical in many testing images. For example, when $QF = 70/80$, the optimal bins-pair selected by the proposed method is more likely to be $(-1,1)$, which is identical to Huang et al.'s selection.

4.2   File Size Preservation Comparisons

During the experiments, to evaluate the preservation of file size, we directly measure the increased file size between the original image file and the embedded image file.

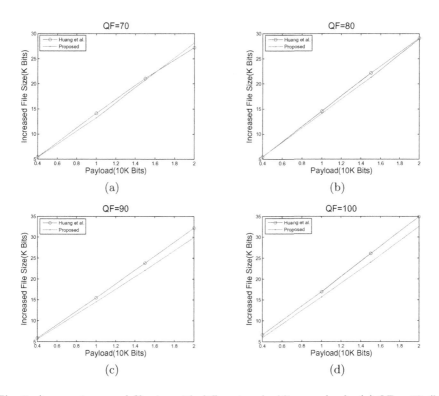

Fig. 8. Average increased file size with different embedding payloads: (a) QF = 70, (b) QF = 80, (c) QF = 90, (d) QF = 100.

The comparison results are shown in Fig. 8, which gives the average increased file size of 1000 test images with different JPEG compression quality factors and different payloads.

According to Fig. 8, as the payload and QF increases, the proposed method shows more improvements compared to Huang et al.'s method. When the payload is large and QF level is high, the proposed method demonstrates a significant advantage for preserving the file size. However, when the QF level is low, the performances are similar between the two methods. The reason is similar to that in Sect. 4.1.

5   Conclusion

In this paper, an adaptive reversible data hiding method for JPEG images is proposed. The proposed method firstly select the optical bins-pair for each cover image by adopting a KNN algorithm. Then, according to the bins-pair and message length, ABBS chooses the appropriate blocks for embedding the message bits. At last, ABBS embeds message bits by the standard histogram-shifting method. During the experiments, the proposed method can excellently keep the file size advantage and visual quality less. It demonstrates a superior performance compared to the state-of-the-art method.

Acknowledgments. This work was supported by National Key Research and Development Plan (No. 2016YFC0801004, 2016YFB0800100), National Natural Science Foundation of China (No. 61332012, 61671448), "Strategic Priority Research Program" of the Chinese Academy of Sciences (No. XDA06010701), and National Program for Support of Top-notch Young Professionals.

References

1. Altman, N.: An introduction to kernel and nearest-neighbor nonparametric regression. Am. Stat. **46**(3), 175–185 (1992)
2. Bas, P., Filler, T., Pevný, T.: "Break our steganographic system": the ins and outs of organizing BOSS. In: Filler, T., Pevný, T., Craver, S., Ker, A. (eds.) IH 2011. LNCS, vol. 6958, pp. 59–70. Springer, Heidelberg (2011). doi:10.1007/978-3-642-24178-9_5
3. Fridrich, J., Goljan, M., Du, R.: Lossless data embedding: new paradigm in digital watermarking. EURASIP J. Appl. Sig. Process. **2002**(1), 185–196 (2002)
4. Hu, Y., Wang, K., Lu, Z.: An improved VLC-based lossless data hiding scheme for JPEG images. J. Syst. Softw. **86**(8), 2166–2173 (2013)
5. Huang, F., Qu, X., Kim, H., Huang, J.: Reversible data hiding in JPEG images. IEEE Trans. Circ. Syst. Video Technol. **26**(9), 1610–1621 (2016)
6. Jaiswal, S.P., Au, O.C., Jakhetiya, V., Guo, Y., Tiwari, A.K., Yue, K.: Efficient adaptive prediction based reversible image watermarking. In: 2013 IEEE International Conference on Image Processing, pp. 4540–4544. IEEE (2013)
7. Li, Q., Wu, Y., Bao, F.: A reversible data hiding scheme for JPEG images. In: Proceedings of 11th Pacific Rim Conference on Multimedia, pp. 653–664 (2010)

8. Mobasseri, B., Berger, R., Marcinak, M.P., NaikRaikar, Y.: Data embedding in JPEG bitstream by code mapping. IEEE Trans. Image Process. **19**(4), 958–966 (2010)

9. Ni, Z., Shi, Y., Ansari, N., Su, W.: Reversible data hiding. IEEE Trans. Circ. Syst. Video Technol. **16**(3), 354–362 (2006)

10. Nikolaidis, A.: Reversible data hiding in JPEG images utilising zero quantised coefficients. IET Image Proc. **9**(7), 560–568 (2015)

11. Pevný, T., Filler, T., Bas, P.: Using high-dimensional image models to perform highly undetectable steganography. In: Proceedings of 12th International Workshop on Information Hiding, pp. 161–177, April 2010

12. Sakai, H., Kuribayashi, M., Morii, M.: Adaptive reversible data hiding for JPEG images. In: International Symposium on Information Theory and its Applications, ISITA 2008, pp. 1–6. IEEE (2008)

13. Subramanyam, A., Emmanuel, S., Kankanhalli, M.: Robust watermarking of compressed and encrypted JPEG2000 images. IEEE Trans. Multimedia **14**(3), 703–716 (2012)

14. Tian, J.: Reversible data embedding using a difference expansion. IEEE Trans. Circuits Syst. Video Techn. **13**(8), 890–896 (2003)

15. Tuncer, T., Avci, E.: A reversible data hiding algorithm based on probabilistic DNA-XOR secret sharing scheme for color images. Displays **41**, 1–8 (2016)

16. Wallace, G.: The JPEG still picture compression standard. IEEE Trans. Consum. Electron. **38**(1), xviii–xxxiv (1992)

17. Wang, K., Lu, Z., Hu, Y.: A high capacity lossless data hiding scheme for JPEG images. J. Syst. Softw. **86**(7), 1965–1975 (2013)

18. Wang, Z.H., Zhuang, X., Chang, C.C., Qin, C., Zhu, Y.: Reversible data hiding based on geometric structure of pixel groups. Int. J. Netw. Secur. **18**(1), 52–59 (2016)

19. Xuan, G., Shi, Y.Q., Ni, Z., Chai, P., Cui, X., Tong, X.: Reversible data hiding for JPEG images based on histogram pairs. In: Kamel, M., Campilho, A. (eds.) ICIAR 2007. LNCS, vol. 4633, pp. 715–727. Springer, Heidelberg (2007). doi:10. 1007/978-3-540-74260-9_64

Separable Multiple Bits Reversible Data Hiding in Encrypted Domain

Yan Ke$^{(\boxtimes)}$, Minqing Zhang, and Jia Liu

Key Laboratory of Network and Information Security Under the Chinese People
Armed Police Force, Department of Electronic Technology,
Engineering University of PAP, Xi'an, China
15114873390@163.com

Abstract. This paper proposes a novel scheme of separable multiple bits reversible data hiding in encrypted domain based on LWE (Learning with Errors). Multi-band data could be embedded by recoding the redundancy of ciphertext, which does enhance the capacity of embedding data. With embedded ciphertext, the additional data can be extracted by using data-hiding key, and the original data can be recovered losslessly by using decryption key, the processes of extraction and decryption are separable. By deducing the error probability of the scheme, parameters in the scheme which directly related to the scheme's correctness is mainly discussed, and reasonable ranges of the parameters are obtained by experiments. When analyzing the security, the probability distribution function of the embedded cipher text is deduced and the statistic features of ciphertext are analyzed, which both proved the embedded data isn't detective. The proposed scheme is based on encryption process, so it can apply to different kinds of media vehicle. Experimental results have demonstrated that the proposed scheme can not only achieve statistical security without degrading the quality of encryption, but realize that 1bit original data can maximally load multiple-bit additional data in encrypted domain.

Keywords: Information security · Reversible data hiding · Public key cryptography · LWE · Multiple bits data hiding

1 Introduction

Reversible data hiding in encrypted domain is one kind of information hiding techniques which can both extract secret messages, and decrypt the embedded ciphertext then restore the original cover vehicle losslessly, possessing privacy protection and data hiding dual function. It is a potential technique in signal processing and data management in the encrypted domain fields [1].

Reversible data hiding in encrypted domain have difficulties realizing such issuses: high capacity embedding, original data losslessly restoring and undetectability [2]. To deal with the difficulties, present algorithms mainly have two categories: one concentrate on leaving some features unencrypted or spare space as additional redundancy for embedding, the data hiding methods are usually based on difference expansion [3], histogram shift [4–6] or image's lossless compression [7] etc. Zhao, etc. [8] proposed

© Springer International Publishing AG 2017
Y.Q. Shi et al. (Eds.): IWDW 2016, LNCS 10082, pp. 470–484, 2017.
DOI: 10.1007/978-3-319-53465-7_35

to encrypt parts of DCT coefficients during compression while other coefficients carried secret message; also, in [9, 10], part of features get encrypted. Strictly speaking, these algorithms and separable algorithms [11] do not truly operate in the encrypted domain, resulting in cover information's divulging.

The other category can guarantee the security of encryption process, operating in the encrypted domain based on homomorphic encryption [12–14], image encryption, compression in encrypted domain etc. Algorithms based on homomorphic encryption can be separable but there is a rocketing computational complexity and an enormous encryption blowup factor; To enhance efficiency, Zhang [15] proposed reversible data hiding in encrypted image combining the technologies of encryption and data hiding, but processes of extraction and decryption are inseparable and embedding capacity and quality of recovered image are unduly constrained; To enhance capacity, algorithms [16–20] made it at the price of degrading the quality of recovered original data; Zhang [21] proposed a separable data hiding method in encrypted image, data was embedded into space spared by compressing encrypted image's LSB, but caver's recovering is based on image neighboring pixels' relativity, so reversibility cannot be well ensured. It is worth noting that the encrypted data, unlike common carrier data, follows the uniform distribution, but present algorithms did little research in the security or undetectability. In our scheme, a multiple bits reversible data hiding in encrypted domain based on LWE is proposed. We achieve such features: Consistent reversibility, that original data can be completely restored; Separablility of extraction and decryption; Accurate correctness of multiple-bit data embedding and extraction. By theoretical analysis and experimental results, the embedded ciphertext in the proposed scheme is proved to follow uniform distribution.

LWE public key cryptography algorithm used in our scheme has three important advantages for reversible data hiding in encrypted domain: 1. Strong security for privacy protection and information security; 2. Generous controllable redundancy for embedding; 3. Brief structure and simple computation which is significant in practical applications. Because the best known algorithms for LWE run in exponential time (even quantum algorithms don't seem to help). And LWE algorithms have the defects of public key size of order n^2 (n is a size parameter of the lattices space) and high encryption blowup factor, but the encryption redundancy can be controllable once knowing the secret key. LWE problem has simple algebraic structure and almost linear operations [22, 23].

Main contributions of this paper are: 1. In the pre-processing, we introducing the stream cipher to maintain the hardness of LWE algorithm; 2. Multi-band data can be embedded by quantifying the encrypted domain and recoding the redundancy of ciphertext; 3. To keep the fully reversibility of data-recovering, we recode the redundancy according to original data's probability distribution during encryption; 4. By dividing the encrypted domain into the sub-regions and introducing different quantifying standards, the processes of extraction and decryption can be separated. Meanwhile, we also give the theoretical analysis and experimental results on the reversibility of the cover-restoring, the feasibility and the security of the proposed scheme.

The rest of this paper is organized as follows. The next Section first introduces Regev's LWE algorithm, then the design idea and the proposed scheme are elaborated; In Sect. 3, three judging standards of reversible data hiding schemes including correctness, security and capacity are discussed theoretically; In Sect. 4, the paper is concluded and future investigation is discussed.

2   Separable Multiple Bits Reversible Data Hiding in Encrypted Domain

2.1   Regev's LWE Algorithm [22]

Cryptosystem is parameterized by integers n (the security parameter), m (number of lattice space's dimension), q (modulus), l (the length of binary data in once encryption operate). Choose q to be a prime, $q \in (n^2, 2n^2) \geq 2$, a real $\varepsilon > 0$, $m = (1 + \varepsilon)(n + 1)\log q$ and on $\mathbb{Z}_q$ as χ, where $\chi = \bar{\Psi}_{\alpha q}$, $\bar{\Psi}_{\alpha q} = \{\lceil qx \rfloor q | x \sim N(0, \alpha^2)\alpha$ is the standard deviation of χ, ($\lceil qx \rfloor$: round to nearest integer). The length of the plaintext data is $l \in \mathbb{Z}_q$, all operations are performed modulo q in $\mathbb{Z}_q$.

Secret Key: choosing a matrix $\mathbf{S} \in \mathbb{Z}_q^{n \times l}$ uniformly; Public Key: choosing a matrix $\mathbf{A} \in \mathbb{Z}_q^{n \times m}$ uniformly. Generate noise matrix $\mathbf{E} \in \mathbb{Z}_q^{m \times l}$ whose elements follow the distribution χ independently. Output the pair $(\mathbf{A}, \mathbf{P} = \mathbf{A}^{\mathrm{T}}\mathbf{S} + \mathbf{E}) \in \mathbb{Z}_q^{n \times m} \times \mathbb{Z}_q^{m \times l}$ as public key. Encryption: the plaintext is $\mathbf{m} \in \{0, 1\}^l$. Output the pair $(\mathbf{u} = \mathbf{Aa},$ $\mathbf{c} = \mathbf{P}^{\mathrm{T}}\mathbf{a} + \mathbf{m}\lfloor q/2 \rfloor) \in \mathbb{Z}_q^n \times \mathbb{Z}_q^l$ as ciphertext. Decryption: To ciphertext $(\mathbf{u}, \mathbf{c})$, calculate $\mathbf{ms} = \mathbf{c} - \mathbf{S}^{\mathrm{T}}\mathbf{u}$. And the decryption of $(\mathbf{u}, \mathbf{c})$ is 0 if the elements of $\mathbf{ms}$ is closer to 0 than to $\lfloor q/2 \rfloor$ modulo q, and 1 otherwise.

The explanation of correctness using graph are as follows:

$$\mathbf{ms} = \mathbf{c} - \mathbf{S}^{\mathrm{T}}\mathbf{u} = \mathbf{P}^{\mathrm{T}}\mathbf{a} + \mathbf{m}\lfloor q/2 \rfloor - \mathbf{S}^{\mathrm{T}}\mathbf{Aa} = (\mathbf{A}^{\mathrm{T}}\mathbf{S} + \mathbf{E})^{\mathrm{T}}\mathbf{a} + \mathbf{m}\lfloor q/2 \rfloor - \mathbf{S}^{\mathrm{T}}\mathbf{Aa} = \mathbf{E}^{\mathrm{T}}\mathbf{a} + \mathbf{m}\lfloor q/2 \rfloor$$

Donate the elements of $\mathbf{ms}$ as ms_i, so $\mathbf{ms} = (ms_1, ms_2, \ldots, ms_l)^{\mathrm{T}}$. Then ms_i can be regarded as points on the circle in Fig. 1. Because of the additive noise $\mathbf{E}^{\mathrm{T}}\mathbf{a}$, the exact locations of ms_i on the circle are uncertain. By cotralling α, $\mathbf{E}^{\mathrm{T}}\mathbf{a}$ have magnitudes less than $\lfloor q/4 \rfloor$, so the bits of $\mathbf{m}$ can be recovered by rounding each ms_i back to either $ms_i = 0$ ($m_i = 0$) or $ms_i = \lfloor q/2 \rfloor$ ($m_i = 1$) whichever is closer modulo q.

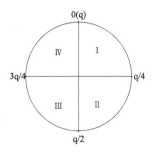

Fig. 1. Distribution of integers in $\mathbb{Z}_q$

2.2   Proposed Scheme

2.2.1   Design Idea

But as for secret-key keeper, the range of $ms = (ms_1, ms_2, \ldots, ms_l)^{\mathrm{T}}$ takes up half of the integer domain $\mathbb{Z}_q$, namely ms_i ranging in $\lfloor q/2 \rfloor$ only corresponds to 1 bit plaintext. As Fig. 2 shows, the integer domain $\mathbb{Z}_q$ has been divided into 4 regions I II III IV averagely, each region is divided averagely into B sub-regions, so the quantization step of sub-region is $\lfloor q/4B \rfloor$. Donate the sub-regions in one region as sub-region0, sub-region1,..., sub-region $B - 1$ ($B = 4$ in the Fig. 2). By adding or subtracting a multiple of quantization step to change the location of ms_i into sub-region i within the same region, B-b and data i can be embedded, thus 1bit plaintext can carry log B bit secret message in encrypted domain.

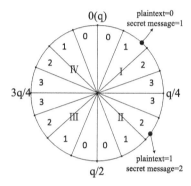

Fig. 2. Distribution of integers in $\mathbb{Z}_q$

Definition 1: The function $L : i = L(x), i \in \{0, 1, 2, 3, \ldots, B - 1\}, x \in \mathbb{Z}_q$, which indicates that x is located in sub-region i.

$$L(x) = \begin{cases} \left\lfloor \frac{64x}{q} \right\rfloor, x \in [0, q/4) \\ 32 - \left\lfloor \frac{64x}{q} \right\rfloor - 1, x \in [q/4, q/2) \\ \left\lfloor \frac{64x}{q} \right\rfloor - 32, x \in [q/4, 3q/4) \\ 64 - \left\lfloor \frac{64x}{q} \right\rfloor - 1, x \in [3q/4, q) \end{cases} \tag{1}$$

Process of proposed scheme in detail as following:

2.2.2   Pre-processing

(1) Choose a security parameter n, a power of 2, which determines the other parameters. Modulus is $q \in (n^2, 2n^2) \geq 2$, the dimension of vectors in lattice space is $m = (1 + \varepsilon)(n + 1) \log q, \varepsilon > 0$, the noise's distribution $\chi = \bar{\Psi}_{\alpha q}$, where the

standard deviation $\alpha = o(1/\sqrt{n} \log n)$. All the reasonable ranges of parameter above-mentioned are analyzed in Sect. 3 in detail;

(2) Donate the plaintext as $pl \in \{0,1\}^l$, the secret message as $me \in \{0,1\}^{l \cdot \log B}$;
(3) Donate the band of the multi-band data to embed as $B = 2^x (x \in \mathbb{Z}_q)$. To maintain the security of encrypted data, the data to encrypt and to embed has to follow random distribution. The exclusive-or sequence m of the plaintext pl and pseudo-random bits $ra1 \in \{0,1\}^l$ and the exclusive-or sequence se of the secret message me and pseudo-random bits $ra2 \in \{0,1\}^{l \cdot \log B}$ are calculated:

$$m = ra1 \oplus pl \tag{2}$$

$$se = ra2 \oplus me \tag{3}$$

Where $m = (m_1, m_2, \ldots, m_l), m_i \in \{0,1\}^l$ is for encryption; $se = (se_1, se_2, \ldots),$ $se_i \in \{0,1\}$. Then encode se as a B-b and vector $sm = (sm_1, sm_2, \ldots, sm_l), sm_i \in \{0, 1, \ldots, B-1\}$ is for embedding.

2.2.3 Data Encryption and Data Embedding

(1) Secret Key: Choose a matrix $S \in \mathbb{Z}_q^{n \times l}$ uniformly. The decryption key is $(S, ra1)$, and the data-hiding key is $(S, ra2)$.
(2) Public Key: Choose a matrix $A \in \mathbb{Z}_q^{n \times m}$ uniformly. Generate a noise matrix $E \in \mathbb{Z}_q^{m \times l}$, whose elements follow the distribution χ independently. Output the pair $(A, P = A^T S + E) \in \mathbb{Z}_q^{n \times m} \times \mathbb{Z}_q^{m \times l}$.
(3) Encryption: Generate a vector $a \in \{0,1\}^m$ randomly. Output $(u = Aa, c = P^T a + m \lfloor q/2 \rfloor) \in \mathbb{Z}_q^n \times \mathbb{Z}_q^l$
(4) Data embedding: Calculate $h = c - S^T u$, where $h = (h_1, h_2, \ldots, h_l)^T$. Donate the vector that decide the plus-minus of ciphertext's change when embedding as $bt = (\beta_1, \beta_2, \ldots, \beta_l)^T, \beta_i \in \{-1, +1\}$, and the change quantity of ciphertext as b_i, the vector $b = (b_1, b_2, \ldots, b_l)^T$.

Calculate vector bt and b:

$$\beta_i = \begin{cases} 1, h_i \in (0, q/4) \cup (q/2, 3q/4) \\ -1, h_i \in (q/4, q/2) \cup (3q/4, q) \end{cases} \tag{4}$$

$$b_i = sm_i - \mathrm{L}(h_i), b_i \in -B+1, -B+2, \ldots, 0, 1, \ldots, B-1\} \tag{5}$$

Output the pair (u, cs) as the embedded ciphertext, where $cs = (cs_1, cs_2, \ldots, cs_l)^T$:

$$cs_i = c_i + \beta_i \cdot b_i \cdot \lfloor q/4B \rfloor \ (i = 1, 2, \ldots, 1) \tag{6}$$

2.2.4   Data Decryption and Data Extraction

Decryption: To ciphertext (u, cs) with decryption key $(S, ra1)$, calculate $h' = cs - S^{\mathrm{T}}u$, where $h' = (h'_1, h'_2, \ldots, h'_l)^{\mathrm{T}}$. Donate the decryption of (u, cs) as a vector $m' = (m'_1, m'_2, \ldots, m'_l)^{\mathrm{T}}$:

$$m'_i = \begin{cases} 0, h'_i \in (0, q/4) \cup (3q/4, q) \\ 1, h'_i \in (q/4, 3q/4) \end{cases} \tag{7}$$

and the decrypted data is:

$$pl' = ra1 \oplus m' \tag{8}$$

Data Extraction: To ciphertext (u, cs) with decryption key $(S, ra1)$, calculate $h' = cs - S^{\mathrm{T}}u$, where $h' = (h'_1, h'_2, \ldots, h'_l)^{\mathrm{T}}$. Donate the extracted data of (u, cs) as a vector $sm' = (sm'_1, sm'_2, \ldots, sm'_l)^{\mathrm{T}}$:

$$sm'_i = L(h'_i) \tag{9}$$

Encode the vector sm' as a binary sequence se', and the extracted message is:

$$me' = ra2 \oplus se' \tag{10}$$

In summary, the embedding process is based on the encryption process, so the proposed scheme can apply to different kinds of media vehicle (e.g., texts, images, and audio).

3   Theoretical Analysis and Experimental Results

3.1   Correctness

The correctness of proposed scheme includes the plaintext's lossless decryption and the secret message's accurate extraction, which are the fundamental principle and criterion of reversible data hiding in encrypted domain. The correctness analysis of proposed scheme's decryption and extraction are as following:

In Sect. 2.2.3(3): if $m_i = 0$, h_i will locate in region I IV in $\mathbb{Z}_q$ shown in Fig. 2, and if $m_i = 1$, h_i will locate in region II III. In Sect. 2.2.3(4): if $sm_i = i$, the corresponding encrypted data will add or subtract a multiple of quantization step $\lfloor q/4B \rfloor$, which results that h_i will locate in sub-region i within the same region as h_i. Hence, the same region can ensure the consistency of decryption after embedding while the sub-region's number carry the information of secret message, the orders of decryption and data extraction aren't fixed. So the necessary condition of the proposed scheme'correctness is that the elements of $E^{\mathrm{T}}a$ (the i-th element donated as $E_i a$) have magnitudes less than $\lfloor q/4 \rfloor$, namely each $E_i a$ ranges within $(0, \lfloor q/4 \rfloor) \cup (\lfloor 3q/4 \rfloor, q)$.

Donate the elements of matrix E as $E = (E_1, E_2, \ldots, E_l)$, $E_i = (e_{i1}, e_{i2}, \ldots e_{im})$, $i = 1, 2, \ldots, l$. e_{ij} follows the distribution χ independently, so $E_i a = \sum_{j=1}^{m} e_{ij} a_j, i = 1, 2, \ldots, l$ can be deduced to follow the Gaussian distribution whose expectation is 0, the standard deviation is $\sqrt{\sum_{j=1}^{m} a_j} \cdot \alpha$.

According to Sect. 2.2.3(3), $a \in \{0, 1\}^m$ is generated randomly, $\sum_{j=1}^{m} a_j \approx \frac{m}{2}$. So:

$$E_i a \sim N(0, \sqrt{m/2} \cdot \alpha) \tag{11}$$

Here is a truncated inequality probability on Gaussian distribution: let $z \sim N(0, 1)$, then:

$$\Pr(|z| > x) = 2 \int_{x}^{+\infty} \frac{1}{\sqrt{2\pi}} \exp(-\frac{1}{2} z^2) dz \leq \frac{1}{x} \sqrt{\frac{2}{\pi}} \exp(-\frac{1}{2} z^2) \tag{12}$$

So the probability of decryption noise in our scheme is:

$$P(|\sum_{j=1}^{m} e_{ij} a_j| \geq \frac{q}{4B}) = P(|\frac{\sum_{j=1}^{m} e_{ij}}{\alpha \sqrt{m/2}}| \geq \frac{q}{4B\alpha\sqrt{m/2}}) \leq \frac{4B \, \alpha\sqrt{m}}{q\sqrt{\pi}} \exp(-\frac{q^2}{16mB^2\alpha^2}) \tag{13}$$

So the decryption failure will occur if the relative total noise to be bigger than $\lfloor q/4 \rfloor$, and the smaller α, the smaller probability of decryption failure. On the other hand, if α is too small, the distribution of noise will be close to a constant 0 with tiny deviation, which seriously affects encryption security. So the schemes based on LWE problem generally require $\alpha q > 2\sqrt{n}$ [22]. Above all, the choice of α directly determines the probability of decryption failure and security. However, the condition $\alpha = o(1/\sqrt{n} \log n)$ can't accurately give the reasonable range of α, therefore, reasonable ranges of α are obtained by experiments as following:

With the security parameter n increasing, there will be a high encryption blowup factor. To reach a balance of security and efficiency of practical use, we set $n \in [100, 320]$. Other parameters are set: $q = n^2 + n + 1, l = 8n$, $B = 2, 4, 8, 16, 32, 64,$ 128. By testing plenty of sample data in conditions that $n = 100, 120, 140 \ldots 320$, we obtained the upper limit value α_{max} that α smaller than can guarantee the correctness of the proposed scheme. The lower limit value α_{min} is set $2\sqrt{n}/q$ to ensure necessary deviation is generated by the additive noise.

The experiment to get α_{max} are as follows shown in Fig. 3: Image Lena sized 512×512 was used as the original image in Fig. 3(a). Then we divided the image into 8 bit planes, the bit-plane is shown in a 2048×1024 binary image as Fig. 3(b).

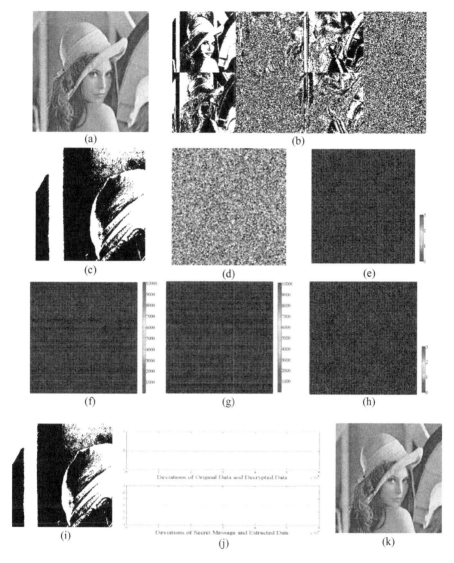

Fig. 3. Experiment the image Lena by the proposed scheme. (a) Lena; (b) Original data' bit-plane image; (c) Original data' first block; (d) Randomly Permuted Original Data; (e) Randomly Permuted Secret Message; (f) Encrypted Data before Embedding; (g) Encrypted Data after Embedding; (h) Secret Message Extracted; (i) Decrypted Data; (j) Deviations of Original Data and Decrypted Data and of Secret Message and Extracted Data; (k) Recovered Data.

To show the experiment results visually and intuitively, we set $n = 100$, $q = n^2 + n + 1$, $l = 8n$, $B = 4$ to encrypt a 7200Byte binary image sized 240×240, embed 14800Byte additional data to test the reasonability of $\alpha = 2.8452 \times 10^{-3}$ as an example: We segment the bit-plane image into a number of no overlapping 240×240 blocks; Then we set $\alpha 2.8452 \times 10^{-3}$ to test on the first block shown in Fig. 3 (c)–(h): First, the bit values of the original data's first block are shown in a 240×240 binary image Fig. 3(c); Second, we calculate the exclusive-or results of the original data and pseudo-random data shown in Fig. 3(d) and generate 4-band randomly permuted data to embedding shown in Fig. 3(e); Then we encrypt the permuted plaintext data, the ciphertext before embedding is Fig. 3(f); Finaly, we embedded 4-band randomly permuted data into ciphertext shown in Fig. 3(g); With embedded ciphertext, the secret message can be extracted from it by using data-hiding key in Fig. 3(h) and the original data can be recovered by using decryption key in Fig. 3(i). The results both in decryption and extraction are lossless by comparing bit by bit shown in Fig. 3(j).

To recover the whole image, we repeated above processes into the rest blocks of Lena's bit-plane. Recovered image is Fig. 3(k). It demonstrated that there is no error in decryption and extraction and $\alpha = 2.8452 \times 10^{-3}$ is a reasonable value for $n = 100$.

Repeat all the processes above to obtain the different reasonable values of α, then we can record the upper limit value α_{max} in Tables 1, 2. So the reasonable range of α should be $[\lambda \alpha_{min}, \nu \alpha_{max}](\lambda > 1, \nu < 1)$ To test the reliability of the ranges, we apply the proposed scheme to text, audio, and other media data, and the results demonstrated that the embedded data can be extracted and the original data can be perfectly recovered with no error.

Table 1. $\alpha_{max}, \alpha_{min}$ by experiments $n \in [220 \sim 320]$

n	100	120	140	160	180	200
α_{max}	2.8597 $\times 10^{-3}$	2.3790 $\times 10^{-3}$	2.1931 $\times 10^{-3}$	1.9867 $\times 10^{-3}$	1.8206 $\times 10^{-3}$	1.7206 $\times 10^{-3}$
α_{min}	1.9801 $\times 10^{-3}$	1.5088 $\times 10^{-3}$	1.1988 $\times 10^{-3}$	9.8204 $\times 10^{-4}$	8.2358 $\times 10^{-4}$	7.0358 $\times 10^{-4}$

Table 2. $\alpha_{max}, \alpha_{min}$ by experiments $n \in [220 \sim 320]$

n	220	240	260	280	300	320
α_{max}	1.6202 $\times 10^{-3}$	1.4857 $\times 10^{-3}$	1.3915 $\times 10^{-3}$	1.3232 $\times 10^{-3}$	1.2629 $\times 10^{-3}$	1.1688 $\times 10^{-3}$
α_{min}	6.1013 $\times 10^{-4}$	5.3568 $\times 10^{-4}$	4.7523 $\times 10^{-4}$	4.2535 $\times 10^{-4}$	3.8362 $\times 10^{-4}$	3.4830 $\times 10^{-4}$

PSNR (Peak Signal-Noise Ratio) in directly decrypted images is a quality metric used to measure the distortion in directly decrypted image caused by data hiding. Figure 4 shows the rate-distortion curves of the four images Lena, Man, Lake and Baboon in classical reversible data hiding algorithms in encrypted domain [15, 21].

In Fig. 4, the values of PSNR within (36, 55) indicate that distortion has been introduced that nearly all the previous algorithms have, while the distortion is

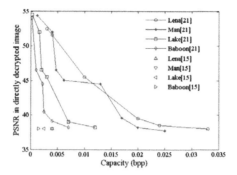

Fig. 4. Rate-PSNR comparison of the methods in [15, 21].

controlled under the degree of the differentiation for the human visual system (PSNR >35). But in our proposed scheme, the PSNR in directly decrypted images is "∞", which indicates that the original images have been recovered without any error.

3.2 Security

The security of data hiding mainly including two aspects: one is to maintain the hardness or security of encryption algorithm, and a crucial criterion on security of the present image encryption and public key algorithms is that encrypted data follows uniform distribution [24]; the other aspect is the undetectability of embedded data, demanding the marked ciphertext is indistinguishable from the original ciphertext by means of either human visual system or analysis methods. So far, there is no acknowledged criterion indicating the security of a reversible data hiding method. In consideration of the main ideology of steganalysis technology which lies in modeling original cover and embedded cover, extracting features of a test image and judging whether the sample data is embedded by using some kind of classifier without knowing any information about the original cover, therefore, it is the change of the statistic features (e.g., distribution function, histograms, information entropy) of ciphertext after embedding that indicates the undetectability [24]. Given all that, we will discuss the statistic features of data after embedding.

First, we'll deduce the distribution function of cs_i: According to (6): $cs_i = c_i + \beta_i \cdot b_i \cdot \lfloor q/4B \rfloor$ $(i = 1, 2, \ldots, l)$, $b_i = sm_i - L(h_i), b_i \in \{-B+1, -B+2, \ldots, B-1\}$.

According to (11) in 3.1: $E_i a \sim N(0, \sigma = \sqrt{m/2} \cdot \alpha)$. We donate the distribution function of $E_i a$ as $F_\sigma(x)$, and to guarantee the correctness, the deviation of $E_i a$ is within $(3q/4, q) \cup (0, q/4)$ Based on the symmetry of Gaussian distribution, we get:

$$P[E_i a \in (0, q/4)] = F_\sigma(0) = P[E_i a \in (3q/4, q)] = 1 - F_\sigma(0) = 1/2 \quad (13)$$

Also, if $\mathbf{E_i a} \in (0, q/4)$, $h_i \in (0, \lfloor q/4 \rfloor) \cup (\lfloor q/2 \rfloor, \lfloor 3q/4 \rfloor)$; if $\mathbf{E_i a} \in (3q/4, q)$, $h_i \in (\lfloor q/4 \rfloor, \lfloor q/2 \rfloor) \cup (\lfloor 3q/4 \rfloor, q)$. So we can deduce the probability of β_i from (4) (13):

$$P(\beta_i = 1) = P(\beta_i = -1) = 1/2 \tag{14}$$

The function $L(e) \in \{0, 1, \ldots B - 1\}, e \in \mathbb{Z}_q$, we donate the probability of the function L's value is x as $P_L(x) = P(L(e) = x)$:

$$P_L(x) = 2 \cdot \{F_\sigma[q \cdot (x+1)/4B] - F_\sigma[q \cdot x/4B]\}, x \in \{0, 1, \ldots, B - 1\} \tag{15}$$

The probability of each element of message sm is

$$P(sm_i = 0) = P(sm_i = 1) = \ldots = P(sm_i = B - 1) = 1/B \tag{16}$$

Also $b_i = sm_i - L(h_i), b_i \in \{-B+1, -B+2, \ldots 0, \ldots, B-1\}, sm_i, L(h_i) \in \{0, \ldots, B-1\}$, we donate the probability of $b_i = x$ as $P_b(x)$ Then all above leads up the distribution rate of b_i using discrete convolution as Table 3 shows, which also establish the variables' values in different cases. The probability expression of the different change quantities after embedding can be deduced:

$$P(cs_i = c_i + \lambda \cdot \lfloor q/4B \rfloor) = P(\beta_i = 1) \cdot P_b(\lambda) + P(\beta_i = -1) \cdot P_b(-\lambda) \tag{17}$$

$$P(cs_i = c_i - \lambda \cdot \lfloor q/4B \rfloor) = P(\beta_i = -1) \cdot P_b(\lambda) + P(\beta_i = 1) \cdot P_b(-\lambda) \tag{18}$$

where $\lambda \in \{0, 1, \ldots, B - 1\}$.

Substitute the probabilities in Table 3 into (17) (18), and it can be deduced that $P(cs_i2 = c_i + \lambda \cdot \lfloor q/4B \rfloor) = P(cs_i = c_i - \lambda \cdot \lfloor q/4B \rfloor)$. Then we can obtain the distribution rate of λ shown in Table 4:

Since the encrypted data $C_i \sim U(a,b)$, we donate the distribution function of C_i as $F_c(x) = x/q, x \in (0, q)$, that of encrypted data after embedding, donated as $F_{cs}(x)$:

Table 3. Distribution ratio of b_i

b_i	(sm_i, L)	$P_b(b_i)$
$-(B-1)$	$(0, B-1)$	$2 \cdot \{F_\sigma[q \cdot B/4B] - F_\sigma[q \cdot (B-1)/4B]\}/B = 2 \cdot \{1 - F_\sigma[q \cdot (B-1)/4B]\}/B$
$-(B-2)$	$(0, B-2), (1, B-1)$	$\frac{2}{B} \cdot \left\{ \begin{matrix} F_\sigma[\frac{q}{4B}B]- \\ F_\sigma[\frac{q}{4B}(B-1)] \end{matrix} \right\} + \frac{2}{B} \cdot \left\{ \begin{matrix} F_\sigma[\frac{q}{4B}(B-1)]- \\ F_\sigma[\frac{q}{4B}(B-2)] \end{matrix} \right\} = \frac{2}{B} \cdot \{1 - F_\sigma[\frac{q}{4B}(B-2)]\}$
...	...	...
-1	$(0, 1), (1, 2),\ldots, (B-2, B-1)$	$\frac{2}{B} \{F_\sigma[\frac{q}{4B}B] - F_\sigma[\frac{q}{4B}]\} = \frac{2}{B}\{1 - F_\sigma(\frac{q}{4B})\}$
0	$(0, 0), (1, 1),\ldots, (B-1, B-1)$	$\frac{2}{B}\{F_\sigma[\frac{q}{4B}B] - F_\sigma[0]\} = \frac{2}{B}\{1 - \frac{1}{2}\} = \frac{1}{B}$
$B-1$	$(B-1, 0)$	$\frac{2}{B}\{F_\sigma(\frac{q}{4B}) - F_\sigma(0)\} = \frac{2}{B}\{F_\sigma(\frac{q}{4B}) - \frac{1}{2}\}$

Table 4. Distribution rate of λ

λ	$P_\lambda(\lambda)$
0	$1/B$
1	$P_\lambda(1) = \{1/2 + F_\sigma[q \cdot (B-1)/4B] - F_\sigma[q/4B]\}/B$
2	$P_\lambda(2) = \{1/2 + F_\sigma[q \cdot (B-2)/4B] - F_\sigma(q \cdot 2/4B)\}/B$
...	...
B–1	$P_\lambda(B-1) = \{1/2 + F_\sigma[q/4B] - F_\sigma[q \cdot (B-1)/4B]\}/B$

$$F_{cs}(x) = P(cs_i < x)$$

$$= P_\lambda(0) \cdot F_c(x) + P_\lambda(1)[F_c(x - \lfloor q/4B \rfloor) + F_c(x + \lfloor q/4B \rfloor)] + \ldots + P_\lambda(B-1)\begin{bmatrix} F_c(x - \lfloor q(B-1)/4B \rfloor) \\ + F_c(x + \lfloor q(B-1)/4B \rfloor) \end{bmatrix}$$

$$= \frac{1}{B} \cdot \frac{x}{q} + P_\lambda(1)(\frac{x + \lfloor q/4B \rfloor}{q} + \frac{x - \lfloor q/4B \rfloor}{q}) + \ldots + P_\lambda(B-1)(\frac{x + \lfloor q(B-1)/4B \rfloor}{q} + \frac{x - \lfloor q(B-1)/4B \rfloor}{q})$$

$$= \frac{x}{Bq} + \frac{2x}{q} \cdot \frac{1}{B} \cdot \frac{B-1}{2} = \frac{x}{q} = F_c(x)$$

$$(19)$$

In (19), it shows that the embedded ciphertext follows the uniform distribution in $\mathbb{Z}_q$ as the original ciphertext does. Next, we analysis the statistic features:

To get the histograms of data before and after embedding, n is given value 100, 200, 300 to test different groups of sample data. Information entropy plays an important role in proving the security of image encryptions that makes entropy become maximum. Average information entropy donated as H (H_{ideal} is the theoretical maximum entropy) of original data and embedded data are calculated. The results are shown in Fig. 5 (the different colors in histograms represent different sample data groups).

The experiment results demonstrate that the histograms hasn't produced obvious changes after embedding. And the average information entropy of embedded data is not less than the original data. Repeat the experiments with different embedding rates, and the conclusion remains the same.

In the probability theory, if $C \sim U(a, b)$, the ideal expectation of C should be $(b-a)/2$. To test the expectation of the embedded ciphertext, we apply the proposed scheme with different embedding rates. The parameters are: $n = 140, 180, 220, 260, 320$; $\log B = 0, 1, 2, 3, 4, 5, 6, 7$, where $\log B = 0$ represents the original data. Figure 6 shows the relationship between the expectations of test data (the asterisks) and the ideal expectations in $\mathbb{Z}_q$ (the horizontal line).

3.3 Capacity

In the previous reversible data hiding schemes, the capacity in [21] is about 0.0328 bpp, an 8-bit pixel can load 0.0328bit additional data; in [18], it has enhanced the capacity about 0.06 bpp by reversing the 6LSB; in [25], the capacity has increased to 0.1 bpp by introducing the LDPC coding technology. In the proposed scheme, the embedding process is based on the encryption process, so it is independence from the

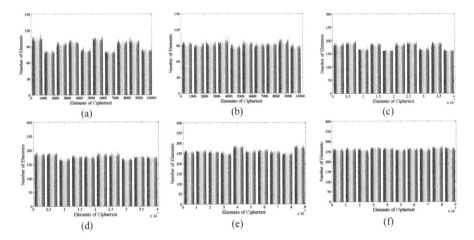

Fig. 5. Histograms and information entropy of encrypted data before embedding and those after embedding: (a) Histogram before embedding with $n = 100$, $H = 10.4885$, $H_{ideal} = 10.5304$; (b) Histogram after embedding with $n = 100$, $H = 10.5084$, $H_{ideal} = 10.5304$; (c) Histogram before embedding with $n = 200$, $H = 11.5586$, $H_{ideal} = 11.5826$; (d) Histogram after embedding with $n = 200$, $H = 11.5702$, $H_{ideal} = 11.5826$; (e) Histogram before embedding with $n = 300$, $H = 12.1686$, $H_{ideal} = 12.1951$; (f) Histogram after embedding with $n = 300$, $H = 12.1816$, $H_{ideal} = 12.1951$.

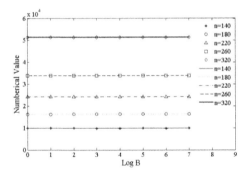

Fig. 6. Relationship between expectation of test data and ideal expectation

context of ciphertext and can apply to different kinds of encrypted media's data hiding. If we donate the band of the multi-band message as B, 1 bit plaintext data can maximally load $\log B$ bit additional data in encrypted domain theoretically. But the value of B can't be set infinitely big, the analysis is as follows:

The quantization step of the sub-region $\lfloor q/4B \rfloor$ will narrow with the increase of B, meanwhile, the effect of data hiding on ciphertext gets greater, which might reduce the hardness of the LWE algorithm, because the random-permuted secret message is usually generated by pseudo-random generator whose randomicity of output might be

Table 5. Embedding Rate (bit per bit of ciphertext)

n	100	140	180	220	260	300	320
Log $B = 1$	0. 0714	0. 0667	0.0667	0.0625	0.0588	0.0588	0.0588
Log $B = 7$	0.5000	0. 4667	0.4667	0.4375	0.4118	0.4118	0.4118

less satisfactory than LWE algorithm. To achieve a balance between security and embedding capacity, we should limit B to a security level. Embedding Rates are shown in Table 5.

According to the results of experiments on amounts of sample data, the proposed scheme can not only realize that 1bit original data can load 1 to 7 bit additional data in encrypted domain when $n > 100$, without degrading the quality of decryption.

4   Conclusion

This paper proposes a novel scheme of separable multiple bits reversible data hiding in encrypted domain. Multi-band data could be embedded by recoding the redundancy of cipher text, the processes of extraction and decryption are separable. Theoretical analysis concentrated on proposed scheme's correctness, security and embedding capacity. Experimental results have demonstrated that the proposed scheme can not only better guarantee the reversibility losslessly than the previous methods, but also realize that 1bit original data maximally load multiple-bit additional data in encrypted domain without reducing the security of encryption. In the future, it deserves further investigation to increase the efficiency and broaden the band of secret message by optimizing the method of recoding the redundancy.

References

1. Barni, M., Kalker, T., Katzenbeisser, S.: Inspiring new research in the field of signal processing in the encrypted domain. IEEE Signal Process. Mag. **30**(2), 16 (2013)
2. Moulin, P., Koetter, R.: Data hiding codes. Proc. IEEE **93**(12), 2083–2126 (2005)
3. Tian, J.: Reversible data embedding using a difference expansion. IEEE Trans. Circ. Syst. Video Technol. **13**(8), 890–896 (2003)
4. Dragoi, L., Coltuc, D.: Local-prediction-based difference expansion reversible watermarking. IEEE Trans. Image Process. **23**(4), 1779–1790 (2014)
5. Caciula, I., Coltuc, D.: Improved control for low bit-rate reversible watermarking. In: IEEE International Conference on Acoustics Speech and Signal Processing, Florence, Italy, pp. 7425–7429 (2014)
6. Zhang, W., Hu, X., Li, X., et al.: Recursive histogram modification: establishing equivalency between reversible data hiding and lossless data compression. IEEE Trans. Image Process. **22**(7), 2775–2785 (2013)
7. Jarali, A., Rao, J.: Unique LSB compression data hiding method. Int. J. Emerg. Sci. Eng. **2**(3), 17–21 (2013)
8. Zhao, B., Kou, W., Li, H., et al.: Effective watermarking scheme in the encrypted domain for buyer–seller watermarking protocol. Inf. Sci. **180**(23), 4672–4684 (2010)

9. Lian, S., Liu, Z., Ren, Z., et al.: Commutative encryption and watermarking in video compression. IEEE Trans. Circ. Syst. Video Technol. **17**(6), 774–778 (2007)

10. Cancellaro, M., Battisti, F., Carli, M., et al.: A commutative digital image watermarking and encryption method in the tree structured Haartransform domain. Signal Process. Image Commun. **26**(1), 1–12 (2011)

11. Xiao, Di., Chen, S.: Separable data hiding in encrypted image based on compressive sensing. Electron. Lett. **50**(8), 598–600 (2014)

12. Kuribayashi, M., Tanaka, H.: Fingerprinting protocol for images based on additive homomorphic property. IEEE Trans. Image Process. **14**(12), 2129–2139 (2005)

13. Memon, N., Wong, P.W.: A buyer-seller watermarking protocol. IEEE Trans. Image Process. **10**(4), 643–649 (2001)

14. Chen, J.H., Wang, C., Zhang, W.M., et al.: A secure image steganographic method in encrypted domain. J. Electron. Inf. Technol. **34**(7), 1721–1726 (2012). in Chinese

15. Zhang, X.: Reversible data hiding in encrypted image. IEEE Signal Process. Lett. **18**(4), 255–258 (2011)

16. Yu, J., Zhu, G., Li, X., Yang, J.: An improved algorithm for reversible data hiding in encrypted image. In: Shi, Y.Q., Kim, H.-J., Pérez-González, F. (eds.) IWDW 2012. LNCS, vol. 7809, pp. 384–394. Springer, Heidelberg (2013). doi:10.1007/978-3-642-40099-5_32

17. Li, M., Xiao, D., Peng, Z., et al.: A modified reversible data hiding in encrypted images using random diffusion and accurate prediction. ETRI J. **36**(2), 325–328 (2014)

18. Wu, X., Sun, W.: High-capacity reversible data hiding in encrypted images by prediction error. Signal Process. **104**(11), 387–400 (2014)

19. Qian, Z., Zhang, X., Wang, S.: Reversible data hiding in encrypted JPEG bitstream. IEEE Trans. Multimedia **16**(5), 1486–1491 (2014)

20. Liao, X., Shu, C.: Reversible data hiding in encrypted images based on absolute mean difference of multiple neighboring pixels. J. Vis. Commun. Image Representation **28**(4), 21–27 (2015)

21. Zhang, X.: Separable reversible data hiding in encrypted image. IEEE Trans. Inf. Forensics Secur. **7**(2), 826–832 (2012)

22. Regev, O.: On lattices, learning with errors, random linear codes and cryptography. J. ACM **56**(6), 34 (2009)

23. Regev, O.: The learning with errors problem (2010). http://www.cs.tau.ac.il/~odedr/papers/lwesurvey.pdf

24. Min-Qing, Z., Yan, K., Ting-Ting, S.: Reversible steganography in encrypted domain based on LWE. J. Electron. Inf. Technol. **38**(2), 354–360 (2016). in Chinese

25. Zhang, X., Qian, Z., Feng, G., Ren, Y.: Efficient reversible data hiding in encrypted image. J. Vis. Commun. Image Representation **25**(2), 322–328 (2014)

Steganography and Steganalysis

Distortion Function for Spatial Image Steganography Based on the Polarity of Embedding Change

Zichi Wang$^{(\boxtimes)}$, Jinpeng Lv, Qingde Wei, and Xinpeng Zhang

School of Communication and Information Engineering,
Shanghai University, Shanghai 200444, China
wangzichi@shu.edu.cn

Abstract. Most of the existing distortion functions for digital images steganography allot a same embedding cost for ± 1 embedding change, which should be different intuitively. This paper proposes a general method to distinguish the embedding cost for different polarity of embedding change for spatial images. The fluctuation after pixels are $+1$ or -1 modified respectively, and the texture of cover image are employed to adjust a given distortion function. After steganography with the adjusted distortion function, the fluctuation around stego pixels become more similar to the fluctuation around their neighbourhoods. This similarity performs less detectable artifacts. Experiment results show that the statistical undetectability of current popular steganographic methods is increased after incorporated the proposed method.

Keywords: Steganography · Spatial images · Distortion function · Polarity

1 Introduction

Steganography aims to secretly convey data through digital media without drawing suspicion by slightly modifying cover data [1–3]. Initially, the steganographic methods hammer at increase the embedding efficiency [4–6], that is to decrease the quantity of embedding changes on cover data for a given embedding payload. With the emergence of the syndrome trellis coding (STC) [7] which can minimize additive distortion between the cover and the stego image under a fixed payload with a user-defined distortion function, the security performance of steganography has been greatly improved and thus the direction of steganography is turn to properly design of the distortion function.

The distortion function allot a embedding cost for each cover element. Where the embedding cost quantifies the effect of modifying a cover element. And the distortion between cover and stego object is expressed as a sum of costs of modified elements. There are many excellent distortion functions for spatial image such as HUGO [8], WOW [9], S-UNIWARD [10, 11], HILL [12], MVGG [13]. Most of the these distortion functions allot a same embedding cost for ± 1 embedding change. But intuitively, the effect of $+1$ change and -1 change on a pixel in a natural image should not

© Springer International Publishing AG 2017
Y.Q. Shi et al. (Eds.): IWDW 2016, LNCS 10082, pp. 487–493, 2017.
DOI: 10.1007/978-3-319-53465-7_36

be equivalent. That means the polarity of embedding change can be brought in distortion function to increase the security of steganography.

This paper proposes a general method to distinguish the embedding cost for different polarity of embedding change for spatial images. The fluctuation after pixels are +1 or −1 modified respectively, and the texture of cover image are employed to adjust a given distortion function. By using the adjusted distortion function, the fluctuation around stego pixels become more similar to the fluctuation around their neighbourhoods. This similarity performs less detectable artifacts and increases the statistical undetectability of current popular steganographic methods.

2 Proposed Method

The sketch of the proposed method is given in Fig. 1. For a uncompressed image and a given distortion function. The image-texture is calculated using the given distortion function. Meanwhile, the local-fluctuation, which reflects the fluctuation after pixels are +1 or −1 modified respectively, is calculated using image pixels. Then the given distortion function is adjusted with the help of image-texture and local-fluctuation. After steganography with the adjusted distortion function, the fluctuation around stego pixels become more similar to the fluctuation around their neighbourhoods. Thereby less detectable artifacts are left. The details are as follows.

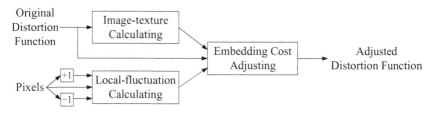

Fig. 1. Sketch of proposed method

For a 8-bit gray-scale cover image sized $M \times N$, the (i, j)th pixel is denoted as $p(i, j)$, where $p(i, j) \in \{0, 1, ..., 255\}$, and $i \in \{1, 2, ..., M\}, j \in \{1, 2, ..., N\}$. The cost of making an embedding change by +1 and −1 of $p(i, j)$ are denoted as $\rho_+(i, j)$ and $\rho_-(i, j)$ respectively. In most steganographic methods based on STC, $\rho_+(i, j) = \rho_-(i, j)$. We denote $\rho_+(i, j) = \rho_-(i, j) = \rho(i, j)$.

A image-texture value $b(i, j)$ is assigned for each (i, j) which is defined in Eq. (1). Where $\rho(u, v)$ is the given embedding cost for $p(u, v)$, and $b(i, j)$ is summational distortion of the $s \times s$ sized block contains neighbourhoods of $p(i, j)$ as shown in Fig. 2. Thus $u \in \{i-(s-1)/2, ..., i+(s-1)/2\}$ and $v \in \{j-(s-1)/2, ..., j+(s-1)/2\}$, s is odd and experimentally determined as 7.

$$
\begin{bmatrix}
p(i-\dfrac{s-1}{2},j-\dfrac{s-1}{2}) & \cdots & p(i-\dfrac{s-1}{2},j+\dfrac{s-1}{2}) \\
\vdots & \ddots & \vdots \\
p(i+\dfrac{s-1}{2},j-\dfrac{s-1}{2}) & \cdots & p(i+\dfrac{s-1}{2},j+\dfrac{s-1}{2})
\end{bmatrix}_{s\times s}
$$

Fig. 2. Neighbourhoods of $p(i, j)$

$$
b(i,j) = \sum\sum \rho(u,v) \tag{1}
$$

To the best of our knowledge, embedding cost is closely related to image-texture. A large embedding cost means smooth texture, and a small embedding cost means complex texture conversely. Image-texture $b(i, j)$ represents the texture of the neighbourhoods around $p(i, j)$. To make the fluctuation around stego pixels become more similar to the fluctuation around their neighbourhoods, the given embedding cost $\rho(i, j)$ is adjusted according to $b(i, j)$. In detail, for a large value of $b(i, j)$, which means smooth texture around $p(i, j)$, we aim to make the location (i, j) of stego image smoothly by adjust the given embedding cost. Otherwise, we aim to make the location (i, j) of stego image complexly for a small $b(i, j)$. The way to adjust the given embedding cost $\rho(i, j)$ is described in Eqs. (2) and (3).

$$
\rho_{+}(i,j) = \begin{cases} \rho(i,j)\cdot[1+w(i,j)], & f_{+}(i,j) > f_{-}(i,j) \\ \rho(i,j), & f_{+}(i,j) \le f_{-}(i,j) \end{cases} \tag{2}
$$

$$
\rho_{-}(i,j) = \begin{cases} \rho(i,j)\cdot[1+w(i,j)], & f_{+}(i,j) < f_{-}(i,j) \\ \rho(i,j), & f_{+}(i,j) \ge f_{-}(i,j) \end{cases} \tag{3}
$$

where $f_{+}(i, j)$ and $f_{-}(i, j)$ which are the local-fluctuation of the location (i, j) will be discussed later. And $w(i, j)$ is determined by $b(i, j)$ using Eq. (4) which is in proportion to $b(i, j)$. Thereinto β_{max} and β_{min} are the maximum and minimum value of all $b(i, j)$ respectively.

$$
w(i,j) = \alpha \cdot \left[\frac{b(i,j) - \beta_{min}}{\beta_{max} - \beta_{min}} - 0.5 \right] \tag{4}
$$

Equation (4) is employed to make the range of $b(i, j)$ symmetrically to zero, which restrained in $-\alpha/2$ to $\alpha/2$. The value of α is experimentally determined as 0.05. The polarity of $w(i, j)$ indicates a increasing or decreasing modification on $\rho(i, j)$. As the adjusting-strategy mentioned above, for a large value of $b(i, j)$, the $w(i, j)$ is positive with high probability. The modification is increasing at this case, and the embedding cost corresponding to larger local-fluctuation is increased. In this way, it is more likely to make the stego image smoothly. That is to choose the smoother embedding pattern.

And vice verse for a small value of $b(i, j)$. To further improve the performance [14], both $\rho_+(i, j)$ and $\rho_-(i, j)$ are set to infinity when $p(i, j) = 0$ or 255.

The local-fluctuation $f_+(i, j)$ and $f_-(i, j)$ are defined by the 1st and 2nd order polarity residuals of pixels. The 1st order polarity residuals in four directions are defined in Eqs. (5) and (6). And the 2nd order polarity residuals in four directions are defined in Eqs. (7) and (8).

$$r_\pm^{\rightarrow}(i,j) = p_\pm(i,j) - p(i,j+1), \; r_\pm^{\leftarrow}(i,j) = p_\pm(i,j) - p(i,j-1) \qquad (5)$$

$$r_\pm^{\downarrow}(i,j) = p_\pm(i,j) - p(i+1,j), \; r_\pm^{\uparrow}(i,j) = p_\pm(i,j) - p(i-1,j) \qquad (6)$$

$$r_\pm^{\Rightarrow}(i,j) = r_\pm^{\rightarrow}(i,j) - r^{\rightarrow}(i,j+1), \; r_\pm^{\Leftarrow}(i,j) = r_\pm^{\leftarrow}(i,j) - r^{\leftarrow}(i,j-1) \qquad (7)$$

$$r_\pm^{\Downarrow}(i,j) = r_\pm^{\downarrow}(i,j) - r^{\downarrow}(i+1,j), \; r_{\pm1}^{\Uparrow}(i,j) = r_{\pm1}^{\uparrow}(i,j) - r^{\uparrow}(i-1,j) \qquad (8)$$

where $p_\pm(i, j) = p(i, j) \pm 1$. $r^{\rightarrow}(i, j) = p(i, j) - p(i, j+1)$, $r^{\leftarrow}(i, j) = p(i, j) - p(i, j-1)$, $r^{\downarrow}(i, j) = p(i, j) - p(i+1, j)$, and $r^{\uparrow}(i, j) = p(i, j) - p(i-1, j)$.

Finally, the local-fluctuation $f_+(i, j)$ and $f_-(i, j)$ are defined in Eq. (9), where $\Theta \in \{\rightarrow, \downarrow, \leftarrow, \uparrow\}$, and $\Xi \in \{\Rightarrow, \Downarrow, \Leftarrow, \Uparrow\}$.

$$f_\pm(i,j) = \left| \sum r_\pm^{\Theta}(i,j) \right| + \sum \left| r_\pm^{\Theta}(i,j) \right| + \left| \sum r_\pm^{\Xi}(i,j) \right| + \sum \left| r_\pm^{\Xi}(i,j) \right| \qquad (9)$$

3   Experiment Results

All experiments are carried out on the BOSSbass ver. 1.01 [15], which contains 10000 uncompressed grayscale images sized 512×512. The payloads range from 0.05 to 0.5 bpp. The steganographic methods S-UNIWARD and WOW are employed to test the effectiveness of the proposed method. All the methods are worked via optimal embedding simulator [8].

In the phase of steganalysis, the feature sets SPAM-686D [16], CSR-1183D [17], SRMQ1-12753D [18], and SRM-34671D [18] are employed in our experiments. The ensemble classifier [19] is used to measure the property of feature sets. In detail, half of the cover and stego feature sets are used as the training set while the remaining half are used as testing set. The criterion to evaluate the performance of feature sets is the minimal total error P_E under equal priors achieved on the testing set [19]:

$$p_E = \min_{p_{FA}} \left(\frac{p_{FA} + p_{MD}}{2} \right) \qquad (10)$$

where P_{FA} is the false alarm rate and P_{MD} is the missed detection rate. The performance is evaluated using the average value of P_E over ten random tests.

When the proposed method is incorporated in S-UNIWARD and WOW, the updated methods S-UNIWARD-P and WOW-P are obtained respectively. Figure 3 shows the comparison of S-UNIWARD with S-UNIWARD-P and WOW with

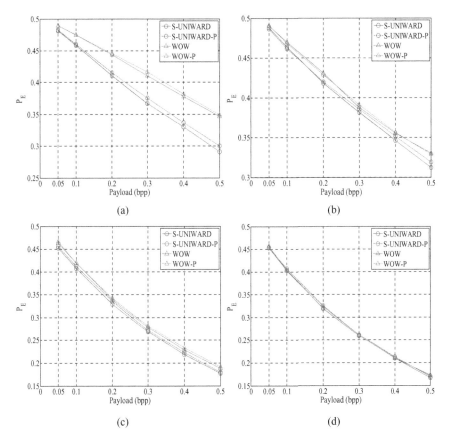

Fig. 3. Testing error for S-UNIWARD, and WOW on BOSSbass 1.01 with ensemble classifier and (a) SPAM-686D, (b) CSR-1183D, (c) SRMQ1-12753D, (d) SRM-34671D

WOW-P under several feature sets. It can be observed that the security performance is improved for most cases by employing the proposed method. This observation attests that the approach to adjust distortion function in this paper is effective.

Numerically, for S-UNIWARD, the P_E can be improved by 0.89% when payload is 0.5 bpp with SPAM-686D, 0.68% when payload is 0.5 bpp with CSR-1183D, and 0.61% when payload is 0.2 bpp with SRMQ1-12753D. For WOW, the improvement is 0.60% when payload is 0.3 bpp with SPAM-686D, 0.34% when payload is 0.3 bpp with CSR-1183D, and 0.46% when payload is 0.4 bpp with SRMQ1-12753D. For SRM-34671D, regrettably, the performance is hardly improved.

The ± 1 embedding costs are also different in the steganographic methods for spatial images based on non-additive distortion such as [3, 20]. But these methods have essential distinction with the proposed method. These methods are embedding in batches and not aim to distinguish the ± 1 embedding costs. Hence these methods can be executed with the adjusted distortion function using the proposed method. That means the two kind methods can be implement independently.

4 Conclusion

This paper proposes a general method to distinguish the embedding cost for different polarity of embedding change. The texture of cover image and the fluctuation of modified image are employed to adjust the given distortion function. Experiment results show that the statistical undetectability of current popular steganographic methods is increased after incorporated the proposed method. For further study, steganographic methods are expected to considered more potential tools such as the knowledge of steganalysis features.

Acknowledgment. This work was supported by the Natural Science Foundation of China (61525203, 61472235, and 61502009), the Program of Shanghai Dawn Scholar (14SG36) and Shanghai Academic Research Leader (16XD1401200).

References

1. Ker, A., et al.: Moving steganography and steganalysis from the laboratory into the real world. In: Proceedings of the First ACM Workshop on Information Hiding and Multimedia Security, New York, NY, USA, pp. 45–58, June 2013
2. Li, B., Tan, S., Wang, M., Huang, J.: Investigation on cost assignment in spatial image steganography. IEEE Trans. Inf. Forensics Secur. **9**(2), 1264–1277 (2014)
3. Li, B., Wang, M., Li, X., Tan, S., Huang, J.: A strategy of clustering modification directions in spatial image steganography. IEEE Trans. Inf. Forensics Secur. **10**(9), 1905–1917 (2015)
4. Frdrich, J., Soukal, D.: Matrix embedding for large payloads. In: Proceedings of the International Society for Optics and Photonics, San Jose, CA, pp. 60721W–60721W-12, February 2006
5. Zhang, X., Wang, S.: Efficient steganographic embedding by exploiting modification direction. IEEE Commun. Lett. **10**(11), 781–783 (2006)
6. Zhang, W., Zhang, X., Wang, S.: Maximizing steganographic embedding efficiency by combining hamming codes and wet paper codes. In: Solanki, K., Sullivan, K., Madhow, U. (eds.) IH 2008. LNCS, vol. 5284, pp. 60–71. Springer, Heidelberg (2008). doi:10.1007/978-3-540-88961-8_5
7. Filler, T., Judas, J., Fridrich, J.: Minimizing additive distortion in steganography using syndrome-trellis codes. IEEE Trans. Inf. Forensics Secur. **6**(3), 920–935 (2011)
8. Pevný, T., Filler, T., Bas, P.: Using high-dimensional image models to perform highly undetectable steganography. In: Böhme, R., Fong, P.W.L., Safavi-Naini, R. (eds.) IH 2010. LNCS, vol. 6387, pp. 161–177. Springer, Heidelberg (2010). doi:10.1007/978-3-642-16435-4_13
9. Holub, V., Fridrich, J.: Designing steganographic distortion using directional filters. In: Proceedings of the IEEE International Workshop on Information Forensics and Security, Binghamton, NY, USA, pp. 234–239, December 2012
10. Holub, V., Fridrich, J.: Digital image steganography using universal distortion. In: Proceedings of the First ACM Workshop on Information Hiding and Multimedia Security, New York, NY, USA, pp. 59–68, June 2013
11. Holub, V., Fridrich, J., Denemark, T.: Universal distortion function for steganography in an arbitrary domain. EURASIP J. Inf. Secur. **2014**(1), 1–13 (2014)

12. Li, B., Wang, M., Huang, J., Li, X.: A new cost function for spatial image steganography. In: Proceedings of the IEEE International Conference on Image Processing, Paris, France, pp. 4206–4210, October 2014

13. Sedighi, V., Fridrich, J., Cogranne, R.: Content-adaptive pentary steganography using the multivariate generalized gaussian cover model. In: Proceedings of the International Society for Optics and Photonics, San Francisco, California, USA, pp. 94090H–94090H-13, March 2015

14. Sedighi, V., Fridrich, J.: Effect of saturated pixels on security of steganographic schemes for digital images. In: Proceedings of the IEEE International Conference on Image Processing, Phoenix, Arizona, USA, pp. 25–28, September 2016

15. Bas, P., Filler, T., Pevný, T.: "Break our steganographic system": the ins and outs of organizing BOSS. In: Filler, T., Pevný, T., Craver, S., Ker, A. (eds.) IH 2011. LNCS, vol. 6958, pp. 59–70. Springer, Heidelberg (2011). doi:10.1007/978-3-642-24178-9_5

16. Pevny, T., Bas, P., Fridrich, J.: Steganalysis by subtractive pixel adjacency matrix. IEEE Trans. Inf. Forensics Secur. 5(2), 215–224 (2010)

17. Denemark, T., Fridrich, J., Holub, V.: Further study on the security of S-UNIWARD. In: Proceedings of the SPIE, Electronic Imaging, Media Watermarking, Security, and Forensics, San Francisco, CA, pp. 902805–902805-13, February 2014

18. Fridrich, J., Kodovsky, J.: Rich models for steganalysis of digital images. IEEE Trans. Inf. Forensics Secur. 7(3), 868–882 (2012)

19. Kodovsky, J., Fridrich, J., Holub, V.: Ensemble classifiers for steganalysis of digital media. IEEE Trans. Inf. Forensics Secur. 7(2), 432–444 (2012)

20. Denemark, T., Fridrich, J.: Improving steganographic security by synchronizing the selection channel. In: Proceedings of the 3rd ACM Workshop on Information Hiding and Multimedia Security, New York, NY, USA, pp. 5–14, June 2015

Embedding Strategy for Batch Adaptive Steganography

Zengzhen Zhao[1,2(✉)], Qingxiao Guan[1,2], Xianfeng Zhao[1,2], Haibo Yu[1,2], and Changjun Liu[1,2]

[1] State Key Laboratory of Information Security,
Institute of Information Engineering, Chinese Academy of Sciences,
No. 89A, Minzhuang Road, Beijing 100093, China
{zhaozengzhen,guanqingxiao,zhaoxianfeng,yuhaibo,liuchangjun}@iie.ac.cn
[2] University of Chinese Academy of Sciences, Beijing, China

Abstract. In this paper, we present a new embedding strategy for batch adaptive steganography. This strategy can make up for the problem when applying batch steganography to adaptive steganography and determine the sub-batch of cover images to carry the total message. Firstly, we define a secure factor α to evaluate the embedding security. Then, we utilize the secure factor α to calculate the corresponding payloads for each image based on distortion-limited sender (maximizing the payload while introducing a fixed total distortion) and fit the relation curve for the secure factor and the corresponding payload. When embedding, the images with large size and more upward convex relation curve are employed to carry the total message. Experimental results show that fitting curves vary according to images and employing images with more upward convex relation curve to carry the total message can improve the secure performance effectively.

Keywords: Steganography · Security · Distortion function

1 Introduction

Steganography aims to deliver secret messages through digital media objects but arouses no suspicion to others. Although digital media objects after embedding is imperceptible visually, the statistical detection as the countermeasure of steganography can reveal the presence well. Especially the steganalysis based on the high-dimensional feature spaces [1–4], is the natural enemy of steganography.

There are two mainstream approaches to minimize the statistical detectability in empirical covers: steganography preserving a chosen cover model and steganography minimizing a well-defined distortion function [5–8]. Although the former strategy has a long history, it can be easily detected by going beyond the chosen model. Nowadays the prevailing strategy is the latter, which abandons modeling the cover source and employs a coding scheme [9–11] to embed messages while minimizing a distortion function. Although the relationship between

© Springer International Publishing AG 2017
Y.Q. Shi et al. (Eds.): IWDW 2016, LNCS 10082, pp. 494–505, 2017.
DOI: 10.1007/978-3-319-53465-7_37

distortion and steganographic security is not so clear, embedding while minimizing a well distortion function truly improve the steganographic security according to the performance of distortion function [7,8]. Actually the additive distortion introduced by embedding can be regarded as the sum of costs of all changed factors in cover objects and the costs value assigned to cover objects evaluate the disturbance of modification. So employing the distortion to evaluate the steganographic security is reasonable.

In [12] A.D. Ker *et al.* has proposed five embedding strategies for the batch steganography which wants to spread a message of total length M among cover $(I_1, \ldots, I_n)$ with capacities $(c_1, \ldots, c_2)$ using the same steganographic embedding algorithm for individual covers. Sorted by the security, they are the max-greedy strategy, the max-random strategy, the linear strategy, the even strategy and the sqroot strategy. The experimental result demonstrates that the max-greedy strategy and the max-random strategy have well performance and the former behaves better than the latter. The max-greedy strategy wants to embed the message into the fewest possible number of covers. Therefore during embedding, the covers with highest capacity are chosen and embedded a portion of the message equalling to the capacity of the cover. The max-random strategy is the same as max-greedy, but the covers used for embedding are chosen in a random order. Ker's method to estimate the capacities is that they set a initial value of capacity, and try to embed a randomly generated message of the length to image. If the embedding fails, value of capacity is decreased and the procedure is repeated until finding the successful value of capacity. For adaptive steganography, This method is not available since the capacity of image is determined by the coding scheme. For example, the single-layered STCs leads to the 0.5 bpp (bits per pixel) capacity for the spatial cover image. That means if all covers have the same size, they have the same capacities and max-greedy is equal to max-random, which is commoner in real life. In [8], B. Li *et al.* has pointed that for image steganography, embedding modifications made in texture areas should be more secure than in smooth areas and for this reason they have proposed the more secure cost function HILL (High Low Low). Therefore the image with more texture areas is more secure than the image with more smooth areas when embedding the same message. Consequently the random order is not the best. As an alternative, choosing the images with more texture areas is a better choice than the random order. But the problem is how to evaluate the complexity of image. We associate it with the embedding distortion and steganographic security.

In this paper, we adopt a new embedding strategy to spread the message among covers. In our work we define a extreme: the most insecure circumstance which is embedded with an upper-bounding length message. Then we define a secure factor $\alpha, 0 \leq \alpha \leq 1$, which will be multiplied by the upper-bounding distortion of the most insecure circumstance to get the α-secure distortion. The corresponding α-secure payload can be calculated by α-secure distortion based on distortion-limited sender. With these, we fit the relation curve of the secure factor α and the corresponding α-secure payload for each image. The images with large size and more upward convex relation curve are employed to carry the total message. To achieve a good performance, the cost function used to derive the payload and the cost function used to embed message are independent. Especially the cost function used to derive the payload should be universal and available for all most the adaptive steganography, which will be determined by experiment. Experimental results demonstrate that batch adaptive steganography based on our embedding strategy can improve the security efficiently, and further demonstrate employing the method derived from distortion to evaluate the complexity of image is available.

The rest of the paper is organized as follows. In Sect. 2, we describe the preparation. In Sect. 3, our proposed embedding strategy is introduced and the detailed embedding procedure is also presented. In Sect. 4, the security of our work is tested using steganalysis based high-dimensional feature spaces. Conclusion is listed in Sect. 5.

2   Preparation

2.1   Notation

Without loss of generality, let $\mathbf{X} = (x_{i,j}) \in \{\mathcal{L}\}^{n_1 \times n_2}$ represent $n_1 \times n_2$ pixels cover image and $\mathbf{Y} = (y_{i,j}) \in \{\mathcal{L}\}^{n_1 \times n_2}$ represent the stego image after embedding operation on cover $\mathbf{X}$. $\mathcal{L}$ is the pixel dynamic range of image. For example, $\mathcal{L} = \{0, \dots, 255\}$ for 8-bit grayscale image and $\mathcal{L} = \{-1024, \dots, 1023\}$ for JPEG image. So $x_{i,j}$ is the pixel or DCT coefficient in (i, j) location.

This embedding strategy can also be applied to other kind of cover if distortion function can be used to it, but for concreteness we employ images to demonstrate the secure performance of our embedding strategy.

2.2   Distortion Function

The impact of image embedding modifications is evaluated by the distortion function D which can be regarded as the sum of costs of all changed pixels or DCT coefficients

$$D(\mathbf{X}, \mathbf{Y}) = \sum_{(i,j)} \rho_{i,j}(x_{i,j} \neq y_{i,j}). \tag{1}$$

where $\rho_{i,j} \in \{0, \dots, \infty\}$ expresses the cost of replacing the cover $x_{i,j}$ with $y_{i,j}$. Actually the prevailing distortion functions are designed based on high-pass filter and low-pass filter. The high-pass filter is used to locate the less predictable parts in an image and the low-pass filter is used to make the low cost values more clustered. For example, HILL [8] employs the 3×3 KB (Ker-Bohme) high-pass filter, the 3×3 low-pass filter and the 15×15 low-pass filter. UNIWARD (Universal Wavelet Relative Distortion) [7] employs a high-pass decomposition wavelet filter and a low-pass decomposition wavelet filter. WOW (Wavelet Obtained Weights) [6] uses the same filters with UNIWARD but has some differences during the filtering process. After further analysis, we can get that KB filter is one of the compositions for the SRM [1] features set and has a outstanding performance for steganalysis. So HILL has such good performance with KB filter as the high-pass filter is reasonable. HUGO (Highly Undetectable steGO) [5] also adopts above method but the high-pass filter is chosen as the SPAM filter in SRM.

To understand the construction of distortion function in detail, we give a brief overview of the distortion functions, i.e., HILL and UNIWARD, which are employed to test our embedding strategy.

For spatial image steganography, HILL algorithm has a good performance of security. Based on the above analysis, the construction of HILL is quite straight-forward and effective. For concreteness, it can be divided into three steps.

a. Calculate the high-pass filter residuals by first using the KB high-pass filter $\mathbf{H}_1$ to the cover image,

$$\mathbf{T}^1 = \mathbf{X} \otimes \mathbf{H}_1. \tag{2}$$

b. Apply the 3×3 low-pass filter $\mathbf{L}_1$ to the absolute value of above residuals to get the new designed embedding suitability,

$$\mathbf{d}^1 = |\mathbf{T}^1| \otimes \mathbf{L}_1. \tag{3}$$

c. Calculate the cost value by using the 15×15 low-pass filter $\mathbf{L}_2$ to the reciprocals of the embedding suitability,

$$\rho = \frac{1}{\mathbf{d}^1} \otimes \mathbf{L}_2. \tag{4}$$

Comparing to HILL algorithm, UNIWARD algorithm only employs two filters which are the high-pass decomposition wavelet filter $\mathbf{g}$ and the low-pass decomposition wavelet filter $\mathbf{h}$. Actually UNIWARD algorithm doesn't apply above filters to the filtering operation directly but use them to generate a bank of directional filters, and then apply the bank of directional filters to obtain the filter residuals. So to describe UNIWARD algorithm in detail, the construction of it can be divided into three steps.

a. Using the one-dimensional low-pass and high-pass wavelet decomposition filters to build filter kernels $\mathbf{B} = \{\mathbf{K}^{(1)}, \mathbf{K}^{(2)}, \mathbf{K}^{(3)}\}$,

$$\mathbf{K}^{(1)} = \mathbf{h} \cdot \mathbf{g}^T, \mathbf{K}^{(2)} = \mathbf{g} \cdot \mathbf{h}^T, \mathbf{K}^{(3)} = \mathbf{g} \cdot \mathbf{g}^T. \tag{5}$$

b. Given a pair of cover and stego images $\mathbf{X}$ and $\mathbf{Y}$, get the corresponding uvth wavelet coefficient $W_{uv}^{(k)}(\mathbf{X})$ and $W_{uv}^{(k)}(\mathbf{Y})$, $k = 1, 2, 3$, $u \in \{1, \ldots, n_1\}$, $v \in \{1, \ldots, n_2\}$ in the kth subband of the first decomposition level,

$$W^{(k)}(\mathbf{X}) = \mathbf{K}^{(k)} \otimes \mathbf{X}, W^{(k)}(\mathbf{Y}) = \mathbf{K}^{(k)} \otimes \mathbf{Y}. \tag{6}$$

c. The UNIWARD distortion function is the sum of relative changes of all wavelet coefficients with respect to the cover image,

$$D(\mathbf{X}, \mathbf{Y}) = \sum_{k=1}^{3} \sum_{u=1}^{n_1} \sum_{v=1}^{n_2} \frac{|W_{uv}^{(k)}(\mathbf{X}) - W_{uv}^{(k)}(\mathbf{Y})|}{\sigma + |W_{uv}^{k}(\mathbf{X})|}. \tag{7}$$

where $\sigma > 0$ is a constant to avoid the denominator equalling to zero.

2.3   Binary Embedding Operation

When we embed the message $\mathbf{m}$ with costs ρ to the cover image $\mathbf{X}$ using binary STCs which is **PLS** (Payload-limited sender), the relationship between the message length $|\mathbf{m}|$ and the costs ρ has been built. The intermediate is the flipping λ. When we get the costs ρ, we can obtain the flipping probability via

$$\beta_{i,j} = \frac{e^{-\lambda \rho_{i,j}}}{1 + e^{-\lambda \rho_{i,j}}}. \tag{8}$$

In theory, with the flipping probability β the embedding message length $|\mathbf{m}|$ is represented as

$$|\mathbf{m}| = \sum_{i,j} H(\beta_{i,j}), \tag{9}$$

where $H(\beta_{i,j})$ is the entropy function of the change probability $\beta_{i,j}$,

$$H(\beta_{i,j}) = -\beta_{i,j} \log_2(\beta_{i,j}) - (1 - \beta_{i,j}) \log_2(1 - \beta_{i,j}). \tag{10}$$

After substituting the variables in (9) with (8) and (10), the embedding message length is further expressed as

$$
\begin{aligned}
|\mathbf{m}| = \sum_{i,j} & -\frac{e^{-\lambda \rho_{i,j}}}{1 + e^{-\lambda \rho_{i,j}}} \log_2 \left(\frac{e^{-\lambda \rho_{i,j}}}{1 + e^{-\lambda \rho_{i,j}}} \right) \\
& - \sum_{i,j} (1 - \frac{e^{-\lambda \rho_{i,j}}}{1 + e^{-\lambda \rho_{i,j}}}) \log_2 (1 - \frac{e^{-\lambda \rho_{i,j}}}{1 + e^{-\lambda \rho_{i,j}}}),
\end{aligned}
\tag{11}
$$

yet the unknown variable in (11) is the flipping lambda λ which can be figured out by a simple binary search because $|\mathbf{m}|$ is monotone with regard to λ.

3   Proposed Work

3.1   Secure Factor α Definition

It is obvious that when we embed a large amount of message to image, the steganographic security can't be assured universally, and using the distortion to evaluate the steganographic security is reasonable. So we assume the most insecure situation occurs to the steganography with a upper-bounding payload p_{max} and the corresponding message $\mathbf{m}_{max}$. With the embedding message $\mathbf{m}_{max}$ and costs ρ which is calculated by the payload-derived distortion function we can figure out the upper-bounding flipping lambda λ_{max} by solving (11). What's more, the flipping probability can be got after substituting λ_{max} and cost ρ to the variables in (8),

$$\beta_{i,j}^{max} = \frac{e^{-\lambda_{max} \rho_{i,j}}}{1 + e^{-\lambda_{max} \rho_{i,j}}}. \tag{12}$$

We define the change of a pixel as a random variable $c_{i,j}$, and it conforms to binary distribution:

$$c_{i,j} \sim \begin{cases} 1, & P(c_{i,j}) = \beta_{i,j}^{max}; \\ 0, & P(c_{i,j}) = 1 - \beta_{i,j}^{max}. \end{cases} \tag{13}$$

So when embedding the message m_{max} to cover, the theoretical upper-bounding distortion D_{max} can be obtained via

$$E(D_{max}) = \sum_{i,j} E(c_{i,j}) \cdot \rho_{i,j} = \sum_{i,j} \frac{e^{-\lambda_{max}\rho_{i,j}}}{1 + e^{-\lambda_{max}\rho_{i,j}}} \cdot \rho_{i,j}. \tag{14}$$

Let $\alpha, 0 \leq \alpha \leq 1$ represents the secure factor which can be multiplied by the upper-bounding distortion D_{max} to evaluate the steganographic security. The distortion with the α-secure performance is D_α, $D_\alpha = \alpha \times D_{max}$. Obviously embedding with the lower α value has the better security. However during the embedding, the input should be the message (payload) but not the distortion. It's easy to associate with **DLS** (Distortion-Limited Sender) to solve this problem. In [10], Filler *et al.* have pointed out the duality of **DLS** and **PLS**. And we give the practical realization of the accurate calculation combining with our work in next section.

3.2 Accurate Calculation for DLS

– **Distortion-limited sender (DLS):** maximize the average payload while introducing a fixed average distortion.

We know that the intermediate between costs and embedding message is the flipping lambda. If we want to calculate the embedding message using distortion, we should get the corresponding flipping lambda firstly. As the cost ρ is known, we can represent the flipping probability via

$$\beta_{i,j}^\alpha = \frac{e^{-\lambda_\alpha \rho_{i,j}}}{1 + e^{-\lambda_\alpha \rho_{i,j}}}. \tag{15}$$

Then the α-secure distortion D_α is described the same as (14) by flipping probability via

$$E(D_\alpha) = \sum_{i,j} \frac{e^{-\lambda_\alpha \rho_{i,j}}}{1 + e^{-\lambda_\alpha \rho_{i,j}}} \cdot \rho_{i,j}, \tag{16}$$

where the only unknown parameter is the flipping lambda λ_α which can be solved by a simple binary search since the α-secure distortion D_α is monotone with regard to λ_α. The embedding message length $|\mathbf{m}_\alpha|$ can be obtained by substituting the λ_α and costs ρ to (11),

$$|\mathbf{m}_\alpha| = \sum_{i,j} -\frac{e^{-\lambda_\alpha \rho_{i,j}}}{1 + e^{-\lambda_\alpha \rho_{i,j}}} \log_2 \left(\frac{e^{-\lambda_\alpha \rho_{i,j}}}{1 + e^{-\lambda_\alpha \rho_{i,j}}} \right)$$
$$- \sum_{i,j} (1 - \frac{e^{-\lambda_\alpha \rho_{i,j}}}{1 + e^{-\lambda_\alpha \rho_{i,j}}}) \log_2 (1 - \frac{e^{-\lambda_\alpha \rho_{i,j}}}{1 + e^{-\lambda_\alpha \rho_{i,j}}}). \tag{17}$$

Finally, we can get the embedding rate p_α by the embedding message $|\mathbf{m}_\alpha|$ and the cover image $\mathbf{X}$ via $p_\alpha = \frac{|\mathbf{m}_\alpha|}{|\mathbf{X}|}$.

3.3   Curve Fitting and Convexity

For a batch of images, our intention is to find a sub-batch of images to carry the total message. Meanwhile, the sub-batch of images should have higher complexity to improve the security. The problem is how to evaluate the complexity. In this section, we describe the solution, curve fitting and convexity.

For each image with the given secure factors $\mathbf{A} = \{\alpha_i | 0 < i < 1\}$, the corresponding payloads $\mathbf{p}_\alpha = \{p_{\alpha_i} | 0 < i < 1\}$ can be obtained based on the method of above two sections. Therefore we can employ the curve fitting to build the relationship between the payloads and the secure factors. Since the relationship is not complicated, the cubic polynomial fitting can meet the requirements sufficiently. The concrete format is described as

$$p(\alpha) = \omega(3) \times \alpha^3 + \omega(2) \times \alpha^2 + \omega(1) \times \alpha^1 + \omega(0) \times \alpha^0, \qquad (18)$$

where ω is the coefficient of fitting function. Since images with more upward convex relation curve are more tolerant to the large payload when the secure factor is given, we select this kind of images as the sub-batch to carry the total message. Theoretically the convexity of relation curve can be measured by the second derivative of payload on secure factor,

$$p'' = \frac{d^2 p(\alpha)}{d\alpha^2} = 6 \times \omega(3) \times \alpha + 2 \times \omega(2). \qquad (19)$$

Combined with the fitting result that the relation curve is upward convex, $\frac{d^2 p(\alpha)}{d\alpha^2} < 0, \forall \alpha \in \{0, \ldots, 1\}$. So when given α, the smaller the value of the second derivative is, the more upward convex the relation curve is. For a batch of images with number N, we can get the fitting curves $\mathbf{P}(\alpha) = \{p_i(\alpha) | 1 \leq i \leq N\}$. Therefore when fixed the value of secure factor as α^*, we can sort the images in ascending order according to the values of second derivative $\{p_1''(\alpha^*), \ldots, p_N''(\alpha^*)\}$ and employ the former sorting images as the sub-batch.

3.4   Embedding Procedure

In this section, to better understand the implementation of our embedding strategy, we describe it using Algorithm 1. The inputs are the batch of cover images $\mathbf{X}^b$, distortion function FUNC1 and FUNC2, upper-bounding payload p_{max}, embedding message $\mathbf{m}$ and the embedding code STCs (ternary STCs [10] or NDSTCs [11]). While the outputs are the batch of stego images $\mathbf{Y}^b$. In Algorithm 1, we distinguish the payload-derived distortion function FUNC1 from the embedded distortion function FUNC2. This is because we find the distortion function with a narrow range of costs is preferable to be the payload-derived distortion function according to the experimental results. The optimum payload-derived distortion function can be got according to experiment.

Algorithm 1. Embedding procedure for batch adaptive steganography. Input the batch of cover images $\mathbf{X}^b$, distortion function FUNC1 and FUNC2, upper-bounding payload p_{max}, embedding message $\mathbf{m}$, and The embedding code STCs.

1. Set secure factors $\mathbf{A} = [0.1, 0.2, \ldots, 1]$
2. for $i = 1$ to Number of $\mathbf{X}^b$
3.   Calculate cost $\rho = \text{FUNC1}(\mathbf{X}^b(i))$
4.   Get the corresponding upper-bounding message length $|\mathbf{m}_{max}|$ according to cover $\mathbf{X}^b(i)$ and p_{max}
5.   Get the upper-bounding flipping lambda λ_{max} by solving the formula (11) with inputs ρ and $|\mathbf{m}_{max}|$
6.   Calculate the upper-bounding distortion D_{max} by solving the formula (14) with inputs ρ and λ_{max}
7.   for $j = 1$ to Number of $\mathbf{A}$
8.   Set $\alpha = \mathbf{A}(j)$, then get the α-secure distortion $D_\alpha = \alpha \times D_{max}$
9.   Get the secure flipping lambda λ_α by solving formula (16) with inputs D_α and ρ
10.   Calculate the secure embedding message length $|\mathbf{m}_\alpha|$ based on the formula (11) with inputs ρ and λ_α, then convert to secure payload p_α
11.   Set $\mathbf{P}(j)(i) = p_\alpha$
12.   end for j
13. end for i
14. for $i = 1$ to Number of $\mathbf{X}^b$
15.   Fit curve for $\mathbf{A}$ and $\mathbf{P}(:)(i)$. Store the fitting curve to $\mathbf{R}(i)$
16.   Given a secure factor, calculate the second derivative of $\mathbf{R}(i)$ and store it to $\mathbf{SD}(i)$
17. end for i
18. Sort the cover images according to the size of image in descending order firstly
19. For the images with the same size, sort them by $\mathbf{SD}$ in ascending order and get the sorting cover images $\mathbf{X}^c$
20. Determine the proper numbers N of images in the former part to carry the embedding message $\mathbf{m}$
21. for $i = 1$ to N
22.   Calculate the cost $\rho^{'} = \text{FUNC2}(\mathbf{X}^c(i))$ and cover size NUM
23.   Embed $p_{max} \times NUM$ bits message into $\mathbf{X}^c(i)$ with costs $\rho^{'}$ using STCs, then store to the stego $\mathbf{Y}^b(i)$
24. end for i

4   Experiment

4.1   Experimental Setup

Since that using images with large size to carry message is more secure is a common view, we just need to test the images with the same size. Therefore in this paper, we utilize the BOSSbase database ver.1.01 [14] consisting

of 10,000 512 × 512 8-bit grayscale images as the testing image set. To assure
the testing adequacy, the testing payload-derived distortion functions and the
testing embedding distortion functions all consist of S-UNIWARD and HILL.
The ternary multilayered version of STCs and NDSTCs are employed to combine with distortion function. Since we just want to demonstrate that using this
embedding strategy to determine the sub-batch for batch adaptive steganography is more secure and practical than max-random strategy (same to max-greedy
strategy) when all images are in the same size meanwhile avoid the embedding
failure when the payload is quite large, when the images need to be embedded
the embedding payloads are selected as 0.2 bpp and 0.4 bpp. The upper-bounding
payload is selected as 0.6 bpp.

To test the embedding security efficiently, we attack the cover and stego images
samples by state-of-the-art feature-based steganalyzers, which consists of the Spatial Rich Model (SRM) [1] and the maxSRMd2 [2]. Both SRM and maxSRMd2 are
34,671D features set. The ensemble classifier described in [13] is employed in our
experiments. For both cover and stego images, we randomly select 5000 images as
the training set and the remaining 5000 images as the testing set. The security of
steganography is measured by the total detection error of steganalysis test. And
detection error is the average error rate for two classes:

$$P_E = \min_{P_{FA}} \frac{1}{2}(P_{FA} + P_{MD}), \quad (20)$$

where P_{FA}, P_{MD} are the probabilities of false alarms and missed detection,
respectively. Actually, we employ the mean value of ten times' test $\bar{P}_E$ to evaluate
the security of steganography.

4.2   Proper Payload-Derived Distortion Function

We employ S-UNIWARD and HILL for both payload-derived distortion functions and embedding distortion functions to execute the payload-derived distortion function testing experiment. The payload is selected as 0.4 bpp, coding
scheme is selected as ternary STCs and the feature set is maxSRMd2. We fix
the number of sub-batch for embedding as 5000. Table 1 shows the experimental
result that selecting S-UNIWARD as the payload-derived distortion function is
more universal and effective than HILL. Therefore S-UNWIARD is adopted in
subsequent experiments.

Table 1. Experiment for determining the proper payload-derived distortion function

Experiment for determining the proper payload-derived distortion function		
Embedding	Payload-derived	
	S-UNIWARD	HILL
S-UNIWARD	0.3786 ± 0.0047	0.3790 ± 0.0022
HILL	0.4052 ± 0.0022	0.3767 ± 0.0030

4.3   Distinction of Fitting Curves

Before showing the experimental result for security, we draw figure showing the convexity of fitting curves for 8 images belonged to BOSSbase database v1.01. Figure 1 shows the result that different images have different fitting curves and using the convexity of fitting curves to distinguish the images is available and meaningful.

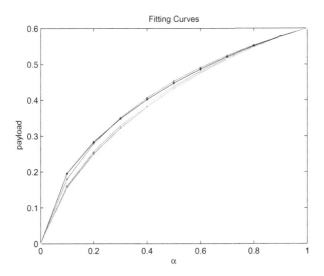

Fig. 1. Fitting curves of 8 images belonged to BOSSbase database v1.01

4.4   Secure Performance

In this section, we compare our embedding strategy with the max-random strategy which randomly selects the sub-batch from cover images. Here we name our strategy as ESBAS (Embedding Strategy for Batch Adaptive Steganography) and the max-random strategy as max-random. The number of sub-batch for both ESBAS and max-random is 5000. Table 2 shows the comparing result that ESBAS has more secure performance than max-random for both S-UNIWARD and HILL distortion functions combined with ternary STCs and NDSTCs when using maxSRMd2 and SRM to detect the security. The average improvement is higher than 3% and for the best performance, the detection error of ESBAS is higher by approximately 4.32% than max-random for embedding rate 0.4 bpp with the feature maxSRMd2, coding scheme NDSTCs and the HILL distortion function. The experimental result means using the method derived from embedding distortion to evaluate the complexity of image and then determining the sub-batch for batch adaptive steganography is feasible.

Table 2. Detection error rate comparison with max-random and ESBAS strategy

maxSRMd2				
Distortion function	Coding scheme	Payload	Detection error	
			max-random	ESBAS
S-UNIWARD	NDSTCs	0.2	0.4112 ± 0.0015	$\mathbf{0.4531 \pm 0.0030}$
		0.4	0.3555 ± 0.0024	$\mathbf{0.3885 \pm 0.0039}$
	Ternary STCs	0.2	0.4074 ± 0.0063	$\mathbf{0.4501 \pm 0.0034}$
		0.4	0.3479 ± 0.0024	$\mathbf{0.3786 \pm 0.0047}$
HILL	NDSTCs	0.2	0.4329 ± 0.0020	$\mathbf{0.4646 \pm 0.0029}$
		0.4	0.3730 ± 0.0018	$\mathbf{0.4162 \pm 0.0037}$
	Ternary STCs	0.2	0.4299 ± 0.0015	$\mathbf{0.4618 \pm 0.0051}$
		0.4	0.3719 ± 0.0023	$\mathbf{0.4052 \pm 0.0022}$
SRM				
Distortion function	Coding scheme	Payload	Detection error	
			max-random	ESBAS
S-UNIWARD	NDSTCs	0.2	0.4151 ± 0.0021	$\mathbf{0.4530 \pm 0.0032}$
		0.4	0.3612 ± 0.0018	$\mathbf{0.3977 \pm 0.0014}$
	Ternary STCs	0.2	0.4105 ± 0.0032	$\mathbf{0.4511 \pm 0.0021}$
		0.4	0.3507 ± 0.0017	$\mathbf{0.3873 \pm 0.0027}$
HILL	NDSTCs	0.2	0.4383 ± 0.0026	$\mathbf{0.4702 \pm 0.0018}$
		0.4	0.3795 ± 0.0033	$\mathbf{0.4157 \pm 0.0019}$
	Ternary STCs	0.2	0.4355 ± 0.0023	$\mathbf{0.4709 \pm 0.0033}$
		0.4	0.3770 ± 0.0019	$\mathbf{0.4178 \pm 0.0042}$

5   Conclusion

In this paper, we propose a new embedding strategy for batch adaptive steganography. The new strategy firstly fits curve between a well-defined secure factor and embedding payload based on embedding distortion. Then the images with large size and more upward convex relation curve are employed as the sub-batch to carry the total message. What more, we utilize the second derivative of payloads on secure factor to accurately evaluate the convexity of relation curve. Our embedding strategy makes up for the problem when applying batch steganography to adaptive steganography. Experimental results show that the new embedding strategy for batch adaptive steganography can achieve a outstanding performance for security. In the future work, we will extend our embedding strategy to other kind of cover that can achieve the adaptive steganography, just like JPEG adaptive steganography, not limit to the field of spatial adaptive steganography.

Acknowledgments. This work was supported by the NSFC under U1536105 and 61303259, National Key Technology R&D Program under 2014BAH41B01, Strategic Priority Research Program of CAS under XDA06030600, and Key Project of Institute of Information Engineering, CAS, under Y5Z0131201.

References

1. Fridrich, J., Kodovsky, J.: Rich models for steganalysis of digital images. IEEE Trans. Inf. Forensics Secur. **7**(3), 868–882 (2011)
2. Denemark, T., Sedighi, V., Holub, V., Cogranne, R., Fridrich, J.: Selection-channel-aware rich model for steganalysis of digital images. In: IEEE International Workshop on Information Forensics and Security (WIFS), pp. 48–53. IEEE (2014)
3. Holub, V., Fridrich, J.: Random projections of residuals for digital image steganalysis. IEEE Trans. Inf. Forensics Secur. **8**(12), 1996–2006 (2013)
4. Holub, V., Fridrich, J.: Low complexity features for JPEG steganalysis using undecimated DCT. IEEE Trans. Inf. Forensics Secur. **10**(2), 219–228 (2015)
5. Pevný, T., Filler, T., Bas, P.: Using high-dimensional image models to perform highly undetectable steganography. In: Böhme, R., Fong, P.W.L., Safavi-Naini, R. (eds.) IH 2010. LNCS, vol. 6387, pp. 161–177. Springer, Heidelberg (2010). doi:10.1007/978-3-642-16435-4_13
6. Holub, V., Fridrich, J.: Designing steganographic distortion using directional filters. In: IEEE International Workshop on Information Forensics and Security (WIFS), pp. 234–239. IEEE (2012)
7. Holub, V., Fridrich, J., Denemark, T.: Universal distortion design for steganography in an arbitrary domain. EURASIP J. Inf. Secur. **2014**(1), 1–13 (2014)
8. Li, B., Wang, M., Huang, J.: A new cost function for spatial image steganography. In: 2014 IEEE International Conference on Image Processing, pp. 4206–4210. IEEE (2014)
9. Fridrich, J., Goljan, M., Lisonek, P., Soukal, D.: Writing on wet paper. IEEE Trans. Sig. Process. **53**(10), 3923–3935 (2015)
10. Filler, T., Judas, J., Fridrich, J.: Minimizing additive distortion in steganography using syndrome-trellis codes. IEEE Trans. Inf. Forensics Secur. **6**(3), 920–935 (2011)
11. Zhao, Z., Guan, Q., Zhao, X.: Constructing near-optimal double-layered syndrome-trellis codes for spatial steganography. In: 2016 ACM Workshop on Information Hiding and MultiMedia Security, pp. 139–148 (2016)
12. Ker, A., Pevný, T.: Batch steganography in the real world. In: ACM Proceedings of the on Multimedia and Security, pp. 1–10 (2012)
13. Kodovský, J., Fridrich, J., Holub, V.: Ensemble classifiers for steganalysis of digital media. IEEE Trans. Inf. Forensics Secur. **7**(2), 432–444 (2012)
14. Bas, P., Filler, T., Pevný, T.: "Break our steganographic system": the ins and outs of organizing BOSS. In: Filler, T., Pevný, T., Craver, S., Ker, A. (eds.) IH 2011. LNCS, vol. 6958, pp. 59–70. Springer, Heidelberg (2011). doi:10.1007/978-3-642-24178-9_5

Adaptive Steganography Using 2D Gabor Filters and Ensemble Classifiers

Yuan Bian$^{(\boxtimes)}$, Guangming Tang, Shuo Wang, Zhanzhan Gao, and Shiyuan Chen

Institute of Information Science and Technology, Zhengzhou 450001, China
bianyuanlara@163.com

Abstract. In order to preserve the statistical properties of image in all scales and orientations when the embedding changes are constrained to the complicated texture regions, a steganography method is proposed based on 2 dimensional (2D) Gabor filters and Ensemble classifiers. First, we use histogram sequence features of filtered images generated by Gabor filters to describe the texture properties of the image. Then, we design the distortion function using the classification results differences of classifiers between cover and stego. The stego images are used to train the ensemble classifiers using the current popular steganography schemes, such HUGO and S-UNIWARD. Then, the message is embedded using STC (Syndrome Trellis Code). The experimental results show that the proposed scheme can achieve a competitive performance compared with the other steganography schemes HUGO, MVG and S-UNIWARD when using the SRM detection.

Keywords: Adaptive steganography · 2D Gabor filter · Ensemble classifiers

1 Introduction

With the rapid development of information technology, more and more security issues become prominent, especially threatening confidentiality of information. Therefore, information security has become a big concern and drawn a wide public attention. It is necessary to keep the confidential information itself secret. In addition, the existence of the communication behavior has to be hidden. And that is what steganography cares about. As the mainstream of steganography, adaptive steganography is defined as heuristic strategy according to the contents of the cover in the embedding process. The distortion function with Syndrome Trellis Code (STC) is a popular framework of adaptive steganography. The STC proposed by the literature [1] could solve the problem of adaptive steganography code. Therefore, the design of distortion function is a focus for researchers. Currently, the design of the adaptive steganography can be mainly classified into three methods based on the types of distortion function. The first method assigns the distortion cost based on the texture distribution of image. The second method designs

© Springer International Publishing AG 2017
Y.Q. Shi et al. (Eds.): IWDW 2016, LNCS 10082, pp. 506–517, 2017.
DOI: 10.1007/978-3-319-53465-7_38

the distortion function using the feature set from steganalysis. Thirdly, we can use image statistical model to define the distortion cost of pixels. As for the first method, the classic schemes are: WOW [2–4]. The main idea is to use the high-pass filters to define the distortion function. The second method, there are mainly two kinds of schemes. One is to assign the distortion cost according to the feature changes between cover and stego. HUGO [5] is a typical scheme following this idea. The scheme introduces the state-of-the-art features of horizontal, vertical, diagonal and anti-diagonal transition probability matrix already used in SPAM [6] into the design of distortion. The cost of changing only one pixel is in the form of a weighted sum of differences between feature vectors extracted from a cover image and the stego one. The other defines the distortion function based on the classification results differences of the classifiers between cover and stego. The scheme ASO [7] defines the distortion cost of the pixels using the result of an ensemble classifier [8]. The pixel distortion cost is in the form of the sum of all base classifiers results differences between covers and stegos. Owing to the fact that the base classifier trained by the feature set of stego images using HUGO [5] scheme, the selection of feature set is limited and incomplete, which affects security of the scheme against other attacks (other feature sets).

In general, the design of distortion function for steganography scheme should satisfy the following principles: the distortion cost of the noise and complex texture region or edge is lower, and the smooth region is higher. The edge of the image has the properties in direction and scale, which has some values for the design of distortion function. In the literature [2–4], the statistical properties of the four directions with the same scale for the local pixels are considered. However, the properties such as edges of the image in different scales and orientations contain more statistical details. Therefore, referring to the literature [7], this paper proposes an adaptive steganography scheme combined Gabor filter [8] with Ensemble classifiers [9]. The proposed scheme is divided into three steps. First, we use the histogram sequence features to describe the fileted image generated by Gabor filters. Then, the distortion function is designed based on the classifiers results. Finally, the secret message is embedded using STC. The experimental results show that the proposed scheme has a strong ability resisting the SRM detection.

2   Related Work

2.1   Gabor Filter

The Gabor filter, widely used in image processing and pattern analysis, is a finite impulse response filter proposed by Gabor. Gabor filters model according to human visual system. They yield desirable properties like spatial locality and orientation selectivity. In the spatial domain, a Gabor filter $g(x, y)$ is a product of the Gaussian and cosine function as Eqs. (1)–(3) show.

$$g(x, y; \lambda, \theta, \psi, \sigma, \gamma) = \exp(-\frac{x^{'2} + \gamma^2 y^{'2}}{2\sigma^2}) \cos(2\pi \frac{x^{'}}{\lambda} + \psi) \tag{1}$$

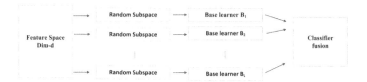

Fig. 1. The illustration of the ensemble classifiers

$$x' = x\cos\theta + y\sin\theta \tag{2}$$

$$y' = -x\sin\theta + y\cos\theta \tag{3}$$

In Eq. (1), λ is the wavelength of the cosine function. σ represents the scale parameter. A small σ means high spatial resolution, and the convolution result reflects the local properties of small scale, while a large σ means low resolution in coarse scale. θ denotes the orientations of 2D Gabor filter. γ is the spatial aspect ratio and specifies the phase offset of the cosine function. When 2D Gabor filter $g(x, y)$ is used for image processing, suppose that the input image is $I(x, y)$, then the Gabor transform is defined as a convolution of a Gabor filter $g(x, y)$ with image $I(x, y)$ as Eq. (4) shows:

$$S(x, y) = g(x, y) * I(x, y) = \sum_{m=0}^{M-1} \sum_{n=0}^{N-1} g(m, n) \cdot I(x - m, y - n) \tag{4}$$

Where $*$ denotes 2D linear convolution while M and N are the size of the filter mask.

In order to capture the local properties of the image, we use the Gabor filter bank composed of a set of multi-scale and multi-direction filters. In Fig. 1, the filtered images are given, which are all generated by convolving the input image with the Gabor filter banks. From the Fig. 1, it can be found that the image local properties are more obvious such as texture and edge when the scale parameter σ is relative small and the spatial resolution is relative high. Moreover, the texture and edge are relative coarse when the scale parameter is relative large with low resolution. The 2D Gabor filters can describe the image texture features from different scales and orientations, therefore the changes of image statistical characteristics caused by embedding operation can be captured more effectively. Hence, we use Gabor filters to design the steganography scheme in Sect. 3.

2.2 Ensemble Classifiers

The essence of the steganalysis is to classify cover and stego images, so as to determine whether the image to be detected is a cover or a stego. Hence, the detection could be considered as a binary classification problem. Therefore, the core parts of the classification are the feature extraction and design of classifier.

Kodovsky, who introduced the idea of ensemble learning to the steganalysis field, designs an ensemble classifier to detect the trace of embedding operation.

The proposed ensemble classifier consists of many base learners independently trained on a set of cover and stego images. Each base learner is a simple classifier built on a (uniformly) randomly selected sub-space of the feature space. The method of ensemble learning is used to reduce the complexity of training, which makes it possible to use high dimensional features to realize the detection of hidden writes. The proposed Ensemble classifier is illustrated in Fig. 1.

3   Proposed Scheme

At present, the standard, which measures the security of the adaptive steganography schemes, is the testing error when resisting the steganalysis scheme. Based on small statistical properties changes of the cover caused by the embedding operation, the blind detection of the embedding trace could be considered as a binary classification problem from pattern recognition. Therefore, a good steganography scheme should limit the statistical properties change of the image between cover and stego. The flowchart of the proposed scheme is shown in Fig. 2.

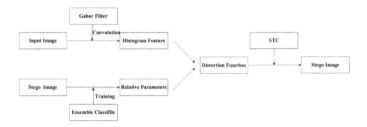

Fig. 2. The flowchart of the proposed scheme

3.1   The Description of the Texture Feature

In this section, a feature extraction method based on Gabor filter is presented. The process of the feature extraction is shown in Fig. 3, which mainly includes the following steps: (1) determining the parameters of Gabor filters and design of the Gabor filter banks and convolving the image with the Gabor filters with different scales and orientations; (2) dividing the fileted image into sub-blocks, then calculating the histogram feature of each sub-block, and putting all the histogram features of the blocks together to get histogram sequences; (3) merging the feature.

Step 1: Generation of Gabor filter bank. For the generation of 2D Gabor filter bank with different scales and orientations, suppose the number of scales equals S (the scale parameter σ has S different values), and the number of orientations equals O. Suppose that $M = N$, the mask size of Gabor filter is $M \times N$. ψ is set to 0 and $\pi/2$, so the number of 2D filters are $2 \cdot O \cdot S$. For example, if S = 4 and O = 32, then the number of the 2D Gabor filters is 256.

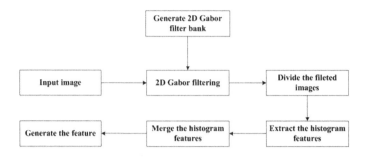

Fig. 3. The process of feature extraction

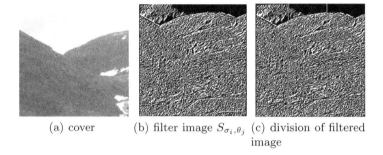

(a) cover   (b) filter image S_{σ_i,θ_j} (c) division of filtered
                                          image

Fig. 4. Divisions of filtered image

Step 2: Extraction of the histogram feature. Suppose the filtered image is S_{σ_i,θ_j} after the input image $I(x,y)$ convolved with the Gabor filter, the scale is σ_i and orientation is θ_j, then the filtered image can be expressed as following.

$$S_{\sigma_i,\theta_j}(x,y) = \sum_{m=0}^{M-1}\sum_{n=0}^{N-1} g(m,n) \cdot I(x-m,y-n) \tag{5}$$

Then, the filtered image S_{σ_i,θ_j} is divided into sub-blocks. Considering the even size of the input image, we divide the input image of $col \times row$ into $t \times t$ blocks, where $t = 2K$. In this paper, we make $K = 2, 4, 8$. And the concrete process of division is shown in Fig. 4.

For example, the U^{σ_i,θ_j} is the four-block of filtered image S_{σ_i,θ_j}, which divided the filtered image of 512×512 into sub-block $U_{11}{}^{\sigma_i,\theta_j}, U_{12}{}^{\sigma_i,\theta_j}, U_{13}{}^{\sigma_i,\theta_j}, U_{14}{}^{\sigma_i,\theta_j}$ (The block is in zig-zag order, which makes the feature more connected, as Fig. 5 shows). And the histogram feature x_n is extracted respectively of the four sub-blocks, where $n = 1, 2, 3, 4$.

$$x_1{}^{\sigma_i,\theta_j} = h_{11}{}^{\sigma_i,\theta_j} = \frac{1}{\left|U_{11}{}^{\sigma_i,\theta_j}\right|} \sum_{u \in U_{11}{}^{\sigma_i,\theta_j}} [Q_T({}^u/_q) = k] \tag{6}$$

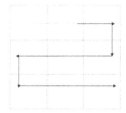

Fig. 5. Horizontal zig-zag order

where $\left|U_{11}^{\sigma_i,\theta_j}\right|$ is the number of pixels in sub-block $U_{11}^{\sigma_i,\theta_j}$, Q_T is a quantizer with integer centroids $0, 1, \ldots\ldots, T$, q denotes the quantization step, and $[P]$ is the Iverson bracket equal to 0 when the statement P is false and 1 when P is true. From the description above, we can get histogram feature of $2 \cdot S \cdot O$ fileted images. We connect all the histogram features in series together.

Step 3: Merging the histogram features. The dimensions of the histogram feature can be reduced further by merging the features extracted by 2D Gabor filters with symmetrical direction and same scale. For example, the histogram features of the filtered image with $\theta = \frac{\pi}{8}, \frac{7\pi}{8}$, $\theta = \frac{2\pi}{8}, \frac{6\pi}{8}$ and so on should be merged by averaging. This merging operation has been used in many feature extraction method because images have similar statistical characteristics in symmetrical orientations and same scale. Hence, the dimension of histogram feature is: $2 \cdot S \cdot (^{O}/_{2} + 1) \cdot (4 + 9 + 16) \cdot (T + 1)$.

3.2 The Design of Distortion Function

In this section, the distortion function is designed to minimize the statistical properties changes made by embedding operation, and to prevent detection by the classifier. Figure 6 shows the concrete procedure.

Step 1: Determination of the parameters. Relating to the ensemble classifiers, the number of base classifiers and the number of feature subspaces are selected and optimized. Referring to the literature [8], the number of classifier L is 30, and the number of feature subspace d_{sub} is 300.

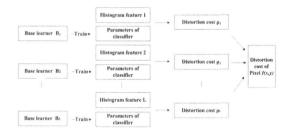

Fig. 6. The flowchart of the distortion cost assignment

Step 2: Training the base classifiers. We choose 2500 cover images and 2500 stego images (using HUGO or S-UNIWARD) randomly to train the classifiers. Based on the method of random sampling, the feature set is selected to generate 300 dimensional training sub-sets. Then, the initial classifier is trained on the training subset to generate a base classifier. The feature of each base classifier is different, which ensures the diversity of the classifiers. The parameters $\omega^{(l)}$ and $S^{(l)}$ of base classifier l ($l = \{1, 2 \cdots, L\}$) are obtained by using the training subset, where $\omega^{(l)}$ is the parameter in base learner of Fisher function, and $S^{(l)}$ is the scaling parameter which satisfies the following Eq. (7):

$$S^{(l)} = (\mu_1^{(l)} - \mu_0^{(l)})\omega^{(l)} + 2(\sqrt{\omega^{(l)T} \sum_0^{(l)} \omega^{(l)}} + \sqrt{\omega^{(l)T} \sum_1^{(l)} \omega^{(l)}}) \quad (7)$$

Step 3: Calculating the change of the feature. Since the training feature of each base classifier is random, the characteristics of each base classifier are different. Given the trained based classifier F_l, the training feature of classifier l is denoted as $\mathbf{X}_{\sigma_i,\theta_j}^{(l)}$ (300 dimensional). Similarly, $\mathbf{X}_{\sigma_i,\theta_j(x,y)}^{(l)(+1)}$ represents the training feature set of classifier l when the pixel is changed by +1. And $\mathbf{X}_{\sigma_i,\theta_j(x,y)}^{(l)(-1)}$ represents the training feature of classifier l when the pixel is changed by −1.

Step 4: Determination of the distortion cost. The goal of steganography is to minimize the statistical characteristics of the image between cover and stego, so as to resist the steganalysis detection. When the pixel $I(x,y)$ is changed by +1, the distortion cost $\rho_{I(x,y)}^{+1}$ of pixel $I(x,y)$ is calculated as the sum of distortion cost from each base classifier, as the Eq. (8) shows.

$$\rho_{I(x,y)}^{+1} = \sum_{l=1}^{L} \rho_{I(x,y)}^{(l)+1} \quad (8)$$

Based on the parameters obtained from the training step, we can use each base classifier to calculate the pixel distortion cost.

$$\rho_{I(x,y)}^{(l)+1} = \frac{\omega^{(l)} \cdot \mathbf{X}_{\sigma_i,\theta_j(x,y)}^{(l)(+1)} - \omega^{(l)} \cdot \mathbf{X}_{\sigma_i,\theta_j(x,y)}^{(l)}}{s^{(l)}}$$

$$= \frac{\omega^{(l)} \cdot (\mathbf{X}_{\sigma_i,\theta_j(x,y)}^{(l)(+1)} - \mathbf{X}_{\sigma_i,\theta_j(x,y)}^{(l)})}{s^{(l)}} \quad (9)$$

Similarly, when the pixel $I(x,y)$ is by −1, the distortion cost $\rho_{I(x,y)}^{-1}$ of pixel $I(x,y)$ is calculated as follows:

$$\rho_{I(x,y)}^{-1} = \sum_{l=1}^{L} \rho_{I(x,y)}^{(l)-1} \quad (10)$$

$$\rho_{I(x,y)}^{(l)-1} = \frac{\omega^{(l)} \cdot (\mathbf{X}_{\sigma_i,\theta_j(x,y)}^{(l)(-1)} - \mathbf{X}_{\sigma_i,\theta_j(x,y)}^{(l)})}{s^{(l)}} \quad (11)$$

Where $\rho_{I(x,y)}^{+1}$ is the distortion cost of pixel $I(x,y)$ for classifier l when the pixel $I(x,y)$ is by $+1$, and $\rho_{I(x,y)}^{(l)-1}$ is the cost of pixel $I(x,y)$ for classifier l when the pixel $I(x,y)$ is changed by -1. Similarly, we can get the meaning of $\rho_{I(x,y)}^{-1}$ and $\rho_{I(x,y)}^{(l)-1}$.

3.3 The Embedding and Extraction

For the sender, the message is embedded using the distortion function and STC code. For the receiver, it is necessary to know the length of the secret message and the relevant STC parameters to extract the message correctly.

4 Experiments and Analysis

In this section, we first illustrate the experimental procedure. Then we realize the proposed scheme using the HUGO, MVG and S-UNIWARD as the training feature sets respectively. Then we subject the proposed steganography by testing on standard image database, and compare the statistical delectability with the HUGO, MG and S-UNIWARD using 34,671-dimension SRM feature set.

4.1 Common Procedure of Experiments

All the experiments in this paper were conducted on the BOSSbase ver. 1.01 image database [10] with 10,000 8-bit gray-scale images coming from eight different cameras. The steganographic security is evaluated empirically using binary classifiers trained on a given cover source and its stego version embedded with a fixed pay-load. The schemes mentioned above will be analyzed using the Spatial Rich Model (SRM) [11] consisting of 39 symmetrized sub-models quantized with three different quantization factors with a total dimension of 34, 671. All classifiers were implemented using the ensemble classifiers [9] with Fisher linear discriminant as the base learner. The security is quantified by the ensemble's minimal total testing error P_E under equal priors.

$$P_E = \min_{P_{FA}} \frac{1}{2}(P_{FA} + P_{MD}) \qquad (12)$$

Where P_{FA} and P_{MD} are false-alarm and missed-detection probabilities.

4.2 Parameters Setting

For the feature description in Sect. 3.1, all the parameters S, O, T, q should be set. In this section, the performances of different parameters settings are discussed.

Table 1. Detection error for the proposed scheme (using S-UNIWARD as training feature set) with different scales

Payload	Parameter S				
	0.5	0.75	1	1.25	Combine
0.1 bpp	0.405	0.403	0.402	0.407	0.406
0.2 bpp	0.329	0.331	0.330	0.329	0.330
0.3 bpp	0.261	0.263	0.259	0.265	0.267
0.4 bpp	0.201	0.197	0.199	0.203	0.213

(1) Scale parameter S

2D Gabor filters with different orientations can capture the changes of the statistical features of image more effectively. In Table 1, the detection performances are given for proposed scheme (S-UNIWARD as training feature set) with the scale parameter S set as 0.5, 0.75, 1, and 1.25 respectively. The orientations of 2D Gabor filters equal 32 for each scale and the threshold T equals 6. The Quantization step q is set to 2, 4, 6, 8 respectively for different scales. The detection performances of combinatorial feature which is formed by combining the histogram features got indifferent scales are also given in Table 1.

(2) Direction parameter O

2D Gabor filters with different orientations can capture the changes of the statistical features of image more effectively. In Table 2, for proposed scheme (S-UNIWARD as training feature set) with payload 0.4 bpp, the detection performances are presented when the orientations of 2D Gabor filters equal 8, 16, 32, 48 respectively. The other parameters for the detection performance are set as S = 1, q = 2, and T = 6.

Table 2. Detection error for the proposed scheme (using S-UNIWARD as training feature set) with different directions

Payload	Parameter O			
	8	16	32	48
0.4 bpp	0.200	0.195	0.194	0.194

(3) Threshold T

For the histogram sequence feature, the feature dimension will be increased when the larger threshold T is set. In Table 3, the effects of the threshold T on testing error are given when scale parameter S is set as 0.5, 0.75,1, 1.25 respectively, the corresponding quantization steps q are 2, 4, 6, 8, and the orientations equal 32 for all scales.

Table 3. Detection error for the proposed scheme (using S-UNIWARD as training feature set) with different thresholds

Payload	Parameter T			
	3	4	5	6
0.4 bpp	0.195	0.197	0.199	0.201

(4) Quantization step q

For the histogram sequence feature, the quantization for the image filtering coefficients can make the feature more sensitive to embedding changes at spatial discontinuities in the image. In Table 4, the effects of the quantization step q on testing error are shown for the proposed steganography at 0.4 bpp with S = 4, the orientations O equal 8, the threshold T = 6.

Table 4. Detection error for the proposed scheme (using S-UNIWARD as training feature set) with different quantization steps

Payload	Parameter q			
	2	4	6	8
0.4 bpp	0.201	0.199	0.197	0.195

4.3 Computation of the Proposed Scheme

The computation of the feature proposed in Sect. 3.1 is cpu-consuming. In our method, the feature is obtained by extracting the histogram feature of the Gabor filtered image. And the distortion cost requires to compute $\rho^{+1}_{I(x,y)}$ and $\rho^{-1}_{I(x,y)}$ for each pixel $I(x,y)$, which requires to compute the feature vector $\mathbf{X}^{(+1)}_{\sigma_i,\theta_j(x,y)}$ and $\mathbf{X}^{(-1)}_{\sigma_i,\theta_j(x,y)}$ resulting from the modification $+1$ or -1 of the pixel $I(x,y)$ (see Eqs. 8–11). Since the vector $\omega^{(l)}$ and $S^{(l)}$ are computed during the leaning phase of classifier, we don't need to calculate them again in the computation of $\rho^{(l)+1}_{I(x,y)}$ and $\rho^{-1}_{I(x,y)}$. And the computation complexity of the distortion cost is mainly from the computation of feature vector $\mathbf{X}^{(+1)}_{\sigma_i,\theta_j(x,y)}$ and $\mathbf{X}^{(-1)}_{\sigma_i,\theta_j(x,y)}$. In order to solve this problem, we extract the feature on a reduced area as Fig. 7 shows, where the red block represents the embedding pixel, the shadow area represents the reduced area and the biggest block represents the image.

In this paper, considering the even number of image segmentation, the reduced area is 9×9 block. Using the parallel tool in C++ of Intel Core TM2 CPU6320@1.86 GHz, with the trick of reduced area, the calculation of the feature vector $\mathbf{X}^{(+1)}_{\sigma_i,\theta_j(x,y)}$ took about 0.0001625 s with the set of $L = 30$, $d_{sub} = 300$, $S = 4$, $O = 8$, $T = 6$ and $q = 2$. Therefore, the computation time of distortion cost for the 10,000 images is $0.0001625 \times 2 \times 512 \times 512 \times 10000 \times 3600 \times 24 = 9.86 \, days$ (almost about ten days).

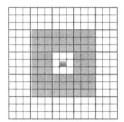

Fig. 7. The illustration of reduced area (Color figure online)

4.4 Comparison to Prior Schemes

In this section, the proposed scheme is compared with schemes HUGO, MG and S-UNIWARD. In Table 5, the testing errors of the four schemes are given. From Table 5, it can be seen that the proposed scheme can achieve the best performance against the SRM detection.

Table 5. Average detection error P_E for S-UNIWARD, MVG, HUGO and the proposed scheme using SRM features.

Scheme	Payload					
	0.05	0.1	0.2	0.3	0.4	0.5
Proposed scheme (S-U)	0.441	0.406	0.331	0.269	0.215	0.176
S-UNIWARD	0.437	0.395	0.323	0.258	0.201	0.162
MG	0.369	0.295	0.215	0.166	0.136	0.112
Proposed scheme (MG)	0.373	0.307	0.221	0.175	0.150	0.123
HUGO-BD	0.425	0.372	0.287	0.225	0.180	0.145
Proposed scheme (HUGO)	0.431	0.388	0.296	0.242	0.192	0.161

5   Conclusion

In this paper, a steganography method based on 2D Gabor filters is proposed, which constrains the embedding changes to complicated texture and edge regions. First, we use histogram sequence features of filtered images generated by Gabor filters to describe the texture properties of the image. Then, we design the distortion function using the classification results differences of classifiers between cover and stego. The stego images are used to train the ensemble classifiers using the current popular steganography schemes, such HUGO and S-UNIWARD. Then, the message is embedded using STC and distortion cost. From the experimental results, it can be seen that the security of the scheme can be improved effectively.

References

1. Filler, T., Judas, J., Fridrich, J.: Minimizing additive distortion in steganography using syndrome-trellis codes. IEEE Trans. Inf. Forensics Secur. **6**(3), 920–935 (2011)
2. Holub, V., Fridrich, J.: Designing steganographic distortion using directional filters. In: 2012 IEEE International Workshop on Information Forensics and Security (WIFS), pp. 234–239. IEEE, December 2012
3. Holub, V., Fridrich, J.: Digital image steganography using universal distortion. In: Proceedings of the First ACM Workshop on Information Hiding and Multimedia Security, pp. 59–68. ACM, June 2013
4. Li, B., Wang, M., Huang, J., Li, X.: A new cost function for spatial image steganography. In: 2014 IEEE International Conference on Image Processing (ICIP), pp. 4206–4210. IEEE, October 2014
5. Gul, G., Kurugollu, F.: A new methodology in steganalysis: breaking highly undetectable steganograpy (HUGO). In: Filler, T., Pevný, T., Craver, S., Ker, A. (eds.) IH 2011. LNCS, vol. 6958, pp. 71–84. Springer, Heidelberg (2011). doi:10.1007/978-3-642-24178-9_6
6. Pevny, T., Bas, P., Fridrich, J.: Steganalysis by subtractive pixel adjacency matrix. IEEE Trans. Inf. Forensics Secur. **5**(2), 215–224 (2010)
7. Kouider, S., Chaumont, M., Puech, W.: Adaptive steganography by oracle (ASO). In: 2013 IEEE International Conference on Multimedia and Expo (ICME), pp. 1–6. IEEE, July 2013
8. Song, X., Liu, F., Yang, C., Luo, X., Zhang, Y.: Steganalysis of adaptive JPEG steganography using 2D Gabor filters. In: Proceedings of the 3rd ACM Workshop on Information Hiding and Multimedia Security, pp. 15–23. ACM, June 2015
9. Kodovsky, J., Fridrich, J., Holub, V.: Ensemble classifiers for steganalysis of digital media. IEEE Trans. Inf. Forensics Secur. **7**(2), 432–444 (2012)
10. Bas, P., Filler, T., Pevný, T.: "Break our steganographic system": the ins and outs of organizing BOSS. In: Filler, T., Pevný, T., Craver, S., Ker, A. (eds.) IH 2011. LNCS, vol. 6958, pp. 59–70. Springer, Heidelberg (2011). doi:10.1007/978-3-642-24178-9_5
11. Fridrich, J., Kodovsky, J.: Rich models for steganalysis of digital images. IEEE Trans. Inf. Forensics Secur. **7**(3), 868–882 (2012)

An Adaptive Video Steganography Based on Intra-prediction Mode and Cost Assignment

Lingyu Zhang[1,2(✉)] and Xianfeng Zhao[2]

[1] State Key Laboratory of Information Security,
Institute of Information Engineering, Chinese Academy of Sciences,
Beijing 100093, China
{zhanglingyu,zhaoxianfeng}@iie.ac.cn
[2] University of Chinese Academy of Sciences, Beijing 100049 China

Abstract. In this paper, we proposed an adaptive video steganography algorithm based on intra-prediction mode. Unlike traditional approaches locating the embedding position referring to the changed mode selection of I4-blocks which are randomly distributed across the whole I frame, our approach applies modifications in an adaptive way. Inspired by Fridrich et al.'s STC, costs assignment of candidate blocks are introduced to perform adaptive embedding perturbations within the optimal cost area which has the characteristic of complex texture. The perturbations are optimized with the hope that these perturbations will be confused with normal mode assignments that cannot be detected by state-of-art steganalytic methods. Experimental results have validated the feasibility of the proposed method.

Keywords: Adaptive video steganography · Intra-prediction mode · Costs assignment · Complex texture

1 Introduction

Steganography is the art and science of covert communication. With the recent advances in digital multimedia and development of network technology, the need for private and personal communication application is necessary to our daily life. Simultaneously, the phenomenon of tampering, counterfeiting and attacking private information is increasingly serious [1]. Conventionally, cryptography can prevent the third parties stealing the private message via a covert channel which can tunnel through secure operating systems and require special measures to control by constructing and analyzing protocols. However, the covert messages from readable state are almost nonsense. Once the transmitting behavior is to be tapped from Eve (eavesdropper), the security of cryptosystem can be attracted. In contrast to cryptography, steganography aims to hide confidential messages inside innocent multimedia covers, e.g., images, videos, or audios etc.

Video steganography has obtained the attraction not only because of the versatility but also the ability of achieving a large capacity with less distortion. However, the form

© Springer International Publishing AG 2017
Y.Q. Shi et al. (Eds.): IWDW 2016, LNCS 10082, pp. 518–532, 2017.
DOI: 10.1007/978-3-319-53465-7_39

of existence of video is compression. H.264/AVC is the most popular forms of video compression on the internet. The compression method of H.264/AVC removes the spatial or time redundancy between inter frames and intra frames to improve coding efficiency. The video steganographic algorithms based on compressed domain include embedding data in the motion vectors [2, 3], quantized the discrete cosine transform (DCT) coefficients [4, 5], variable length code [6, 7], new entropy coding methods of context-adaptive binary arithmetic coding (CABAC) and context-adaptive variable length coding (CAVLC) [8], or prediction modes [9–12] etc.

In the intra-prediction mode of H.264, the similarity feature of pixels in neighborhood provides the spatial redundancy during intra-coding. Its implementation of video steganography is by modulating the intra prediction modes (IPMs). For instance, Hu et al. proposed a data hiding method by modifying intra-prediction modes of H.264/AVC [9]. Its coding method is based on the intra 4×4 prediction modes (I4PM). By beforehand designing the mapping rules, the I4PM of current block is modified based on the mapping, and the corresponding secret bit "0" or "1" can be embedded. Its coding method is based on LSB steganography which has high capacity but large distortion. A similar approach was proposed by Xu et al. [10]. The difference is the chosen embeddable macroblocks are based on a chaotic sequence and most probable prediction modes were manipulated to embed information. Its proposed method can effectively control the capacity for hidden data and the quality of video signals conveying hidden data. Yang et al. [11] improved the algorithm of Hu. It used matrix coding method, the embedding efficiency (message bits/number of flipping) can be increased. However, the embedding rate (message bits/cover length) can be decreased. Bouchama et al. [12] divided 9 prediction modes into four groups according to the prediction direction of I4PM, and modulated the corresponding prediction modes within the same group to embed secret bits. This algorithm ensured both visual quality and steganographic capacity of the video. The IPM-based steganographic algorithms have similar feature which replace optimal with suboptimal IPM according to a certain pre-agreed mapping rules to achieve the embedding. Although the existing IPM-based steganographic algorithms complete the data hiding work with relatively low bit rate, the secure factors of embedding positions are not considered at all. In this paper, an adaptive IPM-based video steganography based on cost assignment is proposed. The proposed method analyzes the texture feature of each candidate intra 4×4 coded block (I4-block), compute entropy of I4-block, and statistics minimum residual between optimal sum of MROSS (absolute transformed differences (SATD) and sub-optimal SATD) in each I4-block. Finally, by combining the above two values, the cost function ρ_{ij} is proposed, and through utilizing STC [13, 14] method an optimal Viterbi flipping path can be obtained. The detection performance results have been significantly improved compared to other existing IPM-based video steganographic algorithms.

The rest of the paper is organized as follows. In Sect. 2, the intra-prediction mode within the H.264/AVC encoder is briefly introduced. In Sect. 3, the proposed data hiding algorithm is discussed in details, including the process of cost function designing, and the steganographic course of the proposed scheme are presented. In Sect. 4, experimental results are presented and discussed. Finally, conclusions and future work are given in Sect. 5.

2   Process of Intra-prediction in H.264/AVC

For uncompressed raw video sequences, there are spatial redundancies within single frames and temporal redundancies among adjacent frames. Spatial redundancy means that the adjacent pixels have the similar gray values in an I frame, that is, there exist high correlation among the adjacent regions. So the intra prediction technique is generally utilized to decrease the spatial redundancy and obtain high compressed rate in a video picture. There are four types of intra prediction mode (IPM) in H.264/AVC including intra_4 × 4, intra_16 × 16, intra_chroma and I_PCM [8]. The intra_4 × 4 prediction mode (I4PM) in intra 4 × 4 luminance blocks (I4_blocks) is utilized to be modified in embedding process. The reason is that the I4PM is qualified for coding regions of I frame with significant details and some complex texture areas being coded well. Furthermore, because the proposed adaptive video steganography needs to be considered the characteristic texture to design the embedding cost, the I4PM can be chosen and should obtain the optimal performance. In practice, the I4PM is utilized in the existing IPM-based steganographic algorithms.

Figure 1 illustrates the intra prediction of I4_block. There are 9 prediction modes for I4_block, and each I4PM corresponds to different image texture direction. It is shown in Fig. 1, 'a' ~ 'p' are predicted pixels incurrent I4_block, 'A' ~ 'M' are already coded pixels which adjoin with the current I4_block. Figure 2 shows the 9 direction modes for 4 × 4 luminance block. The weighted values of 'a' ~ 'p' pixels are computed by the adjacent pixels 'A' ~ 'M'. The dc prediction (mode 2) adopts utilizing the average value of 'a' ~ 'p'.

M	A	B	C	D	E	F	G	H
I	a	b	c	d				
J	e	f	g	h				
K	i	j	k	l				
L	m	n	o	p				

Fig. 1. 4 × 4 luminance block to be predicted

The i th I4_block is denoted as $S_i | S_i \in \Omega$, where Ω denotes the candidate embeddable I4_block set. The chosen optimal IPM for S_i is denoted as $M_i \in \{M_1, \ldots, M_9\}$. For Intra_4 × 4 prediction, the optimal prediction mode decision for each of the I4_block is performed by minimizing the following:

$$J(S_i, M_i | QP, \lambda) = SSD(S_i, M_i | QP) + \lambda R(S_i, M_i | QP). \tag{1}$$

$J(S_i, M_i | QP, \lambda)$ is the rate distortion (RD) cost function which make the RD value of each IPM reach the minimum optimal IPM can be obtained by the metric. QP is the quantization parameter, λ is Lagrange multiplier for mode decision and R is the required number of bits to encode the block. SSD is the sum of squared differences

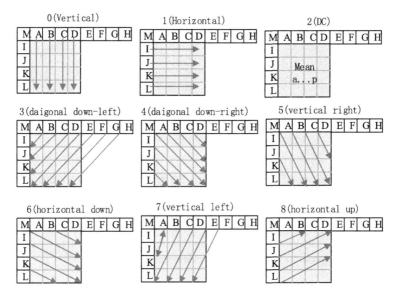

Fig. 2. The 4 × 4 intra prediction modes

between the pixels of reconstructed block-S_i^{REC} and the pixels of original block-S_i^{ORI} for the i th I4_blockgiven by formula (2):

$$SSD = \sum_{1 \leq x,y \leq 4} \left| S_i^{REC}(x,y) - S_i^{ORI}(x,y) \right|, \tag{2}$$

where $S_i^{REC}(x,y)$ and $S_i^{ORI}(x,y)$ denote the gray values of pixel on coordinate (x,y) in the i th reconstructed I4_block and original I4_block respectively. However, because the computation complexity is high, in practice, a better cost computation method with low computation complexity and low video bit rate-SATD (Sum of Absolute Transformed Differences) [15] is used to instead of SSD for selecting optimal IPM.

$$SATD = \sum_{1 \leq x,y \leq 4} \left| H(S_i^{REC}(x,y) - S_i^{ORI}(x,y)) \right|, \tag{3}$$

where $H(\cdot)$ is Hadamard Transform.

There exists a predictive coding to encode the prediction modes more efficiently for each I4_block. For each current I4_block S_i denoted as 'C', the most probable mode (MPM_{S_i}) is estimated based on spatial adjacent upper S_i^{upper} denoted as 'U' and left blocks S_i^{left} denoted as 'L' in Fig. 3 by the follow:

$$MPM_{S_i} = min\left\{M^{upper}, M^{left}\right\}, \tag{4}$$

where M^{upper} and M^{left} are the prediction modes of previously encoded I4_blocks S_i^{upper} and S_i^{left} respectively. If the two blocks are outside the current slice or not coded in Intra

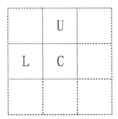

Fig. 3. Current and adjacent 4×4 blocks

4×4 mode, the corresponding value is set to 2 (DC mode). H.264/AV encoder assign an identifier *pre* for each I4_block to indicate whether MPM_{S_i} is estimated by the two adjacent blocks. When the optimal IPM of current I4_block S_i is equal to MPM_{S_i}, *pre* will beset 1.Then the prediction mode of current block will not be stored in code stream, and there is only one bit to record the information. Otherwise, *pre* will be set 0, and OPT_{S_i}(optimal prediction mode of S_i) is indicated by the follow:

$$OPT_{S_i} = \begin{cases} OPT_{S_i}, OPT_{S_i} \leq MPM_{S_i} \\ OPT_{S_i} - 1, OPT_{S_i} > MPM_{S_i} \end{cases} \tag{5}$$

In the proposed IPM-based steganography, the I4_blocks with *pre* = 1 are not coded and their prediction modes need not be stored in code stream. For this reason, the candidate embeddable I4_blocks set is $\Omega = \{S_i | pre_{S_i} = 0\}$.

3   The Proposed Adaptive Embedding Scheme

The proposed algorithm embeds message into qualified I4-blocks of I frames by modulating their prediction modes according to the mapping rules between these modes and binary embedding bits. The distribution of changed prediction modes are randomly in I frame. The behavior of taking no account of texture feature will be vulnerable to certain existing steganalyzers. The residuals between prediction I4-block and raw I4-blockreferring to optimal and sub-optimal mode respectively are different when the embeddable I4-block is located in different kinds of texture regions. Embedding in these smooth regions will easily lead to visible artifacts.

3.1   The Proposed Cost Assignment Scheme Based on I4-Blocksentropy and Its MROSS

However, the storage and quality of videos and the bandwidth-limited of the intranet are important factors affecting the video communication. Raw videos should be compressed into the coded bit streams with less loss of quality. The H.264/AVC standard uses spatial correlation to reduce the spatial redundancy during intra prediction coding. The property of correlation among adjacent pixels achieves compression by predicting the values in a block of pixels from the values in one or more previously coded blocks of pixels. Searching the optimal IPM for evaluating the luminance of predicted pixel from pixels located above and to the left since they have already been encoded and reconstructed in each 4×4 luminance block is the course of intra coding. Up to now, H.264 steganographic algorithms based on intra-prediction modes have utilized LSB or simple linear codes (matrix coding) to embed secret messages by modulating the prediction modes of intra-coded blocks. Usually, their embedding position referring to the changed mode selection of I4-blocks is randomly distributed across the whole I frame. However, the distribution of the embedding positions is important to the security of video steganographic system because the perturbed degree is different between the complex area and the smooth area in a picture. The difference characteristics are discussed in Sect. 3.1, which denotes the fact that if the distortion happened in complex area the steganography is relatively safe. Next, the complexity based on 4×4 luminance block should be further discussed, and the distortion function for these candidate blocks is proposed.

In this section, we restrict our design to additive distortion in the form:

$$D(\mathbf{X}, \mathbf{Y}) = \sum_{i=1}^{n_1} \sum_{j=1}^{n_2} p_{ij}(\mathbf{X}, map(Y_{ij})) \big| map(X_{ij}) - map(Y_{ij}) \big|, \qquad (6)$$

where $\mathbf{X}$, $\mathbf{Y}$ are the cover and stego which are mapped onto the IPMs of candidate I4-blocks in a frame, and $n_1 \times n_2$ is the number of candidate I4-blocks, If the mode of certain I4-block need to be changed, $map(X_{ij})$ is changed to $map(Y_{ij})$. The mapping $map(\cdot)$ denotes the parity of modes X_{ij} and Y_{ij}. ρ_{ij} are the cost of each I4-block with changing mode. To design the practical distortion metric, however, the magnitude of complex texture for each I4-block and its MSE (Mean Variance Measure) of SATD for nine prediction modes should be taken into account.

- **Statistical distribution of I4-blocks entropy**.

As an important property of natural images, texture can be viewed as a repetition of patterns along a region, and the concept that the texture complexity has an important influence on the steganographic security is widely accepted. There are a lot kinds of parameters which describes the characteristic of image texture, i.e., mean, variance, the energy, entropy, contrast, local homogeneity and correlation are main feature statistical measures. Therefore, the entropy of GLCM is the prevailing method of evaluating the properties of texture. In the early 70s, Haralik [16] et al. suggested the GLCM algorithm of texture features. This method constructed the GLCM based on the direction and distance between pixels, and obtained the meaningful statistics from the GLCM as a texture feature vector. Later many scholars have further researched along this method. W. Equitz [17] proposed the Inverse difference moment, Contrast and Entropy as a valid measurement. J.G. Hong [18] proposed Gray-Gradient co-occurrence matrix method which combined filtering operator and the gray value distribution to obtain the better features. GLCM is formed by two order joint conditional probability density function of gray levels. By calculating the correlation between any two gray levels with a certain distance and a certain direction, the information about the direction, interval, and rangeability of image texture is exact reflected. In image, GLCM describes the joint probability of two gray levels l_1 and l_2 with distance $d = (dx, dy)$ in certain direction θ, and the joint probability $p(l_1, l_2, \theta)$ is as follows:

$$\frac{\#\{\{(x,y),(x+dx,y+dy)\} \in S | g(x,y) = l_1 \& g(x+dx,y+dy) = l_2\}}{\#S}, \quad (7)$$

Suppose the gray level of the image is L, the GLCM is a $L \times L$ matrix. (x, y) is the coordinates of the first pixel, $g(\cdot)$ is the gray level of pixel in a certain coordinate, S is the set of pixel pairs with the special spatial relationship, and $\#S$ denotes the number of elements in set S. In practical, $\theta \in \{\rightarrow, \nearrow, \uparrow, \nwarrow\}$ and the corresponding direction set is $d = (0, d), (d, d), (d, 0), (-d, d)$. We utilize the average entropy of GLCMs with $d = (0, d) | d = 1$ and four directions in a certain I4-block to test its texture complexity.

$$\overline{ent}(i,j) = \frac{1}{4} \sum_{\theta \in \{\rightarrow, \nearrow, \uparrow, \nwarrow\}} -\sum_{l_1=0}^{L-1} \sum_{l_2=0}^{L-1} p(l_1, l_2, \theta) \cdot log[p(l_1, l_2, \theta)], \quad (8)$$

where i, j denotes the coordinate of a certain I4-block. Based on the theory of entropy, local entropy reflects the dispersion degree of texture or contained amount of information of image gray-scale values. If the texture is smooth, the corresponding local GLCM is near to zero matrix, the entropy is smaller. On the contrary, if the texture is more complex, the entropy is bigger. The characteristic of local entropy can be utilized to construct the cost ρ_{ij}, the larger the values of $\overline{ent}(i,j)$, the smaller the ρ_{ij} should be. If there exists $\overline{ent}(i,j) = 0$, then $\rho_{ij} = +\infty$.

- **Statistical Minimum Residual Between optimal SATD and sub-optimal SATD**.

   During the intra-coding process, H.264 encoder will comprehensively select optimal IPMs in cover video and in order to maintain the picture quality of video. Therefore, the SATD of the selected optimal IPM is the minimum. However, the existing IPM-based steganography usually uses sub-optimal IPMs to replace the optimal ones. The existing problem is that the magnitudes of the difference between optimal IPM and suboptimal IPM are usually different in all I4-blocks. A new metric of measuring the difference is defined as Minimum Residual between Optimal and Suboptimal SATD (MROSS). If the smaller MROSS values the I4-blocks, the corresponding blocks have more chance to be chosen to embed messages. We suppose symbol $r_{MROSS}(i,j)$ denotes the residual of a I4-block with coordinate (i,j), which is defined as follows:

$$r_{MROSS}(i,j) = |SATD_{OPTIMAL} - SATD_{SUBOPTIMAL}|. \quad (9)$$

   The distortion introduced by embedding mainly caused by the quantization of substantial residuals. The advantage of choosing small value of r_{MRBOSS} is that the stego disturbance caused by modifying IPM can be relative small, which makes the IPM of stego video slightly deviated from the original IPM. The distortion is very weak while the video bit rate is not particularly low, and even can be ignored when the bit rate is sufficiently high. So, the blocks with smaller values of $r_{MROSS}(i,j)$ should be given priority attention. Similarly, the characteristic of MROSS should be considered in the process of constructing cost function. When the value $r_{MROSS}(i,j)$ is smaller, the smaller cost ρ_{ij} should be. Overall, a simple function that meets both requirements is defined as follows:

$$\rho_{ij} = \frac{r_{MROSS}(i,j)^{\lambda_2}}{(\overline{ent}(i,j) + \varepsilon)^{\lambda_1}}. \tag{10}$$

where λ_1 and λ_2 are two parameters that are used to control impacts caused by $r_{MROSS}(i,j)$ and $\overline{ent}(i,j)$, respectively, and the range of the two parameters is $(0,1]$. The parameter ε is utilized to avoid the zero divisors in Eq. (10). When $\overline{ent}(i,j) = 0$, the cost ρ_{ij} is a maximum value. When $r_{MROSS}(i,j) = 0$, the cost ρ_{ij} is zero which means the SATD of suboptimal IPM is the same as optimal one and there is no distortion at

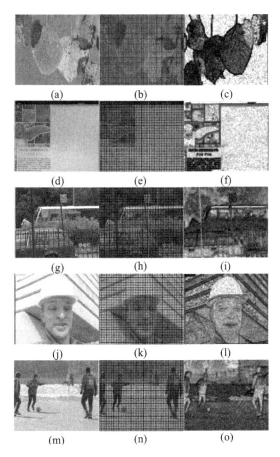

Fig. 4. Costs graphs of the candidate I4-blocks in I-frames: (a)(d)(g)(j)(m) are raw I-frames of chosen sequences; (b)(e)(h)(k)(n) are the luminance pictures divided into 4×4; (c)(f)(i)(l)(o) are the cost graphs of these luminance pictures.

the result. An intra-coded frame of aspen sequence, bowing sequence, bus sequence, foreman sequence and soccer sequence are selected to display the costs of candidate I4-blocks, and the corresponding cost graph is shown in Fig. 4. The picture of the I-frame is divided into 4×4 blocks, the message is only embedded into the I4-block which is denoted as the smaller grid in Fig. 4. The value ρ_{ij} of each I4-block is computed, and it is mapped into gray value. The value ρ_{ij} of each I4-block in the I-frame is shown in Fig. 4. It is shown that the blocks with smaller cost are distributed in complex texture area. If we combine the cost function with STC, the changed IPMs of chosen I4-blocks are convergent to minimum distortion region, and the security can be maintained. The corresponding secure testing will be given in section.

3.2   The Steganographic Course of the Proposed Scheme

The existing IPM-based algorithms only randomly change the I4-blocks, the characteristics of these selected blocks are not considered. In this paper, the proposed method combines binary STC with the designed cost function to form an adaptive IPM-based steganography. Its optimal performance is that this method considers the suitable embedding positions. By modifying the prediction mode of I4-blocks with optimal cost, the security should be improved. Besides, the capacity of STC is 0.5bpp, and the corresponding average distortion is almost less than1/4 on the basis of the results of testing. However, the actual payload of this proposed is higher than the above Hu's

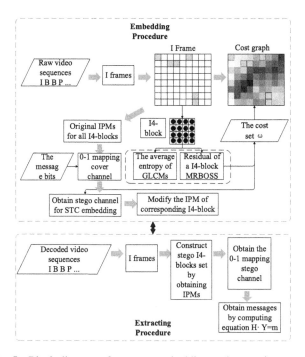

Fig. 5. Block diagram of message embedding and extracting process

algorithms. Because there exists a large number of 4×4 blocks have the same prediction modes within a 16×16 macroblock in Hu's algorithm, the number of candidate I4-blocks are relative smaller than our proposed. In other words, the length of cover channel of our proposed is longer, and the actual payload is larger.

In this section, the adaptive video steganography based on IPM is carried out in the following algorithm. The block diagram of the proposed scheme is illustrated in Fig. 5.

In Fig. 5, the smaller grid denotes the I4-block. Majority of I4-blocks are included in to candidate embeddable I4-blocks set except those blocks marked with yellow background which identifiers *Pre* are set 1. Based on the corresponding cost function, the modified I4-blocks are converged on complex texture region.

Algorithm 1
Embedding:

1. Choose an I-frame from video stream.
2. 4×4 luminance blocks with their corresponding identifiers *Pre*=0 are selected to integrate to the candidate I4-blocks set $\mathfrak{X} = \{X_{ij}|1 \leq i \leq n_1, 1 \leq i \leq n_2\}$ based on chaotic sequence controlled by a key.
3. Compute cost value for each selected I4-block X_{ij} based on formula (7-10). The cost set of set $\mathfrak{X}$ is denoted as $\mathcal{W} = \{\rho_{ij}|1 \leq i \leq n_1, 1 \leq i \leq n_2\}$.
4. Compute the prediction modes for candidate I4-blocks set $\mathfrak{X}$, and construct their corresponding 0-1 mapping cover channel $\widehat{\mathfrak{X}}_{cover} = \{x_{i,j}|x_{i,j} = prediction\_mode (X_{ij}) \bmod 2\}$.
5. Obtain the secret bits from messages, and apply STC and $\{\rho_{ij}\}$for data embedding to generate the modified stego channel $\widehat{\mathfrak{X}}_{stego} = \{y_{i,j}|y_{i,j} = x_{i,j} \pm 1 \bmod 2\}$ where $x_{i,j}$ is needed to be flipped.
6. Compute nine prediction modes set $M = \{M_1, \dots, M_9\}$ for each flipped I4-block X_{ij}, and choose suboptimal prediction mode from set $\{M_i|i \bmod 2 = (prediction\_mode(X_{ij}) \bmod 2 \pm 1) \bmod 2\}$. Repeat the above steps until all I-frames are processed.

Extracting:

1. Decode the stego H.264/AVC video stream to get the prediction modes of all the I4-blocks.
2. Construct stego I4-blocks set $\mathfrak{X}_{stego} = \{Y_{ij}|1 \leq i \leq n_1, 1 \leq i \leq n_2\}$ with identifiers *Pre*=0 based on chaotic sequence controlled by a key.
3. Obtain the corresponding 0-1 mapping stego channel $\widehat{\mathfrak{X}}_{stego} = \{y_{i,j}|y_{i,j} = prediction\_mode(Y_{ij}) \bmod 2\}$.
4. Compute the equation $\mathbf{H} \cdot \mathbf{Y} = \mathbf{m}$, $\mathbf{Y}$ is the stego vector of set $\widehat{\mathfrak{X}}_{stego}$and the secret message $\mathbf{m}$ is obtained.

4 Experiments and Performance Results

Security is important issue for video steganographic schemes. The true positive rate (TP) and true negative rate (TN) are utilized to evaluate detection performance. The IPMC features [20] including the IPM shift probability feature set and the SATD shift distance feature set are chosen to be tested, and the dimension of IPMC features is only 9 + 4 = 13. PMC and TPMC (Truncated PMC) features [19] are also tested. The dimension of the PMC features is 9801, and the dimension of TPMC features is declined to 200. A database of 30 CIF videos in the 4:2:0 YUV format is used for experiments. 500 consecutive frames are randomly intercepted from each video as one experimental sequence. Each 100 consecutive frames are divided into a group as one subsequences and the total number of subsequences sums up to 150. Open source 264 encoder is used to compress the experimental sequences as the set of video cover. In order to test the performance of our proposed method, two video steganographic methods based on IPM, i.e., Yang's and Bouchama's schemes are chosen to be compared with ours. The stego video sets created by the above steganographic methods are denoted as Method1 (ours), Method2 (Yang's) and Method3 (Bouchama's). In Yang's method, a matrix coding algorithm is used, its maximum relative payload rate (embeddable secret message bits/cover length) reaches to 2/3, and its maximum distortion rate (number of modification/cover length) reaches 1/4. The "cover length" denotes the number of I4-blocks in defined candidate set Ω in above section. And the "number of modification" denotes the number of replaced suboptimal IPM for each modified I4-block. In Bouchama's method, LSB coding algorithm is used, there is 1/2 probability for embedding 1 secret bit and 1/2 probability for embedding 2 secret bits. The maximum payload is $\frac{1}{2} \times 1 + \frac{1}{2} \times 2 = 2$ for per modification and the average distortion rate is 1/2. In our proposed method, the upper bound of the relative payload reaches 0.5 and the average distortion almost reaches 0.15. In our experiments, the different relative payload rates $\alpha \in \{0.1, 0.2, 0.3, 0.5\}$ are chosen to produce the stego sets. The set of 150 video subsequences are divided into two sets, one including randomly selecting 100 video subsequences for training, the rest including 50 video subsequences for classification. Repeat 10 times experiments to test the average detection performance.

Table 1 shows the comparative performance results between these IPM-based video steganographic methods and our proposed method. Figure 6 shows the corresponding performance curve of TP. Through analyzing the experimental results, the better performance of ours is shown up prominently, and when the higher the bit rate is, the more significant the performance of ours shows. Among the three kinds of feature sets, the IPMC features have the optimal detection performance. Our proposed method can make the TP or TN rate of IPMC feature decrease around 5 percentage points compared with the other methods, i.e., the TN rate of Method1 is 92.1%, the TN rate of Method2 is 97.3%. It is known from the results that the better performance of one stego scheme is, the lower TP and TN rates would be. When the relative payload rate is given a certain value, the average detection performance of our proposed is better than other IPM-based video stego schemes under all the kind of detection features. Specially, when the bit rate increase, the detection rate can be improved near to

Table 1. Detection performance comparison within different IPM-based video steganographic methods

Steganography methods	Bit rate (Mb/s)	Relative payload rate	PMC features		TPMC features		IPMC features	
			TP (%)	TN (%)	TP (%)	TN (%)	TP (%)	TN (%)
Method1	1.0	0.1	45.7	68.1	45.3	67.9	67.9	92.1
		0.2	47.3		47.6		77.0	
		0.3	55.9		51.8		88.2	
		0.5	62.4		59.5		91.1	
	0.2	0.1	44.1	67.2	46.7	66.5	66.4	90.4
		0.2	46.5		48.1		76.9	
		0.3	55.4		52.8		87.6	
		0.5	63.0		59.7		90	
Method2	1.0	0.1	49.2	74.2	50.6	73.1	70.8	97.3
		0.2	52.6		52.6		80.4	
		0.3	60.3		56.4		91.6	
		0.5	67.8		63.3		94.7	
	0.2	0.1	47.3	73.1	50.3	72.5	68.4	94.2
		0.2	51.7		51.9		79.6	
		0.3	59.5		55.1		90.3	
		0.5	68.3		62.8		93.1	
Method3	1.0	0.1	53.2	74.2	51.2	73.1	79.4	97.6
		0.2	58.1		54.3		86.9	
		0.3	66.9		60.1		94.1	
		0.5	76.7		69.2		91.8	
	0.2	0.1	51.7	73.1	50.2	72.5	77.9	90.1
		0.2	56.6		54.1		84.2	
		0.3	65.7		60.8		85.6	
		0.5	75.8		67.9		90.4	

1% points. The embedding method of IPM-based adaptive video steganography make the changeable I4-blocks be located within complex texture area, which make the embedding cost lower than other methods. And because the STC coding algorithm is utilized, the average distortion is less too. Based on the analysis and experimental results, our proposed method can obtain the better performance than the others.

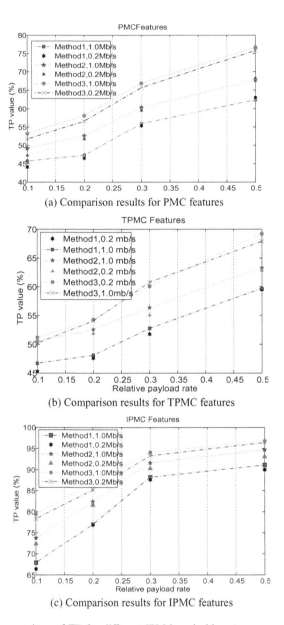

(a) Comparison results for PMC features

(b) Comparison results for TPMC features

(c) Comparison results for IPMC features

Fig. 6. The comparison of TP for different IPM-based video steganographic schemes

5   Conclusion

IPM-based video steganographic schemes hide the secret messages during the I-frame coding. By modulating the suboptimal IPM of each embeddable I4-block, the secret bits are embedded. However, existing algorithms randomly select the embeddable

I4-blocks through choosing a quasi-stochastic scrambling algorithm, and usually ignore the characteristic of I4-block, i.e., texture feature. The choice of embeddable region is important for the security of steganography. In this paper, cost assignments of candidate blocks are introduced to perform adaptive embedding perturbations within the optimal cost area. By using the STC coding algorithm, the modifications to I4-blocks are concentrated in less cost regions which have more complex texture and smaller residual values of STAD between optimal IPM and suboptimal IPM. Finally, according to the experimental results, the proposed method is less detectable compared with the other IPM-based video steganographic schemes. Future research work will be investigation of the possibility of introducing the adaptive IPM-based video steganography for H.265/HEVC so as to further improve the embedding capacity.

Acknowledgement. This work was supported by the NSFC under 61303259 and U1536105, National Key Technology R&D Program under 2014BAH41B01, Strategic Priority Research Program of CAS under XDA06030600, and Key Project of Institute of Information Engineering, CAS, under Y5Z0131201.

References

1. Wu, M., Liu, B.: Data hiding in image and video. I. Fundamental issues and solutions. IEEE Trans. Image Process. **12**(6), 685–695 (2003)
2. Jordan, F., Kutter, M., Ebrahimi, T.: Proposal of a watermarking technique for hiding/retrieving data in compressed and decompressed video. ISO/IEC Doc. JTC1/SC 29/QWG 11 MPEG 97/M 2281 (1997)
3. Liu, Z., Liang, H., Niu, X.: A robust video watermarking in motion vectors. In: Proceedings of the 2004 7th International Conference on Signal Processing, ICSP 2004, vol. 3, pp. 2358–2361. IEEE, Beijing, 31 August–4 September 2004
4. Ma, X., Li, Z., Tu, H.: A data hiding algorithm for H.264/AVC video stream without intra-frame distortion drift. IEEE Trans. Circuits Syst. Video Technol. **20**(10), 1320–1330 (2010)
5. Neufeld, A., Ker, A.: A study of embedding operation and locations for steganography in H.264 video. In: Proceedings of IS&T/SPIE Electronic Imaging, vol. 8665, pp. 86650J:1–86650J:14. International Society for Optics and Photonics (2013)
6. Lu, C., Chen, J., Fan, K.: Real-time frame-dependent video watermarking in VLC domain. Sig. Process. Image Commun. **20**(7), 624–642 (2005)
7. Seo, Y., Choi, H., Lee, C.: Low-complexity watermarking based on entropy coding in H.264/AVC. IEICE Trans. Fundam. Electron. Commun. Comput. Sci. **91**(8), 2130–2137 (2008)
8. Wiegand, T., Sullivan, G.J., Bjntegaard, G., Luthra, A.: Overview of the H.264/AVC video coding standard. IEEE Trans. Circ. Syst. Video Technol. **13**(7), 560–576 (2003)
9. Hu, Y., Zhang, C., Su, Y.: Information hiding based on intra prediction modes for H.264/AVC. In: Proceedings of 2007 IEEE International Conference on Multimedia and Expo, ICME 2007, pp. 1231–1234. IEEE, Beijing, 2–5 July 2007
10. Xu, D., Wang, R., Wang, J.: Prediction mode modulated data-hiding algorithm for H.264/AVC. J. Real-Time Image Proc. **7**(4), 205–214 (2012)

11. Yang, G., Li, J., He, Y.: An information hiding algorithm based on intra-prediction modes and matrix coding for H.264/AVC video stream. Int. J. Electron. Commun. **65**(4), 331–337 (2011)
12. Bouchama, S., Hamami, L., Aliane, H.: H.264/AVC Data hiding based on intra prediction modes for real-time application. In: Proceedings of the World Congress on Engineering and Computer Science, vol. 1, pp. 655–658 (2012)
13. Fridrich, J., Filler, T.: Practical methods for minimizing embedding impact is steganography. In: Proceedings SPIE, EI, Security, Steganography, and Watermarking of Multimedia Contents IX, San Jose, CA, vol. 6505, pp. 2–3, 29 January–1 February 2007
14. Filler, T., Fridrich, J., Judas, J.: Minimizing embedding impact in steganography using Trellis-Coded quantization. In: Proceedings SPIE, EI, Media Forensics and Security XII, San Jose, CA, pp. 05-1–05-14, 18–20 January 2010
15. Kim, J., Jeong, J.: Fast intra mode decision algorithm using the sum of absolute transformed differences. In: Proceedings of 2011 International Conference on Digital Image Computing: Techniques and Applications, DICTA 2011, pp. 655–659. IEEE (2011)
16. Haralick, R.M., Shanmugam, K., Dinstein, I.: Texture features for image classification. IEEE Trans. Syst. Man Cybern. **3**(6), 610–621 (1973)
17. Equitz, W., Niblack, W.: Retrieving images from a database using texture-algorithms from the QBIC system. In: Technical Report. RJ 9805, Computer Science, IBM Research Report (1994)
18. Hong, J.G.: The texture analysis based on gary-gradient co-occurrence matrix. Acta Automatica Sinica **10**(1), 22–25 (1984)
19. Li, S., Deng, H., Tian, H.: Steganalytic of prediction mode modulated data-hiding algorithms in H.264/AVC video stream. Annals of telecommunications-annales des télécommunications, **69**(7–8), 461–473 (2014)
20. Zhao, Y., Zhang, H., Cao, Y., Wang, P., Zhao, X.: Video steganalysis based on intra prediction mode calibration. In: Shi, Y.-Q., Kim, H.J., Pérez-González, F., Echizen, I. (eds.) IWDW 2015. LNCS, vol. 9569, pp. 119–133. Springer, Heidelberg (2016). doi:10.1007/978-3-319-31960-5_11

Segmentation Based Steganalysis of Spatial Images Using Local Linear Transform

Ran Wang[1,2(✉)], Xijian Ping[2,3], Shaozhang Niu[1], and Tao Zhang[2]

[1] Beijing University of Posts and Telecommunications, Beijing, China
[2] Zhengzhou Information Science and Technology Institute, Zhengzhou, China
nemo2007@163.com
[3] Zhengzhou Shengda University of Economics, Business and Management,
Xinzheng, China

Abstract. Most of the traditional image steganalysis techniques are conducted on the entire image and do not take advantage of the content diversity. However, the steganalysis features are affected by image content, and the impact is more serious than embedding. This makes steganalysis to be a classification problem with bigger within-class scatter distances and smaller between-class scatter distances. In this paper, a steganalysis algorithm aimed at spatial steganographic methods which can reduce the differences of image statistical characteristics caused by image content is proposed. The given images are segmented to sub-images according to the texture complexity. Steganalysis features based on local linear transform are separately extracted from each sort of sub-images with the same or close texture complexity to build a classifier. The final steganalysis result is figured out through a weighted fusing process. Experimental results performed on several diverse image databases and circumstances demonstrate that the proposed method exhibits excellent performances.

Keywords: Steganalysis · Image segmentation · Texture analysis · Local linear transform

1 Introduction

Steganography, as an art of covert communication, is carried out by hiding secret data into a cover medium in a manner that the existence of the message is unknown. The most important attribute of a steganography algorithm is security, which expects no existing detect algorithm can determine whether an object medium contains a hidden message. As the counterpart of steganography, steganalysis is to discover the presence of hidden messages in the multimedia objects, such as image, video and music. The success of steganalysis relies on the statistical changes of the cover medium caused by embedding.

Steganalysis methods mainly fall into two categories, namely, specific steganalysis and blind steganalysis. Specific steganalysis is aiming at a particular steganography algorithm by investigating the embedding mechanism and the statistical changes it will cause. Such method can often obtain a high accuracy and sometimes can detect the embedding rate. For example, the least significant bit (LSB) replacement method can

© Springer International Publishing AG 2017
Y.Q. Shi et al. (Eds.): IWDW 2016, LNCS 10082, pp. 533–549, 2017.
DOI: 10.1007/978-3-319-53465-7_40

be easily detected due to the symmetry of pixel value pairs [1, 2]. Many heuristic detectors, such as [3–6], have been proposed for LSB matching steganography, which is a trivial modification of LSB substitution, but is much harder to be detected. Blind steganalysis, which is also named as universal steganalysis, uses machine learning to distinguish the cover and stego images. It is more attractive in practical use because of its ability to offer an overall good performance on diverse steganographic schemes. The most frequently used blind steganalysis features include image quality [7], pixel correlation [8, 9], empirical probability density function (PDF) moments [10, 11] and empirical characteristic function (CF) moments [12, 13].

Although various steganalyzers have been presented, there are still many challenges in the field of steganalysis attacking the spatial domain steganography. The detection accuracy for uncompressed images with low embedding rate is still not satisfactory. In addition, compared to traditional non-adaptive embedding methods, adaptive steganographers [14–18] can constrain their embedding changes to those parts that are difficult to model, such as textured or noisy regions. Consequently, adaptive embedding methods become more and more significant for a high embedding capacity and enhanced security. To improve the steganalysis performances of the adaptive embedding methods, several high-dimensional steganalysis feature sets were investigated in [19–21] and substantial improvement are obtained by merging joint distributions.

Moreover, the basic concept of the current image steganalysis is to analyze the embedding mechanism and the statistical changes of the image data caused by secret message embedding. However, the embedding changes are not only correlated with the steganography methods, but also with the image content and the local statistical characteristics. Compared with the process of embedding, the image contents make a more significant impact on the differences of image statistical characteristics. This makes the image steganalysis to be a classification problem with bigger within-class scatter distances and smaller between-class scatter distances. Furthermore, the steganalysis performance closely tied to the image content and quality of the training and testing database. When the training and testing images are from different databases with dissimilar statistical features, the detection results are obviously affected, which is unfavorable for the practical application of the steganalyzer. Considered the impact of image content on steganalysis results, researchers have proposed some relevant algorithms. Experimental results of LSB matching steganalysis on three databases [22] clearly demonstrated that the performance varied considerably across databases. In [23], the conclusion was drawn that image complexity was an important factor to evaluate the steganalysis performance. Paper [24] proposed a steganalytic method to detect spatial domain steganography in grayscale images from the perspective of texture analysis. Several new frameworks of steganalysis considering image content were proposed in JPEG domain. In [25], the whole input images were first divided into classes according to image content, and then each category of images were classified to obtain a fuzzy result. Paper [26] classified image blocks in a middle size according to the steganalysis features, and built a classifier for each kind of blocks which went through a voting process to get the total results. In the same experimental condition, both content based methods mentioned above can improve the performance.

Based on the analysis of the prior content-based steganalysis methods, we can hypothesize that the steganalysis performance could be improved by considering the texture complexity of the images. In [27], we proposed a JPEG steganalysis method based on image segmentation. The given images are segmented into several overlapped sub-images according to the block texture complexity. Steganalysis feature set is extracted from each sub-images with different texture complexity and independently trained and tested. The experimental results demonstrate that segmentation can obviously improve the steganalysis results to several embedding methods. We tend to combine image segmentation with powerful steganalysis feature set to obtain better detection accuracy in spatial domain.

In this paper, a new blind steganalysis method of spatial image which can reduce the differences of image statistical characteristics caused by image content is proposed. Firstly, the given images are segmented to several sub-images according to the block texture. Then steganalysis features obtained by various local linear transform (LLT) masks are extracted from each sort of sub-images with close texture complexity to build a classifier. The total steganalysis result is obtained through a weighted fusing process. This paper is organized as follows. Section 2 focuses on introducing the LLT based steganalysis features. Section 3 covers the essential idea of the content based spatial image steganalysis algorithm and describes the process in detail. The effectiveness of the proposed method is verified with experimental results under several different practical scenarios in Sect. 4. Finally, the conclusion is drawn in Sect. 5.

2 LLT Based Steganalysis Features

Local linear transform (LLT) is a general computational framework in which an image is convolved with a bank of masks with relatively small sizes for all local neighborhoods in a sliding window fashion. From the view of image texture, the statistical changes caused by embedding can be regarded as the variety of image texture. The LLT can capture the changes of the local stochastic textures.

2.1 Steganalysis Features Obtained by LLT

Given an image I with size $W \times H$, assume ω is the LLT mask, the output D can be obtained as:

$$D = I * \omega \qquad (1)$$

where '*' indicates convolution operation. Considering features extracted from high order of difference pixels are more sensitive to the embedding changes, we define the k-th order of LLT residuals $D^{(k)}$ as:

$$D^{(k)} = D^{(k-1)} * \omega \qquad (2)$$

which means to convolve the image I with mask ω for k times.

The value region of high order LLT matrix will be greatly enlarged. To curb the dynamic range and extract features from the most significant part, each high order of

LLT residuals will be quantized. Moreover, the adaptive steganography methods always embed messages in the pixels with large difference value. Quantization will make the residual more sensitive to embedding changes at spatial discontinuities in the image. Assume $\omega_{i,j}$ represent the element of ω, and the size of the mask ω is $M \times N$, let $QC = \sum_{i=1}^{M} \sum_{j=1}^{N} |\omega_{i,j}|$. The quantized high order LLT residual is defined as:

$$Q^{(k)} = \left[\frac{D^{(k)}}{QC^k} \right] \tag{3}$$

where $[x]$ rounds the element x to the nearest integer.

The elements of quantized LLT residuals distribute around value zero, and there are huge zeros and small values. To decrease the feature dimensionality, we choose a truncated threshold T, and use the truncated $Q^{(k)}$:

$$Q_{i,j}^{(k)} = \text{trunc}(Q_{i,j}^{(k)}) = \begin{cases} T & \text{if } Q_{i,j}^{(k)} > T \\ -T & \text{if } Q_{i,j}^{(k)} < T \\ Q_{i,j}^{(k)} & \text{else} \end{cases} \tag{4}$$

$Q^{(k)}$ can be modeled as a Markov process and we extract three order of adjacent occurrence probability in three directions:

$$M_{u,v,w,x}^{\rightarrow} = \Pr(Q_{i,j}^{(k)} = u, Q_{i,j+1}^{(k)} = v, Q_{i,j+2}^{(k)} = w, Q_{i,j+3}^{(k)} = x) \tag{5}$$

$$M_{u,v,w,x}^{\downarrow} = \Pr(Q_{i,j}^{(k)} = u, Q_{i+1,j}^{(k)} = v, Q_{i+2,j}^{(k)} = w, Q_{i+3,j}^{(k)} = x) \tag{6}$$

$$M_{u,v,w,x}^{\rightrightarrows} = \Pr(Q_{i,j}^{(k)} = u, Q_{i,j+1}^{(k)} = v, Q_{i+1,j}^{(k)} = w, Q_{i+1,j+1}^{(k)} = x) \tag{7}$$

Consequently, the dimension of each adjacent occurrence probability matrix is $(2T+1)^4$.

The elements of LLT residual are approximate symmetric about the 0 value, as a result we can make a plausible assumption that

$$\Pr(u, v, w, x) = \Pr(-u, -v, -w, -x) \tag{8}$$

Thus we can decrease nearly half of the feature dimension by computing:

$$\Pr(u, v, w, x) = \frac{1}{2} (\Pr(u, v, w, x) + \Pr(-u, -v, -w, -x)) \tag{9}$$

and deleting the repeated part. Then the final dimension of each adjacent occurrence probability matrix is $\frac{1}{2} \left((2T+1)^4 + 1 \right)$.

2.2 Selection of LLT Masks

The LLT masks we used in the proposed algorithm are sensitive to image details such as edges, lines, and isolated points. These masks are given as:

1st order of difference matrices:

$$\begin{bmatrix} 1 & -1 \end{bmatrix}, \begin{bmatrix} 1 \\ -1 \end{bmatrix}, \begin{bmatrix} 1 & 0 \\ 0 & -1 \end{bmatrix}, \begin{bmatrix} 0 & 1 \\ -1 & 0 \end{bmatrix}, \begin{bmatrix} 1 & -1 \\ -1 & 1 \end{bmatrix};$$

2nd order of difference matrices:

$$\begin{bmatrix} 1 & -2 & 1 \end{bmatrix}, \begin{bmatrix} 1 \\ -2 \\ 1 \end{bmatrix}, \begin{bmatrix} 1 & 0 & 0 \\ 0 & -2 & 0 \\ 0 & 0 & 1 \end{bmatrix}, \begin{bmatrix} 0 & 0 & 1 \\ 0 & -2 & 0 \\ 1 & 0 & 0 \end{bmatrix}, \begin{bmatrix} 1 & -2 & 1 \\ -2 & 4 & -2 \\ 1 & -2 & 1 \end{bmatrix};$$

3rd order of difference matrices:

$$\begin{bmatrix} 1 & -3 & 3 & -1 \end{bmatrix}, \begin{bmatrix} 1 \\ -3 \\ 3 \\ -1 \end{bmatrix}, \begin{bmatrix} 1 & 0 & 0 & 0 \\ 0 & -3 & 0 & 0 \\ 0 & 0 & 3 & 0 \\ 0 & 0 & 0 & -1 \end{bmatrix}, \begin{bmatrix} 0 & 0 & 0 & 1 \\ 0 & 0 & -3 & 0 \\ 0 & 3 & 0 & 0 \\ -1 & 0 & 0 & 0 \end{bmatrix}, \begin{bmatrix} 1 & -3 & 3 & -1 \\ -3 & 9 & -9 & 3 \\ 3 & -9 & 9 & -3 \\ -1 & 3 & -3 & 1 \end{bmatrix};$$

4th order of difference matrices:

$$\begin{bmatrix} 1 & -4 & 6 & -4 & 1 \end{bmatrix}, \begin{bmatrix} 1 & -4 & 6 & -4 & 1 \\ -4 & 16 & -24 & 16 & -4 \\ 6 & -24 & 36 & -24 & 6 \\ -4 & 16 & -24 & 16 & -4 \\ 1 & -4 & 6 & -4 & 1 \end{bmatrix};$$

2 Laplace matrices:

$$\begin{bmatrix} 0 & 1 & 0 \\ 1 & -4 & 1 \\ 0 & 1 & 0 \end{bmatrix}, \begin{bmatrix} 1 & 1 & 1 \\ 1 & -8 & 1 \\ 1 & 1 & 1 \end{bmatrix};$$

The matrix used in [20]:

$$\begin{bmatrix} -1 & 2 & -2 & 2 & -1 \\ 2 & -6 & 8 & -6 & 2 \\ -2 & 8 & -12 & 8 & -2 \\ 2 & -6 & 8 & -6 & 2 \\ -1 & 2 & -2 & 2 & -1 \end{bmatrix}.$$

This matrix was obtained as a result of optimizing the coefficients of a circularly symmetrical 5×5 kernel using the Nelder-Mead algorithm to minimize the detection error for the embedding algorithm HUGO.

3   Segmentation Based Steganalysis Algorithm

After embedding, the image characteristics change differently according to the image content complexity, while the steganalysis features of the image regions with the same content complexity are similar. As a result, segmenting the given image to several sub-images assorted by the texture complexity will make the steganalysis features of each category of sub-images more centralized, and it will be easier to distinguish the cover images from the stego ones.

The block-diagram of the proposed steganalysis algorithm is shown in Fig. 1. In the training process, the input images are segmented according to the texture features of image blocks. To segment the image, we first categorize the image blocks according to the texture complexity, and then amalgamate the adjacent block categories. LLT based steganalysis features are extracted from each category of sub-images, and a classifier is developed. In the testing process, the image is also segmented, and steganalysis feature set of each sub-image is dealt with the corresponding classifier. The weight value of each steganalyzer will be assigned according to the detection accuracy. The final decision result of the entire image is derived from a weighted fuzzy process.

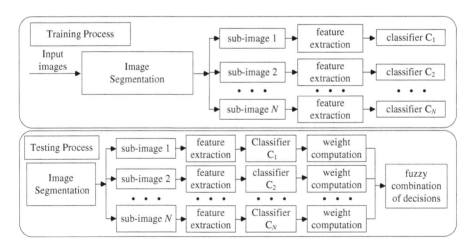

Fig. 1. The block-diagram of the proposed steganalyzern.

3.1   Image Segmentation

The block texture based segmentation includes blocks classification and block category amalgamation, which is summed up in Fig. 2.

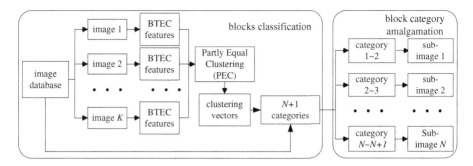

Fig. 2. The process of texture based image segmentation.

3.1.1 Block Texture Based Classification

Given an image I with size $W \times H$, compute the mean value of differences of a pixel to its eight neighbours:

$$DI_{i,j} = \frac{1}{8} \sum_{\substack{m,n = -1 \\ m+n \neq 0}}^{1} \left| I_{i,j} - I_{i+m,j+n} \right| \tag{10}$$

where $i = 2, \ldots, W - 1$, $j = 2, \ldots, H - 1$. Divide the given image into several non-overlapped blocks with fixed size $S \times S$. To each block, we define the mean value of difference pixels as the block texture evaluation criteria (denoted as BTEC):

$$B = \frac{1}{S \times S} \sum_{i,j=1}^{S} DI_{i,j} \tag{11}$$

The block size S needs to best balance the continuity and diversity of the image content, and we will discuss the selection in the experimental part.

To categorize the image blocks, we need to divide the BTEC features into several continuous disjoint clusters. On account of the situation that the difference values of the image pixels are centralized around zero point which causes the nonuniform distribution of the BTEC features in the value region, the most popular clustering method, such as K-means clustering, classifies most blocks into the same category. The number of the blocks in different categories might be dramatically different, which will affect the performance.

To classify the image blocks better, we need a method to make each class have close block numbers. To solve this problem, we propose a partly equal clustering (PEC) method. Denote K randomly picked images in the given data set as $I_1, I_2, \ldots, I_K$ and the image blocks need to be classified into $N + 1$ categories. For each image, sort the BTEC features extracted from each block in ascending order and equally partition the feature vectors into M clusters. Record the demarcation points $P^i, i = 1, \ldots, K$ as the classification vector. Accordingly, we can obtain $(1 \times N)$-dimensional classification vector from each image. To obtain the clustering vector C of the image set, compute as:

$$[C_1 \quad C_2 \quad \ldots \quad C_N] = \left[median_{i=1}^{K}(P_1^i) \quad median_{i=1}^{K}(P_2^i) \quad \cdots \quad median_{i=1}^{K}(P_N^i) \right]$$

(12)

where $median(\bullet)$ refers to computing the median value. The PEC method can classify the given image blocks into $N + 1$ categories with almost equal number of blocks, unless the image is too smooth or too complex.

3.1.2   Block Category Amalgamation

The blocks classified into different categories may have closer steganalysis features when their BTEC features are separated by the boundary. Consequently, we amalgamate the 2 adjacent block categories with contiguous BTEC features. Given K images, assume that we need to classify the blocks into $N + 1$ categories and amalgamate the 2 adjacent block categories to obtain a sub-image, then we can segment the images into N sub-images. $N - 1$ categories, except the smoothest and the most complex one, belong to more than one sub-image. The detailed process of segmentation is summarized as follows: 1. Compute the BTEC features of each image block. 2. For the blocks of each image, sort the BTEC features and compute the classification vector using the PEC clustering method. 3. Classify the blocks of all images in the database into $N + 1$ categories according to the classification vector. 4. Amalgamate the adjacent 2 categories of image blocks to form a sub-image. In such a way, we can obtain N overlapped sub-images.

Figure 3 illustrates an example of segmentation. Assume that the blocks of an image are classified into four categories in the block classification phase. Then, we amalgamate every contiguous two categories of blocks to obtain three sub-images, i.e., categories 1 and 2, categories 2 and 3, and categories 3 and 4 are amalgamated into one sub-image separately.

(a)	(b)	(c)	(d)

Fig. 3. Segmentation results (the blocks with non-zero gray-level compose one sub-image, from (b)–(d), the sub-image complexity increases). (a) An image. (b) The amalgamation results of block categories 1 and 2, (c) The amalgamation results of block categories 2 and 3, (d) the amalgamation results of block categories 3 and 4.

3.2   Segmentation Based Steganalysis Features

We extract the same LLT based features from each segmented sub-image. In the smooth images, there are more zero and small pixel values after difference and quantization, and the quantized LLT residuals tend to distribute more centralized. However, for we extract three order Markov features from the high order of LLT residuals, even in the complex regions, the values of quantized LLT residuals are small. As a result, the truncated threshold T is set to 1 to get rid of the redundancy which can decrease the computing complexity. The dimension of features we extract from each segmented sub-image is 2460. To reduce the computing complexity, we only consider the circumstances that the images are segmented to 3 sub-images. As a result, the total feature dimension is 7380.

3.3   Training and Testing

After extracting LLT based steganalysis features from each class of sub-images, we need to construct the classifier. As is shown in Fig. 1, the steganalysis features of the same category of sub-images are trained separately to form N classifiers. In the testing process, we take the steganalysis features of each sub-image as the input of the corresponding classifier to get the classification result. Thus, we can obtain N determination results for one image.

In order to fuse the N judgments to get a more reliable result, we need to assign a weight value to each classifier. For the sake of the simpleness and validity of the fuzzy approach, we compute the voted weight based on the minimal total error P_E under equal priors of the classifier, which is defined as:

$$P_E = \min_{P_{FA}} \frac{P_{FA} + P_{MD}}{2} \tag{13}$$

where P_{FA} is the false alarm rate and P_{MD} is the missed detection rate. If the value P_E of a specific type of sub-image is relatively low which means more sub-images are correctly detected, it is better to assign a bigger weight, and vice versa. Assume P_{Ei} is the indicator of the i-th classifier, let $a_i = 1 - P_{Ei}$, the weight value of the classifier is

$$w_i = \frac{a_i - 0.5}{\sum\limits_{i=1}^{N} (a_i - 0.5)} \tag{14}$$

where $i = 1, \ldots, N$. In the voting process, we set the predicted results p_i of each sub-image in the value range $\{0,1\}$, which means $p(I = \text{cover}) = 0$ and $p(I = \text{stego}) = 1$. The voting rule is as follows:

$$P = \sum\limits_{i=1}^{N} p_i \cdot w_i \tag{15}$$

The given image is detected as a cover image when $P \leq 0.5$, and stego otherwise. In such a way, we can get the final fuzzy detection result.

4 Experimental Results

4.1 Experiment Setup

To evaluate our proposed algorithm and compare it to prior art under different conditions, we ran the experiments on several image databases that have been previously used in the context of steganography. The used image databases include BOSSbase 0.92 [28], BOWS2 Images [29], UCID Images [30] and the combined database. The combined database including 7000 images is created by concatenating 3000 randomly selected images from the first two databases and 1000 images from the last database. These databases not only contain different images, but more importantly, the image sources are significantly different. The motivation for using more than one database is to determine any variability in performance across databases.

We generate stego images by embedding data with different message lengths and different embedding algorithms. The four steganography embedding methods we considered are: LSBM, AELSB [16], EA [17], WOW and HUGO [18]. We use bits per pixel, or bpp for short to describe message length. The embedding rate is set according to the detection results. The method which is hard to detect is embedded with higher rate. In consideration of the speed and performance, we use ensemble classifier for training and testing. For each database, 50 percent images constructed by cover images and the corresponding stego ones are randomly selected for training and the rest 50 percent are for testing.

4.2 Effect of Block Size S

The block size S is crucial to the performance of the proposed algorithm. If S is too small, there will be too much isolated blocks, and the steganalysis features which capture the dependencies among the pixels. While if S is too large, the image content inside the block tends to become inhomogeneous, which will reduce the experimental accuracy. To decide the block size, we test the proposed algorithm on 1000 randomly chosen images from BOWS2 database with different S. The embedding rate of LSBM, AELSB, EA, WOW, HUGO is respectively 0.1, 0.3, 0.4, 0.5 and 0.6 bpp, and the order of LLT residual is 5. The values of tested S include 4×4, 8×8, 16×16, 32×32, 64×64 and 128×128. The minimal total error is shown in Fig. 4. From the figure it can be seen that although there may be an oscillation, the performances tend to form a concave curve, which means the performance increases with the segmented number S and after reaching an inflexion, the performance will reduce when S is bigger. Considering both the performance and the algorithm complexity, we decide to set the block size to 16 in the following experiments.

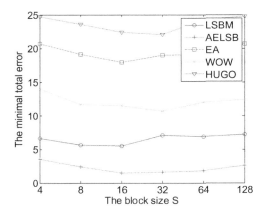

Fig. 4. The minimal total error of the proposed algorithm with different block size S.

4.3 Effect of LLT Residual Order

The order of LLT residual k is also closely related to the algorithm performance. To decide the value k, we test the proposed algorithm on 1000 randomly chosen images from BOWS2 database. The embedding rate of LSBM, AELSB, EA, WOW and HUGO is respectively 0.1, 0.3, 0.4, 0.5 and 0.6 bpp. The minimal total error with different k is shown in Fig. 5. From the figure, it can be seen that the performances increase with the differential order k, especially for AELSB, WOW and HUGO method. This is because the adaptive method embedding messages in the pixels with large difference values. High order of LLT features with appropriate quantized coefficient can better catch the changes. After reaching a point, the detection accuracy almost remain the same. Considering the computing complexity, we choose 8 as the LLT residual order in the following experiment.

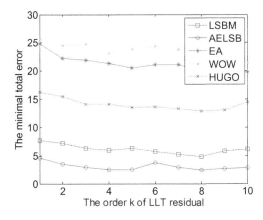

Fig. 5. The minimal total error of the proposed algorithm with different LLT orders.

4.4   Performance Comparison

In this section, we compare the proposed method with SPAM method in paper [9], the algorithm using the local linear transform (LLT) method in [24], and the algorithm based on spatial rich models (SRM) in [20]. The dimensions of the three compared feature sets are 686, 120 and 12753 respectively. The compared methods are representative and have extraordinary performance. We test the algorithms with 5 embedding methods and 2 embedding rates on the databases mentioned above. In order to meet the needs of practical application, we test the algorithms in different conditions, including when the training and testing database are the same and different. For each embedding algorithm, rate, database, and circumstances, an ensemble classifier is constructed to detect cover and stego images. The compared indicator is the minimal total error of all cover and stego images in the testing set. Smaller indicator signifies better performance. The listed indicators are the mean value of 5 repeated experiments, and the bold numbers represent the best results in the same condition.

Table 1 shows the performance of the compared algorithms when the training and testing images are from the same database. The performance illuminates that SRM and the proposed method outperforms the first two on all databases, and the results of steganalysis to adaptive embedding methods exhibit more significant improvement. This verifies the power of high dimensional feature set. Compared with SRM, with smaller feature dimension, the proposed feature set can obtain almost the same or better results when detecting LSBM and AELSB. When detecting EA, WOW and HUGO, the proposed method is a little weaker than SRM. However, the computing time of extracting the steganalysis feature set from one image of the proposed method is much less. In the same experimental condition, the computing time of SRM is 28.316 s, whereas using the proposed method, the time is 6.158 s. The compared codes we used are provided by the author of paper [20].

Table 1. Comparison of detection result when training and testing database are the same (%)

Cover vs	Embedding rate (bpp)	Comparison method	Database			
			BOSS	BOWS	UCID	Combined
LSBM	0.1	SPAM	20.75	16.06	35.31	18.10
		Xiong's	17.77	15.88	31.02	14.07
		SRM	**10.57**	5.64	**20.76**	**11.00**
		Proposed	11.43	**5.53**	21.70	11.20
	0.2	SPAM	14.81	8.60	24.31	13.02
		Xiong's	11.08	7.97	20.07	9.92
		SRM	6.21	2.33	**15.96**	6.43
		Proposed	**5.90**	**2.30**	16.10	**5.71**

(*continued*)

Table 1. (*continued*)

Cover vs	Embedding rate (bpp)	Comparison method	Database			
			BOSS	BOWS	UCID	Combined
AELSB	0.2	SPAM	33.98	34.29	43.06	35.67
		Xiong's	25.42	17.24	36.38	28.88
		SRM	3.15	**1.73**	9.62	3.00
		Proposed	**2.93**	1.83	**8.90**	**2.74**
	0.3	SPAM	21.65	26.87	38.37	24.59
		Xiong's	15.17	20.13	30.54	19.87
		SRM	**1.82**	0.49	5.86	1.89
		Proposed	2.20	**0.47**	**4.40**	**1.63**
EA	0.3	SPAM	29.60	33.54	46.06	33.64
		Xiong's	27.82	28.13	42.48	30.28
		SRM	**13.87**	**16.05**	**29.86**	**17.09**
		Proposed	16.07	18.13	31.70	20.17
	0.4	SPAM	21.04	23.29	39.62	24.62
		Xiong's	17.47	20.38	36.02	21.28
		SRM	**9.93**	**10.77**	**23.76**	**12.09**
		Proposed	11.73	12.73	26.10	14.87
WOW	0.4	SPAM	48.82	45.63	49.83	47.72
		Xiong's	36.83	30.92	43.39	36.59
		SRM	**25.15**	**22.37**	**38.64**	**27.17**
		Proposed	28.03	25.50	40.20	29.98
	0.5	SPAM	42.01	36.24	39.87	38.46
		Xiong's	25.13	21.82	36.97	26.24
		SRM	**15.35**	**12.67**	**29.76**	**16.23**
		Proposed	18.27	15.43	30.83	19.34
HUGO	0.5	SPAM	44.29	41.60	48.69	43.49
		Xiong's	31.77	23.88	41.17	30.08
		SRM	**25.15**	**17.79**	**30.44**	**19.89**
		Proposed	28.03	20.27	32.20	22.53
	0.6	SPAM	66.21	64.67	52.44	63.50
		Xiong's	77.23	82.98	62.12	78.23
		SRM	**8.67**	**8.98**	**19.76**	**10.71**
		Proposed	11.73	11.37	21.30	13.01

Table 2 shows the performance of the compared algorithms when the training and testing images are from different image databases. The listed database indicates the testing set, while the combination of other two sets is used for training. The methods with high dimensional features still outperform the first two weak feature sets. The detection result of the proposed method in most circumstances is better than SRM method. Unlike the traditional steganalysis algorithms, the proposed method is not

Table 2. Comparison of detection result when training and testing database are different (%)

Cover vs	Embedding rate (bpp)	Comparison method	Database		
			BOSS	BOWS	UCID
LSBM	0.1	SPAM	24.18	28.07	37.90
		Xiong's	20.13	17.24	34.21
		SRM	**19.68**	**12.52**	33.90
		Proposed	19.87	13.10	**33.35**
	0.2	SPAM	18.03	23.12	31.15
		Xiong's	14.54	26.17	30.28
		SRM	12.23	6.69	28.80
		Proposed	**9.65**	**5.87**	**25.20**
AELSB	0.2	SPAM	42.77	40.12	44.50
		Xiong's	30.15	32.38	40.02
		SRM	4.12	7.65	10.63
		Proposed	**4.10**	**3.97**	**9.75**
	0.3	SPAM	32.25	28.35	39.25
		Xiong's	23.89	24.58	33.72
		SRM	1.92	2.83	7.59
		Proposed	**1.78**	**1.35**	**6.40**
EA	0.3	SPAM	26.62	35.60	47.15
		Xiong's	32.42	31.08	44.57
		SRM	**21.70**	29.84	**36.30**
		Proposed	22.85	**27.70**	36.95
	0.4	SPAM	26.58	25.92	42.97
		Xiong's	25.57	22.76	59.81
		SRM	15.37	24.70	**28.95**
		Proposed	**15.26**	**22.10**	29.82
WOW	0.4	SPAM	49.23	48.34	49.37
		Xiong's	40.24	40.05	48.92
		SRM	33.10	35.10	43.13
		Proposed	**30.53**	**32.65**	**40.45**
	0.5	SPAM	45.78	43.92	46.25
		Xiong's	29.64	31.35	41.12
		SRM	**17.81**	22.66	28.85
		Proposed	18.78	**20.01**	**26.40**
HUGO	0.5	SPAM	49.97	49.88	48.95
		Xiong's	39.87	38.81	43.38
		SRM	**18.94**	26.95	33.20
		Proposed	19.65	**25.05**	**30.03**
	0.6	SPAM	39.22	41.38	47.33
		Xiong's	26.77	27.82	41.76
		SRM	**12.76**	15.13	23.58
		Proposed	13.13	**14.25**	**20.38**

much affected when the training and testing database are totally different. This is because the proposed algorithm is based on the image content and has sufficient consideration of the characteristics of the image itself. With this advantage, the proposed content based method can work better when there is a considerable diversity in image sources and contents which is quite useful in the practical application.

5 Conclusion

In this paper, a steganalysis method of spatial images based on segmentation and local linear transform is proposed. The proposed method has sufficiently considered the influence of the content difference of images to the steganalysis result. In this algorithm, the input images are segmented according to the block texture. Then, feature set based on local linear transform is extracted from each sub-image with different texture complexity. The steganalysis features of each category of sub-images are independently trained. In the testing phase, the steganalysis features of each segmented sub-image are sent to the corresponding classifier and the final decision is made through a weighted fusing process. The results of the experiments show that the proposed algorithm has a convincing power in improving the performance of blind steganalysis, especially for adaptive embedding methods. Although in some circumstance, the performance is not good as algorithm in paper [20], the proposed method has less features and lower computing complexity. When there is a considerable diversity in image sources and contents, such as the training and testing images are differentiated, the proposed method can also obtain good performance.

Acknowledgments. This work was supported by the National Natural Science Foundation of China under grant No. 61272490 and No. 61602511. The authors would like to thank the reviewers for their insightful comments and helpful suggestions.

References

1. Fridrich, J., Goljan, M., Du, R.: Detecting LSB steganography in color and gray-scale images. IEEE Multimed. **8**(4), 22–28 (2001)
2. Zhang, T., Ping, X.: A new approach to reliable detection of LSB steganography in natural images. Sig. Process. **83**(10), 2085–2093 (2003)
3. Ker, A.D.: Steganalysis of LSB matching in grayscale images. IEEE Sig. Process. Lett. **12** (6), 441–444 (2005)
4. Zhang, J., Cox, I.J., Doerr, G.: Steganalysis for LSB matching in images with high-frequency noise. In: IEEE Workshop Multimedia Signal Processing, pp. 385–388 (2007)
5. Cai, K., Li, X., Zeng, T.: Reliable histogram features for detecting LSB matching. In: IEEE International Conference on Image Processing, , Hong Kong, pp. 1761–1764 (2010)
6. Zhang, T., et al.: Steganalysis of LSB matching based on statistical modeling of pixel difference distributions. Inf. Sci. **80**(23), 4685–4694 (2010)

7. Avcibas, I., Memon, N., Sankur, B.: Steganalysis using image quality metrics. IEEE Trans. Image Process. **12**(2), 221–229 (2003)
8. Sullivan, K., et al.: Steganalysis for Markov cover data with applications to images. IEEE Trans. Inf. Forensics Secur. **1**(2), 275–287 (2006)
9. Pevný, T., Bas, P., Fridrich, J.: Steganalysis by subtractive pixel adjacency matrix. IEEE Trans. Inf. Forensics Secur. **5**(2), 215–224 (2010)
10. Farid, H.: Detecting hidden messages using higher-order statistical models. In: IEEE International Conference on Image Processing, New York, pp. 905–908 (2002)
11. Goljan, M., Fridrich, J., Holotyak, T.: New blind steganalysis and its implications. In: SPIE, Electronic Imaging, Security, Steganography, and Watermarking of Multimedia, pp. 1–13 (2006)
12. Xuan, G., et al.: Steganalysis based on multiple features formed by statistical moments of wavelet characteristic functions. In: 7th International Workshop on Information Hiding, Barcelona, Spain, pp. 262–277 (2005)
13. Wang, Y., Moulin, P.: Optimized feature extraction for learning based image steganalysis. IEEE Trans. Inf. Forensics Secur. **2**(1), 31–45 (2007)
14. Kawaguchi, E., Eason, R.O.: Principle and applications of BPCS-Steganography. In: SPIE Multimedia Systems and Applications, Boston, pp. 464–472 (1998)
15. Wang, C.M., et al.: A high quality steganographic method with pixel-value differencing and modulus function. J. Syst. Softw. **81**(1), 150–158 (2008)
16. Yang, C., et al.: Adaptive data hiding in edge areas of images with spatial LSB domain systems. IEEE Trans. Inf. Forensics Secur. **3**(3), 488–497 (2008)
17. Luo, W., Huang, F., Huang, J.: Edge adaptive image steganography based on LSB matching revisited. IEEE Trans. Inf. Forensics Secur. **5**(2), 201–214 (2010)
18. Pevný, T., Filler, T., Bas, P.: Using high-dimensional image models to perform highly undetectable steganography. In: 12th International Workshop on Information Hiding, Calgary, AB, Canada, pp. 161–177 (2010)
19. Fridrich, J., Kodovský, J., Goljan, M., Holub, V.: Steganalysis of content-adaptive steganography in spatial domain. In: 13th International Workshop on Information Hiding, Prague, Czech Republic, pp. 102–117 (2011)
20. Fridrich, J., Kodovský, J.: Rich models for steganalysis of digital images. IEEE Trans. Inf. Forensics Secur. **7**(23), 868–882 (2012)
21. Holub, V., Fridrich, J., Denemark, T.: Random projections of residuals as an alternative to co-occurrences in steganalysis. In: SPIE, Electronic Imaging, Media Watermarking, Security, and Forensics XV, vol. 8665, , San Francisco, CA, pp. 3–7 (2013)
22. Cancelli, G., Doërr, G., Barni, M., Cox, I.J.: A comparative study of ±1 steganalyzers. In: IEEE International Workshop Multimedia Signal Processing, Cairns, Australia, pp. 791–796 (2008)
23. Liu, Q., Sung, A.H., Chen, Z., Xu, J.: Feature mining and pattern classification for steganalysis of LSB matching steganography in grayscale images. Pattern Recogn. **41**(1), 56–66 (2008)
24. Xiong, G., Ping, X., Zhang, T., et al.: Image textural features for steganalysis of spatial domain steganography. J. Electron. Imag. **21**(3), 033015 (2012)
25. Amirkhani, H., Rahmati, M.: New framework for using image contents in blind steganalysis systems. J. Electron. Imag. **20**(1), 013016 (2011)
26. Cho, S., Cha, B., Gawecki, M., et al.: Block-based image steganalysis: algorithm and performance evaluation. J. Visual Commun. Image Representation **24**(7), 846–856 (2013)

27. Wang, R., et al.: Steganalysis of JPEG images using block texture based rich models. J. Electron. Imag. **22**(4), 043033 (2013)
28. BOSS. http://boss.gipsa-lab.grenobleinp.fr/BOSSRank/
29. Bows-2 (2007). http://bows2.gipsa-lab.inpg.fr/BOWS2OrigEp3.tgz
30. Schaefer, G., Stich, M.: UCID - An Uncompressed Colour Image Database. School of Computing and Mathematics, Nottingham Trent University, U.K. (2003)

Reliable Pooled Steganalysis Using Fine-Grained Parameter Estimation and Hypothesis Testing

Wei Huang[1(✉)] and Xianfeng Zhao[2,3]

[1] Software School, Xiamen University, Xiamen 361005, China
whuang@xmu.edu.cn
[2] State Key Laboratory of Information Security,
Institute of Information Engineering, Chinese Academy of Sciences,
Beijing 100093, China
zhaoxianfeng@iie.ac.cn
[3] University of Chinese Academy of Sciences, Beijing 100049, China

Abstract. Despite the state-of-the-art steganalysis can detect highly undetectable steganography, it is too unreliable to implement in the real world due to its false alarm rate. In pooled steganalysis scenario, multiple objects are intercepted and a reliable collective decision is required. To control the reliability, the confidence intervals of the detectors' false rates are estimated as a parameter and hypothesis testing technology is used to determine the threshold of stego rates. In view of the fact that the false rate is vulnerable to some image properties (e.g. image size, and texture complexity), we propose a novel fine-grained scheme where test sets are divided by its texture measure in both parameter estimation and hypothesis testing processes. The demonstration on public image sets shows the proposed scheme achieves higher reliability in most cases. It confirms that the priori knowledge of image properties is conductive to a accurate threshold and reliable decision.

Keywords: Steganalysis · Steganography · Parameter estimation · Hypothesis testing

1 Introduction

Steganography [1–3] refers to the art and science of concealing messages into mainstream media. Its contrast, steganalysis, is the technology of distinguishing the steganographic behavior from innocent communication. Nowadays, it is convenient for users to hide messages via steganographic tools. However, steganalysis is rather difficult. Although many features [4,5] and classifiers [6,7] for steganalysis have been raised, they are too unreliable to implement because their false alarm rates are not negligible [8,9]. When it alarms, the warden is still at risk to stop the innocent communication because there is a large amount of data transmission in the daily life.

Batch steganography and pooled steganalysis scenario is firstly discussed by Ker [8]. A criminal, Alice, hides information into multiple images on the computer via steganography. Because she is allowed to arbitrarily spread the payload

© Springer International Publishing AG 2017
Y.Q. Shi et al. (Eds.): IWDW 2016, LNCS 10082, pp. 550–563, 2017.
DOI: 10.1007/978-3-319-53465-7_41

among multiple cover objects [10], her disks contain steganographic images as well as innocent ones. So, she can deny the existence of steganography. A warden, Warden, supervises communication and receives a copy of each communicated image. She uses one or more detectors to tell her whether a given image carries hidden messages. Once her collective decision is to accept that the communicated images contain payloads, the communication cannot continue. To simplify the discussion and make the solution general, we suppose a detector outputs its prediction with an observable and predictable accuracy ranging from 0 to 1. As we have known, the detection accuracy of a predictor is particularly affected by many factors [11] which result in inaccurate estimation.

It is reasonable to set up a novel reliable model of multiple communicated objects. In the real world, it is of high importance to have a reliable comprehensive conclusion even if there is an effective steganalysis against a weak steganography. For generality, we discuss the target aware steganalysts, where steganalysts are aware of the cover source and target steganography; otherwise even the outputs of unsupervised methods are not guaranteed if everything is out of control. Supervised classifiers, such as binary classification, quantised steganalysis with a threshold [13], and multi-class classification [14], can be generalised to a binary predictor which indicates steganography exists or not.

In this study, we propose a reliable pooled steganalysis by using fine-grained parameter estimation and hypothesis testing. With the new model of pooled steganalysis where the reliable collective decision must be made, traditional hypothesis testing is utilised to control the false alarm rate. However, steganalysis can also be conditioned by the image properties (e.g. image size, texture complexity, etc.), the estimated false rate is not accurate. To solve this problem, the proposed fine-grained scheme divides the image set into small groups by their properties and tests the image respectively, so as to raise the detection accuracy. Experimental results on public image sets confirm our analysis that the fine-grained version is preferable for its high stability in terms of accepting the null hypothesis for innocent communication.

The contribution of this study is as follows. Firstly, the proposed scheme is effective in reliability in the practical pooled steganalysis scene where steganographers can arbitrarily distribute the payloads, and a reliable collective decision must be made. Secondly, the fine-grained version makes good use of the priori knowledge of the image properties and raised the reliability. Thirdly, it is compatible to two-class classification of image steganalysis.

The rest of this paper is organized as follows. Section 2 revisits the related works and the problem definition is stated in Sect. 3. In Sect. 4, the proposed framework of fine-grained parameter estimation and hypothesis testing is listed. Demonstrations and numeric results are presented in Sect. 5. Finally, we conclude and discuss our work in Sect. 6. .

2   Related Works

Researchers [15] listed some important but unanswered questions of steganography and steganalysis. Pooled steganalysis combines evidence from multiple objects to make a collective decision whether steganographic payload exists. Although there have been a lot of discussion in the field of analysing a single sample, there is limited success to move it to multiple samples.

Batch steganography and pooled steganalysis is firstly discussed by Ker [8]. In the discussion, the false negative rate is fixed to 50% so that the concept of medium p-value can be used to determine the threshold. Although three basic steganographic schemes, a classifier with 50% false negative rate may be under a high false positive rate, and it is still not reliable.

Ker [13] then designed a threshold game and found a Nash equilibrium for it. The approach requires a quantised predictor so that thresholds can be determined by medium p-value, and two strategies for steganography are compared. In fact, not all existing features can indicate the payloads. Hence, it is not general enough to apply to most existed detectors.

Hypothesis testing has been used in the field of not only making decisions in pooled steganalysis, but also detecting within single objects. There are some applications: steganalysis against least significant bit (LSB) based steganography [8,13,16,17], theoretical research [18], and the concept of constrained minimax test to improve the ensemble classifiers [19]. However, as far as we have known, using hypothesis testing in pooled steganalysis has not been discussed adequately.

3   Definition of the Problem

The framework of batch steganography and pooled steganalysis is extended from the traditional model for steganography and steganalysis. The steganographer, Alice, is an actor who participates in steganography. She has a set of N cover images, $x_1, x_2, \cdots, x_N$ to arbitrarily choose part of them to embed hidden messages. Thus, the proportion is called stego rate $r = \frac{1}{N} \sum_{i=1}^{N} v_i$, where $v_i \in \{0, 1\}$ denotes whether Alice embeds the message slice in x_i. The warden, Warden, who makes a collective decision whether steganography exists in these images, intercepts all the communicated images and uses a detector D, which outputs $y_i = D(x_i)$ with a false rate of $\varepsilon \in [0, 1]$, to help her. To avoid too many false alarms, she must control the false alarm rate to a certain level (e.g. 5%).

The scenario we use in this study is distinct from the original version [8] in the following constraints. Initially, our goal is to obtain a collective decision without the prior knowledge of steganographers' strategies. Furthermore, our framework does not require a quantised predictor so that any classifier which can distinguish stego objects is compatible with our framework. Finally, the steganography can choose arbitrary strategies besides average distributing payloads or concentrating on one object.

It makes sense to work on supervised classification. To allow training in steganalysis will help improve the design of steganography. Even if we have no idea about the exact scheme that a steganographer uses, we may have a list of suspicious steganographic schemes so that one-versus-rest or multiclass classifiers can be used. Regardless of the type of detector, the result can be viewed as a binary one that follows binomial distribution. In supervised classification, there are three stages: training, validation and testing stages. In the training stage, Warden prepares a set of cover images $\mathbf{c} = \{c_i\}$ and generates the stego texts $\mathbf{s} = \{s_i\}$ so as to train the classifiers. After that, the validation stage tests the detection accuracy of a predictor. The testing stage is tantamount to put the detector into use. In this stage, the scheme has to output a comprehensive decision with a low false alarm rate.

4   Implementation of Proposed Pooled Steganalysis

4.1   Parameter Estimation of Detection Error

In the validation stage, Warden estimates the detection error of the detector. Although the exact value of the detection error ε is unknown, it can be estimated by preparing a set of samples. Let the observed size of error samples be

$$e = \sum_{i=1}^{n_{\mathbf{c}}} \mathbb{I}\left(D\left(c_i\right) \neq 0\right) + \sum_{i=1}^{n_{\mathbf{s}}} \mathbb{I}\left(D\left(s_i\right) = 0\right) \tag{1}$$

with the indicator function $\mathbb{I}$, the size of cover objects $n_{\mathbf{c}}$ and the one of stego objects $n_{\mathbf{s}}$. Assuming detecting results are independent, the number of error e follows binomial distribution $e \sim \mathrm{Bi}(n, \varepsilon)$, i.e.,

$$\Pr\left(e; n, \varepsilon\right) = \binom{n}{e} \varepsilon^e (1 - \varepsilon)^{n-e}, \tag{2}$$

where $n = n_{\mathbf{c}} + n_{\mathbf{s}}$ and $\binom{n}{e}$ is the combination number. Then, the maximum likelihood estimation (MLE) of ε is the solution of $\frac{\partial \ln \Pr(e)}{\partial \varepsilon} = \frac{e}{\varepsilon} - \frac{n-e}{1-\varepsilon} = 0$, i.e. $\hat{\varepsilon} = \frac{e}{n}$. Such an estimation is unbiased because its expected value $\mathrm{E}\left(\hat{\varepsilon}\right) = \mathrm{E}\left(\frac{e}{n}\right) = \frac{\mathrm{E}(e)}{n} = \frac{n\varepsilon}{n} = \varepsilon$ equals ε. Moreover, the variance of $\hat{\varepsilon}$ is $\mathrm{Var}\left(\hat{\varepsilon}\right) = \frac{\mathrm{Var}(e)}{n^2} = \frac{n\varepsilon(1-\varepsilon)}{n^2} = \frac{\varepsilon(1-\varepsilon)}{n}$.

Because e is binomially distributed, the confidence interval of ε can be calculated from cumulative distribution function (CDF) of e. Thanks to Copper and Pearson's work [20], the 95% confidence intervals $[\varepsilon_1, \varepsilon_2]$ of estimated false rates $\hat{\varepsilon}$ can be found in Fig. 1. In the figure, the length of the confidence interval decreases as the sample size increases. Thus, we suggest $n \geq 1000$ so that the length of confidence interval is no larger than 0.1 for all estimations.

By using MLE, the false rate ε of the detector D is estimated by randomly selecting a large amount of samples and then its bound is used in the testing stages. The steganalyst may have multiple detectors with different accuracies. It can also be viewed as a detector has different performance in different situations. Under the circumstances, the estimation must be proceeded on each detector.

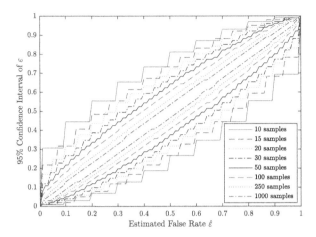

Fig. 1. The 95% confidence intervals of estimated false rate $\hat{\varepsilon}$ as a binomially distributed variable.

4.2   Hypothesis Testing of Pooled Steganalysis

Hypothesis testing is a statistical inference method of testing when the process is modeled via a set of variables. It is used to infer the population from a sample. With the assumption that the cover source is known, we viewed the cover source as the population and the communicated object is a sample that Alice selected. If she has no priori knowledge of the properties which influence detection accuracy, the sample is almost randomly selected. Therefore, it serves to obtain a reliable result from unreliable predictors. Normally, Warden has to decide on the following decision:

$$\begin{cases} H_0 : r = 0; \\ H_1 : r > 0. \end{cases}$$

Using these hypotheses, a reliable steganalytic system is defined. For innocent users, it is expected to accept H_0 at a predetermined high probability $1 - \alpha$; while for steganographers, the probability of failure to reject H_0 is expected to below.

Under the null hypothesis, the stego rate r is supposed to be 0, i.e., for any i, $v_i = 0$. Therefore, the observed size of positive samples $\sum y_i$ is equal to that of error samples $\sum \mathbb{I}(y_i \neq v_i)$. Since confidence interval is defined as the bounds of sampling error, H_0 cannot be rejected only when positive rate (as well as the observed error rate) $r' = \frac{\sum_{i=1}^{N} y_i}{N}$ falls in the confidence interval $[T_1, T_2]$ with a false rate of ε under a predefined error percentile α.

Due to the computational complexity, the approximation of confidence interval is used. The confidence interval can be directly calculated by CDF of binomial distribution, however, it requires a lot of computation. Researchers have provided some approximations on confidence interval for binomial distribution. One of the most commonly used approximation is normal approximation interval [21].

As it suggests, when $N\varepsilon > 5$, $N(1 - \varepsilon) > 5$ and $\varepsilon < 0.5$, the bounds of confidence interval approximate

$$T_1(N, \varepsilon) = \varepsilon - z_{\frac{\alpha}{2}}\sqrt{\frac{1}{N}\varepsilon(1 - \varepsilon)}, T_2(N, \varepsilon) = \varepsilon + z_{\frac{\alpha}{2}}\sqrt{\frac{1}{N}\varepsilon(1 - \varepsilon)}, \qquad (3)$$

with the confidence level $(1 - \alpha)$. Normally, we set $\alpha = 0.05$ with standard normal quantiles $z_{\frac{\alpha}{2}} \approx 1.96$ in the lookup table.

4.3 Factors that Affect Estimations

Intuitively, there are two factors that affect estimations on the confidence interval $[T_1, T_2]$: sample size N and false rate ε. The sample size N affects estimations from the aspect of statistical stability. Under the same stego rate, larger size is more likely to expose. Besides, the false rate ε decides upon both the center and length of the confidence interval. Accurate detectors are preferred to a detector that is not much better than randomly guessing.

From Eq. (3), we know ε is the center of T_1 and T_2, and N affects their difference. In particular, the range of the confidence interval $T_2 - T_1 = 2z_{\frac{\alpha}{2}}\sqrt{\frac{1}{N}\varepsilon(1 - \varepsilon)}$ is inversely proportional to $\sqrt{N}$.

Different from sample size N which is public knowledge to steganalysis, the false rate ε is unknown and it requires estimation. Steganalysts have to estimate the false rates of the detectors before they are used, while steganographers can still roughly estimate it to select a secure stego rate.

4.4 Factors that Affect Strategies

The steganographers' and steganalysts' strategies selection is a trade-off among sample size N, false rate ε and stego rate r. A secure stego rate r_0 is a threshold for Alice to control her payloads, so that for any $r < r_0$, Warden cannot reject the null hypothesis H_0 if she wants to control the false alarm rate below α. In the average sense, $Nr(1 - \varepsilon)$ stego images will be recognised as positive samples correctly, while $N(1 - r)\varepsilon$ cover samples will be predicted as positive samples mistakenly. So, averagely $N[r(1 - \varepsilon) + (1 - r)\varepsilon]$ samples are predictive as positive samples by a detector with a false rate of ε, and the other $N[r\varepsilon + (1 - r)(1 - \varepsilon)]$ ones will be predicted as negative. If H_0 cannot be rejected, the positive rate $r' = r(1 - \varepsilon) + (1 - r)\varepsilon \in [T_1, T_2]$. Thus, a secure stego rate must satisfy

$$r < r_0 = \frac{T_2 - \varepsilon}{1 - 2\varepsilon} = \frac{z_{\frac{\alpha}{2}}\sqrt{\frac{1}{N}\varepsilon(1 - \varepsilon)}}{1 - 2\varepsilon} = \frac{z_{\frac{\alpha}{2}}}{2\sqrt{N}} \cdot \sqrt{\frac{1}{(1 - 2\varepsilon)^2}} - 1, \qquad (4)$$

where r_0 is the upper bound of stego rates. If Alice chooses any $r < r_0$, it is secure enough to have $r' < T_2$ so that Warden cannot reject H_0. As for the lower bound T_1, the conclusion $r \geq 0$ is trivial. Moreover, there is approximately "square root law" $r_0 \propto N^{-\frac{1}{2}}$ in Eq. (4). If Alice wants to use more images, the

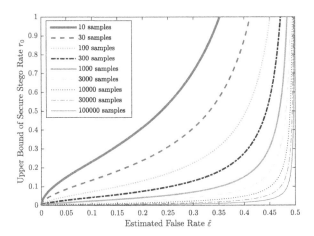

Fig. 2. The relation between approximately secure stego rate r_0 and false rate ε.

secure stego rate will decrease accordingly. The false rate ε affects the threshold in hypothesis testing when Warden makes decisions. For steganalysts, the error in estimating false rate will result in a shift, but the length of confidence interval will be slightly affected when N is large (e.g. $N \geq 100$).

The maximum false rate ε_0 is a threshold above which Warden cannot detect any stego rate $r \geq r_0$ under the given false alarm rate constrain. From another perspective of Eq. (4), if the minimum detected stego rate r_0 and sample size N are known, such a detector cannot provide a reliable prediction if its false rate $\varepsilon \geq \varepsilon_0 = \frac{1}{2} \cdot \left[1 - \left(4N z_{\frac{\alpha}{2}}^{-2} r_0^2 + 1 \right)^{-\frac{1}{2}} \right]$. So, any detector with false rate $\varepsilon > \varepsilon_0$ should be ignored.

The relation between approximately secure stego rate r_0 and the false rate ε is plotted graphically as shown in Fig. 2. The graph illustrates the upper bound of r_0 theoretically. Although ε is unknown to Warden and others, the confidence interval $(\varepsilon_1, \varepsilon_2)$ can be estimated in the validation stage. In Eq. (4), r_0 is advanced with the growth of $\hat{\varepsilon}$. This monotonicity tells that it is significant for Warden to make the detector more accurate. Fortunately, she has a lot of time and computing capacity to prepare.

4.5   Effectiveness of Dividing Images into Small Subsets

It is the key point of a good estimation on false rate in making decision for both steganographers and steganalysts, however, it is difficult because of the lack of stability of a detector. Existed detectors, which use statistical approaches, are easily influenced by some factors. If we utilise this priori knowledge, the estimation will be more accurate. As far as our knowledge, there are mainly two factors proposed: image size [11] and macro characteristics. Nevertheless, additional factors may be disclosed in the future.

Highleyman [22] derived the bound of pattern recognition experimentation. Let m represent the number of the classes that the test set is divided into. In each class ω_i, e_i is the amount of error prediction, and n_i is the sample size. On the assumption that ε_i is independent, the joint distribution of e_i is derived from Eq. (2), i.e.,

$$\Pr(e_1, e_2, \cdots, e_m) = \prod_{i=1}^{m} \Pr(e_i; n_i, \varepsilon_i) = \prod_{i=1}^{m} \binom{n_i}{e_i} \varepsilon_i^{e_i} (1 - \varepsilon_i)^{n_i - e_i}.$$

For each i, the MLE of ε_i can be solved from $\frac{\partial \ln \Pr(e_i)}{\partial \varepsilon_i} = \frac{e_i}{\varepsilon_i} - \frac{n_i - e_i}{1 - \varepsilon_i} = 0$, and $\hat{\varepsilon}_i = \frac{e_i}{n_i}$ is obtained. The estimation of the total false rate $\hat{\varepsilon}' = \sum_{i=1}^{m} \Pr(\omega_i) \hat{\varepsilon}_i$ is the weighted sum of error, where $\Pr(\omega_i)$ is the priori probability of class i. Its expectation $\mathrm{E}(\hat{\varepsilon}') = \sum_{i=1}^{m} P(\omega_i) \mathrm{E}(\hat{\varepsilon}_i) = \sum_{i=1}^{m} P(\omega_i) \varepsilon_i = \varepsilon$. turns out to be unbiased, and its variance $\mathrm{Var}(\hat{\varepsilon}') = \frac{1}{n} \sum_{i=1}^{m} P(\omega_i) \varepsilon_i (1 - \varepsilon_i)$ is the weighted sum of each $\mathrm{Var}(\hat{\varepsilon}_i)$. Noting that $\sum_{i=1}^{m} \Pr(\omega) = 1$, the difference between two variances is

$$\mathrm{Var}(\hat{\varepsilon}) - \mathrm{Var}(\hat{\varepsilon}') = \frac{1}{n} \left[\varepsilon(1 - \varepsilon) - \sum_{i=1}^{m} \Pr(\omega_i) \varepsilon_i (1 - \varepsilon_i) \right]$$

$$= \frac{1}{n} \left[\sum_{i=1}^{m} P(\omega_i) \varepsilon_i^2 + \varepsilon^2 \sum_{i=1}^{m} \Pr(\omega_i) - 2\varepsilon \sum_{i=1}^{m} \Pr(\omega_i) \varepsilon_i \right]$$

$$= \frac{1}{n} \sum_{i=1}^{m} P(\omega_i) (\varepsilon_i - \varepsilon)^2 \geq 0.$$

Therefore, $\hat{\varepsilon}'$ is a preferable estimation to $\hat{\varepsilon}$ for its lower variances.

Even so, it is not always advantageous to divide the entire sample set into small classes. As the validation set of images is separated, there is a decline in sample size and the estimated false rate $\hat{\varepsilon}'$ may be inaccurate. However, steganography and steganalysis are in a game. Nevertheless, steganographers can perform cover selection by which different classes of images do not have the same stego rate. In this situation, the fine-grained strategy is effective.

4.6   Proposed Framework

To raise the accuracy of false rate estimation, we modify the general hypothesis testing approach by adding links of dividing images into specific classes. The new framework has two stages: the validation stage and the testing stage. The framework of validation stage is listed in Algorithm 1. In the validation stage, which requires to run only once and will use in the future, the goal is to calculate confidence intervals of estimated false rate. Then, this information is used to determine the threshold in the testing stage. The framework of testing stage is

Algorithm 1. Framework of the validation stage of fine-grained hypothesis testing based steganalysis.

Input: A large set of cover images $c = \{c_i\}$ and stego images $s = \{s_i\}$ where s_i is generated by concealing messages in c_i using target steganographic algorithms; A detector, D, which outputs a binary decision $y_i = D(x_i) \in \{0, 1\}$; A metric $\phi(x)$ measuring properties of images.

Output: Confidence intervals of estimated false rate $\left[\varepsilon_1^{(k)}, \varepsilon_2^{(k)}\right]$, and thresholds $\left\{t^{(k)}\right\}$ for class division where $k = 1, 2, \cdots, m$.

1. Calculate the metric $\phi(x)$ of any image x in the validation sets c, s.
2. Divide the set $\{\phi(x), x \in c \cup s\}$ into m classes so that each class contains no less than 100 images. For any image $x \in x^{(k)}$, the metric $\phi(x) \in \left(t^{(k-1)}, t^{(k)}\right]$ where $t^{(0)} = -\infty$.
3. Use $x^{(k)}$ to validate the detector, and calculate the amount of error samples $e^{(k)}$ by Eq. (1).
4. The confidence interval $\hat{\varepsilon}^{(k)}$ in the class $x^{(k)}$, $\left[\varepsilon_1^{(k)}, \varepsilon_2^{(k)}\right]$ is obtained using Fig. 1 or the approximated CDF.

Algorithm 2. Framework of testing stage of fine-grained hypothesis testing based steganalysis.

Input: A sequence of test images, $x = \{x_1, x_2, \cdots, x_N\}$; A detector, D, which outputs a binary decision $y_i = D(x_i) \in \{0, 1\}$; A metric $\phi(x)$ measuring images; Confidence intervals of estimated false rate $\left[\varepsilon_1^{(k)}, \varepsilon_2^{(k)}\right]$, and thresholds $\left\{t^{(k)}\right\}$ obtained from Algorithm 1.

Output: The collective decision $d \in \{0, 1\}$ indicating the acceptance of hypothesis H_d.

1. Divide the test set x into m classes $\left\{x^{(k)}\right\}, k = 1, 2, \cdots, m$, so that for any image $x \in x^{(k)}$, $\phi(x) \in \left(t^{(k-1)}, t^{(k)}\right], t^{(0)} = -\infty$. The size of class $x^{(k)}$ is $N^{(k)}$.
2. Detect each image and get the binary decision $y_i = D(x_i)$.
3. Compute the positive rate $r'^{(k)} = \frac{1}{N^{(k)}} \sum_{x_i \in x^{(k)}} y_i$ of each class.
4. Calculate the confidence interval $T_1'^{(k)} = \min\left[T_1\left(N^{(k)}, \hat{\varepsilon}_1^{(k)}\right), T_1\left(N^{(k)}, \hat{\varepsilon}_2^{(k)}\right)\right]$, $T_2'^{(k)} = \max\left[T_2\left(N^{(k)}, \hat{\varepsilon}_1^{(k)}\right), T_2\left(N^{(k)}, \hat{\varepsilon}_2^{(k)}\right)\right]$ by Eq. (3).
5. If there is any $r'^{(k)} \notin \left[T_1'^{(k)}, T_2'^{(k)}\right]$, assign d to 1; otherwise, assign d to 0.

---

shown in Algorithm 2. Its motivation is to obtain the collective decision. In these two stages, both set of images is divided by their properties so that detailed information can play its role. Furthermore, there is no requirement to have a unique detector for all sorts of images, and in most cases detectors can be invoked by properties of the image.

5   Demonstrations

This section contains some demonstrations using the image databases BOSSBase v0.92 (9,074 images) and BOSSRank (1,000 images) [23], which are filled with 512×512 grey-scale innocent images. The stego images are generated using three of modern steganographic schemes (HUGO [1], WOW [2], S-UNIWARD [3]), through embedding randomly generated bytes of embedding rates 0.1, 0.2, 0.3 and 0.4 bpp (bit per pixel). Furthermore, the maxSRM features [5] are extracted from each image and the low-complexity linear classifier [7] is used to output a binary prediction. These detectors are trained by BOSSBase and proposed methods are tested on randomly selected images in BOSSRank.

Because the influences of image size [11] is well studied, in this demonstration we merely focus on macro characteristics, which is open to both steganographers and steganalysts. One of the effective measurement in modern spatial steganography is the second ordered linear pixel prediction error (LPE) [12]. Thus, the image set is divided into an equal amount of two halves by median ranking: low LPE images and high LPE images. To test the fine-grained parameter estimation, the false rate are tested by parameter estimation, and those of randomly selected images (without using prior knowledge of LPE), low-LPE and high-LPE are shown in Table 1. In the table, low-LPE images always have much lower false rates and this phenomenon is stable.

After the false rates of the classifiers in different classes are successfully estimated, we demonstrate the case of Warden's intercepting a set of n images. The proportion of low-LPE images ρ is randomly determined. So, it contains $200(1 - \rho)$ high-LPE images and 200ρ low-LPE images. Each stego rate r is tested in 20,000 rounds. The reliability is defined as probability that the null hypothesis cannot be rejected (PrNH).

Some of the results are recorded in Table 2. The cases of innocent users ($r = 0$) listed shows that fine-grained methods has lower false alarm rate than general hypothesis testing. In these typical cases, the result of fine-grained hypothesis testing is more reliable so that when it alarms, it is very likely that steganography exists. The table also shows cases of stego communication, and in most cases, fine-grained methods accept the null hypothesis with a smaller probability.

Table 1. Estimated false rates and confidence intervals of general, low- and high-LPE cases.

Emb. Rate	General			Low LPE			High LPE		
	$\hat{\varepsilon}$	$\hat{\varepsilon}_1$	$\hat{\varepsilon}_2$	$\hat{\varepsilon}$	$\hat{\varepsilon}_1$	$\hat{\varepsilon}_2$	$\hat{\varepsilon}$	$\hat{\varepsilon}_1$	$\hat{\varepsilon}_2$
0.10	0.384	0.354	0.415	0.299	0.260	0.340	0.470	0.426	0.513
0.20	0.313	0.284	0.341	0.185	0.153	0.221	0.440	0.397	0.483
0.30	0.239	0.213	0.266	0.110	0.085	0.140	0.368	0.326	0.411
0.40	0.174	0.151	0.198	0.052	0.035	0.075	0.296	0.257	0.337

Table 2. Comparison of PrNH of general and fine-grained hypothesis testings under different conditions.

Stego Algo.	Emb. Rate	Stego Rate	PrNH			
			Cover (HT)	Stego (HT)	Cover (FG)	Stego (FG)
HUGO	0.10	0.500	0.952	0.301	0.987	0.211
HUGO	0.20	0.400	0.741	0.269	0.991	0.147
HUGO	0.30	0.300	0.710	0.244	0.990	0.097
HUGO	0.40	0.160	0.690	0.509	0.988	0.211
WOW	0.10	0.900	0.986	0.326	0.991	0.178
WOW	0.20	0.400	0.967	0.424	0.988	0.239
WOW	0.30	0.400	0.844	0.187	0.991	0.125
WOW	0.40	0.300	0.743	0.327	0.989	0.162
S-UNIWARD	0.10	0.600	0.981	0.663	0.980	0.697
S-UNIWARD	0.20	0.400	0.863	0.346	0.969	0.277
S-UNIWARD	0.30	0.400	0.779	0.293	0.990	0.113
S-UNIWARD	0.40	0.300	0.712	0.479	0.989	0.215

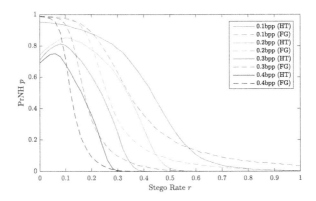

Fig. 3. Probability that H_0 cannot be rejected in different stego rates (200 samples).

The relation between stego rate r and PrNH p is tested using 200 images and the experiment is repeated in 20,000 rounds. In each round, the proportion of low-LPE images is not constant. The result is plotted in Fig. 3. The solid (or dashed) lines present HUGO steganography and from top right to bottom left embedding rates are 0.1 bpp to 0.4 bpp. General hypothesis tests are labeled as HT, while fine-grained hypothesis testing approach is labeled as FG. For innocent users whose stego rate r is 0, PrNH p is close to 1. It is important to keep silent under the null hypothesis H_0 when innocent users are in communication. Fine-grained scheme is preferred to general hypothesis test when $r = 0$ because their PrNH is higher. Although LPE measurement is open to public, general hypothesis testing does not use this priori knowledge. Therefore, this disadvantage causes its inaccuracy in estimating false rates. We repeat the experiment

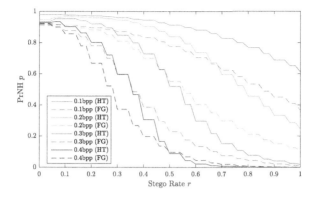

Fig. 4. Probability that H_0 cannot be rejected in different stego rates (20 samples).

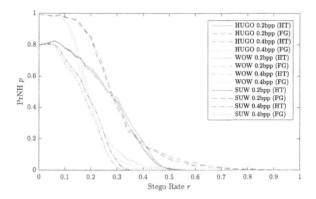

Fig. 5. Probability that H_0 cannot be rejected when target steganographic schemes and embedding rates are not exactly known (200 samples).

by reducing the image size of test set to 20, and the result is shown in Fig. 4. Similar to the 200-image case, the fine-grained hypothesis testing is preferred to general hypothesis testing. Although statistical stability is weaker as the sample size reduced, in the same stego rate, fine-grained hypothesis testing attains a much lower PrNH than general method.

We can also see "square root law" of pooled steganalysis in Figs. 3 and 4. Let us take HUGO 0.4 bpp as an example. If the stego rate is $r = 0.35$ and the image size $n = 20$, the possibility of no alarm is almost 22%. This number r declined to 0.12 as the image amount goes up to 200.

The proposed fine-grain approach is also effective when target steganography is not exactly known. Similar to the conditions in multi-class steganalysis [14], it is reasonable to suppose that the steganalyst knows the set of suspicious steganographic schemes. So, the cover and stego sets (HUGO, WOW and S-UNIWARD in 0.2 bpp and 0.4 bpp respectively) are mixed to train the linear classifier. Then, the estimated false rate is calculated to obtain the confidence intervals as well as the thresholds. As a result, the relation of stego rate r and PrNH p are plotted in Fig. 5. As the figure shows, fine-grained hypothesis testing raised the probability to correctly recognise innocent users. Its PrNH p is close to 1 and much higher than general hypothesis testing. For stego users, proposed fine-grained method has much lower PrNH and is more likely to reject steganographic users. Hence, we can safely conclude that the effectiveness of fine-grained method exists when target steganography is not exactly known.

6   Conclusions and Discussions

In the novel pooled steganalysis scenario, where a comprehensive conclusion is required, it is beneficial to control the false alarm rate to a certain level. To make it controllable, we proposed a framework for pooled steganalysis using fine-grained parameter estimation and hypothesis testing. In the framework, the validation and test sets are split into classes by their characteristics to obtain an accurate prediction. Numeric results from public database confirm our analysis that fine-grained hypothesis testing achieves a reliable and stable result in most cases.

In the future work, we would like to study the bounds under different situations, including quantitative steganalysis where embedding rates are arbitrary selected, and unsupervised steganalysis where steganographic schemes are completely unknown.

Acknowledgments. This work was supported by the National Natural Science Foundation of China (Grant No. 61402390), the National Key Technology R&D Program (Grant No. 2014BAH41B01), and the Strategic Priority Research Program of Chinese Academy of Sciences (Grant No. XDA06030600).

References

1. Pevný, T., Filler, T., Bas, P.: Using high-dimensional image models to perform highly undetectable steganography. In: Böhme, R., Fong, P.W.L., Safavi-Naini, R. (eds.) IH 2010. LNCS, vol. 6387, pp. 161–177. Springer, Heidelberg (2010). doi:10. 1007/978-3-642-16435-4_13
2. Holub, V., Fridrich, J.: Designing steganographic distortion using directional filters. In: IEEE Int'l Workshop on Information Forensics and Security (WIFS 2012), pp. 234–239. IEEE Press, New York (2012)
3. Holub, V., Fridrich, J.: Digital image steganography using universal distortion. In: ACM IH&MMSec 2013, pp. 59–68. ACM, New York (2013)
4. Pevný, T., Bas, P., Fridrich, J.: Steganalysis by subtractive pixel adjacency matrix. IEEE Trans. Inf. Forensics Secur. **5**(2), 215–224 (2010)
5. Denemark, T., Sedighi, V., Holub, V., Cogranne, R., Fridrich, J.: Selection-channel-aware rich model for steganalysis of digital images. In: IEEE WIFS 2014, pp. 48–53. IEEE Press, New York (2014)
6. Chang, C.C., Lin, C.J.: LIBSVM: a library for support vector machines. ACM Trans. Intell. Syst. Technol. **2**(3), 1–27 (2001)

7. Cogranne, R., Sedighi, V., Fridrich, J., Pevný, T.: Is ensemble classifier needed for steganalysis in high-dimensional feature spaces?. In: IEEE WIFS 2015, pp. 1–6. IEEE Press, New York (2015)
8. Ker, A.D.: Batch steganography and pooled steganalysis. In: Camenisch, J.L., Collberg, C.S., Johnson, N.F., Sallee, P. (eds.) IH 2006. LNCS, vol. 4437, pp. 265–281. Springer, Heidelberg (2007). doi:10.1007/978-3-540-74124-4_18
9. Pevný, T., Ker, A.D.: Towards dependable steganalysis. In: Proceedings of Media Watermarking, Security, and Forensics 2015. SPIE, vol. 9409, pp. 94090I–94090I (2015)
10. Ker, A.D.: Perturbation hiding and the batch steganography problem. In: Solanki, K., Sullivan, K., Madhow, U. (eds.) IH 2008. LNCS, vol. 5284, pp. 45–59. Springer, Heidelberg (2008). doi:10.1007/978-3-540-88961-8_4
11. Böhme, R.: Assessment of steganalytic methods using multiple regression models. In: Barni, M., Herrera-Joancomartí, J., Katzenbeisser, S., Pérez-González, F. (eds.) IH 2005. LNCS, vol. 3727, pp. 278–295. Springer, Heidelberg (2005). doi:10.1007/11558859_21
12. Huang, W., Zhao, X.: Novel cover selection criterion for spatial steganography using linear pixel prediction error. Sci. Chin. Inf. Sci. **59**(5), 05910301–05910303 (2016)
13. Ker, A.D.: Batch steganography and the threshold game. In: Proceedings of the International Society for Optical Engineering. SPIE, vol. 6505, pp. 650504–650504 (2007)
14. Pevný, T., Fridrich, J.: Multiclass detector of current steganographic methods for JPEG format. IEEE Trans. Inf. Forensics Secur. **3**(4), 635–650 (2008)
15. Ker, A.D., Bas, P., Böhme, R., Cogranne, R., Craver, S., Filler, T., Fridrich, J., Pevný, T.: Moving steganography and steganalysis from the laboratory into the real world. In: First ACM Workshop on Information Hiding & Multimedia Security (IH&MMSec 2013), pp. 45–58 (2013)
16. Dabeer, O., Sullivan, K., Madhow, U., Chandrasekaran, S.: Detection of hiding in the least significant bit. IEEE Trans. Sig. Proc. **52**(10), 3046–3058 (2004)
17. Qiao, T., Retraint, F., Cogranne, R., Zitzmann, C.: Steganalysis of JSteg algorithm using hypothesis testing theory. EURASIP J. Inf. Secur. **1**, 1–16 (2015)
18. Cachin, C.: An information-theoretic model for steganography. In: Aucsmith, D. (ed.) IH 1998. LNCS, vol. 1525, pp. 306–318. Springer, Heidelberg (1998). doi:10.1007/3-540-49380-8_21
19. Cogranne, R., Fridrich, J.: Modeling and extending the ensemble classifier for steganalysis of digital images using hypothesis testing theory. IEEE Trans. Inf. Forensics Secur. **10**(12), 2627–2642 (2015)
20. Clopper, C.J., Pearson, E.S.: The use of confidence or fiducial limits illustrated in the case of the binomial. Biometrika **26**(4), 404–413 (1934)
21. Brown, L.D., Cai, T.T., DasGupta, A.: Interval estimation for a binomial proportion. Stat. Sci. **16**(2), 101–117 (2001)
22. Highleyman, W.H.: The design and analysis of pattern recognition experiments. Bell Syst. Tech. J. **41**(2), 723–744 (1962)
23. Bas, P., Filler, T., Pevný, T.: "Break our steganographic system": the ins and outs of organizing BOSS. In: Filler, T., Pevný, T., Craver, S., Ker, A. (eds.) IH 2011. LNCS, vol. 6958, pp. 59–70. Springer, Heidelberg (2011). doi:10.1007/978-3-642-24178-9_5

Deep Learning on Spatial Rich Model
for Steganalysis

Xiaoyu Xu, Yifeng Sun$^{(\boxtimes)}$, Guangming Tang, Shiyuan Chen, and Jian Zhao

Institute of Information Science and Technology, Zhengzhou 450001, China
yfsun001@163.com

Abstract. Recent studies have indicated that deep learning for steganalysis may be a tendency in future. The paper novelly proposes a faeture-based deep learning classifier for steganalysis. Analysis shows SRM features are suitable to be the input of deep learning. On this basis, a modified convolutional neural network (CNN) is designed for detection. In the initial layers, taking the thought of ensemble classifier for reference, we extract L subspaces of the entire SRM feature space, and process each subspace respectively. In the deeper layers, two different structures are designed. One is complex in structure and hard to train, but achieve better detection accuracy; the other is simple in structure and easy to train, but the achieved detection accuracy is a little worse. Experiments show that the proposed method achieves comparable performance on BOSSbase compared to GNCNN and ensemble classifier with SRM features.

Keywords: Deep learning · Steganalysis · CNN · RandomData

1 Introduction

Deep learning has been extensively studied in the last decade. It allows computational models that are composed of multiple processing layers to learn representations of data with multiple levels of abstraction [1]. CNN (convolutional neuro network) [2] is a branch of deep learning. It has much fewer connections and parameters, so it is easier to train, while its theoretically-best performance is likely to be only slightly worse [3]. So far, CNN has achieved remarkable success in classification tasks, such as Alexnet [3], DeepID-net [4].

In essence, steganalysis is a task of binary classification problem. The purpose is to detect whether the image is cover or stego. Therefore, deep learning for steganalysis tends to be a hot topic of study in future. At present, the main solution to steganalysis is still the steganalysis features combining with a conventional machine learning classifier, for example, [5–10]. The published papers of deep learning for steganalysis are only a few [11–14]. Tan and Li [11] firstly proposed a CNN for steganalysis which comprises three stages of alternating convolutional and max pooling layers, and sigmoid nonlinear activations. They involved a high-pass kernel [7,15] into parameter initialization of the first convolutional layer,

© Springer International Publishing AG 2017
Y.Q. Shi et al. (Eds.): IWDW 2016, LNCS 10082, pp. 564–577, 2017.
DOI: 10.1007/978-3-319-53465-7_42

and pretraining all of the parameters with unsupervised learning. Qian et al. [12] presented a CNN equipped with a high-pass filtering (HPF) layer, Gaussian non-linear activations, and average pooling for steganalysis. The reported detection error rates of CNNs proposed by Tan and Qian are still inferior to that of SRM with ensemble classifiers. However, along this direction, Xu et al. [14] proposed a CNN that tries to incorporate the knowledge of steganalysis. The reported detection error rates are 1%–4% lower than those achieved by the SRM with ensemble classifiers on the BOSSbase when detecting S-UNIWARD [16] and HILL [17]. This is a significant boost in performance.

CNNs were used directly on spatial noise residual images for steganalysis [12,14]. However the noise residual is too weak for distinguishing cover and stego. If a more powerful signal is used as the input of a designed CNN, it may be more suitable for steganalysis. SRM (Spatial Rich Model) [7] is steganalysis features which reflects the difference between cover and stego better than spatial noise residual images. This paper proposes a deep learning classifier using SRM features as the input of a designed CNN. Applying the thought of ensemble classifier [18] on CNN, a layer called RandomData is proposed and placed at the very beginning to produce L subspaces of the entire SRM feature space. Then each subspace is processed respectively. The random data layer is the key to improving the performance of detection. Using operation such as ReLU [19], Convolution, Dropout [20], FullConnection, the deeper layers take the advantages of deep learning. We propose two different structures for deep processing. One is complex in structure and hard to train, but achieve better detection accuracy; the other is simple in structure and easy to train, but the achieved detection accuracy is a little worse. Experiments show the performance of our designed method approach to the state-of-the-art.

2   Analysis of Deep Learning for Steganalysis

2.1   Neural Network and Deep Learning

In its most general form, a neural network is a machine designed to model the way in which the brain performs a particular task or function of interest. A stand neural net-work consists of many simple, connected processors called neurons. The neuron k can be described as the following equation:

$$y_k = \phi(\sum_{j=1}^{m} \omega_{kj}x_j + b_k) \qquad (1)$$

where $x_1, x_2, \cdots x_m$ are the inputs, which come from the raw input data or may be the outputs of other neurons; $\omega_{k1}, \omega_{k2}, \cdots, \omega_{km}$ is the respective weights; b_k is the bias; $\phi(\cdot)$ is the activation function; y_k is the output of neuron k.

A neural network may have deep hierarchical structure. It is usually called as deep neural network (DNN). In DNN, the first layer is composed of the raw multi-dimensional input data units. The following layers are made of neurons, which transform the lower level data (starting with the raw input data) into a data representation at a higher, slightly more abstract level. The last layer neurons consist of the outputs of DNN, which represent the categories of input data in pattern classification problems. Neural network learning refers to finding the proper weights and bias based on a large quantity of samples. Deep learning is the technology about accurately training the weights and bias of neurons across many layers or stages, in order to discovering intricate structures in high-dimensional data.

2.2 Convolutional Neural Networks and Its Application to Steganaysis

Convolutional neural network (CNN) is a kind of deep learning models. A typical CNN is composed of two kinds of layers: the convolutional layer, which usually follows the activation and pooling operation [2], and the inner product layer, which follows the activation operation, as shown in Fig. 1. Convolutional layers combine two architectural ideas: local regions and shared weights. Firstly, using shared weight and local region strategy, convolutional layers have much fewer connections and weight parameters, compared to standard feed forward neural networks. Hence, CNNs are much easier to train, while theoretically-best performance is likely to be only slightly worse [3]. Secondly, convolutional layers perform filtering operations which search some kind of local feature. Hence, CNNs are very suitable for the input data with strong local correlation, such as images. Furthermore, CNNs usually adopt ReLU [3] activation function in neurons which alleviates gradient diffusion problem. So CNNs can have deeper layers which correspond to more abstract level data representation. As a result, CNNs have exhibited excellent performance in many domains of science and business, such as beating records in image recognition [3].

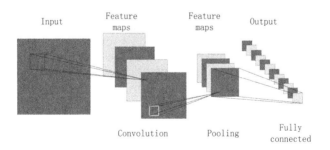

Fig. 1. Convolutional neural network examples

Recently, CNNs are applied to image steganalysis [11–14]. Though CNNs auto-matically extract the abstract level features by training, they still need the data which reflect the difference between different categories. So Qian et al. [12] made a predefined high-pass filtering to the input image, in order to strengthen the weak stego signal and reduce the impact of image content. Denote as the input image, as image after high-pass filtering (also named as noise residual image).

$$R = K * I \tag{2}$$

where the symbol * denotes convolution, and is a shift-invariant finite-impulse response linear filter kernel.

$$K = \frac{1}{12} \begin{pmatrix} -1 & 2 & -2 & 2 & -1 \\ 2 & -6 & 8 & -6 & 2 \\ -2 & 8 & -12 & 8 & -2 \\ 2 & -6 & 8 & -6 & 2 \\ -1 & 2 & -2 & 2 & -1 \end{pmatrix} \tag{3}$$

Then the filtered image is the input layer of CNN, which has five convolutional layers and three fully connected layers (inner product ones). The last fully connected layer has two neurons, which are fed to a two-way softmax activation function, producing a distribution over two class labels: the cover and the stego.

After high-pass filtering, some weak local pixel correlation in filtered image data survives, and the stego signal further destroys the weak correlation. It is the fundamental to distinguish the original image and the stego. But the distinction between the pixel correlations of filtered original image and that of stego image may be too weak. Figure 2 gives an example. The left is the original image, the middle is the filtered original image, and the right is the filtered stego image. Few difference exists between the middle and the right. The impact of image content still obstructs detection. Moreover, only one type of residuals is captured by the filter, and more types can describe the stego signal comprehensively. Maybe there are better choices than the filtered image to be the input of CNNs or other deep neural networks in steganalysis.

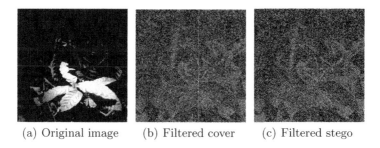

(a) Original image   (b) Filtered cover   (c) Filtered stego

Fig. 2. The filtered image used for the input of CNN

3   Proposed Method

The overall framework of detection can be divided into four general steps, as shown in Fig. 3. Firstly, high-dimension datum of the image are extracted. Secondly, taking the thought of ensemble classifier, L subspaces of the entire datum space are randomly selected. Each subspace is processed with a linear function and a non-linear function. Thirdly, layers of Convolution, ReLU, Dropout, Full-Connection are used in deep processing. Fourthly, a two-way FullConnection combining with softmax outputs the result of detection.

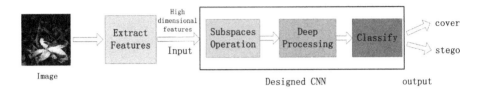

Fig. 3. Overall framework

3.1   High-Dimensional Datum Extraction

We extract high-dimension datum from the image for deep learning. These datum should be suitable for steganalysis. So these datum should represent the difference between stego and cover more remarkably compared with filtered image in Sect. 2.2. The dimension of these extract datum can be high, because neuro networks are able to deal with high-dimension input. Here we adopt SRM [7].

Compared with high-pass filtering operation in [12] (introduced in Sect. 2.2), SRM has two distinct advantages. Firstly, SRM exactly exploits various types of noise residuals with linear and non-linear filters. These noise residuals more comprehensively capture the relationships among neighboring samples. The relationships can be destroyed by embedding operation, which is the fundamental of steganalysis. Secondly, the difference between cover and stego is strengthened by joint distributions (co-occurrence matrices) of neighboring samples from quantized noise residuals.

SRM have high dimensional feature datum, for instance, 34671 dimensions when adopting all three quantization steps. We believe SRM features may be a better choice as the input of deep learning.

3.2   Random Subspaces Based Processing

As we know, the CNNs for image recognition, such as AlexNet, make use of the local correlation of pixels in an image to distinguish objects, such as a cat or a dog. This method is called local regions in convolution operation. However, local correlation of features in SRM feature space may not reflect the difference of cover or stego. Direct use of conventional operation with local regions may not contribute to accuracy of detection. Ensemble classifier is a good solution to SRM. So we imitate ensemble classifier extracting random subspaces (subsets). Datum in each subspace are input of single neuron.

Paper [18] adopt ensemble classifier as shown in Fig. 5. Subspaces are sub-sets of the entire feature space. Each subspace is a input of a base classifier. Base classifiers operate on subspaces and obtain mutual independence results of classification. These results vote for the final result.

Analogously, denote $X = \{x_1, x_2, x_3....x_{34671}\}$ as SRM features. The symbol $d = 34671$ stands for the SRM feature space dimensionality. As shown in Fig. 6, we extract L subspaces (L subsets) of X, as Algorithm RandomData. d_{sub} denotes the dimensionality of the feature subspace. L denotes the number of subspaces. Denote $D_l = \{m_1, m_2, m_3......m_{d_{sub}}\}$ as the lth subspace.

Algorithm *RandomData*:
1:    **for** $l = 1$ **to** L **do**
2:      **for** $d_s = 1$ **to** d_{sub} **do**
3:        select a feature m_{d_s} randomly from feature space of X

$$m_{d_s} \in X, |X| = 34671$$

4:        add the selected m_{d_s} to the subspace D_l

$$f \in D_l, D_l \subset \{1, 2, ..., d\}, |D_l| = d_{sub} \ll d$$

5:      **end for**
6:    **end for**

D_l is input of a neuron. Each subspace, such as D_l, is operated on through expression (4). The result of expression (4) $Y = \{y_1, y_2, y_3, ..., y_L\}$ is input of next layer.

$$y_l = \phi(\sum_{j=1}^{d_{sub}} \omega_{lj} x_{lj} + b_{lj}), l = 1, 2..., L \tag{4}$$

In expression (4), y_l is the result of the lth subspace through computation; is a vector of weight parameter ($|\omega_l| = d_{sub}$), and ω_{lj} is the jth data in ω_l; b_l is a vector of bias parameter ($|b_l| = d_{sub}$), and b_{lj} is the jth data in b_l; x_{lj} is the jth data in the lth subspace. $\phi(.)$ denotes a non-linear function. So the connection between the two layer is not a conventional full-connection but a local-connection, as shown in Fig. 4.

In order to realize the processing above, we add a layer in caffe toolbox [21] called RandomData to produce random-selected subspaces. Following the RandomData layer are a convolutiuon layer and a ReLU layer to perform expression (4) on sub-spaces. In the convolution layer, L different convolutional kernels are used, each convolutional kernel is used on a subspace. That means a bijective mapping between L subspaces and L convolutional kernels. The size of each convolutional kernel is the same as a subspace (global convolution). Expression (5) is the convolutional operation.

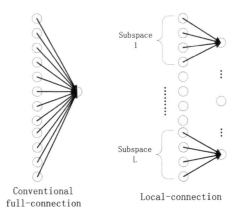

Fig. 4. Comparison between conventional full-connection and local-connection

$$t_l = D_l * C_l = \sum_{i=1}^{d_{sub}} m_l \times x_l, l = 1, 2, 3, ...L \tag{5}$$

In Expression (5), $D_l = \{m_1, m_2, m_3......m_{d_{sub}}\}$ denotes a subspace and $C_l = \{x_1, x_2, x_3......x_{d_{sub}}\}$ is a convolutional kernel, $|D_l| = |C_l| = d_{sub}$. Through convolution layer we obtain L output nodes, $T = \{t_1, t_2, t_3, ..., t_L\}$, which are inputs of ReLU layer. Expression (6) is the ReLU operation.

$$f(t_l) = \max(0, t_l) \tag{6}$$

Operation of ReLU is equal to $\phi(.)$ in expression (4). Obviously, operation of expression (5) then expression (6) on a subspace is equal to expression (4) on a subspace.

Operation of convolution and ReLU are similar to projection and threshold of FLD (Fisher Linear Discriminant) in ensemble classifier in [19]. Difference is that the adopted weight parameters in FLD are computed using means and covariance of features while the adopted weight and bias parameters in our network are computed through backpropagation.

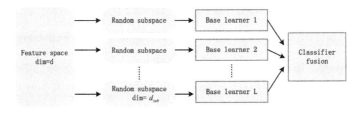

Fig. 5. Ensemble classifier

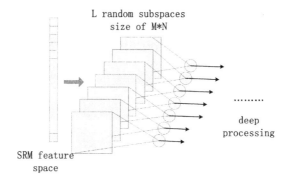

L random subspaces
size of M*N

SRM feature
space

deep
processing

Fig. 6. CNN with random subspace

Figure 5 is the ensemble classifier while Fig. 6 is the subspaces-based processing in our designed CNN. Since each convolutional operation works on a random-selected subspace of entire data space, the L convolution and ReLU operations are similar to the L base classifiers in ensemble classifier. L convolution and ReLU operations work independently and improve the accuracy of classification by integrating together in deep processing module. In order to ensure the mutual independence of the L convolution operations, we initialize the weight parameters in L convolutional kernels with random-generated values which subject to normal distribution with mean of zero and variance of one. The normal distribution will make the values in filters adjusted to much appropriate ones more easily while training the whole CNN.

3.3   Deep Processing

According to the pre-existing examples of CNN in classification tasks [3,4], advisable deep processing could enhance the performance of CNN classifier. In this module, we attempt to make the best of several linear or non-linear operation of CNN, such as Convolution, Fullconnection, ReLU, Droupout and Softmax. While making use of the listed layer operation, we designed two structure of this deep processing module, as shown in Fig. 7, in which each structure has its advantages and disadvantages.

Structure 1: In order to perform another convolution operation, the output of the ReLU layer is reshaped into a square matrix. Then a convolution layer is placed after the reshape layer. The convolution layer is used again for the following reasons: first, local regions, shared weights of convolution reduce the amount of computation, compared with full connection; second, convolutional operation uses different kernels that can extract different factors of the current features. Though the extracted factor may not benefit for steganalysis, adjusting weight parameter in convolution kernels through back propagation in training phase is to adapt the kernels to the speciality of steganography factors so that they can extract factors beneficial to steganalysis from input features. After the second convolution layer are an other non-linear activation function layer of ReLU and a FullConnect layer, then the ReLU layer again. These operations all improve the complexity of the whole network and let the model be able to express a more complex relationship theoretically.

Structure 2: This is a much more simple structure compared with structure 1. The layers used are shown in Fig. 7 clearly. Since training a network with structure 1 needs powerful computing resource, a much simpler structure with only 9 layers is designed.

Obviously, a Dropout layer is used in this structure. Dropout sets the value of a node to zero with a certain probability, and the probability is called dropout ratio. This operation changes the structure a little between iterations. Dropout has been proved good to prevent overfitting. We performed an experiment and found that a Dropout layer with proper dropout ratio improve the accuracy a lot. Our experiment also found a Dropout layer in structure 1 makes the accuracy decrease by 10%–15%.

Comparison: A comparison between structure 1 and structure 2 in some keys points is shown in the following table: Table 1

Table 1. Comparison between whole CNNs with structures 1 and structures 2

	Layers	Nodes	Connections	Weight parameters
Structure 1	11	290944	2613638	2351392
Structure 2	9	290944	713094	458896

The datum in the table show that the connections and weight parameters in structure 1 is much more than that in structure 2. The network with structure 1 is a complex model while the one with structure 2 is a simple one. The complexity ensures the probability of model approaching to an ideal one through training theoretically. However, too much layers, connections and weight parameters cause the gradient diffusion problem much more highlighted, especially in the several primal layers. The complex one may be more difficult to train.

3.4   Classification

A FullConnect layer which has two output nodes with a two-way softmax is the classification module of whole network. The two-way softmax activation function is used to produce a distribution over all the class labels as follows:

$$y_i = \frac{e^{x_i}}{\sum_{j=1}^{2} e^{x_j}} i = 1, 2 \tag{7}$$

The two-way output respectively denotes the decision of cover and stego.

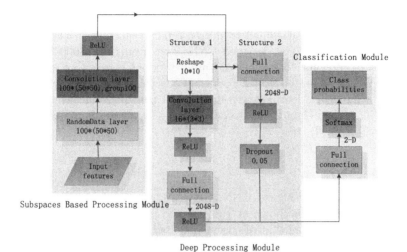

Fig. 7. Structure of designed CNN

4 Experiments and Analysis

4.1 Dataset and Software Platforms

We performed experiments on SRM features using our designed CNN to detect the spatial domain content-adaptive steganographic algorithms: HILL and S-UNIWARD, with embedding rates of 0.4 bpp and 0.1 bpp. The corresponding performance achieved by the GNCNN [12] and the SRM with ensemble classifier is used as references. All of the experiments using the CNN were performed on a modified version of Caffe toolbox [21] and a workstation with Nvidia Tesla K40 GPU.

The dataset used is BOSSbase v1.01 [22] containing 10000 cover images. Image data of the class stego were generated through data embedding into the cover images. Each image was converted into SRM features as the input of our designed CNN.

4.2 Training and Test

The 10000 pairs of images (10000 cover and 10000 stego) were divided into training set of 5000 pairs and test set of 5000 pairs. Different structures of CNN were experimented on to study the effect of RandomData and the performance of the two structures.

4.3 Parameters in the Designed CNN

As many conventional CNN, Mini-batch GD was used in the training phase of our designed CNN, and the batch size for each iteration of training was fix to

2 (1 cover/stego pairs). The momentum was fixed to 0.9. The learning rate was
initialized to 0.01 and scheduled to decrease 0.0005 for every 5000 iterations,
for all the parameters. The designed CNNs was trained for 800000 iterations.
Parameters in convolution kernels and inner product layers were initialized by
random numbers generated from zero-mean Gaussian distribution with standard
deviation of 0.01; bias learning was disabled in convolutional layers and inner
product layers. The weight decay in convolutional layers and inner product layers
was set to 1(disabled).

4.4   Result

The best accuracy of designed CNN, GNCNN (proposed by Qian et al. [12])
and ensemble classifier is shown in Table 2. The accuracy of proposed CNN has
already been approaching that of ensemble classifier.

Table 2. The best detection accuracy of different methods

Payload (bpp)	HILL		S-UNIWARD		
	Proposed CNN	Ensemble classifier	Proposed CNN	Ensemble classifier	GNCNN
0.4	0.7354	0.7201	0.7419	0.7407	0.6910
0.1	0.5601	0.5604	0.5608	0.5734	0.5408

4.5   More Details and Analysis

We have attempted to use different parameters in our CNN in order to learn more
about the theory and regularity of CNN on SRM for steganalysis, especially effect
of size and amount of subspaces. A portion of results of HILL 0.4 bpp detection
are shown in Table 3.

The randomly selected subspaces are extracted to represent the entire feature
space. The size and amount of subspaces influence the accuracy of steganalysis.
A subspace of larger size contains more datum in the entire datum space, and the
statistical property of the subspace can be more similar to the entire one, which
could benefit the classification of our CNN. However, to our knowledge, not all
datum of SRM distinguish the signal of cover and stego perfectly. A subspace of
larger size may increase the probability that useless datum are selected. Moreover, according to the theory of ensemble learning, subspaces selected by different
base learners should have enough difference. Larger subspaces may improve the
similarity of them. Experiments show that 50×50 to 100×100 is the best
domain of size of subspace. To the amount of subspaces, more subspaces may
describe the entire data space roundly. However, according to Sect. 3.2, more subspaces mean more convolutional kernels in the first convolution layer. Since the
first convolution layer is closed to the bottom of the whole structure, problem of

Table 3. Performance of different proposed CNNs

	CNN1	CNN2	CNN3	CNN4	CNN5	CNN6	CNN7	CNN8
Accuracy	0.7354	0.7212	0.6990	0.7019	0.6998	0.6986	0.6808	0.6602
Iterations	355000	395000	505000	355000	400000	335000	425000	395000
Training duration	160 min	590 min	330 min	110 min	108 min	120 min	180 min	210 min

gradient diffusion may appear much more serious. Too many convolutional kernels may make the network hard to train. Experiments show that 100 subspaces may be the best choice.

In CNN1 to CNN3, we experimented on the proposed structure 1. In CNN1, 100 subspaces, 100 kernels in size of 50×50 in the first convolution layer was used, which made the best performance; In CNN2, the parameters was changed to 900 subspaces, and 900 kernels in size of 70×70; In CNN3, that is 400 subspaces, and 400 kernels in size of 50×50.

In CNN4 to CNN6, we experimented on the proposed structure 2. In CNN4, 100 subspaces, 100 kernels in size of 50×50 in the first convolution layer was used; In CNN5, the parameters was changed to 100 subspaces, 100 kernels in size of 75×75; In CNN6, that is 100 subspaces, 100 kernels in size of 55×55. Experiment above shows that CNN with more nodes, connections and weight parameters consumes more time in training phase.

To verify effect of RandomData layer designed in proposed Sect. 3.2, in CNN7 and CNN8, we use a convention convolution layer with 100 kernels in size of 50×50 and a max pooling layer with kernels in size of 137×137 (global pooling) instead of the RandomData layer in CNN1 and CNN4, which makes the structure of CNN back to a conventional one. The result shows that the accuracy decreases and training duration increases compared with CNN1 and CNN4. So the RandomData layer improves the accuracy and shortens the time of training.

Obviously, although comparable detection accuracy was achieved, training a proposed CNN takes much more time than training an ensemble classifier. Besides, the average training time of GNCNN is about 2 h, which is slightly faster than proposed CNN.

5 Conclusion

In this paper, we proposed a feature-based deep learning model for steganalysis. SRM features are used as the input of the designed CNN because SRM features can represent the difference between original and stego images more exhaustively. Taking the thought of ensemble classifier, the operation of RandomData is proposed to improve the detection accuracy and shorten the training time. As the network goes deeper, higher level datum are obtained for classification. The result of experiment shows that the proposed method can achieve comparable performance with ensemble classifier and GNCNN. Feature-based CNN is a good tool for steganalysis and would have the potential to give a better performance in the future for two reasons: firstly, the structure of proposed CNN still has space to optimize; secondly, there could be other features more suitable than SRM to be the input of CNN, for instance maxSRMd2 [23]. Both are follow-up work for the authors.

References

1. LeCun, Y., Bengio, Y., Hinton, G.: Deep learning. Nature **521**(7553), 436–444 (2015)
2. LeCun, Y., Bottou, L., Bengio, Y., Haffner, P.: Gradient-based learning applied to document recognition. Proc. IEEE **86**(11), 2278–2324 (1998)
3. Krizhevsky, A., Sutskever, I., Hinton, G.E.: Imagenet classification with deep convolutional neural networks. In: Advances in Neural Information Processing Systems, pp. 1097–1105 (2012)
4. Ouyang, W., Wang, X., Zeng, X., Qiu, S., Luo, P., Tian, Y., Tang, X.: Deformable deep convolutional neural networks for object detection. In: Proceedings of the IEEE Conference on Computer Vision and Pattern Recognition, pp. 2403–2412 (2015)
5. Zou, D., Shi, Y. Q., Su, W., Xuan, G.: Steganalysis based on Markov model of thresholded prediction-error image. In: 2006 IEEE International Conference on Multimedia and Expo, pp. 1365–1368. IEEE, July 2006
6. Shi, Y.Q., Sutthiwan, P., Chen, L.: Textural features for steganalysis. In: Kirchner, M., Ghosal, D. (eds.) IH 2012. LNCS, vol. 7692, pp. 63–77. Springer, Heidelberg (2013). doi:10.1007/978-3-642-36373-3_5
7. Fridrich, J., Kodovsky, J.: Rich models for steganalysis of digital images. IEEE Trans. Inf. Forensics Secur. **7**(3), 868–882 (2012)
8. Pevny, T., Bas, P., Fridrich, J.: Steganalysis by subtractive pixel adjacency matrix. IEEE Trans. Inf. Forensics Secur. **5**(2), 215–224 (2010)
9. Holub, V., Fridrich, J.: Random projections of residuals for digital image steganalysis. IEEE Trans. Inf. Forensics Secur. **8**(12), 1996–2006 (2013)
10. Chen, L., Shi, Y.-Q., Sutthiwan, P.: Variable multi-dimensional co-occurrence for steganalysis. In: Shi, Y.-Q., Kim, H.J., Pérez-González, F., Yang, C.-N. (eds.) IWDW 2014. LNCS, vol. 9023, pp. 559–573. Springer, Heidelberg (2015). doi:10.1007/978-3-319-19321-2_43
11. Tan, S., Li, B.: Stacked convolutional auto-encoders for steganalysis of digital images. In: 2014 Asia-Pacific Signal and Information Processing Association Annual Summit and Conference (APSIPA), pp. 1–4. IEEE, December 2014
12. Qian, Y., Dong, J., Wang, W., Tan, T.: Deep learning for steganalysis via convolutional neural networks. In: International Society for Optics and Photonics SPIE/IS & T Electronic Imaging, p. 94090J, March 2015
13. Pibre, L., Jérôme, P., Ienco, D., Chaumont, M.: Deep learning is a good steganalysis tool when embedding key is reused for different images, even if there is a cover source-mismatch. In EI: Electronic Imaging, February 2016
14. Xu, G., Wu, H.Z., Shi, Y.Q.: Structural design of convolutional neural networks for steganalysis. IEEE Sig. Process. Lett. **23**(5), 708–712 (2016)
15. Ker, A.D., Böhme, R.: Revisiting weighted stego-image steganalysis. In: Electronic Imaging 2008, p. 681905. International Society for Optics and Photonics, February 2008

16. Holub, V., Fridrich, J.: Digital image steganography using universal distortion. In: Proceedings of 1st ACM Workshop on Information Hiding and Multimedia Security, Montpellier, France, p. 59. C68, June 2013
17. Li, B., Wang, M., Huang, J., Li, X.: A new cost function for spatial image steganography. In: 2014 IEEE International Conference on Image Processing (ICIP), pp. 4206–4210. IEEE, October 2014
18. Kodovsky, J., Fridrich, J., Holub, V.: Ensemble classifiers for steganalysis of digital media. IEEE Trans. Inf. Forensics Secur. **7**(2), 432–444 (2012)
19. Nair, V., Hinton, G.E.: Rectified linear units improve restricted Boltzmann machines. In: Proceedings of the 27th International Conference on Machine Learning (ICML 2010), pp. 807–814 (2010)
20. Hinton, G.E., Srivastava, N., Krizhevsky, A., Sutskever, I., Salakhutdinov, R.R.: Improving neural networks by preventing co-adaptation of feature detectors. arXiv preprint arXiv:1207.0580 (2012)
21. Jia, Y., Shelhamer, E., Donahue, J., Karayev, S., Long, J., Girshick, R., Darrell, T.: Caffe: convolutional architecture for fast feature embedding. In: Proceedings of the 22nd ACM International Conference on Multimedia, pp. 675–678. ACM, November 2014
22. Bas, P., Filler, T., Pevný, T.: Break our steganographic system: the Ins and Outs of organizing BOSS. In: Filler, T., Pevný, T., Craver, S., Ker, A. (eds.) IH 2011. LNCS, vol. 6958, pp. 59–70. Springer, Heidelberg (2011). doi:10.1007/978-3-642-24178-9_5
23. Denemark, T., Sedighi, V., Holub, V., Cogranne, R., Fridrich, J.: Selection-channel-aware rich model for steganalysis of digital images. In: 2014 IEEE International Workshop on Information Forensics and Security (WIFS), pp. 48–53. IEEE, December 2014

A High Embedding Capacity Data Hiding Scheme Based upon Permutation Vectors

Chin-Chen Chang[1], Jen-Chun Chang[2], Yun-Hong Chou[2],
and Hsin-Lung Wu[2(✉)]

[1] Department of Information Engineering and Computer Science,
Feng Chia University, Taichung, Taiwan
alan3c@gmail.com
[2] Department of Computer Science and Information Engineering,
National Taipei University, New Taipei City, Taiwan
{jcchang,hsinlung}@mail.ntpu.edu.tw, coolyupo@gmail.com

Abstract. Reference-matrix-based data hiding is a way to embed secret data within cover images according to a secret reference matrix. Existing schemes such as exploiting-modification-direction-based method, Sudoku-based method, and magic-cube-based method provide several means to construct reference matrices and embed secret data by modifying the LSBs of cover images according to generated reference matrices. In order to obtain better embedding capacity and stego-image quality, we propose a novel data hiding scheme based on permutation vectors. In this proposed scheme, a 1-dimensional reference matrix is constructed by concatenating a secret permutation vector repeatedly. Experimental results show that the proposed scheme achieves higher embedding capacity and better stego-image quality. To further improve the visual quality when the embedding capacity is less than 1.5 bpp, we also propose an improved version where a 2-dimensional reference matrix is constructed based on a secret permutation vector. The experimental result also demonstrates nice visual quality of our improved scheme.

Keywords: Data hiding · Reference matrix · LSB · Permutation vectors

1 Introduction

Data hiding on images [1,4–6,8] is a technique to embed a secret data string into an image with two requirements. First, it is hard to distinguish between the embedded image and the host image. Second, the embedded secret data string should be extracted losslessly. In the domain of data hiding on images, the embedding capacity (the number of bits embedded into the host image) and the visual quality of the embedded image are two important factors. The goal of data hiding is to construct a scheme which obtains high embedding capacity while preserving good stego-image quality.

Turner [9] proposed a data hiding scheme called the least significant bit (LSB) replacement which embeds secret data into the least significant bits of the cover

© Springer International Publishing AG 2017
Y.Q. Shi et al. (Eds.): IWDW 2016, LNCS 10082, pp. 578–587, 2017.
DOI: 10.1007/978-3-319-53465-7_43

pixels. However, the embedded data by using this method may be detected by a steganalysis detector. To have a better resistance against steganalysis detectors, some reference matrices are applied in constructions of data hiding schemes based on the LSB replacement. Zhang and Wang [11] proposed a method based on exploiting modification direction (EMD) which constructs a magic matrix as a reference to modify the least significant bits of the cover pixels. Chang et al. [3] presented a Sudoku-based method which uses a well-known Sudoku matrix to construct a reference matrix. In addition, Sudoku-based data hiding scheme obtains higher embedding capacity and security than the EMD method. Inspired by the Sudoku method, Lin et al. [7] proposed an improved method which constructs a similar secret reference matrix. Chang and Wu [2] proposed a 2-level EMD method whose maximum embedding capacity is 2.32 bpp. Wu et al. [10] presented a magic-cube-based method which applies a magic cube as a 3-dimensional reference matrix. Their scheme can obtain higher embedding capacity than other existing methods while preserving high stego-image quality.

In this paper, we propose a new data hiding scheme (called PV) which uses a permutation vector to construct a 1-dimensional reference vector. Each cover pixel can be embedded at least 1 secret bit by modifying its LSBs according to the secret data and the generated reference vector. Experimental results show that our proposed scheme outperforms existing schemes in visual quality of stego-images when the embedding capacity is between 1.5 bpp and 3.32 bpp. In order to improve the stego-image quality with embedding capacity from 1 bpp to 1.5 bpp, we propose an improved permutation-vector-based data hiding scheme (called IPV). In this improved scheme, a 2-dimensional reference matrix is constructed based on permutation vectors. Experimental results show that the IPV scheme obtains high stego-image quality when the embedding capacity is between 1 bpp and 1.5 bpp.

The remaining part of the paper is organized as follows. In Sect. 2, we survey some existing data hiding schemes based on reference matrices. Next, in Sect. 3, we show our proposed data hiding scheme based on permutation vectors. In Sect. 4, we give experimental results for our proposed scheme and compare it with existing data hiding schemes. Finally we give a conclusion in Sect. 5.

2   Previous Works

In this section, we review recent data hiding schemes based on exploiting modification direction [11], Sudoku [3], and magic cube [10], respectively.

We view each cover image as a vector

$$X = \{x_i : 0 \leq x_i \leq 255 \,\&\, 0 \leq i < (H \times W)\}$$

for a fixed order where H and W are the height and width of the cover image, respectively.

2.1 Data Hiding Based on Exploiting Modification Direction (EMD) [11]

Assume that the secret message $s = (s_1, s_2, \ldots, s_m)$ is a vector in the base-$(2n + 1)$. The cover image X is partitioned into m consecutive pixel sets $\{(x_{i1}, x_{i2}, \ldots, x_{in}) : 1 \leq i \leq m\}$ of size n. For the i-th pixel set $(x_{i1}, x_{i2}, \ldots, x_{in})$, the scheme first computes

$$\alpha_i = \sum_{j=1}^{n} (i \times x_{ij}) \mod (2n + 1).$$

To embed the i-th digit s_i into the i-th pixel set $(x_{i1}, x_{i2}, \ldots, x_{in})$, the scheme does the following steps:

1. If $s_i = \alpha_i$, then keep $(x_{i1}, x_{i2}, \ldots, x_{in})$ unchanged.
2. If $s_i \neq \alpha_i$ and $0 < (s_i - \alpha_i) \leq n$, then increase the value of x_{it} by 1 where $t = s_i - \alpha_i$.
3. If $s_i \neq \alpha_i$ and $n < (s_i - \alpha_i)$, then decrease the value of x_{it} by 1 where $t = 2n + 1 - s_i + \alpha_i$.

2.2 Data Hiding Based on Sudoku [3]

Chang et al. proposed a data hiding scheme based on Sudoku [3]. A Sudoku is a 9×9 matrix like the one shown in Fig. 1 where each row contains every digit from 1 to 9 exactly once, and so do each column and each 3×3 block.

In their method [3], Chang et al. extended a 9×9 Sudoku grid to a 256×256 reference matrix M first. Assume that the secret message $s = (s_0, s_1, \ldots, s_m)$ is a vector in the base-9. The cover image X is partitioned into m consecutive pixel pairs $\{(x_{2i}, x_{2i+1}) : 0 \leq i \leq m - 1\}$. For the i-th pixel pair (x_{2i}, x_{2i+1}), their scheme first computes

$$\alpha_i = M(x_{2i}, x_{2i+1}).$$

8	3	5	4	1	6	9	2	7
2	9	6	8	5	7	4	3	1
4	1	7	2	9	3	6	5	8
5	6	9	1	3	4	7	8	2
1	2	3	6	7	8	5	4	9
7	4	8	5	2	9	1	6	3
6	5	2	7	8	1	3	9	4
9	8	1	3	4	5	2	7	6
3	7	4	9	6	2	8	1	5

Fig. 1. An example of 9×9 Sudoku grid

To embed the i-th digit s_i into the i-th pixel pair (x_{2i}, x_{2i+1}), their scheme does the following steps:

1. If $s_i = \alpha_i$, then keep (x_{2i}, x_{2i+1}) unchanged.
2. If $s_i \neq \alpha_i$, then do the following:
   (a) In the 9×9 Sudoku grid containing the (x_{2i}, x_{2i+1})-entry of the matrix M, find the row vector SR, the column vector SC, and the 3×3 block SB which contain the (x_{2i}, x_{2i+1})-entry.
   (b) Find the (x_R, y_R)-entry in SR, the (x_C, y_C)-entry in SC, and the (x_B, y_B)-entry in SB such that $M(x_R, y_R) = M(x_C, y_C) = M(x_B, y_B) = s_i$.
   (c) Let $SU = \{(x_R, y_R), (x_C, y_C), (x_B, y_B)\}$. Modify (x_{2i}, x_{2i+1}) as $(x', y') = \arg\min\{|x - x_{2i}| + |y - x_{2i+1}| : (x, y) \in SU\}$.

2.3   Data Hiding Based on Magic Cubes (MC) [10]

Wu et al. proposed a data hiding scheme based on magic cubes [10]. For $1 \leq k \leq 8$, a 2^k-magic cube is a three-dimensional matrix of size $2^k \times 2^k \times 2^k$ in which every number from 0 to $2^{3k} - 1$ appears exactly once in the matrix. Given a 2^k-magic cube M as a reference matrix, the scheme of Wu et al. [10] embeds the secret message into the cover image X in the following way.

Given a number t, let $(t)_2$ denote the binary representation of the number t. Assume that the secret message $s = (s_0, s_1, \ldots, s_{3m-1})$ is a vector where each entry s_i is a k-bit string. The cover image X is partitioned into m consecutive pixel triplets $\{(x_{3i}, x_{3i+1}, x_{3i+2}) : 0 \leq i \leq m - 1\}$. To embed the i-th secret message triplet $(s_{3i}, s_{3i+1}, s_{3i+2})$ into the i-th pixel triplet $(x_{3i}, x_{3i+1}, x_{3i+2})$, their scheme first computes the coordinate vector (u_i, v_i, w_i) such that

$$M(u_i, v_i, w_i) = SN_i$$

where SN_i is the number whose binary representation is equal to $s_{3i} \circ s_{3i+1} \circ s_{3i+2}$ where $\circ$ denotes the concatenation. Now, their scheme modifies the pixel triplet $(x_{3i}, x_{3i+1}, x_{3i+2})$ by replacing the least k bits of $x_{3i}, x_{3i+1}, x_{3i+2}$ with $(u_i)_2, (v_i)_2, (w_i)_2$, respectively. This completes the embedding procedure in their scheme.

3   The Proposed Data Hiding Scheme Based on Secret Permutation Reference Vectors

In this section, we describe the proposed embedding and extraction processes of our proposed scheme based on permutation vectors.

3.1   The Data Embedding Process

For a natural number k, let P_k denote the set of permutations on $\{0, 1, \cdots, k-1\}$. The process randomly chooses a permutation $\pi = (\pi_0, \pi_1, \ldots, \pi_{k-1}) \in P_k$. In order to construct a reference vector V of length 256, the proposed scheme expands the permutation vector π by repeating it until the length is at least 256. That is,

$$V = (\pi_0, \pi_1, \ldots, \pi_{k-1}, \pi_0, \pi_1, \ldots, \pi_{k-1}, \ldots).$$

Assume that the secret message $s = (s_0, s_1, \ldots, s_{m-1})$ is a vector in the base-k. The cover image X is viewed as a vector $X = (x_0, x_1, \ldots, x_{m-1}) \in \{0, 1, \ldots, 255\}^m$. For the i-th pixel x_i, the proposed scheme first computes $\alpha_i = V(x_i)$. To embed the i-th digit s_i into the i-th pixel x_i, the proposed scheme does the following steps:

1. If $s_i = \alpha_i$, then keep x_i unchanged.
2. If $s_i \neq \alpha_i$, then do the following:
   (a) Find the index $t \in \{0, 1, \ldots, 255\}$ such that $|t - x_i|$ is minimum and $V(t) = s_i$.
   (b) Replace the original pixel x_i by t.

3.2   The Data Extraction Process

In this subsection, we describe the extraction process of the proposed scheme. Let $X' = (x'_0, x'_1, \ldots, x'_{m-1})$ denote the stego-image after embedding the secret message $s = (s_0, s_1, \ldots, s_{m-1})$ into the original cover image X.

To extract s_i from x'_i, the proposed scheme does the following steps:

1. Generate the permutation vector $\pi = (\pi_0, \pi_1, \ldots, \pi_{k-1}) \in P_k$ which was previously constructed by the embedding process.
2. Generate the vector V which was previously constructed by the embedding process.
3. Compute $V(x'_i)$ and output it.

3.3   Expected Stego-Image Quality of the Proposed Scheme

We assume that the secret message $s = (s_0, s_1, \ldots, s_{m-1})$ is a random vector in the base-k since we always embed the secret message into the cover image after encrypting this message. In addition, PSNR is a known way to measure the similarity between the cover image $X = (x_0, x_1, \ldots, x_{m-1})$ and the stego-image $X' = (x'_0, x'_1, \ldots, x'_{m-1})$. The PSNR definition is as follows:

$$PSNR(X, X') = 10 \log_{10} \frac{255^2}{MSE(X, X')},$$

where

$$MSE(X, X') = \frac{1}{m} \sum_{j=0}^{m-1} (x_j - x'_j)^2.$$

Table 1. Expected value of MSE and $PSNR$ in the proposed scheme based on permutation vectors and the corresponding embedding capacity (EC).

k	2	3	4	5	6
MSE	1/2	2/3	3/2	2	19/6
$PSNR$	51.14	49.89	46.37	45.12	43.12
EC	1	1.59	2	2.32	2.59
k	7	8	9	10	11
MSE	4	11/2	20/3	17/2	10
$PSNR$	42.11	40.73	39.89	38.83	38.13
EC	2.81	3	3.17	3.32	3.46

Given any cover image X, let X' be its stego-image after the proposed scheme embeds a random message into X. Then the expected value of $MSE(X, X')$ is

$$\frac{2}{k}\left(\sum_{i=1}^{\lfloor (k-1)/2 \rfloor} i^2\right) + \frac{k}{4}(\lceil \frac{k-1}{2} \rceil - \lfloor \frac{k-1}{2} \rfloor).$$

For $2 \leq k \leq 10$, we list the expected MSE and $PSNR$ in Table 1.

We remark that the stego-image quality of the scheme of Zhang and Wang [11] is better than that of our proposed scheme when the embedding capacity is 1.16 bpp. In fact, the expected MSE and $PSNR$ of their scheme are 2/5 and 52.11, respectively when the embedding capacity is 1.16 bpp. However, their scheme does not provide the expected MSE and $PSNR$ when the capacity is 1 bpp.

3.4 The Improved Data Hiding Scheme Based on Permutation Vectors

In this subsection, we describe our improved scheme based on permutation vectors. The improved scheme is designed for improving the stego-image quality when the embedding capacity is from 1 bpp to 1.5 bpp.

The Data Embedding Process. We consider $k = 4$ or 5. The scheme randomly chooses a permutation $\pi = (\pi_0, \pi_1, \ldots, \pi_{k-1}) \in P_k$ and constructs a reference vector V of length W as in the previous construction. Note that

$$V = (\pi_0, \pi_1, \ldots, \pi_{k-1}, \pi_0, \pi_1, \ldots, \pi_{k-1}, \ldots).$$

Next, we define the reference matrix M such that the i-th row vector of M is V^i where V^i is defined in the following way:

$$V^i(j) = \pi_{((j-2i) \mod k)}, \text{ for } 0 \leq j \leq W - 1.$$

Note that V^0 is identical to V. Assume that the secret message $s = (s_0, s_1, \ldots, s_{m-1})$ is a vector in the base-k. The cover image X is partitioned into m consecutive pixel pairs $\{(x_{2i}, x_{2i+1}) : 0 \le i \le m-1\}$. For the i-th pixel pair (x_{2i}, x_{2i+1}), the improved scheme first computes

$$\alpha_i = M(x_{2i}, x_{2i+1}).$$

To embed the i-th digit s_i into the i-th pixel pair (x_{2i}, x_{2i+1}), the improved scheme does the following steps:

1. If $s_i = \alpha_i$, then keep (x_{2i}, x_{2i+1}) unchanged.
2. If $s_i \ne \alpha_i$, then do the following:
   (a) Find the (x', y')-entry in the matrix M such that $M(x', y') = s_i$ and $|x' - x_{2i}| + |y' - x_{2i+1}|$ is the minimum value.
   (b) Replace the original pixel pair (x_{2i}, x_{2i+1}) by (x', y').

The Data Extraction Process. Let $X' = (x'_0, x'_1, \ldots, x'_{2m-1})$ denote the stego-image after embedding the secret message $s = (s_0, s_1, \ldots, s_{m-1})$ into the original cover image X. To extract s_i from the pixel pair (x'_{2i}, x'_{2i+1}), the proposed extracting scheme does the following steps:

1. Generate the permutation vector $\pi = (\pi_0, \pi_1, \ldots, \pi_{k-1}) \in P_k$ and the reference matrix M such that $M(i, j) = \pi_{(j-2i) \bmod k}$.
2. Compute $M(x'_{2i}, x'_{2i+1})$ and output it.

We discuss the expected MSE and $PSNR$ of our improved scheme in the next subsection.

Expected MSE and $PSNR$ of Our Improved Scheme. For $k = 5$, for any (i, j)-entry of the reference matrix M, the set

$$\{M(i, j), M(i+1, j), M(i-1, j), M(i, j+1), M(i, j-1)\}$$

is exactly the set $\{\pi_0, \pi_1, \pi_2, \pi_3, \pi_4\}$ where we assume that $i, j \ne 0$ or 255. Thus, the expected MSE of stego-image is approximately $2/5$, the corresponding expected $PSNR$ is approximately 52.11, and the embedding capacity is $(\log_2 5)/2 \approx 1.16$ bpp.

For $k = 4$, for any (i, j)-entry of the reference matrix M, the set

$$\{M(i, j), M(i+1, j), M(i-1, j), M(i, j+1), M(i, j-1)\}$$

must contain the set $\{\pi_0, \pi_1, \pi_2, \pi_3\}$ where we assume that $i, j \ne 0$ or 255. Based on this observation, the expected MSE of the stego-image is approximately $3/8$, the corresponding expected $PSNR$ is approximately 52.39, and the embedding capacity exactly equals 1 bpp. For reader's convenience, we give a comparison in Table 2.

Table 2. Expected value of MSE and $PSNR$ in the original and the improved proposed schemes and the corresponding embedding capacity (EC).

Method	The improved scheme	The origin scheme
k	4	2
MSE	3/8	1/2
$PSNR$	52.39	51.14
EC	1	1
Method	The improved scheme	The origin scheme
k	5	3
MSE	2/5	2/3
$PSNR$	52.11	49.89
EC	1.16	1.59

4   Experimental Results

In this section, some experimental results are provided to demonstrate the performance of the proposed schemes. In our experiment, we use four 512×512 test images shown in Fig. 2.

The stego-images are generated by embedding the randomly generated secret data stream. We compare the embedding capacity measured by bit per pixel (bpp) and the stego-image quality measured by PSNR. In Table 3, the performance of the proposed scheme is shown. The experimental result shows that the PSNR value is at least 40 dB when the embedding capacity is 3 bpp.

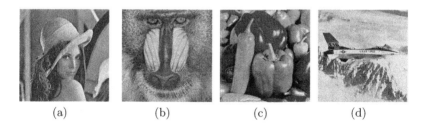

(a)   (b)   (c)   (d)

Fig. 2. Four test images (a) Lena (b) Baboon (c) Peppers (d) Airplane

Table 3. Embedding Capacity versus $PSNR$ in the proposed (improved) scheme.

Image	EC	PSNR	EC	PSNR	EC	PSNR	EC	PSNR	EC	PSNR	EC	PSNR	EC	PSNR	EC	PSNR
Lena	1	52.40	1.16	52.11	1.59	49.90	2	46.37	2.32	45.14	3	40.72	3.17	39.89	3.32	38.86
Baboon	1	52.38	1.16	52.12	1.59	49.89	2	46.37	2.32	45.13	3	40.74	3.17	39.88	3.32	38.84
Pepper	1	52.39	1.16	52.10	1.59	49.89	2	46.37	2.32	45.12	3	40.72	3.17	39.88	3.32	38.81
Airplane	1	52.40	1.16	52.11	1.59	49.88	2	46.39	2.32	45.13	3	40.72	3.17	39.89	3.32	38.84

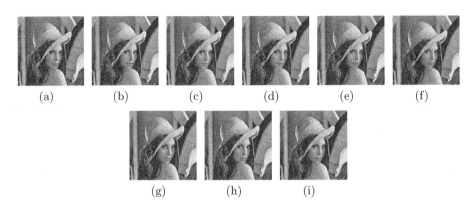

(a)   (b)   (c)   (d)   (e)   (f)

(g)   (h)   (i)

Fig. 3. The cover Lena image and stego-images of our proposed scheme. (a) Original image (b) Stego-image (k=3) (c)Stego-image (k=4) (d) Stego-image (k=5) (e) Stego-image (k=6) (f) Stego-image (k=7) (g) Stego-image (k=8) (h) Stego-image (k=9) (i) Stego-image (k=10)

Table 4. The comparison of the EMD method [11], the Sudoku method [3], the improved Sudouk method [7], the two-level EMD method [2], and the MC method [10].

Method	[11]		[3]		[7]		[2]		[2]		[10]		[10]	
Image	EC	PSNR	EC	PSNR	EC	PSNR	EC	PSNR	EC	PSNR	EC	PSNR	EC	PSNR
Lena	1.16	52.12	1.5	44.67	1.58	49.91	1.58	44.66	2.32	42.10	2	45.13	3	38.76
Baboon	1.16	52.10	1.5	44.68	1.58	49.92	1.58	44.66	2.32	42.10	2	45.15	3	38.91
Pepper	1.16	52.11	1.5	44.66	1.58	49.91	1.58	44.65	2.32	42.11	2	45.15	3	38.90
Airplane	1.16	52.11	1.5	44.68	1.58	49.90	1.58	44.66	2.32	42.10	2	45.14	3	38.89

In Fig. 3, the original Lena image and its stego-images generated by our proposed scheme are shown. Figure 3(a) is the original image and Fig. 3(b), (c), (d), (e), (f), (g), (h), (i) are with embedding capacity (in bpp) 1.59, 2, 2.32, 2.59, 2.81, 3, 3.17, 3.32, respectively. The visual quality of these stego-images are quite good as shown in Fig. 3.

In Table 4, we show comparison results of the EMD method [11], the Sudoku method [3], the improved Sudouk method [7], the two-level EMD method [2], and the magic-cube-based method [10]. By comparing experimental results presented in Tables 3 and 4, it is shown that our proposed schemes outperforms mentioned methods when the embedding capacity is less than or equal to 3 bpp. In particular, the stego-image quality of our proposed scheme ($\geq$ 40 dB) is much better than that ($\leq$ 39 dB) of the scheme in [10] when the embedding capacity is 3 bpp.

5   Conclusion

In this paper, we construct two novel data hiding schemes based on permutation vectors. In our proposed schemes, a permutation vector is expanded to a reference vector and a reference matrix, respectively. By using the generated reference vector or matrix, the proposed schemes can embed the secret data into the cover image. Experimental results show that our proposed schemes outperform previous schemes on image quality when the embedding capacity is at most 3 bpp. Furthermore, the proposed schemes obtain high PSNR which is at least 40 dB when the embedding capacity is 3 bpp while known methods only achieve at most 39 dB under the same capacity restriction.

Acknowledgements. This work was supported in part by the Ministry of Science and Technology under the Grant Number 102-2221-E-305-008-MY3.

References

1. Chan, C.K., Cheng, L.M.: Hiding data in images by simple LSB substitution. Pattern Recogn. **37**(3), 469–474 (2004)
2. Chang, C.C., Wu, H.L.: A large apyload information hiding scheme using two-level exploiting modification direction. In: 10th International Conference on Intelligent Information Hiding and Multimedia Signal Processing, pp. 512–515 (2014)
3. Chang, C.C., Chou, Y.C., Kieu, T.D.: An information hiding scheme using sudoku. In: 3rd International Conference on Innnovative Computing Information and Control, p. 17 (2008)
4. Kim, H.J., Kim, C., Choi, Y., Wang, S., Zhang, X.: Improved modification direction methods. Comput. Math. Appl. **60**(2), 319–325 (2010)
5. Lan, T.H., Tewk, A.H.: A novel high-capacity data-embedding system. IEEE Trans. Image Process. **15**(8), 2431–2440 (2006)
6. Lee, S., Yoo, C.D., Kalker, T.: Reversible image watermarking based on integer-to-integer wavelet transform. IEEE Trans. Inf. Forensics Secur. **2**(3), 321–330 (2007)
7. Lin, C.N., Chang, C.C., Lee, W.B., Lin, J.A.: A novel secure data hiding scheme using a secret reference matrix. In: Fifth International Conference on Intelligent Information Hiding and Multimedia Signal Processing, pp. 369–373 (2009)
8. Tai, W.L., Yeh, C.M., Chang, C.C.: Reversible data hiding based on histogram modification of pixel differences. IEEE Trans. Circuits Syst. Video Technol. **19**(6), 906–910 (2009)
9. Turner, L.F.: Digital data security system. Patent IPN WO **89**, 08915 (1989)
10. Wu, Q., Zhu, C., Li, J.J., Chang, C.C., Wang, Z.H.: A magic cube based information hiding scheme of large payload. J. Inf. Secur. Appl. **26**, 1–7 (2016)
11. Zhang, X.P., Wang, S.Z.: Efficient steganographic embedding by expliting modificatioin directioin. IEEE Commun. Lett. **10**(11), 781–783 (2006)

Data Hiding in H.264/AVC Video Files Using the Coded Block Pattern

Hong Zhang[1,2]([✉]), Yun Cao[1,2], Xianfeng Zhao[1,2],
Haibo Yu[1,2], and Changjun Liu[1,2]

[1] State Key Laboratory of Information Security,
Institute of Information Engineering, Chinese Academy of Sciences,
No. 89A, Minzhuang Road, Beijing 100093, China
{zhanghong,caoyun,zhaoxianfeng,yuhaibo,liuchangjun}@iie.ac.cn
[2] University of Chinese Academy of Sciences,
No. 19A, Yuquan Road, Beijing 100049, China

Abstract. This paper presents a novel data hiding method for H.264 which employs the coded block pattern (CBP) as the data carrier. The CBP is defined in the H.264/AVC standard, and indicates which luma and chroma blocks in a macroblock contain non-zero transform coefficients. To the best of our knowledge, little research has been conducted on exploiting the CBP for information hiding. In the proposed method, the four least significant bits of each CBP are mapped to a single bit to form the embedding channel. In addition, an embedding distortion function is specifically designed to evaluate the impacts of CBP manipulation on visual quality and compression efficiency. Combined with the suitably defined distortion function, the syndrome-trellis codes are employed to minimize the overall embedding impact. The experimental results show that only a slight reduction in visual quality would be caused, even when large payload is embedded. In addition, the compression efficiency could be maintained with insignificant fluctuation in bitrates.

Keywords: Data hiding · Coded block pattern · H.264/AVC · Compressed video

1 Introduction

In recent years, with the rapid development of broadband Internet services and practical video compression techniques, high-quality digital video can be conveniently downloaded and broadcast through social networking services such as YouTube, Facebook and Weibo. Therefore, digital video has become one of the most influential media in the entertainment industry. With the increasing popularity of digital video, copyright protection for video grows in importance and receives a lot of attention. Information hiding is one of the possible solutions for protecting copyrighted video from illegal copying and distribution.

Information hiding refers to the process of inserting information into a host to achieve certain features or serve specific purposes. Information hiding in video

© Springer International Publishing AG 2017
Y.Q. Shi et al. (Eds.): IWDW 2016, LNCS 10082, pp. 588–600, 2017.
DOI: 10.1007/978-3-319-53465-7_44

can be divided into two main categories according to the domain where data embedding takes place. One category is spatial domain-based information hiding. Under this embedding scheme, raw pixel values are directly modified using those conventional information hiding methods designed for digital image, such as Least Significant Bit (LSB) Matching [1] and Spread Spectrum (SS) [2,3]. However, researchers refrain from taking these approaches due to the inevitable loss of hidden data caused by video compression. The other category is usually referred to as compressed domain-based information hiding. Methods of this type manipulate entities of compressed video to realize data embedding. Commonly used entities include motion vectors (MVs) [4–8], intra prediction modes [9–11], inter prediction modes [12,13], quantized DCT coefficients (DCTCs) [14–16], quantization parameters [17,18], reference frame indices [19] and variable length codes [20,21].

Prior to H.264/AVC [22], there are numerous information hiding methods proposed for MPEG-1/2 standards. However, the data carriers (hiding venues) are restricted to DCTCs and MVs, mainly because other entities of MPEG-1/2 compressed video are not quite suitable for information hiding purposes. With the advent of the H.264/AVC standard in 2003, information hiding in video has then received much attention due to the introduction of various new technical features in H.264/AVC, which provides plenty of opportunities for information hiding. For instance, in Hu et al.'s work [9], 4×4 intra prediction modes (I4-modes) were exploited for data embedding, which is based on a predefined mapping rule between I4-modes and hiding bits. Kapotas and Skodras [12] proposed forcing the encoder to choose a particular inter prediction mode according to the information to be embedded. In [21], a specific type of codeword in CAVLC (Context-based Adaptive Variable Length Coding) was employed as the data carrier to realize information hiding.

In the H.264/AVC standard, the coded block pattern (CBP) is a syntax element contained in the Macroblock Layer[1], and indicates which luma and chroma blocks within a macroblock contain non-zero transform coefficients. To the best of our knowledge, the CBP is never utilized as the data carrier for information hiding, contrasting with other entities of H.264/AVC compressed video. Nevertheless, the CBP has the potential to be exploited for data embedding, and the reasons are listed as follows. First, CBPs are losslessly coded to form an integral part of compressed bitstreams. Thus it is reasonably practicable to employ the CBP as the data carrier for information hiding. Second, for CBP-based data embedding, any crucial process in video compression would not be influenced except for entropy coding. Consequently, only a slight reduction in compression efficiency and visual quality would be caused. Last but not least, compressed video usually contains a substantial quantity of CBPs, which ensures the high embedding capacities that CBP-based data hiding methods can have.

In this paper, we propose a novel data hiding method for H.264/AVC which exploits the CBP as the data carrier. In the proposed embedding scheme, the

---

[1] The Macroblock Layer contains all the syntax elements necessary to decode a single macroblock.

four LSBs of each CBP are mapped to a single bit to form the embedding channel. In addition, an embedding distortion function is specifically designed to evaluate the impacts of CBP manipulation on visual quality and compression efficiency. With the suitably defined distortion function utilized, the Syndrome-Trellis Codes (STC) [23] are further exploited to minimize the overall embedding impact. The experimental results show that the proposed method is capable of performing data hiding at the expense of a fairly slight reduction in visual quality, even when large payload is embedded. More importantly, the problem of bitrate overhead caused by data embedding could be considerably alleviated, enabling an efficient use of transmission and storage resources. As a result, the proposed method is suitable to be used in practice.

The rest of this paper is organized as follows. In Sect. 2, the basic concepts of H.264/AVC syntax and the CBP are introduced. In Sect. 3, the embedding distortion caused by modification of CBPs is analyzed, and our CBP-based data hiding method is presented. In addition, the practical implementation of the proposed method is discussed. In Sect. 4, comparative experiments are conducted to demonstrate the effectiveness of our method. Finally we draw conclusions in Sect. 5.

2   The Coded Block Pattern in H.264/AVC

H.264/AVC syntax is defined in the H.264/AVC standard and specifies the exact structure of an H.264/AVC-compliant bitstream in terms of syntax elements.

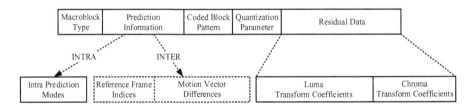

Fig. 1. The basic structure of the Macroblock Layer in the H.264/AVC standard.

According to H.264/AVC syntax specifications, the CBP is a syntax element for macroblocks that are not coded using 16×16 intra prediction modes. Contained in the Macroblock Layer (Fig. 1), the CBP indicates which luma and chroma blocks in a macroblock contain non-zero transform coefficients. In addition, the CBP can be expressed as a 6-bit binary number, and can take values between 0 and 47.

As shown in Fig. 2, given a CBP represented by $\overline{b_5 b_4 b_3 b_2 b_1 b_0}$ where b_i ($i = 0, 1, \ldots, 5$) denotes a binary digit, it is constructed as follows:

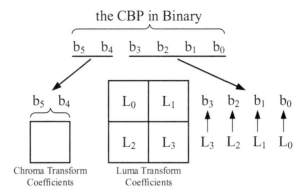

Fig. 2. The relationship between the CBP and the corresponding transform coefficients. b_i ($i = 0, 1, 2, 3$) indicates whether there are non-zero coefficients present in L_i, one of the four 8×8 luma blocks. b_5 and b_4 closely correlate with the presence of non-zero chroma transform coefficients.

1. Each of the four LSBs of the CBP, i.e. b_i ($i = 0, 1, 2, 3$), indicates whether there are one or more non-zero transform coefficients within the corresponding 8×8 luma block (denoted by L_i in Fig. 2). Specifically, the value of b_i is given by

$$b_i = \begin{cases} 1 & \text{non-zero coefficient(s) present} \\ 0 & \text{no non-zero coefficients present} \end{cases} \tag{1}$$

where $i = 0, 1, 2, 3$.

2. The two MSBs (Most Significant Bit) of the CBP, b_5 and b_4, are associated with chroma transform coefficients, and can take the values specified by

$$\overline{b_5 b_4} = \begin{cases} 00_2 & \text{no non-zero chroma coefficients present} \\ \\ 01_2 & \text{non-zero chroma DC coefficient(s) present,} \\ & \text{no non-zero chroma AC coefficients present} \\ \\ 10_2 & \text{non-zero chroma AC coefficient(s) present} \end{cases} \tag{2}$$

Residual data for a macroblock is transmitted according to the corresponding CBP. If the CBP indicates a block contains no non-zero coefficients, that block would be bypassed. In addition, since the CBP is losslessly entropy coded and inserted into H.264/AVC bitstreams, the decoding of the residual data for a macroblock could be facilitated by referring to the corresponding CBP.

3   The Proposed Method

As introduced in Sect. 2, the CBP indicates which luma and chroma blocks in a macroblock contain non-zero transform coefficients. In addition, residual data for a macroblock is transmitted according to the corresponding CBP.

In this section, we propose a data hiding method for H.264/AVC which utilizes the CBP as the data carrier. An embedding distortion function is designed to evaluate the reduction in visual quality and compression efficiency caused by modification of CBPs. In addition, combined with the suitably defined distortion function, the STC [23] is adopted in the embedding channel construction to minimize the overall embedding impact. Consequently, the proposed method can embed the payload with very limited embedding distortion introduced.

3.1   The Embedding Channel Construction

Given the cover with N CBPs denoted by $\mathbf{C} = (C_1, C_2, \ldots, C_N)$, the embedding channel construction is carried out by exploiting the STC as follows.

Each CBP C_i $(i = 1, 2, \ldots, N)$ is mapped to a single bit according to the parity check function given by

$$P(C) = \oplus_{i=0}^{3} c_i \tag{3}$$

where c_i denotes one of the four LSBs of C and satisfies $\overline{c_3 c_2 c_1 c_0} = C\%^2 16$. The symbol $\oplus$ represents the bitwise exclusive OR operation. Based on the parity check function P, the embedding channel $\mathbf{p} = (p_1, p_2, \ldots, p_N)$ can then be obtained, where $p_i = P(C_i)$ $(i = 1, 2, \ldots, N)$.

Assume that modifications of CBPs are mutually independent and let p_i $(i = 1, 2, \ldots, N)$ be assigned a positive scalar γ_i expressing the impact of making an embedding change at the corresponding CBP C_i, the STC is adopted to minimize the overall embedding impact $D(\mathbf{p}, \mathbf{p}') = \sum_{i=1}^{N} \gamma_i [p_i \neq p_i']$ [3], where $\mathbf{p}' = (p_1', p_2', \ldots, p_N')$ denotes the embedding channel with hidden data. Given an αN-bit message $\mathbf{m}$ to be embedded, where α denotes the embedding payload, the STC-based data embedding and extraction can be formulated as

$$\text{Emb}_{\text{STC}}(\mathbf{p}, \mathbf{\Gamma}, \mathbf{m}) = \arg \min_{\mathbf{p}' \in \mathcal{C}(\mathbf{m})} D(\mathbf{p}, \mathbf{p}') = \tilde{\mathbf{p}}, \tag{4}$$

$$\text{Ext}_{\text{STC}}(\tilde{\mathbf{p}}) = \tilde{\mathbf{p}} \mathbf{H}_{\text{STC}}^T = \mathbf{m}. \tag{5}$$

Here, $\mathbf{\Gamma} = (\gamma_1, \gamma_2, \ldots, \gamma_N)$ denotes the distortion scalar vector, $\mathcal{C}(\mathbf{m})$ represents the coset corresponding to the syndrome $\mathbf{m}$, and $\mathbf{H}_{\text{STC}} \in \{0, 1\}^{\alpha N \times N}$ is the parity check matrix of the STC which should be shared between communication parties. For detailed information about the STC, please refer to [23].

The design of embedding distortion is an essential part of the distortion minimization framework, and could directly affect the performance of the embedding algorithm. Given a CBP C and one of its four LSBs c, the embedding distortion caused by modification of c is analyzed as follows. If c is modified from 1 to 0, as mentioned in Sect. 2, those non-zero transform coefficients within the corresponding 8×8 luma block (Fig. 2) would be bypassed, leading to a decrease in bitrates

---

[2] $\%$ denotes the modulo operator, i.e., $a \% b$ denotes the remainder of a divided by b.
[3] The Iverson bracket $[I]$ is defined to be 1 if the logical expression I is true and 0 otherwise.

but a reduction in reconstructed visual quality. On the other hand, if c is modified from 0 to 1, although reconstructed visual quality could be maintained, bitrate overhead would be caused inevitably because 64 extra zero coefficients have to be entropy coded and transmitted. In addition, the number of bits required for representing C could also be affected if c is modified. Consequently, both visual quality and compression efficiency could be influenced by modification of c. The distortion caused by modification of c (denoted by $\Psi(C, c)$) can then be defined in terms of the fluctuation in visual quality and bitrates, i.e.

$$\Psi(C, c) = |\mathcal{J}(\mathbf{S}, \mathbf{S}_{\text{rec}}, R) - \mathcal{J}(\mathbf{S}, \mathbf{S}'_{\text{rec}}, R')|. \tag{6}$$

Here, $\mathbf{S}$ denotes the original macroblock associated with C, $\mathbf{S}_{\text{rec}}$ and $\mathbf{S}'_{\text{rec}}$ represent the corresponding reconstructed (decoded) macroblock with c unaltered and that with c modified, respectively. R denotes the number of bits required for coding $\mathbf{S}$ when c is unaltered, and R' modified. $\mathcal{J}$ denotes the Lagrangian cost function given by

$$\mathcal{J}(\mathbf{A}, \mathbf{B}, R) = D(\mathbf{A}, \mathbf{B}) + \lambda R \tag{7}$$

where D represents the visual distortion measured as SSD (Sum of Squared Differences), and λ is the Lagrange multiplier determined by the employed H.264 encoder that is used for controlling the tradeoff between D and R.

According to the analysis above, for a CBP C, the corresponding embedding distortion scalar γ can be intuitively defined as

$$\gamma = \begin{cases} \min\left\{\Psi(C, c_i) \mid i = 0, 1, 2, 3\right\} & \mathbf{S} \text{ is inter-coded.} \\ \infty & \text{else} \end{cases} \tag{8}$$

where $\mathbf{S}$ denotes the macroblock associated with C. c_i $(i = 0, 1, 2, 3)$ represents one of the four LSBs of C, and satisfies $\overline{c_3 c_2 c_1 c_0} = C \% 16$.

3.2   Practical Implementation

In practice, almost all available H.264/AVC CODECs can be customized to implement the proposed method. Typically, I-frames are not used for the data embedding, and secret message bits are embedded into P- or B-frames in a frame-by-frame manner. Without loss of generality, the processes of embedding and extraction with one single P- or B-frame are described as follows.

1. **Data Embedding**
   First, the raw frame is subdivided into macroblocks to be fed into the customized encoder. For each macroblock not coded using 16×16 intra-prediction modes, record its associated CBP determined by the encoder, and calculate the corresponding distortion scalar according to (8). Afterwards, the cover with N CBPs $\mathbf{C} = (C_1, C_2, \ldots, C_N)$ and the distortion scalar vector $\mathbf{\Gamma} = (\gamma_1, \gamma_2, \ldots, \gamma_N)$ are obtained.

Second, the embedding channel $\mathbf{p} = (p_1, p_2, \ldots, p_N)$ is constructed according to the parity check function (3). As described in (4), the STC is subsequently exploited to embed an αN-bit message $\mathbf{m}$ by turning $\mathbf{p}$ into $\tilde{\mathbf{p}}$, where $\mathrm{Emb}_{\mathrm{STC}}(\mathbf{p}, \mathbf{\Gamma}, \mathbf{m}) = \tilde{\mathbf{p}} = (\tilde{p_1}, \tilde{p_2}, \ldots, \tilde{p_N})$.

Third, the raw frame is fed into the encoder again. Each CBP C_i in $\mathbf{C}$ is then subject to the possible modification controlled by $\tilde{p}_i$. Specifically, if $\tilde{p}_i = p_i$, C_i is left unaltered. In case $\tilde{p}_i \neq p_i$, C_i is modified by flipping one of its four LSBs $\tilde{c}$ that satisfies

$$\tilde{c} = \arg\min_{c \in \mathcal{X}} \Psi(C_i, c). \tag{9}$$

where $\mathcal{X}$ denotes the set of the four LSBs of C_i.

Finally, the compressed frame with an αN-bit message embedded is inserted into the compressed bitstream.

2. **Data Extraction**

Compared with the embedding process, data extraction is much easier. Received by the recipient, the compressed frame can be decoded by any H.264 decoder to parse a total of N CBPs from the Macroblock Layer (Fig. 1). With $\tilde{\mathbf{p}}$ reconstructed, the message can be extracted by computing $\mathbf{m} = \tilde{\mathbf{p}}\mathbf{H}_{\mathrm{STC}}^T$.

4   Experiments

In this section, experiments are conducted to demonstrate that the proposed method is capable of embedding the payload with very limited embedding distortion introduced.

4.1   Experimental Setup

In the experiments, x264 [24], a highly practical H.264 encoder, is customized to prepare the compressed video samples, with only the *Baseline Profile* adopted. For each compressed video sample to be prepared, the quantization parameter (QP) is set as 20 or 28. In addition to the proposed method, Kapotas and Skodras [12] and Aly's [6] methods are also implemented for comparison, and are referred

Fig. 3. The raw sequences used for performance evaluation.

Table 1. The impacts of data embedding on visual quality and compression efficiency under different experimental settings. RC_{PSNR} defined in (10) is used for evaluating the impacts on visual quality, and RC_{BR} given by (11) is employed for evaluating the impacts on compression efficiency. (NF (the Number of Frames), IM (Impact Measure)).

Sequence	NF	IM	QP = 20			QP = 28		
			Ours	ALG1	ALG2	Ours	ALG1	ALG2
Bus	150	RC_{PSNR}	−0.3947	0.0529	−0.0312	−0.3252	−0.0343	−0.1454
		RC_{BR}	−1.4219	6.3199	2.4008	−1.4552	11.6714	5.5127
City	300	RC_{PSNR}	−0.2203	0.0652	−0.0024	−0.3662	−0.0314	−0.0428
		RC_{BR}	−1.4853	14.2124	6.6469	−2.1621	19.3939	16.3481
Coastguard	300	RC_{PSNR}	−0.5229	0.0290	−0.0169	−0.3103	−0.0575	−0.1120
		RC_{BR}	−1.5379	4.8642	3.8725	−1.4821	8.7027	7.7539
Crew	300	RC_{PSNR}	−0.4400	−0.0210	−0.0397	−0.3900	−0.0910	−0.0908
		RC_{BR}	−1.1542	2.4761	5.6439	−1.5194	2.9023	11.1871
Flower	250	RC_{PSNR}	−0.8790	0.2352	−0.0306	−0.4450	0.2469	−0.0229
		RC_{BR}	−1.2293	9.1775	2.9747	−1.2171	16.1361	5.3261
Football	260	RC_{PSNR}	−0.4943	−0.0165	−0.0306	−0.3418	−0.0605	−0.0932
		RC_{BR}	−0.9673	1.7062	3.3846	−0.9351	2.3373	6.8543
Foreman	300	RC_{PSNR}	−0.2437	0.0572	−0.0238	−0.4193	−0.1266	−0.0989
		RC_{BR}	−1.6034	9.7714	6.5952	−2.1021	17.7053	18.2170
Harbour	300	RC_{PSNR}	−0.5503	0.0483	−0.0145	−0.2770	−0.0058	0.0029
		RC_{BR}	−1.5228	3.9207	2.0061	−1.4535	7.2136	4.6024
Ice	240	RC_{PSNR}	−0.2561	0.0358	−0.0893	−0.5677	−0.0782	−0.1632
		RC_{BR}	−0.8086	9.4638	15.1377	0.4275	11.8305	26.7857
Mobile	300	RC_{PSNR}	−0.3518	0.1210	0.0169	−0.3083	0.1328	0.0206
		RC_{BR}	−0.9311	5.5549	1.8686	−1.5534	11.9526	4.0792
Soccer	300	RC_{PSNR}	−0.2269	−0.0119	−0.0237	−0.3597	−0.0830	−0.1270
		RC_{BR}	−1.0695	3.9515	5.0369	−1.3647	4.9959	11.9280
Stefan	90	RC_{PSNR}	−0.5985	0.1132	0.0306	−0.3304	−0.0420	−0.0503
		RC_{BR}	−1.3692	6.1065	2.6727	−1.4838	13.8216	7.0889
Tempete	260	RC_{PSNR}	−0.3252	0.1052	−0.0310	−0.3141	0.0344	−0.0258
		RC_{BR}	−1.0634	4.7759	2.1870	−1.5454	10.1810	5.6177
Walk	376	RC_{PSNR}	−0.4400	0.0230	−0.0391	−0.4569	−0.0877	−0.1113
		RC_{BR}	−0.9860	4.2180	4.0630	−1.4641	7.4054	10.2806

to as ALG1 and ALG2 respectively. Since these three methods are not applicable to I-frames, the embedding strength is measured by average embedded bits per inter-coded frame (bpf), and is fixed at 190 bpf in the experiments. As shown in Fig. 3, 14 CIF-resolution raw test sequences are used in the experiments to evaluate the impacts of data embedding on visual quality and compression efficiency. All of them are progressively scanned and with YUV 4:2:0 color sampling.

4.2   Impacts on Visual Quality

PSNR (Peak Signal-to-Noise Ratio) is a commonly used objective measurement of picture quality. In YUV domain, human visual system is more sensitive to luminance (Y) than to chrominance (U or V). Thus, the picture quality in the experiments is measured by PSNR to luminance (PSNR_Y). Accordingly, given a stego video sequence V_s and the corresponding cover V_c, the impacts of data embedding on visual quality can be evaluated by computing the relative change between the average PSNR_Y values of V_s and V_c, i.e.

$$\text{RC}_{\text{PSNR}}(V_\text{s}, V_\text{c}) = \frac{\text{PSNR}_\text{Y}(V_\text{s}) - \text{PSNR}_\text{Y}(V_\text{c})}{\text{PSNR}_\text{Y}(V_\text{c})} \times 100 \qquad (10)$$

where $\text{PSNR}_\text{Y}(V)$ denotes the average PSNR_Y value of the sequence V.

It can be observed from Table 1 that, our proposed method always has an adverse impact on visual quality. The reasons are explained as follows. As described in Sect. 3, the modification of a given CBP is performed by flipping one of its four LSBs. If that bit is modified from 1 to 0, those non-zero residual coefficients within the corresponding 8×8 luma block would be bypassed, which could easily result in a reduction in visual quality. If that bit is modified from 0 to 1, the 64 zero coefficients in the corresponding 8×8 luma block need to be entropy coded and transmitted. In this case, only compression efficiency would be negatively influenced. Therefore, when the embedding payload is large enough, a reduction in visual quality would always be caused by our proposed method.

Nevertheless, for our proposed method, visual quality is regarded as a crucial factor in evaluating the embedding distortion. In addition, by virtue of the STC, a practical distortion minimization framework, our proposed method could embed the payload with very limited embedding distortion introduced. Thus, although the impacts on visual quality could always be made by our method, it could be considerably alleviated and reduced to a fairly low level. As shown in Table 1, for the proposed method, the minimum value of RC_{PSNR} is given by -0.8790 for QP = 20, and -0.5677 for QP = 20.

As can be seen in Table 1, compared with our method, both ALG1 and ALG2 seem to cause a minor reduction in visual quality. However, this is achieved at the expense of significant bitrate overhead, leading to poor rate-distortion performance in general.

As shown in Fig. 4, we take a closer look at the specific sequence named "stefan", and RC_{PSNR} is computed for each frame. It can be observed that, for the proposed method, although a reduction in visual quality is caused, it can always be maintained at a low level. In contrast, with the increase in QP, the impact of data embedding on visual quality becomes more obvious and severe for ALG1 and ALG2.

4.3   Impacts on Compression Efficiency

Compression efficiency, also known as "compression capability", is the most fundamental driving force behind the adoption of modern video compression tech-

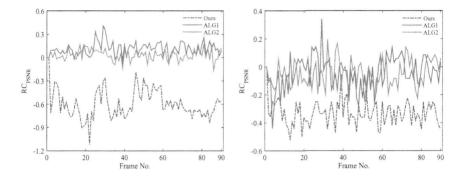

Fig. 4. Impacts on visual quality are evaluated in a frame-by-frame manner for sequence "stefan", with QP set as 20 (left) and 28 (right).

niques. Since compression efficiency is a crucial factor in assessing the performance of video encoders, the impacts of data embedding on compression efficiency could suggest whether or not the corresponding data hiding method is suitable to be used in situations where limited transmission and storage resources are available.

With compression efficiency represented as bitrates, given a a stego video sample V_s and the corresponding cover V_c, the impacts of data embedding on compression efficiency can then be evaluated by computing the relative change between the bitrates of V_s and the V_c, i.e.

$$RC_{BR} = \frac{BR(V_s) - BR(V_c)}{BR(V_c)} \times 100 \tag{11}$$

where $BR(V)$ denotes the bitrate of the sequence V.

As described in Sect. 3, a distortion function is defined in terms of the fluctuation in visual quality and compression efficiency. In addition, by using the STC, our method can embed the payload while minimizing that suitably defined distortion function. Therefore, compared with traditional video data hiding methods, the proposed approach can perform data embedding with minor fluctuation in bitrates, even when large payload (190 bpf) is embedded.

As can be seen in Table 1, for our proposed method, the problem of bitrate overhead is considerably alleviated, enabling more efficient use of transmission and storage resources. Therefore, our method is capable of maintaining compression efficiency at the cost of a fairly slight reduction in visual quality. As expected, both ALG1 and ALG2 are subject to marked bitrate overhead, leading to reduced compression efficiency.

Given a single frame F_s of a stego video sequence, the impacts on compression efficiency could be evaluated as

$$RC_{frmSize} = \frac{size(F_s) - size(F_c)}{size(F_c)} \tag{12}$$

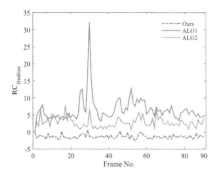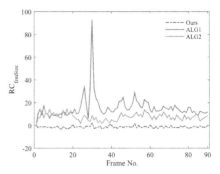

Fig. 5. Impacts on compression efficiency are evaluated in a frame-by-frame manner for sequence "stefan", with QP set as 20 (left) and 28 (right).

where F_c denotes the frame of the cover video sequence which corresponds to F_s, and size(F) represents the size of the frame measured in bytes.

As shown in Fig. 5, our proposed method can always provide well maintained compression efficiency, but, by contrast, significant bitrate overhead could be caused by ALG1 and ALG2. Thus, compared with ALG1 and ALG2, our method is capable of performing data embedding with rate-distortion efficiency well maintained, even when large payload is embedded.

5   Conclusion

In this paper, we propose a novel data hiding method which utilizes the CBP as the data carrier. An reasonable embedding distortion is designed by considering the reduction in visual quality and compression efficiency caused by CBP manipulation. Combined with the distortion function, the STC is employed to minimize the overall embedding impact. Thus, the proposed method is capable of conducting data embedding with limited distortion introduced.

The experimental results demonstrate that, compared with traditional video data hiding methods, the proposed approach is capable of embedding large payload with only a slight reduction in visual quality produced. In addition, the problem of bitrate overhead could be considerably alleviated, thus well maintaining the compression efficiency. Therefore, our method enables more efficient use of transmission and storage resources, and is suitable to be used in practice.

Acknowledgments. This work was supported by the NSFC under 61303259 and U1536105, Strategic Priority Research Program of CAS under XDA06030600, National Key Technology R&D Program under 2014BAH41B01, and Key Project of Institute of Information Engineering, CAS, under Y5Z0131201.

References

1. Mielikainen, J.: LSB matching revisited. IEEE Signal Process. Lett. **13**(5), 285–287 (2006)
2. Hartung, F., Girod, B.: Watermarking of uncompressed and compressed video. Signal Process. **66**(3), 283–301 (1998)
3. Cox, I.J., Kilian, J., Leighton, F.T., Shamoon, T.: Secure spread spectrum watermarking for multimedia. IEEE Trans. Image Process. **6**(12), 1673–1687 (1997)
4. Jordan, F., Kutter, M., Ebrahimi, T.: Proposal of a watermarking technique for hiding/retrieving data in compressed and decompressed video. Tech. rep. M2281, ISO/IEC Document, JTC1/SC29/WG11, Stockholm, Sweden, July 1997
5. Xu, C., Ping, X., Zhang, T.: Steganography in compressed video stream. In: Proceedings of 1st International Conference on Innovative Computing, Information and Control, pp. 269–272. Beijing, China, September 2006
6. Aly, H.A.: Data hiding in motion vectors of compressed video based on their associated prediction error. IEEE Trans. Inf. Forensics Secur. **6**(1), 14–18 (2011)
7. Cao, Y., Zhang, H., Zhao, X., Yu, H.: Video steganography based on optimized motion estimation perturbation. In: Proceedings of the 3rd ACM Workshop on Information Hiding and Multimedia Security, pp. 25–31. Portland (June 2015)
8. Zhang, H., Cao, Y., Zhao, X.: Motion vector-based video steganography with preserved local optimality. Multimed. Tools Appl. **75**, 13503–13519 (2015)
9. Hu, Y., Zhang, C.: Yuting: information hiding based on intra prediction modes for H.264/AVC. In: Proceedings of 2007 IEEE International Conference on Multimedia and Expo, pp. 1231–1234. Beijing, China, July 2007
10. Yang, G., Li, J., He, Y.: Zhiwei: an information hiding algorithm based on intra-prediction modes and matrix coding for H.264/AVC video stream. AEU Int. J. Electron. Commun. **65**(4), 331–337 (2011)
11. Xu, D., Wang, R., Wang, J.: Prediction mode modulated data-hiding algorithm for H.264/AVC. J. Real Time Image Process. **7**(4), 205–214 (2012)
12. Kapotas, S.K., Skodras, A.N.: A new data hiding scheme for scene change detection in H. 264 encoded video sequences. In: Proceedings of 2008 IEEE International Conference on Multimedia Expo, pp. 277–280. Hannover, Germany (2008)
13. Zhang, H., Cao, Y., Zhao, X., Zhang, W., Yu, N.: Video steganography with perturbed macroblock partition. In: Proceedings of the 2nd ACM Workshop on Information Hiding and Multimedia Security, pp. 115–122. Salzburg, Austria, June 2014
14. Ma, X., Li, Z., Tu, H., Zhang, B.: A data hiding algorithm for H.264/AVC video streams without intra-frame distortion drift. IEEE Trans. Circ. Syst. Video Technol. **20**(10), 1320–1330 (2010)
15. Lin, T., Chung, K., Chang, P., Huang, Y., Liao, H.M., Fang, C.: An improved DCT-based perturbation scheme for high capacity data hiding in H.264/AVC intra frames. J. Syst. Softw. **86**(3), 604–614 (2013)
16. Chang, P., Chung, K., Chen, J., Lin, C., Lin, T.: A DCT/DST-based error propagation-free data hiding algorithm for hevc intra-coded frames. J. Vis. Commun. Image Representation **25**(2), 239–253 (2014)
17. Wong, K., Tanaka, K., Takagi, K., Nakajima, Y.: Complete video quality-preserving data hiding. IEEE Trans. Circ. Syst. Video Technol. **19**(10), 1499–1512 (2009)
18. Shanableh, T.: Data hiding in MPEG video files using multivariate regression and flexible macroblock ordering. IEEE Trans. Inf. Forensics Secur. **7**(2), 455–464 (2012)

19. Li, J., Liu, H., Huang, J., Zhang, Y.: A robust watermarking scheme for H.264. Digital Watermarking, January 2009. http://dx.doi.org/10.1007/978-3-642-04438-0_1
20. Kim, S.M., Kim, S.B., Hong, Y., Won, C.S.: Data hiding on H.264/AVC compressed video. In: Kamel, M., Campilho, A. (eds.) ICIAR 2007. LNCS, vol. 4633, pp. 698–707. Springer, Heidelberg (2007). doi:10.1007/978-3-540-74260-9_62
21. Liao, K., Lian, S., Guo, Z., Wang, J.: Efficient information hiding in H.264/AVC video coding. Telecommun. Syst. **49**(2), 261–269 (2012)
22. Wiegand, T., Sullivan, G.J., Bjontegaard, G., Luthra, A.: Overview of the H.264/AVC video coding standard. IEEE Trans. Circuits Syst. Video Technol. **13**(7), 560–576 (2003)
23. Filler, T., Judas, J., Fridrich, J.: Minimizing additive distortion in steganography using syndrome-trellis codes. IEEE Trans. Inf. Forensics Secur. **6**(3), 920–935 (2011)
24. VideoLAN-x264, The Best H.264/AVC Encoder. http://www.videolan.org/developers/x264.html

A Study of the Two-Way Effects of Cover Source Mismatch and Texture Complexity in Steganalysis

Donghui Hu[1]([✉]), Zhongjin Ma[1], Yuqi Fan[1], and Lina Wang[2]

[1] School of Computer Science and Information, Hefei University of Technology,
Hefei 230009, Anhui Province, People's Republic of China
{hudh,yuqi.fan}@hfut.edu.cn, 1272885181@qq.com
[2] School of Computer Science, Wuhan University,
Wuhan 430072, Hubei Province, People's Republic of China
lnawang@163.com

Abstract. Cover source mismatch (CSM) occurs when a detection classifier for steganalysis trained on objects from one cover source is tested on another source. However, it is very hard to find the same sources as suspicious images in real-world applications. Therefore, the CSM is one of the biggest stumbling blocks to hinder current classifier based steganalysis methods from becoming practical. On the other hand, the texture complexity (of digital images) also plays an important role in affecting the detection accuracy of steganalysis. Previous work seldom conduct research on the interaction between the two factors of the CSM and the texture complexity. This paper studies the interaction between the two factors, aiming to improve the steganalysis accuracy. We propose a effective method to measure the texture complexity via image filtering, and use the two-way analysis of variance to study the interaction between the two factors. The experimental results have shown that the interaction between the two factors affects the detection accuracy significantly. We also design a method to improve the detection accuracy of steganalysis by utilizing the interaction of the two factors.

Keywords: Cover source mismatch · Texture complexity · Analysis of variance · Steganalysis

1 Introduction

Currently, steganography tools and software can be easily found online and used by ordinary people. Most of the current steganography tools are based on LSBR [9] or LSBM [12] algorithms, such as BMP Secrets, EzStego, Hide and Seek95v1.1. These tools have low computation cost and can be easily used. Steganalysis methods are developed to detect the various kinds of steganography algorithms. Although high detection accuracy of steganalysis is reported in lab, we face many difficulties in modeling and designing steganalysis methods, such

© Springer International Publishing AG 2017
Y.Q. Shi et al. (Eds.): IWDW 2016, LNCS 10082, pp. 601–615, 2017.
DOI: 10.1007/978-3-319-53465-7_45

as cover source mismatch (CSM), when the steganalysis is used in more general real-world environment [6].

CSM happens when training set is trained on a source of images and the suspicious examples are from a different source [8]. Many researchers have been aware of the negative impact of the CSM [2,3]. Recently CSM has become more and more widely recognized and many algorithms are proud of higher accuracy rate in CSM cases [1,10]. [8] refutes some of the common misconceptions that the severity of the CSM is tied to the feature dimensionality or their fragility. Ker et al. [7] presents an in-depth study of a particular instance of model mismatch, aiming to separate different effects of mismatch in feature space and find methods of mitigation where possible.

It seems an indisputable fact that the smooth regions in the cover images will inevitably be contaminated after data hiding even at a low embedding rate [4] in non-adaptive circumstances. Therefore, the texture complexity (of digital images) plays an important role in both steganography and steganalysis. Do the two factors of texture complexity and CSM both affect the accuracy the steganalysis? Do the two factors interact with each other in the situation of steganalysis? Can we improve the detection accuracy in the case of CSM by considering the interaction of the two factors? In this paper, we study the two-way effects of CSM and texture complexity in steganalysis. We hope the findings of our study can be utilized to reduce the negative affects of CSM in the real-world applications.

We use the two-way analysis of variance to study the interaction between texture complexity and CSM. We propose a method to measure the texture complexity based on the residual of image filtering. Varying degrees of texture complexity are measured by TC (texture complexity). We find that the higher TC the higher texture complexity. So we use TC to describe the factor of texture complexity. The factor CSM is described using different brands of cameras in the two-way analysis of variance. We then give a brief mathematical description of the two-way analysis of variance. Experiments are carried out to test the two-way analysis of variance with five brands of cameras and five kinds of TC ranges. We also design a method and do corresponding experiments to prove that we can improve the detection accuracy in the case of the CSM by utilizing the interaction of the two factors.

In the next section, we propose the method to calculate the value of TC, which can measure the degree of the texture complexity of a given image. In Sect. 3, we give a formal description of two-way analysis of variance. We then present the experimental results and analysis in Sect. 4. As an example, in Sect. 5, we give an accuracy enhancing steganalysis method by utilizing the interaction of the CSM and texture complexity. The paper is concluded in Sect. 6, where we also outline some possible directions for future research.

2   A Texture Complexity Measuring Method

In this section, we propose a simple method that measure the degree of the texture complexity of an image. In image processing, the average filter is a simple yet effective filter that can make an image more smooth. After the average filtering operation, some noisy or trivial part of the image will be removed. So we can design a method to measure the degree of the texture complexity based on the difference of the filtered image and the original one.

Let $x = (x) \in \{0, ..., 255\}^{m \times n}$ represent a pixel values of an 8-bit grayscale image, where m and n represent the length and width of the image (pixels), respectively. Let $f(x)$ represent the filtered image, and $g(x)$ represent the original one.

$$f(x) = average\_filter(g(x)) = \sum x \times w \qquad (1)$$

The equation of the average filter can be described in Eq. (1), where w is the filtering template which is often set to a 3×3, 5×5 or 7×7 matrix. In this paper, we set the w to as a 3×3 matrix. After the image edge region is filtered, the edge region will become vague, while the smooth region of an image will be changed. So we can use the residual of the original image and filtered image to measure the smooth degree of a given image. Let $I(x)$ denote the residual of the original image $g(x)$ and the filtered image $f(x)$. Then we can use the proportion of the value 0 in the residual matrix $I(x)$ to represent the smooth degree, which means the more 0 left in the residual matrix, the more smooth the original image is. Finally, the degree of texture complexity is the difference between 1 and the smooth degree, as shown in Eq. (3). Apparently, the higher the value of $I^{\{0\}}$ is, the more complex an image is. To keep things simple, in this paper, we call $I^{\{0\}}$ as the TC (Texture Complexity).

$$I(x) = |f(x) - g(x)| \qquad (2)$$

$$I^{\{0\}} = 1 - \frac{\sum\limits_{1 \leq i \leq m, 1 \leq j \leq n} I(x)_{(i,j)} = 0}{m \times n} \qquad (3)$$

We conduct experiments and found the TC value defined in Eq. (3) can measure the degree of image texture complexity and satisfy the human visual perception. Figure 1 gives some selected pictures with different TC values of 0 ± 0.01, 0.1 ± 0.01, 0.2 ± 0.01, 0.3 ± 0.01, 0.4 ± 0.01 and 0.5 ± 0.01, we can see that, when the human eye perceived texture complexity from image (1) to image (6) becoming more and more complex, the TC values from image (1) to image (6) also become increasingly larger.

To find the distribution range of TC in the real-world image sets, we do experiment on 19074 images in image sets of BOSSBase-1.01[1] and BOSSBase-v0.92[2]. Figure 2 shows the experimental result, where the X axis in the histogram represents different TC ranges (with step of 0.001), the Y axis represents the

---

[1] http://agents.fel.cvut.cz/stegodata/.
[2] http://agents.fel.cvut.cz/boss/index.php?mode=VIEW\&tmpl=materials.

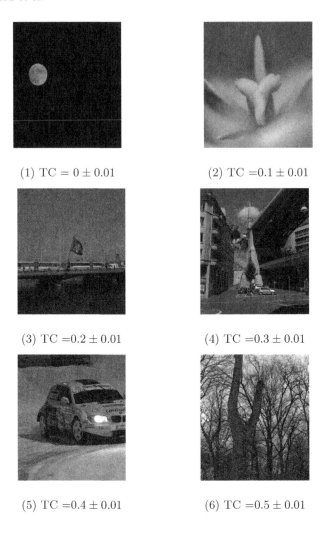

(1) TC = 0 ± 0.01   (2) TC =0.1 ± 0.01

(3) TC =0.2 ± 0.01   (4) TC =0.3 ± 0.01

(5) TC =0.4 ± 0.01   (6) TC =0.5 ± 0.01

Fig. 1. Examples of different TC values, (1), (2), (3), (4), (5) and (6) correspond to 0 ± 0.01, 0.1 ± 0.01, 0.2 ± 0.01, 0.3 ± 0.01, 0.4 ± 0.01 and 0.5 ± 0.01, respectively

number of images which has different TC ranges. From the figure we can find that the TC values are nearly distributed from 0.02 to 0.55. So in Sect. 4, we use $(0, 0.1)$, $(0.1, 0.2)$, $(0.2, 0.3)$, $(0.3, 0.4)$ and $(0.4, 0.5)$ to describe different scales of texture complexity.

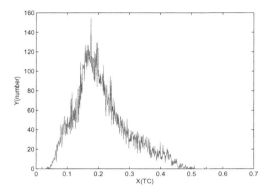

Fig. 2. The figure contains 19074 images downloaded from BOSSBase-1.01 and BOSSBase-v0.92. The X axis in the histogram represents different TC ranges (with step of 0.001), and the Y axis represents the number of images which has different TC ranges.

3   Two-Way Analysis of Variance

Variance analysis is one of the best statistical methods used to study whether certain factors affect the results [5]. In this section, we briefly introduce the two-way analysis of variance to readers, although this is a very mature statistical theory. The detail of the theory and related proofs can be found in some literatures material such as [5, 11, 13]. We use A and B to represent the two influencing factors. Two-way analysis of variance is used to explore the interaction between factors A and B, as well as it can test effect of a factor A or B alone on the result. We assume that factor A has r levels value and B has s levels value. We use X_{ij} to denote the test results from $(A_i, B_j)(i = 1, 2, \cdots, r; j = 1, 2, \cdots, s)$, where every X_{ij} is independent and $X_{ij} \sim N(\mu_{ij}, \sigma^2)$; we use $X_{ijk}(k = 1, 2, \cdots, t)$ to denote the kth result from the t independent repeated tests. Table 1 shows the data needed for the two-way analysis of variance.

Table 1. The data needed for the two-way analysis of variance.

	B_1	B_2	...	B_s
A_1	$X_{111},...X_{11t}$	$X_{121},...X_{12t}$	...	$X_{1s1},...X_{1st}$
A_2	$X_{211},...X_{21t}$	$X_{221},...X_{22t}$	...	$X_{2s1},...X_{2st}$
...	...	...	...	...
A_r	$X_{r11},...X_{r1t}$	$X_{r21},...X_{r2t}$	...	$X_{rs1},...X_{rst}$

For the convenience of description, we further introduce the symbols shown in Eq. (4), where μ denotes the ensemble average of μ_{ij}; μ_i and μ_j denote the

ensemble average of A and B levels, respectively; α_i denotes the effect of experimental results of the level A_i of factor A; β_i denotes the effect of experimental
results of the level B_j of factor B.

$$\begin{cases} \mu = \frac{1}{rs} \sum_{i=1}^{r} \sum_{j=1}^{s} \mu_{ij} \\ \mu_i = \frac{1}{s}\mu_{ij} \\ \alpha_i = \mu_i - \mu \quad (i = 1, 2, ...r) \\ \mu_j = \frac{1}{r}\sum_{i=1}^{r} \\ \beta_j = \mu_j - \mu \quad (j = 1, 2, ..., s) \end{cases} \tag{4}$$

The interaction influence can be described via Eq. (5), where γ_{ij} denotes the
interaction effect of level A_i and level B_j.

$$\gamma_{ij} = (\mu_{ij} - \mu) - \alpha_i - \beta_j \tag{5}$$

Then, we get the following three original hypotheses as shown in Eq. (6),
where H_{01} is the original hypothesis support that the different levels of factor
A have no effect on the result; H_{02} is the original hypothesis support that the
different levels of factor B have no effect on the result; and H_{03} is the original
hypothesis support that the different levels of both factor A and factor B have
no effect on the result. Equation (7), H_{11}, H_{12} and H_{13} are the corresponding
three alternative hypotheses.

$$\begin{cases} H_{01} : \alpha_1 = \alpha_2 = ... = \alpha_r \\ H_{02} : \beta_1 = \beta_2 = ... = \beta_s \\ H_{03} : \gamma_{ij} = 0 \quad (i = 1, 2, ..., r; j = 1, 2, ...s) \end{cases} \tag{6}$$

$$\begin{cases} H_{11} : \alpha_1 \neq \alpha_2 \neq ... \neq \alpha_r \\ H_{12} : \beta_1 \neq \beta_2 \neq ... \neq \beta_s \\ H_{13} : \gamma_{ij} \neq 0 \quad (i = 1, 2, ..., r; j = 1, 2, ...s) \end{cases} \tag{7}$$

Next, we give the theorem to describe under what conditions we can accept
or refuse the original hypotheses. Before presenting the theorem, we introduce
some basic formulas as shown in Eqs. (8–12), where Q_A, Q_B and $Q_{A \times B}$ represent
the sum of the square of deviations caused by factor A, factor B and interaction
effects of factors B and A, respectively; Q_T is the sum of the total sum of square
of deviations, and Q_e is the sum of squared error.

$$Q_T = \sum_{i=1}^{r} \sum_{j=1}^{s} \sum_{k=1}^{t} X_{ijk}^2 - \frac{1}{rst}\left(\sum_{i=1}^{r} \sum_{j=1}^{s} \sum_{k=1}^{t} X_{ijk}\right)^2 \tag{8}$$

$$Q_A = \frac{1}{st} \sum_{i=1}^{r} \left(\sum_{j=1}^{s} \sum_{k=1}^{t} X_{ijk}\right)^2 - \frac{1}{rst} \times \left(\sum_{i=1}^{r} \sum_{j=1}^{s} \sum_{k=1}^{t} X_{ijk}\right)^2 \tag{9}$$

$$Q_B = \frac{1}{rt} \sum_{j=1}^{s} \left(\sum_{i=1}^{r} \sum_{k=1}^{t} X_{ijk}\right)^2 - \frac{1}{rst} \times \left(\sum_{i=1}^{r} \sum_{j=1}^{s} \sum_{k=1}^{t} X_{ijk}\right)^2 \tag{10}$$

$$Q_e = \sum_{i=1}^{r}\sum_{j=1}^{s}\sum_{k=1}^{t} X_{ijk}^2 - \frac{1}{t}\left(\sum_{i=1}^{r}\sum_{j=1}^{s}\sum_{k=1}^{t} X_{ijk}\right)^2 \tag{11}$$

$$Q_{A\times B} = Q_T - (Q_A + Q_B + Q_e) \tag{12}$$

The theorem can be described as:

Theorem 1. *If the error is independent and follows the normal distribution with the mean of 0 and variance of σ^2, then we have:*

a. $Q_e/\sigma^2 \sim \chi^2(rs(t-1))$;
b. If H_{01} is true, $Q_A/\sigma^2 \sim \chi^2(r-1)$, and Q_e and Q_A are independent of each other, then:

$$F_A = \frac{Q_A/(r-1)}{Q_e/rs(t-1)} \sim F[r-1, rs(t-1)] \tag{13}$$

c. If H_{02} is true, $Q_B/\sigma^2 \sim \chi^2(s-1)$, and Q_e and Q_B are independent of each other, then:

$$F_B = \frac{Q_B/(r-1)}{Q_e/rs(t-1)} \sim F[s-1, rs(t-1)] \tag{14}$$

d. If H_{03} is true, $Q_{A\times B}/\sigma^2 \sim \chi^2((r-1)(s-1))$, and Q_e and $Q_{A\times B}$ are independent of each other, then:

$$F_{A\times B} = \frac{Q_{A\times B}/(r-1)(s-1)}{Q_e/rs(t-1)} \sim F[(r-1)(s-1), rs(t-1)] \tag{15}$$

Accordingly, we give conditions under which the original hypotheses will be refused. Let α denotes the significant level, then we can get $F_\alpha[r-1, rs(t-1)]$, $F_\alpha[s-1, rs(t-1)]$ and $F_\alpha[(r-1)(s-1), rs(t-1)]$, and we have:

a. H_{01} should be refused if:

$$F_A \geq F_\alpha[r-1, rs(t-1)] \tag{16}$$

b. H_{02} should be refused if:

$$F_B \geq F_\alpha[s-1, rs(t-1)] \tag{17}$$

c. H_{03} should be refused if:

$$F_{A\times B} \geq F_\alpha[(r-1)(s-1), rs(t-1)] \tag{18}$$

For the convenience of computation and analysis, we give the structure of the analysis of variance table as shown in Table 2, which will be used in the experimental section.

Finally, we use the p value to measure the meaning of the calculated F value. The p value describes the results of the analysis from probability calculation. p value can be calculated by Eqs. (19, 20 and 21), where $p1$ and $p2$ values test effect of factors A and B alone on the result, respectively; $p3$ value tests the

Table 2. The structure of the analysis of variance, including source of variance (Sources), sum of squares of deviations (SS), degree of freedom (df), and the mean sum of squares of deviations (MS).

Sources	SS	df	MS	value F
A	Q_A	$r-1$	$Q'_A = \frac{Q_A}{r-1}$	$F_A = \frac{Q'_A}{Q'_e}$
B	Q_B	$s-1$	$Q'_B = \frac{Q_B}{s-1}$	$F_B = \frac{Q'_B}{Q'_e}$
$A \times B$	$Q_{A \times B}$	$(r-1)(s-1)$	$Q'_{A \times B} = \frac{Q_{A \times B}}{(r-1)(s-1)}$	$F_{A \times B} = \frac{Q'_{A \times B}}{Q'_e}$
e	Q_e	$rs(t-1)$	$Q'_e = \frac{Q_e}{rs(t-1)}$	
sum	Q_T	$rst-1$		

interaction between factor A and factor B. The smaller the p value, the more sufficient reason we reject the original hypothesis and accept the alternative hypothesis. The significant level of p value can be set according to the application requirement.

$$p1 = 2 * P(F_A \geq F_\alpha[r-1, rs(t-1)]|\alpha_1 = \alpha_2 = ... = \alpha_r) \qquad (19)$$

$$p2 = 2 * P(F_B \geq F_\alpha[s-1, rs(t-1)]|\beta_1 = \beta_2 = ... = \beta_s) \qquad (20)$$

$$p3 = 2 * P(F_{A \times B} \geq F_\alpha[(r-1)(s-1), rs(t-1)]|\gamma_{ij} = 0) \qquad (21)$$

In this paper, we use the two-way analysis of variance to analyze the interaction between CSM and texture complexity. The experiments involve two independent variables which are CSM and texture complexity and one dependent variable, detection accuracy. Each independent variable corresponds to a different level, for example, different image sources represent different CSM levels and different TC ranges represent different texture complexity levels. In the next section, experiments will be conducted to test the three hypotheses.

4   Experiments for the Two-Way Analysis of Variance Study

4.1   Experimental Setup

In this paper, we do not use the raw format images as used in [8] for the following two reasons. One is that we think the raw format requires greater storage capacity and we rarely see this format images in real-world life; the other is that we cannot find the downloading website of raw format image set from used in [8]. In our experiments, we use 5 × 2300 of 8-bit grayscale images transformed by true-color JPEG images taken by five different brands of cameras (with each camera has 2300 images). The detail information of the image sources are shown in Table 3.

We focus on the texture complexity and CSM problems in this paper, so the experiments are conducted in the spatial domain. The function "rgb2gray" is

Table 3. Five cover sources for experiments.

	Cover source	Format	Size
1	SonyN1X5T	JPEG	4912 × 2760
2	SonyDSCW5	JPEG	1280 × 960
3	NikonD7100	JPEG	2992 × 2000
4	NikonD7000	JPEG	2464 × 1632
5	CanonSX60HS	JPEG	4608 × 3456

used to convert a true-color image to a 8-bit grayscale one in Matlab. A block of 512×512 is selected from the original image. We can see that the distribution of the texture complexity is similar to the Gaussian distribution in Fig. 2, where we also can find that when TC is small than 0.02 there are few images and when TC greater than 0.55 there are almost no images. So we set the TC ranges in (0,0.1), (0.1,0.2), (0.2,0.3), (0.3,0.4) and (0.4,0.5). We divide each 512×512 image from the image sources into several 128×128 sub images, and totally we get $16 \times 5 \times 2300$ images. For each 128×128 image set (taken by one band of cameras) and each TC range, we choose 1000 images as testing images, on the condition that no two images come from the same original 512×512 image. For each testing image set, we randomly choose six training images sets with each set composes of 2000 images. Among the six training sets, one is no CSM (with the camera brand same to that of the testing image set), four are CSM (with the camera brand different with that of the testing image set). The left one is a 'mixture' of four CSM ones (4×500 images uniformly and randomly selected from the other four different image sources). Therefore, we have 25 test image sets with different camera brands and TC ranges, each set having 1000 images; we have six training image sets with five set are from different brands of camera and one set from 'mixture', with each set having 2000 images. In order to be more close to practical, although we use Support Vector Machine(SVM) as the classifier, we are not to adjust the parameters to make higher accuracy of experiment.

4.2 Experimental Results and Analysis

We do experiments of steganalysis with the training images sets and test image sets mentioned above. We conduct each experiment five times. Tables 4, 5 and 6 are experimental results (detection accuracy) of test image sets with different camera brands of NikonD7100, SonyN1X5T and NikonD700, respectively. For example, the first cell (in the top left corner of the table) of Table 5 denotes five experimental results (detection accuracy) of using the training set of SonyD-SCW5 to detect the test set of NikonD7100 with TC range of (0, 0.1).

Table 4. Experimental results of test image sets with camera brand of NikonD7100.

Training sets	Test sets: NikonD7100 with different TC ranges				
	(0, 0.1)	(0.1, 0.2)	(0.2, 0.3)	(0.3, 0.4)	(0.4, 0.5)
SonyN1X5T	98.77;98.21;99.67;99.37;98.74	83.23;83;80.13;78.88;82.95	65.63;65.5;65.18;64.63;67.9	53.95;54.05;55.35;53.38;52.83	51.33;52.28;51.58;52.00;52.15;
SonyDSCW5	90.30;94.23;78.87;91.74;93.08;	73.68;75.53;76;79.78;73.1;	77.28;81.33;77.20;77.3;76.6;	60.75;59.1;64.63;60.83;61.08;	55.25;54.28;53.58;54.48;53.5;
NikonD7100	99.96;100;99.96;99.96;100	99.88;99.93;99.95;99.95;100	94.35;94.98;94.58;99.23;95.48	77.58;78.25;78.68;78.28;79.15	62.33;62.45;60.15;61.73;61.48;
NikonD7000	99.96;100;100;100;99.93;	95.68;94.13;95.05;94.75;93.83	74.9;75.73;75.25;74.48;73.4	60.35;60.65;60.3;57.18;59.9	51.83;52.03;52.68;52.78;52.63
CanonSX60HS	99.96;99.29;99.37;99.93;99.44;	82.55;85.9;84.8;87.5;85.5;	64.7;56.83;70.58;64.08;71.2;	55.63;55.3;56;55.03;54.6;	51.65;52.58;51.93;51.45;51.8;
mixture	99.697;99.24;99.85;99.55;99.85	96.75;97.7;95.25;94.9;95.8	74.7;73.5;74.45;75.75;73.7;	56.3;57.3;57.75;57.15;56.15	50.9;50;52.2;51.85;52.35;

Table 5. Experimental results of test image sets with camera brand of SonyN1X5T.

Sources	Test sets: SonyN1X5T with different TC ranges				
	(0, 0.1)	(0.1, 0.2)	(0.2, 0.3)	(0.3, 0.4)	(0.4, 0.5)
SonyN1X5T	100;99.81;100;100;99.90;	99.23;100;100;100;100;	99.98;100;99.98;100;99.98;	99.28;99.43;99.18;99.23;99.43;	83.9;84.15;85.05;84.68;84.45;
SonyDSCW5	93.94;96.46;98.64;90.84;86.14;	93.43;95.63;93.58;91.2;88.78;	78.45;85.2;79.23;82;77.95;	66.05;55;62.78;63;66.85;	53.55;52.8;53.35;57.1;52.4;
NikonD7100	96.75;99.42;95.40;99.90;98.74;	94.8;97.6;95.9;94.63;96.8;	63.43;63.9;61.93;59.68;63.03;	51.43;51.08;51.68;50.83;50.8;	52.95;54.53;53.52;52.43;53.6;
NikonD7000	100;100;100;100;99.95;	99.83;99.88;99.8;99.83;99.83;	94.9;96.2;97.08;97.35;94.53;	89.13;86.63;85.88;87.2;87.65;	75.3;75.05;75.85;74.38;74.45;
CanonSX60HS	100;99.85;99.03;99.81;98.4;	99.78;99.23;99.2;99.88;99.63;	99.33;98.98;98.98;98.95;99.43;	96.43;97.13;97.5;97.58;97.93;	80.38;78.5;79.1;77.9;79.58;
mixture	100;100;100;100;100;	98.75;99.45;99.8;98.5;99.45;	93.05;95.3;93.95;99.35;99.45;	82.85;84.45;85.75;75;75.2;81.2;	66.2;69.35;68.95;75.05;69.6;

Table 6. Experimental results of test image sets with camera brand of NikonD7000.

Sources	Test sets: NikonD7000 with different TC ranges				
	(0, 0.1)	(0.1, 0.2)	(0.2, 0.3)	(0.3, 0.4)	(0.4, 0.5)
SonyN1X5T	100;100;99.98;99.63;99.95	96.78;96.5;95.5;97.75;98.5;	87.3;89.75;89.9;88.85;88.35;	75.85;77.5;76.83;79.18;77.38;	62.63;64.35;64.08;62.2;90.8;
SonyDSCW5	76.15;89.05;86.63;93.43;79.075;	89.4;85.05;81.65;89.6;96.05;	86.48;82.88;83.35;80.95;84.58;	63.83;65.53;60.35;66.8;61.45;	55.53;54.65;53.73;53.95;54.48;
NikonD7100	99.75;99.65;97.83;99.88;99.2;	95.63;97.98;97.58;97.7;97.13;	73.15;73.95;72.78;73.95;71.13;	56.13;54.63;55.95;56.575;57.05;	52.55;51.58;52.13;52.75;54.43;
NikonD7000	100;100;100;100;100;	99.95;99.88;99.93;100;99.98;	99.25;99.5;99.45;99.5;99.4;	89.68;91.23;90.35;89.78;89.95;	67.58;67.1;67.18;67.73;67.33;
CanonSX60HS	99.05;99;99.95;100;99.6;	96.2;94.85;97.98;95.83;96.68;	87.7;84.35;85.25;79.43;82.55;	76.85;77.23;77.4;78.03;78.38;	60.98;58.98;59.35;59.16;59.75;
mixture	100;100;100;99.92;99.84;	99.23;98.59;97.96;99.23;98.24;	95.35;95.25;94.85;93.75;92.2;	77.45;78.15;77.4;79.25;77.2;	59.3;60.75;58.6;61.65;60.35;

In our experiments, the steganalysis accuracy is defined as Eq. (22):

$$P_A = (P_{TP} + P_{TN})/2 \tag{22}$$

where P_{TP} and P_{TN} are true positive rate and true negative rate, respectively.

We further calculate the experimental results in Tables 4, 5 and 6 using formulas given in Table 2 and Eqs. (19 – 21), where the final p value of each experiment is shown in the last columns of Tables 7, 8 and 9. In our experiments, the significant level of p value is set to 0.05. If the p value is smaller than the significant level, original hypothesis will be rejected; otherwise, the original hypothesis will be accepted. At the same time, the smaller the p value, the more likely we reject the original hypothesis. There are three p values in each two-way analysis of variance table. The p values in the first and second row of each table denote the factors of TC and CSM, respectively. The p value in the third row of each table denotes the factor of interaction.

In the three tables above mentioned, we can find that the p values are extremely small. These results imply that we need to reject the three original hypothesis as described in the Eq. (6), and accept the three alternative hypothesis described in the Eq. (7). We can get the following conclusions from Tables 7, 8 and 9. First, the complexity of the texture has a significant effect on the results of steganalysis; second, CSM has a significant effect on the results of steganalysis; third, the interaction between CSM and the texture complexity has a significant effect on the results of steganalysis. These conclusions is achieved by mathematical analysis based on a large number of experimental results.

Table 7. Two-way analysis of variance of test image sets with camera brand of NikonD7100.

Sources	SS	df	MS	F	Prob > F
Columns (TC)	40869.9	4	10217.5	2766.16	$4.1145e - 117$
Rows (CSM)	4795	5	959	259.63	$1.40655e - 62$
Interaction	3327.1	20	166.4	46.26	$3.08397e - 46$
Error	443.2	120	3.7		
Total	49435.3	149			

Table 8. Two-way analysis of variance of test image sets with camera brand of SonyN1X5T.

Sources	SS	df	MS	F	Prob > F
Columns (TC)	18436.5	4	4609.12	1275.6	$2.84488e - 97$
Rows (CSM)	12752.3	5	2550.46	705.85	$3.58199e - 87$
Interaction	6588.9	20	329.45	91.18	$8.78822e - 63$
Error	433.6	120	3.61		
Total	38211.3	149			

Table 9. Two-way analysis of variance of test image sets with camera brand of NikonD7000.

Sources	SS	df	MS	F	Prob > F
Columns (TC)	29588.1	4	7397.02	821.99	$3.72566e - 86$
Rows (CSM)	5261.5	5	1052.29	116.94	$2.03697e - 44$
Interaction	2946	20	147.3	16.37	$1.85089e - 25$
Error	1079.9	120	9		
Total	38875.4	149			

5   An Accuracy Enhancing Steganalysis Strategy

Though we know now that the interaction between CSM and the texture complexity affects the detection accuracy of steganalysis, but how the the interaction between the two factors affects the steganalysis till further to be researched and utilized. We visualize the Tables 4, 5 and 6 into figures. Here, we just show one of the figure. Figure 3 is the visualization figure of Table 4, where the X axis is the different TC ranges (in descending order), the Y axis is the detection accuracy of steganalysis, and 6 lines are the detection accuracy of test images (NikonD7100) under different line with different training images. We can find that: (1) no matter whether there is CSM or not, the lower the texture complexity of the test image is, the higher the detection accuracy it can achieve; (2) when the texture complexity of the test images is the same, different levels of CSM (including no CSM) have different detection accuracy; (3) when there is no CSM (in this case when both test images and training images are taken by NikonD7100), the detection results are the highest (which is shown in the top line); (4) the second highest detection accuracy is achieved when the training images are 'mixture', which is consistent with the state-of-the-art understanding that the mixture set can be used as the training set to improve the accuracy of steganalysis.

For the finding (1), we propose a simple approach to improving the detection accuracy when CSM exists. In this method, we divide the original image into small size sub-blocks, and calculate the TC of each sub-block. We select the sub-block with the lowest TC as the original image as test image. We do experiment to show the effectiveness of this improved method. The cover sources and the information hiding method are the same as to the previous subsection (with image brand of NikonD7100). We compare the original test sample of a 512×512 image and the selected 128×128 sub-blocks with the lowest TC. Figure 4 is the comparison result. We can see that except when the test image and the training image are both taken by NikonD7100, the detection accuracy of the selected 128×128 sub-block improves a lot compared with the original 512×512 image.

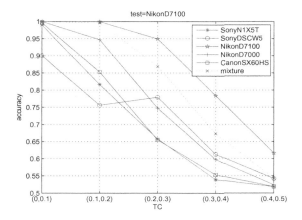

Fig. 3. The visualization figure of Table 4 (with test set of NikonD7100)

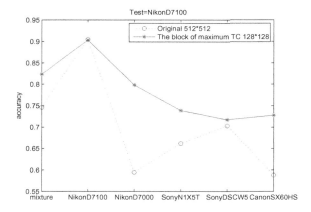

Fig. 4. Comparison result of the improved method and the original method.

6   Conclusions and Future Work

Besides CSM, many factors may affect the detection accuracy of steganalysis. In this paper, we study the interaction effect of CSM and the texture complexity with two-way analysis of variance. Firstly, we propose a new texture complexity measurement method based on statistical analysis, and design different scales of TC values through experimental observation. Secondly, we introduce the statistical method of two-way analysis of variance and how to use it in our study. Thirdly, we conduct experiments for two-way analysis of variance to show whether there exist interaction effects between CSM and the texture complexity. The experimental results demonstrate that the image texture complexity and CSM alone have a significant effect on the steganalysis; what's more, the interaction effect between the texture complexity and CSM is very significant.

We also design a method to improve the detection accuracy by considering the interaction effect of the texture complexity and CSM.

The future work may be as follows: (1) the texture complexity measurement method proposed in this paper is effective, but we think there is still room for improvement to measure the texture complexity; (2) in this study, the experiments are conducted in the spatial domain; we will explore the interaction effect of CSM and other factors in the JPEG domain; and (3) in this paper, we design a simple method to improve the detection accuracy by utilizing the interaction effect of the texture complexity and CSM; however, the proposed improved approach aims to detect the non-adaptive steganography in the spatial domain; we also need to study how to detect the adaptive steganography by utilizing the interaction between CSM and the texture complexity.

Acknowledgment. This work was supported in part by the National Natural Science Foundation of China (No. 61272540, No. U1536204), the National Key Technology R&D Program (No. 2014BAH41B00, No. 2015AA016004), and in part by the Natural Science Foundation of Anhui province (No. 1508085MF115, No. 1608085MF142).

References

1. Bas, P., Filler, T., Pevný, T.: Break our steganographic system: the ins and outs of organizing BOSS. In: Filler, T., Pevný, T., Craver, S., Ker, A. (eds.) IH 2011. LNCS, vol. 6958, pp. 59–70. Springer, Heidelberg (2011). doi:10.1007/978-3-642-24178-9_5
2. Cancelli, G., Doërr, G., Barni, M., Cox, I.J.: A comparative study of±steganalyzers. In: 2008 IEEE 10th Workshop on Multimedia Signal Processing, pp. 791–796. IEEE (2008)
3. Goljan, M., Fridrich, J., Holotyak, T.: New blind steganalysis and its implications. In: Electronic Imaging, pp. 607201–607201. International Society for Optics and Photonics (2006)
4. Huang, F., Zhong, Y., Huang, J.: Improved algorithm of edge adaptive image steganography based on LSB matching revisited algorithm. In: Shi, Y.Q., Kim, H.-J., Pérez-González, F. (eds.) IWDW 2013. LNCS, vol. 8389, pp. 19–31. Springer, Heidelberg (2014). doi:10.1007/978-3-662-43886-2_2
5. Iversen, G.R., Gergen, M.: Statistics: the Conceptual Approach. Springer Science & Business Media, New York (2012)
6. Ker, A.D., Bas, P., Böhme, R., Cogranne, R., Craver, S., Filler, T., Fridrich, J., Pevný, T.: Moving steganography and steganalysis from the laboratory into the real world. In: Proceedings of the First ACM Workshop on Information Hiding and Multimedia Security, pp. 45–58. ACM (2013)
7. Ker, A.D., Pevný, T.: A mishmash of methods for mitigating the model mismatch mess. In: IS&T/SPIE Electronic Imaging, pp. 90280I–90280I. International Society for Optics and Photonics (2014)
8. Kodovský, J., Sedighi, V., Fridrich, J.: Study of cover source mismatch in steganalysis and ways to mitigate its impact. In: IS&T/SPIE Electronic Imaging, pp. 90280J–90280J. International Society for Optics and Photonics (2014)
9. Petitcolas, F.A., Anderson, R.J., Kuhn, M.G.: Information hiding-a survey. Proc. IEEE **87**(7), 1062–1078 (1999)

10. Qian, Y., Dong, J., Wang, W., Tan, T.: Deep learning for steganalysis via convolutional neural networks. In: IS&T/SPIE Electronic Imaging, pp. 94090J–94090J. International Society for Optics and Photonics (2015)
11. Rice, J.: Mathematical Statistics and Data Analysis. Nelson Education (2006)
12. Sharp, T.: An implementation of key-based digital signal steganography. In: Moskowitz, I.S. (ed.) IH 2001. LNCS, vol. 2137, pp. 13–26. Springer, Heidelberg (2001). doi:10.1007/3-540-45496-9_2
13. Walpole, R.E., Myer, R., Myers, S.I., Keying, E.Y.: Essentials of Probabilty & Statistics for Engineers & Scientists. Pearson Higher Ed., Upper Saddle River (2012)

Erratum to: Speech Authentication and Recovery Scheme in Encrypted Domain

Qing Qian, Hongxia Wang[✉], Sani M. Abdullahi, Huan Wang,
and Canghong Shi

School of Information Science and Technology,
Southwest Jiaotong University, Chengdu 611756, China
hxwang@swjtu.edu.cn

Erratum to:
Chapter "Speech Authentication and Recovery
Scheme in Encrypted Domain" in: Y.Q. Shi et al. (Eds.):
Digital Forensics and Watermarking
DOI: 10.1007/978-3-319-53465-7_4

By mistake the name of the third author – Sani M. Abdullahi – was misspelled in the original version.

The updated original online version for this chapter can be found at
DOI: 10.1007/978-3-319-53465-7_4

© Springer International Publishing AG 2017
Y.Q. Shi et al. (Eds.): IWDW 2016, LNCS 10082, p. E1, 2017.
DOI: 10.1007/978-3-319-53465-7_46

Author Index

Printed in the United States
By Bookmasters